A Grammatical Aid
to the
Greek New Testament

A Grammatical Aid
to the
Greek New Testament

Robert Hanna

1983

Baker Book House

Grand Rapids, Michigan 49506

This edition was originally published in 1980 by the Summer Institute of Linguistics in two volumes.

Permission has been granted by the following publishers to quote from their works: Cambridge University Press, The University of Chicago Press, and T. & T. Clark.

Contents

Preface

I have compiled this material in order to provide an aid for all interested in doing in-depth New Testament exegesis, be they ministers, students, or translators. This work is not intended to be exhaustive; comments are included not on every grammatical construction, but only on those that call for particular clarification and are discussed in the eight reference grammars on which I have drawn (the grammars of Blass/Debrunner, Robertson, and Moulton/Howard/Turner, Turner's *Grammatical Insights into the New Testament*, Burton's *Moods and Tenses of New Testament Greek*, and Moule's *An Idiom Book of New Testament Greek*). In these individual works numerous valuable comments are hidden away from all but the specialist in Greek grammar. I have attempted to make these comments available to a much wider audience by collating them in a verse-by-verse order, thus reducing the time required to obtain the information, and by clarifying them.

The criteria for inclusion of a comment in this work are as follows: (1) The comment aids one's understanding of the passage of Scripture under discussion. (2) It is not common knowledge for the New Testament exegete (who, it is assumed, has approximately three years of Greek); e.g., the comment "this accusative is used as a direct object" would never be included unless there were substantial variant translations. Or (3) it aids in understanding the reason for the occurrence of an unusual construction (this criterion deals with the author's structure and style more specifically than does the first criterion).

When a comment has been included, I either state it verbatim or reword it, specifying the principle it illustrates so as to facilitate an understanding of the more difficult observations. When a contradiction or question arises, I include in brackets my own opinion as an editorial comment. The references that are included after a comment fall into two categories: those that agree with and support the comment (e.g., "cf. M56"), and those that add further information to or contradict it (e.g., "this preposition has an instrumental sense—R590").

I am greatly indebted to Harold Van Broekhoven for performing the laborious tasks of typing and editing, and to William Lane for his evaluation and constant encouragement. I would also like to express special gratitude to June Hinken and many others too numerous to mention here for their typing, suggestions, and criticism, which made the work possible. Finally, I am grateful to the publishers of the reference grammars for permission to use these books.

A Grammatical Aid
to the
Greek New Testament

Sources and Abbreviations

BD   Blass, F., and Debrunner, A. *A Greek Grammar of the New Testament*. Translated and revised by Robert Funk. Chicago: The University of Chicago Press, 1961.

B   Burton, E. D. *Moods and Tenses of New Testament Greek*. Edinburgh: T. & T. Clark, 1898.

H   Howard W. F. *A Grammar of New Testament Greek*. Vol. 2. Edinburgh: T. & T. Clark, 1928.

M   Moule, C. F. D. *An Idiom Book of New Testament Greek*. New York: Cambridge University Press, 1959.

MT   Moulton, J. H. *A Grammar of New Testament Greek*. Vol. 1. Edinburgh: T. & T. Clark, 1908.

R   Robertson, A. T. *A Grammar of the Greek New Testament*. Nashville: Broadman Press, 1934.

T   Turner, N. *A Grammar of New Testament Greek*. Vol. 3. Edinburgh: T. & T. Clark, 1963.

TGr   ———. *Grammatical Insights into the New Testament*. Edinburgh: T. & T. Clark, 1965.

Matthew

2   T167 The article τόν is used to determine the case in vv. 2ff. (it is used with indeclinable proper names, but without the usual meaning).

6   R501 Τῆς τοῦ Οὐρίου is used as a genitive of relationship, referring to the wife of Uriah.

11   R501 Βαβυλῶνος is used as an objective genitive, "to Babylon" ("leading to"-- T212).

17   R576 There is nothing un-Greek about the construction ἀπο Ἀβραὰμ ἕως Δαυίδ (the preposition ἀπό has a temporal meaning, "from" or "since").

18   R1184 A new topic may be introduced by δέ in entire harmony with the preceding discussion, "Now the birth of Jesus Christ."
       T78 Πρὶν ἤ with the aorist infinitive means "before they ever came together."
       T176 Omission of the article may occur with a preposition, even when the reference is to the Holy Spirit (cf. Luke 1:15 and M113).

19   R1128 The participles ὤν and θέλων have a causal sense, "because he was just and unwilling."

20   R418 The verb occurs between the substantive and adjective in ἐκ πνεύματος ἐστιν ἁγίου, to give unity to the clause.
       TGr19 Since πνεύματός ἁγίου is anarthrous the third person of the Trinity is not referred to, but an undefinable and holy power of God (note that this occurs in a prepositional phrase; cf. 1:18 and the discussion on Luke 1:15 and 35).
       T77 In this verse we expect the present prohibition "stop fearing," instead of the aorist "never fear" (μὴ φοβηθῇς means "do not forbear out of fear"--BD336 [3]).
       T151 Τὸ ἐν αὐτῇ γεννηθέν means "her unborn baby."

21   R575 The idea of "off" or "away from" is present in the preposition ἀπό here.
       R679 The pronoun αὐτός is emphatic, "For he it is that shall save."
       R874 Notice the volative future καλέσεις, "you shall call."

22   R534 Ὑπό is used to refer to the direct agent and διά is used to refer to the intermediate agent, "what the Lord had spoken through the prophet."
       R1428 The participle λέγοντος simply means "when saying."
       B222 The writer of the first gospel never uses ἵνα to express result, either actual or conceived; and that he by this phrase at least intends to express purpose is made especially clear by his employment of ὅπως (which is never consecutive) interchangeably with ἵνα (the clause indicates divine purpose-- R998).
       M15 In the phrase τοῦτο . . . πληρωθῇ, the perfect tense denotes that the event

stands recorded in the abiding Christian tradition. This type of interpretation viewed the Old Testament narrative as contemporary.

23 M17 Ἐστίν may be regarded as independent, with an explanatory participle
(rather than periphrastic). [Ed. This clause may be translated "which means
God with us."]

MATTHEW 2

1 R408 Ἀνατολῶν is used as an idiomatic plural, simply meaning "east" (directions
are generally plural--T26).

2 R1062 The infinitive has the notion of purpose here, "we came for worshipping."
TGr26 The question in this verse should be translated, "Where is the new-born
king of the Jews?" The Magi did not ask, "Where is he that is born to be king
of the Jews?"
T172 The articular singular noun ἀνατολῇ apparently does not refer to a compass-
point but means "in its rising," in vv. 2 and 9.
T189 Notice the position of the pronoun αὐτοῦ (emphatic, "his star").

3 B439 The participle ἀκούσας has a causal sense, "because Herod the king heard
this."

4 R795 In the Gospels ὁ χριστός is usually a verbal adjective meaning "the Anointed One, the Messiah."
M7 Γεννᾶται is used as a futuristic present, "is to be born?" (cf. BD323[2]).
TGr27 Surprisingly, the verb ἐπυνθάνετο is in the imperfect tense, which means
that Herod hardly expected his demand to be implemented. Tentative requests
are often described in the imperfect tense. King Herod suspected plotting
against him, especially those nearest his throne, and his suspicion comes out in
Matthew's report. "Where? But I expect you will not tell me."

5 R1109 Although the participle ἡγούμενος is anarthrous it is used as a substantive here ("prince"--T151).

6 T48 One should not read too much of a consecutive sense into the pronoun ὅστις
(probably more accurately "who" rather than "that").

7 R530 Λάθρᾳ is used as a dative of manner, "secretly."

8 R860 The aorist participle πέμψας refers to action which is simultaneous to
that of the principal verb (πέμψας εἶπεν means "sent with the words"--T156).

9 T279 Ἐπάνω is adverbial here, "before."

10 B439 The participle ἰδόντες has a causal sense, "because they saw the star,
they rejoiced."
M32 Ἐχάρησαν χαρὰν μεγάλην σφόδρα means "they rejoiced with very great joy."

11 M68 The participle with the following prepositional phrase ἐλθόντες εἰς τὴν
οἰκίαν simply means "entering the house."

13 R1088 Τοῦ with the infinitive ἀπολέσαι is used to express purpose (the examples
        of this chiefly occur in Matthew, Luke and Acts).
        BD321 Φαίνεται is used as an historical present, "an angel appeared."

14 T235 The genitive νυκτός means "during the night."

15 R636 Ὑπό is used to refer to the direct agent and διά is used to refer to the
        intermediate agent (cf. 1:22).
        R1428 Λέγοντες simply means "when saying."
        B222 The ἵνα clause expresses purpose (cf. 1:22).

16 R834 Ἐθυμώθη is used as an ingressive aorist, "he became angry."

20 R392 The plural τεθνήκασιν purposely conceals the identity of the person re-
        ferred to (Herod the Great; the plural of generalization--BD141).
        B127 The present participle οἱ ζητοῦντες is used as an imperfect to denote a
        continued action antecedent to that of the principal verb (cf. M206; "those
        who were seeking are dead").
        T75 The present imperative πορεύου occurs here, where one would expect the
        aorist, "go."

22 R574 Ἀντί has the idea of succession, as son succeeds father on the throne.

23 TGr27 "He shall be called a Nazarene" is not in fact part of any prophecy and
        may even be a scribal gloss or a comment by the evangelist (preferably the
        latter).
        T7 The plural τῶν προφητῶν simply refers to Hosea.

                                MATTHEW 3

2   R895 The perfect verb ἤγγικεν refers to an act which is durative-punctiliar,
        with a backward look, "is near."

4   T41 In αὐτός δὲ ὁ Ἰωάννης the proleptic pronoun is followed by a resumptive
        noun, "he that is John" (emphatic--BD277[3]).

7   R213 Γεννήματα has the sense of "living creatures."
        R602 Aim or purpose is expressed by the preposition ἐπί, "for baptism."
        R848 The verb ὑπέδειξεν may be translated "has warned," but "warned" is suf-
        ficient.
        T66 The preceding imperfects (vv. 44ff) contribute to a vivid picture against
        the background of which John utters his rebukes (aorist).

9   R834 Δόξητε is used as an ingressive aorist (cf. Luke 3:8), "do not begin to
        think."
        BD392(1a) The infinitive λέγειν is complementary to the principal verb, "do not
        get the idea of saying."

10 R881 The present verb κεῖται has a perfective sense, "the axe lies at the root
        of the tree" (i.e., it has been placed there; cf. T62).
        M107 Πᾶν οὖν δένδρον μὴ ποιοῦν probably means "every tree that does not" (attri-

butive participle) rather than "every tree when," or "if, it does not" (πᾶς
δένδρον means "any tree"--T199).

11 R520 The prepositional phrase ἐν ὕδατι is used as a locative, "in water."
    R679 The pronoun αὐτός is emphatic here, referring to ὁ ἐρχόμενος.
    T266 Εἰς seems to have a causal sense in this verse, "because of repentance."

12 R533 Πυρὶ ἀσβέστῳ may be used as a locative or instrumental (probably refer-
    ring to judgment by and at the coming of the Messiah [cf. v. 11]).
    R575 The compound noun ἀποθήκη means "a treasure-house for putting things
    away."
    R581 The compound verb here διακαθαρίζω has a perfect sense, "he will thor-
    oughly cleanse."

13 T141 Τοῦ with the infinitive denotes the idea of purpose, "to be baptized."

14 R234 The pronoun is emphatic in the phrase πρός με (cf. T39).
    R885 Διεκώλυεν is used as a conative imperfect (i.e., action begun, but inter-
    rupted; cf. B23; "wished to hinder"--T65).
    T334 In this verse καί has the sense of "and yet," where we expect καὶ μήν or
    καίτοι.
    H302 In the compound verb here διά has a perfective notion, actually John was
    for "stopping him altogether."

15 B384 The infinitive πληρῶσαι is used as the subject of the verb ἐστίν, "it is
    fitting for us to fulfill."
    T200 Πᾶσαν means "the whole of."

16 T25 Οἱ οὐρανοί in vv. 16f. is an exceptional use of the plural; generally the
    singular is used for the material sense of "sky."

17 R372 The verbal adjective ἀγαπητός has the idea of completion, "beloved."
    M7 The aorist verb εὐδόκησα means "I approve" (i.e., "I am pleased with" --
    referring to an immediate reaction; cf. 2 Pet. 1:17).

MATTHEW 4

1 R990 The simple infinitive πειρασθῆναι has the idea of purpose, "to be tempted."

2 R1112 The aorist participle νηστεύσας denotes the reason for the hungering ex-
    pressed by the principal verb, "because he fasted."

3 R781 Υἱὸς τοῦ θεοῦ and ὁ υἱὸς τοῦ θεοῦ (John 1:49) do not mean the same thing.
    Υἱός is anarthrous here because it is indefinite (υἱός in vv. 3 and 6 is anar-
    throus because it precedes the verb--T183). [Ed. Generally when a predicate
    nominative precedes the verb it is anarthrous even though it may be definite,
    as it appears to be here, "the Son of God"; cf. 14:33 and 27:40.]
    B200 Ἵνα is used to introduce an object clause after the verb of exhorting
    εἰπέ, "command that."

4 R604 The preposition ἐπί has the notion of basis here, "live on bread."

B68   The verb ζήσεται appears to be used as an imperatival future (volitive,
"man shall not live"), although the Hebrew of the passage quoted (Deut. 8:3) is
apparently gnomic rather than imperatival.

5   R756   Τὸ πτερύγιον should not be translated "a pinnacle." The whole point lies
in the article -- "the wing of the Temple overlooking the abyss."

7   R874   Ἐκπειράσεις is used as a volitive future, "you shall not tempt."
R895   The perfect verb γέγραπται means "it was written (punctiliar) and still
is on record" (durative).

9   R705   There no doubt is some difference between ταῦτα πάντα (this verse) and
πάντα ταῦτα (6:32). In the first expression, πάντα is a closer specification
of ταῦτα; in the second πάντα is pointed out demonstratively by means of ταῦτα.

11   R847   The tenses are interesting in this verse; ἀφίησιν is used as an historical
present, προσῆλθεν begins the action (aorist), while διηκόνουν (imperfect) continues it, "angels came and were ministering."

14   B222   Ἵνα denotes purpose (cf. 1:22).

15   R500   The genitive θαλάσσης means "by the sea" ("seawards"--T247).

18   R1190   In this verse γάρ introduces an explanation by way of appendix to the
train of thought.

23   T51   The compound verb περιάγω means "go about, traverse."
T211   Τῆς βασιλείας is used as an objective genitive, "about the kingdom."

MATTHEW 5

1   R756   The articular expression τὸ ὄρος refers to the mountain right at hand, not
a mountain (that great hill which stood like a throne behind the sea).

2   R885   Ἐδίδασκεν is used as an inchoative imperfect, "he began to teach."

3   R443   The Beatitudes (in vv. 3-12) have no connectives at all, and are all the
more effective because of the asyndeton (i.e., the lack of connectives).
M46   Does οἱ πτωχοὶ τῷ πνεύματι mean "the poor" used in its spiritual (i.e., religious) connotation; cf. James 2:5 (τῷ πνεύματι is used as a dative of respect
--T221; a locative--R523). [Ed. In this verse, πνεῦμα appears to refer to the
inner life of man (cf. Mark 2:8 and Luke 1:47). The whole phrase seems to mean
"those who are poor in reference to their inner life," this attitude is in direct contrast to the pharisaical pride in their own spiritual riches.]

7   R872   The future verb ἐλεηθήσονται has an ingressive sense, "obtain mercy."

8   T220   Τῇ καρδίᾳ is used as a dative of respect (locative--R523). [Ed. The
resultant meanings of "in reference to the heart" and "in the sphere of the
heart" have similar connotations.]

10 T85 The perfect tense is used in οἱ δεδιωγμένοι because of the tendency to connect a past action with its present consequences, "who are persecuted."

12 M74 The preposition has a temporal sense in τοὺς πρὸ ὑμῶν, "those who were before you."

13 R590 The preposition in ἐν τίνι has an instrumental sense, "by what?"
BD390(3) The infinitives here have the notion of purpose, "to be cast out and
trampled under foot."

15 R757 In τὸν μόδιον . . . τὴν λυχνίαν, the article singles out the bushel and
the lampstand present in the room.
R1183 After the conjunction in καὶ λάμπει we may add "so" (καί has a consecutive sense, "and so"--BD442[2]).

16 T72 Λαμψάτω appears to be used as an ingressive aorist, "let your light begin
to shine."

17 R833 The verb ἦλθον is used as a simple, constative aorist (just punctiliar and
nothing more), describing the purpose of Christ's mission.
R857 The infinitives καταλῦσαι and πληρῶσαι are used as effective aorists
(stressing the end of the action), "I did not come to destroy but to fulfill."
TGr32 The prohibition here has the aorist tense and means "Do not think for one
moment that I have come in order to destroy the Law."

18 R405 The singular verb παρέλθη with the compound subject here emphasizes the
totality.
BD474(1) Ἓν is in an emphatic position here; the emphasis lies on the number
due to the repetition.

19 T107 The aorist tense in the relative clause refers to action which is antecedent to that of the principal verb, "he will be called least, who (by that time
shall have) relaxed."

20 R666 Note the ellipsis in this verse, "than that of the Scribes and Pharisees"
(the comparison here is heightened by the addition of πλεῖον--BD246).

21 R844 The aorist verb ἠκούσατε should be translated, "you have heard" (similar
to the perfect, "ye have heard that it was said to the ancients": the reference
is doubtless to the frequent occasions on which they had heard such teachings
in the synagogue--B52).
R889 Οὐ φονεύσεις is used as a volitive durative future in vv. 21, 27, 33 and
48, "you shall not kill" (a prohibition).
MT186 The aorist subjunctive φονεύσῃ has the sense of a future perfect, "the
man who has committed murder."

24 R428 The absence of a connective between ὕπαγε and διαλλάγηθι gives life and
movement to the expression, "go, first be reconciled."
TGr30 The latter part of this verse should be translated, "First be reconciled
once and for all (aorist) to your brother, and then come and offer (present)
as many gifts as you like" ("then you may resume bringing"--BD336[3]).

25 B330 Ἕως ὅτου is in effect a compound conjunction having the same force as
the simple ἕως ("while"--T110).

BD353(1) The participle εὐνοῶν appears as though it is periphrastic, but is
actually adjectival (it is a periphrastic construction--MT249). [Ed. There
seems to be very little support for separating the participle from the verb
by making the participle adjectival, since the participle is dependent upon the
verb and together they mean "making friends."]

28 R1003 In this verse πρὸς τό with the infinitive may express either the notion
of purpose or result (aim unless it is explanatory of βλέπων--R1075; simple
accompaniment, "and"--T144; "with respect to"--BD402[5]; it seems to explain
βλέπων--MT218). [Ed. In this context πρὸς τό with the infinitive refers to
the result that follows from a set of circumstances, with the resultant meaning, "the one who looks at a woman in such a way that desire for her is aroused"
(cf. the use of πρός with the accusative in 1 Cor. 14:26; Col. 2:23 and John
4:35). In this rendering it is explanatory of βλέπων.]
T73 Ἐμοίχευσεν is used as a gnomic aorist, ie., a well known fact.

29 R992 The ἵνα clause here is used as the subject of συμφέρει (cf. B214), "it is
better for you that . . ."
R1018 The condition expressed by εἰ σκανδαλίζει is considered as a present
reality (cf. Mark 9:43-47), "since . . . "
T32 Note the comparison here without ἤ (καὶ μή means "rather than that"--BD
442[1]).
T42 The simple personal pronoun occurs in the phrase ἀπὸ σοῦ instead of a reflexive pronoun, "from yourself."

31 MT186 At first sight this verse raises some difficulty, but ἀπολύσῃ denotes not
so much the carrying into effect as the determination to do.

32 M103 Πᾶς ὁ . . . αὐτοῦ means "anyone who divorces his wife" (cf. the relative
clause).
T107 Part of this verse should be translated "he makes his wife an adulteress
who divorces her" (i.e., "has already divorced," the present participle ἀπολύων
refers to action antecedent to that of the main verb).

34 R1094 The negative aorist infinitive μὴ ὀμόσαι is used in an indirect command,
"but I say to you not to swear at all."
TGr31 Jesus uses the aorist tense to prohibit swearing by heaven, etc. For
some reason, his listeners may already have renounced oath-swearing (through
the teaching of John the Baptist) and his commandment was that they should never
in the future resume the practice.
BD445(1) The continuation of negatives in this context has the resultant meaning
"not at all . . . (in particular) not . . . not . . ." (i.e., μήτε is equivalent
to μηδέ here).

35 R594 After ὀμόσαι, εἰς with the accusative has the sense of a dative ("by"--T255)

37 M42 The genitive is used to express comparison in τὸ δὲ περισσὸν τούτων, with
the meaning "anything more than these" (i.e., "in excess of").

38 R573 In ὀφθαλμὸν ἀντὶ ὀφθαλμοῦ there is exact equivalence ("eye for eye").

39 T77 The aorist imperative στρέψον is used for a precept valid until the coming
of Christ (cf. BD337[2]; cf. also in vv. 40 and 42).

42 R809 The aorist infinitive δανίσασθαι means "to have money lent" (i.e., "to
    borrow").
    R855 Note the distinction between the tenses in τῷ αἰτοῦντι . . . δός ("give
    to him that is asking"; the aorist imperative refers to a definite occasion
    and person--T76).

43 R646 The adverb πλησίον is used with the article as a substantive, meaning
    "neighbor."
    R943 The future indicative ἀγαπήσεις and the present imperative ἀγαπᾶτε (v. 44)
    appear to be equivalent (cf. BD362).

44 T86 The Old Testament quotations often use the future to express commands (cf.
    v. 43), but Jesus' own commands employ the imperative.

45 R801 The verb ἀνατέλλει is strictly causative ("cause to rise"--T53; parallel
    to "cause to rain"--BD309[1]).

46 R1181 In καὶ οἱ τελῶναι and καὶ οἱ ἐθνικοί, the καί has an ascensive sense,
    "even."
    M122 The final question in this verse should be translated, "Do not even the
    tax collectors do as much" (i.e., "the same thing"--αὐτό).

47 MT186 The aorist subjunctive has the sense of a future perfect, "if you have
    only saluted" (a practical turn is given by the pointed question in the change
    from aorist to present--R1019).

                              MATTHEW 6

1   R1003 Πρὸς τό with the infinitive expresses the notion of purpose here ("in
    order to be seen by them"--M140).
    R1172 Μήγε is an intensive compound negative (γε occurs in this context simply
    to strengthen the other words--M164).
    H471 In vv. 1ff., δικαιοσύνην ποιεῖν means "to give alms" (semitic).

2   R687 In this verse σοῦ is used instead of a reflexive pronoun (cf. T42), "before
    yourself."
    R853 The aorist prohibition μὴ σαλπίσῃς means "don't begin to sound" ("on no
    account sound a trumpet before you when you do alms"--TGr32).
    R866 In vv. 2, 5, and 16, the combination of the aoristic present and the per-
    fective use of ἀπό (in ἀπέχουσι) makes the description very vivid. "The hypo-
    crites have as it were their money down, as soon as their trumpet has sounded."
    MT186 The present tense in ὅταν ποιῇς ἐλεημοσύνην has a durative sense, "when-
    ever you are for doing alms."

4   T334 Καί appears to have the meaning "for" (cf. Dan 10:17; a consecutive usage,
    semitic--H422).

5   R552 Certain grammarians conceive that in φιλοῦσιν . . . προσεύχεσθαι, we may
    translate "gladly pray." But what advantage has this over "love to pray," "are
    fond of praying?"
    R874 Ἔσεσθε is used as a volitive future (cf. 1:21), "you shall be."

                              18

R963 The causal sentence with ὅτι is paratactic (co-ordinate; "and when you pray, you shall not be as the hypocrites; because they love to stand and pray in the synagogues and in the corners of the streets [cf. v. 16, where in a closely similar sentence, γάρ is used instead of ὅτι]--B231; cf. Luke 11:32).

6   R1186 Notice the contrast indicated by σὺ δέ.
    T77 The aorist imperative εἴσελθε is used for a precept valid until the coming of Christ (cf. 5:39).

7   R589 The preposition ἐν gives the occasion here (i.e., causal; "by [means of] their many words"--M77; "because of"--T253). [Ed. There is a very fine line between the instrumental and causal usage of ἐν, and they often blend into one, as in this occurrence.]

9   R459 Notice that the nominative is in apposition with the vocative here (cf. T35), "our father, the one in heaven."
    BD277(1) Ὑμεῖς occurs with the imperative here with some degree of emphasis (in contrast to the Gentiles).

10 R1181 In its occurrence here καί means "just so" (or "even so").
    T75 The aorist imperative ἐλθέτω has the sense "continue to come" (the Kingdom being present already as a grain of seed).

11 BD123(1) The most plausible explanation for ἐπιούσιος is the assumption that there is a substantivization of ἐπὶ τὴν οὖσαν (supply ἡμέραν), meaning "(determined) for the day in question."
    M135 Luke has the present imperative δίδου (11:3), whereas Matthew uses the aorist δός because σήμερον is added, "give us this day."

12 T37 The pronoun ἡμεῖς has a definite emphasis here.
    BD453(2) Ὡς has a causal sense here (cf. R963), "as" or "because."

13 R653 Τοῦ πονηροῦ does not refer to evil in general, but διάβολος is apparently meant (i.e., "the evil one").

16 B457 The participle νηστεύοντες is used as the subject of the verb φανῶσιν (not only they, but their fasting, is to be seen; cf. v. 18).

17 T37 The pronoun σύ has emphasis here.

18 R589 The prepositional phrase with ἐν has the notion of manner, "who sees secretly."
    BD414(3) The participle νηστεύων is an addition to the subject of the verb (cf. v. 17), "that you may not be seen by men fasting."

19 R853 The present tense used in the prohibition μὴ θησαυρίζετε indicates that they were already storing treasure on earth.

22 R768 When the article occurs with the subject and predicate nominative, both are definite, treated as identical, one and the same, and interchangeable, as here (the predicate nominative [ὀφθαλμός] has the article because it is a notable instance, "the eye alone is the light of the body"--T183).

24   R573   The compound verb ἀνθέξεται has an interesting meaning, "cleave to," "cling to," "hold one's self face to face with."

25   R539   Τῇ ψυχῇ is used as a dative of advantage, "for your life."
      R853   The present prohibition μὴ μεριμνᾶτε implies that they already were anxious.

26   R581   Actually the compound verb διαφέρω means "bear apart," "differ."
      BD246   The comparative is heightened by μᾶλλον, "of more value."

27   R1128   In the participle μεριμνῶν the notion of manner shades off into means, "by being anxious" (cf. B443: it may mean either "by worrying" or "even if he does worry" [conditional]--MT230). [Ed. The participle appears to be describing the means by which benefit is not gained.]

28   T76   The aorist imperative καταμάθετε refers to a command now, once and for all, to look at the lilies, probably during a walk in the fields.

29   R807   Περιεβάλετο is apparently used as a direct middle, "clothe himself."

30   T115   The conditional clause with εἰ and the indicative here has the meaning "since he clothes."

32   R403   Usually a neuter plural noun in the New Testament that has a personal or collective meaning has a plural verb (ἔθνη, "the Gentiles," cf. T313).
      R419   In πάντα ταῦτα the first word carries the emphasis (cf. 4:9 and Luke 12: 30), "all these."

34   TGr30   Jesus uses the aorist tense in the prohibition here because he brings this particular discussion to a close (cf. R853), and his words refer to the future. At this point his presence and his discourse may have calmed their fears, and he tells them not to let this occur in the future. "Do not ever begin to be anxious again. Tomorrow will look after itself."

MATTHEW 7

1   R890   The present prohibition μὴ κρίνετε is used to forbid an action already taking place, "stop judging."

2   R590   The preposition ἐν has an instrumental sense here, "with" or "by."

3   R685   The possessive pronoun (τῷ σῷ) occurs where a reflexive pronoun may have been used (the possessive adjective has a reflexive sense--T191), "your own."

4   R931   In the first person singular, the New Testament always has ἄφες or δεῦρο with the hortatory subjunctive (cf. Luke 6:42; "allow me"--MT176).

5   R1088   The infinitive ἐκβαλεῖν has the notion of purpose, "to take out."

6   R1185   Μηδέ occurs here with a continuative sense (continuing the negation), "and do not."

TGr32   The aorist tense is used in a categorical prohibition, "on no account give dogs."
BD111(3)   The noun κύνες is used to designate profane men.

11   R1053   The construction with the infinitive in οἴδατε διδόναι means "you know how to give."
R1129   The context calls for the adversative idea (i.e., concessive participle) in πονηροὶ ὄντες (cf. T157), "although being evil."

12   R427   In this verse ὅσα ἐὰν θέλητε is an adjective sentence and describes πάντα, with the resultant meaning "all things, whatever you desire."
T107   The present tense is interesting in this verse: the main verb means "do so to them" and the relative clause means "what you wish them to do to you" (i.e., at the time when you are doing it to them).

13   B124   The present participle οἱ εἰσερχόμενοι has a generic sense referring to a distinct class of people (cf. οἱ εὑρίσκοντες in v. 14), "those that are entering through it."

14   BD299(4)   Τί has an adverbial sense, "how" (the best text includes ὅτι with a causal sense--R730). [Ed.   The text that includes τί has the greatest manuscript support. The resultant meaning seems to be "how straight is the gate!"]

15   R589   The preposition ἐν has the idea of accompanying circumstance, "with."

17   M8   The present tense is used here with a gnomic sense (introducing a maxim or generalization), "a good tree [always] bears good fruit" (cf. B12).

20   R1148   The particle ἄρα γε has a climactic force here (clearly illative--R1190; cf. 6:1), "as a result."

21   R752   Οὐ merely negates πᾶς here. Jesus did not mean to say that no one who thus addressed him could enter the kingdom of heaven. He merely said that not every one would (the harshness of οὐ πᾶς is mitigated by the following positive clause with ἀλλά containing the main point of the sentence--T196).

23   MT174   The verb ἀποχωρεῖτε   may have a quasi-ingressive sense even in the present tense, "depart."
H469   In its occurrence here ὅτι appears to have the meaning "verily."

24   R727   Πᾶς . . . ὅστις is indefinite, "everyone who hears."

25   BD202   In the compound verb προσπίπτω, πρός has a very literal sense, "fall down before."

26   T151   Πᾶς ὁ ἀκούων means "any hearer."

28   R532   The preposition ἐπί has a causal sense here, "at," or "because of his teaching."

MATTHEW 8.

2   R1018 The present verb in ἐὰν θέλῃς is future in concept (a lively sense of
    present need is evident--R1019; "if you wish [but in modesty I leave that open]"
    --BD372[1a]).
    T65 The imperfect verb προσεκύνει means "request."

4   R595 The preposition εἰς in this verse has the notion of purpose, "for."
    R854 The imperative ὅρα is used almost like a particle adding emphasis to the
    statement, "see that you do not speak to anyone."

8   R653 The neuter adjective μόνον has an adverbial usage here, meaning "only"
    (contrast μόνος in 14:23).
    R681 Note the position of μοῦ here (cf. T189; unemphatic [enclitic] pronouns
    tend to be placed as near the beginning of the sentence as possible--BD473[1]).
    M65 The preposition ὑπό is used with the accusative in this verse to signify a
    motion beneath, "I am not worthy that you should come under my roof."
    BD442(2) Καί in the latter part of this verse has a consecutive sense, "then."

9   BD336(1) The aorist imperative πορεύθητι means "be off"; whereas the present
    imperative ἔρχου could mean "come with me" or "come back."

10 R844 Εὗρον should be translated "I have found" (cf. 5:21).

11 R357 The future passive verb ἀνακλιθήσομαι occurs without the passive sense
    (it is possible to find a passive sense here--R819). [Ed. Generally in the
    New Testament the passive form of this verb simply means "lie down," or "re-
    cline at a meal," without any passive notion. This apparently is the meaning
    of the verb here (cf. 14:19 and Mark 6:39).]
    T26 The nouns for direction generally have the plural in Biblical Greek, as
    ἀνατολῶν and δυσμῶν here, "east" and "west."

12 T29 The comparative adjective ἐξώτερος is used for a true superlative, "far-
    thest."
    T173 In the latter part of this verse, the article ὁ has the notion "that mem-
    orable" or "greatest of all."

16 R533 Λόγῳ is used as a dative of means, "with a word."
    R653 The noun ὥρα is to be supplied with ὀψίας, "late hour."

17 R1428 The participle λέγοντος simply means "when saying."
    T40 The pronoun αὐτός has a degree of emphasis here, "he himself carried."

19 R674 Εἷς is used as an indefinite article, "a scribe" (we must not follow Meyer
    [in location] in denying that εἷς is ever used in the New Testament in the
    sense of τις: it is dangerous to import exegetical subtleties into the New Tes-
    tament against the known history of the koine Greek--MT97; cf. M125).

20 R757 The article τοῦ in ὁ υἱὸς τοῦ ἀνθρώπου is used in a representative sense
    for the whole class, thus Jesus calls himself the Son of Mankind.

21 T334 Καί in this verse has a final sense (consecutive--H422). [Ed. On occasion
     the Jewish mind did not distinguish between purpose and result (cf. Rom. 1:20).
     Καί with the infinitive may introduce the idea of conceived result, but not ac-
     tual result.]

24 R679 There is strong emphasis evident in the pronoun αὐτός here.
     R883 Notice the narrative imperfect ἐκάθευδεν ("he kept on sleeping until final-
     ly ἤγειραν αὐτόν"--T66).

25 R941 The imperative σῶσον has the notion of appeal rather than command.
     MT114 The compound verb ἀπολλύμεθα has the sense of an inevitable doom, under
     the visible conditions, although the subsequent story indicates that it was
     averted.

27 T318 Ὅτι has an almost consecutive sense here, "so that."
     BD444(3) In this verse καὶ . . . καί means "even . . . and."

28 M141 Ὥστε with the infinitive has a consecutive sense (indicating the result;
     it may be potential rather than actual).
     BD291(3) The pronoun ἐκείνης designates something previously mentioned; in this
     instance the reference is to the dwelling place of the demoniacs, because the
     road itself had not yet been mentioned.

29 M74 The temporal phrase πρὸ καιροῦ actually means "too soon."
     TGr43 The context requires the question in this verse to have the meaning, "why
     are you troubling us?"

31 R948 The imperative ἀπόστειλον has the notion of entreaty ("send us") and
     ὑπάγετε (v. 32) denotes permission ("Go," cf. B182).
     B256 The general supposition εἰ ἐκβάλλεις ἡμᾶς has a futuristic reference, "if
     you cast us out."

32 R570 Κατά is used with the ablative genitive here, "down from the cliff" ("down
     along"--M60; the preposition has a local sense "over and down"--BD225). [Ed.
     Actually all of these explanations are similar. Within the context this prepo-
     sition is used with a genitive of place, "they rushed down (from) the bank."]

34 R995 Ὅπως introduces an indirect question after the verb παρεκάλεσαν, "they
     begged him to."
     M70 The preposition εἰς has a final-consecutive sense here, "with a view to,"
     or "resulting in" (cf. 25:1).

                              MATTHEW 9

1   R691 Ἰδίαν is used as a reflexive pronoun, "his own city" (there is definite
     emphasis here--R692; cf. MT90).

2   T64 The present verb ἀφίενται has a punctiliar sense, herewith "sins receive
     forgiveness."

5   R1190 The particle γάρ denotes a degree of scorn here (cf. John 7:41).

8 R409   In this verse there is a double sense in δόντα, for Jesus had the ἐξουσίαν
in a way not true of ἀνθρώποις who received the benefit of it.

13 R1429   The first οὐ in this verse negates the implied θέλω, "I desire mercy and
not sacrifice."

15 T208   Υἱός is used figuratively with a noun in the genitive to express a certain
quality, "the bridegroom's friends."

17 R1025   Εἰ δε μήγε is such a fixed phrase that it occurs even when the preceding
sentence is negative, having the meaning "otherwise."

18 T65   The imperfect verb προσεκύνει means "request" (cf. 8:2).
T330   Before the command here, ἀλλά should be translated as an interjection,
"well" (cf. Mark 9:22).

20 B131   The present participle αἱμορροῦσα refers to a past action still in progress,
"a woman who had been bleeding for twelve years."

21 TGr33   When Jesus spoke to the hemorrhage victim about her present health, he
used the perfect tense deliberately. He said, in effect, "You have received
healing and are now in perfect health. Your faith has accomplished this."
Then, the tense becomes aorist as the evangelist looks back upon the event and
records it historically. "At that very moment the woman did receive healing."

25 B53   The aorist verb ἐξεβλήθη should be translated as a pluperfect (it is antecedent to another aorist verb), "when the crowd had been put outside."

29 R609   The preposition κατά is used to introduce a standard or rule of measure.

34 M77   Ἐν has an instrumental sense here, "by means of the prince of the demons"
(cf. BD219[1]).

35 BD150   The compound verb περιάγω means "to go about in an area."

36 M62f.   Περί has a metaphorical sense in the clause ἐσπλαγχνίσθη περὶ αὐτῶν,
meaning "he was moved with compassion for them."

38 R995   Ὅπως introduces an indirect question after the verb δεήθητε (cf. 8:34 and
T106), "pray that."

MATTHEW 10

1 R500   Ἐξουσίαν with the genitive here means "authority over."
R809   The middle participle προσκαλεσάμενος portrays Jesus as calling the disciples to himself.
R1089   Ὥστε with the infinitive in this verse has the notion of purpose, meaning
"so as," not "so that" (cf. M140 and T136; it denotes tendency or conceived result thought of as such, "to cast them out"--B371). [Ed. Burton's suggestion
is similar to the previous comment.]

2   R657 Πρῶτος is used as an adjective here, referring to the fact that first in
     the list is Simon.

4   R859 The articular aorist participle ὁ παραδούς refers to an act past with ref-
     erence to the time of writing, although future with reference to the action of
     the principal verb (cf. B142; "Judas who was to betray him"--T80).

5   R500 In ὁδὸς ἐθνῶν the genitive has an objective sense, "the way to the Gen-
     tiles."

6   R881 The perfect participle ἀπολωλότα is used as a present in the New Testament,
     "the lost sheep."

7   H469 In this context ὅτι appears to have the idea of assertion, "verily" (cf.
     7:25).

8   R488 Δωρεάν is used as an adverbial accusative, "freely" or "as a gift."

9   R810 Κτήσησθε means "provide for yourselves (procure)."
     MT125 The aorist prohibition μὴ κτήσησθε would be answered with "we will avoid
     doing so."

13   R948 A notion of permission is apparent in the imperative here, "let your peace
     come upon it."

14   TGr89 The accusative with ἀκούσῃ here indicates that it is not enough that the
     householders merely hear the apostles, but they must take heed and understand.

18   R1185 Δὲ καί means "and also."

19   BD368 The subject of δοθήσεται is actually "to know."

21   R403 The neuter plural subject τέκνα has a plural verb because τέκνα has a per-
     sonal sense (cf. 6:32).

23   R776 Εἰς τὴν ἑτέραν is an incorrect way of saying "the next."

24   R632 In this verse the preposition ὑπέρ has the metaphorical sense of "above" or
     "over."

25   B214 The ἵνα clause is used as the subject of the impersonal word ἀρκετόν, "it
     is enough . . . that."

26   T77 In this verse we would expect the present tense (rather than the aorist),
     since the context requires the translation "stop fearing."

28   R473 Φοβηθῆτε ἀπό imitates the Hebrew idiom, which is best translated as "be
     afraid of" (cf. H460).
     BD444(3) Καὶ ψυχὴν καὶ σῶμα means "even body and soul."

29   R751 Ἕν . . . οὐ is distinctly emphatic, "not one."
     M39 The genitive ἀσσαρίου with the verb of selling means "for an assarion."
     M82 Ἄνευ with the genitive perhaps means "without the cognizance" or "permis-
     sion of."

31 R853 The present prohibition μὴ φοβεῖσθε means "quit being afraid."

32 R957 Ὅστις is indefinite in vv. 32f. (derived from the sense of τις), "any one."
R588 The use of ἐν after ὁμολογέω is apparently due to a literal translation of the Aramaic (cf. MT104; it simply means "to acknowledge [someone]"--M183).

35 R581 The compound verb διχάζω means "set at variance (cleave asunder)."
M143f. The infinitive in ἦλθον γὰρ διχάσαι is perfectly represented by the plain infinitive in English, and is equally ambiguous: is it a grim hyperbole, as though it meant "I came [in order] to . . ?" In any case its basic, literal meaning actually must be consecutive (i.e., expressing the result).

37 R633 The preposition ὑπέρ has the comparative sense "more than."

41 M79 The preposition εἰς has a causal sense here, "because he is a prophet" (ὄνομα brings out the notion that one has the name or character of prophet-- R649).

MATTHEW 11

1 B459 The participle διατάσσων is used as the object of the verb ἐτέλεσεν, "when Jesus had finished directing his disciples."
TGr150 The antecedent of the pronoun αὐτῶν is omitted, "their cities" (i.e., in someone else's cities).

2 BD420(2) Πέμψας εἶπεν here means "he sent word."

3 T63 The present participle ὁ ἐρχόμενος has a futuristic sense, "the Messiah."

6 T253 The preposition ἐν has a causal sense in this verse, "at" or "because of me."

7 R1088 The infinitives θεάσασθαι and ἰδεῖν in vv. 7f. have the sense of purpose (cf. T134), "to behold . . . to see."

9 R1150 Ναί introduces the clause with the meaning "yea" or "verily."

10 BD378 The future relative clause here has a final sense (the messenger is sent for the purpose of preparing the way).

11 T29 The comparative adjective μικρότερος is used as a true superlative here (this adjective means "younger" [possibly referring to Jesus?]--BD61[2]). [Ed. Christ's primary concern was not to get the people to think highly of himself, but to gain a greater appreciation of the kingdom. Consequently, the adjective μικρότερος refers to any one in the kingdom with the resultant superlative sense (cf. the similar use of μικρότερος in 13:32 and Luke 9:48).]

12 TGr59f. Although the verb βιάζεται is generally deponent, it has a passive sense here, "The kingdom suffereth violence."

16 T86 Note the deliberative future ὁμοιώσω meaning "am I to compare?"

19 T258 The preposition ἀπό has a causal sense here (cf. H461).

20 M95 In this verse αἱ πλεῖσται δυνάμεις αὐτοῦ should, strictly, mean "his very
    great miracles" (i.e., an elative superlative; cf. R670; actually an intensi-
    fying superlative), but the context makes it probable that the meaning is "the
    majority of his miracles" -- as though it were αἱ πλεῖσται τῶν δυναμένων αὐτοῦ,
    with πλεῖσται in a pronominal position (the adjective here is used as an elative
    superlative, thus Jesus upbraids the cities in which "his very many mighty works"
    were performed--TGr34; "numerous"--BD245[1]). [Ed. Generally in the New
    Testament, the plural of πλεῖστος has the sense of "most of" or "the majority
    of," as the sense appears to be in this verse (cf. Acts 27:12).]

21 B142 The articular aorist participle αἱ γενόμεναι refers to an event past with
    reference to the time of writing, but future with reference to the action of
    the principal verb (cf. 10:4), "which were done in you."

22 R646 Πλήν is used as an adversative conjunction, "but."

23 T37 The pronoun σύ occurs here without much emphasis.

25 MT136 The aorist verbs here have the sense of the perfect, "thou has hid . . .
    thou has revealed."

27 R682 Emphasis may be present even though the short form of the pronoun is used
    (μου).
    T107 The latter part of this verse should be translated "to whom the Son has
    been willing (from time to time, present) to reveal Him."

28 R235 In πρὸς με, the pronoun "me" is emphatic (cf. 3:14).
    R873 The future verb ἀναπαύσω may have a predictive ("shall . . .") or volitive
    sense ("will . . ."; solemnly predictive--B65). [Ed. Apparently this verb has
    a predictive sense dependent upon the previous command, "I will give you rest"
    (Robertson's rendering of a volitive is inappropriate).]

29 R687 The personal pronoun in ἐξ' ὑμᾶς is used as a reflexive pronoun, "upon
    yourself."

MATTHEW 12

1 T27 The plural σάββασιν simply means "sabbath" in vv. 1 and 5.

3 R844 To translate the aorist verb ἀνέγνωτε the English requires a perfect sense,
    "Have you not read?"

4 R611 The phrase τοῖς μετ' αὐτοῦ refers to one's attendants or followers (com-
    panions, cf. οἱ μετ' αὐτοῦ in v. 3).
    R1032 Πῶς is used in an indirect question here, "how he entered" (instead of
    ὅτι; cf. Mark 2:26).
    M27 In ὃ οὐκ ἐξον ἦν αὐτῷ φαγεῖν, there seems to be a mixed construction -- the

relative ὅ, which refers to the eating of the shewbread, being the subject of
ἐξον ἦν, and then φαγεῖν appearing as a reiterated subject, as though the sentence had begun with ἀλλά or καίπερ instead of ὅ (εἰ μή is used for ἀλλά--H468).

6   T21   Μεῖζον appears to mean "something greater."

7   R904   Present perfect verbs that had come to be mere present verbs through accent
on the durative idea and loss of emphasis on the aoristic notion (punctiliar)
are virtual imperfects when used in the pluperfect (so ἐγνώκειτε, "if you had
known"; cf. MT148).

10   R1176   Εἰ is used to introduce a direct question here, "is it lawful . . ?"
T195   In this verse ἄνθρωπος is used as a substitute for τις, "a certain one."

12   R292   Πόσος is used as a direct interrogative in a quantitative sentence, with
the meaning "how much?"
M144   Ὥστε is used as an inferential particle (as if it were ὥς τε), meaning
"and so, accordingly" (cf. 19:6; "therefore"--R999).

14   B207   Ὅπως is used in an object clause with the meaning "that" (similar to an
indirect deliberative question).

17   R1428   The participle λέγοντος simply means "when saying" (cf. 8:17).

18   B55   The aorist verb εὐδόκησεν apparently refers to past time (cf. 3:17; the
Hebrew perfect is represented by the Greek aorist--H458).
T43   Ἡ ψυχή μου is equivalent to ἐγὼ αὐτός, "I myself."

21   T238   The dative occurs with ἐλπίζω here with the resultant meaning "to hope in"
(cf. Isa. 42:4).

24   BD219(1)   Ἐν has an instrumental sense, "by means of" (cf. "with"--R590).
T152   The attributive participle must be distinguished from a simple apposition.
Thus, οἱ δὲ Φαρισαῖοι ἀκούσαντες does not mean "the Pharisees who heard," but
"when they heard." [Ed. Actually this is not an attributive participle but
an adverbial one. Turner's translation is consistent with this observation.]

25   R1116   The perfect participle εἰδώς has a linear notion similar to the present
tense, "knowing."

26   R602   Ἐπί has the notion of hostility, "against" (cf. v. 25).
R1008   In εἰ ὁ . . . ἐμερίσθη there is a change of tense in the apodosis. "He
was already divided against himself, in that case, before he casts himself out."
But the aorist tense may be merely due to a quick change of viewpoint as accomplished (timeless aorist in reality). This point is quite vivid in v. 28.

27   R1008   Εἰ with the indicative in this verse refers to an assumption which is
untrue in fact, although assumed to be true by Jesus for the sake of argument.

30   R611   The notion of fellowship in the preposition μετά has developed into the
idea of followers or partisans in this verse.

31   R494   Ἡ τοῦ πνεύματος βλασφημία actually means "the Spirit-blasphemy." From

the context we know that it is blasphemy against the Spirit, although the genitive alone does not mean "against."

32 R1165 The negative οὐ is amplified here by οὔτε . . . οὔτε (emphasizing their condemnation).

36 R436 Observe how πᾶν ῥῆμα is carried on by περὶ αὐτοῦ (a suspended subject; either πᾶν ῥῆμα ἀργόν is an unusual usage of the nominative or it is an accusative attracted to the pronoun ὅ--M30). [Ed. It is more probable to consider it as an accusative attracted to the pronoun ὅ, and together it is the direct object of λαλήσουσιν (cf. Robertson's explanation).]

38 R579 The preposition ἀπό has a sense similar to ὑπό, "by."

39 T214 The appositional genitive occurs in the phrase τὸ σημεῖον Ἰωνᾶ, with the meaning "the sign which was Jonah" (cf. TGr60).

41 R593 The preposition εἰς here has the sense of ἐν. It is absurd to take εἰς as meaning "into," "unto" or even "to" (similar to ἐν, "at the preaching"--M204; εἰς has a causal sense; they repented because of the preaching of Jonah--T255). [Ed. The rendering "to repent at the preaching" is similar to a causal translation (cf. Luke 11:32 and Rom. 4:20).]

42 BD253(5) The anarthrous νότου refers to a definite land in the south (it is almost a proper name here).

44 T319 The participle has a conditional sense. Thus καὶ ἐλθὸν εὑρίσκει means "if he comes and finds."

45 R749 The notion of difference is present in ἕτερα.
    T43 The reflexive pronoun ἑαυτοῦ is not dependent on the verb, "more evil than himself."

50 R679 Αὐτός μου ἀδελφός is resumptive, referring to ὅστις, and is distinctly emphatic, "my brother himself" (cf. T41).

                              MATTHEW 13

1   M51 The preposition παρά generally designates movement to a position alongside of, thus the latter part of this verse should be translated "Jesus left the house and sat by the lake."

2   T154 Ἐμβάντα is used as a modal-temporal participle, but with no stress on the temporal relationship ("when he had entered, he sat down"--MT230).

3   R764 The articular participle ὁ σπείρων has a representative sense, "the sower" (actually any sower that sows the word).
    R1088 The infinitive τοῦ σπείρειν portrays the notion of purpose (cf. T141).

4   R747 The construction ἂ μὲν . . . ἄλλα δέ means "some . . . others."
    M77 The expression ἐν τῷ σπείρειν has a temporal sense, "while he was sowing."

5   BD364(3) In this verse καί denotes a consecutive sense, "with the result that."

8   R838 In ἔπεσεν . . . καὶ ἐδίδου, the aorist lifts the curtain, whereas the im-
    perfect continues the play.

12 R957 The pronoun ὅστις has an indefinite sense, "whoever."
    T292 The future verb περισσευθήσεται apparently has a passive impersonal sense
    (not "he" but "it shall be made to abound"), because of the parallel passive
    verb.

13 BD369(2) The particle ὅτι is causal in this context.

14 R539 Αὐτοῖς is used as a dative of disadvantage, "for them."
    R1110 Both ἀκοῇ ἀκούσετε and βλέποντες βλέψετε are attempts to translate the
    Hebrew infinitive absolute (the infinitive absolute was used to strengthen the
    verbal idea), "you shall indeed hear . . ."
    B167 The double negatives with the aorist subjunctives συνῆτε and ἴδητε are
    probably to be understood as prohibitory (as in the Hebrew quotation of Isa.
    6:9), and not as emphatically predictive, "do not understand and do not per-
    ceive." [Ed. This is a direct quote from the LXX.]

15 R844 The aorist verbs ἐπαχύνθη, ἤκουσαν and ἐκάμμυσαν have a perfect sense. Con-
    sequently the English translation would employ "have."
    R1173 In this verse καί is used to continue the negation ("nor") introduced by
    μήποτε (with the subjunctive, μήποτε presents the notion of negative purpose
    --B199).

18 R501 Τοῦ σπείραντος is used as an objective genitive, "the parable about the
    sower."

21 R623 The compound πρόσκαιρος has the meaning "for a time."

23 R1149 In this context, the particle δή occurs in a relative clause, "who is
    just the man who bears fruit" (ὅς δή means "whoever"--T333; it means "he is
    just the man who"--BD451[4]). [Ed. The emphatic particle δή does not have the
    indefinite sense that Turner ascribes to it. Actually, it denotes that the
    statement is definitely established, "who indeed bears fruit." This is similar
    to the explanations presented by Robertson and Blass and Debrunner.]

24 T179 The prepositional phrase ἐν τῷ ἀγρῷ has the article because a definite
    field is referred to.

25 R571 Together ἀνὰ μέσον have the idea of "between."
    M77 The clause ἐν τῷ καθεύδειν τοὺς ἀνθρώπους has a temporal sense, "while the
    men were sleeping."

26 T72 The aorist verb ἐποίησεν may have an ingressive sense, "began to make grain."

27 R1157 In the question here οὐχί is slightly more emphatic than οὐ would have
    been (the point is that the servants definitely knew that good seed had been
    sown).

28 M139 θέλεις . . . συλλέξωμεν αὐτά means "do you want us to . . . collect them?"

T195   In this verse ἄνθρωπος is used as a substitute for τις, with an indefinite sense, "an enemy" or "a certain enemy."

29   M81   This verse contains the only occurrence of ἅμα used in the New Testament as a preposition, meaning "simultaneously with."

31   R836   The redundant expression λαβὼν ἔσπειρεν means "took and sowed" (the occurrence of the participle is justified because it has a slight temporal sense--T154).

32   R1205   The figure of speech hyperbole occurs in this verse (i.e., **exaggeration** for effect, cf. John 21:25).

33   B330   Ἕως οὗ is in effect a compound conjunction, having the same force as the simple ἕως, "while" (cf. 5:25).

35   R1106   Διὰ τοῦ προφήτου λέγοντος is apparently an example of an articular attributive participle, "through the prophet who says," since the Greeks did not always place the attributive participle between the article and the substantive (the participle may simply mean "when saying"--R1428). [Ed. When the noun has the article and the participle does not, the participle is almost always adverbial. There has to be a very strong reason in the context for translating the participle any other way in such a construction. Consequently, Robertson's latter suggestion is preferable.]
B222   Ὅπως πληρωθῇ denotes the notion of pure purpose (cf. 1:22).

38   R698   The resumptive pronoun οὗτοι differs in number and gender from σπέρμα (the masculine gender refers to people).
T208   Figuratively υἱός is used with a noun in the genitive in order to express a certain quality, "men of the kingdom . . . men of evil."

41   R598   The preposition ἐκ in this verse has the idea of "out from among." Just as cockle grows in among the wheat in the same field, the two kingdoms co-exist in the same sphere (the world).

44   R580   The preposition ἀπό has a causal idea (cf. H461).
R837   The verbs ἔκρυψεν (in v. 44), ἠγόρασεν (in v. 46) and συνέλεξαν and ἔβαλον (in v. 48) are used as gnomic aorists, referring to a customary or known truth (these aorists may simply be narrative aorists--M13). [Ed. The fact that these aorists are timeless in nature does not necessarily prove that they are gnomic, as Robertson assumes. On the contrary, they appear to be simple narrative (historical) aorists, merely stating the events of the narrative.]
R868   The historical present often occurs in parables (as ὑπάγει, πωλεῖ, ἔχει and ἀγοράζει in this verse; simply relaying the narrative).
BD255(1)   In ἐν τῷ ἀγρῷ the article is incorrect (D and Chrysostom omit τῷ), where the rendering "a field" is to be understood. [Ed. On occasion Blass uses an unusual method of determining the original text. The manuscript that omits the article has very weak textual support, consequently it is necessary to explain its usage here. The article apparently is generic, indicating the field, as the locality, which is distinct from other places where treasures were placed.]

45   T195   Ἀνθρώπῳ is used as a substitute for τινί, referring to an indefinite person (cf. v. 28 and H433).

31

46 R900 The dramatic historical perfect πέπρακεν occurs in a vivid parable (the
        participle and verb are used together with the meaning "he has gone and sold"
        --R1110; there is no aorist of the same root of this verb, but still there may
        be a point in the use of the perfect tense--BD344).

48 T14 The adjectives τὰ καλά and τὰ σαπρά are used substantivally with the noun
        "fish" implied.

52 R656 Οἰκοδεσπότῃ is used in apposition to the noun ἀνθρώπῳ (ἀνθρώπῳ is used as
        a substitute for τινί, cf. v. 45--T195; cf. H433). [Ed. Ἀνθρώπῳ is used as
        a substitute for τινί in apposition to οἰκοδεσπότῃ, "a householder."]
        H400 Μαθητεύομαι is used as a deponent verb, meaning "to be a disciple."

54 R1091 Ὥστε with the infinitive portrays actual result in this verse, "so that
        they were astonished."

55 R757 The use of the article in ὁ τοῦ τέκτονος υἱός denotes that he is the son
        of the (well known to us) carpenter.

56 M52 The preposition πρός denotes position here, "all with us."

57 H464 The prepositional phrase ἐν αὐτῷ is used in place of a simple dative,
        "they were offended at him" (this is similar to a causal clause).

                                  MATTHEW 14

2 R694 In this verse, the article αἱ is nearly equivalent to a demonstrative
        pronoun meaning "these."

3 R840 The aorist verbs ἔδησεν and ἀπέθετο refer to action which is antecedent
        in time to that of ἤκουσεν (in v. 1) and εἶπεν (in v. 2), but the story of the
        previous imprisonment and death of John is introduced by γάρ in a reminiscent
        manner (the aorists in this verse are similar to a pluperfect, "for Herod
        having laid hold on John had bound him"--B48; cf. M16).

4 B29 The imperfect verb ἔλεγεν refers to an action which precedes an event al-
        ready mentioned and is best translated into English by a pluperfect, "for John
        had been saying to him."

5 R1129 The participle θέλων has a concessive sense, "although he desired."
        BD157 Ὡς occurs with a predicate accusative with εἶχον, meaning "they regarded
        him as a prophet."

6 M44f. The dative expression γενεσίοις δὲ γενομένοις is equivalent to a genitive
        absolute, with the resultant meaning "when his birthday celebrations had come."

7 R963 Ὅθεν has a causal sense in the context here.
        R1047 The aorist infinitive δοῦναι of indirect discourse is used to represent
        the future verb δώσω in the direct discourse(cf. Mark 6:23; the aorist infini-
        tive preserves the aktionsart (punctiliar) but abandons the future time ele-
        ment--BD350).
        M61 The prepositional phrase μεθ᾽ ὅρκου has the idea of association, "with an
        oath."

8   R866 Φησίν is used as an aoristic present, "she said," referring to a punctil-
    iar action which takes place at the moment of speaking (cf. T64).

9   R1129 The participle λυπηθείς portrays a concessive sense, "although the king
    was grieved" (cf. B437).
    T26 The idiomatic plural τοὺς ὅρκους simply means "the oath," but the plural
    is used to emphasize the individual's action.
    BD442(16) The second καί in this verse may be used in place of a dependent
    genitive, "because of the oath taken before his guests."

13 R609 Κατ' ἰδίαν is used with an adverbial sense, meaning "privately."

14 T40 Αὐτοῖς varies from ὄχλον in number and gender because of the sense implied
    (the masculine plural refers to the individual people of the crowd).

15 R613 Ἡ ὥρα ἤδη παρῆλθεν should be translated "the hour is already far spent"
    (the compound verb actually means "gone by").

16 M127 Perhaps τι should be understood with φαγεῖν, meaning "something to eat,"
    rather than to take the infinitive as an anarthrous noun, "food."

22 R857 The aorist infinitive ἐμβῆναι is used with a constative sense, describing
    an action as a simple point, whereas the present infinitive προάγειν has a dura-
    tive sense, "go on ahead of him."
    R976 Ἕως with the aorist subjunctive has the meaning "while," instead of "un-
    til."

23 R657 Μόνος is used as an adjective, "he was there alone."

25 M49f. Ἐπί with the accusative presents the notion of position rather than ul-
    timate goal, "upon the sea" (cf. the parallel accounts).

26 R580 The preposition ἀπό denotes a causal idea here (cf. H461).
    H469 Ὅτι has an assertative force in this verse, "certainly," or "verily."

28 T27 Τὰ ὕδατα is an idiomatic plural simply meaning "the water."

29 T75 The aorist imperative ἐλθέ either is ingressive, "start to come," or per-
    fective, "come here" ("the imperative means 'come [back] here'"--BD336[1]).

31 R739 Εἰς τί is employed to express purpose ("in order to what"--T267, or simply
    "why").

33 T183 The predicate nominative θεοῦ υἱός precedes the verb, and consequently is
    anarthrous (although definite in sense).

35 R827 The compound participle ἐπιγνόντες has a perfective sense, "recognizing."

36 R958 Ὅσοι has an indefinite sense (cf. Mark's parallel account), "as many as."
    B200 Ἵνα introduces the content of παρεκάλουν, "they begged him, that."

MATTHEW 15

2   R739 In vv. 2f., διὰ τί means "because of what" (or "why").

5   R874 Οὐ μὴ τιμήσει is probably volitive although some exegetes consider it as
    predictive (the idea   requires the imperative [volitive] sense; cf. the fre-
    quent usage of οὐ μή with a future in an imperative sense in the LXX--B67; it
    has an imperatival meaning, "he need not honor," since it is a quotation of a
    saying of the rabbis--BD365[2]).
    T91 Ὅ ἐὰν ἐξ ἐμοῦ ὠφεληθῇς apparently means "you would have gained (if it were
    not δῶρον)." Thus, the resultant translation would be "Δῶρον is the benefit
    you would have received from me." But ἐάν is not elsewhere used for ἄν in this
    unreal sense (this is the correct rendering of the clause; ἐάν is used for ἄν
    because ὃ ἄν would have resembled a generalizing relative clause [the manu-
    script D replaces ἐάν with ἄν]--BD360[1]).

6   R845 The aorist verb ἠκυρώσατε should be translated into English by a present
    perfect, "you have made void."

11 R1172 The position of οὐ gives it emphasis in this verse (a sharp antithesis--
    R1066).

19 R427 The omission of a connective here gives emphasis to the individual words
    ("evil thoughts, murder . . .").

20 R1058 The articular infinitive τὸ . . . φαγεῖν is used as the subject of κοινοῖ
    (cf. B393), "to eat . . . does not defile."

22 T195 Γυνή appears to be used as a substitute for τις, "a certain Canaanite wo-
    man" (cf. 12:10).

23 R645 Ὄπισθεν literally means "from behind," and so in this verse it has the
    meaning "after."

25 T65 The imperfect verb προσεκύνει has the meaning "request" (cf. 9:18).

26 R757 By using the articular noun τοῖς κυναρίοις, Jesus points to the little
    dogs by the table.

27 R577 The prepositional phrase ἀπὸ τῶν ψιχίων expresses a partitive notion,
    "some of the crumbs."

28 TGr40 The response of Jesus is filled with emotion, "your faith is great in-
    deed," for the unusual position of the word μεγάλη lends feeling and emphasis
    to his appreciation of the woman's attitude. This is further underlined by the
    occurrence of ὦ in the vocative exclamation, "O woman!" (cf. BD146[1]).

29 R615 In παρὰ τὴν θάλασσαν, the preposition has the sense of "near to" or "along-
    side of" ("he came to the shore of the Lake of Galilee"--M51).

30 R1127 Ἔχοντες μετά together simply have the meaning "with" (cf. T154).

32 R602 The preposition ἐπί is used in this verse to denote Christ's emotion,
    "on the crowd."
    T49 In this context a form of τίς occurs instead of ὅστις, with the resultant
    meaning "anything to eat."

33 R710 The pronoun τοσοῦτοι is used to denote quantity, "so many loaves."
    R1089 Ὥστε with the infinitive expresses the notion of purpose, "so as to
    feed."

MATTHEW 16

1   B121 The participle πειράζοντες expresses the idea of purpose, "for the pur-
    pose of testing."

3   R1062 Γινώσκετε διακρίνειν apparently means "you have knowledge for discerning."
    T27 The idiomatic plural τῶν καιρῶν means "this period (of time)."

6   R1183 In ὁρᾶτε καὶ προσέχετε the conjunction has the meaning of "that," "see
    that you beware."

7   R1028 The ὅτι in v. 7 is recitative (i.e., introducing direct speech), while
    the ὅτι in v. 8 is probably causal (the ὅτι in v. 7 has the resultant meaning
    "with reference to the fact that"--BD480[6]; this particle is used as an in-
    terrogative pronoun meaning "why?" Therefore the Lord was not scolding them,
    but the disciples were scolding one another.--TGr68). [Ed. The last sugges-
    tion does not seem to be probable since in the very next verse Christ rebukes
    his disciples. The comment in v. 11 indicates that the disciples were attemp-
    ting to explain (in v. 7) Christ's comment (in v. 6). This limits the usage
    of ὅτι to either the suggestion Blass offers above, or to a causal sense. In
    view of the more usual meaning of ὅτι in the New Testament, it seems prefer-
    able to consider it as causal (cf. Mark 8:16), with the resultant meaning "he
    says that, because."]

12 R1047 The infinitive προσέχειν introduces an indirect command, "to beware."

18 R1185 Κἀγὼ δέ means "and also I."
    M50 Ἐπί with the dative here designates movement ending in a definite spot,
    "I will build upon this rock."
    TGr181 The ingenious combination of πέτρος and πέτρᾳ points to the fact that
    Jesus was actually speaking in Greek (not Aramaic).
    T27 Πύλαι seems to be an idiomatic plural referring to one gate (cf. R408).

19 B94 Ἔσται δεδεμένον is a future perfect periphrastic construction (the parti-
    ciple is virtually an adjective, and more naturally means "shall be bound"
    rather than "shall have been bound" [although it may be stretched to mean
    "shall be found to be bound"]--M18; the whole clause should be translated
    "whatsoever you bind shall already have been permanently bound"--TGr80; it
    is used as a future perfect periphrastic--T89). [Ed. There is little dis-
    agreement here if Moule's alternate rendering is considered preferable, which
    seems to be the case ("shall be found to be bound").]

20   R679   The pronoun αὐτός denotes emphasis here.
     R1046   Ἵνα introduces the content of the verb of exhortation διεστείλατο, "he ordered his disciples to tell no one."

21   R579   The prepositional phrase ἀπὸ τῶν πρεσβυτέρων should be translated by a free rendering of the idea of agency or source, "at the hands of" (ἀπό has a causal sense here--T258). [Ed. On occasion, ἀπό has a meaning similar to ὑπό in the New Testament (the manuscript D replaces ἀπό with ὑπό; Mark uses ὑπό instead of ἀπό in 8:31 because of the inclusion of the passive infinitive, whereas Luke includes both the infinitive and ἀπό in 9:22). Consequently, the former suggestion is preferable, especially since the reason for Christ's suffering was not the evil of the religious leaders, but because of the sin of all mankind.]

22   R541   Σοί is used with ἔσται as a dative of possession, "yours" (this has the meaning "it shall not happen to you"--T240; cf. BD189[3]). [Ed. In essence both suggestions are similar in meaning.]
     R809   The middle participle προσλαβόμενος is used as an indirect middle, indicating that "Peter takes Jesus to himself."
     R875   In οὐ μὴ ἔσται, the double negative occurs with a volitive future, expressing a prohibition (the verb is predicate and emphatically negated--B66). [Ed. The volitive, "it must not happen," and the predictive, "it will not happen," are similar, but in the latter the idea of confidence is much more pronounced. The latter rendering seems preferable since Peter was overly confident and required a severe rebuke (v. 23; cf. 26:35).]
     T309   Apparently ὁ θεὸς εἴη is to be supplied with ἵλεως σοί, "God be merciful to thee" (cf. MT240; apparently ἵλεως does not mean "merciful," but "far be it from"--BD128[5]). [Ed. The rendering "may God be merciful to you" actually means "may God in his mercy spare you from this."]

24   R742   Τις is used as a substantive here, "if any one."
     H421   The imperatives have a conditional sense with an implied apodosis, "then he will be my disciple."

25   T43   Τὴν ψυχὴν αὐτοῦ is used as a reflexive pronoun, "himself" (cf. Luke 9:25).
     T107   The aorist verb ἀπολέσῃ has the meaning "who by that time has already lost it."

26   R501   The genitive τῆς ψυχῆς with the noun ἀντάλλαγμα has the idea of "exchange for his soul."
     M185   The noun ψυχή simply means "self" in this verse (cf. v. 25).

27   B72   Μέλλει is used with an infinitive in a sense similar to a future, but with the indication that the action is certain to take place.

28   R743   In this verse τινες is the antecedent of οἵτινες; the latter is more definite than relative pronoun οἵ would have been, "some of those who are standing here."
     R955   The subjunctive verb γεύσωνται has a futuristic sense, "will not taste."
     T241   Ἐν occurs with the associative dative here, "with his kingdom" (cf. BD 198[2]; the whole clause means "bringing his kingdom"--H464).

MATTHEW 17

3 R405 The compound subject has a singular verb here (ὤφθη), "Moses and Elijah appeared to them."

4 R661 In this verse the positive adjective καλόν is fervently employed by Peter as the highest absolute good (similar to a superlative).
T115 Εἰ with the indicative verb θέλεις indicates that this is a foregone conclusion for Peter ("if, as appears to be the case"--BD372[1a]; it possibly has the connotation "please, shall I make"--BD372[2c]).

5 B55 The aorist verb εὐδόκησα is best understood as an inceptive aorist referring to some indefinite, imagined point of past time at which God is represented as becoming well pleased with Jesus (cf. 2 Pet. 1:17).

6 R409 The idiomatic singular πρόσωπον occurs for the plural, "fell on their faces."

8 R657 Μόνον is used as an adjective, not an adverb, with the resultant meaning "Jesus alone."

9 R597 With the use of the preposition ἐκ in this verse, we are not to suppose that they had been in a cave, but merely up in the mountain. The term "mountain" denotes more than the earth and rock.
MT125 The aorist prohibition μηδενὶ εἴπητε would be answered by "we will avoid doing so."

11 R870 The futuristic present ἔρχεται portrays the certainty of the expectation.

12 M76 The prepositional phrase ἐν αὐτῷ is used for the simple dative, with the meaning "to him" (cf. R588; T264).

15 T189 The genitive μου occurs in an unusual position here, indicating a certain degree of emphasis, "my son."

17 T33 Great emotion is expressed by the use of ὦ here.

19 T37 The pronoun ἡμεῖς occurs in this verse with some degree of emphasis.

25 R531 In προέφθασεν λέγων, the participle expresses the chief idea and the verb is subordinate in meaning, "he spoke to him first" (specimen of literary style).

27 R573 The prepositional phrase ἀντὶ ἐμοῦ καὶ σοῦ refers to the tax that is due by Christ and Peter ("take the coin and give it to them on behalf of myself and you"--M71; cf. TGr173; similar to ὑπέρ--T258).
R657 Πρῶτον is used as an adjective, referring to the first fish that came up.
T292 The active participle ἀναβάντα is actually used instead of a passive verb, because the fish is taken up" (cf. BD315).

MATTHEW 18

1 T29 In vv. 1 and 4, the comparative adjective μείζων probably has a superlative
   sense, "greatest" (or possibly an elative sense "very great"). [Ed. The superlative rendering fits the context more readily.]

2 T65 With the participle of requesting προσκαλεσάμενος, the aorist tense denotes
   the request as peremptory, demanding obedience, "begged."

4 BD380(2) Ὅστις ταπεινώσει is indefinite, similar to ἄν with a subjunctive verb
   ("whoever humbles," cf. vv. 5f.).

6 R992 Ἵνα introduce the subject of the verb συμφέρει, "it would be better for
   him that."

7 R580 The preposition ἀπό has a causal sense (cf. H461), "woe to the world because of temptation to sin."

8 T31 The positive adjective καλόν has a comparative sense here, "better" (cf.
   BD245[3]).

9 R496 Τοῦ πυρός is used as a descriptive (adjectival) genitive, "into the hell
   of fire," or "the fiery hell."

10 R995 Μή with the subjunctive denotes the content of the verb ὁρᾶτε, "see that
   you do not . . ."

12 R541 Ἀνθρώπῳ is used as a dative of possession, "if a man has a hundred sheep."
   T63 The present verb ζητεῖ has a futuristic sense (denoting certainty).

14 R993 Ἵνα introduces the content of ἔστιν θέλημα, "it is not the will . . .
   that . . ."
   BD214(6) Ἔμπροσθεν τοῦ πατρός is used for the simple genitive, "the will of
   your father" (semitic).

15 R428 The absence of a connective between ὕπαγε and ἔλεγξον gives life and vi-
   tality to the description.
   R687 The personal pronoun σοῦ is used instead of the reflexive pronoun, "between
   yourself and him" (cf. v. 16 and T42).
   R1020 In the conditional clause ἐάν σου ἀκούσῃ, ἐκέρδησας τὸν ἀδελφόν σου, the
   protasis looks to the future, while the apodosis views the past, "if he listens
   to you, you have gained your brother" (an aorist after a future condition is
   to a certain extent futuristic--BD333[2]).

16 R604 In this verse, the preposition ἐπί has the meaning of "on the basis of."
   T57 The aorist passive verb σταθῇ actually has the meaning "stand."

18 B94 Ἔσται λελυμένα is a periphrastic future perfect, expressing a future
   state (cf. T89; the participle is virtually an adjective, cf. the discussion
   on 16:19; "shall be found to be loosed"--M18).

20 R593 In this verse, εἰς has the meaning "in" similar to the preposition ἐν.

21   R889 In the interrogative statement, the future verb ἁμαρτήσει has a durative
      sense.

22   T188 Ἑβδομηκοντάκις ἑπτά actually means "70 times (and) 7," not "70 times 7"
      (D amends the text with ἑπτάκις; cf. BD248[2]).

23   T195 The noun ἄνθρωπος occurs as a substitute for τις, "a certain king" (cf.
      12:10 and H433).

24   R674 The numeral εἷς is used instead of the indefinite pronoun τις in this
      verse (cf. v. 23).

26   R605 Ἐμοῦ is used as a simple dative but with ἐπί supplementing it, "have
      patience with me."

27   T234 The genitive τοῦ δούλου should be taken with ὁ κύριος, not with the
      participle σπλαγχνισθείς (the phrase "the master of that servant" is to be
      taken together--BD176[1]).

28   R883 The imperfect tense is descriptive in ἔπνιγεν, describing the debtor as
      "choking him in his rage."
      T321 Εἴ τι has the meaning "whatever."

30   R834 Ἔβαλεν is used as a constative aorist, "he threw" (this type of an aorist
      refers to an act as punctiliar which is not in itself point-action).
      R885 The negative imperfect οὐκ ἤθελεν denotes resistance to pressure (undoubt-
      edly persistent pressure), "he refused."
      B324 Ἕως with the subjunctive ἀποδῷ is dependent upon a verb of past time and
      refers to what was at that time conceived of as a future contingency, "until
      he should pay."

32   BD328 The aorist verb παρεκάλεσας indicates that the simple request sufficed.

33   R919 The imperfect verb ἔδει refers to a past necessity, although the obliga-
      tion still exists at the time of speaking ("ought you not to have pitied"--
      T90).
      R1181 Καί occurs with both parts of the comparison, resulting in a studied bal-
      ance of the two members of the sentence, "ought not you . . . as I also."

                              MATTHEW 19

3   R1176 Εἰ is used to introduce a direct question (cf. 12:10 and T33), "is it
      lawful?"
      M59 Κατά has a transferred sense here, "on the ground of any cause" (the pre-
      position has a causal sense--T268; the anarthrous πᾶσαν has the meaning "any"
      --TGr61).

4   B52 The aorist verb ἀνέγνωτε refers to an event of which the time is entirely
      indefinite, "have you not read?"

5   T253 The preposition εἰς with the accusative is used with ἔσονται as a predi-
      cate nominative, "the two shall become one" (this is due to semitic influence).

6 R845 The aorist verb συνέζευξεν should be translated into English by "has
   joined together" ("those whom God joined together" is preferable--MT140).
   [Ed. It is difficult to convey the idea of the aorist here without using a
   form of "have" in English.]
   M144 Ὥστε is simply used as an inferential particle, meaning "and so," "accordingly" (cf. 12:12).

8 R626 The preposition in πρὸς τὴν σκληροκαρδίαν has a causal sense ("in view
   of your stubbornness"--M53; "in view of" is equivalent to "because of"--BD239
   [8]).
   H469 Ὅτι appears to have an assertative force in this verse, meaning "certainly," or "verily" (cf. 14:26).

10 B243 & 264 The conditional sentence here depends upon the truth of a general
   principle. Thus, the disciples say that if the principle stated by Jesus is
   true, it follows as a general principle that it is not expedient to marry"
   (εἰ with the indicative denotes a foregone conclusion--T115).
   BD5(3b) Αἰτία appears to be used as a Latinism (cf. M192), meaning "relationship" or "case." The whole clause should then read "if the relationship of a
   man with his wife is like this."

11 R752 In this verse οὐ merely negates πάντες, with the resultant meaning "not
   every one."

12 R727 The pronoun οἵτινες expresses quality, similar to οἷοι, "which were so . ."

14 B387 The infinitive ἐλθεῖν is used to complete the meaning of the verb of hindering, "forbid them not to come unto me."

16 M125 The numeral εἷς is used with a sense, "one," similar to τις (cf. BD247
   [2]).

17 R738 Τί has an adverbial sense, "why."

18 T182 The article τό is used to introduce a quotation, similar to quotation
   marks.

20 BD154 In τί . . . ὑστερῶ the pronoun appears to be used as an accusative of
   general reference, "in what am I deficient?"

21 R949 Δεῦρο is used as an interjection, "Come! follow me."
   R1038 The nominative τέλειος occurs with the infinitive εἶναι, because in essence it is a predicate nominative, "if you desire to be perfect."

22 T154 The participle λυπούμενος portrays the manner in which the young man left,
   "in sorrow."

24 R192 For κάμηλος in this verse a few late cursive manuscripts substitute κάμι-
   λος, "rope" (this is only an attempt to simplify the illustration).
   T216 The particle ἤ is used here because the genitive of comparison would not
   have been sufficiently clear.

25 BD440(2) Ἄρα is an inferential particle in vv. 25 and 27, meaning "now, then."

26   R1096 The adjective ἀδύνατον here means "impossible."

27   MT140 The aorist verb ἀφήκαμεν in v. 27 and ἀφῆκεν in v. 29 refers unmistak-
ably to the day of the sacrifice, "we have left everything."

28   T214 Note the position of αὐτοῦ, when actually the pronoun modifies θρόνου and
the whole phrase means "his glorious throne" (a semitism).

29   T48 Ὅστις is used as a simple relative pronoun, "everyone who."
BD460(3) The repetition of the particle ἤ is not necessarily rhetorical, since
the concept could not very well be expressed any other way.

MATTHEW 20

1   R728 At the beginning of the parable, ὅστις has the meaning "now he" or "now
that one."
R809 The middle infinitive μισθώσασθαι means "to let out for wages" ("to hire").
M82 In ἅμα πρωΐ, ἅμα is practically equivalent to a preposition and πρωΐ is
practically equivalent to a noun, with the resultant meaning "at dawn."
H433 Ἀνθρώπῳ is used as equivalent to τινι in an indefinite sense, "a house-
holder" (cf. 13:28).

2   R470 The accusative τὴν ἡμέραν denotes the extent of time, referring to the
agreement between the landlord and the laborers (with a distributive sense,
"per day"--BD161[2]; the article is distributive, "for the day in question"--
BD252).
R599 The preposition in ἐκ δηναρίου portrays the notion of price, "at" or "for
a denarius."

3   M62 The prepositional phrase περὶ τρίτην ὥραν means "at about the third hour."

4   T107 The relative clause is dependent upon a future principal verb, "I will
pay you whatever (at that time) is the right payment."

6   R738 Τί has an adverbial sense, "why" (cf. 19:17).

7   MT140 The aorist verb ἐμισθώσατο actually means "has hired."

8   T155 Ἀρξάμενος occurs with the sense of "from . . . onwards."

9   M67 The prepositional phrase ἀνὰ δηνάριον has a distributive notion, "a denarius
each."

10   T14 The articular prepositional phrase τὸ ἀνὰ δηνάριον (supported by S, C, L,
N and Z) means "everyone a penny."

13   M39 Δηναρίου is used as a genitive of quality, "at a denarius."
BD495(2) The use of ἑταῖρε here appears to be an example of irony, "my friend."

18   T240 θανάτῳ is used as an instrumental dative, "they will condemn him to death"
(cf. BD195[2]).

41

BD323(3) Ἀνα βαίνομεν is used as a futuristic present, "Behold, we will go" (indicating certainty).

19 R595 Εἰς τό with the infinitive is used in this verse to denote purpose (cf. T143; it is used as the indirect object of the verb--B410). [Ed. Actually, τοῖς ἔθνεσιν is the indirect object of παραδώσουσον. The three infinitival clauses in this verse all express purpose (εἰς τό is not repeated, but the idea is carried on by καί).]

20 MT160 It appears to be difficult to distinguish between the middle and active of αἰτέω in vv. 20 and 22. [Ed. Αἰτεῖσθε in v. 22 is used as a direct middle meaning "ask for yourselves."]

22 B72 Μέλλω occurs with the infinitive indicating that the action is certain to take place (cf. 16:27).

23 B393 The articular infinitive τὸ καθίσαι is used as the subject of ἔστιν("to sit . . . is not mine to give").
BD448(8) In this verse ἀλλά is similar to εἰ μή, meaning "except."

24 M63 Ἠγανάκτησαν περί means "they were indignant about."
T178 The article in οἱ δέκα marks the contrast of one fraction from another; "the ten" are the remaining ten disciples.

. 26 R874 The volitive future occurs three times in vv. 26f., expressing a command, "let him be" (cf. B68; this may be due to the semitic use of the imperfect for both the jussive and future in the Septuagint--H458).

27 T108 The present subjunctive θέλη with ἄν refers to an action which is antecedent interative, with the meaning "whoever desires from time to time."

28 R573 The phrase λύτρον ἀντὶ πολλῶν denotes the substitutionary conception of Christ's death, not because ἀντί of itself means "instead," which is not true, but because the context renders any other resultant idea out of the question ("instead of"--M71).
T43 Τὴν ψυχὴν αὐτοῦ is used as a reflexive pronoun meaning "himself" (semitic; cf. BD283[4]).
T134 The infinitives following ἦλθεν express the idea of purpose, "the Son of man came not to be served but to serve."

32 R994 The aorist verb ποιήσω seems to portray an imperatival sense following θέλετε here, "what do you want me to do to you?"

33 T94 Ἵνα ἀνοιγῶσιν has an imperatival sense, "open our eyes."

MATTHEW 21

1 R834 The aorist verb ἤγγισαν has an ingressive sense, "when they came near" (cf. T72).

3 R742 Τι is equivalent to a substantive, meaning "anything."

R874 'Ερεῖτε is used as a volitive future, expressing a command, "say" (cf. the parallel account in Mark 11:3; cf. 20:26--H458).

4   R1428 The participle λέγοντος appears to simply mean "when saying."
    B222 The clause ἵνα πληρωθῇ was intended to express purpose (cf. 1:22).
    M15 The perfect verb γέγονεν seems to indicate that the Old Testament narra-
    tive was viewed as contemporary. This may be called a perfect of allegory
    (cf. 1:22 and 26:56).

7   R409 It is probable that αὐτῶν refers to τὰ ἱμάτια, not to τὴν ὄνου καὶ τὸν
    πῶλον (Matthew describes the placing of garments upon both animals and appar-
    ently states that Jesus was mounted upon both--TGr69; this clause involves a
    text-critical problem; either αὐτῶν is to be omitted or it is to be replaced
    with αὐτόν [as in S^C]--BD141[8]). [Ed. The omission of αὐτῶν or the replace-
    ment of it by αὐτόν is only evidence of a later editorial attempt to eliminate
    the apparent difficulty of the use of the plural. On the other hand, the
    phrases ἐπ' αὐτῶν and ἐπάνω αὐτῶν seem to be parallel. Thus, Turner's render-
    ing appears to be preferable. Matthew was apparently more specific in his de-
    tailed description of the account, attempting to show the fulfillment of the
    Old Testament prophecy ἐπιβεβηκὼς ἐπὶ ὄνον, καὶ ἐπὶ πῶλον.]

8   R838 In this verse the aorist verb ἔστρωσαν lifts the curtain and the imperfect
    verbs ἔκοπτον and ἐστρώννυον continue the action.
    M98 In the context here the superlative πλεῖστος has an elative sense, "huge"
    ("a very large crowd"--T31).

9   R670 'Υψίστοις is used as a true superlative, denoting the abode of God,
    "highest."

11 T210 Τῆς Γαλιλαίας is a geographic genitive, indicating the country within
    which Nazareth lies, "in Galilee."
    BD209(3) The preposition ἀπό is used instead of ἐκ to denote the place of ori-
    gin.

13 T86 The future verb κληθήσεται expresses a command,"my house shall be called."

16 MT140 The aorist verb ἀνέγνωτε should be rendered similar to the perfect tense
    (the adverb οὐδέποτε introduces the element of time), "have you never read."

19 R603 The prepositional phrase ἐπὶ τῆς θαλάσσης indicates that the fig tree was
    not on the path, but on the edge of the road.
    B167 The aorist subjunctive verb γένηται has an emphatic predictive sense,
    "there shall be no fruit from thee henceforward forever" (it appears to be a
    volitive subjunctive--R943). [Ed. The rendering with the predictive meaning
    seems to be preferable since οὐ μή is unusual in prohibition and the volitive
    subjunctive is rare in the third person.]
    BD247(2) The numeral μίαν is used in place of the indefinite pronoun τινα, "a
    certain fig tree" or "a fig tree" (cf. H432).

21 T16 Τὸ τῆς συκῆς actually means "the fig tree."

23 R740 In vv. 23f., ποίᾳ seems to retain its qualitative force, "what authority."

24 M33   A double accusative occurs with the verb ἐρωτήσω, "I will ask you one
      thing."
      BD247(2)   The numeral ἕνα appears to be used instead of an indefinite pronoun
      (the parallel account in Luke 20:3 has only λόγον, which seems to equate ἕνα
      with an indefinite article; "a question," cf. v. 19).

26 BD157(3)   The verb ἔχω occurs with ὡς with a meaning similar to λογίζομαι ὡς,
      "they considered John as a prophet."

28 T32   The superlative πρῶτος in vv. 28 and 32 is used as a comparative, meaning
      "elder."

31 BD245a(3)   The concept of exclusion is contained in the verb προάγουσιν, "go
      into the Kingdom, but you do not."

32 R1066   It is possible to regard τοῦ πιστεῦσαι as expressing result, although in
      reality it gives the content of μετεμελήθητε (cf. R1090), "you did not repent
      that you might believe."

33 R575   The compound verb ἀπεδήμησεν actually means "a man went off from home"
      (ἄνθρωπος apparently has an indefinite sense here [cf. 11:19]--H433).

34 T135   Matthew tends to substitute an infinitive for Mark's ἵνα with a subjunc-
      tive verb, denoting purpose (as with λαβεῖν here).

36 R516   Notice the comparison in πλείονας τῶν πρώτων, "more than the first."

37 R819   The future passive verb ἐντραπήσονται has an active sense, "they will re-
      spect my son."

38 B161   Δεῦτε is prefixed to a hortatory subjunctive verb without affecting the
      meaning of the verb, "come, let us kill."

41 B317   The relative clause with the future indicative here expresses the notion
      of purpose, "he will let out the vineyard unto other husbandman, which shall
      render him the fruits" (the relative clause may be either final, "so that they
      may render," or purely affirmative, "who shall render"--M139). [Ed. Moule's
      second suggestion seems preferable here, since it is very unusual for the pro-
      noun ὅστις to have the idea of purpose. Οὕτινες is primarily descriptive of
      the noun γεωργοῖς (cf. R247 and Matt. 19:12).]
      TGr181   The vigorous phrase κακοὺς κακῶς seems to indicate that Jesus actually
      spoke these words originally in Greek. The resultant meaning is "he will de-
      stroy those miserable men miserably" (cf. 16:18; the phrase portrays popular
      iteration as well as good classical style--BD488[1a]).

42 M182   Since Hebrew did not have the neuter gender, the feminine was used to
      refer to abstract ideas. Consequently, αὕτη is used in this verse as trans-
      lation Greek, with the resultant meaning "this thing came from the Lord" (cf.
      T21 and BD138[2]).
      BD220(1)   The prepositional phrase ἐν ὀφθαλμοῖς ἡμῶν means "in our judgment."

45 R787   The article οἱ is repeated because the two groups are treated as separate.
      BD324   The present tense in λέγει is used in indirect discourse to refer to re-
      lative time, "that he was speaking of them."

46 M70 The preposition εἰς with the accusative has a predicative sense, "they
    reckoned (or considered) him as a prophet" (cf. v. 26).

                              MATTHEW 22

1   R409 The plural ἐν παραβολαῖς is followed by only one parable, but there were
    doubtless others not recorded.

2   R408 Γάμους is an idiomatic plural referring to only one wedding (cf. T27).
    R957 The pronoun ὅστις has a definite sense here, "some one in particular."
    MT140 The aorist verb ὡμοιώθη may have been used because the working out of
    the comparison included action partially past, "may be compared."
    H433 Ἀνθρώπῳ has an indefinite sense, with the resultant meaning "a king."

3   R919 The negative imperfect οὐκ ἤθελον brings out sharply the element of will,
    "they refused to come."

5   T192 Ἴδιον is used as a simple possessive pronoun (cf. the following αὐτοῦ,
    BD286[1] and M121), "his farm."

7   R834 The verb ὠργίσθη is used as an ingressive aorist, "became angry" (cf. T72).
    R835 The aorist verb ἐνέπρησεν has an effective sense, emphasizing the end of
    the action, "he burned their city."
    T26 Στρατεύματα is an idiomatic plural, referring to "his army."

11 R485 The accusative ἔνδυμα with the passive participle would have been a dative
    with the active voice, "not being clothed with a wedding garment."
    R1138 In v. 11, οὐκ occurs with the participle ἐνδεδυμένον, while in v. 12, μή
    is used with the participle ἔχων. The first instance lays emphasis on the ac-
    tual situation in the description (the plain fact) while the second instance
    is the hypothetical argument about it (οὐ with the participle is classical--
    BD430[1]; the first negation is a plain fact, the second is an application of
    it--MT232). [Ed. Οὐκ is used with the participle to emphasize that the object
    of the king's vision was perceptively affirmed (i.e., the man definitely did
    not have on wedding clothes). But μή with the participle does not have to be
    explained in the New Testament. Throughout the New Testament this negative is
    used with a participle to negate simple facts as well as many other types of
    ideas. It appears that the author had in mind the same objective negation
    that he previously stated (but with less stress -- possibly less shock).]
    T161 The participle ἐνδεδυμένον is used with the verb εἶδεν with the resultant
    meaning "he saw a man and he had not on" (the object participle is similar to
    a relative clause; cf. BD416[1]).

13 BD62 In the New Testament, ἐξώτερον only has a superlative sense, "the darkness
    farthest out."

15 B207 Ὅπως is used to introduce an object clause, meaning "that" (cf. 12:14).

16 R550 The prepositional phrase ἐν ἀληθείᾳ is used with an adverbial sense,
    "truthfully."
    M28 The impersonal verb μέλει is followed by the prepositional phrase with περί,
    meaning "it does not matter to you concerning."

17   R1058   The infinitive δοῦναι is used as the subject of the verb ἔξεστιν, "is it lawful to pay?"

27   R668   The comparative adjective ὕστερον is used with πάντων as a superlative, "last of all" (cf. BD62).

28   B39   The aorist verb ἔσχον refers to a series of acts viewed as constituting a single fact, "for they all had her" (a constative aorist--R833).

30   R392   In the occurrence of the verbs γαμοῦσιν and γαμίζονται, men should be as the subject of the former and women should be supplied with the latter verb (the passive verb actually has a transitive sense, "get married"--T57).

36   R740   Ποῖος doesn't have a qualitative force in this verse, but has a meaning similar to τίς, "which."
       T31   The positive adjective μεγάλη has a superlative sense, "the greatest commandment" (cf. Mark 12:28 and M97f.).

37   T39   The notion of rhythm may be present in the repetition here, "with all your heart and with all your soul and with all your strength."

MATTHEW 23

2   R866   In v. 2, ἐκάθισαν is a gnomic aorist verb ("they sit") and in v. 3, the present verbs λέγουσιν and ποιοῦσιν are gnomic also, "for they preach but they do not practice" (the gnomic usage denotes a customary well-known truth; ἐκάθισαν seems to be a perfective aorist, "they took their seat and still sit" --T72; cf. BD342[1]; this verb is ingressive and expresses the self assertion of the would-be Moses more rigorously than the present tense could; and it is iterative, for it applies to many individual scribes--H458). [Ed. The initial suggestion seems to be the most preferable since the scribes and pharisees are extensively recognized as the exponents of the Mosaic law.]

4   R1184   Two instances of δέ occur in this verse; the first is copulative and should be translated "yea" and the second occurrence is adversative and means "but."

5   R1075   Πρὸς τό with the infinitive denotes purpose, "to be seen."

8   M135   The subjunctive verbs κληθῆτε, καλέσητε and κληθῆτε in vv. 8ff. are equivalent to an imperative, expressing a command, "you are not to be called . . . and call no man . . . neither be called."
       T189   There is some degree of emphasis indicated by the pronoun ὑμεῖς here.

9   M166   There appears to be emphasis on the words brought toward the beginning of the last clause in this verse. It may be rendered "for, for you there is only one Father -- the heavenly Father."

12   R957   Ὅστις is used with an indefinite sense in both instances in this verse, with the meaning "whoever."

13 T81 The present participle τοὺς εἰσερχομένους refers to action that occurs
    prior to that of the principal verb, "those who were entering" (or trying to
    enter; it is conative, "trying to"--R1116).

15 M174 The semitic idiom υἱός with the genitive simply means "people worthy of,"
    or "associated with hell" (cf. H441).
    BD150 The compound verb περιάγω means "to go about in the area."

16 M60 Ἐν with the dative is used to designate the guarantee of an oath, "to
    swear by" (semitic; cf. H464).
    T51 In vv. 16 and 18, the verb ὀφείλει is used with an absolute sense, "he is
    bound by his oath."

20 R859 The aorist participle ὀμόσας refers to an action that occurs at the same
    time as that of the main verb ὀμνύει, "he who swears . . . swears" (ὁ ὀμόσας
    seems to be equivalent to ὅς ἂν ὀμόσῃ, "whoever sweareth"--B150).

23 T90 The imperfect verb of obligation ἔδει means "it was necessary" (but it is
    not happening, although it is still a present obligation).

25 M72 Γέμουσιν ἐκ with the genitive is virtually partitive, meaning "they are
    full of."

26 M83 Τὸ ἐντός is apparently an adverbial expression, meaning "that which is
    inside" (in contrast to τὸ ἐκτός).

28 R633 In the compound noun ὑπόκρισις, the notion of an actor under a mask
    (ὑπό) lies behind the resultant idea.

31 R538 Ἑαυτοῖς is used as a dative of disadvantage, meaning "against yourselves."
    M144 In this context, ὥστε is simply an inferential particle meaning "and so,"
    "accordingly."

32 R948 There is the notion of irony in πληρώσατε, although it is used as an im-
    perative of permission, "fill up."

33 BD366(1) The subjunctive is used in the deliberative question, "how shall (can)
    you escape?" (the subjunctive has more of a potential sense than the future
    indicative).

34 T209 The partitive prepositional phrase ἐξ αὐτῶν is used as a direct object,
    "some of them."

35 M206 The present participle ἐκχυννόμενον refers to action which preceded that
    of the principal verb, "which has been poured out."

37 R689 Notice that αὐτήν is used here instead of σέ (a change occurs from the
    second person to the third person).
    M34 Ὃν τρόπον is practically an adverbial accusative, meaning "in the way in
    which."

47

MATTHEW 24

2 M159 Οὐ βλέπετε ταῦτα πάντα is best translated into English by "do you see all
these things?" (not "do you not see . . .?"

4 B209 Μή introduces a subordinate clause, dependent on βλέπετε, "take heed that
no one."

5 R604 In ἐπὶ τῷ ὀνόματι μου the preposition portrays the notion of basis.

6 B209 Μὴ θροεῖσθε is an imperative expression co-ordinate with ὀρᾶτε (cf. R949),
"look out for the wars, but do not be scared by them."

9 R899 The future periphrastic participle ἔσεσθε μισούμενοι has a continuous
sense (stressing the duration of the hate), "you will be hated."

12 B108 Τὸ πληθυνθῆναι τὴν ἀνομίαν apparently refers to the multiplication of in-
iquity as a fact of that time without exlusive reference to its preceding the
action of the principal verb.

13 B150 The articular aorist participle ὁ ὑπομείνας may be used instead of the
relative clause ὃς ἂν ὑπομείνῃ, "whoever shall endure" (cf. 23:20).

15 R434 Ὁ ἀναγινώσκων νοείτω is actually a parenthetical command, "let the reader
understand."

17 M74 Ἆραι τὰ ἐκ τῆς οἰκίας αὐτοῦ   provides an illustration of a pregnant sense of
the preposition ἐκ, meaning "to take from his house the things which are in it"
(ἐκ is used for ἐν--BD437).

18 M86 Ὀπίσω is used as an adverb, "let him not turn back."

20 R522 In the temporal expressions χειμῶνος and σαββάτῳ, the genitive refers to
time within which winter occurs ("in winter"--M39; as opposed to summer), while
the dative refers to a point of time, "on the Sabbath."
B200 Ἵνα introduces an object clause, denoting the content of προσεύχεσθε,
"pray that."

21 T70 The perfect verb γέγονεν occurs with the sense of an aorist in the narrative
(S, D, θ and other manuscripts correct to ἐγένετο; cf. BD343[3]), "such as was
not."

22 R752 In οὐκ . . . πᾶσα, οὐκ negates the verb and the resultant meaning is that
no flesh would be saved.
B469 Εἰ μή does not mean "except," but μή negates the conditional clause, "if
those days would not have been."
T268 Διά with the accusative may indicate the idea of purpose, "for the elect's
sake."

24 R990 Ὥστε with the infinitive πλανῆσαι appears to be used to denote pure purpose (cf. R1428; a consecutive train of thought may underlie the usage--M143).

48

27 T26 Ἀνατολῶν is an idiomatic plural, referring to a direction, "east."

30 T214 In τὸ σημεῖον τοῦ υἱοῦ τοῦ ἀνθρώπου the genitive is either appositive,
     "the sign which is the son of man," or possessive, "the sign which the son of
     man will give."   [Ed. The latter rendering seems preferable since there is
     a response (κόψονται) of all the tribes to the sign before the son of man is
     actually seen. In addition, if the former suggestion was accurate, the second
     καὶ τότε in this verse would seem superfluous and the following clause would
     be redundant.]

31 T25 Οὐρανῶν in this verse is an exceptional use of the plural; generally the
     singular is used for the material sense of "sky."
     T234 The genitive in τοὺς ἐκλεκτους αὐτοῦ designates the agent, "the chosen by
     God."
     BD474(4) The variant text with μετὰ σάλπιγγος φωνῆς μεγάλης means "with loud
     trumpet call" (in essence this is equivalent to the shorter reading).

33 M50 The preposition in ἐπὶ θύραις has a locative sense, "at the doors."

40 R675 The numerals εἷς in v. 40 and μιά in v. 41 have an indefinite sense sim-
     ilar to τις, "one."
     T319 In vv. 40f., the future verb ἔσονται and the present participle ἀλήθουσαι
     have a conditional meaning "if there are two in the field . . ., if there are
     two women grinding" (cf. BD418[2]).

42 R740 In vv. 42f., the pronoun ποία merely has the force of an interrogative
     with very little qualitative sense, "on what day?"

43 R870 The futuristic present verb ἔρχεται is used to portray the certainty of
     expectation.
     BD291(5) Ἐκεῖνο has the meaning of "that other thing."

45 R777 The force of the article ὁ is carried over to the second adjective φρόνι-
     μος by the conjunction καί (cf. BD269[5]).
     R845 The aorist verb κατέστησεν is best translated into English with a perfect,
     "he has set over."
     B397 Τοῦ with the infinitive δοῦναι is used to express the purpose of the ac-
     tion denoted by the principal verb, "to give to them" (cf. T141).

51 T226 Ἐκεῖ has a temporal sense in this verse, "then" (cf. Luke 13:28).

                                  MATTHEW 25

1 R727 The pronoun αἵτινες has a definite sense similar to the relative pronoun
     , "who."
     R1127 The participle λαβοῦσαι is used with the notion of manner (having the
     resultant meaning "they came with lamps"--T154).
     M70 The preposition εἰς has the sense of "with a view to" (cf. v. 6).

5 R838 In this verse the aorist verb ἐνύσταξον lifts the curtain and the imper-
     fect verb ἐκάθευδον continues the play, "they fell to nodding and went on
     sleeping."

6   R897 Γέγονεν is used as a vivid perfect, referring to a sudden cry (γέγονεν
     is used for the aorist in narrative [B corrected the text with ἐγενέτο]--BD
     343[2]. The evidence seems to show clearly that Matthew regularly uses γέγονα
     in the sense of an aorist; some of the instances cannot, without violence, be
     otherwise explained, and all are naturally so explained. Mark's use of the
     word is possibly the same, but the evidence is not decisive. All other writ-
     ers of the New Testament use the form as a true perfect.--B88; cf. 24:21).
     T235 The genitive is used in μέσης νυκτός to indicate the point of time, "at
     midnight" (unclassical; it denotes the kind of time--R495). [Ed. There is
     no need to force the classical genitive of kind of time upon this phrase,
     especially since the genitive designating the point of time occurs occasion-
     ally in the New Testament.]

9   R1161 A verb of fearing is implied with the use of μήποτε here (cf. B225; per-
     haps the meaning is "go and buy . . . lest"--T99; "it will hardly be enough"
     --BD428[6]).
     T75 The present imperative πορεύεσθε may be used to portray politeness (it is
     less peremptory than the aorist; the present imperative portrays going here
     and there, wherever they may find one, whereas the aorist imperative indicates
     the goal, "and buy"--BD336[1]).

10   T27 Γάμους is an idiomatic plural referring to one wedding feast (cf. 22:2).

11   R1200 Strong emotion is expressed by the repetition of Κύριε here.

14   T192 Ἰδίους is used as a simple possessive pronoun, "his servants" (cf. 22:5).
     BD453(4) Ὥσπερ γάρ is used to introduce a parable with neither a following
     correlative nor any close connection to what precedes, with the resultant mean-
     ing "it is indeed so that" (the main clause is to be assumed with the compari-
     son--BD482).

16   B150 The articular participle ὁ λαβών has a sense similar to a relative clause,
     "he that received" (cf. 24:13).
     MT116 The verb ἠργάσατο is used as a constative aorist (a series of events is
     simply referred to).

20   R835 Ἐκέρδησα is used as an effective aorist, stressing the end of the action,
     "I gained."

21   M49 The change from ἐπί with the accusative to ἐπί with the genitive seems to
     be merely a stylistic variation (with no difference in meaning).
     BD102(3) Εὖ is used as an interjection meaning "bravo!" in vv. 21 and 23.

24   BD342(1) The perfect tense is used in εἰληφώς to denote a continuing effect,
     "the possessor" (cf. R909 and MT238).
     BD437 "Whence" (ὅθεν) is used instead of "Where" (ἐκεῖθεν οὖ) in vv. 24 and
     26.

27   T90 The imperfect verb of obligation ἔδει means "it was necessary" (cf. 23:23).

30   BD62 In the New Testament, the comparative adjective ἐξώτερον only has a super-
     lative sense, "the darkness farthest out" (cf. 22:13).

32   T313 The plural verb is used with the neuter plural subject τὰ ἔθνη because
     the subject has a personal sense, "all the nations."

33   R408 Δεξιῶν and εὐωνύμων are idiomatic plurals simply denoting direction,
     "right . . . left."

34   M73 The preposition ἀπό has a temporal sense here, "since."
     T152 The articular participle τὴν ἑτοιμασμένην is equivalent to a relative
     clause, meaning "which has been prepared."
     BD183 The genitive τοῦ πατρός is used to indicate the agent of the passive
     participle, "by my father."

35   BD390(2) Φαγεῖν is used as an infinitive of purpose, "to eat."

40   R963 The prepositional phrase ἐφ' ὅσον has a causal sense, "since you did it"
     (the aorist verb ἐποιήσατε is similar to a perfect--MT138).
     T31 The superlative adjective ἐλαχίστων has an elative sense in vv. 40 and 45,
     "very small" (cf. 5:19).

41   R1096 The perfect passive participle κατηραμένοι means "having become the sub-
     jects of a curse," and is not to be rendered as a verbal adjective κατάροι,
     "cursed" (cf. MT221).

MATTHEW 26

2   R869 The present verb γίνεται has a futuristic punctiliar sense (the verb
     γίνομαι has an aoristic tendency), denoting the certainty of expectation (the
     present verb παραδίδοται is futuristic also--M7; "the passover will come" and
     "the Son of man will be delivered").
     R1090 Εἰς τό with the infinitive is used to express a hypothetical result (the
     meaning is very near that of purpose--T143), "to be crucified."

4   R811 The middle voice of συνεβουλεύσαντο has a reciprocal idea, "they coun-
     selled with one another."

8   R739 Εἰς τί expresses purpose, "for what purpose?"

10   M69 Εἰς ἐμέ is used instead of a simple dative, "to me."
     MT116 Ἠργάσατο is used as a constative aorist, stressing the activity rather
     than its product.

12   R1075 Πρὸς τό is used with the infinitive to denote purpose, "to prepare me for
     burial."

15   R951 In this verse the conjunction καί is almost equivalent to ἐάν (καί almost
     has the sense of ὅτι or ἵνα, "that"--R1183; it may have a final sense--T334;
     cf. BD442[2]). [Ed. Καί appears to be used to complete the interrogative
     statement (similar to Robertson's former suggestion), "what will you give to
     me if I hand him over to you?" The final rendering "that" doesn't fit into
     the interrogative statement as smoothly.]

18 R744 Τὸν δεῖνα is a rare pronoun and means "Mr So-and-So."
R870 Ποιῶ is a futuristic present, indicating the certainty of expectation
(cf. B15; "I will celebrate the Passover"--M7).
M52 The preposition πρός denotes position, "with."

24 R707 The pronoun ἐκείνῳ portrays the notion of contempt in this verse.

25 R1168 Judas introduced his question with μήτι (expecting a negative answer)
because he did not dare to use οὐ (he receives the unexpected answer συ εἶπας
--BD427[2]).
T87 The present participle ὁ παραδιδούς is used for the future, "the one who
would betray him."

28 R595 The preposition εἰς has the meaning "for."
M206 The present participle has a futuristic sense, "which will be shed."
T269 In this verse περί seems to be used for ὑπέρ, meaning "on behalf of, on
account of" (it is equivalent to ὑπέρ, D has ὑπέρ--BD229(1); the preposition
περί approaches the death of Christ from a different angle--R567). [Ed. Occasionally in the New Testament, περί has a meaning similar to ὑπέρ (cf. Acts
26:1 and Heb. 10:26), which appears to be the meaning here in view of the parallels (cf. Mark 14:24; Luke 22:20 and Paul's treatment of this subject).]

29 BD382(3) Ὅταν has the meaning of "that day when."

33 R1026 Εἰ introduces a concessive clause here, "although" (cf. B279; the feeling
of definiteness in εἰ with the future indicative almost results in a causal
sense--T115). [Ed. Actually the concessive sense fits the context more readily.]

35 R208 Κἄν means "even if" (concessive--R1026; the concessive idea is stressed
more when καί is included--B279).
R875 Ἀπαρνήσομαι is used as a volitive future (predictive and emphatically ne-
gated--B66). [Ed. The last suggestion seems to be preferable, since Peter
was overly self-confident (cf. 16:22).]
T265 Σὺν σοί appears to mean "in your company."

36 R976 Ἕως has the meaning "while," cf. 14:22 (it has the meaning "until" with
the aorist subjunctive, "sit here until I pray" or "have prayed"; "while I
pray" is slightly periphrastic--B325). [Ed. Actually, "until I have prayed"
has a resultant idea that is similar to "while I pray."]

38 R856 Μείνατε is used as a constative aorist, referring to a durative action
but treating it as punctiliar ("do not go and continue to watch"--T77).

39 T338 Πλήν is used as an adversative particle in πλὴν οὐχ instead of Mark's
ἀλλ' οὐχ, "nevertheless, not."

43 B91 The imperfect of the stative verb ἦσαν with the perfect participle βεβαρ-
ημένοι forms a periphrastic pluperfect, "their eyes were heavy" (literally, it
means "were having been weighed down"--M19).

44 M122 The pronoun is used as an adjective in τὸν αὐτὸν λόγον εἰπών, which means
"saying the same word" (actually "words").

45 R807 Ἀναπαύεσθε may be considered as a direct middle, "rest yourselves."
    R882 Παραδίδοται is used as a futuristic present, indicating the certainty of
    expectation, "will be betrayed."
    R948 Καθεύδετε and ἀναπαύεσθε are imperatives denoting permission. This is
    not a question nor necessarily a case of irony. It is too late to do Christ
    any good by keeping awake. Consequently, he withdraws his plea for watchful-
    ness ("all that is left to do is to sleep"--M161; τὸ λοιπόν has the sense of
    an inferential "therefore," with the resultant meaning "so you are still a-
    sleep!"--BD451[6]).
    T334 The last καί in this verse is used in place of temporal subordination,
    "when" (equivalent to ὅτε; cf. R1183, BD442[4] and H421).

46 R428 The absence of a connective in ἐγείρεσθε ἄγωμεν portrays life and move-
    ment in the narrative, "arise, let us go."
    T151 The articular participle in ὁ παραδιδούς is virtually a proper name,
    meaning "my betrayer."

48 B310 In "whomsoever I will kiss, that is he," the supposition with ὃν ἄν is
    particular, referring to a specific occasion and event.
    T77 The aorist imperative κρατήσατε means "arrest him!"

50 R602 The preposition in ἐφ' ὃ πάρει expresses the notion of aim, "for what pur-
    pose" (the relative pronoun is actually used as an interrogative, "why have you
    come?"--TGr69ff.; cf. T50, R725 and MT93; this clause denotes irony, "that is
    why you are here"--BD300[2]). [Ed. The phrase ἐφ' ὃ was used during the first
    century A. D. in an interrogative sense, and is apparently so used in this
    verse (cf. the interrogative statement in the parallel account in Luke 22:48).
    The point is that the Master makes known to the betraying disciple that he is
    not taken up by the public display of affection.]

52 R1191 The conjunction γάρ is used here to indicate the major premise.

53 T334 In this verse καί is employed to express a result, "that."
    BD440(1) Ἤ introduces an interrogative statement, "or."
    MT50 Πλείω is an indeclinable comparative adjective, "more than twelve legions"
    later manuscripts include the emendation πλείους).

55 R602 The preposition ἐπί portrays the notion of hostility in this verse, "a-
    gainst."

56 M17 The perfect verb γέγονεν seems to indicate that the Old Testament narrative
    was viewed as contemporary. This may be called a perfect of allegory (cf. 21:4).

60 R1129 The participle προσελθόντων has a concessive sense, "although many false
    witnesses came forward."

61 R581 Διά has the meaning "after" (cf. M56; διά with the genitive refers to time
    within which something takes place, "within three days"--T267; cf. BD223[1]).
    [Ed. The temporal genitive generally indicates the time within which. That
    appears to be the meaning of the prepositional phrase here (cf. John 2:19).]
    R697 The pronoun οὗτος is used with the notion of reproach, "this fellow."

63 R883 The imperfect tense of ἐσιώπα has a descriptive durative sense, "kept
    silent" ("Jesus kept silent until the high priest said"--T66).

T64   The present verb ἐξορκίζω refers to a punctiliar action taking place at
the time of speaking, "I charge you."

64   T72ff.   The response σὺ εἶπας simply means "you say it" (cf. Mark 15:2 and MT86;
the pronoun is emphatic--T37).

67   BD250   Οἱ δέ means "but others" (the article is similar to a demonstrative pro-
noun--R694; cf. 28:17).

69   R674   The numeral μιᾶ is used as an indefinite article, "a maid" (cf. M125).
R1182   In καὶ σὺ ἦσθα, καί begins the sentence because the connection is with
an unexpressed idea, "you also were with."

71   R697   The pronoun οὗτος carries a note of reproach in this verse (cf. v. 61).

72   H469   In vv. 72 and 74, ὅτι introduces a strong assertion, with the resultant
meaning "verily" (cf. 19:18).

73   R28   The brogue that Peter revealed in this verse was probably due to his Gali-
lean accent of Aramaic.

MATTHEW 27

1   R1089   Ὥστε with the infinitive is used here to express purpose (cf. M140,
T136 and MT207; it is used to express intended result, similar to purpose--
BD391[3]; this construction stands in definitive apposition with συμβούλιον,
defining the content of the plan, rather than expressing the purpose of making
it--B371). [Ed. Συμβούλιον ἔλαβον apparently does not mean "receive a plan,"
but "gather for a consultation." Two meetings of this type were required by
law in grave criminal cases. Consequently, ὥστε with the infinitive denotes
the purpose for this consultation against Jesus (cf. 10:1).

3   R858   The aorist participle μεταμεληθείς has an ingressive sense (the repentance
began at that point).

4   R874   The futuristic and volitive future are occasionally similar, as in σὺ ὄψῃ,
meaning "you will see to that" (cf. MT177; it is volitive, "see to it yourself"
--BD362).
R1128   The participle παραδούς presents the ground or reason for the action of
the principal verb ἥμαρτον (i.e., causal; the participle refers to action which
is simultaneous with that of the main verb--R1113; cf. B139; the participle is
modal-temporal, "by betraying"--T154; the participle expresses identical action, "in that I . . ."--BD339[1]). [Ed. The last suggestion seems to be the
preferable one, since the sinning and the betraying are one. In essence there
isn't much difference between the resultant meanings of these suggestions.]
BD299(3)   The elliptical construction τί πρὸς ἡμᾶς means "what is that to us?"
(the verb is omitted).

5   T54   Ἀπήγξατο is used as a direct (reflexive) middle, "he hanged himself" (the
verb may have the meaning of "choke"--MT155).

7   M73 In ἠγόρασαν ἐξ αὐτῶν the preposition has an instrumental sense, "they pur-
    chased with them" (i.e., "the pieces of silver").

8   R848 The aorist verb ἐκλήθη is connected to the present time in a way that is
    similar to the English perfect, "has been called" (cf. B52; it may mean "was
    called [then] and has retained the name until today"--M14; cf. T71; this is a
    more specific rendering of the aorist verb).

11 TGr73 Σὺ λέγεις means "you say it" (cf. 26:64; the pronoun σύ is emphatic--T37).
    BD277(1) In σὺ εἶ ὁ βασιλευς the pronoun is emphatic (a man like you).

15 R884 Ἤθελον is used as an iterative imperfect, denoting repetition, "whom they
    wanted."
    M59 The preposition κατά has a distributive sense in a temporal expression, "at
    feast-time," or "at every feast" (cf. T268).

18 R888 The pluperfect verb ᾔδει has the force of an imperfect, "he knew."

19 R396 The verb ἔστω should be supplied with μηδὲν σοί (the idea of concern is
    predominant in this statement, "let there be nothing to you and that innocent
    man:"--TGr46).

20 R805 The middle voice of αἰτήσωνται seems to refer to a request as in a business
    transaction.
    R835 Ἔπεισαν is used as an effective aorist, emphasizing the end of the action
    ("they succeeded in persuading"--T72; cf. B42).

22 M35 The accusative Ἰησοῦν is used predicatively, "what shall I do with Jesus?"
    ("to do something to"--T246).

23 R1149 In this verse, γάρ is used as an intensive particle ("Why, what evil has
    he done?"--BD452[1]).

24 R644 Ἀπέναντι has the meaning of "in the presence of."
    R810 The middle verb ἀπενίψατο probably means "he himself washed his hands."
    R874 In ὑμεῖς ὄψεσθε the future has a volitive sense, "you yourselves see to
    it" (cf. T86, BD362 and v. 4; the pronoun is emphatic--R678).
    BD182(3) With ἀθῷος the preposition ἀπό has the sense of "free from."

30 R593 In this verse, the second instance of εἰς has the sense of "on" (similar
    to ἐπί--T256).
    R884 The imperfect verb ἔτυπτον has an iterative meaning, "they repeatedly
    struck."

31 B48 When an aorist verb is used in a narrative passage, referring to a past e-
    vent which precedes another past event in the context, it should be translated
    into English with a pluperfect,"when they had ridiculed him" (cf. M16).
    M33 The verbs ἐξέδυσαν and ἐνέδυσαν have double accusatives here, with the re-
    sultant meaning "they stripped him of the cloak and put his own garments on
    him."

32 R993 Ἵνα introduces the content of the requisition, "to carry his cross."

33 B20 The clause ὅ ἐστιν κρανίου τόπος λεγόμενος provides an instance of a periphrastic present tense (it is a question whether ἐστιν should not rather be regarded as standing independent, with an explanatory participle, "which means
[literally "is, when said" or "translated"] Skull Place" [instead of "which is
being translated"]--M17). [Ed. Moule's rendering is more appropriate, since
it is incorrect to force a periphrastic sense from this construction. "Ο
ἐστιν is occasionally used in the New Testament as an explanatory formula (cf.
Mark 12:42; John 1:41 and Eph. 5:5).]

34 R1087 The close connection between the epexegetical infinitive and the purpose
infinitive can be seen in the first occurrence of πιεῖν here, "for drinking"
and "to drink" (although the latter rendering with the notion of purpose seems
preferable).

35 R690 The middle verb διεμερίσαντο has a reflexive sense, "they divided his garments among them."

37 R604 Ἐπάνω has the idea of "over."

40 T81 The participles καταλύων and οἰκοδομῶν refer to action prior to that of the
main verb, "you who were trying to destroy . . . and rebuild" (cf. BD339[3] and
MT127).
T183 The noun υἱός is anarthrous because it is a predicate nominative and it
precedes the verb (cf. βασιλεύς in v. 42 and John 1:1), "the Son of God."

42 T237 Ἐπί with the accusative is used with the verb πιστεύσομεν, meaning "we
will believe in him."

43 B75 The perfect tense in the verb πέποιθεν denotes existing state, "he trusteth
on God."
H469 Ὅτι has the force of assertion in this verse, meaning "verily" (cf. 26:
72).

44 R409 Οἱ λησταί is not to be taken as a plural for the singular. Probably both
reproached Jesus at first and afterwards one became sorry and turned on the
other (cf. MT58; this is an idiomatic plural, actually only one robber reproached
Jesus--TGr76). (Ed. Robertson's suggestion seems to be preferable, especially in view of Mark's account in Mark 15:32 (οἱ συνεσταυρωμένοι).
M34 Τὸ αὐτό is used as an adverbial accusative, "in the same way."

46 R705 Τοῦτ' ἔστιν is an explanatory phrase without any regard to the number,
gender or case of the noun it explains.
M11n.1 The aorist verb ἐγκατέλιπες refers to an event in the past, the results
of which are not prominantly contemplated by the writer. But this does not
mean that the rendering by the English perfect, "hast thou forsaken," is incorrect (it is perfective--T72).
M62 Περί has a temporal sense here, "at about."

49 R1128 The future participle σώσων expresses the purpose for the action of the
verb ἔρχεται (cf. T157), "will come to save."
MT175 The combination of ἄφες and ἴδωμεν simply means "let us see."

54 T183 θεοῦ υἱός is anarthrous because it is a predicate nominative and it precedes the verb, with the resultant meaning "the Son of God" (cf. v. 40).

55 R727 Αἵτινες introduces an explanatory clause (describing the women).

57 T53 Ἐμαθητεύθη has a causative sense, "he was made a disciple."
    BD160 Τοὔνομα means "by name" (with respect to name).

61 R1104 The participle καθήμεναι has an adjectival notion ("sitting opposite the
    grave"), especially since it varies in number from the verb ἦν (Mr. Scott con-
    siders this a periphrastic construction--R1406). [Ed. This seems highly im-
    probable especially in view of the previous observation.]

63 R870 The present verb ἐγείρομαι has a futuristic sense, portraying the certain-
    ty of expectation, "I shall rise" (prophetic--T63).

64 T32 The superlatives πρῶτος and ἔσχατος are used as comparatives, meaning "for-
    mer" and "latter" (cf. BD62).

                              MATTHEW 28

1   R646 Ὀψὲ σαββάτων may mean either "late on the sabbath" or "after the sabbath"
    (cf. M86; according to what follows and in view of the parallel in Mark, it
    means "after the sabbath"--BD164[4]; cf. H471).
    T27 Σαββάτων is used as an idiomatic plural, meaning "the sabbath."

2   R840 Ἐγένετο refers to action which is antecedent to (prior to) that of ἦλθεν
    in v. 1.

4   H461 The preposition ἀπό has a causal sense in this verse.

6   R845 The aorist verb ἠγέρθη should be translated into English by the perfect
    tense, "he has risen."
    B295 The clause with ὅπου ἔκειτο identifies the place, "where he lay."

9   TGr76 In the latter segment of this verse the plural is idiomatic, since only
    Mary Magdalene held him by the feet (cf. John 20:14-18).
    BD260(1) The article is omitted with Ἰησοῦς because it refers to the first
    appearance after the resurrection; in John's account the anaphoric article is
    included because of the context (it is best to accept the variant text with
    ὁ Ἰησοῦς supported by D and L, which is in accord with the Gospel usage--
    T167). [Ed. Although Blass may be ascribing too much significance to the
    anarthrous occurrence of Ἰησοῦς, one is not forced to accept the doubtful
    text that Turner suggests. Generally, Ἰησοῦς is articular in the Gospels,
    but it is considered a proper name and it does not require an article to be
    definite. Matthew frequently employs Ἰησοῦς in an anarthrous construction
    (cf. 1:16, 21; 17:8; 20:17, 30; 21:1, 12; and 27:17).]

10 R993 Ἵνα introduces the content of the command, "tell my brethren to go to
    Galilee."

13 M56 The genitive νυκτός means "by night."

15 R614 The preposition παρά has the idea of "among."

MT139   The aorist verb διεφημίσθη is used as a narrative aorist, but with the added words "and continues."

17   BD250   Οἱ δέ means "but others" (the article is similar to a demonstrative pro-
noun--R694; cf. 26:67).

19   R649   In this verse ὄνομα has the idea "the authority of" (baptism into the name,
i.e., a relationship as a goal of baptism--T255).
R684   The pronoun αὐτούς has the masculine gender, because it refers to the
people included in ἔθνη.
R1128   Βαπτίζοντες and διδάσκοντες are modal participles describing the manner
in which disciples are made.
BD148(3)   The active verb μαθητεύσατε has the meaning of "make disciples of"
(cf. H400).

20   M34   Πάσας τὰς ἡμέρας should perhaps strictly be translated as "the whole of
every day."

Mark

1 R781 Although ἀρχή is anarthrous, it is definite because it is used as part of
the title of the book.
TGr27f. Verses 1 and 4 should be taken together, with the intervening material
regarded as a parenthesis. Thus, the resultant meaning is "John the Baptist,
baptizing . . . and preaching . . . , was the beginning of the gospel of Jesus
Christ."
T211 Ἰησοῦ Χριστοῦ is used as an objective genitive, "about Jesus Christ."
T307 Mark's fondness for including the verb "to be" is against the interpretation, "the beginning of the gospel is as it is written . . ." (when Mark
omits the stative verb, it is best to translate the text as such).

2 R960 The relative clause with the future verb, ὅς κατασκευάσει . . ., portrays
the idea of purpose (cf. Luke 7:27).

3 T151 The participle here has a substantival usage, "voice of a herald."

4 R1127 The participle κηρύσσων has the notion of manner (the participle is not
the periphrastic construction with ἐγένετο), "John appeared . . . preaching."
T151 The participle βαπτίζων has a substantival force ("the baptizer"; cf. BD
413[1]).
T211 Μετανοίας is used as a subjective genitive; baptism does not lead to, but
springs from, repentance (an appositional genitive, "baptism involving repentance"?--T214; cf. R496). [Ed. Turner's comment may not be inaccurate, but
this particular genitive specifies John's unique type of baptism (cf. Matt.
31:ff).]

7 B376 The infinitive λῦσαι is used to limit the adjective ἱκανός, "the latchet
of whose shoes I am not worthy to stoop down and unloose."
T67 In the aorist expression ἐκήρυσσεν λέγων the reference may be to some definite occasion and actual saying (not a summary of his total ministry).
BD418(5) The participle κύψας is used to express the notion of manner, "even
by stooping."

8 T41 The pronoun αὐτός apparently has some emphasis here (in contrast to ἐγώ).

9 M68 The preposition εἰς appears to be used for ἐν in a local sense (cf. BD205),
perhaps with the meaning "He came to the Jordan and was baptized in it."
T166f. The anarthrous Ἰησοῦς is to be taken closely with the phrase which follows, "Jesus of Nazareth in Galilee." If it meant "Jesus came from Nazareth
in Galilee," it would have to be ὁ Ἰησοῦς to accord Mark's practice.

10 R577 The assertion is made by the preposition ἐκ that Jesus had been in the
water.

T25   Generally the singular οὐρανός is used for the material sense of "sky"
(but not in vv. 10f.).

11   R532   The prepositional phrase ἐν σοί is used to express a causal idea.
B55   Εὐδόκησα appears to be an ingressive aorist, "joy comes at the thought of
you" (cf. T72; it probably means "on thee I have set the seal of my approval":
literally "I set," at a time which is not defined—MT134; cf. the discussion
on 2 Pet. 1:17).

15   TGr121   The latter part of this verse should not be translated, "I believe in
the gospel," but "in this gospel dispensation, you must repent and believe"
("believe, in the sphere of the gospel"—T237 and MT67).
T75   The present imperatives μετανοεῖτε and πιστεύετε mean "persevere in repentance and belief."

17   R1023   In this verse the adverb δεῦτε has the force of an imperative, "come."

19   R659   The adjective ὀλίγον in the accusative case is used as an adverb, "a little further."
BD442(9)   The conjunction in καὶ αὐτούς is emphatic here, "who also."

21   M7   Εἰσπορεύονται is used as an historical present (very frequent in Mark),"they
went into."
M9   Ἐδίδασκεν is used as an inceptive imperfect, "he began to teach."
T27   The plural σάββασιν is used for the singular, "on the sabbath."
H446   Εὐθύς (εὐθέως) is not only extremely frequent in Mark, but is sometimes
an inferential conjunction, meaning "so then" (as in vv. 21, 23, 29 and 30).

22   R1127   ᾽Ως ἔχων expresses the notion of manner (cf. B445), "he taught as one
who had authority."

23   R784   The anarthrous prepositional phrase ἐν πνεύματι ἀκαθάρτῳ is attributive
to the noun ἄνθρωπος (cf. T221 and BD272; the ἐν of accompaniment here implies
the idea of manner (cf. BD219[4]0, with the meaning "the man with the unclean
spirit," unless we take the dative as meaning "in the power of"—T252).   [Ed.
Turner's former suggestion seems preferable in view of Christ's command in v.
25.]

24   M154   The clause σε τίς εἶ is used as the object of οἶδα (thus σέ is in the accusative rather than the nominative), meaning "I know who you are" (cf. T149;
prolepsis occurs [i.e., the subject is brought forward]—T325).
TGr43   Τί ἡμῖν καὶ σοί means "Leave us alone!" (cf. Luke 4:34).

25   TGr42   The aorist imperative φιμώθητι means "be harmless" (i.e., "become harmless").

27   R1181   In καὶ τοῖς πνεύμασι, the καί has an ascensive sense, meaning "even" (cf.
Rom. 13:5).

28   BD103   Πανταχοῦ means "in all directions."

31   T67   Διηκόνει is used as an iterative imperfect, meaning "began to wait on them."

33 M53 The preposition πρός may have a pregnant sense, seemingly combining linear
motion with punctiliar rest on arrival, "toward" (although it is questionable
whether this can be distinguished Mark 11:4 or 13:29 with ἐπὶ θύραις).

34 M72 With the compound verbs in vv. 34 and 42, there seems to be very little
distinction between ἐκ and ἀπό.

35 M72 A general distinction in Mark (although not consistently observed, cf. v.
34), may be that a man will go out of a house (ἐκ), but from a country (ἀπό);
thus in this verse, "he left the house and went away to an uninhabited place."

36 R606 In the compound verb καταδίωξεν, the preposition has a perfective force,
"hunt down" (cf. MT116).

38 R595 The prepositional phrase εἰς τοῦτο has the idea of purpose.
B103 Ἀλλαχοῦ means "in another direction" (cf. v. 28).
H276 The compound noun κωμοπόλεις means "village-town" (i.e., a πόλις that
is little more than a κώμη).

39 BD205 Εἰς is used instead of ἐν in a local sense (εἰς occurs here because of
the verb ἦλθεν--R593). [Ed. The preposition does have a local sense ("they
went preaching in their synagogues"), but the verb of motion ἦλθεν tends to
prefer εἰς; notice the variant with the stative verb ἦν, which construction
Luke prefers.]

44 R619 The preposition περί here implies a causal notion (cf. BD229[1]).
MT124 In this verse, ὅρα is only a sort of particle adding emphasis to the imperative, "see that you say nothing to anyone."

45 H446 Πολλά is used with an adverbial sense, "to talk freely."

MARK 2

1 R581 The preposition in δι' ἡμερῶν has a temporal sense, meaning "interval of
days," "days between," "after some days" (cf. BD223[1]), although surely no one
would think that διά in itself means "after."
T261 The local expression ἐν οἴκῳ means "at home" ("in a house"--MT82).

2 M27 Ὥστε μηκέτι χωρεῖν μηδὲ τὰ πρὸς τὴν θύραν appears to mean "so that there
was no longer room, not even in the part near the door" (unless τὰ πρὸς τὴν
θύραν is not an accusative of respect but the subject of χωρεῖν, which seems
quite unlikely with the intervening μηδέ).

4 H470 Because of the reversed order and the redundancy in ἀπεστέγασαν τὴν
στέγην καὶ ἐξορύξαντες χαλῶσι, Wellhausen retranslates the first clause in a
way which might also mean "they brought him to the roof." [Ed. This reconstruction of the text is actually unnecessary, since the participle is often
redundant in New Testament Greek (generally indicating some degree of emphasis).]

5 MT119 Ἀφίενται is used as an aoristic present, "they are this moment forgiven"
(cf. Luke 5:23 and BD320).

7   R697 Οὗτος is used to express the notion of reproach (by the Pharisees about
    Jesus; cf. Luke 15:2).

8   M75 Ἐν ἑαυτοῖς is used in v. 8 (cf. v. 6) as equivalent to ἐν ταῖς καρδίαις
    αὐτῶν (this is a semitism of vocabulary to be expected in the sayings of Jesus
    --H432).

10 R434 The insertion λέγει τῷ παραλυκτικῷ in the speech of Jesus to the paralytic
    is a very interesting parenthesis.

11 R428 The absence of the conjunction in ἔγειρε ἆρον gives life and movement to
    the expression, "rise, take."
    R855 The present imperative ὕπαγε is exclamatory (cf. John 9:7), "go!"

12 BD434(2) The adverb οὕτως is used here instead of an accusative object, "like
    this."

15 R1190 Γάρ introduces an explanation by way of an appendix to the train of
    thought, "for there were many."
    T348 In vv. 15f., the punctuation should run as follows: "For they were many.
    There followed him some scribes of the Pharisees. They noticed him eating . ."
    BD471(4) Notice the co-ordination of the two finite verbs ἦσαν. . . ἠκολούθουν
    rather than a participle.

16 R1029 The second occurrence of ὅτι in this verse has an interrogative sense,
    "why" (cf. διὰ τι in Matt. 9:11; the first occurrence of ὅτι introduces indi-
    rect discourse, "that").
    M43 Τῶν Φαρισαίων may be a partitive genitive, "of the Pharisees" (cf. T209;
    Luke 5:30 has "their scribes").

17 R990 The infinitive καλέσαι expresses the notion of purpose, "to call."

18 T292 In this verse the undefined plural may be impersonal or it may refer to
    the subject of the preceding sentence. [Ed. The subject of ἔρχονται and λέγου-
    σιν is apparently provided as the subject of the previous sentence, οἱ μαθηταὶ
    Ἰωάννου καὶ οἱ Φαρισαῖοι.]

19 M174 The adjectival genitive can be seen in οἱ υἱοὶ τοῦ νυμφῶνος, meaning "the
    bridal party" (semitic).

20 B316 The relative clause with ὅταν is conditional in form, but definite in
    force, "but days will come when the bridegroom shall be taken away from them"
    (cf. BD382[3]).

21 R1025 Εἰ δὲ μή has the sense of "but if not" or "otherwise" (cf. John 14:11).
    T209 The partitive genitive with ἀπό here has the sense of "some of it" (the
    best reading from a syntax point of view is αἴρει ἀπ᾽ αὐτοῦ ["some of it"]
    τὸ πλήρωμα τὸ καινὸν ["the new fulness"] ἀπὸ τοῦ παλαιοῦ ["namely, some of the
    old"]). [Ed. The correct text appears to be αἴρει ἀπ᾽ αὐτοῦ τὸ πλήρωμα τὸ
    καινὸν τοῦ παλαιοῦ supported by A, K, Δ and certain Syriac miniscules, which
    was slightly rearranged to conform to the text in Matt. 9:16. This clause
    should then be rendered "the new patch of the old (garment) breaks away from
    it."]

23   R1043   Outside of Luke's writings the infinitive with ἐγένετο is confined to
     this verse, which Moulton (MT17) calls a primitive assimilation of Luke 6:1.
     T56   The active infinitive ποιεῖν occurs where we would expect the middle (cf.
     MT159, the active ὁδὸν ποιεῖν actually means "construct a road").

25   T41   Αὐτός carries emphasis here, "he himself" (cf. R679, showing contrast).
     T49   Τί is equivalent to a relative pronoun here, meaning "what."

26   R603   Ἐπί with the genitive here has the idea of "in the time of," or "during
     the time of" (cf. Acts 11:28).
     T137   Πῶς is used to introduce an object clause, "how."

27   M55   Διά appears to have a prospective sense here, with the resultant meaning
     "the sabbath was made for man, and not man for the sabbath" (aim or purpose
     --R584; cf. T268).

28   B237   Ὥστε introduces an independent sentence, and has the meaning "therefore,
     accordingly" (an inferential particle meaning "and so, accordingly"--M144),
     "so that the Son of Man is lord even of the sabbath."

                                 MARK 3

1   R902   Ἐξηραμμένην ἔχων is similar to a perfect periphrastic, "who had a with-
     ered hand."

2   R1024   Εἰ is used to introduce an indirect question here, "whether."

4   B384   The infinitives here are used as the subject of the finite verb ἔξεστιν
     ("is it lawful . . . to do good . . . to do harm").
     T32   Notice the comparative idea in ἔξεστιν . . . ἤ (the comparative particle
        is used after a verb as though by itself it meant "more than"--H442).

5   R813   Περιβλέπομαι is always middle in the New Testament, accenting the movement
     of the eyes or concern expressed in the look.
     H325   The meaning of συλλυπέομαι in this verse is difficult to determine, since
     the word in its earlier record involves "sympathy" which is somewhat forced
     here: can it be perfective, meaning "utterly distressed"?   [Ed.   The preposi-
     tion σύν strengthens the simple verb, with the resultant meaning "deeply grieved
     at the hardening of their heart."]

6   B207   Ὅπως occurs with object clauses (with the meaning "that") in the New
     Testament only in Matt. 12:14; 22:15 and in this verse, and in all these cases
     after a phrase meaning "to plan."

7   R1183   In this verse the second καί comes near taking the place of the relative
     pronoun ὅ, for in the next verse there are five instances of καί co-ordinate
     with each other, but subordinate to καί in v. 7.

8   M62   Περί with the accusative here means "in the region of."

9   MT208   The first ἵνα in this verse introduces the content of the command, "that."

                                      63

11 R884 The imperfect verbs in this verse have an iterative sense (thus the mean-
    ing is "Whenever the unclean spirits saw him, they used to fall down before
    him, and cry out . . . Then he would habitually charge them not to make him
    known"--TGr34).
    B290 The first part of this verse should be translated, "If at any time, they
    saw him, they were wont to fall down before him." That is, while the class of
    events is actual, the relative clause presents the successive instances distrib-
    utively as suppositions.

12 H446 Πολλά is used with the adverbial sense, "he strictly ordered" (cf. 1:45).

13 T179 The formula τὸ ὄρος means "the highlands."

14 R1088 The simple infinitive here expresses the notion of purpose ("to proclaim
    continually [present infinitive]"--T78).

16 R488 The dative and accusative appear to be in apposition. [Ed. Actually,
    ἐπιτίθημι may be used with ὄνομα and a dative to indicate the giving of a sur-
    name to someone (cf. v. 17).]

17 T208 Υἱοὶ βροντῆς actually means "thunderbolts" (cf. BD162[6]).

21 R614 Οἱ παρ' αὐτοῦ refers to one's family or kinsmen ("his relatives"--M52).
    B47 The aorist verb ἐξέστη has the force of a perfect, denoting a present
    state, the result of a past action ("he has become mad"--BD342[1]).
    TGr56 In this verse, many versions imply that the mother and kinsmen of Jesus
    considered him mad. But ἔλεγον has an impersonal subject, common in Mark. It
    was rumor, not his own family, that spread the doubts of his sanity. The fam-
    ily was anxious, having heard he had taken no food, and they wished to have a
    quiet word with him, especially when they heard the rumors (cf. T292).

24 R602 The preposition ἐπί has the sense of "against" in vv. 24ff.

28 R732 The pronoun ὅσα has both ἁμαρτήματα and βλασφημίαι as antecedents and natu-
    rally is neuter.

31 R991 The present participle καλοῦντες implies the notion of purpose, with the
    meaning "they sent to him calling him."

                                      MARK 4

1   M51 Παρά has the notion of rest, "he began to teach by the sea."
    M98 The superlative adjective πλεῖστος is used as an elative superlative (i.e.,
    it is used to intensify), with the meaning "huge" ("very large"--T31).

4   M125 Ὁ μέν is used as a demonstrative pronoun here, meaning "some."
    BD447(3) The occurrence of ὁ μέν . . . καὶ ἄλλο is occasioned by an intervening
    development of the story.

8   M77 If the preposition ἐν is the correct reading here, it apparently has the
    meaning "at the rate of sixty and a hundred" (i.e., to one; cf. T265 and MT103).

This, according to one reading, is preceded by εἰς τριάκοντα, which may be an instance of the blurring of the distinction between ἐν and εἰς, or may, conceivably represent a real shade of difference -- "to the extent of thirty to one, and at the rate of sixty," etc. (cf. T266).

M187 The anomalous εἰς . . . ἐν . . . ἐν has been tentatively explained as due to a literal translation of Aramaic (literally "one") as εἷς ("one"), whereas it should have been treated as a mere idiomatic usage of εἰς and ἐν with multiples (cf. the comment above).

BD248(3) Ἐν τριάκοντα is an Aramaism, meaning "thirty fold" (ἐν is an inferior reading). [Ed. The text with εἰς . . . ἐν . . . ἐν has the best manuscript support. The prepositions were altered to numerals as an attempt to conform with Matthew's parallel account. Whereas the change to ἐν throughout is in conformity with v. 20.]

9 R720 The relative clause (ὅς . . .) is the subject of ἀκουέτω.

10 T16 Οἱ περὶ αὐτόν means "his disciples" (cf. Luke 22:49).
    T26 The plural τὰς παραβολάς means "the parable" (cf. TGr47).

11 M77 Ἐν παραβαλαῖς means "by parables" (instrumental ἐν).

12 R1413 When the construction with ἵνα is continued in a further clause by μή, the negative alone is repeated (cf. John 6:50).
    M142f. The radical view which interprets the whole phrase -- ἵνα and μήποτε alike -- as strictly final, so that parables are to prevent any who are not predestined for salvation from hearing, is too incongruous with any part of the New Testament period to be plausible. It is far more reasonable to take both ἵνα and μήποτε as instances of the Semitic blurring of purpose and result, so that Matthew's change of ἵνα to ὅτι is essentially true to the sense, while his illogical retention of the μήποτε is true to the semitic idiom (cf. 2 Cor. 4:4).
    M187 T. W. Manson tried to soften the apparent harshness of this verse by assuming that it was a mistranslation of the Targumic form of Isa. 6:9f. in which the original should have been translated not as ἵνα but as οὔ (this is improbable-- TGr48).
    TGr49 Ἵνα means "in order that" and μήποτε means "lest." The prophet (Isaiah) saw the darkening of the national mind as part of God's inscrutable providence and it looks as if Mark, and indeed Jesus, did so too. Jesus took pains according to the synoptic gospels, to hide his true identity from most of the Jews throughout his ministry (ἵνα is final--BD369[2]).
    T102 The ἵνα of v. 12 (and Luke 8:10) is transformed into a causal ὅτι in the Matthew parallel, but this would not prove identity of meaning.
    BD471(3) This verse means "although they look with perceptive eyes, yet they will not perceive," and the latter part of this verse means "in case they repent." [Ed. The initial particle of verse 12 is used as a quotation formula, meaning "that it may be fulfilled" (cf. the similar construction in Matt. 18:16). In this usage, ἵνα portrays the notion of purpose. Teaching by means of parables was intended to fulfill the sentence of judicial blindness pronounced on those who will not see.]

13 T200 Πάσας τὰς παραβολάς means "any parables," not "all the parables" (cf. BD 275[3]).

17 R880 Σκανδαλίζονται is used as a conative present, referring to an act just be-
    ginning (cf. T63).

22 R999 Ἵνα is used here like ὥστε and the infinitive (consecutive; cf. BD382[1]),
    "that."
    R1185 Οὐδέ has a continuative sense, carrying on the negative with no idea of
    contrast.
    T330 Ἀλλά has the meaning of "except" (cf. BD448[8] and H468).

24 M33 Ἐν occurs with the dative of judgment here, "with which measure."

26 M23 The subjunctive is used in a comparison, "as though he might throw." This
    has been claimed as unique; but Luke 11:5f. looks uncommonly like the same
    usage (it may be called a parabolic subjunctive).

27 R470 In νύκτα καὶ ἡμέραν, the sleeping and rising go on continually from day
    to day.

28 R549 The Greek prefers the personal connection of the adjective with the subject
    to the adverbial connection with the verb (thus the adjective αὐτομάτη is used
    as an adverb in English; cf. T225 and Acts 12:10), "all by itself."

30 R407 By using the plural in this verse Christ associates others with himself
    in a very natural manner (cf. BD280).
    T257 Ἐν with the dative has an instrumental sense here.

32 M65f. The preposition ὑπό seems to portray the notion of "rest beneath," with
    the resultant meaning "so that the birds of the sky could nest under its sha-
    dow."

33 R884 Ἐλάλει is used as an iterative imperfect, "he spoke repeatedly."

36 T321 Ὡς ἦν ἐν τῷ πλοίῳ either means "when he was in the boat" or "as he was,
    in the boat" (these two translations are similar).

37 R868 The realistic present γίνεται (historical) is followed by the imperfect,
    "a great storm arose."
    R1000 Ὥστε with the infinitive has the sense of actual result, "so that."
    T52 The compound verb ἐπιβάλλω means "rush upon."

38 R679 The pronoun in καὶ αὐτός is emphatic, denoting Jesus as the chief person
    in the story.
    R1034 Ὅτι introduces a subject clause here (the subject of μέλει), "is it not
    a concern to you that."

39 R428 The absence of the conjunction in σιώπα, πεφίμωσο gives life and movement
    to the expression.
    R908 The durative idea is in both σιώπα (linear present) and πεφίμωσο, "put the
    muzzle on and keep it on" (πεφίμωσο is probably a solemn stereotyped phrase used
    in adjurations--T85; an emphatic command--BD346).

41 R699 In this verse, ὅτι is almost equivalent to ὥστε (with a consecutive sense,
    "so that"; cf. T318).

R1182 In the latter section of this verse καὶ . . . καί means "both . . . and"
(cf. T335; "even . . . and"--BD444[3]). [Ed. the conjunctions appear to be
used with a climatic sense, stressing Christ's majestic ability, "even . . .
and."]
M58 The verb ὑπακούει is singular even though the subject is a compound.

MARK 5

2 T252 The prepositional phrase with ἐν has the idea of manner, "a man with an
unclean spirit" (cf. 1:23).

4 R533 Πέδαις and ἀλύσεσιν are used as instrumental datives (accompanying circumstance or manner--T241). [Ed. These explanations have a similar sense; the
dative nouns have the resultant meaning "with fetters and chains."]
R581 The root idea of the preposition is present in the compound verb διασπάω,
"rend in two."
B108 The infinitive δεδέσθαι denotes an action whose result was existing, not
at the time of speaking, but at an earlier time.
B408 Διὰ τό with the infinitive expresses the evidence (for his condition of
being bound) rather than the cause strictly so called (cf. R1071).

5 M39 The temporal prepositional phrase here means "continually, night and day."

7 R669 Ὕψιστος is a true superlative referring to God, "Jesus, son of the most
high God."

10 T65 There is a distinction between v. 10 and v. 12; the request is successful
and therefore aorist in v. 12 (but the imperfect tense is used in v. 10, in
which verse the request is incomplete).
MT208 Ἵνα introduces the content of the command here, "that."
H446 Πολλά is used with an adverbial sense, "eagerly" (cf. 1:45).

11 M54 The prepositional phrase here means "on the hill."

13 R607 Κατὰ τοῦ κρημνοῦ has the idea "down from the cliff."
R884 In this verse the separate details are well described by the vivid imperfect tense (ἐπνίγοντο is used as an iterative imperfect--T67; the action was
repeated until every pig had drowned).
R968 The adverb ὡς has the sense of "about."

14 TGr57 The impersonal subject occurs here, "they (i.e., "people") came to see
what had happened."

15 R868 The historical present verbs ἔρχονται καὶ θεωροῦσιν occur between aorists,
"they came and saw."
R1117 The perfect participle ἐσχηκότα is not used as a simple perfect and describes the state of the man before Jesus cast out the demon, which casting-out
is itself in the past (as an aorist--BD343[2]; cf. MT145).
T21 The masculine λεγιῶνα occurs for a feminine, because it is the demons' name.

16 R1032 Πῶς is used instead of a declarative ὅτι (after διηγήσαντο), "they told
what had happened."

18 B200 Ἵνα is used to introduce an object clause after παρεκάλει, with the meaning "he besought him that he might be with him."
T322 Mark should have made the genitive absolute construction ἐμβαίνοντος αὐτοῦ
agree with the accusative αὐτόν (cf. BD423[2]). [Ed. This isn't absolutely
necessary, since the genitive absolute is a segment of the sentence which lacks
close connection with the rest of the sentence. Apparently a simple temporal
expression was desired. Having written the temporal expression as a genitive,
Mark then had to change to αὐτόν as the object of the verb παρεκάλει, "while
he was getting into the boat, the man who had been demon possessed was begging
him.]

19 B350 The pronoun ὅσα is used in an indirect question in vv. 19f, "how much."
TGr34 An accurate distinction of the tenses is maintained in this verse (cf.
R901). "Go home," said Jesus, "and show your family the kind of man the Lord
has made of you." The perfect tense indicates the abiding result of what God
had done for the demented sufferer. When Jesus spoke again, he used the aorist
tense: "and tell them God has given you a touch of his love."

21 T229 The text is doubtful at this verse where both πάλιν εἰς τὸ πέραν and εἰς
τὸ πέραν πάλιν occur; perhaps the fact that Mark usually has πάλιν near its
verb sways the balance in favor of the latter.

22 H432 Εἷς is used as an indefinite pronoun here, "one of the rulers of the synagogue."

23 R933 Ἵνα seems to be merely an introductory term with the volitive subjunctive
(i.e., with imperatival force) in ἵνα . . . ἐπιθῇς (it is an imperatival ἵνα,
"do please come and lay your hands"--M144; cf. T95).
H446 Πολλά has an adverbial sense, "eagerly" (cf. v. 10).

25 R892 The present participle οὖσα refers to a past action still in progress (cf.
B131), "had been bleeding."
R1105 Wescott and Hort indicate by the comma after ἐλθοῦσα that they regard the
participles with γυνή (οὖσα, παθοῦσα, δαπανήσασα, ὠφεληθεῖσα, and ἐλθοῦσα) as
attributive. They describe the woman who comes. Then the sentence proceeds
with the predicate-circumstantial participles (ἀκούσασα, ἐλθοῦσα in v. 27) before ἥψατο, "after she heard . . ., coming . . ., she touched."
M78 The prepositional phrase ἐν ῥύσει αἵματος denotes attendant circumstance,
with the meaning "suffering from a hemorrhage."

26 R1111 In παθοῦσα ὑπὸ πολλῶν ἰατρῶν, the active participle has the construction
of the passive, but this is due to the verb πάσχω (and the preposition ὑπό),
not to the voice of the participle.
M51 Δαπανήσασα τὰ παρ' αὐτῆς means "having spent all that she had"(literally
"the things from beside her," with a suggestion, perhaps, of emphasis on the
disastrous movement away of all her small savings; cf. Luke 10:7).

27 T257 The prepositional phrase ἐν τῷ ὄχλῳ after the verb ἔρχομαι does not express
motion from place to place, but rather the accompanying circumstances on the
sphere in which motion occurs (cf. 8:38 and 13:26), "in the crowd."

28 R208 Ἐὰν . . . κἄν has the sense "if only" (cf. T321).

32 R838 The imperfect tense has significance in περιεβλέπετο, with the sense "he
    began to look around because of the touch" (Jesus was looking around him until
    the woman came [ἦλθεν] --T66).

33 R858 Φοβηθεῖσα is used as an ingressive aorist (only the inception of the act
    precedes the action of the principal verb--B137), "began to fear."
    R897 The use of the perfect verb εἰδυῖα preserves the vividness of the woman's
    consciousness.

34 BD206(1) The preposition εἰς here has a sense similar to ἐν, "in peace."

35 R502 In ἀπὸ τοῦ ἀρχισυναγώγου, it is possible that οἴκου is to be supplied
    ("from the ruler's house," cf. v. 38), since the man himself has already come
    (v. 22).
    B47 The aorist verb ἀπέθανεν occurs with the proper force of a Greek perfect
    (i.e., to denote a present state, the result of a past act; cf. Luke 8:49).

36 TGr87 The first part of this verse should be translated, "Jesus overheard the
    word that was spoken" (despite the fact that the accusative is used).
    T75 The imperatives here are interesting, meaning "stop being frightened, but
    go on having faith" (perhaps corrected in Luke 8:50 with πίστευσον, "start to
    have faith"). In Mark the command is to continue to have as much faith as be-
    fore; in Luke it is to begin to have faith, or to have a better faith than be-
    fore the child died. Perhaps Luke felt the subtle difference.

38 H446 Πολλά has an adverbial sense, "wailing loudly" (cf. v. 10).

40 BD277(3) The pronoun αὐτός is emphatic here, "but he."

41 R29 The fact that Mark twice (5:41 and 7:34) uses Aramaic quotations from the
    words of Jesus does not prove that Jesus always spoke in that tongue, nor that
    he did so only on these occasions.
    R684 In this verse αὐτῇ agrees with the natural gender of παιδίον rather than
    the grammatical gender (the child was a girl).
    B20 The present periphrastic construction occurs here (it is debatable whether
    εἰμί should not rather be regarded as standing on its own feet, with an explana-
    tory participle--M17). [Ed. In the New Testament, ὅ ἐστιν μεθερμηνευόμενον
    does not have the full force of a periphrastic construction, but is used as an
    explanatory formula, "which means (when translated)"; cf. Matt. 1:23; Mark 15:
    22, 34 and John 1:41.]

42 R1190 Γάρ is explanatory here (γάρ is not explanatory in this context. No one
    ever suspected that the child was too young to walk. Mark misplaces a paren-
    thesis--TGr66). [Ed. The particle γάρ here has its usual explanatory sense,
    although this clause is similar to a parenthesis in usage.]

43 H446 Πολλά has an adverbial sense, "strictly" (cf. v. 10).
    H450 The infinitive δοθῆναι occurs after εἶπεν in a jussive sense, denoting the
    content of a request, "he said, give her to eat."

MARK 6

1   R880 'Ακολουθοῦσιν seems to be used as a durative historical present, "his dis-
    ciples followed him."

2   R735 Τίς is equivalent to ποῖος here ("where does it come from?"--BD298[2]).
    T31 Πολλοί means "the majority" (even without the article).
    H462 The prepositional phrase διὰ τῶν χειρῶν is obviously modelled upon the
    vernacular phrase διὰ χειρός, referring to money paid "directly."

3   M52 Πρός denotes position here ("with"; cf. H467).
    BD273(1) Τέκτων has the article because Jesus was known by this designation
    (well known), "the carpenter."

6   M108f. Τὰς κώμας κύκλῳ is best understood as equivalent to τας κύκλῳ, rather
    than taking κύκλῳ with περιῆγεν (κύκλῳ may define the verb as in Rom. 15:19--
    T221). [Ed. If Mark would have intended κύκλῳ to be used as an adjective, he
    probably would have used the article with it, as he did in v. 36 of this chap-
    ter. The anarthrous κύκλῳ doesn't appear to be used as an adjective, especially
    since the noun it occurs with is articular, "he was going around."]

7   M67 'Απέστειλεν αὐτοὺς ἀνὰ δύο means he sent them out in pairs, i.e., perhaps
    "at the strength of, up to, two."

8   R1042 The indirect discourse in vv. 8ff. begins with ἵνα and concludes with the
    infinitive (a change for the sake of variety), "he charged them to take."
    T225 There is some confusion of μόνος with the adverb μόνον (D has μόνην), "ex-
    cept a staff."

12 R993 Ἵνα introduces an object clause after ἐκήρυξαν here, "they preached that
    men should repent."

13 R483 Ἐλαίῳ is used as an instrumental dative, "with oil."

14 R694 The article αἱ is nearly equivalent in meaning to "these."
    R1111 In 'Ιωάννης ὁ βαπτίζων, it is not present time that is here given by this
    tense, but the general description of John as the Baptizer without regard to
    time. It is actually used of him after his death (the participle is equivalent
    to ὁ βαπτιστής--BD413[1]; the phrase is less of a technical term that the noun
    --MT127).

15 TGr66 With the delayed parenthesis here, the meaning is "John the Baptist is
    risen and therefore mighty powers are at work in him, like one of the prophets.
    Some said that he was Elijah and others that he was a prophet."
    T320 Ὡς is used to soften a statement "as it were, perhaps, approximately."

17 T41 The proleptic pronoun (placed forward) followed by a resumptive noun is an
    Aramaic peculiarity; the meaning here is "he, that is Herod" (cf. M176).

18 M10 The imperfect tense here is equivalent to an English periphrastic perfect
    or pluperfect, with the resultant meaning "for John had been saying" (cf. T67).

19 R539 Αὐτῷ is used as a dative of disadvantage, "against him."
    T52 The compound verb ἐνέχω means "hate, persecute" (cf. Luke 11:53).

20 H445f. Ἀκούσας αὐτοῦ πολλὰ ἐποίει means "he listened to him often " (πολλά has
    an adverbial sense; cf. 1:45 and BD414[5]).

21 M43 Τοῖς γενεσίοις is used as a temporal dative, "at his birthday feast" (cf.
    R523; names of feasts are often plural--R408).

22 M33 Αἴτησόν με ὁ ἐὰν θέλῃς with the double accusative means "request of me
    whatever you like."
    MT160 There is a distinction between αἰτέω and αἰτέομαι maintained in vv. 22 -
    25. The middle was used in business transactions, while the active in requests
    of a son from a father, etc. Consequently, the daughter of Herodias, after the
    king's declaration, stands in a kind of business relation to him (cf. R805 and
    BD316[2]).

25 R943 Ἵνα with the subjunctive has an imperatival sense after θέλω (θέλω ἵνα
    . . . δῷς is paralleled in Matt. 14:8 by δός; cf. BD387[3]), "I want you to
    give."
    BD425(2) The modal-temporal participle with εὐθύς means "she came in immediate-
    ly."

26 T26 The plural ὅρκους simply means "oath."
    T335 A chain of dependent genitives which are not appreciated by New Testament
    writers, is avoided by the use of καί here. Thus it does not mean "oaths and
    guests," but "oaths sworn before the guests" (cf. BD442[16]).
    T350 The middle part of this verse should be interpreted "he was grieved because
    of" (not "he was unwilling . . . because of").

28 T40 Αὐτῆς has the feminine gender according to the sense, referring to the girl
    (instead of the neuter, which would be in concord with κοράσιον).

33 R530 Πεζῇ is used as a dative of manner, "on foot" or "by land."

34 R1140 Ὡς merely has the notion of comparison here, "they were as."
    BD155(1) A double accusative does not occur in αὐτοὺς πολλά but πολλά is rather
    an accusative of content, "many things."

37 R678 The pronoun ὑμεῖς is emphatic here (cf. T37), "you give them."

38 R916 The pronoun πόσος is used in an indirect question here, "how many."

39 R487 Συμπόσια συμπόσια may be considered as nominative or accusative, as well
    as πρασιαὶ πρασιαί in the following verse (adverbial nominatives--T231; the
    accusative of result--B158). [Ed. According to form συμπόσια may be either
    nominative or accusative. In view of the repeated nominative for distribution
    in v. 7 and v. 40, it appears as though this distributive repetition may be
    nominative as well, "by parties."]
    BD493(2) The doubling of words for a distributive sense is not rhetorical but
    vulgar (a semitism--MT97).

40 M59 Κατά is used distributively with the accusative here. Κατὰ ἑκατον καὶ
    κατὰ πεντήκοντα is usually explained as meaning "in groups, (some) of a hundred

and (some) of fifty;" but the context, with its προσιαὶ προσιαί, implies that
they were seated "in rows, consequently they formed a great rectangle, "a hundred by fifty"; the κατά will then be equivalent to our "at" in the idiom: "one
side of the rectangle was reckoned at a hundred, the other at fifty." This interpretation is not inconsistent with Luke 9:14, if κλισία is a "rank" or "row"
rather than a "group."

41 TGr67f. Part of this verse should be translated "He gave thanks (aorist), broke
    the loaves (aorist), and kept on distributing it to the disciples" (imperfect).
    The disciples came to Jesus repeatedly for more food, and they handed it to the
    people. Then Mark returns to the aorist tense when he writes "He divided the
    two fish among them all." The aorist describes the action as a whole, without
    considering any of the parts (cf. Luke 9:16).

43 TGr57 The initial part of this verse should be translated "they took up twelve
    baskets."

45 R975 Ἑως with the present indicative has the notion "while" (not "until") and
    it refers to a contemporaneous event (cf. B328).

47 R686 Αὐτός is emphatic in this verse, "he was alone."

48 M62 Περί with the accusative has the sense of "about."
    T146 Ἐν τῷ ἐλαύνειν means "by the rowing" (cf. BD404[3]).

50 B165 The present imperative φοβεῖσθε with μή forbids the continuation of the
    action already in progress.

52 R604 The sense of ἐπί with the dative here wavers between occasion and time,
    "they did not understand about."

54 TGr57 The indefinite plural ἐπιγνόντες should be translated "they (i.e., "peo-
    ple") recognized him."

55 R884 Ἤκουον is used as an iterative imperfect, "where they would hear."

56 R969 In ὅπου ἄν εἰσεπορεύετο, ἄν emphasizes the notion of repetition in the
    imperfect tense "wherever he would enter."
    M138 Ἵνα κἄν τοῦ κρασπέδου has the sense "even if it were no more than the
    fringe" ("so that even if"--T100; cf. Acts 5:15).

                                    MARK 7

4 R807 Βαπτίσωνται is used as a direct middle, "unless they wash themselves."
    TGr57 The preposition ἀπό means "after" in a temporal sense, "when (after) they
    come from the market-place they Pharisees do not eat, unless they wash them-
    selves" (cf. BD209[4]).
    T135 The infinitive κρατεῖν is used to denote purpose, "to keep."

5 T185 The adjective appears to be used predicatively, "with hands unwashed" (D
    and W have ταῖς before χερσίν).

                                    72

9   R1198 Note the use of irony by Jesus here (cf. BD495[2]).

11 R599 'Εϰ has the notion of cause or occasion here, "because of me."
    M131 The relative clause has an adverbial sense, "anything in regard to which
    you would have received benefit."
    M151 The latter section of this verse has an implied protasis, "if the money
    had not been dedicated."

12 B482 The compound of οὐ occurs with an infinitive, because it is dependent upon
    a principal verb negated by οὐ.

15 M84 "Εξωθεν is used as a preposition here ("from outside," cf. v. 18--BD104[2]).

19 BD111(6) 'Αφεδρῶνα means "latrine" (D softens the text to εἰς τον ὀχετόν, mean-
    ing "through the intestinal canal").
    BD126(3) The meaning "stench" or "filth" for βρώματα has been accepted by many
    exegetes on the basis of Modern Greek, but this does not suit Mark 7:19, in
    which verse it has the meaning of "foods."

20 BD291(4) 'Εϰεῖνο means "that other thing."

21 BD104(2) "Εσωθεν is used as a preposition in vv. 21 and 23, meaning "from in-
    side."

26 R884 'Ηρώτα is used as an iterative imperfect, "she begged him (repeatedly)."

28 H345 The diminutive ψιχίον is used for "food."

30 R1123 Note the indirect discourse after the verb εὖρεν, "she found the child
    lying on the bed."

31 M67 Generally the phrase ἀνὰ μέσον means "among" or "in the midst," but this
    verse is problematic: does it mean "right through"? [Ed. In this context,
    the phrase has the meaning of "through the region."]

35 R838 In the latter part of this verse the aorist lifts the curtain and the im-
    perfect continues the play (with an inchoative imperfect, "began"--R885).

36 T29 The comparative is doubled here for emphasis (cf. BD246).
    BD154 The relative ὅσον has the sense of "the more," properly "as much as."

37 T26 The idiomatic plural occurs here; a single case seems to be in mind, "the
    deaf . . . the dumb." [Ed. Actually the people appear to be making a general-
    ized statement.]

MARK 8

1   B346 An indirect question is introduced by τί after ἐχόντων, "not having some-
    thing."

7   R1047 The infinitive is used in an indirect command after εἶπεν (cf. H450), "he
    commanded that these . . . "

11 R614 Both παρά and ἀπό are used with the ablatival genitive, "from."

12 R1024 Εἰ occurs with the sense of "not," in the solemn oath here (with the force
of an emphatic negative assertion or oath--B272; cf. M179), "there certainly
shall not be given" (a result of semitic influence--H468).

14 B48 The aorist verb ἐπελάθοντο is used to refer to a past event which precedes
another past event mentioned in the context (similar to a pluperfect), "they
had forgotten."

19 T236 Εἰς with the accusative is used for the simple dative, meaning "for."

22 R807 Ἅφηται is really a direct middle, meaning "fasten himself to," "touch."

23 R916 Εἰ introduces a direct question, "do you see anything?" (this is unclassical and may be due to the tendency of the Septuagint to render the Hebrew with
εἰ as well as μή).

24 H436 Ὅτι is equivalent to the relative pronoun οὕς.

26 BD445(2) Because of the position here, μηδέ means "not even" (the sense of this
clause requires εἴπῃς instead of εἰσέλθῃς). [Ed. The weightiest manuscript
support includes εἰσέλθῃς in the text, although an injunction to silence may be
implicit within the prohibition.]

34 H421 The imperatives here present the notion "then he will be my disciple."

38 T257 Ἐν τῇ δόξῃ with the verb ἔλθῃ portrays the idea of accompanying circumstance, "with the glory of his father" (cf. 5:27).

MARK 9

1   R742 The plural τινες means "some."
TGr42f. The latter part of this verse should be translated "till they see the
kingdom of God already established (perfect participle) with power." His words
appear to be spoken immediately before the Transfiguration and that is where the
significance lies. Either the Transfiguration itself was "the kingdom already
established" or it provides the clue to it.
T82 The perfect participle ἐστηκότων is used as a present participle (often in
the New Testament), "standing."

6   T117 According to Latin standards, the initial part of this verse would mean
"he did not know what he was saying."

8   R809 Περιβλεψάμενοι is used as an indirect middle, meaning "the disciples themselves suddenly looking around."
BD448(8) Ἀλλά means "except" in this verse (equivalent to εἰ μή).

9   B204 The ἵνα clause is used to denote the object of the command, "he commanded
them that they should tell no one."

10 M110 The article τό is used to introduce a quotation, so that the disciples
ask what is meant by "rising from the dead" (unless here the article merely
turns the infinitive into a noun; the articular infinitive is used as the subject of the verb ἐστιν--B393). [Ed. Occasionally in the New Testament, the
neuter article is used to introduce a whole clause as a quotation (cf. 9:23),
and is probably so used in this verse.]
BD239(1) Πρός is used instead of παρά, "among themselves."

11 M132 The first ὅτι in this verse introduces direct speech, similar to an interrogative adverb, meaning "why" (cf. Matt. 17:10 and BD300[2]).

12 BD233(2) The preposition ἐπί in vv. 12f means "concerning."
BD442(8) Καὶ πῶς γέγραπται means "how is it that it is written (how is this to
be reconciled with . . .)?"
BD447(6) In vv. 12f., μέν means "certainly, of course," and ἀλλά is an emphatic "but."

15 R597 Ἐκ has a perfective sense in the compound verb here, "greatly amazed."

18 BD101 The verb ῥήσσει means "to dash to the ground."
MT186 The aorist subjunctive in ὅπου ἐὰν αὐτὸν καταλάβῃ has a future-perfect
sense, "wherever it has seized him" (but this may be reading English or Latin
into the Greek--R850). [Ed. Over refining this clause may be due to reading
Latin or English into the Greek, but the tentative aspect of the subjunctive
occasionally has a futuristic sense.]
H409 Τρύζω is a word found from Homer onwards for the utterance of any sharp
sound. In this verse, it means "to grind the teeth."

19 T33 There is great emotion expressed in the use of ὦ here (Jesus used the exclamation ὦ as a sort of groan, "O faithless generation"--TGr40).
H467 Πρός with the accusative here means "with."

20 R436 In view of the participle ἰδών, the noun πνεῦμα is considered as masculine here (cf. v. 26; the masculine gender designates a personal being--BD134
[3]).
R883 The imperfect verb ἐκυλίετο with the present participle ἀφρίζων is very
descriptive in the narrative (he kept rolling about, and presumably they
watched him awhile, until Jesus spoke [ἐπερώτησεν]--T66).

21 R974 The temporal aspect of ὡς is sharp in this verse where it means "since"
(one would expect something like ἀφ' οὗ--M133).
M73 Ἐκ is redundant here since the ending -θεν implies "from" (the strengthening with ἐκ points to the fact that the original force of the suffix is wearing
thin--H164).

22 B181 The imperative βοήθησον is used in a petition, with the resultant meaning
"help us."
T330 Ἀλλά is used as an interjection before the command in this verse, with
the meaning "well."

23 M110 Τὸ εἰ δύνῃ seems best treated as an exclamatory or questioning repetition
by Jesus of the anxious father's words: "'If you can. . .!' Why, anything is
possible . . ." (or "'If you can?' Do you ask such a question?").

75

T182 The article τό is used to mark a quotation, with the sense "so far as the εἰ δύνῃ is concerned" (cf. BD267[1]).

25 R465 There appears to be a sort of insistence in the article in τὸ ἄλαλον καὶ κωφὸν πνεῦμα, "thou dumb and deaf spirit."

26 R1091 Ὥστε with the infinitive here expresses the notion of actual result (cf. B371).
H446 Πολλά has an adverbial usage here, "terribly" (cf. 1:45).

28 M159 Ὅτι is used as an interrogative adverb, "why" (cf. v. 11).

30 T282 Οὐκ ἤθελεν has the force of "he was reluctant."

31 B15 Παραδίδοται is used as a futuristic present to describe vividly a future event (cf. M7; in a prophetic sense--T63).

34 R529 Πρός has an associative idea here, "with."
R811 The passive deponent verb διελέχθησαν is used with a reciprocal pronoun here, "they had discussed with one another."
M97 Τίς μείζων probably means "who was greatest," although it may conceivably mean that they discussed their relative greatness -- "who was greater" (than another; the comparative is used for the true superlative, "who was greatest" --T30). [Ed. The comparative μείζων may be used with more than two objects of comparison with the resultant force of a superlative, as is the case in this verse; cf. Matt. 23:11 and Luke 22:24.]

35 R874 Ἔσται is used as a volitive future, "he must be last" (cf. H458).

37 T282 The negative in οὐκ ἐμέ forms a single idea, "it is not me" (the antithesis is also present with ἀλλά).

38 M9 Ἐκωλύομεν is probably used as a conative imperfect, with the meaning "we tried to prevent him" (cf. TGr41; the man refused to be stopped in his good work--MT129).

40 M64 Ὅς γὰρ . . . ἔστιν means "for he who is not against us is on our side."

41 R795 In the words of Jesus, Χριστοῦ is used as a proper name.
M33 Note the double accusative here, "for whoever gives you a cup of water to drink."
M79 Ἐν ὀνόματι ὅτι Χριστοῦ ἐστε is nearly equivalent to διὰ τὸ Χριστοῦ εἶναι, "on the score of your being Christ's" (this use of ὀνόματι is not unknown to classical Greek; ἐν ὀνόματι means "on the claim, on the basis that"--BD397[3]).

42 R997 Εἰ is equivalent to ὅτι here (in this verse εἰ with the indicative is an encroachment on the unreal condition, cf. ἐάν with the subjunctive--BD372[3]). [Ed. Matthew, in his parallel account (18:16), employs the ἵνα of content. Consequently, the clause with εἰ in Mark present part of the content of the comparison, but at the same time it indicates an unreal supposition.]

49 R534 Πυρί and ἐν τίνι are used as datives of means in vv. 49f., "with fire . . . with what."

MARK 10

5   M53 The prepositional phrase πρὸς τὴν σκληροκαρδίαν ὑμῶν means "in view of your stubbornness" (the preposition has a transferred sense; "in view of" is equivalent to "because of"--BD239[8]).

8   M144 Ὥστε is used merely as an inferential particle here, meaning "and so, accordingly" (cf. 2:28).

9   TGr60f. Some exegetes have pleaded that ἄνθρωπος μὴ χωριζέτε means "let not a husband put asunder." This, however, is to overlook that whereas in v. 2 the word ἀνήρ ("husband") is used, our Lord changed to the word ἄνθρωπος when he said, "let no man put asunder" in v. 9 and ἄνθρωπος means a member of the human species, but never "a husband" (thus, Jesus completely forbade divorce).

10 B205 The preposition εἰς is used instead of ἐν in a local sense, "in."

11 T272 The preposition ἐπί has the sense of "with" after the verb μοιχᾶται.

14 T214 Τῶν τοιούτων is not necessarily a possessive genitive (as Matthew [18:3] and John [3:3, 5] understand it), but it has the sense "consists of such"; children are the very nature of the kingdom.

17 R675 Εἷς here has practically the same sense as τις (indefinite), "a man."

18 R176 In this verse, Jesus himself insists on the use of ἀγαθός for the idea of absolute goodness.

20 R597 With expressions of time, ἐκ gives the point of departure, "from my youth." T55 In this verse, the middle occurs where one expects the active, "observe" (cf. M24n.1).

21 R834 Ἠγάπησεν is used as an ingressive aorist, "he began to love" (cf. T72).

22 B432 Ἔχων appears to be an attributive participle used substantively, "for he was one that had great possessions" (cf. John 18:30; ἦν ἔχων is used as a periphrastic construction--R888; cf. H452). [Ed. Apparently, ἦν ἔχων κτήματα πολλά is used as a periphrastic construction, emphasizing the adjectival idea inherent in the participle, "he was very rich." The frequency of the periphrastic construction in Mark and the proximity of the stative verb and participle support this rendering.]

23 R741 Πῶς has an exclamatory sense here (as though it were ὡς; cf. M207; similar to a declarative ὅτι--T137; cf. BD396), "how."

30 R1020 Ἐὰν μή almost has the sense of the relative ὃς μή here, "who will not receive." M61 The prepositional phrase μετὰ διωγμῶν means "with (i.e., "among" or "accompanied by") persecutions."

32 T37 In this verse, where οἱ δέ does not mark a change of subject, the reading with οἱ δέ is probably to be rejected in favor of καί). [Ed. Actually, the

article οἱ seems necessary to signify the participle ἀκολουθοῦντες as attributive.]

33 R882 'Αναβαίνομεν is used as a futuristic present (stressing the certainty of the action.)

35 MT160 There is a distinction between the active αἰτέω (v. 35) and the middle αἰτέομαι (in v. 38; cf. 6:22).
MT179 In this verse, ἵνα seems to coalesce with θέλομεν rather than being used imperatively, "we desire that."

36 B171 Notice the deliberative subjunctive ποιήσω (ἵνα never occurs when the verb θέλω is in the second person, and the following verb is in the first person), "what do you want me to do?"

38 R717 In τὸ βάπτισμα ὃ ἐγὼ βαπτίζομαι, the relative pronoun is in the cognate accusative retained with the passive verb, with the resultant meaning "the baptism with which I am baptized."

40 R1058 Δοῦναι appears to be the original dative, meaning "for giving."

41 BD480(1) Οἱ δέκα means "the other ten."

43 H458 The future verb ἔσται is used for the imperative, equivalent to a volitive future (cf. 9:35 and Luke 22:26, γινέσθω).

45 R573 This verse (cf. Matt. 20:28) teaches the substitutionary conception of Christ's death, not because ἀντί of itself means "instead", which is not true, but because the context renders any other resultant idea out of the question (the Son of Man came to give his life as a ransom "in exchange for many", since the price to be paid for them is the laying down of his life--TGr172).
M139 The infinitives following ἦλθεν are used to express purpose, "to serve . ."
BD283(4) Through semitic influence, τὴν ψυχὴν αὐτοῦ may be used instead of the reflexive pronoun, "to give himself."

51 R933 ῞Ινα appears to be merely an introductory expletive here with the volitive subjunctive (cf. 5:23; ἵνα ἀναβλέψω may mean "Let me recover my sight" rather than "I want to recover . . .", an imperatival --M145; cf. T95). [Ed. Actually, Robertson explains this grammatical construction in a way which only slightly differs from the explanation offered by the other grammarians. But in the final product, both interpretations have an imperatival sense.]

MARK 11

1 R971 'Εγγίζουσιν is used as an historic present (cf. Matt. 21:1), "when they drew near."

5 T82 The perfect participle ἑστηκότων is used as a present participle (cf. 9:1).
T154 The participle λύοντες has a modal-temporal sense, with no stress on the temporal relationship, "what do you mean by loosing?"

13 R1190 In this verse, εἰ ἄρα has the idea of "if haply."
    T161 The participle ἔχουσιν actually means "which had" (similar to a relative
    clause).

14 R854 The aorist optative φάγοι has an ingressive sense (it expresses prohibi-
    tion here--R913; this verse contains the most vehemently prohibitive optative
    in all the New Testament--M136), "may no one ever eat."

16 T138 The ἵνα denoting content is used after a verb ἤφιεν, "he would not allow
    anyone to carry."

19 T93 Ὅταν ὀψὲ ἐγένετο means "whenever it was evening, every evening" (probably
    denoting a habit--BD367), not as some translators take it "when it was evening"
    (of that day).
    MT248 The papyrus examples of ὅταν as meaning "when" make it an open question
    whether in this verse it is best to translate "when evening fell," that is the
    evening before the πρωΐ of v. 20. In such a writer as Mark, this is at least
    possible, and the other rendering produces an awkward sequence. [Ed. It is
    difficult to determine whether ὅταν is definite or indefinite. Even though
    the aorist indicative verb ἐγένετο occurs, the adverb appears to be indefinite
    (cf. v. 25, and also the usual meaning of ὅταν). Christ apparently made it a
    habit not to spend evenings in Jerusalem; cf. v. 11. The resulting transla-
    tion is not awkward at all if the imperfect verb is retained as the accurate
    verb of the following clause, "whenever evening came they would go out of the
    city."]

22 R500 Ἔχετε πίστιν θεοῦ should be translated "have faith in God," although the
    genitive does not mean "in," but only the God-kind-of-faith (cf. TGr110).

23 R880 Γίνεται is used as an inchoative present, referring to an act just begin-
    ning (cf. T63; "will begin to take place").

24 T73 Ἐλάβετε is used as a gnomic aorist (an act valid for all time; "if you ask
    for, you received it"--BD333[2]).

25 R958 Ὅταν may have a general reference here (even though it occurs with the
    indicative it is still indefinite--M133), "whenever you stand."

28 B220 The ἵνα clause here appears to have the notion of conceived result (cf.
    R999), "to do these things."

31 R613 The preposition πρός suggests the idea of "facing one another."

32 T67 The imperfect verb ἦν in this verse is equivalent to a periphrastic perfect
    or pluperfect, meaning "that John had been a prophet" (cf. 6:18 and BD330).

                                  MARK 12

1   R409 Ἐν παραβολαῖς λαλεῖν (cf. Matt. 22:1) is followed by only one parable,
    but there were doubtless others not recorded.
    BD123 The compound noun ὑπολήνιον refers to "the vessel placed under a wine-
    press."

2   R614   The prepositional phrase παρὰ τῶν γεωργῶν has an ablatival sense, "from
    the tenant farmers."
    T209   Ἀπό is used with the genitive with a partitive notion, "some fruit."

11 R655   The feminine gender in αὕτη and θαυμαστή is probably due to Hebrew influ-
    ence.   The Hebrew used the feminine for abstract ideas, since it had no neuter
    gender (cf. M182; αὕτη is not to be referred to κεφαλὴν γωνίας --BD138[2]).

12 B387   The infinitive κρατῆσαι is used as the object of the verb ἐζήτουν, "and
    they sought to lay hold on him."
    M53   The preposition πρός has a transferred sense here, "he had spoken the para-
    ble with reference to (perhaps almost "against") them" (cf. BD239[6]).
    BD324   The aorist verb is used of relative time in ὅτι . . . τὴν παραβολὴν ἔιπεν,
    meaning "that he had told the parable."
    BD442(1)   The second καί is used in this verse with the idea of actual contrast,
    "and yet."

13 R786   The article τῶν is repeated to indicate distinct groups of people.

14 M22   The deliberative subjunctive δῶμεν has the meaning "are we to give or are
    we not to give?"

15 M145   In this verse, ἵνα probably has a final sense (purpose) rather than imper-
    atival sense, "bring me a penny that I may look at it."

19 BD470(1)   Ἵνα λάβῃ . . . is used as an imperatival clause, "his brothers must."

23 MT145   The aorist verb ἔσχον has an ingressive idea; the forming of the marriage
    tie is the issue.

24 R700   The causal participle εἰδότες is actually explanatory of τοῦτο, "because
    you do not know."

25 BD101   Generally the active of γαμέω refers to the man and the passive refers to
    the woman, as in this verse (γαμίζονται means no more than the simple passive
    γάμουνται--H410).

26 R603   In ἐπὶ τοῦ βάτου an ellipsis in thought occurs, "in the passage about the
    bush."
    R1032   Πῶς is used in this verse instead of a declarative ὅτι, "how God said."

28 R740   Ποῖος seems to have lost its qualitative force here, "which commandment"
    (cf. 11:28; the pronoun is equivalent to τίς).
    R1042   The genitive following ἀκούσας seems to be used with the notion that what
    was heard was also understood ("he heard them reasoning together"--TGr87).
    M113   Perhaps in both instances of πρώτη . . . πρώτη (in vv. 28f.) the article
    is dispensed with because of the sufficiently determinative force of what fol-
    lows.
    T31   Note the masculine adjective πάντων with the superlative πρώτη (the feminine
    πασῶν to be in concord with the feminine noun ἐντολή would be beside the point
    as it is rather the general idea of omnium [all] that is involved--R410).

32 R1187   Πλήν is used as a preposition, meaning "near by" (similar to "there is
    no other but he").

33 R1058 Τὸ ἀγαπᾶν is used as a subject infinitive (the subject of ἐστιν; the
     durative force is evident in the present tense--R1081), "to love . . . is bet-
     ter."

34 R546 The adverb μακράν is similar to an adjective here (predicate adjective),
     "you are not far."

38 R441 It looks like a sudden change to find ἀσπασμούς here, but actually this
     noun and the infinitive περιπατεῖν are in the accusative as the object of
     θελόντων, "the scribes who desire to (or "love to") walk about with robes and
     to have greetings."
     R589 The preposition in ἐν στολαῖς has the notion of accompanying circumstance,
     "with."
     T227 Τῶν θελόντων means "who love to."

40 TGr55f. The articular participles οἱ κατεσθίοντες and προσευχόμενοι do not re-
     fer specifically to the scribes, but they have a general reference, "those who
     . . ." (these nominatives refer to the distant genitive ἀπὸ τῶν γραμματέων in
     v. 38--R413; the nominative case [as the naming case] is sometimes left unal-
     tered in the sentence instead of being put in the case of the word with which
     it is in apposition--R458).

41 R838 In vv. 41-44, the general scene is presented by the descriptive durative
     imperfect ἐθεώρει and the durative present βάλλει. It is visualized by the
     πολλοί . . . ἔβαλλον. But the figure of the widow woman is singled out by the
     aorist ἔβαλεν. The closing reference by Jesus to the rest is by the consta-
     tive aorist πάντες ἔβαλον. Note also the precise distinction between εἶχεν
     and ἔβαλεν at the end. Where the aorist and imperfect occur side by side, it
     is to be assumed that the change is made on purpose and the difference in idea
     to be sought ("many that were rich were casting in much"--B21; ἔβαλλον describes
     the scene in progress, ἔβαλον merely states the fact--B56).

42 R674 Μία is used as an indefinite article here (cf. H432), "a certain widow"
     (cf. 14:66).

                              MARK 13

2   R1174   The force of οὐ μή is probably weakened to some degree in this verse
     (Luke drops the μή[21:6]).

3   BD205 Εἰς is used instead of ἐν in a local sense, "on."

5   R996 The clause following βλέπετε is clearly dependent upon that imperative,
     denoting the content of the command ("see to it that no one leads you astray").

7   M21 The reason for the use of the present tense with the imperative is difficult
     to detect in μὴ θροεῖσθε of v. 7 and μὴ πιστεύετε of v. 21 (when an action is
     not yet begun, the present prohibition demands continued abstinence from it
     when it does begin--B165). [Ed. In both instances Luke (in 21:9 and 17:23)
     corrects the text with an aorist tense, and changes the verb as well. Matthew,
     on the other hand, retains the present tense for v. 7 (in 24:6), but he changes
     πιστεύετε of v. 21 to an aorist (in 24:23). In view of this degree of variety,

Burton offers the best solution.]

8   M59 The preposition in κατὰ τόπους denotes close connection (of place), meaning "in (certain) places" (cf. T268).

9   T37 The pronoun ὑμεῖς is used in this verse without much emphasis.
BD205 Εἰς is used instead of ἐν in a local sense, "in" (cf. Matt. 10:17).

10 M69 The preposition εἰς with the accusative seems to be equivalent to a simple dative, "to all nations."

12 T313 When a personal neuter plural subject occurs in the New Testament, the plural verb is generally used (as with ἐπαναστήσονται τέκνα, cf. Luke 12:30).

13 R889 The periphrastic future is used to express the durative notion, "you will continue to be hated."
MT150 The future verb σωθήσεται may be used to express a promise (a volitive use), "this one shall be saved."

14 R429 Τοτέ accents the logical connection of thought, "then."
T82 The perfect participle ἐστηκότα is used as a present participle (cf. 9:1; "standing").

16 BD205 Εἰς is used instead of ἐν in a local sense, "in" (cf. R525 and Matt. 24:18).

17 T51 The participle of ἔχω with ἐν γαστρί means "be pregnant."

18 B200 Ἵνα introduces an object clause after προσεύχεσθε (cf. 5:18), "pray that."
T235 The temporal genitive χειμῶνος refers to time within which an act occurs, "in winter."

19 R1390 Αἱ ἡμέραι ἐκεῖναι may be regarded as the subject or as the nominative of time. [Ed. It is preferable to consider αἱ ἡμέραι ἐκεῖναι as the subject of ἔσονται. This makes the statement very harsh, emphasizing the prolonged calamity; the parallel accounts soften the description.
T70 The perfect tense in γέγονεν is used for the aorist (cf. BD343[3] and Matt. 24:21), "such as has not been."

20 R752 In οὐκ . . . πᾶσα, a negative statement is made as to πᾶσα. The result is the same as if οὐδείς had been used with an affirmative verb; the idea is "no flesh," not "not all flesh" (i.e., "some flesh"), would have been saved.

21 B165 The present imperative μὴ πιστεύετε commands continued abstinence from an action that had not yet begun (cf. v. 7).

23 T37 The pronoun ὑμεῖς occurs in this verse without much emphasis (cf. v. 9).

24 MT150 The future tense in vv. 24-27 is merely futuristic (not volitive), and is best translated by "will . . ."

25 R889 The periphrastic future ἔσονται πίπτοντες expresses a durative notion (cf. v. 13), "will be falling."

T130 The plural οὐρανοῖς is used to convey the dwelling-place of God. Consequently, this verse reads "the stars shall fall from the sky, and the powers
in heaven shall be shaken."

28 R613 Παραβολή in this verse means "placing of one thing beside another."
R827 The meaning of γινώσκετε is durative here, "gaining knowledge."

29 T27 The idiomatic plural ἐπὶ θύραις refers to one door, "he is near" or "at
your door."

31 R873 The future verbs in this verse have a volitive sense, "shall . . ."

34 B204 The ἵνα clause is used to denote the object of the command (cf. 9:9),
"commanded to watch."
BD453(4) Ὡς is used to introduce a parable with neither a following correlative nor any close connection to what precedes, "it is like a man."

36 T99 Μή occurs here to introduce a subordinate clause, "watch therefore . . .
lest" (cf. M139).

MARK 14

1 R408 Names of feasts are often plural as in the case of τὰ ἄζυμα (cf. 6:21),
"the feast of unleavened bread."
TGr66f. The latter part of v. 1 and the initial part of v. 2 should be translated, "the chief priests and the scribes sought how they might take him by craft
and put him to death, to avoid an uproar of the people (for the people said,
"not on the feast day!" (γάρ gives the reason for the decision of the scribes
and chief priests, therefore the subject of ἔλεγον is someone else--T292).
T252 The prepositional phrase ἐν δόλῳ has an adverbial sense similar to an instrumental dative, meaning "by means of guile" or "guilefully."
BD323(4) The imperfect verb ἦν is used in this verse with the meaning "was to
take place."

2 R988 Μήποτε introduces a negative purpose clause here, "lest there may be" (cf.
B199).

3 R607 Κατέχεεν means "pour down on."
R1127 The participle ἔχουσα expresses the notion of manner, "with" (cf. T154).

4 R739 Purpose is expressed by εἰς τί, "for what purpose."
T70 The perfect verb γέγονεν is used for the aorist, "was."
T153 Notice the periphrastic construction that occurs in this verse (cf. H452;
ἦσαν . . . ἀγανακτοῦντες means "they were greatly agitated"--BD239[1]).

6 T264 The prepositional phrase ἐν ἐμοί is used for a dative of advantage, "to
me."
MT175 This verse favors the sense "Let her alone: let her keep it."

7 BD102(3) Εὖ ποιῆσαι means "to do good."

8   R551   The infinitive presents the chief idea in προέλαβεν μυρίσαι (the verb has
     an adverbial sense, "beforehand"--T227; προέλαβεν μυρίσαι may be a result of
     semitic influence, because nowhere else does this verb have the sense of antic-
     ipating the action of a subsequent verb--H445).

9   BD206(4) The first εἰς in this verse seems to be used for ἐν, "in" (cf. Matt.
     26:13).

10   R675   In ὁ εἷς τῶν δώδεκα, the article initially looks incongruous, "the one of
     the twelve," but the early papyri give illustrations of this usage also. Εἷς
     is to be construed as a pronoun (ὁ εἷς is used for τις--BD247[2]).

13   R873   Ἀπαντήσει is merely futuristic here, "will meet" (this compound verb has
     the notion of face-to-face--R573).

14   R442   Ὅτι is merely recitative and is equivalent to quotation marks.
     R969   In ὅπου . . . φάγω the subjunctive is probably deliberative, answering to
     ποῦ φάγω in the direct question (cf. B319).

18   MT111 The participle is durative in ὁ ἐσθίων μετ᾽ ἐμοῦ, meaning "he who is
     taking a meal with me."

19   M60   Is εἷς κατὰ εἷς an adverbial use of the preposition, or sheer bad grammar
     (the phrase κατὰ εἷς or καθεῖς has become stereotyped as an adverb in the New
     Testament--T268; as an adverb distributively--MT105; cf. John 8:9; "one by one")?

20   R525   Εἰς is used with the sense of ἐν, "in" (cf. Matt. 26:23).

21   R1016 The negative of the contrary to fact conditional clause is always μή in
     the New Testament except twice, here and the parallel in Matt. 26:24. Here
     the οὐ is very emphatic (it is only the ultimate sense that makes this unreal
     at all--MT200).

23   T209   The prepositional phrase ἐξ αὐτοῦ has a partitive sense, "some of it."

24   R632   Ὑπέρ conveys the notion of "instead" (cf. M64 and 10:45).

25   R708   The phrase τῆς ἡμέρας ἐκείνης refers to "the Last Day."
     R930   Notice the emphatic denial with the futuristic subjunctive πίω, "I will
     drink no more."

28   R871   The future verb προάξω is durative ("I shall go before you"--MT149).

29   B280   Καί seems to have an intensive force with πάντες here, suggesting that the
     supposition is an extreme one, "even though they all."
     T37   There is emphasis in the use of ἐγώ here.
     T115 The feeling of definiteness and actual realization accompanies εἰ with the
     future indicative. Thus, in εἰ καὶ πάντες σκανδαλισθήσονται, Peter grants the
     assumption, "let us suppose that all will actually be offended."
     T330 After the conditional clause here, ἀλλά has the sense of "at least" (cf.
     BD448[5]).

30   R873   The future verb ἀπαρνήσῃ is often misunderstood because of the rendering

"you shall deny me." It could not therefore be Peter's fault if Jesus commanded him. Here the translation with "will" is free from that peril (cf. Luke 22:
61).

31 R875 The future verb ἀπαρνήσομαι has a volitive sense in this verse "I shall . ."
     (emphatically negative here--B66).

32 B325 Ἕως with the aorist subjunctive denotes a simple event. Thus, the latter
     part of this verse means "sit here till I pray," or "have prayed" (cf. MT169).
     H342 Χωρίον in this verse means "an enclosed piece of ground."

34 R856 The durative action referred to by the aorist imperative is treated as
     punctiliar ("do not go away but be on guard always"--T75).

35 R883 The descriptive imperfect tense in ἔπιπτεν . . ., καὶ προσηύχετο portrays
     the realistic scene in Gethsemane (Peter's description probably).

36 R737 Τί is used for ὅ in this verse, meaning "what."
     T330 In this verse ἀλλά has the sense "not so much . . . as."
     BD211 Παρένεγκε . . . ἀπό means "let . . . pass by" (hence "depart from").

40 R1183 The second καί in this verse almost has the sense of ὅτι, "that."

41 M161 Καθεύδατε τὸ λοιπόν means "all that is left to do is to sleep."
     T291 The problematic verb ἀπέχει may be impersonal, for the classical ἀρκεῖ,
     "it is receipted, the account is settled (consistent with the meaning of the
     variant in D and W; ἀπέχει τὸ τέλος, "it has its end, the matter is settled";
     cf. BD129).
     T336 In this verse Jesus says, "are you going to continue sleeping?" To intro-
     duce "still" (as many translations do, cf. BD451[6], but τὸ λοιπόν does not
     mean "still") is to throw emphasis on the past, but the point is that they must
     not be asleep when the betrayer arrives (future). Ἀπέχει will then have a
     direct reference to Judas. "He has been paid; he is here. Henceforth, it is
     no time for sleep" (ἀπέχει is used as an impersonal verb, meaning "it is enough
     [enough of this]--M27). [Ed. Ἀπέχει is a difficult verb to translate, but
     "it is settled" seems preferable.]

42 T82 Conceivably ἤγγικεν is a true perfect, "has drawn near."

44 R679 The pronoun αὐτός has strong emphasis here ("he is the man"--T41).
     R905 In this verse the perfect tense of δεδώκει refers to Judas' previous
     arrangement.

45 R606 In the compound verb κατεφίλησεν, κατά seems to be weakened, although the
     Authorized Standard Version has "kissed him much" in the margin.

47 R810 In σπασάμενος τὴν μάχαιραν the possessive notion for the article is prob-
     ably sufficient, "drawing his own sword" (cf. Matt. 26:51).
     BD111(3) Ὠτάριον means "ear lobe."

49 M52 The preposition πρός denotes position "with" (cf. H467).
     BD448(7) The elliptical ἀλλ’ ἵνα means "on the contrary (but) this happened, in
     order that."

51   BD337(1)   Κρατοῦσιν is used as an historical present, "they seized him."

54   R807   θερμαινόμενος is used as a direct middle, "warming himself."
      M85   In this verse εἰς τὴν αὐλήν may be an explanation of ἔσω, and ἔσω may be virtually equivalent to a noun, "as far as inside -- that is, to the courtyard."

55   R883   The change from the aorist to the imperfect (ηὕρισκον) in the narrative here is due to the desire to avoid monotony (this imperfect verb means "they could find none" [in spite of repeated attempts]--BD327).
      M60   The prepositional phrase κατὰ τοῦ Ἰησοῦ means "against Jesus" (cf. v 57).
      T143   Εἰς τό with the infinitive here expresses the notion of purpose ("to put him to death").

58   R1042   The genitive following ἠκούσαμεν seems to be used with the notion that what was heard was also understood (cf. 12:28; "we heard him say" not "that he said"--TGr87).
      T267   The prepositional phrase διὰ τριῶν ἡμερῶν means "within three days" (cf. BD223[1]).

60   R917   The use of οὐ may suggest indignation in this verse (cf. v. 61).
      T49   Τί appears to be equivalent to ὅ here (but this involves understanding πρός before οὐδέν; we must therefore divide into two sentences οὐδὲν ἀποκρίνῃ; τί οὗτοι . . .; "are you not going to answer? What is it that these men are testifying against you?"

61   T67   In this context the imperfect verb ἐπηρώτα is equivalent to an aorist ("again the high priest asked him").

62   TGr73f.   The best reading of Jesus' answer is, "you have said that I am" (as in the Matthew and Luke parallel).

65   R617   Περικαλύπτειν means "to cover all round."

66   H432   Μία is used for τις (with an indefinite sense), "one of the maids" (cf. 12:42).

72   R885   Ἔκλαιεν is used as an inchoative imperfect, "began to weep."
      TGr71f.   The participle ἐπιβάλων has an intransitive sense. Peter pushed (βάλλω) himself onwards (ἐπί). Perhaps he threw himself on the ground (C. H. Turner), but it is more likely that he threw himself outside, for that is how Matthew chose to interpret it.
      T137   Ὡς is used as ὅτι here, "that."
      BD308   Ἐπιβάλων is correctly glossed by Theophylactus and Euthymius as ἀρξά-μενος, therefore "he began to weep." [Ed. The weightiest manuscript support includes ἐπιβάλων in the text. Ἀρξάμενος and ἤρξατο are introduced by later manuscripts as an attempt to simplify the text. This is not necessary since ἐπιβάλων may be understood with a valid meaning; cf. TGr71.]

MARK 15

2   TGr73f.   Σὺ λέγεις means "you are saying this, not me." The emphasis is on the personal pronoun (cf. Luke 23:3).

3   R884 Κατηγόρουν, as well as ἀπέλυεν and παρῃτοῦντο in v. 6, is used as an itera-
     tive imperfect (there were repeated charges).
     H446 Πολλά has an adverbial usage here, "earnestly."

4   R917 An exclamation is expressed by the interrogative pronoun πόσα, "see how
     many" (cf. T50).

6   T268 The preposition in καθ' ἑορτήν has a distributive sense, "at each feast"
     (cf. R608).

10 R841 With the use of the pluperfect παραδεδώκεισαν (Matthew has παρέδωκαν),
     Mark draws the distinction ("the chief priests had delivered") which Matthew
     did not care to make.

16 T216 The adverb ἔσω has the genitive τῆς αὐλῆς, meaning "further into the pal-
     ace." (used as a preposition--R643).

18 MT71 The occurrence of βασιλεῦ in this verse is merely an evidence of the writ-
     er's deficient sensitivity to the more delicate shades of Greek idiom.   This
     vocative form seems to admit the royal right, whereas the articular nominative
     could have been used with a descriptive sense (cf. John 19:3 and R465).

20 T191 Τὰ ἴδια has the old classical meaning here, "peculiar, private."

23 R885 Ἐδίδουν is used as a conative imperfect, referring to an action begun,
     but interrupted (contrast οὐκ ἔλαβεν; cf. T65), "they tried to give."

24 BD298(5) The double interrogative τίς τί has a distributive sense, "what each
     one."
     H456 The historical present verb σταυροῦσιν in vv. 24 and 27 provides a pictorial
     description, "they crucified."

25 R1183 The fondness for co-ordination in the Gospels causes the use of καί where
     a temporal conjunction (ὅτε) would be more usual, "when they crucified him."

30 R861 The aorist participle καταβάς refers to an action which is simultaneous to
     that of the principal verb σῶσον, "save yourself by coming down."

32 T102 Ἵνα has a consecutive sense here, "with the result that."

34 R29 For the quotation from Psa. 22:1, spoken on the cross, Matthew (27:46) gives
     the Hebrew, while Mark (15:34) has an Aramaic adaptation.
     M11n.1 According to strict grammar the aorist verb ἐγκατέλιπες should refer to
     an event in the past, the results of which are not prominently contemplated by
     the writer. But, even if this is to be pressed here, it does not mean that the
     rendering by the English perfect, "hast thou forsaken," is incorrect (it is a
     perfective aorist, the present results of the action are much in mind--T72).
     T267 Εἰς τί means "in order to what" rather than "because of what."

36 B161 The sense of ἄφετε is doubtful here (cf. MT175). [Ed. Ἄφες and ἄφετε may
     be used with the hortatory subjunctive ἴδωμεν with the resultant meaning "let
     us see," cf. Matt. 27:49.]

42   R965 'Επεί has a temporal sense here. [Ed. Actually this particle gives the
     reason for immediate action on the part of Joseph, "because it was the day of
     preparation."]

44   R1045 Εἰ is used (twice) to introduce an indirect question here (after θαυμάζω,
     the clause introduced by εἰ has nearly the force of a clause introduced by ὅτι
     --B277), "Pilate wondered if . . ., he asked whether."
     M154 In ὁ δὲ Πιλᾶτος ἐθαύμασεν εἰ ἤδη τέθνηκεν, the sense is not "wondered whe-
     ther . . .," in the modern sense of "wonder" as equivalent to "speculate";
     but rather, "expressed surprise that he was already dead, if he were," that is,
     Pilate's words might have been, "I shall be surprised if . . ."
     T69 Mark is very careful in maintaining the distinction in the tenses in this
     verse. Pilate marvels that Jesus "is already dead" (τέθηνκεν); Pilate then
     enquires when "he died" (ἀπέθανεν; τέθνηκεν means practically "to be dead" while
     ἀπέθανεν means "died," "has died"--R845).

47   T168 The genitive 'Ιωσῆτος is used to identify a mother by her son, "the mother
     of Jesus."

                                    MARK 16

2   R602 'Επί has the sense of "as far as."
     T227 An adverb usually follows the adjective or verb which it determines in
     the New Testament, but this verse contains an exception (λίαν πρωΐ, meaning
     "very early").

3   TGr78 The following reconstruction is more logical than the present order of
     vv. 3f.: "and they said among themselves, who shall roll us away the stone
     from the door of the sepulchre (for it was very great)? and when they looked
     they saw that the stone was rolled away" (an instance of Mark's misplaced pa-
     renthesis).

5   R408 Note the idiomatic plural τοῖς δεξιοῖς, meaning "on the right side."

6   R817 Apparently ἡγέρθη in this verse is merely intransitive, rather than pas-
     sive, in idea (cf. MT163; it has a very active nuance--T57), "He has risen."
     MT137 The aorist verb ἡγέρθη states the past complete fact, the astounding news
     of what had just happened (cf. 1 Cor. 15:4).

7   TGr79 The angels' reported words in this verse are incompatible with what Jesus
     is reported to have said, except on the hypothesis of delayed parenthesis.
     Technically, the parenthesis "as he said to you" should occur immediately after
     Galilee, since Christ hadn't specifically stated that they would see him (cf.
     14:28).
     T330 'Αλλά is best translated as an interjection here, "See the place where they
     laid him. Well, go to his disciples . . ." (actually with a consecutive notion).

10   BD291(6) The pronoun ἐκείνη simply means "she," with reference to the immediate-
     ly preceding subject.

13   BD291(6) The pronoun ἐκείνοις simply means "them" (cf. v. 10).

18   T52   Ἔχω with the adverb καλῶς means "to be well."

19   M162   Μὲν οὖν is purely resumptive or transitional here, "so then."

20   R1127   The participle ἐξελθόντες expresses a temporal notion, "after they went
     out they preached."
     BD291(6)   The pronoun ἐκεῖνοι simply means "they" (cf. v. 10).

Luke

1   BD456(3) Ἐπειδήπερ means "inasmuch as," with reference to a fact already well
    known (it occurs only here in the New Testament; undoubtedly a literary touch--
    R965).
    BD464 Verses 1-4 exhibit moderate length of the members of the sentence and a
    beautiful relationship between the protasis with its three members and the cor-
    responding structure of the apodosis. Πολλοί corresponds to κἀμοί, ἀνατάξασθαι
    διήγησιν to γράψαι, καθώς . . . to ἵνα ἐπιγνῷς . . ., so that the last clause,
    though appended to an idea already completely expressed, is called forth at
    least by the stylistic correspondence.

3   R392 The infinitive γράψαι is used as the subject of the verb ἔδοξε, "to write
    seemed good."
    T31 Κράτιστε is elative meaning "most excellent" (as a title).
    H20 Παρηκολουθηκότι ἄνωθεν refers to the fact that he revised the materials
    afresh.

4   BD294(5) In this verse the antecedent λόγων follows the relative pronoun περι
    ὧν. This is equivalent to either περὶ τῶν λόγων οὕς or to τῶν λόγων περὶ ὧν.

5   R743 The most common use of τις with the substantives is equivalent to "certain"
    (actually rather uncertain).

7   M18n.1 It is striking that there are so many periphrastic tenses within so few
    verses (cf. Luke 1:7, 10, 18[?], 20, 21 and 22), all the more so in view of
    Luke's avoidance of periphrasis in 17:27 as against Matt. 24:38 (the perfect
    periphrastic construction προβεβηκότες ἦσαν has an intensive force--R906, "had
    gone far in their days").
    T220 Ἐν is used with the dative of respect (cf BD197; the preposition is used
    where it is unnecessary--MT75), "in days."

8   M76 Note especially the characteristic Lucan usage of ἐν τῷ with an infini-
    tive, which is to be classed not as a Hebraism but as unidiomatic Greek. But
    if it is true Greek, there is a lack of parallels for its occurrence in the
    sense of "during." In the context here, it has the resultant sense of "in the
    course of his performing his priestly duties."
    M174 The use of ἐγένετο to introduce another verb reflects a degree of semitic
    influence, "it came about . . . that he received as his lot" (in the continua-
    tion of a narrative it may be classical--BD472[3]).

9   B401 The infinitive with τοῦ here is used as the object of ἔλαχε which takes a
    noun in the genitive as the object, "it was his lot (probably he obtained it by
    lot) to burn incense."

10   R888   The imperfect periphrastic construction ἦν προσευχόμενον has a descrip-
     tive notion (it is used to emphasize the durative nature of the action--M17),
     "were praying."

12   BD472(2) Φόβος is placed before the verb because it is parallel with ἐταράχθη.

14   R871   The future verb χαρήσονται has an ingressive punctiliar sense, " will
     begin to rejoice."

15   R933   Οὐ μή occurs with the subjunctive verb πίῃ in a prohibitive sense (cf.
     MT 177), "he shall not drink."
     TGrl9   Since πνεύματος is anarthrous (in vv. 14, 41 and 67), the implication
     is given that neither John the Baptist nor his mother and father were inspired
     directly by the Holy Spirit, but that they were guided by a more vague and less
     personal divine spirit (the anarthrous use of πνεῦμα may refer to the Holy
     Spirit--M113). [Ed. It is incorrect to develop a strict rule concerning
     Greek grammar and then make each example of literature comply with that rule
     (the final judge over any grammatical principle is the context). Although
     πνεῦμα is anarthrous, it still has the adjective ἁγίου, which would seem
     to carry more significance than whether or not the article occurs. Conse-
     quently, the Holy Spirit is referred to.]

17   R679   The pronoun αὐτός is used to express emphasis.
     M76   Ἐν with φρονήσει is used in place of εἰς with an accusative (meaning
     "with the thought," or "so that they have the thought"--BD218; or is
     instrumental?--T257). [Ed. The prepositional phrase is used with an infini-
     tive denoting motion. Consequently, the suggestion of Moule and Blass and
     Debrunner is preferable.]

18   M59   Κατὰ τί means "in view of what? whereby?" (the preposition has a transfer-
     red sense; or causal?--T268). [Ed. In essence the initial rendering "in
     which Zechariah asks for a sign" has a causal notion and is preferable.]
     T37   The pronoun ἐγώ does not express much emphasis.

20   R889   The very failure of the future tense to express durative action clearly
     led to the use of the present participle with a future form of the stative
     verb to express such action (ἔσῃ σιωπῶν means "you shall be dumb" [not σιωπή-
     σεις, "you shall become dumb"; cf. M18; the participle is adjectival and only
     seemingly periphrastic--BD353[1]). [Ed. It is better to explain this as a
     periphrastic construction, since the future generally does not have a durative
     meaning, but this construction is used to descriptively portray an action
     which took place during a period of time consisting of several months.]
     M68   The preposition εἰς has a pregnant use here, combining the ideas of motion
     and rest, "at their proper time" (similar to ἐν; cf. BD206[1]).
     M71   Ἀνθ' ὧν has a true causal sense, "since" or "because."
     MT92   The pronoun οἵτινες means "which for all that" (almost adversative; care
     must be taken so that one does not read in too much of a concessive meaning
     into this pronoun--T48).

21   R532   The preposition ἐν has a causal idea here, "because he delayed."
     M17   The imperfect periphrastic construction is used to emphasize the durative
     nature of the action, "the people were expecting."

22 R680 If there is any emphasis in the use of αὐτός here, it is very slight.
    R888 The imperfect periphrastic construction ἦν διανεύων has an iterative notion
    (emphasizing the durative sense—M17), "he repeatedly made signs to them."
    TGr39 Ὅτι may convey either the proof of a proposition or the reason for
    stating it, and between the two only the context can decide, together with any
    other relevant circumstances, such as Luke's literary style in similar situa-
    tions. In fact this is a feature of Lucan style. In v. 22, "they perceived
    that Zechariah had seen a vision in the temple, because (ὅτι) he beckoned to
    them and remained speechless." Obviously, ὅτι refers back to the first verb
    ("perceived"), just as in Jesus' remark to Simon (in 7:47), it refers back to
    the verb "I tell you." Jesus is saying, "I can tell you she is forgiven, and
    I can tell you because she loves."

28 MT183 There is nothing conclusive to show whether an imperative, optative, or
    indicative form of the stative verb is implied in the latter part of this verse.
    [Ed. The context seems to favor a simple statement of the indicative, "the
    Lord is with you."]

29 R741 Ποταπός is the late form for ποδαπός. In the New Testament it no longer
    means "from what country," but merely "of what sort" (equivalent to ποῖος, cf.
    7:39).
    R1031 An optative verb occurs here in an indirect question where the direct
    question had the indicative verb, "this might be."

30 M52 The preposition παρά has a metaphorical sense, meaning "in the sight of."

31 T86 Notice the future verb καλέσεις used here to express a command, "you shall
    call."

33 T25 The plural noun αἰῶνας means "eternity."

35 M107 In this verse, τὸ γεννώμενον ἅγιον κληθήσεται υἱὸς θεοῦ may mean "the
    (child) which is to be born shall be called holy, the Son of God," in which
    case no problem arises as to the article; but if the meaning is "the holy
    (child) which is to be born shall be called the Son of God," then it is a dis-
    tinctly irregular usage: τὸ ἅγιον τὸ γεννώμενον . . . would perhaps be the only
    clear way of saying it. [Ed. In view of the absence of the article here, the
    former suggestion seems to be more probable.]
    TGr19 Since πνεῦμα is anarthrous, the implication is given that it was not the
    third person of the Trinity that overshadowed Mary and empowered her to conceive
    the Messiah; it was this indefinable and holy power of God, which strengthened
    human beings in a supernatural way as it had done to the heroes of Israel in
    Old Testament times (the anarthrous use of πνεῦμα may refer to the Holy Spirit
    —M113). [Ed. Although πνεῦμα is anarthrous, the adjective ἅγιον is used,
    which would seem to carry more significance than whether or not the article
    occurs, cf. v. 15.]
    T87 The present participle γεννώμενον is used to describe a future event (to
    show certainty).

37 T196 Οὐκ . . . πᾶν means "nothing," rather than "not all."

38 M96f. Δούλη is declined as an adjective and used as a noun, "the handmaid."

39 R652 The adjective ὀρεινήν is used as a noun, "the hill country." The feminine
    gender is used because the omitted noun is feminine (γῆ).
    H471 The difficulty in εἰς πόλιν Ἰούδα(i.e., Judah is not a city) is best ex-
    plained as due to the Hebrew word for "province" which later came to mean "city".

41 TGr19 The anarthrous πνεύματος does not refer to the Holy Spirit (cf. the dis-
    cussion on vv. 15 and 35).
    TGr89 Nothing more than the physical sound of Mary's voice, as she entered her
    cousin's house, inspired the unborn babe to leap in her cousin's womb; nothing
    that Mary had said caused the flutter of excitement, simply the sound of her
    voice (despite the fact that ἀσπασμόν is in the accusative following ἤκουσεν).

42 R422 The speeches of Elisabeth (vv. 42-45), Mary (vv. 46-55) and Zachariah (vv.
    67-79) all contain poetic strains with something of Hebrew spirit and form
    (Hebrew parallelism).
    T31 The use of εὐλογήμενη as a superlative seems to be the result of semitic
    influence, "blessed are you among women" in essence the most blessed of all
    women).

43 BD189(3) An ellipsis of the stative verb εἰμί takes place with the dative pro-
    noun μού (the sense is "to happen to me").
    BD394 Ἵνα introduces an epexegetical clause, further explaining the previous
    statement. The use of ἵνα here does not seem to be correct since the action
    referred to is already a fact; ἵνα is generally used if the epexegesis is theory
    rather than fact; ὅτι is usually used when it is actual fact that is referred
    to (cf. T134), "that."

44 BD205 The preposition εἰς is used for ἐν in a local sense here, "in my ears."

45 T35 It has been suggested that the speech of Elisabeth in v. 45 becomes more
    intelligible if we understand ἡ πιστεύσασα as a vocative, meaning "blessed are
    you because you have believed (cf. the Vulgate). But the difficulty then is
    the αὐτῇ which follows, making the whole verse in the third person. [Ed. It
    seems best to take the articular participle as nominative. Consequently, the
    whole verse is in the third person, referring to the second person, although
    more indefinite, "blessed is she who believed."]
    BD237(1) Παρά is used correctly here with the genitive noun κυρίου, since it is
    not God himself who had spoken, but an angel by his command (the phrase por-
    trays the agent of the passive participle here--R615).

48 M96f. Δούλης is declined as an adjective and used as a noun (cf. v. 38), "hand-
    maiden."

49 BD442(6) The use of καί to co-ordinate words with independent clauses is Hebra-
    izing and slovenly vernacular (καί . . . ἅγιον).

50 BD493(2) Distributive doubling is not rhetorical, but vulgar. Thus, εἰς γενεάς
    καί γενεάς more nearly means "on many generations to come" rather than "for
    every generation."

51 R590 Ἐν has the meaning of "with."
    T23 The distributive singular occurs here referring to something (καρδίας) that
    belongs to each person in a group of people (αὐτῶν).

T74 The aorist verbs in vv. 51-53 may be gnomic (i.e., referring to an action well known).

T228 The adverbial phrase διανοίᾳ καρδίας goes closely with ὑπερηφάνους (i.e., "haughty in heart") and not with διεσκόρπισεν which is further from it in reference to word order.

54 R508 The verb ἀντελάβετο takes an object in the genitive because of its similarity with the idea of "taking hold of."
R1001 The infinitive μνησθῆναι is used to express the idea of result (cf. T136; conceived result--B375; this infinitive is used epexegetically [even with this usage there may be a consecutive sense]--M127).

55 T238 In ἐλάλησεν πρὸς τοὺς πατέρας ἡμῶν, τῷ Ἀβρααμ καὶ τῷ σπέρματι, the datives can hardly be in apposition to the accusative. Thus the datives are probably used as datives of advantage, meaning "he spoke to our fathers in favour of Abraham . . ." (cf. Zerwick, section 40).

57 B400 Τοῦ τεκεῖν has an appositional usage in reference to χρόνος, "the time to give birth."
BD472(2) Ἐλισάβετ is placed forward in the sentence here thus expressing emphasis.
H417 Verses 57ff. may be cited as illustrating the semitic style of narrative, both by the position of the verb, and by the linking of parallel clauses with καί.

58 M183 Μετά is used in a phrase in which the whole cast is semitic (cf. MT106; it may not be semitic--R611) -- ἐμεγάλυνεν κύριος τὸ ἔλεος αὐτοῦ μετ' αὐτῆς -- where regular koine would more naturally have used at least a plain dative, if not a different verbal phrase altogether -- ἠλέησεν αὐτὴν πολλά, perhaps, or at any rate ἐμεγάλυνεν αὐτῇ τὸ ἔλεος αὐτοῦ. The whole phrase represents an entirely natural Hebrew expression, although, curiously enough, it appears not to occur in the Septuagint (except 1 Macc. 1)27 and Tob. 12:6), "the Lord had shown His mercy to her."

59 B23 Ἐκάλουν is used as a conative imperfect (referring to an action attempted but not accomplished), "they wished to name him" (cf. M9).

60 R1164 Notice the occurrence of the intensified negative οὐχί (here there is a sharp antithesis).

62 R683 Αὐτό and αὐτοῦ both refer to παιδίον.
R766 The article τό makes no essential difference in the meaning of the question But it makes clearer the substantival idea of the indirect question and its relation to the principal clause.
R884 Ἐνένευον seems to be used as an iterative imperfect, "they were repeatedly making signs."

63 T153 In this verse, λέγων has the sense of "as follows" (semitic--BD420[2]).

64 R885 Ἐλάλει is used as an inceptive imperfect, meaning "he began to speak."
R1127 The participle εὐλογῶν has the notion of manner, "he was speaking, sing God."

65 M96 The adjective ὀρεινῇ is used as a noun "hill country" (cf. v. 39).
    BD472(2) The reason for moving πάντας forward in this verse is to give the
    adjective (πάντες in v. 66) stress and preserve the parallelism.

67 TGr19 The anarthrous πνεύματος does not refer to the Holy Spirit (cf. the dis-
    cussion on vv. 15 and 35).
    BD472(2) The noun Ζαχαρίας is moved forward to specifically put Zechariah in
    contrast with the neighbors who are the subject of the preceding narrative.

71 T24 The singular noun χειρός is used in a distributive sense (cf. v. 51), "from
    the hand of all."

72 T136 The infinitive ποιῆσαι is used to express result (cf. BD391[4]; the infin-
    itives in this verse appear to be used with epexegetical sense [i.e., further
    defining the action of the previous clause]--M127 and B375). [Ed. In this
    context, these infinitives seem to have the more simplistic meaning of result
    (indicating the result of salvation), "to show mercy . . ., and remember."]

73 BD295 The occurrence of ὅρκον ὅν ὤμοσεν instead of τοῦ ὅρκου οὗ is peculiar
    (here the phrase does not precede the main clause, but follows as an appositive;
    the whole passage is strongly colored by Hebrew influence), "the oath which he
    swore."
    BD400(8) Τοῦ with the infinitive δοῦναι has very little consecutive force, "to
    give."

74 T24 The singular noun χειρός is used with a distributive sense (cf. v. 51),
    "the hand of our enemies."

75 M43 The dative is used temporally with a durative sense here, "all our days."

76 R1185 There is continuation, not opposition in the use of καὶ . . . δέ, where
    δέ means "and" and καί means "also."

77 BD400(6) A simple infinitive may be used to express purpose, but for the sake
    of clarity τοῦ may be added to a second final infinitive (only in passages with
    an Old Testament setting), as in ἑτοιμάσαι . . . τοῦ δοῦναι and ἐπιφᾶναι . . .
    τοῦ κατευθῦναι (cf. MT217 and B397; especially in writings with a pretense to
    style, viz., Matthew, Luke and Acts--T142), "to prepare . . ., to give . . .,
    to give light . . ., to guide."

79 R1086 The infinitives in this verse are used epexegetically (cf. M127). [Ed.
    The simple infinitives in vv. 76f. and 79, occur in Old Testament quotations,
    whereas the infinitive with τοῦ immediately follows. In each instance, the
    articular infinitive portrays the final purpose of the preceding verb (i.e.,
    προπορεύσῃ and ἐπισκέψεται respectively.]
    T52 Ἐπιφαίνω means "show oneself" (the stars).

80 BD165 The genitive ἀναδείξεως is used as a genitive of quality (the Hebraistic
    ἡμέρα is equivalent to χρόνος; "the day of his manifestation").

LUKE 2

1   R1086 The infinitive ἀπογράφεσθαι is in apposition to the noun δόγμα, "a decree that . . ."
BD317 The middle voice is used in ἀπογράφεσθαι with the sense "have oneself en-rolled" (this is taken as middle because of the aorist middle form in v. 5; it has an intrasitive sense in vv. 1, 3 and 5, "register"--T57). [Ed. The two renderings seem to be nearly equivalent in actual meaning.]

2   R657 The exact idea of πρώτη in this verse is not certain, but most probably Luke's idea is that there were two enrolments under Cyrenius (πρώτη is not used in the sense of πρότερος--R669; this adjective refers to the census before the [greater] census made by Cyrenius--TGr23f.). [Ed. Robertson contradicts him-self in these two statements. Compare Luke's use of the superlative πρώτη in Acts 1:1.]

4   R578 In this verse both ἀπό and ἐκ are used for one's home (ἀπὸ τῆς, Γαλιλαίας ἐκ πόλεως Ναζαρέθ).
T142 Διὰ τό with the infinitive is almost equivalent to ὅτι or διότι, denoting cause.

5   R804 In this verse the middle voice of ἀπογράψασθαι means "to enroll oneself in" (it may be causative "have himself enrolled").

6   B400 Τοῦ τεκεῖν is used as appositional to αἱ ἡμέραι (cf. 1:57), "the days that she deliver."

7   R541 Note the use of αὐτοῖς as a dative of possession ("a place to them" in es-sence means "a place for them").

8   M17 Ἦσαν . . . ἀγραυλοῦντες is not a periphrastic construction, but it means "there were (i.e., existed) shepherds, staying in the fields" not "shepherds were staying . . ." (first their presence then their activity is expressed).
T235 The genitive νυκτός is used to refer to time "during the night."
BD153(3) Φυλάσσοντες φυλακάς means "to stand guard."

13   T312 The singular collective noun occurs with a plural participle (according to sense), "a multitude . . . praising . . . and saying."

14   M175 Εὐδοκίας seems to be used as a descriptive genitive (semitic) probably meaning "men on whom God's good will rests," "men who are pleasing to God" (al-though one would, if so, expect [τῆς] εὐδοκίας αὐτοῦ; it has the sense of "among men of whom God approves"--T213; this phrase means "among men to whom God's gracious approval applies"; it is clear that the genitive is the correct reading "men of God's good pleasure," i.e., his chosen ones [the Qumran com-munity thought of itself as the elect of God living in the end time]--BD165).

16   R1113 The aorist participle σπεύσαντες expresses action coincident with the main verb, "they came hurrying."

18   R532 Περί with the genitive has a causal notion following the verb ἐθαύμασαν.

B57 There is a specific distinction in meaning between the aorist verb ἐθαύμασαν and the imperfect, which is used in 4:22, "all who heard wondered."

19 R828 Συντηρέω means "to keep together (safely)."

21 B400 Τοῦ περιτεμεῖν is used in apposition to ἡμέραι, meaning "and when eight
days were fulfilled for circumcising him" (the articular infinitive has a final
consecutive sense--T141; it tends toward a consecutive sense--BD400[2]). [Ed.
The articular infinitive appears to be in apposition to the noun ἡμέραι, equivalent to the similar phrase in 1:57 and 2:6.]
M74 The temporal infinitive is used with πρό meaning "before he was conceived."
BD442(7) The use of καί to introduce an apodosis [of a conditional clause] is
due primarily to Hebrew, although it appears as early as Homer (καὶ ὅτε . . .
καί), "then."

22 R609 The preposition in κατὰ τὸν νόμον refers to a standard or rule of measure.
B397 The initial infinitive παραστῆσαι expresses purpose which is continued by
καὶ τοῦ and a second infinitive (v. 24), "they brought him up to Jerusalem,
to present him to the Lord, . . . and to offer a sacrifice" (cf. T142).

25 TGr19 Simeon was subject to a supernatural influence. The presence of the
article in vv. 26f is due to anaphora, referring back to the immediately
preceding reference in v. 25 (the anarthrous πνεῦμα appears to refer to the
Holy Spirit--M113; cf. the discussion on 1:15 and 35).

26 R1047 In ἦν αὐτῷ κεχρηματισμένον . . . μὴ ἰδεῖν θάνατον, the construction is
like that of an indirect command, but the sense comes nearer to the mere object
infinitive, "it had been revealed . . . that he would not see death."
B114 The aorist infinitive ἰδεῖν refers to what is future with reference to the
principal verb.
B333 The New Testament contains two instances of a finite verb after πρίν, here
and Acts 25:16. In both cases the clause is in indirect discourse, and expresses what was from the point of view of the original statement a future contingency.
M19 The periphrastic pluperfect construction here (i.e., a perfect participle
and an imperfect stative verb) denotes completed action, referring to the past
act as well as the existing result, with the sense "and it had been revealed
to him."

27 R504 The genitive τοῦ νόμου is used with the participle τὸ εἰθισμένον, because
the participle is regarded as a substantive (i.e., a noun), "according to the
custom of the law" (cf. 1:8).
B109 The action denoted by the infinitive εἰσαγαγεῖν, strictly speaking, precedes the action of the principal verb, yet may be thought of by the writer as
marking more or less exactly the time at which the action of the verb takes
place ("after they entered"--T145).
B397 Τοῦ with the infinitive expresses the notion of purpose.
M63 The preposition περί has an absolute sense here, "to do . . . in connection
with him" ("with him"--BD229[2]).

28 R593 Εἰς is used after a verb of motion with the meaning "in."
BD277(3) Αὐτός is used to show emphasis here.

29 R1199 Hebrew parallelism is manifest in the song of Simeon (vv. 29-32).

31 T25 Κατὰ προσώπου and similar Semitisms are always singular (a distributive singular with a plural), "in the presence of all the peoples."

33 R405 The auxiliary verb is singular but the participle is plural because of the compound subject, "were amazed."
   M17 The imperfect periphrastic construction ἦν . . . θαυμάζοντες is used to emphasize the durative nature of the action.

34 T87 The present participle ἀντιλεγόμενον is used for the future (perhaps under Hebrew or Aramaic influence), "will be spoken against."

35 R687 Σοῦ . . . αὐτῆς is intensive, meaning "your own soul."

37 R680 Αὐτὴ χήρα may mean a "widow by herself."
   M45 Note the use of the dative in νηστείαις καὶ δεήσεσιν λατρεύουσα, meaning "serving with fastings and petitions" (this seems more like a dative of accompaniment than of means).

38 R574 'Αντί has the idea of "in return" in the compound verb here.
   R686 Αὐτῇ is strengthened to mean "that very" (similar to a demonstrative pronoun; this is a mannerism of Luke's style, not a result of semitic influence--H432).

39 MT130 The aorist verb ἐτέλεσαν is used with an effective notion, "finish."

41 R523 Τῇ ἑορτῇ is used as a locative dative, "at the feast."
   R884 Notice the iterative use of the imperfect tense in ἐπορεύοντο (i.e., they did it repeatedly).

42 M101 The present participle ἀναβαινόντων seems to refer to an action that takes place before the action of the main verb ὑπέμεινεν (though possibly the participle refers to the whole occasion, rather than to the journey up to the feast as distinct from the return journey; thus Zerwick translates ἀναβαινόντων αὐτῶν as "on the occasion of the pilgrimage"). It is interesting to note that the present participle is followed by an aorist participle before the main verb is introduced. [Ed. The present participle is apparently used to portray previous action in relation to the main verb.]

43 M76 The temporal infinitive means "as they were returning" ("because they were returning"--T145). [Ed. Generally this construction has a temporal sense in Luke's writings (cf. 1:8), and that rendering more readily fits the context here, "while they were returning."]

44 R1060 The accusative with the infinitive is that of general reference, while the infinitive itself is the object of the verb of thinking, "supposing him to be."
   B37 In this verse "supposing him to be in the company, they went a day's journey," it was not the holding of the opinion that he was in the company that preceded the day's journey but the forming of it, and the aorist participle νομίσαντες is inceptive.
   T212 'Ημέρας is used as a genitive of time referring to duration, "a day's journey" (classical).

47   T66   The imperfect verb ἐξίσταντο was intended to make the narrative interesting
           and continuous until some action is expected in the aorist to give point to the
           whole description; but the description is left without climax here (common in
           the New Testament), "were amazed."
           BD442(16)   In this verse καί is used to co-ordinate two ideas, one of which is
           dependent on the other (to avoid a series of genitives), "at his intelligent
           answers."

48   M8   The imperfect verb ἐζητοῦμεν should be considered as a present, referring
           to past action still in progress, "were seeking you" (and still are, or "have
           been looking").

49   B28   The imperfect verb ἐζητεῖτε refers to an action that is not separated from
           the time of speaking by a recognized interval, thus it is best to translate it
           as an English perfect (cf. v. 48).
           M75   There is some papyrus support for the Revised Version translation of ἐν
           τοῖς τοῦ πατρός μου as "in my Father's house"; although the Authorized Version's
           translation, "about my Father's business" seems to be more natural (it is more
           likely that ἐν τοῖς implies "house" rather than "business"--R502; cf. T261 and
           MT103).   [Ed.   The suggestion of "house" seems more probable, especially since
           Jesus answers the question as to his locality rather than the question of his
           purpose or mission, thus negating the necessity of their search.]

50   BD347(2)   If an action takes place without a lasting consequence in the subse-
           quent past, the aorist must be employed (although there is a durative result,
           it was unnecessary to stress it in συνῆκαν).

51   R828   The compound verb with the imperfect tense means "to keep continually."

                                    LUKE 3

2   R603   Ἐπί with the genitive is used with the sense of "during the time of."

5   R595   Εἰς with the accusative is used as a predicate nominative with ἔσται, "the
           crooked shall be straight."

9   R870   The present tense of the verbs ἐκκόπτεται and βάλλεται has a futuristic
           sense (the certainty of the action is expressed).
           T199   Πᾶν δένδρον means "any tree," not "every tree."

13   M51   Παρά is used in comparison here, "more than the appointed amount."
           T151   Τὸ διατεταγμένον ὑμῖν means "your assessment."

14   R532   Τοῖς ὀψωνίοις is used as a dative of means (instrumental), "with your
           wages."
           R582   The preposition διά has a perfective notion in the compound verb here,
           "rob by violence."
           R853   The constative aorist occurs in διασείσητε and συκοφαντήσητε rather than
           the present imperative (the soldiers were present; if John spoke in Greek to
           them, it is more restrained at any rate).

                                      99

T151 The anarthrous participle στρατευόμενοιis used as a substantive (a noun), "soldiers."

15 B111 An optative verb occurs here in an indirect question where the direct question would have had an indicative (cf. R1044 and 1:29; what they actually asked themselves may be expressed by the optative--T123; the tone of remoteness and uncertainty given by the optative is well seen in the reported question here--MT199). [Ed. It seems unusual to consider the verb as originally being an indicative since the subjective particle μήποτε is used.]
BD370(3) Μήποτε means "whether perhaps," or "if possible" (with no negative notion involved).

16 R722 The redundant personal pronoun αὐτοῦ is incorporated into the relative clause in vv. 16f. (cf. H434).
TGr19 John the Baptist announced that the One coming after him would baptize with a holy spirit and with fire, but when the dove descended upon Jesus, Luke probably intended to convey that this was the Holy Spirit, as the definite article appears in 3:22. However, this may be due to anaphora (referring to a previous mention), in spite of the fact that v. 16 is some distance away (cf. the discussion on 1:15 and 1:35).
T240 "To baptize with" usually has ἐν, but ὕδατι is used alone here (i.e., instrumental; also the manuscripts have ἐν πνεύματι by contrast; cf. BD195[1d]; ὕδατι is used as a locative--R521). [Ed. The first suggestion appears to be more probable especially in view of the following ἐν πνεύματι ἁγίῳ καὶ πυρί, cf. Matt. 3:11 where the two are parallel.]

18 M162 Μὲν οὖν has a purely resumptive or transitional sense, "then," or "so then" (this is the only occurrence of μεν οὖν in the Gospel of Luke).
T197 Ἕτερος has the sense of ἄλλος here, "another" (without the distinction of kind).

20 BD235(3) Ἐπί with the dative has the notion "in addition to."

21 B109 Ἐν τῷ βαπτισθῆναι ἅπαντα τὸν λαόν can not (in view of the aorist tense) be rendered "while all the people were being baptized," nor (in view of the preposition ἐν), "after all the people had been baptized," but must be understood as affirming that the baptism of Jesus occurred at the time (in general) of the baptism of all the people (equivalent to ὅτε ἐβαπτίσθη--BD404).

22 B55 Εὐδόκησα appears to be used as an inceptive aorist, "I have become well pleased" (cf. 2 Pet. 1:17).

LUKE 4

1 R1185 The resumptive use of δέ occurs here, after a parenthesis, to continue on with the main story.
M205 The second occurrence of ἐν in this verse seems to be used for εἰς (cf. T257), "into the wilderness."
TGr19 It seems probable that the Holy Spirit did not lead Jesus into the wilderness, since the articular ἐν τῷ πνεύματι is clearly anaphoric reference to the previous line of the narrative: "Jesus, full of holy spirit, . . . was led by the same spirit . . ." (cf the discussion on 1:15 and 35).

3 R1009 An imperative verb is used in the apodosis here. This verse contains a
   first class condition. The devil would not, of course, use the second class
   (assumed to be untrue), for that would be an affront to Christ. The third and
   fourth classes would throw doubt on the point. The temptation, to have force,
   must be assumed to be true. The devil knew it to be true. He accepts the fact
   as a working hypothesis in the temptation. He is anxious to get Jesus to prove
   it, as if it needed proof for Christ's own satisfaction and for his reception.
   If the devil used Aramaic, then we have Christ's own translation of it or that
   of the Evangelist.
   T183 The predicate nominative υἱός precedes the verb and so is anarthrous, "if
   you are the son."

7 BD187(2) Προσκύνω may take either a dative or accusative object, but ἐνώπιον
   ἐμοῦ is the result of Hebraizing, "worship me."

9 R834 Βάλε is used as an ingressive aorist, meaning "hurl."

10 R582 The sense of "thoroughly" occurs in the preposition διά of the compound
   verb, "preserve."
   R1068 Τοῦ with the infinitive is used as the object of ἐντελεῖται, "he will command to guard."

14 R607 Κατά is used with ὅλης with the resultant meaning "throughout."

15 B449 The participle δοξαζόμενος is used to describe an attendant circumstance
   of the principal verb, "and he taught in their synagogues, being glorified of
   all."
   BD277(3) Αὐτός has very little emphasis here. It occurs with the verb ἐδίδασκεν, thereby eliminating the preceding φήμη as the continuing subject.

16 B295 The relative clause in this verse is explanatory, "and he came to Nazareth,
   where he had been brought up."
   T27 The plural σαββάτων has a singular sense.
   T151 The substantival participle (as a noun) τὸ εἰωθός with αὐτῷ means "his custom" (with a dative of possession, stressing the object possessed--BD189[1]).

17 R27 In this verse it is not clear whether it was the Hebrew text or the Septuagint that was read in the synagogue at Nazareth.

18 M83 Οὗ εἵνεκεν means "because."
   M177 Πνεῦμα κυρίου actually means "the Spirit of the Lord"; the omission of the
   article is due to the Hebrew construct state.
   MT143 In this verse it seems best, with some versions, to put a period after
   ἔχρισεν μέ so that ἀπέσταλκε is the governing verb of all the infinitives, and
   is not parallel with ἔχρισεν (cf. New English Bible).

19 M40 The genitive κυρίου in this verse (from the Septuagint) is presumably a
   possessive, "the acceptable year belonging to the Lord"; but no doubt the κυρίου also combines in a special way with the idea behind δεκτόν, to convey the
   meaning that it is "the year when the Lord will accept man" (i.e., there is a
   tinge of subjective meaning in the genitive noun).

20 R757 The articles in τὸ βιβλίον ἀποδοὺς τῷ ὑπηρέτῃ denote that the roll was the

usual one and the attendant was there at his place. [Ed. The first instance
of the article here appears to be anaphoric, (i.e., denoting previous reference; cf. the reference in v. 17).]

M102 The two participles πτύξας and ἀποδούς refer to two successive actions
without a connecting καί, "he rolled up the book and gave it back . . . and
sat down" (Luke introduces participles quite effectively and thus presents a
flowing style which is refreshing in comparison with the jerky epistolary style
of Paul).

BD275(1) The omission of the article before the adjective is unclassical in
πάντων ἐν τῇ συναγωγῇ, "all those who were in the synagogue" (cf. v. 28; this
distinction applies chiefly to literary style--R773; the omission may have
given cause for the manuscripts to change the position of ἐν τῇ συναγωγῇ in
various ways--T200).

21 BD341 The perfect verb πεπλήρωται expresses a state or condition, and thus has
the sense of a present verb, "is fulfilled."

22 R532 Ἐπί is used with the dative here to express a causal idea, "they wondered
because of."

23 B146 The aorist participle γενόμενα is used as an integral part of the object
of the verb of perception ἠκούσαμεν, representing the action which it denotes
as a simple event without defining its time. Since the action denoted by the
participle is learned, it is antecedent to the action of the principal verb,
"whatever things we have heard to have been done."

BD205 Εἰς is used instead of ἐν in a local sense, "happened in Capernaum."

25 R604 Ἐπ' ἀληθείας has the idea of basis, "on the basis of truth."

26 R1187 Εἰ μή means "but only" in vv. 26f. (εἰ μή serves for ἀλλά -- a confusion
which may be traceable to Aramaic influence--T330).

27 R603 Ἐπὶ ἐλισσαίου means "in the time of Elisha."

28 R1127 The participle ἀκούοντες gives the occasion of the main verb (this notion
actually wavers between a temporal and causal idea), "when they heard."

29 R1089 Ὥστε with the infinitive expresses the notion of purpose, "they led him
unto the brow of the hill that they might throw him down headlong" (cf. B371).

32 BD198(2) Ἐν with the dative ἐξουσίᾳ has an associative sense, "with authority."

35 M32 Μηδὲν βλάψαν may present a cognate accusative (as though it were μηδεμίαν
βλάβην); but this might equally well be an accusative of respect. [Ed. The
latter suggestion is more probable since βλάψαν is in the text, "without doing
any harm to him."]

36 R735 Τίς is equivalent to ποῖος in this verse, "what kind."

R1001 Ὅτι is used with a consecutive sense here, "so that" (through semitic influence; cf. T318).

38 R619 Περὶ αὐτῆς has the idea of advantage, "for her."

BD260(2) Is the peculiar anarthrous use of πενθερά treated as a proper name, or does it mean "a mother-in-law was there, namely Simon's"? [Ed. This is of special interest when the parallel accounts of Matthew and Mark are taken into consideration. Luke's account provides the only instance of an anarthrous πενθερά and an articular Σίμωνος. In view of these unique phenomena, the latter suggestion seems preferable.]

41 B90 The pluperfect tense of ἤδεισαν denotes a past state, thus "they knew that he was the Christ."

42 R1089 Τοῦ μή with the infinitive is used as the object of κατεῖχου, with an ablative sense, "kept from leaving" (the negative μή is redundant since the verb of hindering is used--R1171).

43 T197 In classical Greek ὁ ἕτερος is never used for anything but a definite division into two parts, but here ταῖς ἑτέραις πόλεσιν means "the remaining cities."

LUKE 5

1 M76 The temporal clause ἐν τῷ τὸν ὄχλον ἐπικεῖσθαι αὐτῷ, means "while the crowd was pressing on him."
M121 The pronoun αὐτός is unemphatic here (i.e., simply "he was standing").

3 R597 In ἐκ τοῦ πλοίου ἐδίδασκεν the teaching is represented as preceding out of the boat (Jesus was in the boat).

4 R1121 Λαλῶν is used as a complementary participle with παύσατο (the participle is used as the subject of the verb--B457), "when he ceased speaking."

5 R604 ʼΕπὶ τῷ ῥήματί has the idea of basis (i.e., causal; cf. T272), "because of your word."
R1181 Δέ is used with an adversative sense here, "we took nothing, but."
M56 Διά is occasionally used in expressions of time, "the whole night through."

6 R885 Διερήσσετο is used as an inceptive (inchoative) imperfect, "their nets began to break."

7 R748 ʼΕτέρῳ refers to the second of a pair.
R1039 The change from the dative μετέχοις to the accusative ἐλθόντας is due to anacoluthon (a shift in the sentence structure, but referring to the same people, cf. 1:74).
R1068 Τοῦ συλλαβέσθαι is the object of κατένευσαν (cf. B404), "they signaled to help."
BD338(1) The present infinitive in ὥστε βυθίζεσθαι αὐτά has a durative sense, "so that they were in danger of sinking."

10 R889 The force of ἔσῃ . . . ζωγρῶν is that of a progressive future, with the thought of continuance or customariness somewhat emphasized, meaning "thou shalt catch men," i.e., "shalt be a catcher of men" (cf. 1:20).
T239 Κοινωνοὶ τῷ Σίμωνι (D has the genitive) means "Simon had in them partners" (to his credit).

12 H433 Μιᾷ with the partitive genitive τῶν πόλεων is equivalent to τινί, "one of the cities."

14 T40 Αὐτοῖς follows the antecedent ἱερεῖ unless the pronoun indicates a general reference, not to the priests but to the public. [Ed. The pronoun αὐτοῖς seems to refer to the general public, since ἱερεῖ is singular.]
BD229(1) Περί is used here with the sense of ὑπέρ, "for your cleansing."
BD470(2) It is quite impossible for a New Testament author to do what is so common in classical Greek, namely, to maintain indirect discourse in an extended passage. Instead, Luke reverts without failure to the direct discourse, a tendency which is not at all unusual in classical authors as well.

17 T143 Εἰς τό with the infinitive ἰᾶσθαι portrays a sense of purpose.
H433 Μιᾷ is equivalent to τινί (cf. v. 12).

19 M34 The genitive in ποίας (supply ὁδοῦ) εἰσενέγκωσιν αὐτόν refers to place, "by what way they might bring him in" (cf. T235).

21 BD142 The plural noun βλασφημίας here refers to the words of the one blasphemy that was spoken.
BD420(2) The use of the participle in this verse is certainly pleonastic (i.e., redundant), ἤρξαντο διαλογίζεσθαι ("to respect") . . . λέγοντες.

24 R1203 In this verse the Evangelist has inserted εἶπεν τῷ παραλελυμένῳ before the conclusion to make it more clear. The same thing is done in the parallel passages (Matt. 9:6 and Mark 2:10; an incidental argument for a common document for this paragraph).
T75 The present imperative πορεύου occurs here where the rule strictly taken seems to demand the aorist, "go to your house."
BD336(1) In πορεύου εἰς τὸν οἶκόν σου the command refers more to direction than goal; whether he arrives or not is beside the point.

26 B52 The aorist verb εἴδομεν is similar to a perfect, since the event is so recent as to make the thought of an interval between the action and the time of speaking seem unnatural, "we have seen strange things today."

28 H453 The participle ἀναστάς is used in a redundant way with a verb of motion following, "he stood up and followed."

33 M120 It is not clear whether σοί is nominative plural of the adjective or dative of the singular personal pronoun. [Ed. In this context σοί is apparently the nominative plural of the possessive adjective. The adjective distinguishes this group of disciples from the previous two groups, οἱ δὲ σοί means "but yours."]

34 R978 The temporal use of ἐν ᾧ is similar to ἕως, meaning "while."
R1085 The infinitive νηστεῦσαι is dependent on another infinitive (common in the New Testament), "are you able to make . . . fast?"

35 B316 Ὅταν ἀπαρθῇ is conditional in form but definite in force, with the sense "when the bridegroom shall be taken away from them" (at least definite in Christ's mind).

36 BD444(3) The repetition of καί before οὐ συμφωνήσει means "on the one hand . . . on the other" (i.e., a double loss).

37 T41 The pronoun αὐτός seems to have some emphasis in this context, "<u>it</u> will be poured out."

38 R1097 The verbal adjective βλητέον is more like the verb than the adjective (i.e., it takes the accusative case). The agent is not expressed here, "one must put" (ἐστίν has been omitted--BD127[4]).

39 M97 Ὁ παλαιὸς χρηστός ἐστιν should probably be translated "the old is better" (the positive adjective has the sense of a comparative; cf. T31).

LUKE 6

1 R533 Ταῖς χερσίν is used as an instrumental dative, "with their hands."
R1043 Outside of Luke's writings the infinitive with ἐγένετο occurs only in Mark 2:23 (but in that instance it is a primitive assimilation of Luke 6:1--MT17). In Luke 6:1, the infinitive is used as the subject of ἐγένετο, "It came about . . . that he was passing through."

3 R1045 Both ὅ and ὡς are used (in vv. 3f1) to introduce indirect questions, "how"!

4 R714 The relative pronoun οὕς refers to the preceding sentence.

6 R393 The infinitive εἰσελθεῖν is used as the subject of the verb ἐγένετο, "it came about . . . that he entered."
R748 Ἑτέρῳ has the meaning of "next."

7 T55 The verb παρετηροῦντο occurs in the middle voice where one expects the active, "watch closely."

8 R680 Αὐτός portrays only slight emphasis (cf. 1:20).

11 R885 The imperfect verb διελάλουν is used with an inceptive connotation, "they began to discuss."
R940 Moulton (198) suggests that τί ἂν ποιήσαιεν in the indirect question is the hesitating substitute for the direct τί ποιήσομεν. Why not rather suppose a hesitating (deliberative) direct question (cf. Acts 17:18; the optative with ἂν is taken unchanged from the direct discourse--B111)?

12 R500 The genitive τοῦ θεοῦ is used as an objective genitive, "prayer to God."
R1058 The infinitive ἐξελθεῖν is used as the subject of ἐγένετο (cf. v. 6).

16 R501 The genitive of relationship Ἰακώβου probably means "the brother of" rather than "the son of" in view of Jude 1 (although usually "son of" is the relationship to be understood).

18 R574 The idea of removal is present in ἰαθῆναι ἀπό and agency (instrumental) in ἐνοχλούμενοι ἀπό (the latter is causal-instrumental--M73), "to be healed

from" and "those who were troubled with."

R714   The relative pronoun οἵ does not agree with its antecedent (πλῆθος) in number, but has the number according to sense.

20   R1393   The preposition εἰς is used here, where ἐπί would have been used in earlier Greek, "on."

21   TGr39   The same style lies behind this verse as that behind 1:22, where Jesus says, "Blessed are ye that hunger now; (this I know) because ye shall be filled." It can not be interpreted as, "Ye hunger now because ye shall be filled".

22   R834   Μισήσωσιν is used as an ingressive aorist, "begin to hate" (cf. T72).

23   MT174   The ingressive idea is present in the imperatives of this verse, "be glad . . ."

24   R1187   As a conjunction, πλήν is always adversative, as it is in this verse, "but."

25   R459   Οἱ ἐμπεπλησμένοι is actually a vocative, rather than a nominative in apposition to the subject, "woe to you that are full now."

29   T235   The verb κωλύω is used with ἀπό to mean "refuse someone something."
     MT125   The aorist prohibition here would be answered with "I will avoid doing so."
     MT174   The present imperative πάρεχε has a durative sense, "hold out," "offer."

30   T76   Δός in Matt. 5:42 refers to a definite occasion and person, but δίδου in Luke 6:30 refers to anyone who asks. (The present imperatives have a conative sense; i.e., "start giving," and "don't ask again.")

32   B282   In καὶ εἰ, the particle εἰ maintains its conditional force and καί means "and."
     T115   Εἰ is used with the indicative to express a statement, "since" (εἰ is used here with the sense of ἐάν with the subjunctive [cf. v. 33]--BD372).
     [Ed. Ἀγαπᾶτε may be either indicative or subjunctive in form. But since it is unusual for εἰ to occur with the subjunctive, the verb is apparently indicative here.]

34   R576   The compound verb ἀπολάβωσιν has the idea of a recipient getting back what is his due (a debt or reward).
     R720   Παρ' ὧν has an ablative idea, "from whom."

35   TGr35ff.   In view of the sense of this passage, the text with μηδένα seems to be the most accurate. Thus the meaning of the participle ἀπελπίζοντες is "despairing of no man."
     MT65   Ἀπελπίζω generally takes the accusative object, as it seems to do here if μηδένα is correct (it is quite probable that elision occurs in this verse, μηδὲν ἀπελπίζοντες, thus making the variant manuscripts agree in sense--H62).

38   R184   The Doric form πιάζω is used in the New Testament everywhere except here, where, however, πεπιεσμένον has the original idea, "pressed down," not "seized."
     T240   The dative noun μέτρῳ is used in an instrumental sense "to measure <u>with</u> the same measure."

39 BD427(2) Μή is used with a question expecting a negative answer, "a blind man
    can't lead a blind man, can he?" The expected answer is "certainly not." But
    οὐχί expects the answer "of course."

41 MT90 There is emphasis in the use of ἰδίῳ here, "your own."

42 R932 Ἄφες occurs with the first person singular hortatory subjunctive ἐκβάλω
    (with this type of construction, the New Testament always has ἄφες or δεῦρο),
    "allow" or "let me . . ." (cf. M22).
    T139 The infinitive ἐκβαλεῖν is used in loose connection with the verb, meaning
    "see to cast out."
    T285 The negative οὐ is used with the participle βλέπων because of Luke's ten-
    dency towards classical style. [Ed. By using οὐ with the participle βλέπων,
    Luke emphasizes the total spiritual blindness of the hypocrite. The hypocrite
    is so concerned about the minor faults in others, that he completely fails to
    see the major inconsistencies in his own manner of life.]

47 T79 Zerwick (section 184) goes so far as to distinguish ὁ ἀκούων ("he who hears
    with lasting effect") from ὁ ἀκούσας ("who hears ineffectively and momentarily")
    in vv. 47ff. (this is an improbable distinction of the tenses).
    T233 In general, the accusative is used to refer to the hearing of speech in
    the New Testament (except in this verse, which corrects Matt. 7:24).

48 R1136 The expression ἔσκαψεν καὶ ἐβάθυνεν means "he dug and deepened," which
    is equivalent to "he dug deep" (βαθύνας would be smoother, but καί can be taken
    as "and indeed").
    BD293(2) Ὅστις is generally used in connection with a substantive of indefinite
    reference. But Luke overrides this limitation and uses ὅς in vv. 48f., "a man
    . . , who."

                                     LUKE 7

1   T321 Ἐπειδή has a temporal sense only in this occurrence (note the variant
    readings).

2   B73 The imperfect of μέλλω with an infinitive is used to affirm that at a past
    point of time an action was about to take place or was intended or destined to
    occur.

3   T106 Ὅπως with the subjunctive after ἐρωτῶν is used to express the idea of
    purpose (instead of denoting content), "that he might heal."

4   R724 Ὧ introduces a relative clause that expresses a consecutive notion (it
    is a complementary relative clause limiting the adjective ἄξιος--B318). [Ed.
    Actually, these comments do not contradict each other.]
    R884 Παρεκάλουν is used as an iterative imperfect (i.e., the action occurs re-
    peatedly).

6   B216 The ἵνα clause is used as a complementary limitation of the adjective
    ἱκανός, "I am not worthy that come."

T66 The imperfect verb ἐπορεύετο is followed by the aorist ἔπεμψεν, presenting the idea that Jesus was going when the centurion sent friends.
T157 The participle λέγων has a final idea (purpose; cf. BD418[4]), "the centurion sent friends in order to say to him."

8 R856 The present indicatives that follow the imperative are used in an aoristic sense, "he goes . . . he comes . . . he does."

11 R547 In the phrase ἐν τῷ ἑξῆς, the adverb is treated as an adjective, "on the next day."

12 R1116 The perfect participle τεθνηκώς is intensive, having primarily a linear aspect in the present sense, "a man who had died."

14 M26 It is doubtful whether there is any substantial difference between ἐγέρθητι and ἔγειρε (in 8:54): they both appear to be simply intransitive in sense, "arise."

17 T257 The preposition ἐν is used with an interesting sense here. Nain is certainly some distance away from Judaea, but the addition of surrounding districts makes "in" more natural than "to" ("spread in"--BD218).

18 T195 Δύο τινάς does not mean "about two" but "a certain pair."

19 R1118 The present participle ἐρχόμενος has an anticipatory sense (futuristic), "the one who is to come."

22 T58 The deponent verb εὐαγγελίζονται is used with a passive sense, "the poor have good news preached to them."

24 R857 The aorist infinitive θεάσασθαι has a constative sense (i.e., a simple statement summarizing a series of events).

27 R960 The relative clause ὅς κατασκευάσει . . . is used to portray a final notion (purpose; cf. BD378).

28 M42 The genitive of comparison occurs in μείζων . . . Ἰωάννου οὐδείς ἐστιν, "there is none greater than John."
T30 The comparative adjective ὁ μικρότερος is used for the true superlative, meaning "the least."

30 BD192 Εἰς ἑαυτούς is used for the dative of advantage, "for themselves" (semitic).

32 MT82 The anarthrous prepositional phrase ἐν ἀγορᾷ does not mean "in a market-place," but "in the market-place."

35 M13 Ἐδικαιώθη makes excellent sense if translated as a gnomic aorist, "Wisdom is (always) justified . . .," but it could nevertheless be a statement of a single past fact, "Wisdom received her justification . . ." (gnomic--B43 and T73).
M178 Καί has an adversative use in this verse, "yet wisdom . . ."
H461 The use of the preposition ἀπό is taken as an Aramaism by Wellhausen. But

it seems far better to take this ἀπό as equivalent to ὑπό (as so often in the koine), marking the agent after a passive verb, "by" (ἀπό with the genitive expresses an instrumental idea--M73).

38   R525 The preposition παρά is used in a locative sense, "at his feet."
      R533 Ταῖς θριξίν is used as an instrumental dative, "with the hair."
      M86   Ὀπίσω is used as an adverb only twice in the New Testament (here and in Matt. 24:18), "standing behind."

39   R727 The pronoun ἥτις does not differ greatly from οἷος and expresses quality.
      R741 Ποταπός means "of what sort," equivalent to ποῖος (cf. 1:29).
      R1012 In this verse the condition (determined as fulfilled) has only to do with the statement, not with the actual fact. Thus the Pharisee here assumes that Jesus is not a prophet because he allowed the sinful woman to wash his feet. Jesus is therefore bound to be ignorant of her true character. The form of the condition reveals the state of mind of the Pharisee, not the truth about Jesus' nature and powers. As a matter of fact it is the Pharisee who is ignorant (cf. B241).

40   B368 The infinitive εἰπεῖν is used as an indirect object of ἔχω (similar to an infinitive of purpose), "I have something to say to you."

45   R978 Ἀφ' ἧς is used with the meaning "since" (the noun ὥρας can be supplied with the phrase ἀφ' ἧς--BD241[2]).
      B459 The substantival participle καταφιλοῦσα is used as the object of the verb διέλιπεν, "she did not cease to kiss."

47   R647 This instance is the only occurrence of χάριν in the Gospels with the meaning "for the sake of."
      M147 In this verse complete consistency is reached if the ὅτι clause is taken as depending, in respect of logical connexion, on λέγω σοι: "I can say with confidence, because her love is evidence of it" (cf. 1:22, 6:21 and TGr37ff.). But some commentators take it with ἀφέωνται, making her love the ground of her forgiveness, not of the assurance that she has been forgiven, a non-Christian conclusion which throws the sentence into complete opposition both to the preceding parable and to the second half of this very verse.

50   BD206(1) Εἰς with the accusative εἰρήνην is used for ἐν with the dative (this phrase is due to the Septuagint influence--H463), "go in peace."

                                    LUKE 8

1   R608 The preposition in κατὰ πόλιν καὶ κώμην has the notion of distribution, "through cities and villages."

3   R749 Ἕτεραι refers merely to another, with more than two people in mind and with no idea of difference.

4   R583 The prepositional phrase διὰ παραβολῆς reveals the manner of the speaking, "with a parable."

5 R990 Τοῦ with the infinitive is used to express purpose.
T145 The frequent use of ἐν τῷ with an infinitive in Luke's writings is due to the influence of the Septuagint (temporal here), "while he was sowing."
BD447(3) The use of ὁ μὲν . . . καὶ ἕτερον to express contrast is occasioned by an intervening development of the narrative.

7 R749 It is surprising that Luke should change the correct ἄλλος (Mark 4:5-8 = Matt. 13:5-8) to ἕτερος in Luke 8:6-8 (referring to more than two; cf. v.3), "and other seed."

9 R1031 An optative verb occurs here in an indirect question where the direct question had the indicative verb, "his disciples asked him what this parable was" (cf. 1:29).

10 T102 The ἵνα in this verse is transformed into a causal ὅτι in Matthew, but this does not prove that the two particles are equal, "in order that."
BD369(2) The final ἵνα (which seems to support the theory that some are incapable of repentance) is softened by Matthew (13:13) to a causal ὅτι.

12 T23 The distributive singular occurs in vv. 12 and 15 (cf. 1:51), referring to an object in the singular that belongs to each person in a group, "their hearts."

13 R625 Πρός is used in an expression of time with the notion of extension ("for a time," denoting duration—M53).

14 M209 The participle of motion πορευόμενοι may be used to give progressive force to the finite verb συμπνίγονται, "as they go they are choked."

15 TGr181 There is evidence in this verse which may establish an original Greek composition. Jesus uses a phrase which looks anything but semitic: "in a beautiful and good heart." It is well known that "beautiful and good" (καλὸς κ' ἀγαθός) is the traditional Greek phrase for a gentleman; it has no parallel in either Hebrew or Aramaic (it is similar to Socrates' use of καλὸς κ' ἀγαθός --R176).

17 R764 Εἰς φανερόν may be anarthrous, because the thing is not yet in existence. But it is rather a fine point to make (especially since the preposition is used, which may make the noun definite without the article).

20 R881 The perfect verb ἕστηκα is used as a practical durative present in the New Testament, "are standing."

23 R834 Ἀφύπνωσεν is used as an ingressive aorist, "he fell asleep" (cf. T72).
R884 Ἐκινδύνευον is used as a progressive imperfect expressing peril or danger.
R885 Συνεπληροῦντο is used as an inceptive imperfect, "they began to be filled with water."

24 R1200 The repetition of ἐπιστάτα portrays strong emotion.

25 T318 Ὅτι is used with a consecutive sense in this verse, "so that" (cf. BD456 [2] and 4:36).
BD444(3) The use of καὶ . . . καὶ in the latter part of this verse means "even . . . and."

26 R639 The meaning of ἀντιπέρα here is disputed . It is either a pure genitive,
"over against," or an ablatival genitive, "on the other side of" (it apparently means "on the opposite side of"--M82).

27 R809 The indirect middle can be seen in ἐνεδύσατο, "he did not put a garment
on himself."
B29 The action denoted by the imperfect ἔμενεν evidently preceded an event already mentioned. Thus, it is best to translate it into English by the past perfect (so also with the aorist verb ἐνεδύσατο--B48), "who had not been living."
M43 In χρόνῳ ἱκανῷ the dative is clearly durative, "for a long time."

29 R527 Πολλοῖς χρόνοις may be used as an instrumental dative, "of a long time,"
but the locative would give a good sense, "on many occasions" (the most natural translation seems to be "on many occasions [the evil spirit]   had seized
him"--M43).
R581 The compound verb διαρήγνυμι means "rend asunder."
R827 In συνηρπάκει the perfective sense of σύν combines with the past perfect
tense and the locative, (or instrumental) πολλοῖς χρόνοις to denote the estab-
lishment of a permanent hold ("the demon had long ago obtained and now kept complete mastery of him"--MT113).
M9 The iterative imperfect occurs in this verse, "he used to (would) be bound
. . . and he used to (would) break the bonds and be driven . . . into the uninhabited parts."
M10 The imperfect verb παρήγγελλεν means "he had been commanding" (the aorist
is expected--T65). [Ed. The idea that Turner introduces is that we expect the
aorist because the command was carried out and completed. But this is not absolutely necessary.]

33 R607 The prepositional phrase κατὰ τοῦ κρημνοῦ means "down from the cliff."

35 M72 Notice that ἀπό is used here instead of ἐκ, "from whom."

36 R1045 Πῶς is actually used to introduce an indirect question, with the meaning
"how."

37 T65 The aorist verb ἠρώτησεν here means "insisted" (cf. Matt. 8:34 and Mark
5:17).

38 BD392(1c) Ἐδεῖτο . . . εἶναι σὺν αὐτῷ means "he asked . . . to be allowed to
be with him."

42 R827 The imperfect verb ἀπέθνησκεν has the sense of "dying."

43 B131 The present participle οὖσα is used to refer to a past action that is still
in progress.
MT102 The second occurrence of ἀπό refers to the agent of a passive verb (similar to the use of ὑπό), "healed by anyone."

45 R828 The compound verb συνέχω means "to hold together" or "press."

46 R1041 The perfect participle is used to express the content (object) of the
verb ἔγνων, where Christ thus graphically describes the terrible nervous loss
from his healing power. He felt the power "gone" from out of him (the tense
and participle both accent the vivid reality of the experience--R1103; it should

be translated "I felt that power had gone out"--T160).

47 R1045 Both δι' ἥν αἰτίαν ("why") and ὡς ("how") are used to introduce an indirect question (the noun αἰτίαν is in apposition to the relative pronoun ἥν--
R718).

48 H463 The occurrence of the preposition in πορεύου εἰς εἰρήνην must be due to the
Septuagint, where it often represents the Hebrew (similar to ἐν with the dative,
cf. 7:50), "in peace."

49 R867 Luke's manifest reluctance to use the historical present (changing Mark's
historical presents except in this verse) is due to the fact that in Luke's
time the construction was regarded as too familiar for his liking (ἔρχεται, cf.
B14), "came."
M125 The present prohibition μηκέτι σκύλλε prohibits the continuation of an
action, "do not trouble the Teacher any longer."

50 T75 The aorist imperative πίστευσον means "start to have faith" (Luke perhaps
corrects the present imperative πίστευε in Mark 5:36).

52 R809 In ἐκόπτοντο αὐτήν, the verb has really changed meaning, "they beat themselves for grief as to her" ("bewailed her"), actually a direct middle (the word
has practically crystallized into a colorless sense, "they mourned for her"--
M24).

54 R465 The nominative article ἡ is used with παῖς for the vocative (a touch of
tenderness is evident here), "child."
M26 Ἔγειρε means "be roused" (cf. 7:14 and T52).

56 T151 The neuter substantival (i.e., used as a noun) participle τὸ γεγονός means
"the occurrence."

LUKE 9

1 T55 The middle voice occurs (συγκαλεσάμενος) where one expects the active,
"called together."

3 R1092 The infinitive ἔχειν occurs between two imperatives (giving it an imperatival sense; cf. M126, T78 and BD389). Moulton objects (MT179) on this point,
proposing that this infinitive is due to a mixture of indirect and direct discourse. That is true, but it was a very easy lapse, since the infinitive itself has this imperatival usage, "take nothing . . ., do not have two tunics."

4 B310 In this verse, "into whatsoever house you enter, there abide, and thence
depart," the supposition is general, referring to any one of a class of actions.

8 BD306(5) Luke improves Mark's semitic statement in 6:15, by stating προφήτης
τις τῶν ἀρχαίων, which means "one of the other old prophets."

9 BD322 The present verb ἀκούω has a perfective sense, "I have heard."

10   R691 Κατ' ἰδίαν occurs here in the sense of "private."
     R733 Ὅσα is used in an indirect question, "what they had done."

12   H455 The redundant auxiliary verb ἤρξατο occurs here, cf. 4:21 (i.e., the same
     idea could have easily been expressed by the simple imperfect), "the day began
     to decline."

13   B253 The reason for εἰ occurring with the subjunctive here is that there is pro-
     bably a mixture of a conditional clause and a deliberative question: "unless
     indeed -- are we to go?" ("unless indeed we are to go").

14   R968 Ὡσεί is used in the sense of "about" in vv. 14 and 28.
     M35   The double accusative occurs here, meaning "make them recline in parties."
     T266 Ἀνά is used as a distributive preposition here (classical), "make them
     sit down in groups."

16   TGr67f. There is an interesting distinction of the tenses in this verse. So
     we read first that Jesus "gave thanks" (aorist); that was a completed action.
     He then "broke the loaves" (aorist); a completed action. But then followed an
     action which was not finished for a long time. It went on and on, and is there-
     fore expressed by the imperfect tense. "He kept on distributing to the disci-
     ples." The disciples came to Jesus repeatedly for more food, and they handed
     it to the people.

18   R891 A periphrastic present infinitive occurs twice in the Gospel of Luke
     (here and in 11:1) -- εἶναι . . . προσευχόμενον, stressing the continuation
     of an action, "while he was praying."
     R1035 The second infinitive occurs with a declarative sense after λέγουσιν,
     "say that I am."

22   R579 Ἀπό has the sense of "agency" here (similar to ὑπό with the passive), "be
     rejected by."

23   TGr31 "Whoever desires to follow me must once and for all deny himself and seize
     his cross" (aorist verbs; omit the harmonizing variant reading καθ' ἡμέραν);
     then "let him follow me as a continuous disciple" (present). [Ed. The phrase
     καθ' ἡμέραν does not occur in the parallels of Matthew and Mark. But that is
     not reason enough to omit it here, since the major manuscripts support its in-
     clusion. It may have been added by Luke to point to the continual trials of
     the christian life, cf. 11:2f.]
     H421 The two imperatives linked by καί represent the protasis and apodosis of
     an implied condition (καὶ ἀκολουθείτω μοι is equivalent to "then he will be my
     disciple"; cf. 7:7).

25   R1023 Note the implied condition in the participle κερδήσας, "if he gains."

28   R107 Λόγους has the sense of "things."
     R968 Ὡσεί means "about" (cf. v. 14).
     T231 The nominative occurs with time designation here (ἡμέραι), where the ac-
     cusative is expected, "about eight days."

29   T145 Ἐν τῷ προσεύχεσθαι (present) αὐτόν means "while he was praying," but
     ἐγένετο ἐν τῷ ἐλθεῖν (aorist) αὐτὸν εἰς οἶκον means "after he had gone into the
     house" (in 14:1).

113

30 R957 "Οἵτινες is definite here, with the sense of "somebody in particular."

31 R884 Μέλλω with the imperfect has a progressive sense, but without a backward
        look, "which he was about to accomplish."

32 R533 "Ὕπνῳ seems to be used as a dative of means, "with sleep."
    R582 Διά has a perfective idea ("clear through") in the compound verb διαγρη-
        γορέω.
    M13   Does διαγρηγορήσαντες mean "when they were thoroughly roused," or "having
        kept awake all through" (in which case the δια- imparts a linear sense not
        akin to the aorist itself; the linear sense of the verb is preferable--T71).

34 R885 Ἐπεσκίαζεν is used as an inceptive (inchoative) imperfect, "and began
        to overshadow them."
    BD404(3) Ἐν τῷ with the aorist infinitive εἰσελθεῖν expresses action which
        is simultaneous to the main verb, "they were afraid as they entered the cloud"
        (cf. B109).

36 R657 Μόνος is used as an adjective here (not an adverb), "Jesus was found alone."
    R834 Ἐσίγησαν is used as an ingressive aorist, "they became silent" (cf. T70).
    R897 Ἑώρακαν refers to virtually reported speech (i.e., the dramatic histor-
        ical present perfect; cf. M144 and B78; ἑώρακαν is probably an aoristic per-
        fect, although it is possible that the thought of an existing result is more
        or less clearly in mind and gives occasion to the use of the perfect tense--
        B88).
    B109 Ἐν τῷ with the aorist infinitive γενέσθαι can only mean "when the voice
        came," a meaning entirely appropriate for the context ("after"--BD404[2]).
        [Ed. It is not necessary to consider the infinitive as portraying action which
        is antecedent to that of the finite verb merely because the aorist tense is
        used, cf. 3:21.]

38 R541 Μοί is used as a dative of possession, "my."

41 M52   Πρός denotes position (i.e., it has a punctiliar sense), "with you."
    BD146(2) Ὦ is used in an exclamation intended as a rebuke.

42 T322 Luke should have had the participle agree with the accusative rather than
        the genitive (grammatically). [Ed. This is not necessarily correct. Luke
        initially refers to the demoniac with the pronoun αὐτοῦ, but changes to αὐτόν
        because he is the direct object of the verb ἔρρηξεν.]
    BD101 The old Epic verb ῥήσσω "to strike" or "stamp" corresponds to the Attic
        verb "to dash to the ground."

44 B72   Μέλλω is used with an infinitive to refer to an action which is certain to
        take place, "for the Son of Man is to be delivered up into the hands of men."

45 M142 Despite the opinion of some scholars to the contrary, it is still worth
        while to ask whether the ἵνα clause in this verse is not logically consecutive
        (it is consecutive rather than final--T102; it is consecutive but does not por-
        tray an actual result--BD391[5]; the ἵνα clause is not consecutive, for the
        thought of a purpose of Providence seems demanded by παρακεκαλυμμένον --MT210;
        it shows purpose--B222 and R998). [Ed. It may seem preferable in this verse
        to take ἵνα as consecutive, but in many instances it is not definite, cf. Rom.
        5:20.]

T234 Αἰσθάνομαι means "understand" with the accusative.

46 R585 Ἐν occurs here after a verb of motion where εἰς might at first seem more
    natural (cf. M76; "came into them"--BD218; cf. v. 47).
    T130 The optative verb εἴη is used in an indirect question and should not be
    translated "might be"; it is not indefinite, deliberative, or future, but means
    simply "was" (the neuter article introduces the indirect question--R739).

47 M52 Παρά with the dative occurs after a verb of motion in a locative sense, "he
    stood him (a child) beside him."

48 T30 The comparative adjective ὁ μικρότερος is used for the superlative, "the
    least" (cf. 7:28).
    T31   The positive adjective μέγας has the sense of a superlative, "greatest."

49 TGr41 The imperfect tense is used here to refer to an action attempted (repeat-
    edly) but not accomplished (cf. R884), "we tried to discourage him." In reply
    to this, Jesus answers with a present imperative, "Stop discouraging him!" It
    was not a general prohibition, never to discourage the man, for that would be
    aorist. The disciples must change their course of action immediately. There
    are accents in his voice saying, "change your attitude. Go at once to this
    man. Shake hands with him."
    BD193(1) Ἀκολούθει μεθ' ἡμῶν does not mean "follow me," but "follow (you) to-
    gether with us."

51 R951 In ἐγένετο δὲ . . . καί, the καί clause has the meaning "that . . ."
    R1068 Τοῦ with the infinitive is used as the object of the verb ἐστήρισεν, "he
    set his face to go."
    M76 Ἐν τῷ συμπληροῦσθαι τὰς ἡμέρας may mean "while the days were being com-
    pleted (simply temporal; but see Acts 2:1).

52 R1091 Ὡς with the infinitive ἑτοιμάσαι denotes purpose, "in order to prepare"
    (cf. T134 and B372).

56 R748 Ἑτέραν has the sense of "next" (cf. 6:6).

57 B304 Ἐάν occurs in the conditional relative clause here instead of the simple
    ἄν, "wherever you go."

58 B346 An indirect deliberative question follows the verb ἔχει, "the Son of Man
    hath not where to lay his head" (" . . . anywhere to lay . . ."--M139).

59 BD306(2) Ἕτερος refers to a second and third party in vv. 59 and 61 (unclas-
    sical), "to another."

60 R582 Διά in the compound verb here has a perfective idea, "thoroughly."

LUKE 10

1 R884 The imperfect verb ἤμελλεν has a progressive sense, but without a back-
    ward look, "he was about to" (cf. 9:31).

M67 'Ανά has a distributive sense here, "he sent them out in pairs" (i.e.,
perhaps "at the strength of, up to, two").

2   B200 "Οπως introduces an object clause, "pray ye therefore the Lord of the harvest that he send forth laborers into his harvest."

4   R853 The present imperative μὴ βαστάζετε means "don't keep carrying . . . " and
the aorist subjunctive μηδένα . . . ἀσπάσησθε means "don't stop to salute anyone" ("cease carrying" and "never salute"--T77). [Ed. Both suggestions in reference to the present tense appear to be accurate since their actions were to
change from their previous life style, and they were to act accordingly through
out the completion of this mission.]

6   R394 The verb is always absent with εἰ δὲ μήγε, so the idiom becomes a set phrase
meaning "otherwise" (i.e., "if not").
R819 It is possible to find a passive sense in ἐπαναπαήσεται (it has a note of
permission--R948), "your peace will rest."
T208 Υἱὸς εἰρήνης means "man of peace."

7   R615 Τὰ παρ' αὐτῶν refers to one's resources or property.
R709 The personal pronoun αὐτῇ has the force of a demonstrative pronoun, "in that
house" (cf. M93 and T194).
R757 The singular ὁ ἐργάτης is representative, in which case the laborer represents all laborers.
MT125 The iterative force of the present imperative occurs in μένετε (i.e., staying at the houses that are open to them).

8   R1115 The articular present participle τὰ παρατιθέμενα shows the absence of
time, "what is set before."

11 R539 'Υμῖν is used as a dative of disadvantage, "against you."

13 BD134(2) In τύρῳ καὶ Σιδῶνι . . . καθήμενοι, the participle has the gender according to the sense (although the variant reading καθήμεναι is perhaps better
because the cities as whole communities and not the inhabitants are meant; cf.
Matt. 11:21ff.).

16 R418 Occasionally the words in contrast are brought sharply together (as with
ὑμῶν ἐμοῦ), "the one that hears you hears me."

17 R1181 Καί is used in an ascensive sense ("even"). The addition is out of the
ordinary and rises to a climax.

18 R883 The imperfect tense of the verb ἐθεώρουν draws the picture in the narrative here, "I have been watching."
B146 The aorist participle used as an integral part of the object of a verb of
perception represents the action which it denotes as a simple event without defining its time (complementary to the verb; ἐθεώρουν τὸν Σατανᾶν . . . πεσόντα
may perhaps mean "I have been seeing how Satan is overthrown"--M206).

19 B400 Τοῦ with the infinitive is appositional to the noun ἐξουσίαν, "authority
to walk" (cf. 1:57).

20 T25 The plural οὐρανοῖς has a figurative sense referring to heaven as God's
   abode.
   MT125 The present prohibition μὴ χαίρετε is commanding them to stop an action
   already begun.

21 R709 The pronoun αὐτῇ has the force of a demonstrative pronoun "in that hour"
   (cf. v. 7).

23 T38 There can not be any difference between ἃ βλέπετε and ἃ ὑμεῖς βλέπετε standing side by side in vv. 23ff., "what you see."

24 R843 Note the sharp contrast between the aorist and present tense in this verse.

25 R743 Sometimes it is difficult to give more force to τις than the English indefinite article (as with νομικός τις), "a certain lawyer."
   M103 The present participle ἐκπειράζων may possibly be understood as expressing
   purpose, "stood up to test him" (cf. T157).
   H309 Ἐκπειράζω (perfective with the compounded preposition) may suggest the
   daring of the act or the effort to put to a "decisive test" as the meaning.

29 R1182 Sometimes καί begins a sentence when the connection is with an unexpressed
   idea (as here).
   M102 The present participle θέλων has a causal notion, "because he wished" (cf.
   T157).

30 R521 The idea of the dative in λησταῖς περιέπεσεν is "among."
   R634 In ὑπολαβὼν . . . εἶπεν the notion of interrupting or following a speech
   comes from the idea of "up" in ὑπό, "taking up the talk."

31 R565 When a double compound verb occurs, the point to emphasize is that each
   preposition as a rule adds something to the picture. The idea here is that
   the priest and Levite passed along on the other side of the road, facing (ἀντί)
   the wounded traveller.

34 R691 Ἴδιον has a reflexive sense here (cf. 6:41), "on his own beast."

35 R602 In the expression of time ἐπὶ τὴν αὔριον, the preposition merely fills out
   the idea of the accusative, "on the next day."
   T145 Ἐν τῷ ἐπανέρχεσθαι με means "at my return" ("on my return journey"--BD
   404[2]).

36 R908 In δοκεῖ . . . γεγονέναι, we can see the vivid present of story-telling
   (a present verb with a perfect infinitive), "seems to have shown himself as a
   neighbor."

37 M103 The articular participle in this verse is equivalent to a relative clause,
   "the one who showed the mercy."

38 R633 The idea of hospitality (under one's roof) is natural in the compound verb
   ὑπεδέξατο.

39 T44 The demonstrative τῇδε is not equivalent to ταύτη, but καὶ τῇδε ἦν means
   "behold there was."

40 R573 In the double compound verb, each preposition adds an additional aspect to the root idea (cf. Rom. 8:26).
R618 The compound verb περισπάω has a metaphorical sense of "drawn away," or "from around" (hence, "was distracted about much serving"; cf. M62).
R1090 The infinitive διακονεῖν is used to express actual result (cf. BD392[1]; it is used as an indirect object of the main verb--B368). [Ed. Actually the accusative pronoun μέ is the object of the verb κατέλιπεν, while the infinitive portrays the notion of result, "my sister left me to serve."]

42 MT92 The pronoun ἥτις represents what in English would be expressed by a demonstrative pronoun and a conjunction, with the meaning "and it shall not be taken away from her" (cf. R728).

LUKE 11

2 M135 The imperatives in the Lord's prayer are all aorists in Matt. 6:9-13. Luke follows in vv. 2ff. except for the present δίδου (for δός in Matt.). However, Luke's present is exactly right in his context which is a frequentative one, and Matthew's aorist is right in the different context there provided ("continue to give" is used because "day by day" is added--T77; cf. 9:23).

3 R159 There is a controversy over the meaning of ἐπιούσιον. It has been derived successively from ἐπί and οὐσία, "bread for sustenance," although οὐσία only has the sense of ὕπαρξις in philosophical language (another theory is that of "bread of substance" in the spiritual sense); but the context here seems to present the meaning "bread for the present (ἐπί and ὤν are equivalent to ἐπούσιος; cf. BD123[1]).

4 R744 Παντί with the participle here has the idea of "any one" no matter who.
R880 The present verb ἀφίομεν is probably best understood as an iterative present, "we forgive" (whenever the occasion arises).

5 M23 The subjunctive verb in vv. 5f. looks uncommonly like the same usage as that in Mark 4:26 (it may be called a parabolic subjunctive). Being introduced in this case by τίς ἐξ ὑμῶν ἕξει φίλον, the construction passes over this hypothetical subjunctive, with a twice repeated εἴπῃ (vv. 5ff. contain an awkwardly expressed thought, for which the conditional form [ἐὰν φίλος πορευθῇ] with a future in the apodasis would have been more appropriate [cf. vv. 11f.]--BD366[1]), "if a friend goes and says."

6 R960 The relative pronoun ὅ is used to introduce an explanatory clause here (Attic Greek would have used ὅτι), "something to set before him."

7 R853 Μή μοι κόπους πάρεχε means "quit troubling me."
M68 The preposition in εἰς τὴν κοίτην seems to be used with a local sense, "they have got into bed" (cf. BD205).
BD104(2) The ending -θεν is stereotyped and meaningless for the most part in the New Testament, but -θεν has its true force in ἔσωθεν in this verse, "from inside" (cf. R300).

8 B285 The concessive clause introduced by εἰ καί and a future indicative refers

to what is regarded as certain or likely to occur, "although he will not rise and give him because he is his friend, yet because of his importunity he will arise and give him as many as he needeth" (cf. BD372[3]).
T331 Διά γε with the following accusative means "at least because of."

11 M35 The accusative noun τὸν πατέρα is used to predicate (complement) the accusative pronoun τίνα, thus it means (literally) "which of you shall the son ask as the father."
T259 The preposition in ἀντὶ ἐχθύος clearly has a substitutionary sense, "instead of a fish."

13 R599 The concept of the sending of the Holy Spirit by the Father has caused ἐξ to be used instead of ἐν which would otherwise have been regular, "from heaven."
TGr19f. The good gift which God the Father offers to those who ask him is not likely to be God the Holy Spirit because it is anarthrous; it is that powerful spiritual unction which Jesus himself was anointed with and which enabled him to counter the activities of evil spirits (Acts 10:38; cf. the discussion on Luke 1:15 and 35).

15 R749 Ἔτερος is used in contrast to τις, simply meaning "the other."

18 B282 Εἰ καί is not concessive here, but εἰ is conditional and καί means "also."

19 T37 There is some sort of emphasis (antithesis) in the use of the pronoun ἐγώ (in contrast to οἱ υἱοί).

22 R904 Present perfects that had come to be used as mere presents through accent on the durative idea and loss of emphasis on the aoristic notion are virtual imperfects when turned into the past perfect (as ἐπεποίθει here), "upon which he was trusting."
M98 The genitive αὐτοῦ is used for comparison after the comparative adjective here, "stronger than he."

28 M163 Μενοῦν is used as an introduction to a new statement correcting or modifying a foregoing statement, "nay rather" (seldom is it used to begin a sentence; "much more, in fact"--T338).

29 TGr60 Ἰωνᾶ is used as an epexegetical genitive. It has little to do with possession; it explains, expands and defines. The sign which Jesus promised to his generation was Jonah himself -- not the sign of Jonah, but the sign which is Jonah. Jesus therefore is represented as both Jonah and "more than Jonah" (not "greater than," in view of the neuter gender). He is the prophet to the Gentiles, but without the lack of sympathy which curtailed Jonah's usefulness (it may be an objective genitive referring to the sign shown in Jonah--R500). [Ed. Turner's explanation appears to be more feasible in view of the following context.]

32 B232 The distinction between a subordinate causal clause and an independent sentence affirming a cause or reason is usually one of the degree of emphasis on the causal relation between the two facts. When the chief thing asserted is the existence of the causal relation, as happens, for example, when one fact or the other is already present as a fact before the mind, the causal clause

is manifestly subordinate. When the emphasis is upon the separate assertions as assertions, rather than on the relation of the facts asserted, the causal clause easily becomes an independent sentence, as in this verse with ὅτι; "because they repented."

M204 The preposition in εἰς τὸ κήρυγμα seems to be used in a metaphorical sense, "at the preaching" (εἰς has a causal sense here, "they repented because of [but "at" is sufficient] the preaching of Jonah--T266).

35 MT192 Μή is used in a cautious assertion, "Look! Perhaps the light . . . is darkness" (it is co-ordinate not subordinate; like an indirect question--R1045).

37 B109 In ἐν τῷ λαλῆσαι, the action denoted by the aorist infinitive, strictly speaking, precedes the action of the principal verb, yet may be thought of by the writer as marking more or less exactly the time at which the action of the verb takes place ("after"--BD404[2]).

38 R1035 Ὅτι is used after the verb ἐθαύμασεν in a declarative sense, "he was astonished that."

BD317 Ἐβαπτίσθη seems to occur in an entirely different sense of the passive; more probably ἐβαπτίσατο is correct with p[45] and minuscule 700 (Blass has eccentric notions of textual criticism--R808). [Ed. The passive form has much more textual support and should be maintained. This passive verb appears to have an active connotation.]

39 R505 The adverb in τὸ ἔσωθεν ὑμῶν may be looked at more as a noun, "your inner nature."

41 M34 A desperately problematic passage is πλὴν τὰ ἐνόντα δότε ἐλεημοσύνην. It could conceivably be interpreted "but as for what is inside, give alms," in which case τὰ ἐνόντα is an accusative of respect. Alternatively, the τὰ ἐνόντα may be in apposition to ἐλεημοσύνην: "give, as alms, what is inside" (or, following a suggestion made verbally by Professor C.H. Dodd, "give, as alms, what you can" [that which is within your power]); or the passage may be corrupt or mistaken (Jesus exhorts,"Give alms from the heart [sincerely]." He has in mind the Pharisees, who parade almsgiving before the public eye. Generosity must be genuinely felt -- an adverbial accusative--TGr57; the participle may be an attributive accusative, "alms relating to what is within", or an accusative of respect, but neither rendering makes as much sense as the adverbial accusative --T247).

42 R499 Ἀγάπην is used with an objective genitive in this verse (i.e., "they have neglected to love God").

T90 The imperfect verb ἔδει has a present sense referring to the fact that it was necessary but is not happening, "ought you not to have done."

46 M32 The cognate accusative φορτία occurs here, with the meaning "you load people with burdens."

48 R529 The dative τοῖς ἔργοις has an associative idea, "you agree with the works of your fathers."

R1190 Ἄρα is used to express the notion of correspondence, "so you are witnesses."

49   R1202 Τινές should be supplied with ἐξ αὐτῶν, "some of them" (cf. T209).

53   T52 The compound verb ἐνέχω means "to hate" or "persecute."

LUKE 12

1   R587 Ἐν οἷς is used in a temporal sense, "meanwhile," "at which juncture" (the clause introduces a principal sentence—R952).
    B371 Ὥστε is used with the infinitive to express a tendency, which by implication is realized in actual result, "that."
    MT157 The active verb with the reflexive pronoun προσέχετε ἑαυτοῖς ("pay attention for yourselves") differs little from the reflexive middle verb φυλάσσεσθε in meaning (in v. 15, "be on your guard"), but the former seems to be more emphatic.

2   R627 Σύν in the compound verb here has a perfective force, "completely covered."

3   M71 In this context, ἀνθ' ὧν means "and so, accordingly, therefore" (cf. T258; this clause introduces a principal sentence—R952).

4   R704 Sometimes the plural demonstrative ταῦτα occurs where a single object is really in mind. The adverbial phrase μετὰ ταῦτα in this verse can refer either to one or more incidents, "after that."
    B368 The infinitive ποιῆσαι is used as an indirect object (similar to an infinitive of purpose, cf. 7:40), "any more to do."
    BD60(3) Περισσότερόν τι is equivalent to πλέον τι, "any more."

5   R232 Note the difference between φοβήθητε (imperative) and φοβηθῆτε (subjunctive (both the direct [imperative] and indirect command [deliberative subjunctive] occur here—R1046), "I will warn you whom to fear, fear the one."

6   R1157 Οὐχί is slightly sharper in tone than the simple negative οὐ.

7   R1186 Ἀλλὰ καί is not contradictory, but is continuative, carrying on the narrative, "but also."
    M42 The verb of comparison occurs with the genitive here with the meaning "you are of more value than many sparrows."

8   R684 Ὁ υἱὸς τοῦ ἀνθρώπου is used for the sake of emphasis, rather than ἐγώ.
    R1114 The relative clause ὃς ἂν ὁμολογήσει is parallel with the articular participle ὁ ἀρνησάμενος.
    M183 The use of the preposition in ὁμολογήσει ἐν as meaning "acknowledge (someone)" is a result of translating from the Aramaic original (for more natural Greek, a dative, simple accusative, or double accusative is expected after ὁμολογέω; cf. R524 and MT104).

10 R473 Βλασφημέω occurs with εἰς in Attic Greek. If one entertains hostile feelings the resultant idea with εἰς is "against," although the preposition does not of itself mean that (cf. κατά in Matt. 12:32).

11 R787 Because the article is repeated with συναγωγάς, ἀρχάς and ἐξουσίας, it is contended that these groups are all absolutely distinct, but they receive sepa-

rate treatment in this narrative.

12 R709 Αὐτῇ has the sense of a demonstrative pronoun (cf. Mark 13:11 with ἐκείνῃ), "in that hour."

15 R598 The preposition ἐκ is used for the notion of origin or source, "in the abundance."
R807 In v. 14, φυλάσσεσθε means "guard yourselves from."
R974 Ἐν τῷ with the infinitive here is not temporal, but expresses the content of the verb ἔστιν, "a man's life is not in the abundance."
R1183 Καί here seems to have the sense of ὅτι or ἵνα ("that"; it denotes co-ordination--MT178).

19 M185 The rich fool is probably only addressing himself in an exclamatory tone when he says ψυχή, ἔχεις . . . (ψυχή simply means "self").

20 R392 The plural verb ἀπαιτοῦσιν is used purposely to conceal the identity of the person referred to (Luke writes concerning the soul, which "is required" [that "they require it"]).

23 R654 The adjective πλεῖον is neuter because the abstract idea of thing is expressed, "life is more than (things)."

24 R1183 In this verse, καί is almost equivalent to ἀλλά (the context presents contrast), "but."
BD246 The comparison is heightened by the use of μᾶλλον, "how much more."
MT117f. The Revised Version Translation retains the durative sense of the verb κατανοήσατε, "consider." It may however mean "understand," "take in this fact about" (κατα- is perfective here, "take note of"--R606).

25 BD417 The participle μεριμνῶν seems to mean "by being anxious" (although it may have a conditional sense). [Ed. The former suggestion is more probable, since Christ stresses that one does not accomplish anything through anxiety.]

26 R1160 There is no justification for taking εἰ οὐδέ as causal (but rather, it has a conditional sense), "if then."
T31 Ἐλάχιστον is used as an elative superlative meaning "very small" (cf. R670).

28 T227 In the New Testament an adverb usually follows the adjective or verb which it determines, so the initial part of this verse means "which exists today" not "which is in the field today."

29 R609 The compound verb μετεωρίζεσθε (from μετ-έωρος meaning "in mid-air") is used in a metaphorical sense here.

30 T313 Neuter plural subjects have singular verbs in classical Greek. But the New Testament usually breaks this classical rule with words used in a personal sense, as in this verse (ἔθνη).

31 R1187 Πλήν is used as a conjunction in an adversative sense (it means "nevertheless," "however"--BD449[1]; the manuscript D changes to δέ).

32 R465 The vocative τὸ μικρὸν ποίμνιον means "you little flock" (the addition of
τὸ μικρόν shows that there is no consciousness of diminutive force in ποίμνιον,
simply meaning "flock"--H346). [Ed. On the other hand, Luke may be stressing
the minuteness of the flock.]
T72 The aorist verb means "it was his happy inspiration to give you."

33 R1100 Τὰ ὑπάρχοντα ὑμῶν means "your belongings."

35 TGr41 The perfect periphrastic imperative construction does not mean "Gird up
your loins," but "Be the kind of person who never needs to be told to gird them
up, because he will always live in this condition."
T190 The possessive pronoun ὑμῶν occurs before the two nouns to eliminate repetition, "your loins and lamps."

39 R740 Ποίᾳ has lost its original qualitative force, "at what hour."

42 R604 'Επί with the genitive has the metaphorical idea of "over."

45 T139 The infinitive is used in loose connection with the verb (perhaps under
Semitic influence), with the meaning "be a long time in coming" (cf. B405).

47 M32f. Note the retention of the accusative with a passive verb in vv. 47f. (it
occurs only with verbs that have the double accusative in the active voice),
"beaten with much beating."

49 M137 It has been proposed to take εἰ ἤδη ἀνήφθη as expressing a wish, "Oh that
it were already kindled!" But both the construction and the meaning of this
famous "crux" are far from established (τί θέλω, . . . meaning "how I wish . . ."
is equivalent to "I would be glad if it were already kindled!"--BD360[4]; τί
means "how," as an adverb--R739; cf. H472).

50 M207 Πῶς is used in an exclamation here (as though it were ὡς), "how."
T138 "Εχω with the infinitive here has the sense of "must."

51 BD448(8) Οὐχί, . . . ἀλλ' ἤ means "nothing but."

52 R605 'Επί with the dative has the idea of "against" in this verse.
B94 A periphrastic future perfect construction expressing a future state occurs
here, "there will be five divided."

54 R1180 The adjunctive use of καί ("also") is more frequent in Luke than elsewhere
in the New Testament, as with δὲ καί.
BD323(1) "Ερχεται is used as a futuristic present, " a shower is coming."

55 T172 Νότος means "south wind."

57 T258 'Από seems to take the place of ὑπό in a causal sense, "because of yourselves."

58 R967 'Ως has a temporal notion here, "when."
R1062 The infinitive ἀπηλλάχθαι carries the idea of purpose, "give diligence
for being reconciled" (with a passive notion--R1079; it denotes a continuing
effect upon the subject, "to become and remain free"--BD342[1]).

R1147 In μήποτε the notion of time has been replaced by that of contingency, "lest perchance."

M20 The aorist imperative δός is an example of the aoristic <u>aktionsart</u>, "give diligence" (the aorist δός is natural with the phrase ἐν τῇ ὁδῷ--MT174).

LUKE 13

1   R686 In Luke's writings (as in this verse) αὐτός followed by an article is some-times a pure demonstrative pronoun as it comes to be in later Greek, with the meaning "that very."

2   R616 The preposition παρά is used for the notion of comparison here (i.e., "more sinful than," cf. v. 4).
    M147 The Galileans were not pre-eminent sinners because they suffered; but they might (erroneously) have been thought to be pre-eminent sinners because of it (i.e., ὅτι logically depends on δοκεῖτε).

6   R1129 The present participle ζητῶν (in vv. 6f.) has the notion of purpose.

7   R879 The durative present verb ἔρχομαι involves both the past and present time in one phrase (i.e., past action still in progress; cf. B17).
    BD442(14) Καί is used after the interrogative ἰνατί with the meaning "why at all" or "for why?"

8   M32 Περί is used with the accusative in a spatial sense, "until I have dug around it."

9   R394 Εἰ δὲ μήγε is a set phrase meaning "otherwise" (cf. 10:6).
    R874 The future verb ἐκκόψεις has a volitive sense, "you shall cut it down."
    M68 The preposition in εἰς τὸ μέλλον is used metaphorically, "in the future."
    M151 There is an implied apodosis in this verse, "and if it does bear fruit in the future (well and good)."

11 R627 Σύν has a perfective notion in the compound verb here, "she was bent dou-ble."
    M164f. In this context εἰς τὸ παντελές may mean "completely."

13 R770 The article τάς is equivalent to a possessive pronoun, "his hands."
    R885 The imperfect verb ἐδόξαζεν has an inceptive sense, "she began to praise God."

14 M44 The simple dative is used in a temporal sense, "on the sabbath day (cf. ἐν τοῖς . . . in v. 10).

16 T90 The imperfect verb ἔδει has a present sense referring to the fact that it was necessary but is not happening (cf. 11:42).

17 R605 The verb of emotion ἔχαιρεν has ἐπί with the locative use of the dative, "all the people began to rejoice at."

19 T253 Εἰς with the accusative δένδρον is used for the predicate nominative here (semitic), "it became a tree."

23 R916 The use of εἰ to introduce a direct question is due to the Septuagint ren-
    dering of the Hebrew original by εἰ as well as by μή.
    B125 In εἰ ὀλίγοι οἱ σῳζόμενοι, the participle is undoubtedly a general pre-
    sent, the inquiry being neither on the one hand as to the number of "those
    that are already saved" (perfect of existing state) or "that have been saved"
    (perfect of completed action) nor, on the other, with reference to "those that
    are being saved" (progressive present of simultaneous action), but with refer-
    ence to "those that are (i.e., become) saved."

24 BD465(2) Λέγω ὑμῖν is used as a parenthesis, "I tell you."

25 B303 The relative clause (οὗ . . .) in this verse states a supposition which
    refers to the future, suggesting some probability of its fulfillment, "when
    once the head of the house gets up."

28 B316 Ὅταν ὄψεσθε is indefinite in form but definite in force (cf. 5:35), "when
    you will see."
    T226 Ἐκεῖ has a temporal sense, "then" (rare in the New Testament).

31 T194 Αὐτῇ has the sense of a demonstrative pronoun (cf. 12:12 and 13:1), "at
    that hour."

32 R1202 The noun ἡμέρᾳ has been omitted from the adjective τρίτῃ.
    M7 The present verbs in this verse have a futuristic sense, "I shall cast out
    . . . perform . . . be perfected."

33 R393 The infinitive ἀπολέσθαι occurs as the subject of the verb ἐνδέχεται, "for
    it cannot be that a prophet should be destroyed."
    R1198 Notice the use of irony in the words of Jesus, ὅτι οὐκ ἐνδέχεται προφήτην
    ἀπολέσθαι ἔξω Ἰερουσαλήμ (cf. BD495[2]).

34 M65 Ὑπό with the accusative is used with a verb of motion for the idea of
    beneath, "as a hen [gathers] her brood under her wings."
    M132 Ὃν τρόπον represents a compound adverbial phrase such as ἐκεῖνον τρόπον
    ὅν . . ., meaning "in that manner in which."
    M180 It is possible that a semitic tendency to change from second to third per-
    son or from third to second may be behind the shift in this verse (Ἰερουσαλήμ
    . . . ἡ . . . ἠθελήσατε), "O Jerusalem . . ., the one who is killing the
    prophets . . ., you did not desire."

35 R972 Ἄν is always present with ὅτε, when this adverb is used with a subjunc-
    tive, except in this doubtful text (thus, suggesting an alternate reading).
    BD382(2) Ἕως . . . ὅτε means "until the time when."

LUKE 14

1   R613 The compound verb παρατηρέω is used here with the idea of "envious watch-
    ing" ("watch closely"--T55).
    R811 Αὐτοί wavers between a mere personal and intensive sense, "they."
    T145 Ἐν τῷ ἐλθεῖν αὐτὸν εἰς οἶκον means "after he had gone into the house" (it
    is improbable that ἐν τῷ with the aorist infinitive refers to an action anteced-
    ent to that of the principle verb, in view of the imperfect tense which follows

--B109; cf. 9:34; it is antecedent in meaning, "after"--BD404[2]). [Ed. Actually the incident in the following verses occurs after he entered the house, but while he was in it.]

3 R787 The two groups νομικούς and φαρισαίους are treated as one group (because the article is not repeated).

4 T39 The normal tendency of a Greek writer (especially a stylistic writer) was to omit the repetition of personal pronouns (αὐτόν is not repeated in this verse).
BD170(2) The verb ἐπιλαμβάνομαι usually takes an object in the genitive. The use of the accusative here is only an apparent exception; the accusative actually belongs to the finite verb ἰάσατο on which the participle depends.

6 R574 In the double compound verb here, ἀντί has the meaning of "in return" and ἀπό the meaning of "back" (cf. v. 14), "answer back in return."

7 R811 Ἐξελέγοντο is used with a reciprocal notion of the middle voice, "they selected the first seats for themselves" (cf. MT157; the imperfect tense portrays the picture of the narrative--R883).
R1032 Πῶς is used in place of a declarative ὅτι, "he noticed how."

8 R907 In this verse there appears to be a conscious change in tense from κληθῇς to μήποτε . . . ἦ κεκλημένος, possibly suggesting a long-standing invitation by the latter form.
BD337(3) The aorist subjunctive κατακλιθῇς is used for a categorical prohibition, "do not sit."

10 B199 On occasion the future indicative occurs in a pure final clause (purpose) introduced by ἵνα in the New Testament, as here (it never occurs in Classical Greek), "inorder that he may say."
T154 The participle πορευθείς has a temporal sense (cf. 13:32; "when you go, sit").

12 MT125 The present prohibition μὴ φώνει has the connotation, "stop inviting. . ." as well as "continue not to invite. . ."

14 R574 In the double compound verb here, ἀντί has the meaning of "in return" and ἀπό the meaning of "back" (cf. v. 6).

17 T173 In the articular construction τὸν δοῦλον, the servant is the one whose particular task it was to do the activity referred to in this verse.

18 R809 The causative or permissive sense occurs in the middle participle παρητημένον (in vv. 18f.), "consider me as excused."
R1122 Ἔχε in vv. 18f. means "consider as" (cf. T246).
BD241(6) It seems that ἀπό μιᾶς means "unanimously, with one accord."

19 T63 The present verb πορεύομαι has a futuristic sense (i.e., "to be in the process of going," for which reaching the destination still lies in the future--BD323[3]).

21 R787 The groups are treated as one because the article τούς is not repeated with the nouns connected by καί.

23 M20 The aorist imperative simply means "come out" (cf. T76).
    T181 The nouns ὁδούς and φραγμούς are treated as one unified whole, because
    the article occurs only with the first (even though the gender varies; cf.
    v. 21).

26 T43 The reflexive pronoun ἑαυτοῦ is attributive in both occurrences in this
    verse (i.e., it modifies the nouns πατέρα and ψυχήν), "his own."

27 B313 This verse contains a present general supposition, "whoever does not bear
    his own cross and come after me, cannot be my disciple."

28 R1045 Εἰ is used in indirect discourse here, meaning "to see if" (or "whether").

29 R1173 In this verse μήποτε is used with the verb ἄρξωνται and μή with the par-
    ticiple ἰσχύοντος.
    T322 Luke should have written the participle in the dative instead of the gen-
    itive (the manuscript p⁴⁵ attempts to make the correction by omitting αὐτῷ;
    cf. 12:36). [Ed. Actually the genitive case of the participle is necessary to
    be in agreement with αὐτοῦ. Then Luke changes the pronoun to the dative
    to serve as the object of ἐμπαίζειν, "begin to ridicule him.]

31 R589 Ἐν with the numeral expresses the notion of accompanying circumstance,
    "with ten thousand" (similar to μετά and σύν; cf. M78).
    R748 Ἑτέρῳ refers to the second of a pair (cf. 5:7), "another king."
    R1045 Εἰ is used to introduce indirect discourse, "to see if" (cf. v. 28).
    B376 The infinitive ὑπαντῆσαι is used to limit the adjective δυνατός, denoting
    that which one is able to do.
    M49 Ἐπί with the accusative generally designates movement towards (i.e., in a
    linear sense), "the one who . . . is coming towards (against) him."
    T87 The present participle πορευόμενος refers to an event in the future (cf.
    1:35, indicating the certainty of the expectation).

32 BD155(2) Ἐρωτᾷ τὰ πρὸς εἰρήνην means either "he inquires after his well-being"
    (as several times in the Septuagint), or "he greets him (and pays homage to him."
    [Ed. In view of the context the latter suggestion seems preferable.]

33 R744 Πᾶς means "anyone," no matter who (it carries an almost indefinite sense).
    T43 The reflexive pronoun ἑαυτοῦ is not dependent upon the verb, but it is
    attributive, modifying the articular participle τοῖς ὑπάρχουσιν (cf. 11:21),
    "all his own possessions."

34 H402 Μωραίνομαι means "to become foolish" in Rom. 1:22, but "to be tasteless"
    in this verse.

LUKE 15

2 R697 There is a sense of reproach in the use of οὗτος here.

6 R563 The idea is very clear here without the repetition of σύν in συνκαλεῖ τοὺς
    φίλους, meaning "he calls his friends together."
    R786 The two groups φίλους and γείτονας are distinguished in their treatment
    here because of the repetition of the article, "his friends and his neighbors."

7 R661 A comparison is implied by the use of ἤ in this verse, "more . . . than."

9 R787 The two groups φυλάς and γείτονας are treated as one for the discussion at hand, because of the single article (cf. v. 6).

12 M103 The articular participle τὸ ἐπίβαλλον in το . . . τῆς οὐσίας, has the meaning "the share of the property which falls to me" (cf. T152).

13 T282 The negative expression μετ' οὐ πολλὰς ἡμέρας (D has οὐ μετὰ . . .) forms a single idea, "not many days."
MT130 ᾿Απεδήμησεν means "he went abroad."

14 R680 If there is any emphasis in the use of the pronoun αὐτός it is very slight, "he began to lack."
M58 Κατά with the accusative is used in a local expression here, meaning "in (perhaps "throughout") that land" ("throughout"--T268).

15 R817 ᾿Εκολλήθη can be explained as passive or middle in sense, "joined himself with."
BD247(2) The numeral εἷς has the sense of τις here (as an indefinite article), "one of."

16 R885 The negative imperfect οὐδεὶς ἐδίδου denotes resistance to pressure, "no one would give."
T66 The imperfect verbs ἐπεθύμει and ἐδίδου were intended to make the narrative interesting and continuous until some action is expected in the aorist to give point to the whole description; but the description is left without climax here (i.e., an aorist verb does not occur).

17 R532 The dative λιμῷ is used with a causal sense, "because of hunger."
MT114 The verb ἀπόλλυμι refers to "dying," not absolutely barring the possibility of a recovery, but implies death as the goal in sight (ἀπο- has a perfective sense--R828).

18 R594 The preposition εἰς merely accents the accusative case which happens to be in a hostile atmosphere, thus meaning "against."
T154 The use of the participle ἀναστάς with a verb of departure is justified because it has a temporal sense in vv. 18 and 20 (cf. 13:32), "after I arise."
BD214(6) ᾿Ενώπιόν σου is equivalent to εἰς σέ (in vv. 18 and 21; consequently, he has sinned against his father also).

19 T320 In Biblical Greek, ὡς may serve to soften a statement: "as it were, perhaps, approximately," as in this verse.
BD247(2) The numeral εἷς has the sense of τις in this context (cf. v. 15), "one of your hired men."

20 T322 Luke should have made the participle agree with the accusative pronoun, rather than have it in the genitive case, agreeing with the following αὐτόν (cf. 9:42 and BD423[2]). [Ed. It is not necessary for the participle to be accusative since it is in agreement with the previous genitive pronoun αὐτοῦ. The following pronoun αὐτόν changes to the accusative because it is the direct object of the verb εἶδεν.]

21 R845 The aorist verb ἥμαρτον has the notion of an English perfect, "I have
sinned."

22 T256 The use of εἰς for περί is the result of Hebraic (or Aramaic) influence,
"on his hand."
M135 The aorist imperatives in vv. 22f. are interrupted by the present imperative φέρετε with seemingly very little distinction, "bring."

24 B92 In English it is difficult to distinguish between the past perfect of existing state (ἦν ἀπολωλώς) and the historical aorist (εὑρέθη), "was lost and is
found."

25 T154 The participle ἐρχόμενος has a temporal sense (cf. v. 18), "while he came."

26 T65 The imperfect verb of asking, ἐπυνθάνετο, has the idea of incomplete action
in the past, awaiting a fulfillment in a further action by another agent, "he
was inquiring."
T130 The deliberative question with ἄν and the optative is equivalent to an indirect question, "what he meant."
BD247(2) The numeral εἷς has the sense of τις (cf. v. 15).

27 R881 The present verb ἥκει has the sense of a perfect tense, "has come" (actually this is equivalent to "is here").

28 R885 The negative imperfect οὐκ ἤθελεν denotes resistance to pressure (cf. v.
16), "he was not willing" (or "refused").

29 R879 The durative present δουλεύω gathers the past and present time into one
phrase (i.e., past action still in progress; cf. 13:7), "and I still do serve
you" (cf. B17 and M8).

30 R697 There is a sense of reproach in the use of οὗτος here (cf. BD290[6]; con-
temptuously stated--T44).

32 R834 The aorist verb ἔζησεν has an inceptive idea, "became alive" (perhaps "come
to life"--M10; it refers to the fact that he was dead and "began to live"--
TGr150).
R887 The imperfect verb ἔδει applies to both the past and present, probably
with an implication against the attitude of the elder brother.

LUKE 16

1 R703 In this verse only the context makes it clear that οὗτος refers to οἰκόνο-
μον (instead of ἄνθρωπός), "this manager."
R966 Ὡς may occur with the participle to give the alleged reason, which in
essence may be the real one or mere assumption (in this instance the charge is
given by Jesus as that of the slanderer [διεβλήθη] and the context implies that
it is untrue [only alleged]--R1140).
BD193(4) Αὐτῷ seems to be used as a genuine dative with the passive verb διε-
βλήθη, "to be made suspect with him."

3   R600 Ἐπί has a perfective sense in the compound verb here, "beg."
    R1102 The disinction between a participle and infinitive is sometimes quite
    important. In ἐπαιτεῖν αἰσχύνομαι the idea is "I am ashamed to beg and do not
    do it," while ἐπαιτῶν αἰσχύνομαι would mean "I beg and am ashamed of it."
    B387 The infinitives σκάπτειν and ἐπαιτεῖν are used as objects of the verbs
    ἰσχύω and αἰσχύνομαι respectively, meaning "I have not strength to dig" and "to
    beg I am ashamed."

4   R827 The aorist verb ἔγνων is used with an effective notion, "grasping the
    point" (the verb refers to an action just completed, "I found out -- a moment
    ago--M11; this aorist gives the statement greater vividness than is given by
    the more usual present--B45).

8   R496 Τῆς ἀδικίας is used as an attributive genitive (denoting quality--T213),
    "the unjust steward."
    M64 Ὑπέρ with the accusative has a comparative sense, "wiser than (literally
    "wiser beyond") the sons of light."
    M174 The adjectival genitives (semitic) that occur with υἱοί and υἱούς simply
    mean "people worthy of," or "associated with this age" and "of light" (cf. T208).
    T43 The reflexive pronoun is not dependent upon the verb, but attributive to
    γενεάν (cf. 11:21), "their own generation."

9   M28 The subject of δέξωνται may be οἱ φίλοι (the subject seems to be God, "that
    God may receive you into eternal dwellings"--T293). [Ed. The plural verb
    apparently takes the plural subject suggested by Moule; the context and the
    analogy of v. 4 seems to support this.]
    M38 The adjectival genitive in the expression τοῦ μαμωνᾶ τῆς ἀδικίας has the
    meaning "the dishonest Mammon" (denoting quality--T213; cf. v. 8).
    T260 The prepositional phrase ἐκ τοῦ μαμωνᾶ has an instrumental sense, "make
    friends by means of mammon," denoting cause or occasion.

10 T31 Ἐλαχίστῳ is an elative superlative meaning "very small" (hence it is not
    surprising to see ἐν ἐλαχίστῳ and ἐν πολλῷ side by side--R660).

13 R748 Ἕτερος simply refers to a second of a pair, cf. 14:31.

15 B433 An adjectival participle used substantivally with the article may of
    course occur as a predicate nominative with a copula (ἔστε here). This, how-
    ever, is not properly a predicate participle. The presence of the article makes
    its use as a noun easily evident (cf. 7:14), "you are those who justify your-
    selves before men."

16 R975 Μέχρι means "up to the point of."
    T58 The deponent verb εὐαγγελίζεται is used with a passive sense in this verse
    (cf. 7:22), "the kingdom is being preached."

18 B124 The construction with the present participle πᾶς ὁ ἀπολύων does not mean,
    "every one that is wont to divorce"; still less probable is "every one that has
    divorced'; it is "every one that divorces" (a certain class of people).

19 R810 Ἐνεδιδύσκετο seems to be used as an indirect middle, "he put clothes on
    himself," although this may be a direct middle with the accusative of thing ad-
    ded (this is a passive with an accusative--T247). [Ed. This verb appears to

be used with a passive idea, "who was clothed with purple," since the middle
rendering seems awkward with the following accusatives. It is not uncommon
for the accusative to occur with a passive in the New Testament, cf. 1 Cor. 12:13
and 2 Thess. 2:15 and Heb. 6:9.]
T66   The imperfect verb ἐνεδιδύσκετο was intended to make the narrative interesting and continuous (cf. 2:47).

20   R905   The past perfect tense of the verb ἐβέβλητο suggests that the poor man
had been at the door some time (we may use the imperfect "he was lying"--T86;
"[had been prostrated and] lay"--BD347[1]).

21   R1186   The story is carried on by the use of ἀλλὰ καί (these conjunctions do not
indicate any degree of contrast here), "and yet."
BD11(3)   Κύνες refers to "stray dogs."

23   R408   Note the idiomatic plural κόλποις (singular in v. 22), "bosom."

24   R495   The genitive ὕδατος emphasizes the **kind** of material which the speaker
clearly has in mind (S has ὕδατι; ὕδατος is perhaps virtually partitive--M43).

25   R1379   The preposition ἀπό in the compound verb ἀπέλαβες has the force of "in
full."
M123   Occasionally ὅδε gains a slight emphasis by context, and means "this one"
in contrast to someone else; one suspects that it was an eager and emphatic
reader who, desirous of emphasizing it thus, caused the scribe in Luke 16:25
(the best reading?) to write ὧδε ("here") when an emphatic ὅδε ("he" as opposed
to   , "you") is obviously the sense required (cf. T44 and BD289).
TGr63f.   Although the spatial element of heaven and hell is already implicit in
the parable, the text which inserts "here" without justification gives the
impression that the comfort has some necessary connection with the place as such.
The places, heaven and hell, are introduced only as details to help the narra-
tion of the story. One may still believe in heaven and hell as states or conditions, not localities. The kingdom (of God or Satan) is still "within" you.
[Ed.   Actually, one is not forced to push the point as far as Turner attempts
to do.]

26   R896   The perfect tense is used with the verb στηρίζω to stress the fact that the
chasm still stands.

31   B59   Πεισθήσονται has the sense of an aoristic future which conceives of an action
simply as an event, and affirms that it will take place in future time; "neither
will they be persuaded if one arise from the dead" (resultative; "they will not
be open to persuasion"--B101).

LUKE 17

1   R721   Δι' οὗ is equivalent to τούτῳ δι' οὗ, meaning "to him by whom."
R1040   Τοῦ with the infinitive is used as the subject of the finite verb, "that
hindrances should not come is impossible" (cf. M129; the genitive is apparently
suggested by the idea of "hindering" or "avoiding" in the adjective ἀνένδεκτον
--B405).

2   R997 Both εἰ and ἵνα introduce subject clauses (signifying, "it is profitable";
      cf. B214).
      H442 The comparative particle ἤ is used after a verb (λυσιτελεῖ), as though by
      itself it meant "more than."

4   B98 An aorist subjunctive after ἐάν is sometimes properly translated by a per-
      fect or future perfect, but only because the context shows that the action is
      to precede that of the principal verb, "and if he sins against you seven times
      in the day . . . you shall forgive him."

5   B181 The imperative πρόσθες is used in a petition, "and the apostles said to
      the Lord, 'Increase our faith.'"

6   R1022 A mixed conditional sentence occurs here; the protasis is of the first
      class (determined as fulfilled) and the apodosis is of the second class (deter-
      mined as unfulfilled; the conditional sentence seems to mean, "if you have
      faith, you would say"; the real condition, present indicative, may be due to
      politeness, for the disciples had claimed to have some faith, when they asked
      for it to be increased. "If you had faith" would seem to deny this too blunt-
      ly--T92; cf. TGr51f.; The conditional sentence here means "if you really have
      (but you do not; yet if you had), then . . . "--BD372[1a]). [Ed. Jesus does
      not necessarily imply that the disciples had no faith at all. Nevertheless,
      he presented their need as being not more faith, but the right kind of faith.
      They did not have the vigorous, living faith that was necessary to live a vic-
      torious Christian life; cf. vv. 3f. and Matt. 17:20.]

8   R976 The sense of ἕως is really "while" rather than "until" (slightly peri-
      phrastic--B325).
      M135 The aorist imperative ἑτοίμασον refers to a specific action, "make ready
      something for my dinner"; whereas the present imperative refers to a continued
      action, "wait on me."
      T49 Τί seems to be used as a relative pronoun, "that which."
      BD448(4) 'Αλλ' οὐχί means "and not rather" (D omits οὐχί, in which case this
      verse would not be interrogative).

11   R581 Διά and the accusative has the sense of "through" in this verse (cf. διὰ
      μέσου in 4:30); note the genitive after μέσον (the prepositional phrase διὰ
      μέσου has a strictly local sense, "between Samaria and Galilee" [however the
      reading is uncertain; A has διὰ μέσου and D has only μέσον]--M55).
      T170 Γαλιλαία is generally articular except here, where the omission of the
      article with Σαμαρείας has caused the omission with Γαλιλαίας for balance (cf.
      BD261[4]).

15   R611 The preposition μετά has an instrumental sense (denoting the manner of the
      δοξάζων--BD198[3]), "praising God with a loud voice."

17   T178 Usually cardinal numerals are anarthrous, but if the article occurs it
      indicates (as in classical Greek) a certain fraction or part; thus οἱ ἐννέα
      means "the nine of them."

21   M83f. On the meaning of ἐντός commentators have long been divided between "with-
      in you" (i.e., in each individual's heart) and "among you" (i.e., present, in
      the person of Jesus and his work, among those whom he was addressing). The

majority of evidence appears to favor the meaning "within you" (cf. R641 and TGr61f.).

24 BD241(1) It is better to supply μερίδος than γῆς with ἐκ τῆς . . ., "out of one part."

25 R579 The preposition ἀπό has the sense of ὑπό (cf. 6:18), "by this generation."

27 T66 The imperfect verbs describing Noah's time are employed to make the narra-tive interesting and continuous with expectation of an aorist verb to give a point or climax to the whole description (cf. 2:47).
BD101 Ἐγαμίζοντο refers to women, "they were given in marriage."

29 M27n.1 The noun θεός should be supplied as the subject of the impersonal verb ἔβρεξεν.

31 R724 In this verse Luke has καὶ ὁ rather than καὶ αὐτός.
R957 The relative pronoun ὅς has an indefinite sense in vv. 31 and 33 (similar to "whoever").

34 R749 Ἕτερος is used in contrast here, "the one . . . the other."

35 R889 The present participle and future form of the stative verb ἔσονται are used together to portray a durative action (cf. 1:20), "two women will be grind-ing."

LUKE 18

1 R1075 Πρὸς τό with the infinitive is not used to express purpose, but means "with reference to the duty" (cf. B414 and MT218).

2 R743 The English word "certain" seems to be too emphatic for the use of τις and τινι here, "a city."
BD445(4) Καὶ . . . μή does not indicate correlation but an independent kind of parallelism (also καὶ οὐκ in v. 4), "and did not respect man."

4 B284 The concessive clause introduced by εἰ καί corresponds to a first class conditional sentence. The event referred to is in general not contingent, but conceived of as actual, "though I . . . "

5 R1148 The particle γε has the notion of "at least."
BD207(3) Εἰς τέλος means "in full" here; thus the final clause in this verse should be translated, "in order that she may not gradually (present ὑπωπιάζῃ!) wear me out completely by her continued coming (present!)."

7 R495 The genitive of time ἡμέρας καὶ νυκτός refers to the time within which an action occurs (kind of time).
R930 The question in this verse is rhetorical rather than deliberative (the subjunctive verb ποιήσῃ may be explained as occasioned by the emphatic negative or by the rhetorical nature of the question--B172), "will not God . . ."
M178 Καί seems to be used as an adversative particle; thus καὶ μακροθυμεῖ per-

haps means "despite his patience" or "deferring of judgment."
T56   The active form of ποιέω occurs in vv. 7f., where we expect the middle
(cf. MT159).

8   R589   The notion of manner is present in the prepositional phrase ἐν τάχει
("shortly"--M78).
M164   The interrogative particle ἆρα introduces a question meaning "is he,
then, going to find faith . . .?"

9   R605   In ἐφ' ἑαυτοῖς the true dative seems to be used with ἐπί supplementing it,
"in themselves."

10   B366   The infinitive expresses purpose, "two men went up into the temple to
pray" (cf. BD390[1]).

11   R697   There is a sense of reproach of the Pharisee at the Publican evident in
the use of οὗτος here (cf. 5:2).
T57   No one placed the Pharisee in the temple, even though the passive σταθείς
is used, "he stood there."

12   M39   Δὶς τοῦ σαββάτου means "twice each week."

13   T57   Ἱλάσθητι is intransitive active in idea, rather than passive, "be merci-
ful" (cf. BD101; this verb has the sense of permission, "let yourself be dis-
posed to grace"--BD314).   [Ed.   The former suggestion appears to be more correct
in view of the petition presented to God in this verse, and since occasionally
in the New Testament a passive verb may have an intransitive sense.]
T173   The articular phrase τῷ ἁμαρτωλῷ must mean "the sinner of sinners."

14   R703   The two pronouns οὗτος and ἐκεῖνον occur in sharp contrast, one pointing
out the publican, the other the Pharisee (it is unusual for these pronouns
to be used in contrast--BD291[2]).
T31   The preposition παρά is used to express comparison here (actually contrast;
D adds μᾶλλον), "rather than."

18   M173   It is well known that Hebrew was prone to use parataxis (i.e., the placing
side by side of complete sentences with main verbs, instead of the use of subordinate clauses).   The Greek custom was at least more ready to use subordinate
clauses.   The following examples reveal Luke's tendency to subordinate, in contrast to Mark and Matthew:

Mark	Matthew	Luke
10:17	19:16	18:18
10:28	19:27	18:28
11:7	21:7	19:35
14:49	26:55	22:53
	25:29	19:26

22   BD189(3)   The dative pronoun in ἕν σοι λείπει, seems to express antithesis, "one
thing you still lack."

25   B384   The infinitive εἰσελθεῖν is used as the subject of a finite verb, "for it
is easier for a camel to enter in through a needle's eye."

29 BD365(3) Οὐδείς ἐστιν . . . ὃς οὐχὶ μὴ ἀπολάβῃ is equivalent to ὃς οὐκ ἀπο-
λήψεται (the emphasis of the saying rests on the positive content of the whole
"everyone will certainly . . .").

35 R743 Both τυφλός and τις are adjectives (although τυφλός is used as a substantive, "blind man").

36 R1031 The optative verb εἴη occurs in the indirect question where the direct
discourse had an indicative verb.
TGr87 The genitive after the participle ἀκούσας indicates that the blind man actually heard the noise of the multitude passing by, not that it was passing by
(i.e., rather than having the movement reported to him).
T65 The imperfect verb of asking ἐπυνθάνετο has the idea of incomplete action
in the past, awaiting a fulfillment in a further action by another agent (cf.
15:26), "he began to inquire."

39 R664 The instrumental adjective πολλῷ strengthens the adjective μᾶλλον, "all
the more."
T41 Αὐτός seems to have some degree of emphasis in its occurrence here.

41 M145 Ἵνα with the subjunctive verb ἀναβλέψω seems to be virtually imperatival
meaning "let me recover my sight" rather than "I want to recover my sight" (cf.
T95).

LUKE 19

2 R679 Καὶ αὐτός has some degree of emphasis in both occurrences in this verse.

3 R580 The preposition ἀπό has a causal sense, "because of the crowd."

4 M39 The genitive pronoun ἐκείνης refers to place, "he was about to go through
by that way" (cf. 5:19; the genitive in 5:19 and 19:4 does not have the sense
in which the classical genitive of space has, designating the whole area within
which something took place--BD186[1]).

5 R861 The aorist participle σπεύσας refers to an action which is simultaneous
(occurring the same time) with the principal verb.
R1127 Σπεύσας expresses the notion of manner, "come down with haste."

7 T273 Παρά with the dative in this verse has the meaning "in the house of."

8 R880 The present verbs δίδωμι and ἀποδίδωμι may be used as iterative or customary presents, although they more likely refer to a new purpose for Zacchaeus
(they are used as futuristic presents--T63). [Ed. The present verbs do not
describe that which Zacchaeus had been accustomed to, but the action which he
would spontaneously carry out; the vivid futuristic present is used.]

9 B46 The aorist verb ἐγένετο occurs in this verse where the English idiom
requires a perfect, "has come."

11 T227 It is not certain whether προσθεὶς εἶπεν παραβολήν means "he told another
parable," or "he also told a parable" (προσθεὶς εἶπεν means "he continued and

told a parable" [i.e., something he had not just previously done]--BD435[b];
it may mean either "say again" or "say further"--M177; this participle is
equivalent to πάλιν--H445). [Ed. Apparently this construction should be rendered, "he proceeded to tell a parable" since a substantial amount of discourse has taken place between this parable and the preceding one in 18:9-14.]

13   M76   The temporal expression ἐν ᾧ ἔρχομαι presumably means "while I am coming"
      (i.e., "until I return").
      BD285(2)   The pronoun ἑαυτοῦ has the sense "of his."
      MT118   Luke has the simplex verb πραγματεύομαι ("trade") in this verse and the
      perfective compound verb διαπραγματεύομαι ("gained by trading") in v. 15.

15   B109   In ἐν τῷ ἐπανελθεῖν, the action of the aorist infinitive precedes the
      action of the principal verb, yet it may be thought of by the writer as mark-
      ing more or less exactly the time at which the action of the verb takes place
      (it has the meaning "after his return"--T145; cf. 11:37).

17   T31   The superlative ἐλάχιστος has an elative sense, "very small."
      BD102(3)   Εὖγε is an interjection meaning "bravo!"
      MT174   Since the stative verb has no aorist, it is not surprising that its
      imperative is sometimes quasi-ingressive ("begin"), as ἴσθι here.

20   T197   Ὁ ἕτερος apparently means "the third" (A omits the pronoun).

21   R997   In this verse, the rare use of ὅτι with φοβούμην may be causal, "I was
      afraid of you, because."

30   M20   The aorist participle and imperative in λύσαντες αὐτὸν ἀγάγετε means "untie
      it and bring it."

33   T22   The plural οἱ κύριοι may refer to a man and woman owner.

37   R623   Πρὸς τῇ καταβάσει may possibly be regarded as a true dative with ἐγγίζον-
      τος, but it is better to supply "even" and consider it as a locative (as the
      Revised Version has it; πρός occurs with the dative implying position, and
      meaning "at"--M54).

41   R834   Ἔκλαυσεν is used as an ingressive aorist meaning "burst into tears" (cf.
      T72).

42   R834   The aorist verb ἔγνως has an ingressive sense, "came to know."
      R842   Ἐκρύβη is an aorist verb which refers to what has just happened, "now
      they have been hidden."
      BD482   The apodosis is omitted from the conditional sentence in this verse ("it
      would be pleasing to me" is implied).

43   M87   In the compound verb here περί does not govern an object but strengthens
      the idea of encirclement, "surround."

44   M71   The prepositional phrase ἀνθ'ὧν means "since" or "because."
      H423   Καί introduces a circumstantial clause (καὶ ἐδαφιοῦσιν . . .) referring
      to the fact that the enemy will besiege the city while the children are in it --
      not only the regular population, but all Jews from far and near who have fled
      to the metropolis.

47 B34 Repeated action is referred to in the periphrastic imperfect ἦν διδάσκων "he was teaching daily."

48 R1127 The participle ἀκούων expresses the notion of manner ("all the people hung on the words of Jesus, listening" -- for hope and guidance in a world of disorder and despair--R1430).

LUKE 20

6 R891 This verse contains the only instance in the New Testament of a present infinitive in indirect discourse representing an imperfect indicative (contrary to what Burton implies in B112), "that John was a prophet."
M18 The periphrastic perfect construction here is perfect in form more than in meaning, "(the people) are convinced." Here πεπεισμένος is virtually an adjective, with little or no reference to the time at which the convincing was done, and it would be misleading to translate "has been persuaded" (it stresses the existing state--B84).

9 R470 The accusative χρόνους ἱκανούς refers to the duration of time, "for a long time."

10 B198 Note the pure final clause with a future indicative verb, "that they might give."

11 R551 In προσέθετο . . . πέμψαι, the infinitive presents the chief idea, meaning "to go on and do" or "do again" ("do again," or "further"--M177; προσέθετο πέμψαι, by the parallel in Mark 12:4 and 5 [which has πάλιν], means "he sent again"--T227; cf. BD435(a) and H445).

19 R626 The preposition πρός adds nothing to the accusative case, and the idea is simply "with reference to" (i.e., "meant for"; cf. BD239[6]).
R1183 The last καί in this verse is almost equivalent to ἀλλά (the context calls for contrast).

20 M143 ᾿Ωστε with the infinitive here has the sense of purpose (although this context may mean "such words as would enable them to hand him over"). [Ed. The Textus Receptus text has εἰς τό instead of ὥστε, which is an interpretation.]

23 MT117 The aorist participle κατανοήσας refers to the completion of a mental process, "he detected their craftiness."

25 T16 Τά with the genitive here means "property of."

26 M13 The aorist tense with the verb σιγάω which seems to be essentially linear, expresses an extended act or state, however prolonged in time, viewed as constituting a single fact without reference to its progress, "they relapsed into silence."
BD170(2) The genitive construction αὐτοῦ ῥήματος apparently means "a word of his" (but some other manuscripts include the article).

27　R1171　Some manuscripts have ἀντιλέγοντες,　(others omit the prefix ἀντί), in
which case the negative μή is redundant because the compound participle denotes
a negative idea, "who say that there is no resurrection."

32　BD62　In this verse, ὕστερον means "later."

35　T232　On occasion the genitive occurs with the verb τυγχάνω in the writings of
the more cultured authors, "to attain that age and the resurrection."

36　T208　Sons of the resurrection refers to those who will arise.
BD118(1)　'Ισο- in ἰσάγγελος corresponds to a participle, like "being equal to."

37　R1034　Declarative ὅτι occurs with the verb μηνύω (indicating the content of the
verb), "Moses revealed that."
BD234(3)　The preposition ἐπί with the genitive here has the sense of "at, near,
by" (unless it means "on the occasion of" in this instance). [Ed.　The phrase
ἐπὶ τῆς βάτου appears to refer to a segment of history, "in the passage about
the bush" (Ex. 3), which is later quoted from.]

46　T227　The articular participle τῶν θελόντων means "who love to."

47　R564　Κατεσθίω literally means "to eat up (down)."

LUKE 21

1　B138　Frequently the aorist participle of Greek is best reproduced in English
by a finite verb with "and," "he looked up and saw."

8　MT125　The prohibition in this verse would be answered with "we will avoid being
led astray."

11　TGr181　The clever juxtaposition of λιμοί and λοιμοί (i.e., "famines" and "pes-
tilences") is less likely to be the creation of a translator than to be original.
BD443(1)　In both occurrences here, τε simply means "and" (unless perhaps asyndeton is to be assumed since τε is not very suitable as a connective particle).
[Ed.　There is no reason to assume that a connective is omitted when τε　and
τε καί occur.　The particle τε may be used as a connective in the New Testament,
cf. Acts 2:33 and 10:22.]

13　M70　The preposition εἰς has the sense of "resulting in."
M89　The compound verb ἀποβαίνω has the meaning "turn out to be, eventuate."

14　R1094　The infinitive προμελετᾶν introduces the object of the verb θέτε, "settle
it in your minds not to meditate."
BD392(3)　Τίθημι . . . ἐν τῇ καρδίᾳ has the sense "to intend to," "to think of."

16　T209　'Εκ with the genitive here expresses a partitive sense, "some of you."

17　R889　The periphrastic future is used to express a durative action (cf. 1:20),
"you will continue to be hated."

22 R1088 Τοῦ with the infinitive expresses the notion of purpose (limiting a noun
    here--B400), "to fulfill."

24 R534 Στόματι is used as an instrumental dative (cf. T240), "by the edge of the
    sword."
    B71 The periphrastic future expresses a durative idea, "Jerusalem shall (contin-
    ue to) be trodden under foot" (cf. v. 17).
    T27 The plural καιροί is an idiomatic construction referring to "this period of
    time."

26 R566 The preposition ἀπό is not repeated with προσδοκίας because the two ideas,
    φόβου and προσδοκίας, are taken together since they are similar, "from fear
    and from expectation" (the preposition ἀπό has a causal sense here--H461).

33 R873 Οὐ μή occurs with the predictive future here (οὐ μὴ παρελεύσονται is appar-
    ently a conflation of Matt. 24:35, οὐ μὴ παρέλθωσιν, and Mark 13:31, οὐ παρε-
    λεύσονται--T97), "my words will not pass away."

34 H379 Βιωτικός (from βιόω) as first used by Aristotle meant "fit to live, live-
    ly," and showed an analogy with most words in this group (-τικός). But its
    regular usage in Hellenistic writings appears in Luke 21:34 and 1 Cor. 6:3,
    where it is adjectival, corresponding to βίος. This meaning of "worldly," "secu-
    lar," "business," "everyday" can be illustrated from the unliterary as well
    as the literary koine.

36 BD97(1) There is no sufficient reason to attribute a passive sense to the sim-
    ple intransitive infinitive σταθῆναι, which means "to stand before."

37 M9 The imperfect verb ηὐλίζετο means "he used to spend the night" (parallel
    to ἦν . . . διδάσκων; cf. T67).
    BD205 The preposition εἰς seems to be used instead of ἐν in a local sense, "on."

LUKE 22

1   T27 The idiomatic plural ἀζύμων refers to a specific festival.

2   R427 Τὸ πῶς ἀνέλωσιν is the object of the verb ἐζήτουν (the article is used
    with an indirect question in vv. 2 and 4, "how"--R766). [Ed. In essence these
    two comments are similar in meaning.]

4   T181 The article τοῖς is not repeated because the two groups are regarded as a
    unified whole.

6   B400 Τοῦ with the infinitive is used to further define the noun εὐκαιρίαν,
    "an opportunity to betray."

7   R887 The imperfect ἔδει refers to a past obligation, "had to be sacrificed."

9   M139 The plain subjunctive is used in a final clause in this verse, "where do
    you wish us to prepare . . . ?"

11 T109 The subjunctive verb φάγω has a final sense (it is equivalent to ἵνα φάγω--BD378), "that I may eat."

15 M178 Ἐπιθυμίᾳ ἐπεθύμησα probably means "I have (or perhaps "had") earnestly desired" (similar to the infinitive in Hebrew).

19 T87 The present participle διδόμενον occurs for the future (perhaps from Hebrew or Aramaic influence; it literally means "has the characteristic of"-- BD 339[2b]).

20 M31n.1 Ἐν τῷ αἵματί μου, . . . ἐκχυννόμενον looks uncommonly like a "false concord" -- as though τῷ . . . ἐκχυννομένῳ were the sense intended; but it might be argued that the participle is intended to refer to τὸ ποτήριον.
   [Ed. The latter suggestion seems preferable, "this cup which is poured out."]
   M64 The preposition ὑπέρ has a meaning which is similar to ἀντί here, "in your place" (for you).
   M78 The prepositional phrase ἐν τῷ αἵματί μου perhaps means "sealed" or "rati-fied by my blood."
   T301 Luke's parallel of 1 Cor. 11:25 omits the copula ἐστίν; Cadbury remarks on the strangeness of this, in view of Luke's regular practice of inserting the copula, especially if he found it in his sources. It is probably not a Pauline phrase, but one which Luke inherited.

23 R427 Τὸ τίς εἴη is the object of συζητεῖν (the article introduces an indirect question--T131; cf. v. 2, "they began to question one another, which of them it was").

24 M75 Ἐν αὐτοῖς evidently means "among them."

25 R510 The verb κυριεύω takes the genitive object because it has a certain sub-stantive-likeness, "be a ruler of."

26 BD480(5) An ellipsis of the verb occurs in the initial part of this verse (i.e., "should not act").

29 R581 The compound verb διατίθημι has the meaning "dispose."

30 BD369(3) The future verb καθήσεσθε connected by καί and following ἵνα with the subjunctive, designates some further consequence (as an extension of ἵνα with the subjunctive), "and that you will sit."

32 M63 The prepositional phrase περὶ σοῦ means "for you."

37 M61 Μετά has the idea of "association with."

40 R603 Ἐπί with the genitive has the sense of "towards" (classical).
   BD336(1) The present imperative προσεύχεσθε in vv. 40 and 46 refers to an action which hangs in the balance with no definite goal envisaged (i.e., "pray," with no anticipated time when they should stop).

41 M34 The accusative βολήν indicates extent (of space), "about a stone's throw."

42 T115 Εἰ with the present indicative verb βούλει has the notion of "since."

BD211 The compound verb παρένεγκε with the preposition ἀπό following has the idea of "(let) . . . pass by (and hence depart from)."

BD284(1) The possessive pronoun μου occurs in a construction with contrast here (probably not intended at first). The emphasis above all is on the negative "not."

45 R580 Ἀπό has a causal idea ("he found them sleeping because of grief"--M73).

46 B200 Ἵνα is used with an object clause, denoting the content of προσεύχεσθε, "pray that you may not enter."

48 R533 Φιλήματι is used as a dative of means, "with a kiss."

49 M77 The phrase ἐν μαχαίρῃ is instrumental, "shall we strike with the sword?"
M151 Εἰ is used to introduce a question (with the future, asking what ought to be done--B70).
T270 Οἱ περὶ αὐτόν means "his disciples" or "those who were around him" (cf. M62; "those about him"--R620; "his disciples"--BD228). [Ed. At this time, those who were around Jesus would be his disciples.]

50 T195 Εἷς τις means "a certain one."
BD111(3) Οὖς refers to the organ of hearing; Luke Atticizes when he uses οὖς for a part of the body. In v. 50, οὖς occurs in a simple emphatic statement while in v. 51, ὠτίον is emotionally charged.

51 M99 The aorist participle with the aorist indicative verb means "by touching his ear, he healed him."

53 T190 The position of the pronoun in ὑμῶν ἡ ὥρα   shows special emphasis.

55 M89 Περιάπτω refers to lighting a fire.

59 R550 Ἐπ' ἀληθείας is an adverbial phrase meaning, "certainly."

61 R873 Ἀπαρνήσῃ is often misunderstood because of the rendering "shalt deny me." It could not therefore be Peter's fault if Jesus commanded him. In this verse the rendering with "you will deny me" is free from that peril.
T137 Ὡς is equivalent to ὅτι here (it indicates the content of the verb ὑπεμνήσθη).

65 B121 The present participle βλασφημοῦντες actually specifies the inner significance or quality of the principal verb ἔλεγον, "they were saying . . ., blaspheming."

66 R1179 The connective τε and καί are used to show an inner bond, although no hint is given as to the relative value of the matters united.
M101 In vv. 66f., the present participle λέγοντες refers to what was taking place after the action of the main verb ἀπήγαγον.
BD444(4) Ἀρχιερεῖς τε καὶ γραμματεῖς is an explanatory phrase in apposition to the previous phrase τὸ πρεσβυτέριον τοῦ λαοῦ, since otherwise the article would have been used to designate the two groups, "the council of the elders . . . both chief priests and scribes."

70 R678 Ὑμεῖς λέγετε is not the equivalent of "that is right," but means "you
    say it yourself, not I" (cf. B441[3]).

71 M121 Αὐτοί appears to be emphatic here, "for we ourselves have heard."

                              LUKE 23

3   MT86 Σὺ λέγεις means "you say it," "the word is yours" (the emphasis is on the
    personal pronoun, "You are saying this, not me"--TGr73; cf. 22:70).

4   H341 Αἴτιον means "crime" in vv. 4, 14 and 22 (from the adjective meaning
    "blame-worthy").

5   T155 Ἀρξάμενος occurs with the meaning "from . . . onwards."
    BD225 The preposition κατά has the sense of "throughout" in this context.

11 M37 Ἐξουθενέω means "to set at nought."

12 R625 Hostile disposition towards one another is expressed by the preposition
    πρός here, "enmity with each other."

14 R966 Ὡς occurs with the pariticiple to refer to an alleged charge; Pilate
    does not believe the charge against Jesus to be true.

15 R534 The only true example in the New Testament of a simple dative used to refer
    to the agent (equivalent to ὑπό with the genitive) of a passive verb or parti-
    ciple occurs in this verse (unless the dative pronoun αὐτῷ is to be otherwise
    explained, such as meaning "in his case"--M204; it portrays a dative agent--
    BD191; cf. T240).
    R903 The periphrastic perfect construction here is an extensive use of the per-
    fect tense, referring to a completed act, "has been done."

19 R860 Ἦν βληθείς is a punctiliar aorist periphrastic construction, meaning "had
    been thrown."
    M76 Ἐν with the dative τῇ φυλακῇ is used for εἰς and the accusative, "into
    prison."

28 BD449(1) Πλήν is used for ἀλλά following a negative here (the manuscript D
    has ἀλλά), "but."

31 B169 This verse contains a rhetorical question of fact, "for if they do these
    things in a green tree, what will be done in the dry?"
    T293 The suppression of the subject of ποιοῦσιν seems to bring emphasis on the
    action of the verb.

32 BD306(5) Ἕτεροι is used pleonastically, thus καὶ ἕτεροι δυό means "and, besides,
    two malefactors" (the adjective implies the idea of difference--R749).

38 R604 The preposition in ἐπ' αὐτῷ has the idea of "over."

41 M122 Οὗτος is used in contrast, emphasizing "this one."

42 BD198(2) 'Εν with the dative is used in an associative sense, "with your
    kingdom" (the manuscripts B and L change to εἰς).

49 T185 Γυναῖκες αἱ συνακολουθοῦσα means "women, namely those who had followed
    . . . stood" (the present participle refers to an action which takes place be-
    fore the action of the main verb, cf. v. 55--M101).

51 T40 Αὐτῶν refers to the members of the council (understood from the previous
    statement).

54 R885 'Επέφωσκεν is used as an ingressive aorist ("was about to dawn"--BD323[4]).

55 R726 'Ως introduces an indirect question here, with the meaning "how."

56 BDp.5n.1 In the context here, ἡτοίμασαν actually means "to purchase."

LUKE 24

1   M39 The genitive expression ὄρθου βαθέως means "at early dawn."
    T187 The use of μιᾷ to mean "first" may be semitic.

4   T56 The middle verb ἀπορεῖσθαι has an active sense, "be in doubt."
    BD140 'Εσθής is a collective singular meaning "clothing."

6   R1032 'Ως is used to introduce an indirect question, "how" (cf. 23:55).

7   T325 The subject of the infinitives (τὸν υἱόν) is brought forward in this verse
    from its usual position (possibly indicating emphasis).

10 R501 The genitive of relationship in Μαρία ἡ 'Ιακώβου refers to James's Mary;
    whether mother, wife, daughter or sister, the context must decide (in this verse
    mother is meant).

11 BD214(6) 'Ενώπιον αὐτῶν occurs here for the simple pronoun αὐτοῖς, "seemed to
    them."

13 M34 The accusative σταδίους indicates the extent of space, "about sixty stades"
    (i.e., seven miles; cf. 22:41).
    M93 'Εν αὐτῇ τῇ ἡμέρα presents an exception to the usual idiomatic use of αὐτός;
    here the meaning seems to be "in the same day," rather than "in the day itself."
    [Ed. Possibly the prepositional phrase ἐν αὐτῇ was considered as definite with
    out the article, cf. the similar construction in 23:12.]

14 R625 Πρός with the accusative is used in vv. 14 and 17 to refer to a very per-
    sonal intercourse (an intimate conversation).

15 BD260(1) The anarthrous 'Ιησοῦς may be used because it is his first resurrection
    appearance (it is being too subtle to explain the anarthrous 'Ιησοῦς in some
    manuscripts of Matt. 28:9 and Luke 24:15 on the ground that it is his first
    appearance as the risen Christ; rather, it is better to accept the reading ὁ
    'Ιησοῦς in D and L, which accords with the Gospel usage--T167). [Ed. To take

the interpretation that Blass offers, may be too subtle, but one is not forced
to accept the doubtful variant reading that Turner prefers. Actually, Ἰησοῦς
is considered a proper name and it doesn't require an article to be definite.
In addition to this, Luke frequently employs Ἰησοῦς in an anarthrous construction (cf. 4:1; 8:41; 9:36, 50; 18:37, 40; 22:48 and 23:28).]

16 B403 The infinitive with τοῦ μή after a verb of hindering is closely related
to the infinitive of result. Meyer's interpretation of τοῦ μὴ ἐπιγνῶναι αὐτόν
in this verse as expressing a divine purpose (the English translation of his
grammar does not correctly represent the meaning of the German original), is
not required by New Testament usage. The Greek most naturally means "their
eyes were held from knowing him" (an ablative sense--R1061).

17 R572 Note the compound verb ἀντιβάλλετε in this verse, where the two disciples
were exchanging words (casting them from one to the other as they faced each
other -- ἀντί) with one another, an intimate and vivid picture of conversation.
R735 Τίς is equivalent to ποῖος, here (cf. ποῖα in v. 19; "what").
R835 Ἐστάθησαν is used as an effective aorist (i.e., stress is on the end of
the action), "they stood still."

18 R172 Κλεοπᾶς is apparently an abbreviation of Κλεόπατρος (it is also equivalent to κλωπᾶς in John 19:25--BD125[2]).
R1183 Καί has a consecutive sense here, "and as a result you do not know."

20 R731 This is the only instance of ὅπως in the New Testament introducing an
indirect question, "how."

21 R628 Σύν occurs in this context with the idea of "besides."
R701 The predicate accusative occurs in τρίτην ταύτην ἡμέραν. The meaning
is not "this third day," but "this a third day."
R1148 The particle γε has the sense of "this much," "as much as" in this verse,
where the force of the particle is accented by καί, σύν, and ἀλλά, which is
affirmative here not adversative (all together the meaning is "yes, and besides
all this"--M81).
M27 "This is the third day" is perhaps equivalent to "it is spending the third
day."
T66 The imperfect verb ἠλπίζομεν was intended to make the narrative continuous
until some action in the aorist tense is expected to give point to the whole
description, but the description is left without climax here (i.e., an aorist
verb does not follow; cf. 2:47).
T291 Jesus is the subject of the verb ἄγει; he has already allowed three days
to pass.

22 R1186 The narrative is carried on by the use of ἀλλὰ καί (these particles are
continuative here, rather than adversative, "moreover").

23 B343 The latter part of this verse should be translated "they came saying that
they had also seen a vision of angels, which said that he was alive." The
principal clause of the direct discourse is expressed in the indirect discourse
after a verb of past time by an infinitive, while the subordinate clause retains
the tense and mood of the original discourse (cf. M133).

25 B399 Toῦ with an infinitive is used to limit the adjective βραδεῖς, "slow
    to believe."
    TGR40 Emotion was in the words of the risen Lord when he joined Cleopas and
    his friend on the road to Emmaus (because of his use of ὦ). He was surprised
    at their failure to understand the significance of Old Testament prophecy and
    exclaimed "O foolish ones, and slow of heart!"
    BD187(6) Ἐπί with the dative here means "on the basis of."

26 R919 The imperfect verb ἔδει refers to the fact that it was a necessity and the
    statement may be confined to that phase of the matter, although the necessity
    still exists (cf. B30; it refers to a past obligation, "would it not have
    been necessary?"--T90; simply a past necessity--BD358[1]). [Ed. The imperfect
    verb ἔδει refers to a past necessity which was fulfilled. There appears to be
    no reason for maintaining that the necessity still exists.]

27 M63 Τὰ περὶ ἑαυτοῦ means "what concerned himself."
    M181 There is a peculiarity in the use of ἀρξάμενος here; the full meaning may
    be "he expounded to them from Moses (where he began) and then from all the
    prophets (with which he continued)."

29 R1088 Toῦ with the infinitive μεῖναι expresses purpose, "he went in to remain
    with them."

30 B109 In ἐν τῷ with the aorist infinitive, the action denoted by the infinitive
    precedes the action of the principal verb, yet may be thought of by the writer
    as marking more or less exactly the time at which the action of the verb takes
    place ("after"--BD404[2]; cf. 11:37).
    T68 It is an interesting point that, when Luke described the scene at Emmaus
    after the resurrection, he preserved the same sequence as that in Mark 6:41;
    aorist-aorist-imperfect. Before Jesus was recognized by Cleopas and the other
    disciple, he "gave thanks, blessed, and kept on distributing the bread to them."

31 TGr79f. There is double emphasis on the pronoun αὐτῶν: first, to use it at all,
    and secondly, to place it so emphatically at the beginning of the sentence.
    However, the emphasis is not pointless when we view the sentence in relation
    to what goes immediately before. The evangelist has placed the two like-sound-
    ing pronouns together, αὐτοῖς and αὐτῶν; and the clue to correct interpretation
    is mentally to unite the pronouns as closely as possible and to understand the
    concept underlying the story of the Emmaus road to be the enlightening capacity
    of the breaking of bread. As many as (αὐτοῖς) receive the broken bread, these
    are the ones (αὐτῶν) who gain enlightenment.

32 R974 Ὡς is used with a temporal sense here, "when."
    B22 The Authorized Version rendering "did not our heart burn within us?" is
    better than the Revised Version translation, "was not our heart burning within
    us?" Although the verb is a periphrastic imperfect (καιομένη ἦν), the English
    suggests action in progress to render it adequately.

35 R587 Ἐν wtih the dative κλάσει has the notion of "in the case of."
    R726 Ὡς is used to introduce an indirect question, meaning "how" (cf. 23:55).

36 B435 The participle has a temporal sense, "and as they spoke these things, he
    himself stood in the midst of them."

38 R739 Actually there is very little difference between τί meaning "why" and
διὰ τί meaning "because of what."

39 M121 'Εγώ εἰμι αὐτός is very emphatic, meaning "it is I myself."

41 R580 The preposition ἀπό has a causal idea (cf. H461), "because of the joy."

46 R1080 The timeless aorist infinitives παθεῖν and ἀναστῆναι refer to future
events in reference to the principal verb (cf. B114).
B75 The perfect verb γέγραπται refers to an existing state, "thus it is written" (i.e., "stands written").

47 M69 Εἰς with the accusative here appears to be equivalent to a simple dative,
"to all the nations" (this phrase denotes the recipients of the preaching--
BD207[1]).
T78 It seems quite likely that the infinitive κηρυχθῆναι is imperatival, with
the meaning "should be preached."
MT182 With great hesitation, ἀρξάμενοι may be taken as imperatival, punctuating
the verse with the margin of Wescott and Hort: "Begin ye from Jerusalem as witnesses of these things." The emphatic ὑμεῖς repeated in v. 49, thus marks the
contrast between the Twelve, for whom Jerusalem would always be the centre, and
the one to be raised up soon who would make the world his parish (either the
participle is imperatival or anacoluthon occurs--R1203; the participle has the
meaning "from . . . onwards"--T155; "beginning with"--BD419[3]). [Ed. It is
not necessary to render this participle as an imperative; especially since its
more usual meaning of "beginning with" provides a valid sense.]

50 BD239(3) "Εως with the preposition πρός means "as far as, to within sight of,"
since an actual entry is out of the question.

John

1 R623 In this verse the literal idea of πρός is evident, "face to face with God."
M116 Is the omission of the article in θεὸς ἦν ὁ λόγος nothing more than a matter of idiom? Middleton takes it as an instance of the article being omitted
simply because θεός is the predicate of a proposition which does not recipro-
cate (cf. v. 4). Similarly, Stauffer (T.W.N.T., III, 106) speaks of the omission of the article as merely grammatically conditioned.
TGr17 Moffatt translates the latter segment of this verse as, "the Logos was
divine." The implication is that even human persons may be called divine, in
a sense. Dr. Moffatt considered that he had Greek grammar on his side. The
word for God (θεός) does not have the definite article; therefore θεός is not
a noun but a kind of adjective; therefore it must be translated "divine" and
not "God." The fallacy of this has been exposed since Dr. Moffatt's time, but
he has never lacked a following. The one he would doubtless be most anxious to
disown is the utterly unsuitable translation of a German ex-Roman priest, "the
Word was a god." The fact that θεός has no article does not transform the word
into an adjective. It is a predicate noun, of which the subject is λόγος, and
it is a fairly universal rule in New Testament Greek that when a predicate noun
precedes a verb it lacks the definite article. Grammatical considerations therefore require that there need be no doctrinal significance in the dropping of the
article, for it is simply a matter of word order (when a form of the stative
verb occurs, the article does not occur with a predicate nominative unless it
is interchangeable with the subject. The occurrence of ὁ θεὸς ἦν ὁ λόγος would
have supported Sabellianism [cf. the comment on v. 4 and the similar construction in 1 John 4:16]--R767).

3 R751 Οὐδὲ ἕν is more emphatic than οὐδέν, "not one thing."
TGr138f. The best translation of vv. 3f. is "nothing was made without him. As
to that which has been made, he was its life." This translation is based upon
the grammatical idiom that a word in the nominative case occurs at the beginning
of a sentence but is syntactically isolated from the rest of it (cf. v. 12).
T70 There seems to be little distinction in the tenses here between the aorist
and perfect (cf. Col. 1:16; the perfect verb γέγονεν denotes a continuing effect
on the subject, "of the things created," which is equivalent to "existing" [how-
ever, some versions put a full stop before ὅ]--BD342[1]; by placing a full stop
before ὅ and taking ὃ γέγονεν as equivalent to a similar Hebrew construction,
the result is "inasmuch as in Him was life"--H436). [Ed. The manuscript evidence is almost equally divided between placing a period before ὅ and placing
it before ἐν. The context seems to support the punctuation with the period
before ἐν, since the relative clause can be translated in its more usual sense
referring to creation (cf. Blass' rendering).]

4 R768 When the article occurs with the subject and the predicate nominative, both
are definite, treated as identical, one and the same, and interchangeable (cf.
v. 1), "the life was the light."

5   R1183   The use of καί as meaning "and yet" occurs frequently in the Gospel of John (as with the second occurrence of καί in this verse; actual contrast-- BD442[1]).
       M197   Κατέλαβεν seems to mean both "to grasp with the mind (comprehend)" and "to grasp with the hand (overcome)."
       T73   The aorist verb κατέλαβεν in this verse is used with a gnomic sense (expressing an axiom which avails for all time).

6   R534   The preposition παρά with the genitive is used to express the agent here, "by God."

7   R850   The aorist verb μαρτυρήσῃ has merely a constative sense (summary, cf. 15:7), "that he may bear witness."

8   R708   Abbott notes (283) that in John's Gospel, outside of dialogue, ἐκεῖνος usually has considerable emphasis, as in vv. 8, 18 and 33.
       R1187   Ἀλλ' ἵνα is elliptical in this verse (cf. Mark 14:49; "but on the contrary"--BD448[1]).
       M144   The ἵνα clause here may have an imperatival sense, "he had to bear witness" (cf. Mark 14:49; doubtful in John 1:8--T95). [Ed. It seems preferable to consider the ἵνα clause as final repeating the identical clause in v. 7, especially since John's tendency is to repeat words, phrases and clauses.]

9   T87   Although ἦν and the participle are separated by a whole clause, they still form a periphrastic construction (cf. H452), "the true light . . . was coming."

10   R834   The aorist verb ἔγνω has an ingressive sense, "The world did not cease to be ignorant, or begin to recognise" (cf. 16:3 and T71).
       H469   The use of καί in contrasted statements, meaning "but," is a characteristic of the Fourth Gospel (as in vv. 10f.; cf. v. 5).

11   R691   Τὰ ἴδια refers to "one's home" and οἱ ἴδιοι refers to "one's own people."

12   B290   In this verse, "but as many as received him, to them gave he the right to become children of God," we are doubtless to understand the relative clause as definite, not because of the expressed antecedent, "them," but because the clause refers to a certain class who actually received him.
       MT115   In New Testament Greek, the preposition in a compound verb may be omitted without weakening the sense, when the verb is repeated; ἔλαβον carries on the notion introduced by παρέλαβον in v. 11 (cf. R563).

13   T27   Αἱμάτων is a literal plural referring to one's ancestors, of husband and wife (this is merely an idiomatic plural--R408). [Ed. Turner's suggestion is more probable since the construction here denotes the natural transmission of the physical life by procreation.]

14   R829   Ἐσκήνωσεν is used as a constative aorist referring to the whole earthly life of Jesus, while ἐγένετο is ingressive, accenting the entrance of the Logos upon his life on earth (ἐθεασάμεθα is probably effective, accenting the result).
       T315   Πλήρης is indeclinable only when followed by the genitive. In this verse it may be taken either with δόξαν or with αὐτοῦ (D has it as declinable). [Ed. Πλήρης seems to be in apposition with the substantive μονογενοῦς, because of

its close proximity, and because John describes him with the noun πληρώματος in v. 16.]

15 R438 The digression of this verse is considered by Abbott as an example of impressionism due to the writer's desire to make his impression first and then to add the explanatory correction.

R640 Ἔμπροσθεν has the notion of rank in this verse, "ranks before me."

R896 Certainly κέκραγεν (perfect) here is a vivid historical tense even if only intensive in sense (cf. Luke 9:36; equivalent to the historical present --BD321), "he cried."

R964 In vv. 15 ff., causal ὅτι occurs three times in succession.

M42 The superlative πρῶτος is used as a comparative, "before me" (unclassical; or "superior to me"--T32).

16 R574 The explanation of χάριν ἀντὶ χάριτος seems to be that as the days come and go a new supply takes the place of the grace already bestowed as wave follows wave upon the shore. Grace answers (ἀντί) to grace ("we have received one favor in place of another--a succession of favors"--M71).

R829 Ἐλάβομεν is used as an effective aorist, accenting the result (cf. v. 14), "we all have received."

R1181 Καί is used to introduce a phrase which is an explanatory addition ("that is to say"--BD442[9]).

M72 Ἐκ is used with the genitive here with a partitive sense, "of his fulness."

T258 Is ἀντί in this verse substitutionary (i.e., the Spirit in place of Jesus' presence) or does it imply a succession of graces? [Ed. The notion of succession seems to be preferable, cf. R574.]

18 R708 The pronoun ἐκεῖνος denotes emphasis (cf. v. 8).

R829 Ἐξηγήσατο is used as a constative aorist, referring to the whole of the earthly ministry of Christ, "he has made him known" (cf. v. 14).

B88 The use of an adverb of past time with a perfect verb (ἑώρακεν) serves to give more prominence to the past action than is usually given by a perfect tense.

M69 Εἰς τὸν . . . must not be assumed to be subtly different in meaning from ἐν τῷ . . . (εἰς in a local sense occurs instead of ἐν--T254), "in the bosom."

20 R918 Note the progressive abruptness of John the Baptist's three denials in vv. 20ff.

22 BD483 A final clause with ἵνα occurs after a question here (supply "answer," cf. 9:36), "answer, that we may."

26 R550 Μέσος ὑμῶν στήκει means "there stands in the midst of you" (a variant).

27 R961 A non-final use of ἵνα occurs in ἄξιος ἵνα λύσω. Burton (216) prefers to call this a complementary limitation of the principal clause, a sort of secondary purpose. But the notion is rather that of contemplated result (ἵνα introduces a qualitative-consecutive clause equivalent to an infinitive --BD379), "I am not worthy to untie."

29 T151 Ὁ αἴρων actually means "the sin-bearer."

T231 Ἴδε occurs with a nominative as the object because, like ἰδού, ἴδε
has become a stereotyped particle of exclamation (cf. 1926f.), "behold!"

30   R677 Ἐγώ denotes a degree of emphasis in vv. 30 and 33, "I myself . . . "
M42   The superlative πρῶτος has a comparative sense (cf. v. 15).
M65   The preposition ὑπέρ here has a meaning similar to περί, "about whom I
said."

31   R904 Present perfect verbs that had come to be mere presents in the New
Testament through accent on the durative idea and loss of emphasis on the
aoristic notion (punctiliar), are virtual imperfects when they occur with the
pluperfect form, as with ᾔδειν here, "I did not know him."

32   R440 The verb ἔμεινεν is used instead of the participle (cf. v. 33) to give
special emphasis to that point, "the Spirit remained on him."
R893 The perfect verb τεθέαμαι in the mouth of John the Baptist refers to the
baptism of Jesus some weeks before, but he still had the vision (τεθέαμαι τὸ
πνεῦμα καταβαῖνον literally means "I have seen the Spirit descending," but the
English idiom [contemplating an interval] demands "I saw . . . [if not a
clumsy paraphrase such as "I saw . . . and therefore I am now convinced," to
bring out the result which the Greek perfect suggests]--M14).

33   B299 The relative clause here does not express a general principle applying
to any one of many cases, but a supposition and an assertion referring to a
particular case, "upon whomsoever . . ."
T135 The infinitive βαπτίζειν has the notion of purpose, "to baptize."

35   BD321 In vv. 35-43, the circumstances, or all that is secondary, are given
in a past tense; on the other hand the main action is likely to be represented by the present, while the concluding events are again put into the
aorist because here an historical present would not be natural (the pluperfect εἱστήκει is equivalent to an imperfect, "was standing").

39   R813 The middle voice of ἔρχομαι is very hard to explain. [Ed. The middle
form of this verb is understandable, since ἔρχομαι is deponent and the
middle and passive form(s) are used with an active sense, "come."]

41   R549 In this verse, the manuscripts vary between πρῶτος and πρῶτον. One
can but wonder here if after all πρῶτος is not the correct text with the
implication that John also found his brother James. The delicate implication may have been easily overlooked by a scribe. But the use of πρῶτον
would mean that Andrew finds his brother Simon as the first thing which
he does (cf. R657). [Ed. The difference is that πρῶτος is an adjective,
but πρῶτον is an adverb. The adverb is supported by the best manuscript
evidence.]
R692 Emphasis is beyond dispute in the occurrence of τὸν ἴδιον here (practically no more than a possessive adjective--M121). [Ed. Moule's suggestion
seems more probable, since ἴδιον is occasionally used with this sense in
the New Testament; cf. John 4:44, "his brother."]
R795 In the Gospels, ὁ χριστός is usually a verbal adjective meaning "the
Anointed One, the Messiah" (as here).
R893 When Andrew said to Peter εὑρήκαμεν, his discovery was recent and
vivid (cf. the perfect in v. 32).

42   R835   Ἤγαγεν is used as an effective aorist (i.e., emphasis is on the end of
        the action as opposed to the beginning; cf. Luke 19:42), "he brought him."
        T37   Σύ occurs without much emphasis here (this pronoun is used for contrast;
        this particular person in contrast to others—BD277[1]).

44   R598   Ἐκ expresses the idea of origin or source in vv. 44 and 46 (both ἀπό and
        ἐκ are so used here—T259; cf. BD209[3]).

45   R578   With the use of ἀπό here, no effort is made to express the idea that they
        came from within Nazareth (cf. v. 46).

46   T75   The present imperative ἔρχου means "start to come."

48   R634   The accusative with ὑπό here takes the place of the genitive (ὄντα . . .
        means "when you were under the fig tree"—M66; cf. v. 50).

50   R871   The future verb ὄψῃ has a durative sense here, "you shall see greater
        things than these."
        R1028   In this verse the first ὅτι is causal, but the second introduces indirect
        discourse, "because . . ., that."

                                    JOHN 2

4   R539   Certain scholars interpret τί ἐμοὶ καὶ σοί to mean "what is it to me and
        thee?" That is, "what have we to do with that?" In a word, "never mind!" (an
        ethical dative; "of what concern is that to you or me"—BD299[3]); the remark
        of Jesus to his mother appears to be a polite request to refrain from inter-
        ference and to leave the whole matter to him. Perhaps that is why she thought
        that he had a definite plan in mind and asked the servants to be ready for any
        orders—TGr43ff.).

5   R855   In the midst of the aorists in vv. 2-8 (effective aorists ποιήσατε, γεμί-
        σατε, and ἀντλήσατε, with emphasis on the end of the action), the present verb
        φέρετε stands out. It is probably a polite offer to the master of the feast.
        T107   The present subjunctive in the relative clause ὅ τι ἂν λέγῃ means "what-
        ever he will be saying to you" do it at the time he is saying it (Zerwich[235]
        explains it differently, making it equivalent to universal ἄν with the subjunc-
        tive in a conditional clause, "whatsoever at any time he says to you"; "what-
        ever he says" from time to time—MT186).

6   R571   Ἀνά seems to have a distributing sense here (the only example in John,
        cf. Rev. 4:8), "each holding."

9   R1184   Ὡς δέ means "and when" or "so when" (cf. 23).

10   M97   Καλόν perhaps means "best" in both occurrences in this verse (cf. T31).
        T37   There is a degree of emphasis in the antithesis between σύ and πᾶς ἄνθρωπος.

11   R701f.   The initial part of this verse should be translated, "this Jesus did as
        a beginning of miracles" (the absence of the article with the noun makes ταύ-
        την a real predicate—R771).

                                    151

12 R680 With the occurrence of αὐτός here, there is emphasis indicated.

13 H422 Καί seems to be used in a temporal sense, "when."

16 R855 Notice the distinction between the aorist and present imperatives here, "get these things out of here! Stop making . . ."

17 R500 'Ο ζῆλος τοῦ οἴκου σου means "zeal concerning thy house" (an objective genitive).
      R903 Γεγραμμένον ἐστίν is used as an intensive perfect periphrastic (i.e., equivalent to a present; it is virtually an adjective in meaning--M18), "it is written."

18 R433n.3 John is fond of the resumptive οὖν after a parenthesis as in 2:18; 3:25 and 4:28, "then."
      R964 Ὅτι wavers between an objective and causal sense here (it seems to imply εἰς ἐκεῖνο--R1034; it has an almost consecutive sense, "so that"--T318). [Ed. Robertson's third suggestion appears to be the most probable, since the Jews were questioning the authority by which Christ was able to do such things; cf. Mark 11:28 and Luke 20:20 and the similar construction in John 9:17.]

19 R586 By the phrase ἐν τρισὶν ἡμέραις, it is clear that Jesus meant the resurrection will take place within the period of three days.
      R948 Λύσατε is not used as a strict command; it is much the same as ἐὰν λύσατε (the imperative merely proposes an hypothesis--B182), "if you destroy this temple."

20 R833 The verb οἰκοδομήθη is used as a constative aorist, the whole period of forty-six years is treated as a point ("this temple took 46 years to build"--M11).
      R1183 Καί is used in a context of contrast, with the meaning "and yet" (cf. 1:5).

21 R498 Τοῦ σώματος is used as an appositional genitive (temple and body are meant to be identical--R399).
      R708 The pronoun ἐκεῖνος is used to portray emphasis (cf. 1:8).

23 T171 The articular noun 'Ιεροσολύμοις is anaphoric here (i.e., indicating previous reference).

24 R476 Πιστεύω means "entrust" with the accusative here, "Jesus did not entrust himself to them."
      R686 The emphasis of the pronoun in αὐτὸς δὲ 'Ιησοῦς, portrays Jesus himself in distinction from those who believed on him.
      R885 The negative imperfect commonly denotes resistance to pressure or disappointment, as in this verse (ἐπίστευεν).

25 R1029 In this verse, ἦν is used in indirect discourse where ἐστιν would have occurred for the direct discourse (there is either an assimilation of tense instead of ἐστιν which would apply universally, or ἦν refers to that particular time; cf. v. 24--BD330). [Ed. In this particular narrative, the relative clause is dependent upon an imperfect verb, which apparently refers to that time; although this does not eliminate the truth of it at the present time.]

JOHN 3

1   R1185 It is not clear whether δέ is copulative or adversative. Is Nicodemus
    an illustration or an exception? [Ed. This particle appears to indicate a
    contrast, since Nicodemus was an exception to the type of men that Jesus did
    not entrust himself to, such as described in the previous verses.]

2   R611 The preposition μετά has the notion of help or aid (cf. 8:29).

3   TGr182 Supposing that Jesus conversed with Nicodemus in Greek, we are confronted
    with the truth that conversion is not only a new birth (being born again) but
    also a birth from God (being born from above; i.e., the double meaning of ἄνω-
    θεν. In spite of general reluctance to believe that Jesus would speak to a
    rabbi in Greek, it should be remembered that this occurred probably in Gali-
    lee, and not in Jerusalem (cf. v. 22); and Nicodemus, whose name is thorough-
    ly Greek, may have been a rabbi of a very liberal kind, probably a "Hellenist"
    like Stephen.

7   T77 The aorist prohibition μὴ θαυμάσῃς seems unnatural as meaning "cease to mar-
    vel" (referring to an action already begun--R852).

8   BD323(3) Ὑπάγει apparently means "will go," or rather "goes each time."

10 BD273(1) The articular predicate nominative ὁ διδάσκαλος means "the great
    (true) teacher."

11 R407 Notice the use of the literary plural by Jesus in this verse.
    H469 Καί is used with contrasted statements in vv. 11 and 13 (a characteristic
    of the Fourth Gospel; cf. 1:5).

12 B244 The first conditional clause in this verse refers to a fulfilled condi-
    tion, "since I have."

15 TGr121 This verse does not mean "everyone who believes in him has eternal life,"
    but "every believer whose life is hid in Christ possesses eternal life (from
    the ἐν Χριστῷ formula, and the fact that ἐν αὐτῷ is to be taken closely with
    ἔχῃ ζωήν--T237).

16 R762 The adjective μονογενῆ indicates definite significance, because the article
    is repeated with it (cf. 1:9).
    R1413 When a ἵνα clause is continued with ἀλλά (meaning "but on the contrary"),
    ἵνα is not repeated.
    TGr143f. John actually wrote ὥστε with the indicative in this verse (rather than
    ὅτι, as proposed by Blass, 391[2]). The construction makes the result co-ordi-
    nate with the cause expressed in the main verb and relatively more important;
    the infinitive would have subordinated the effect to the cause. The apostle
    then intended the meaning to be: "whence comes this act of incarnation? It
    originates in the love of God." More emphasis is on the incarnation itself
    than on the love which caused it. The question therefore is not, "how does
    the love of God reveal itself?" but, "what caused the incarnation?"
    BD466(3) When writing πᾶς, the second positive clause was probably in the au-
    thor's mind (cf. 6:39). [Ed. Apparently both clauses were in the author's

mind, since πᾶς is the subject of both the negative and positive clause.]

18 R897 Κέκριται and πεπίστευκεν are used as gnomic perfects, denoting customary truths.
R963 The negative in co-ordinate causal sentences is usually οὐ, but μή occurs in one instance (ὅτι μὴ πεπίστευκεν, cf. 1 John 5:10), the clause with μή states the charge, and the clause with οὐ states the simple fact (Moulton (MT 171) and others explain the negative in ὅτι μὴ πεπίστευκεν as due to a hypothetical element: it states the ground of condemnation rather than the fact of disbelief. But all this could have been expressed grammatically instead of by this solecism. 'Ο μὴ πιστεύων just before makes it sound less harsh (cf. 1 John 4:3--M155). [Ed. Although the previous participial negation may make this construction less harsh, the occurrence of μή with an indicative verb in a co-ordinate causal sentence requires explanation, such as Moulton attempts to provide.]

19 R426 Καί has the meaning "and yet" (cf. 4:20).
R964 In this verse, Chrysostom takes ὅτι as meaning "because," but this particle apparently has a declarative sense here, "that" (cf. R1028).
R1184 Δέ occurs in an explanatory parenthesis here, "And this is . . ."

21 TGr11 This verse is best translated, "The man who is a disciple of the Truth comes to the light so that it may be clearly seen that God is in all he does" (because ἀλήθειαν is articular, and for John the verb ποιέω may have some specialized religious significance, like "to worship" or "to be a disciple of").

22 R884 'Εβάπτιζεν is used as an iterative imperfect (customary).

23 T27 The idiomatic plural ὕδατα simply refers to "water."

25 R433n.3 Note the resumptive οὖν after a parenthesis (cf. 2:18), "then."
R515 In ἐκ τῶν μαθητῶν, the preposition makes clear the ablative notion (a partitive genitive [supply ἐν τοῖς]--T208). [Ed. This prepositional phrase appears to have an ablative connotation, since the dispute arose from the disciples of John. The preposition appears to denote the source of the dispute.]
R610 Μετά probably occurs here in a hostile sense, although Abbott (267) argues for the idea of alliance between the Baptist's disciples and the Jews to incite rivalry between the Baptist and Jesus. [Ed. The former suggestion is preferable, since this preposition may be used with this meaning following concepts of quarreling and fighting (cf. Rev. 2:16, 12:7, and 13:4.]

27 R907 Ἦ δεδομένον portrays a punctiliar durative idea, "what is given."

28 R707 John the Baptist uses ἐκείνου to refer to Christ in distinct contrast to himself in vv. 28 and 30.
T326 Note the peculiar position of ὅτι in this verse (ὅτι is omitted before οὐκ because ὅτι already occurs before εἶπον; the omission is rectified after ἀλλά--BD470[1]).

29 R530 Notice the cognate instrumental use of the dative in χαρᾷ χαίρει (cf. the cognate accusative in Matt. 2:10), "rejoices greatly."

31 R598 'Εκ denotes the idea of origin or source.

32 BD342(2) In ὁ ἑώρακεν καὶ ἤκουσεν, John puts the chief emphasis on seeing
    (the occurrence of a perfect with an aorist in the same context does not por-
    tray a confusion of the tenses, but proves the distinction between them--R901;
    cf the discussion on Acts 22:15).
    H469 The second καί in this verse occurs in a contrast statement, meaning "but"
    (cf. 3:11).

33 R859 'Ο λάβων probably refers to the Baptist.

35 R585 In this verse, ἐν occurs with the locative dative (cf. 2 Cor. 8:16; ἐν
    with the dative apparently is similar to εἰς with the accusative here--M76),
    "into."

                                    JOHN 4

1   R684 The substantive 'Ιησοῦς is repeated because the mere pronoun would be
    ambiguous.
    R1034 Note that one ὅτι clause is dependent on another ὅτι clause (double
    indirect discourse--R1421), "Jesus knew that the Pharisees had heard that."

2   R1148 The concessive minimizing idea is expressed by καίτοι γε 'Ιησοῦς αὐτός,
    "although Jesus himself."

3   BD327 'Απῆλθεν has an unusual use of the aorist tense, because vv. 4ff. present
    what happened on the way, and the arrival in Galilee does not actually take
    place until v. 45 (one would expect the imperfect tense).

5   R547 This verse contains the only instance of πλησίον as a preposition in the
    New Testament (with the genitive), meaning "near."
    R596 Notice the preposition in ἔρχεται εἰς πόλιν, where the point is not "into"
    but "to" (similar to πρός).

6   R599 'Εκ has the notion of cause or occasion, "because of the journey."
    R909 The perfect participle κεκοπιακώς represents a state (intensive), "being
    wearied."
    M50 'Εκαθέζετο . . . ἐπὶ τῇ πηγῇ means "he sat at the well."

7   M127 The infinitive πεῖν is used as a noun, "give me a drink."
    T135 The infinitive ἀντλῆσαι has the notion of purpose, "for the purpose of
    drawing water" (cf. v. 15).

9   R434 The particle οὖν makes reference to the context preceding the parenthesis
    of v. 8, "then."
    R482 In παρ' ἐμοῦ the preposition occurs with an ablative genitive, "of me" or
    "from me."

10 T37 There is some degree of emphasis or antithesis in the occurrence of σύ here
    (cf. BD277[1], for emphasis).

11 R762 The article with ὕδωρ has an anaphoric sense, referring to the previous
    reference in v. 10.

R1179 In οὔτε . . . καί, actually the τε . . . καί construction is present, "both . . . and" (the correlation of negative and positive members is admissable, although it is not common in the New Testament--BD445[1]).

14 R889 Διψήσει is used as a durative future with οὐ μή, "will never thirst."

15 R1413 Ἵνα is not repeated in the continuation of the ἵνα μή clause here (cf. 3:16), "that I may not."

16 BD336(1) Ἐλθε ἐνθάδε means "come (back) here."

18 R702 In the translation of τοῦτο ἀληθες εἴρηκας, the English relative pronoun is necessary, "this is a true thing that you did say," or "you did speak this as a true thing."
R843 Note the sharp contrast between the aorist and present tense in ἔσχες . . ἔχεις (the aorist may be rendered "you have espoused"--MT145).

19 M7 θεωρῶ appears to be used as a simple present (punctiliar), meaning "I perceive" (θεωρῶ may be used for no better reason than that there is no convenient aorist of this particular verb).

20 R426 Καί has the meaning "and yet," denoting contrast (cf. 3:19).

22 R713 The neuter pronoun ὅ is used twice to refer to the object of worship (i.e., God).

23 R1186 Abbott (p. 100) considers ἀλλά as inexplicable, because it always has to mean "but." [Ed. It is not necessary to consider ἀλλά as inexplicable since Christ presents a distinction in periods of time.]

27 R604 The preposition in ἐπί τούτῳ conveys the notion of ground or occasion (this phrase has a transferred sense, "at this [juncture]"--M50; cf. T272).
R756 The King James translators missed the point of μετὰ γυναικός when they wrote "the woman." It was "a woman," any woman, not the particular woman in question.
R1188 Μέντοι is a combination of two intensive particles (μέν and τοί), and is used to mean "however."

29 R1167 In the interrogative sentence here, οὐ would have challenged the opposition of the neighbors by taking sides on the question whether Jesus was the Messiah. The woman does not mean to imply flatly that Jesus is not the Messiah by using μήτι, but she raises the question and throws a cloud of uncertainty and curiosity over it with a woman's keen instinct.

31 R645 Μεταξύ occurs as a mere adverb here, in the sense of "meanwhile" (cf. Acts 13:42).

33 BD427(2) The interrogative sentence with μή here means "surely no one could have brought him food" (yet it appeared as if someone had).

34 R1078 Ἵνα introduces an appositional clause (especially common in the writings of John; the clause defines the content of the noun βρῶμα--B213), with the resultant meaning "doing the will of him that sent me is my food."

35 R626 Πρός occurs here in the general sense of fitness.
    R870 Ἔρχεται is used as a futuristic present. It is not merely prophecy, but
    certainty of expectation that is involved (cf. T63).

36 R659 The adjective ὁμοῦ is used as an adverb here, "rejoice together."

38 T135 The infinitive θερίζειν portrays the notion of purpose (cf. v. 7), "to
    reap."

39 R1123 Burton (B461) describes μαρτυρούσης as a substantive participle used as
    an integral part of a genitive limiting phrase ("of the woman testifying," i.e.,
    of the woman's testimony), but actually it is an attributive participle (cf.
    Matt. 21:4). [Ed. These explanations of this construction result in a similar
    rendering.]

41 R1179 In this verse, καί and τέ are not co-ordinate. Καί introduces the whole
    sentence and τέ connects the two parts.

43 R762 In τὰς δύο ἡμέρας, the article refers to the preceding occurrence in v.
    40.

45 R1128 The participle ἑωρακότες has a causal sense, "because they had seen."

52 R470 Ὥραν ἑβδόμην is a difficult example of the accusative, because a point
    of time is indicated (cf. Rev. 3:3). One may conjecture that this use of ὥραν
    was not regarded as essentially different from the idea of extension. Either
    the action was regarded as going over the hour or the hour was looked at more
    as an adverbial accusative (an unusual use of the accusative occurs here to
    indicate at what time--M34).
    R665 Κομψότερον ἔσχεν (a comparative adverb with ἔχω) means "better than before
    the word of Christ was spoken."
    M10 The aorist verb ἔσχεν has an ingressive sense, "took a turn for the better"
    (cf. B41; "started to mend"--T72).
    T65 The aorist verb ἐπύθετο merely presents a question, but an urgent one,
    and the answer known (cf. Luke 15:26; the aorist is incorrect in John 4:52--
    BD328). [Ed. Blass's proposal is highly improbable, since the aorist may be
    explained and the imperfect has very little manuscript support.]

                                    JOHN 5

3   R427 Asyndeton (omission of the connective) occurs in this verse between the
    nouns to give emphasis.

4   R585 Ἐν occurs in the place of εἰς in this spurious verse, "into."

5   B131 The present participle ἔχων refers to an action beginning before the action
    of the principal verb and continuing in progress at the time denoted by the
    latter, "who had been ill for 38 years."

6   B17 The present verb ἔχει refers to past action still in progress, "had been
    there."

7 R960 Ἵνα occurs in ἵνα . . . βάλῃ, where a relative pronoun may have been used (it is used for a qualitative-consecutive relative clause, meaning "such that"--BD379).

8 R855 In the two imperatives ἆρον and περιπάτει the aorist has an ingressive sense "take," and the present expresses a durative notion, "go on walking" (the same tense distinction is preserved in v. 9, ἦρε . . . περιπάτει).

10 H422 The second καί in this verse has a consecutive sense in a co-ordinate construction, "as a result."

11 T37 Ὁ δέ occurs frequently in the New Testament to continue a narrative, even in John where it occurs least often (A and B have ὃς δέ).

18 R884 Ἔλυε is used as an iterative imperfect (cf. 3:22; repeatedly).
MT90 There is undeniable emphasis in the use of ἴδιον here (cf. 1:41), "his own father."

19 R1181 Καί in the latter part of this verse and in v. 26 means "just so."

24 R897 Μεταβέβηκεν is used as a gnomic perfect, denoting a customary truth (cf. 3:22).

27 R781 In this verse υἱὸς ἀνθρώπου may mean either "the son of man" or "a son of man" (apart from Old Testament quotations, this anarthrous construction occurs only here; the omission of the article may be a semitism--M177; the anarthrous form of υἱὸς ἀνθρώπου is probably due to the writer's sense that the title is here used qualitatively--H441). [Ed. Generally when a predicate nominative precedes the verb it is anarthrous (cf. E. C. Collwell, "A Definite Rule for the Use of the Article in the Greek New Testament," J.B.L., I[1933], 12-21). Consequently, there is no reason to make a point of the anarthrous construction here.]
T49 If ὅ is separate from τι the clause seems to mean "to judge what a man is" (or is ὅτι to be read?). [Ed. The reading with ὅτι is preferable .]
T56 The active voice occurs with ποιεῖν, where we expect the middle. [Ed. The active infinitive may be translated as such without forcing the sense of the middle voice upon it. The infinitive occurs with the noun κρίσιν, forming a periphrasis of a simple verb of doing, "to judge."]

28 R890 The present prohibition here, forbids something that is already being done (it may mean either "do you perhaps marvel at this, that [as the rabbis say] . . .?" or "No! You do not wonder, although it is just as astonishing as what I said earlier"--BD427[2]; this presents a question, "do you marvel at this?" --T283). [Ed. The verb θαυμάζετε may be either an indicative or imperative in form. The imperative rendering seems preferable since Christ instructs the people not to marvel at this because even greater things are coming; cf. v. 20 and 3:7.]

29 BD166 The nouns ζωῆς and κρίσεως are used as genitives of purpose (or result), meaning "to life" and "to judgement."

30 B482 The compound negative οὐδέν with the infinitive may be explained as due to the dependence upon a finite verb with οὐ. [Ed. Actually, οὐδέν does not

negate the infinitive, but is used as the object of the infinitive, "I can
myself do nothing."]

31 R1010 It is possible to treat ἐὰν ἐγὼ μαρτυρῶ as a present indicative, "as I
    said before" (if it is a present subjunctive, the meaning would be "if perchance
    I bear witness," cf. 8:14--R1018). [Ed. According to form this verb may be
    either indicative or subjunctive, but since the indefinite particle ἐάν occurs,
    the subjunctive was more probably the mood intended.]

32 BD306(3) The use of ἄλλος here seems to be similar to ἕτερος (with the second
    of two parts), "another."

34 R866 The present verbs λαμβάνω and λέγω have an aoristic sense here, "receive
    . . . say."

35 BD273(1) Predicate nouns as a rule are anarthrous. Nevertheless, the article
    is inserted if the predicate noun is presented as something well known or as
    that which alone merits the designation (the only thing to be considered), as
    with ἐκεῖνος (John) ἦν ὁ λύχνος ὁ καιόμενος καὶ φαίνων (he who alone really
    deserves the designation "light").

36 R516 It is not clear whether the genitive τοῦ Ἰωάννου refers to the witness
    born by John or to him. [Ed. Τοῦ Ἰωάννου appears to be used as a genitive
    of comparison, "than John," following the comparative adjective. If the alter-
    nate rendering would have been desired, the apostle John would have repeated
    the article τῆς or the article and noun τῆς μαρτυρίας (as his tendency was to
    repeat). In addition, John the Baptist was considered a witness; cf. v. 35
    and 1:8.]
    B86 Although each tense retains its own proper force, the two approximate
    very closely, and are used side by side of what seem to be quite co-ordinate
    facts. Instances of this approximation of the two tenses are especially fre-
    quent in the writings of John (vv. 36, 38; 1 John 1:1; 4:9, 10; there is a
    sharp distinction between the present and the following perfect verbs--R894).
    [Ed. Although the aorist πέμψας immediately follows the perfect tense of the
    same verb and the tenses seem to be inter-mingled, the author apparently employs
    the perfect tense in vv. 36ff. for a vivid distinction, especially since the
    perfect verb ἀκηκόατε seldom occurs in the New Testament.]
    T186 Μείζω is used predicatively here, with the meaning "a witness which is
    greater."

37 BD342(2) Ἑώρακα and ἀκήκοα are co-ordinated by the perfect tense, where hear-
    ing and seeing are equally essential (cf. 3:32).
    BD445(4) Καὶ οὐ in v. 38 after the negative clauses (οὔτε . . . οὔτε . . .)
    does not indicate correlation but an independent continuation, "and you do not
    have his word."

38 R703 Notice the contrast denoted by the pronouns ἐκεῖνος and τούτῳ.
    T37 There is not much emphasis in the occurrence of ὑμεῖς in vv. 38, 39 and 44
    (some corrected manuscripts have omitted the pronoun in v. 44; in v. 38, the
    pronoun is used to show contrast; in v. 39, it means "you yourselves, and in
    v. 44, it means "people like you"--BD277[1]).

39 R329 Ἐραυνᾶτε apparently is an indicative verb here, "you do search."

R1183 Καί has the meaning "and yet" (cf. 1:5).
BD273(3) The articular participle αἱ μαρτυροῦσαι is used as a predicate nominative, "they that testify."

40 H469 Καί has the meaning "and yet" in vv. 40 and 43f. (cf. 1:5).

42 R499 The genitive in ἀγάπην τοῦ θεοῦ has either a subjective or objective
sense. [Ed. The genitive is apparently objective referring to the fact that
the Jews did not love God (cf. 1 John 2:5, 15; 3:17; 4:12 and 5:3) because they
rejected His messenger.]

43 R762 The article τῷ occurs with the adjective to portray special significance
(cf. 1:9), "in his own name."

44 R1128 The causal participle λαμβάνοντες is co-ordinate with the verb ζητεῖτε,
"because you receive glory from one another and do not seek the glory only from
God."
TGr6 The spiritual danger facing the Jewish people was, according to Jesus,
that they were accepting glory from other sources as well as God. He reminded
them that glory should be sought only from him (despite the fact that μόνου is
in an attributive position; it is used as an adverb, meaning "only from God,"
rather than as an adjective, meaning "from him who alone is God"--T226).

45 R853 In the present prohibition μὴ δοκεῖτε, it is implied that they had been
thinking just that ("cease to imagine"--T76).
T80 The parallel verb κατηγορήσω just before makes it inevitable that the
present participle ὁ κατηγορῶν has a future sense (therefore the end of the
age is meant--BD339[2b]).

47 R1012 The conditional clause here is determined as fulfilled, "since you do not
believe his writings."

JOHN 6

1 R444 This chapter opens with μετὰ ταῦτα, a connective that refers to the incidents in chapter 5, which may have been a full year before.

6 B121 The verb and participle of identical action (ἔλεγεν πειράζων), though
denoting the same action, usually describe it from a different point of view.
In this instance, the verb expresses the act and the participle expresses the
purpose or result (cf. Matt. 16:1), "to test him."

7 R998 Ἵνα with the subjunctive here expresses a contemplated result (ἵνα is
equivalent to ὥστε--BD393[2]), "that."

9 R713 In παιδάριον . . . ὅς, the change is made according to the real gender
rather than the grammatical one (the masculine pronoun is used referring to a
person).
BD111(3) John uses ὀψάριον to refer to fish as food, but ἰχθύς for fish as a
living animal.
BD299(1) Τί is used predicatively with ταῦτα here, meaning "what good are they?"

10   R486   Τὸν ἀριθμόν is used as an adverbial accusative (actually it is an accusa-
        tive of respect or reference, "about 5,000 in number"--M33).

12   R974   Ὡς has a temporal sense in vv. 12 and 16, "when" (cf. Acts 8:36).

16   R602   Ἐπί with the accusative here has the meaning "as far as."

17   R904   The verb ἤρχοντο is used as a descriptive imperfect and the verb following
        this verse διεγείρετο is used as an inchoative imperfect, "the sea began to
        rise." But the two intervening pluperfects indicate stages in the going before
        they reached the shore. Both ἤδη and οὔπω help to accent the interval between
        the first darkness and the final appearance of Jesus which is soon expressed
        by the vivid historical present, θεωροῦσιν (v. 19).
     T179   The phrase εἰς πλοῖον means "aboard."

19   BD233(1)   Ἐπὶ τῆς θαλάσσης should be understood as meaning "by the sea" (cf.
        21:1 and Matt. 14:25f.).

22   T67   The imperfect tense (ἦν) in indirect discourse here, expresses relative
        past time (similar to a pluperfect), with the meaning "had been there."
     BD467   The textual tradition in John 6:22ff. is too diverse to enable us to
        discern the hand of the author; according to the customary reading, τῇ ἐπαύρον
        ὁ ὄχλος at the beginning is resumed by ὅτε οὖν εἶδεν ὁ ὄχλος in v. 24, in a
        way which is not unknown among classical writers and where there is no question
        of a lapse of memory (cf. 1 John 1:1ff.). [Ed. This is in essence an expla-
        nation for the text which seems to have stronger external support. Conse-
        quently, we are able to ascertain the original text.]

25   R896   The perfect verb γέγονας has both the punctiliar and durative ideas,
        "came and are here" ("when camest thou here?"--B82; this perfect is a combina-
        tion of "when did you come?" and "how long have you been here?"--MT146).

27   R471   Ἐργάζομαι in this context means "work for."

29   R400   The ἵνα clause in this verse is in apposition to the previous clause (cf.
        vv. 39f and 4:34), "this is the work of God, that."

30   R850   The aorist subjunctive verb πιστεύσωμεν has an ingressive sense, meaning
        "come to believe" (cf. πιστεύητε in v. 29).
     T37   The pronoun σύ occurs without much emphasis here.

32   M14   Δέδωκεν is used as a perfect of allegory (cf. Heb. 7:6), "has given."

35   R889   Διψήσει is used as a durative future with οὐ μή (cf. 4:14), "shall never
        thirst."

36   T335   It appears that καί . . . καί is the Biblical Greek equivalent of τε . . .
        καί, which is extremely rare, "and yet do not believe."

37   R409   Πᾶν ὅ in this verse refers to believers (i.e., the neuter is used in a
        collective sense for the sum total, "the all," cf. v. 39--R653).

39   R400   Ἵνα is in apposition to the previous τοῦτο in vv. 39f. (cf. v. 29; in its

occurrence in v. 39 it seems to have an imperatival sense--T95), "this is the will . . ., that."
R1413 When a ἵνα clause is continued with ἀλλά, meaning "but on the contrary," ἵνα is not repeated (cf. 3:16).

42 R697 Οὗτος carries the notion of reproach here, of the Jews against Christ (cf. Luke 15:2).

43 R610 Μετά has a hostile sense with γογγύζω, "against" (cf. 3:25).

45 R614 Παρά occurs with the ablative use of the genitive in vv. 45f., "from the father."

49 R1183 Καί has the meaning "and yet" (cf. 3:19).

51 R1185 In the καί . . . δέ construction, the καί means "also" and the δέ means "and."

52 R811 The middle voice in ἐμάχοντο has a reciprocal sense, "disputed among themselves."

57 R584 Διά with the genitive portrays the personal ground in this verse ("by someone's merit"--BD222).
    H422 In this verse, καί has a consecutive sense in a co-ordinate clause, "as a result" (cf. 5:10).

59 MT236 "In church" is a valid translation of ἐν συναγωγῇ (Westcott over presses this phrase by translating it as "in time of solemn assembly").

61 R587 The preposition in ἐν ἑαυτῷ has the notion of "in the case of."

62 R487 Τὸ πρότερον is used as an adverb, "earlier."
    BD482 The apodosis has been omitted in this verse; supply "would you then still take offense?"

64 R597 With expressions of time, ἐκ gives the point of departure, as in this verse, "from the beginning."

66 R597 Ἐκ τούτου is a temporal expression (ἐκ τούτου may be translated causatively, "because of this," rather than temporally--M72f.). [Ed. This phrase appears to have both a temporal and causal sense here. A major desertion of Christ's disciples occurred from that time (cf. the following οὐκέτι) and because of his previous discussion.]

68 R790 The phrase ῥήματα ζωῆς αἰωνίου should be translated, "words of eternal life" (indefinite since it is anarthrous; stressing the quality or character --MT83).

69 B77 The perfect tense occurs in this verse as an emphatic present, thus, "we have believed and know that thou art the Holy One of God" (intensive perfect).

70 T55 Ἐκλέγομαι occurs in the middle voice where one expects the active. [Ed. Ἐκλέγομαι does not occur with the active voice in the New Testament; cf. the discussion on 1:39.]

H469 Καί is used in a contrast here, "but" (cf. 1:5).

71 B73 The imperfect of μέλλω with the infinitive portrays that at a past time an action was about to take place (cf. 7:39).

JOHN 7

1 R885 The negative imperfect (οὐ ἤθελεν) generally denotes resistance to pressure or disappointment (cf. Luke 15:28).

4 BD372(1a) Εἰ occurs with the indicative of reality, meaning "if, as you say, you want to do that . . ."
MT212 The nominative occurs as the subject of the infinitive here, because the subject of the infinitive is the same as that of the main verb.
H469 In vv. 4 and 19, καί has an adversative sense, "but" (cf. 1:5).

5 R1185 Οὐδέ has the meaning, "not even."

8 BD323(3) Οὐκ ἀναβαίνω is a futuristic present, if οὔπω is not to be preferred nor εἰς . . . ταύτην omitted, "I am not going up."

9 BD332(1) If the aorist of a verb like μένω is used without a time limit, it indicates merely the fact of a stay in contrast to a departure (ἔμεινεν ἐν τῇ Γαλιλαίᾳ is equivalent to οὐκ ἀνέβη εἰς Ἰεροσόλυμα).

11 T46 The pronoun ἐκεῖνος carries a contemptuous notion, "that fellow."

13 R500 The genitive τῶν Ἰουδαίων refers to fear towards or in reference to the Jews.

14 R885 Ἐδίδασκεν is used as an inchoative imperfect, "began to teach."

17 R551 θέλῃ . . . ποιεῖν means "is willing to do."
R757 The article occurs in τῆς διδαχῆς, because reference is made to the teaching concerning which they were puzzled.

18 R762 The article τήν is repeated with the adjective, indicating special significance (cf. 1:9 and 6:70), "his own glory" (as opposed to God's glory).

22 R1429 Οὐχ ὅτι does not mean "not only," but "not that."

23 R774 Ὅλον ἄνθρωπον ὑγιῆ means "a whole man sound."
B244 Εἰ introduces a conditional clause that refers to a fulfilled condition (cf. 3:12), "since."

26 B47 The aorist indicative of a few verbs is used in the New Testament to denote a present state, the result of a past act, hence with the proper force of a Greek perfect; so ἔγνωσαν here, "know."

28 BD442(1) Καί is used with a contrast here, "yet I did not really come . . ." (cf. v. 30).

30 R1183 Καί has the meaning "and yet" (cf. 3:19).

33 H422 Καί has a temporal sense, "then" (cf. 2:13).

35 R501 Τὴν διασπορὰν τῶν Ἑλλήνων means "the dispersion among the Greeks."

38 M30f. The nominative ὁ πιστεύων is not used as the subject here, unless a full
    stop should be placed after ὁ πιστεύων εἰς ἐμέ, in which case it becomes the
    grammatical subject of the preceding verb πινέτω (in nearly every instance where
    there is no ambiguity, a καθώς clause follows its governing verb, and the strong
    presumption is that such is the position here--TGr144). [Ed. Turner seems to
    be forcing an issue, since καθὼς εἶπεν ἡ γραφή is used as a quotation formula
    (cf. 6:31 and 12:14), introducing an Old Testament concept (cf. Prov. 18:4 and
    Isa. 58:11). The articular participle here is used as a nominative absolute
    in apposition to the previous subject, although independent of what precedes
    as well as what follows (cf. Rev. 2:26; 3:12 and 21), "The one that believes
    in me, as the Scripture said, rivers of living water . . ."]

39 R859 The aorist tense in πιστεύσαντες has a constative sense (the whole action
    is treated as a point).
    B73 The imperfect of μέλλω with an infinitive portrays that at a past time an
    action was about to take place, "were to receive" (cf. 6:71).

40 M72 The preposition in ἐκ τοῦ ὄχλου has a partitive sense, "some of the crowd"
    (the apostle John is addicted to the partitive ἐκ and uses it frequently when
    he wishes to express the closest identification [cf. 15:19]--TGr6).

41 R1190 The use of γάρ here portrays a degree of scorn (cf. 9:30).

45 T46 Ἐκεῖνοι refers to the officers who were away from the scene of action.

51 R1168 Note vv. 51f., where Nicodemus cleverly uses μή in a question and the
    other members of the Sanhedrin sharply retort with μὴ καὶ σύ (i.e., μή with a
    question expects a negative response; Nicodemus is rather subtle in using μή--
    T283).

52 R866 Ἐγείρεται is used as a gnomic present (referring to a well known fact).
    R949 On occasion two imperatives are connected by καί when the first suggests
    a concessive sense, "although you search, you will see" (cf. Eph. 4:26).

                                JOHN 8

4   M99 The present participle occurs with an aorist, "she was caught in the very
    act of committing."

7   T226 The verb in ἐπέμενον ἐρωτῶντες has an adverbial notion, "incessantly" (the
    participle portrays the main verbal idea).

9   BD419(3) Ἀρξάμενοι has a classical usage, meaning "beginning with" (some manu-
    scripts add the unclassical ἕως τῶν ἐσχάτων).

14 R870 'Υπάγω is used as a futuristic present in vv. 14 and 21, indicating the
certainty of expectation (cf. 4:35), "where I will go."
BD372(1a) Κἂν ἐγώ means "even if I."

16 B281 Καὶ ἐάν in a concessive sense occurs somewhat rarely in the New Testament
(cf. Gal. 1:8). The force of καί is apparently intensive, representing the
supposition as actual or from a rhetorical point of view an extreme case, improbable in itself, or specially unfavorable to the fulfillment of the apodosis
(καὶ ἐάν κρίνω δὲ ἐγώ means "even if I however judge"--BD475[2]).

20 H469 Καί occurs in contrast here, meaning "but" (cf. 1:5).

25 R487 The expression τὴν ἀρχήν is close to a mere adverb ("from the beginning"
or perhaps "at all, in the first instance," cf. ἀπ' ἀρχῆς in the first epistle
of John--M34).
TGr140ff. For the latter part of this verse, there are two interpretations,
neither of which requires us to suppose that the Lord's words are a mistransla-
tion of Aramaic. Both are intelligible from the Greek. Both are early in date.
Either may have arisen as a reaction to the other. The two possibilities are:
"I am the Beginning, as I have told you," or "Why do I even speak to you!"
(this clause has the meaning "why do I speak to you at all"; εἶπον ὑμῖν is
simply an insertion to make things more easily understood--T49).

26 R1186 'Αλλά has the meaning "now" or "yea" ("but yet"--BD448[3]).

28 R837 'Εδίδαξεν is used as a gnomic aorist (a supposedly well known fact).

29 R549 The adjective μόνον occurs with the meaning "he did not leave me alone."
R611 Μετά has the notion of help or aid (cf. 3:2).

31 B263 The conditional clause should be translated, "if you shall abide in my
word, (you will show that) you are truly my disciples."

32 R872 The future verb ἐλευθερώσει has an effective sense, "set free."

33 R896 Δεδουλεύκαμεν is used as a perfect of broken continuity (cf. 1:18; the
perfect probably conveys the thought of existing result--B88). [Ed. The inclusion of the negation οὐδενὶ . . . πώποτε favors Burton's rendering. The
Jews expressed (however true or false) that they had never been in bondage to
any man, and as a result were presently free.]

37 M75 It is difficult to determine whether ἐν means "within" (an individual) or
"among" (a number of persons). [Ed. The translation of this prepositional
phrase is dependent upon the meaning of χωρέω. In this context, the verb appears to refer to growth and movement, with the resultant meaning "has no progress in you"; cf. vv. 31f.]

39 TGr52ff. The most accurate text seems to be "if you are Abraham's children,
you would do the works of Abraham." This may be a condensed construction,
capable of expansion into, "if you were justified in claiming that you are
Abraham's children . . ."

44   R551   θέλετε ποιεῖν means "you are willing to do" (cf. 7:17; "you gladly do his will"--T227).

     R683   In this verse the αὐτοῦ refers to the ψεῦδος suggested by ψεύτης (cf. T40), "of lies."

     TGr8   The second segment of this verse should be translated "your father the Devil was a murderer from the beginning and has no standing whatever in (Christ) the Truth, because there is no true sincerity in him."

     TGr148ff.   The latter part of this verse should be translated "he is a liar and the father of lies" (note that to be predicative ["the devil is your father"] πατρός ought not to have the article; τοῦ διαβόλου is therefore in apposition or else a possessive genitive.

     BD97(1)   Οὐκ ἕστηκεν probably means "he has not persisted, he does not stand fast."

52   B47   The aorist indicative ἀπέθανον has the force of a perfect (cf. 7:26), "died."

     H469   The second καί in this verse has the notion of contrast, meaning "but" (cf. 1:10).

53   R441   In this verse the continuity of the interrogative form of sentence is abruptly broken by the short clause καὶ οἱ προφῆται ἀπέθανον; a very effective interruption, however.

     R728   Ὅστις seems to have a causal sense, "seeing that he died" (ὅστις refers to a definite person and expresses the general quality, "who nevertheless was a man who died"--BD293[2]). [Ed. John makes use of this pronoun infrequently in his writings, and generally with the sense of a relative pronoun. Its occurrence in this context also appears to have this meaning (similar to Blass's suggestion), although the reason for the questions from the Jews is implied in the relative clause.]

54   R1034   Ὅτι is used epexegetically in this verse (portraying the content of the previous clause), "whom you say that."

56   B217   Ἵνα is used as an epexegetical limitation of the verb ἠγαλιάσατο (expressing the content), "rejoiced to see my day" (cf. M146; ἵνα has a causal sense, "Abraham rejoiced because . . ."T102). [Ed. The former rendering has the support of the more common use of ἵνα. In addition to this, the fact that Abraham did not completely see the day of Christ tends to discredit the latter suggestion.]

     H475   Burney, observing that "rejoiced to see" does not give a satisfactory meaning of the verb, suggests that "longed to see" is what we should expect in this context.

57   R1183   Καί occurs in contrast with the meaning "and yet" (cf. 1:5).

59   BD471(4)   Ἐκρύβη καὶ ἐξῆλθεν is equivalent to ἐκρύβη ἐξέλθων meaning "he eluded them" or rather "he hid himself among the people and so escaped."

JOHN 9

1   M73   In the temporal expression here, ἐκ portrays the point of departure (cf. v. 24 and 6:64), "from his birth."

2   B218 "Ἵνα is used to express a conceived result, "that he should be born blind?"
     (the effect is actual and observed, but it is the cause that is inferred--B219;
     "with the result that," i.e., actual result--BD391[5]; it is consecutive result,
     but the weak variant with ὅτι indicates that scribes understood it as a causal
     ἵνα--T102).

3   TGr145f. "Ἵνα occurs here with an imperatival sense, thus the second part of
     Jesus' answer is "but let the works of God be made manifest in him" (Cadoux
     tentatively notes ἵνα here as imperatival--M145).

4   R976 In this context ἕως means "while," not "until" (Westcott and Hort have
     ὡς in the margin).

5   R972 This verse contains the only instance of ὅταν expressing the idea of dura-
     tion in the New Testament, "as long as."

6   R420 In this verse αὐτοῦ is entirely removed from ὀφθαλμούς and is without
     particular emphasis. It was probably felt that the genitive of the pronoun
     made a weak close of a sentence, "his eyes."

7   R592 The idea of motion is retained in νίψαι εἰς (cf. Mark 1:5; εἰς occurs in-
     stead of ἐν in a local sense--BD204). [Ed. The latter suggestion seems to
     be preferable, since the prepositional phrase indicates the place in which the
     blind man was commanded to wash.]

8   BD330 The participle θεωροῦντες refers to the same prepast (pluperfect) time
     that is expressed in the dependent clause by προσαίτης; since definite past
     time is not expressed by participles at all, it had to be indicated by the im-
     perfect in the ὅτι clause, "who had seen him as a beggar."

9   B345 The presence of ὅτι before a quotation in the New Testament is not even
     presumptive evidence that the quotation is indirect, as here, "he said, I am
     he." The ὅτι is of course redundant.
     BD291(6) John frequently uses ἐκεῖνος in a weakened sense ("he") with reference
     to the immediately preceding subject (cf. vv. 11, 25 and 36).

10   R419 Personal enclitic pronouns (σοῦ) have a tendency to occur relatively early
     in the sentence without emphasis, as in vv. 10 and 17 (cf. 9:6), "your eyes."

15   R681 No undue emphasis is to be put upon the pronoun μου in this verse (cf. v.
     6).

16   T26 The plural σημεῖα may simply mean "sign." [Ed. Actually, the plural here
     seems to be a literal plural, "signs." The Pharisees were undoubtedly refer-
     ring to more than just the preceding sign; cf. 3:2.]

17   R964 The first ὅτι in this verse may be either objective or causal (ὅτι ἠνέῳξέν
     σου τοὺς ὀφθαλμούς should be translated "thou whose eyes he hath opened"--MT94).
     [Ed. In this context, ὅτι appears to have a causal notion, "since"; cf. v. 16
     and 8:22.]

18   B330 "Ἕως ὅτου is in effect a compound conjunction having the same force as the
     simple ἕως, "until."

M121f. The latter occurrence of αὐτοῦ in this verse is strange; the context seems to require "the parents themselves" (τοὺς γονεῖς αὐτούς), not "the parents of the man himself."

T67   In "that he had been blind and made to see," the imperfect occurs in indirect discourse to indicate relative past time, whereas the aorist is used to refer to punctiliar action (cf. 6:22).

21   M121   Αὐτὸς περὶ ἑαυτοῦ λαλήσει means "he himself shall speak for himself."

22   R811   Συνετέθειντο is used as a reciprocal middle verb, "they have agreed among themselves."
B217   In this verse, the ἵνα clause defines the content of the agreement mentioned in the preceding portion of the sentence (cf. 5:7), "for the Jews had already agreed that."
BD120(2)   The compound adjective ἀποσυνάγωγος means "expelled from the synagogue."

25   R892   The present participle ὤν is used to refer to an action which is antecedent to that of the main verb (similar to an imperfect), "I was blind."
M154   Εἰ is used here to give a tentative and cautious tone, "whether he is a sinner or not, I do not know."

27   T78   Generally θέλω is followed by an aorist infinitive (with the meaning "to hear the same thing endlessly"--BD338[2]).

28   R707   A gesture may also have accompanied the remark of the Pharisees (σὺ μαθητὴς εἶ ἐκείνου;   the notion of contempt is evident, cf. 7:11).

30   R1190   In ἐν τούτῳ γάρ, the man uses γάρ with the fine scorn, with the meaning "why, just in this" (it is the equivalent of an interrogative οὐ γάρ ἐν τούτῳ --BD452[2]).
H469   The second καί in this verse has an adversative sense, "but" (cf. 8:52).

32   R497   The preposition ἐκ denotes the point of departure (ἐκ τοῦ αἰῶνος perhaps means "from time immemorial"--M73).

33   B249   The particle ἄν is omitted from the apodosis here, "if this man were not from God, he could do nothing" (cf. 1 Cor. 5:10).

36   R960   Ἵνα occurs in this verse, where a relative pronoun may have been used (cf. 5:7), "such that."
BD442(8)   When the apodosis is a question and καί occurs (as here), the conjunction has an unusual sense, "who then."

40   R611   The phrase οἱ μετ' αὐτοῦ with the participle here refers to Jesus' attendants or followers (companions, cf. Matt. 12:4).

JOHN 10

5   R418   The genitive generally follows the noun it modifies, unless it is emphatic, as in τῶν ἀλλοτρίων τὴν φωνήν.

R889 The future ἀκολουθήσουσιν has a durative sense, "they will not follow."

6   BD291(6) The pronoun ἐκεῖνοι occurs with a weakened sense, "they" (cf. 9:9).

7   R501 The genitive in θύρα τῶν προβάτων has an objective sense, "door to the sheep" (or subjective, "where the sheep enter?"--T212). [Ed. The genitive appears to be used as a subjective genitive, especially in view of Christ's further explanation in v. 9.]

8   R507 Ἤκουσαν has the sense of "hearken" with the genitive (often in John's Gospel).
     R622 The preposition πρό has a temporal sense, "before."

10   R1387 Περισσός is used as a positive here, "in abundance" (cf. 2 Cor. 9:1).
     T180 The generic use of the article occurs in ὁ κλέπτης with the meaning of "thieves."

11   R623 Ὑπέρ conveys the idea of "instead" in vv. 11 and 15 (cf. Rom. 5:6f.).

12   R1163 We may simply accent the fact that the encroachment of μή on οὐ with the participle (in the New Testament) gives all the greater emphasis to the examples of οὐ which remain (the occurrence of οὐ with the participle here is tentatively explained by Abbott (p. 545f.) as due either to μισθωτός -- καὶ ποιμήν coalescing (but, if so, why is ὤν thus intruded?) or to οὐ ποιμήν being a sort of title (cf. Rom. 9:25), but again the intrusion of ὤν is strange--M105; in καὶ οὐκ ὤν ποιμήν, μή would be more correct since it refers to no definite person; but καὶ μή (in close association) is not appreciated in Koine Greek--T285; οὐ is due to the emphasis on the negation--BD430[1]). [Ed. The negative οὐ is used with the participle to express emphatically that the hired man was certainly not the shepherd.]

13   M28 Μέλει followed by περί with the genitive means "it matters to someone concerning."

15   R870 Τίθημι is used as a futuristic present, "I will lay down" (indicating certainty).

17   R965 Note the correspondence between διὰ τοῦτο and ὅτι here, "for this reason . . . because."

21   T26 The plural τυφλῶν simply means "blind man." [Ed. The Jews apparently used the plural noun in a general statement of Christ's crediibility ("the blind") rather than in a reference to the specific miracle in chapter 9.]

24   M209 Is τὴν ψυχὴν ἡμῶν αἴρες in this verse a semitism for "raise our hope?" There does not appear to be much evidence for "keep us in suspense," whereas the Hebrew equivalent can mean "set one's hopes on," and the Septuagint sometimes has ἐλπίζειν, etc., in such contexts (see C.K. Barrett, in location, who however, is inclined to follow Pallis in suggesting "trouble" or "annoy"). [Ed. This clause appears to have the meaning "keep us in suspense" in view of the following comment from the Jews and Christ's response in vv. 25ff.]

30   T37 There is a certain degree of emphasis in the use of ἐγώ here.

32 R880 The present verb λιθάζετε has an inchoative sense referring to an act just beginning (attempted action, "try to stone"--B11; cf. M8; "do you want to stone me"--T63).

35 M35 The accusative θεούς is used predicatively, "he called them gods."

36 R425 A somewhat tangled sentence occurs in this verse because the antecedent of ὅν is not expressed. Here λέγετε is the principal verb, the apodosis of the condition, and has two objects (the relative clause and the ὅτι clause) with a causal clause added (notice the recitative ὅτι in λέγετε ὅτι βλασφημεῖς, instead of βλασφημεῖν which would connect up much better with the preceding ὅν--BD470[1]), "do you say of him whom . . . 'you blaspheme' . . . ?"

37 T284 When εἰ has the meaning "if, as you hope," οὐ is always the negative used in the New Testament (as here).

38 R850 John employs the two forms γνῶτε and γινώσκητε to distinguish between the beginning of knowing and the development of it.

39 R885 Ἐζήτουν is used as an inchoative imperfect, referring to an action begun but interrupted, "they tried."

40 BD332(1) The aorist verb ἔμεινεν occurs here with the meaning "he settled down there (therefore somewhat ingressive) without returning (for the time being) to Judea" (cf. 7:9).

JOHN 11

2 B142 The aorist participle ἡ ἀλείψασα used attributively as the equivalent of a relative clause refers to an action subsequent (after) to that of the principal verb, although antecedent (before) to the time of writing ("Mary who was to anoint" unless a previous anointing is referred to, viz., Luke 7:38, in which case Mary of Bethany is identified with the sinful woman from the street. The aorist participle is usually explained however of time past in relation not to the events described but to the time of writing--T80; the use of the aorist participle ἀλείψασα is understandable: "Mary was ("is" would be more exact) the one who is known (cf. Matt. 26:13) to have anointed him," for that, which in the past, was future ("who later [12:1ff.] anointed, who was to anoint"), the future tense was not common in Greek, so the author makes his parenthetical statement from his own point of time--BD339[1]).

9 B240 In this verse, "if a man walk in the day, he stumbleth not," the supposition refers to any instance of walking in the day, and is general, "the "if" is similar to "since."

11 R895 The perfect verb κεκοίμηται portrays a present state, "has fallen asleep, and is asleep."

14 BD459(2) John uses τότε οὖν as a connective particle to introduce a subsequent event, meaning "thereupon," not "at that time."

18 BD161(1) The occasional replacement of the accusative by ἀπό and a genitive in response to the question "how far away" is actually good Greek.

20 R521 Ἐν τῷ οἴκῳ simply means "at home."

27 R891 The present participle ὁ ἐρχόμενος has a futuristic sense (indicating a degree of certainty).

28 R881 The present tense in ὁ διδάσκαλος πάρεστιν has a perfective usage, meaning "the Teacher is come" (cf. T72).
    T156 The second occurrence of εἰποῦσα in this verse is not pleonastic, but it is equivalent to "with the words."

32 R722 Ὅπου in this verse is equivalent to ἐκεῖσε ὅπου, "there, where."

35 R834 Ἐδάκρυσεν is used as an ingressive aorist, "Jesus began to weep."

36 T68 In vv. 36f., there is no perceptible difference between ἔλεγον οὖν οἱ Ἰουδαῖοι and τινὲς δὲ ἐξ αὐτῶν εἶπαν ("they began to say"); each introduces speech in the same way, and indeed scribes have standardized the εἶπαν to ἔλεγον. The general practice was to use λέγων not εἰπών, after another verb of saying.

37 R920 Ἐδύνατο refers to the present time.
    B206 Ἵνα μή introduces an object clause here, "could he not have kept?"

39 R856 Note the impressive aorists ἄρατε . . . λύσατε . . . ἄφετε in vv. 39 and 44. The aorist is more authoritative and solemn than the present would have been. The aorist here accords with the consciousness of Jesus (v. 41, ἤκουσας).

44 R910 The intensive perfect participle τεθνηκώς refers to an action which is antecedent to that of the principal verb ("had been," equivalent to a pluperfect--B156), but δεδέμενος denotes coincident action in reference to the pricipal verb.

47 R880 The implication of the question in this verse is that nothing was being done, "what are we doing?" (the present indicative rarely is used in a deliberative sense in place of the future--BD366[4]).

48 R681 The position of ἡμῶν is emphatic in this verse (the pronoun occurs before the two nouns to eliminate repetition--T190). [Ed. The pronoun ἡμῶν is in distinct contrast to the noun Ῥωμαῖοι, although it may not be used to portray definite emphasis since the phenomenon that Turner suggests does occur occasionally in the New Testament; cf. Luke 12:35; Acts 21:11; 1 Thess. 1:3 and Rev. 2:19.]
    T63 The future verbs ἐλεύσονται and αἰτοῦσιν have a prophetic or oracular sense.
    H422 The first καί in this verse has a consecutive sense in parataxis (co-ordination), "as a result" (cf. 5:10).

49 T195 Εἷς τις means "a certain one."

50 R631 Ὑπέρ occurs with the notion of substitution "for" (cf. ἀντί, and Rom. 5:7f.).

R993 The parallel between ἵνα denoting content and ὅτι is evident in this verse, "that."

53 B210 Ἵνα denotes an object clause after a verb of striving in this verse (cf. B205; "they took counsel that," or "how").

56 M61 The idea of communication-with is predominant in the preposition μετά here (cf. 4:27).
MT191 Οὐ μή with the subjunctive ἔλθῃ seems to have obvious emphasis.

57 R986 The one example of ὅπως in John's writings occurs parallel to ἵνα in this verse, and may be used for the sake of variety, "that . . . in order that."

JOHN 12

1 M74 Evidently πρὸ ἓξ ἡμερῶν τοῦ πάσχα means "six days before the passover"; but what is the construction? Is ἓξ ἡμερῶν a genitive of time, leaving πρό to govern τοῦ πάσχα? And, if so, is the curious order a Latinism? (Moulton argues against this--MT100f.; cf. 2 Cor. 12:2; it is best to translate this phrase with "before six days of the passover"--T248; cf. BD213). [Ed. This phrase presents difficulty for translation because πρό occurs before ἓξ ἡμερῶν, rather than after it. Since this transposition of πρό occurs in Amos 1:1, Josephus' writings and in the papyri, it is not necessarily a Latinism. Consequently, Moule's rendering seems preferable.]

3 R598 Perhaps the notion of cause or occasion is conveyed by ἐκ τῆς ὀσμῆς ("because of the fragrance").
BD113(2) Πιστικός may well mean "genuine" and be derived from πιστός or πίστις ("fit to be trusted, genuine"--H379).

4 R1118 Note the use of μέλλων here to express intention (cf. 6:64 and Acts 18: 14).

6 M28 The verb μέλει used with περί with the genitive, meaning "it matters to someone concerning" (cf. 10:13).

7 MT175 It is possible that ἄφες αὐτὴν . . . ἵνα τηρήσῃ means "Let her keep it" (so practically the Revised Version text), as an auxiliary. Although the alternative "Let her alone; let her keep it" is favored by Mark 14:6 (it is hardly probable that ἄφες is just an auxiliary verb--R932).

9 R656 The unusual position of the attributive adjective, like ὁ ὄχλος πολύς, where the substantive and adjective form a composite idea, may be illustrated from the papyri (cf. Heb. 9:1; ὁ ὄχλος πολύς evidently means "the great crowd," although by the rules it ought to have meant "the crowd is [or "was"] great" --M107 [A, B and D omit ὁ; W adds ὁ to πολύς]; cf. T186 and v. 12).

10 B205 Ἵνα denotes an object clause after a verb of striving here (cf. 11:53).
T54 The middle verb has a reflexive sense, "took counsel with one another."

12 R762 The article in ὁ Ἰησοῦς is anaphoric, referring to previous reference (cf. v. 1).

16 R605 The preposition ἐπ᾽ αὐτῷ denotes the idea of "about."

17 R892 The present participle ὤν refers to an action which is antecedent to that
of the main verb ("the crowd that was with him"--B127; cf. 9:27).
M16 The aorist verbs here are used as pluperfects, "when he had called . . .
and raised."

18 R1103 The infinitive is used as the object of ἤκουσαν (the infinitive [instead
of ὅτι] occurs here because of the preceding ὅτι--BD388), "because they heard
that."

21 R923 The vocative with the present tense here is felt to be so strong that it
should be translated, "Sir, we would see Jesus."

23 B216 Ἵνα introduces a complementary limitation of the noun ὥρα (cf. T139; in
its usage here, ἵνα may be considered as a temporal particle--H470), "the hour
has come when."

26 R870 The present verb εἰμί is used with a futuristic sense, referring not merely
to prophecy, but to the certainty of expectation (cf. 4:35).

27 R895 The perfect verb τετάρακται refers to a present state (an intensive perfect, cf. 6:38), "now my soul is troubled."

30 T268 Διά with the accusative here denotes the idea of purpose (cf. 11:42), "for
you."

32 B62 Since the verb ἑλκύσω denotes effort, the future will naturally be considered conative if it is judged to be progressive, and resultative if it is taken
as aoristic. In the latter case the meaning will be, "I will by my attraction
bring all men to me." In the former case the words will mean, "I will exert on
all men an attractive influence" (which is preferable).

33 R740 Ποίῳ definitely has a qualitative force here, "by what kind."

34 R697 The pronoun οὗτος has the idea of reproach (cf. 6:42).
H423 Καί in this verse introduces an interrogative phrase, with the meaning
"and yet" (cf. 1:5).

35 M197 Καταλάβῃ unambiguously means "overtake, overcome" in this verse (cf. 1:5
and MT158).
BD455(3) Ἕως and ὡς are seldom confused in the New Testament, so in this verse
ἕως probably ought to be read "as long as," but in v. 36, ὡς is best, "now
while." [Ed. The weightiest manuscript support favors the occurrence of ὡς
in both verses. This adverb appears to have a similar meaning in both
instances, "while, as long as" (cf. 2:23).]

40 MT117 The aorist νοήσωσιν may be constative or ingressive, "realize" (cf. Eph.
3:4).

41 H469 Ὅτι is used as a temporal particle here (cf. 9:8). [Ed. It is very unusual for ὅτι to have a temporal sense such as "when" (similar to ὅτε) in the
New Testaemnt. But even if the temporal rendering is correct, it would still
have a causal notion. The causal ὅτι is preferable here.]

42 R1188 Μέντοι is a combination of two intensive particles (μέν and τοί), and
    is used with the meaning "however" (cf. 4:27).
    BD120(2) 'Αποσυνάγωγος actually means "expelled from the synagogue" (cf. 9:22).

48 R698 'Εκεῖνος is actually in apposition to ὁ λόγος, "the word which I have
    spoken will judge him."

49 R698 Αὐτός is in apposition to πατήρ, "the Father . . . has himself."

                                JOHN 13

1   R691 Τοὺς ἰδίους refers to "one's own people" (cf. 1:11).
    T266 Εἰς τέλος means "with a view to the end," or "fully" (cf. Luke 18:5; "he
    gave them the perfect love-token"--BD207[3]).

2   T139 Ἵνα is used to denote the content of "put into the heart."

4   T27 The plural ἱμάτια means "upper garment" (cf. 19:23 and Acts 18:6).

5   R757 The use of the article with νιπτῆρα indicates that the basis was the one
    there in the room.

6   R418 There may be some contrast expressed by σύ and μοῦ here.
    R880 The present verb νίπτεις has an inchoative sense, referring to an act just
    beginning ("are you trying to wash?"--T63).

9   R1162 Μή occurs with μόνον here, because it is dependent upon the implied imper-
    ative νίπτε (cf. B479), "don't wash my feet only."

11 B126 Τὸν παραδιδόντα αὐτόν probably means simply "his betrayer."

12 M16 The aorist verb ἔνιψεν is used as a pluperfect (cf. 12:17), "when he had
    washed."

17 R1019 In this verse the first and third class conditions are happily combined
    but with clear distinction. Jesus assumes the knowledge as a fact, but the
    performance is doubtful (the latter part is referring to the future--BD372[1a]).

18 TGr147f. Ἵνα here has an imperatival sense, with the meaning "however, let the
    scripture be fulfilled." It is not that Judas is excluded for a purpose, but
    that Judas has excluded himself (cf. M145 and John 9:3 and 15:25).

19 BD12(3) Ἀπ' ἄρτι is equivalent to ἀμήν, and means "definitely."

21 R675 Εἷς is equivalent to τις, "one of you."

22 T56 The middle form ἀπορούμενοι is active with an intransitive sense ("because
    they were uncertain"), but the active form also occurs in the New Testament
    (cf. Luke 24:4).

27 R664 The latter part of this verse may mean that Judas is to do this more quick-

ly than he would have done without the exposure (i.e., the notion of comparison is evident; the comparative adverb τάχιον is used for a positive, "quick-
ly--T30; it may be elative, "as quick as possible"--BD244[1]). [Ed. This
comparative is probably used as a positive, meaning "quickly," or "without
delay," since it has this notion occasionally in the New Testament; cf. 1 Tim.
3:14 and Heb. 13:23.]
R880 The present verb ποιεῖς has an inchoative sense, "what you want to do"
(cf. T63 and v. 6).

28   R626 Πρὸς τί expresses the notion of aim or end, meaning "for what purpose"
(cf. R739).

29   R595 The preposition εἰς expresses the notion of purpose, "for the feast."
T318 Ἐπεί has a purely causal sense here (cf. Rom. 3:6).

32   M119 The reflexive pronoun seems more natural than αὐτῷ (note the variant
reading), "in himself."

34   T225 The adjective καινήν has an adverbial sense, with the meaning "I give it
anew."

35   TGr121 The latter part of this verse should be translated, "if you have love
among (ἐν with the plural) one another," for the sphere in which the love is
exercised is Christ's redeemed community.

36   R857 Ἀκολουθῆσαι is apparently used as a constative aorist (i.e., referring
to an act as punctiliar which is not in itself confined to a particular incident).

JOHN 14

2   R869 The New Testament uses the present with the verbs ἔρχομαι and πορεύομαι in
a futuristic sense (as in vv. 2f., "I will go . . . I will come"), but not
with εἰμι (cf. BD323[3]).
T135 The simple infintive here expresses the notion of purpose, "to prepare."

3   T334 The third καί in this verse has the idea of purpose (cf. BD442[2]).

6   R429 John is rather fond of repetition with asyndeton (omission of the conjunction) in his report of Jesus' words, as here and in 15:13.
M112 It is difficult to build much on the presence of the article in this verse.
The definite article seems to be required (by the context) before ὁδός; but are
the others merely examples of the Greek usage by which an abstract noun often
has the article, or even mere accomodation to that first article? In the English equivalent "I am the Way, I am Truth, I am Life" (the articular ἀλήθεια
is personalized and is synonymous with Jesus himself--TGr8; cf. 8:44 and T178).
[Ed. It is best not to make too much of the article in this verse, but there
appears to be more definiteness expressed than that indicated by Moule's rendering.]

9   R879 The progressive present verb εἰμι refers to both past and present time
(cf. T62).

10 M104n.1 The Authorized Version and the Revised Version translations are no
    doubt intended to represent different texts (not different interpretations of
    the same text); The Authorized Version, "the Father that dwelleth in me, he
    doeth the works," is a translation of ὁ δὲ πατὴρ ὁ ἐν ἐμοὶ μένων, αὐτὸς ποιεῖ
    . . ., while the Revised Version, "the Father abiding in me does his works,"
    is a translation of ὁ δὲ πατὴρ ἐν ἐμοὶ μένων ποιεῖ . . . (the difference is
    made by the omission of the article, irrespective of the αὐτός). [Ed. The
    latter rendering is supported by the best manuscript support.]

11 R856 The present imperative πιστεύετε in this verse stresses the continuance
    of faith.
    R1016 Εἰ δὲ μή without a verb means "otherwise, but if not."

16 R613 In the compound noun παράκλητον, the preposition has the notion of "be-
    side."
    BD306(5) The pronoun in ἄλλον παράκλητον occurs where the idea of two is pre-
    sent, with the meaning "another, namely a counselor."
    H422 Καί has a consecutive sense in this verse (cf. 5:10), "and as a result."

17 TGr10 The association of the Truth with the Spirit in phrases such as τὸ
    πνεῦμα τῆς ἀληθείας probably assumes the close relationship of Christ with the
    Spirit and especially his promise to send the Holy Spirit to believers and by
    this Agency to guide them into the fulness of himself, the Truth. [Ed. Notice
    that Turner assumes that when John uses ἀληθεία with an article it generally
    refers to Christ; cf. 8:32.]

21 BD291(4) Ἐκεῖνος is weakened and indefinite here, and simply means "he."

22 R739 In τί . . . ὅτι here, τί still retains the meaning "why."
    R1001 Abbott (Johannine Grammar, p. 534) takes ὅτι as consecutive in this
    verse, "what has happened, so that" (cf. 2:18).

26 R708 Ἐκεῖνος seems to denote emphasis here.
    R795 The article occurs in τὸ πνεῦμα τὸ ἅγιον where the Holy Spirit is spoken
    of in distinction from the Father and the Son.

27 R777 In εἰρήνην τὴν ἐμήν, the substantive is indefinite and general, while
    the attribute makes a particular application (cf. BD270[3]), "peace, that is
    my peace."

29 BD442(15) Καὶ νῦν means "now then."

31 M144 Ἵνα has an imperatival sense here, thus ἵνα γνῷ ὁ κόσμος means "the world
    must learn" (cf. T95).

                              JOHN 15

2   M104 It is conceivable that πᾶν κλῆμα ἐν ἐμοὶ μὴ φέρον καρπόν means "any branch,
    if it does not bear," rather than "which does not bear," while πᾶν τὸ καρπὸν
    φέρον means "which bears"; but it is a questionable distinction (cf. 14:10; this
    distinction seems valid, however, John's method is often to have variety of voca-

bulary and syntax in close proximity--T157).

T182 There is a play on words in this verse (αἴρει . . . καθαίρει). The best
translation in English is: "Every branch that beareth not fruit, he removeth;
and every branch that beareth fruit, he reproveth." But this has nothing of
the brilliance of the Greek and in any case is not quite accurate.

BD101 Καθαίρω occurs seldom in the New Testament and means "to clean, clear
away" or "prune."

5 R1165 The compound negative occurs here with an intensifying "you can do nothing."

6 M181 The unexpressed subject in this verse is slightly ambiguous (the Authorized
Version has "men gather them," and the Revised Version has "they gather them").

T74 A proleptic aorist (ἐκβλήθη and ἐξηράνθη) looks like a future, taking place
after some actual or implied condition, "if a man will not abide in Christ he
will be cut off and withered" (the aorists may be merely gnomic, referring to
a well known truth--R847; cf. B43; these aorist verbs appear to be dramatically
suggesting immediacy, "he has forthwith been thrown out"--M12). [Ed. Christ
describes the Judgment as already present, as an attempt to emphasize that it is
inevitable. The tenses indicate that the individuals which did not remain in
Christ have already been cast out and are now being gathered and burned.]

8 R837 Ἐδοξάσθη seems to be used as a gnomic aorist (expressing a general truth).

M146 Ἵνα is used to denote content, with the meaning "(my Father is glorified)
in your bearing much fruit" (cf. R992; John is particularly fond of using ἵνα
in apposition with a preceding demonstrative pronoun, especially if the actual
meaning is theory rather than fact [as in this verse]--T139).

BD369(3) The future verb γενήσεσθε (the variant is γένησθε) expresses a further
consequence with a notion of independence, "and then you become."

11 R784 The prepositional phrase ἐν ὑμῖν is used with the verb ᾖ, not with ἡ χαρὰ
ἡ ἐμή, "my joy may be in you."

12 R992 Ἵνα ἀγαπᾶτε is in apposition with ἐντολή (cf. B213), "this is my commandment, that you love."

18 T32 The superlative πρῶτον ὑμῶν is used for the comparative, "before you" (cf.
MT79).

19 R1013f. The addition of ἄν to an indicative hypothesis produces much the same
effect as an italicized "if" or the phrase "in that case" added to an apodosis.
This is the definite use of ἄν, "in that case, the world would love."

T345 The causal ὅτι is almost always post-positive, but not in this verse (in
this verse the ὅτι clause precedes the main clause; cf. 8:45), "because you
are not of the world."

21 M69 Εἰς with the accusative here seems to be equivalent to a simple dative (εἰς
occurs here where one expects ἐν--T256; cf. Matt. 26:10). [Ed. Moule's suggestion appears to be preferable, since the prepositional phrase easily fits
as the indirect object of the verb ποιήσουσιν (the Textus Receptus, A, D² and
N have ὑμῖν).]

24 BD444(3) The second καί in this verse means "and yet," whereas καὶ ἐμὲ καὶ τὸν
πατέρα μου sharpens the distinction between the two persons (they appear to

them to be altogether different persons), "both me and my father."

25 M145 Ἵνα may be taken in an imperatival sense, "the word . . . had to be fulfilled" (in this verse, Jesus was simply provoked to a sad sigh of resignation,
   introduced by an imperatival ἵνα, "Let the Torah be fulfilled" [cf. 13:18]--
   TGr147f).

27 R1185 There is continuation, not opposition expressed in the use of καὶ . . .
   δέ here, where δέ means "and" and καί means "also."
   MT119 Ἔστε occurs with a perfective sense, "you have been with me from the
   beginning."

                                    JOHN 16

2 R859 The articular aorist participle portrays a simple punctiliar action in a
   timeless manner ("every slayer"--B148).
   R998 In its occurrence here, ἵνα is almost temporal (it introduces a temporal
   clause, "when"--T321).
   R1186 Ἀλλ' ἔρχεται ὥρα means "yea, the hour comes" (ἀλλά introduces an additional point in an emphatic way--BD448[6]; cf. T330).
   BD120(2) The compound adjective ἀποσυνάγωγος means "expelled from the synagogue."

3 R834 The aorist tense in οὐκ ἔγνωσαν may have an ingressive sense, with the
   meaning "they did not recognize" (cf. T71 and 1:10).
   B232 The causal clause in this verse is subordinate, thus ταῦτα refers to an
   assertion already made, and the intent of the sentence is to state why they
   will do these things (cf. the comment on Luke 11:32).
   BD448(3) Ἀλλά appears to belong in v. 3, not v. 4. [Ed. Actually, this conjunction appears to have a valid sense in the position in which it occurs in
   the best manuscripts. Ἀλλά breaks off the enumeration of vv. 2f., and re-in-
   troduces the thought of v. 1.]

5 H469 Καί has an adversative sense here, "but."

7 B65 The future verbs πέμψω (in v. 7), ὁδηγήσει, λαλήσει and ἀναγγελεῖ (in v.
   13) refer to a promise and are imperatival or solemnly predictive, "I shall,"
   "he shall."

8 B435 The adverbial participle here is equivalent to a temporal clause, "and he,
   when he is come, will convict the world" (it is modal-temporal with no stress
   on the temporal relationship--T154).

9 M147 It is a fine point whether the ὅτι clauses in vv. 9-11 mean "in that"
   (i.e., they define sin, the δικαιοσύνη, and the judgment) or are consequential
   (i.e., they indicate that the sin, etc., are the result of the conditions in the
   ὅτι clause; this particle has the causal meaning--R964). [Ed. In this context, ὅτι apparently has the more usual causal sense, and is explanatory of
   the reason for each specific area of conviction.]

13 R709 In his use of ἐκεῖνος, John insists on the personality of the Holy Spirit,
   when the grammatical gender so easily called for the neuter form ἐκεῖνο.

T151 Τὰ ἐρχόμενα means "the future."

20 R871 The future verbs λυπηθήσεσθε and γενήσεται appear to have an ingressive
sense, "will begin to . . . "
T253 Εἰς with the accusative occurs in place of a predicative nominative (semitic, with the meaning "as" or "for"--R458).

23 R708 Ἐν ἐκείνῃ τῇ ἡμέρᾳ refers to the Last Day.

24 R907 In the periphrastic construction ᾖ πεπληρωμένη, the consumation is emphasized.
B52 The aorist verb ᾐτήσατε has a sense similar to a perfect, "you have asked
nothing."

27 R614 The preposition παρά has the meaning "from" (cf. 1:18).
M121 Αὐτός is emphatic here, meaning "for the Father himself" (cf. T41).

30 R589 The preposition in ἐν τούτῳ gives the occasion of the action of the main
verb (cf. Acts 7:29; causal--T253 and H463; "for that reason"--BD219[2]).

32 H470 Ἵνα appears to be used as a temporal particle, "when" (cf. 12:23).

JOHN 17

2 R500 Ἐξουσίαν πάσης σαρκός means "authority over all flesh."
R963 Καθώς appears to have the force of a causal particle (cf. ὡς in 19:33).
T21 The neuter adjective πᾶν is used to refer to people because the emphasis
is less on the individual than on some outstanding general quality (the men are
first considered under σάρξ, then under πᾶν, and finally are designated by
αὐτοῖς--BD138[1]).

3 MT206 The sentence "and this is eternal life, that they should know thee . . ."
exhibits a form which under other circumstances would make a purpose clause.
Are we to insist on recognizing the ghost of a purpose clause here? Westcott
(in location) says that ἵνα here expresses an aim, an end, and not only a fact.
The ἵνα clause, then, as compared with (τὸ) γινώσκειν, adds the idea of effort
or aim at acquiring knowledge of God (the ἵνα clause is merely in apposition
with αὕτη, and consequently not a purpose clause, cf. 6:40 and Luke 1:43--R992).
[Ed. John is especially fond of using ἵνα in apposition with a demonstrative
pronoun (cf. 6:29, 39; 1 John 3:11, 23 and 4:21). In view of this tendency,
ἵνα apparently has an appositional usage in 17:3.]

4 R418 Sometimes the words in contrast are brought sharply together, as ἐγώ σέ
in v. 4 and με σύ in v. 5.
R843 The aorist verb ἐδόξασα points backward, "I did glorify you."

5 M44 The dative τῇ δόξῃ has an instrumental sense, "glorify me . . . with the
glory" (cf. v. 17, ἐν τῇ ἀληθείᾳ).

6 M120 The possessive dative in σοὶ ἦσαν is ambiguous. [Ed. The context indicates
that σοῦ is a possessive dative of the singular personal pronoun, "they are
yours.]

11 H469 The initial καί in this verse has an adversative sense, "but" (cf. 1:10).

12 T208 'Απωλείας is used as an adjectival genitive with ὁ υἱός (portraying a characteristic of a person; cf. Acts 3:25).

15 R598 The tense of the verb in τηρήσης . . . ἐκ τοῦ πονηροῦ may imply that the evil one once had power over them (cf. Jesus' prayer for Peter).

17 TGr9 It must not be presumed that there are two distinct meanings of the word ἀλήθεια in this verse, which means "sanctify them in the Truth; thy Logos is the Truth." It is an instance of the predicate nominative occurring before the verb ἔστιν and losing its definite article in consequence (cf. 8:32).

19 R908 In the periphrastic construction ὦσιν . . . ἡγιασμένοι, the consummation is emphasized (cf. 16:24), "that they may be sanctified."

20 T87 The present participle here has a futuristic sense (describing a common characteristic--BD339[2b]), "those who will believe."

23 BD205 Εἰς denotes purpose-result ("perfected into one"--MT234).

24 T21 In this verse the gift is depicted first in its unity (ὅ; i.e., the neuter singular pronoun is used to refer to people), then individually (κἀκεῖνοι). MT179 θέλω ἵνα nearly coalesces in this verse (a sort of quasi-imperative usage, cf. Mark 6:25), "I desire that."

25 M167 Καὶ ὁ κόσμος . . . καὶ οὗτοι is interpreted by E. A. Abbott (Johannine Grammar, 2164) as meaning "both the world . . . and these . . ." but the first καί does not seem so easily explicable (it should be translated "both the world . . . and these," cf. 6:36--T335). [Ed. the difficulty in translating the conjunction here arises from the antithesis that is portrayed by the clauses. In the New Testament, καί . . . καί may be used to introduce a contrast with the meaning "although . . . yet," which seems preferable here; cf. John 6:36 and Acts 23:3.]
MT113 The aorist verb ἔγνων has a constative sense, gathering into one perspective all the successive moments of γινώσκωσιν σέ in v. 3.

JOHN 18

1 R680 The pronoun αὐτός means "he himself" (cf. 2:12).

2 R859 The articular aorist participle ὁ παραδιδούς ("the betrayer") refers to an act which is past with reference to the time of writing, although future with reference to the action of the principal verb.

3 R1127 In this verse, the participle λαβών is used in practically the same sense as μετά in Matt. 26:27 (of manner, "with a detachment"--T154).

5 R888 The pluperfect εἱστήκει is used as an imperfect (the perfect of this verb has the sense of a present), "was standing."

11   MT189   In a question which amounts to a positive assertion, an emphatic negative
     seems wholly out of place (οὐ negates the questions, expecting a positive answer
     but μή negates the verb).

13   T235   The temporal genitive τοῦ ἐνιαυτοῦ ἐκείνου simply means "that year."

16   M54   Πρός with the dative here implies position, "at."

18   R909   The perfect participle ἑστώς represents a state, "standing," whereas
     πεποιηκότες represents a completed act, "having made."

20   R589   The preposition in ἐν κρυπτῷ expresses the notion of manner, "secretly."
     MT236   Ἐν συναγωγῇ simply means "in church" (cf. 6:59).

22   R1116   The perfect participle παρεστηκώς has lost the notion of completion but
     maintains the linear idea alone in the present sense, "standing."

24   B48   The aorist verb ἀπέστειλεν does not express antecedence (i.e., similar to
     a pluperfect) because of the following reasons: the aorist is the only tense
     that can be used if an event is thought of simply as an event, the presence of
     οὖν, which is, in John's writings especially, generally continuative, and there
     is an absence of any intimation in the context that the events are related out
     of their chronological order. The resultant rendering is "therefore Annas sent
     him."

28   R1413   When a ἵνα clause is continued by ἀλλά (meaning "but on the contrary"),
     ἵνα is not repeated (cf. 3:16).
     B14   Ἄγουσιν is used as an historical present, referring to a past event with
     vivid description (cf. Luke 8:49), "they led."

30   M18   In this verse, the question arises whether κακὸν ποιῶν is not virtually a
     noun, "an evildoer."
     M122   The pronoun οὗτος refers to an unemphatic "he," with the resultant meaning
     "if he had not been a criminal."
     T92   The conditional sentence in vv. 30 and 36 has the meaning "if he were not
     . . . we would not have."

32   R740   Ποίῳ has a qualitative force in this verse, "by what kind of death."

33   T37   The personal pronoun σύ does not have much emphasis here.

37   M165   If the particle must be taken as οὐκοῦν (inferential), it seems preferable
     to translate the statement as an exclamation rather than a question: "Then thou
     art a king!" Westcott's paraphrase seems to make the best sense in the context,
     which seems to call for an inference from Christ's mention of his kingdom:
     "so you are a king, are you?"
     T37   The pronoun σύ is emphatic here with the sense, "you have said it, not I"
     (cf. BD277[2]).
     BD441[3]   Ὅτι does not mean "that," but "because."

39   B213   Ἵνα is used in apposition to the noun συνήθεια (cf. 15:12), "a custom that."

40   R1173   Notice the contrast indicated here by μή . . . ἀλλά (instead of the usual
     οὐ . . . ἀλλά).

JOHN 19

1 BD459(2) John uses τότε οὖν as a connective particle to introduce a subsequent
   event, meaning "thereupon," not "at that time" (cf. 11:14).

3 R884 Ἐδίδοσαν is used as an interative imperfect, "they repeatedly struck him."
   TGr76 The articular construction ὁ βασιλεύς is used to express scorn in the context here, "This king of the Jews!" ("Hail, you King!" cf. Acts 26:7--MT70).

6 R1200 Repetition occurs to indicate emphasis here (σταύρωσον).
   T182 The article οἱ is repeated with the two groups of people, because the
   chief priests and officers are not a unified whole like the chief priests,
   elders and scribes of Matt. 16:21 (cf. BD276[2]).

11 MT148 The aorist verb ἐδόθη (instead of ἦν δεδομένον) would have only pictured
   the original gift and not the presence of it with Pilate at the moment.

12 R885 Ἐζήτει is used as a conative imperfect (i.e., an action begun but interrupted).
   M72f. Ἐκ τούτου has a causal sense "because of this" (cf. 6:66).

14 R501 Ἡ παρασκευὴ τοῦ πάσχα probably means "the day before Sabbath" (Friday).

18 R775 Μέσον τὸν Ἰησοῦν means "Jesus in the midst."

19 T88 No real difference can be detected between ἦν γεγραμμένον here and ἐπεγέ-
   γραπτο in Acts 17:23.

21 R707 The pronoun ἐκεῖνος carries the notion of contempt here (cf. 9:28; "this
   fellow"--T46).
   T76 The present prohibition μὴ γράφε means "stop writing" (i.e., "alter what
   you have written").

23 R1184 Δέ introduces an explanatory parenthesis here, "now the coat . . ."

24 M63 Περί is used of casting lots here, "for it."
   M162 Μὲν οὖν is purely resumptive or transitional, "so" (cf. T337).

25 R501 In the construction ἡ τοῦ κλωπᾶ it is the wife (γυνή) that is understood
   from the feminine article.
   R904 The pluperfect εἰστήκεισαν is used as an imperfect (cf. 18:5), "standing."
   M52 The preposition παρά has a local sense, "beside the cross."

26 TGr40 The absence of ὦ with a vocative reduces the emotion. Thus on the cross,
   where emotion was likely to be in evidence, it was in a matter-of-fact manner
   that Jesus commended his mother to the care of John. Christ had in mind the
   provision of an elder son for a mother's needs and simply states, "woman, behold
   thy son."
   T231 Ἴδε occurs with the nominative as the direct object, because it has become
   a stereotyped particle of exclamation (cf. 1:29).

27 R691 Τὰ ἴδια has the sense of "one's home."

28 R425 The final clause with ἵνα in this verse somewhat interrupts the flow of
the sentence (the purpose clause is shifted forward—BD478; possibly indicating
a degree of emphasis).

30 M16 The aorist verb ἔλαβεν has a sense equivalent to an English past perfect,
"when therefore Jesus had recieved the vinegar, he said, 'It is finished.'"

33 R909 Generally when the perfect participle refers to action which is coincident with that of the principal verb, it has an intensive sense, as in this
verse, "they saw that he was already dead."
R963 Ὡς has almost the force of a causal particle (cf. 17:2).

35 TGr138 The pronoun ἐκεῖνος is merely anaphoric here, meaning "he." It definitely does not introduce a new subject. Thus it is best to understand ἐκεῖνος as
referring neither to a mysterious author, nor to God, nor to Jesus. It more
naturally refers to the eye-witness previously mentioned who is the author as
well. "An eye-witness," he says, "has written this record. A true record it
is; the eye-witness can vouch for its truth" (cf. T46).

39 R495 The temporal genitive refers to the time within which (kind of time),
thus νυκτός means "by night" (cf. M56).
R1127 The participle φέρων is used with the notion of manner, "came bringing."

40 R1076 The infinitive ἐνταφιάζειν complements the noun ἔθος, "as the custom of
the Jews is to prepare for burial."

JOHN 20

1 R868 The present verbs ἔρχεται, βλέπει, τρέχει, and ἔρχεται in vv. 1f. all
seem to indicate the excitement of Mary.
T187 It seems to be a result of semitic influence to use μιᾷ for "first" (cf.
H439).

2 R1202 The indefinite subject of Ἦραν apparently means "people took away."

3 R838 With the two tenses in close proximity here, the aorist (ἐξῆλθεν) lifts
the curtain and the imperfect continues the play.

7 R593 In this verse, εἰς has a local sense similar to ἐν, "in" (cf. M68).
R648 This occurrence of χωρίς is the only time that it occurs as an adverb in
the New Testament, with the meaning "by itself."

8 BD459(2) In this verse, τότε οὖν has the sense of "now," in contrast to the
preceding time (cf. 11:14).

11 R624 The preposition πρός has a locative sense in vv. 11f., meaning "near" or
"facing" ("at"—M54).

12 R868 The present verb θεωρεῖ shows the surprise of Mary at seeing the angels,
as in v. 14, the present tense is used when she sees Jesus (cf. v. 1f.).

R906 "Οπου ἔκειτο τὸ σῶμα means "where the body had lain" or "had been placed."

14 R133 The second καί in this verse has the sense of "and yet" or "but."
T167 The risen Christ is referred to by the articular phrase τὸν ᾽Ιησοῦν on his first resurrection appearance.

15 R1009 Εἰ is used with the aorist indicative here because Mary assumes this as a fact, "since."
BD282(3) The masculine pronoun αὐτόν is used for the neuter antecedent σῶμα (Christ as a person was in mind).

17 R853 In the present prohibition μή μου ἅπτου, Jesus indicates that Mary must cease clinging to him ("stop touching me"--T76).
R870 In the futuristic present ἀναβαίνω, it is not merely prophecy, but certainty of expectation that is indicated (cf. BD323[3]).

18 R438 In this verse, καὶ ταῦτα εἶπεν αὐτῇ does not fit in exactly after ὅτι ἑώρακα τὸν κύριον. The added clause is the comment of John, not of Mary.

19 M68 In vv. 19 and 26, εἰς has a local sense, "he came and stood among them" (cf BD205).
T187 Μιᾷ is used with the meaning "first" (cf. 20:1).

20 R1128 The participle ἰδόντες occurs with a causal sense here (the participle may well mean "when they saw the Lord"--BD415). [Ed. Blass's rendering portrays a causal sense also, indicating the reason for their rejoicing.]

21 R429 The use of κἀγώ in the apodosis here accents the logical connection of thought (cf. 7:10), "even so I."

23 M152 There is a latent conditional sense in the indefinite particle ἄν. Thus there are two equally accurate renderings, "whosesoever sins ye forgive" (Revised Version) and "if you remit the sins of any" (Moffatt). [Ed. The indefinite aspect referred to by this particle appears to be the number of people that will be beneficiaries of the ministry of the disciples rather than whether or not they decide to use the power Christ offers to them.]

25 M15 The perfect verb ἑωράκαμεν appears to contemplate the result "We have seen the Lord."

28 R462 When Thomas said ὁ κύριός μου καὶ ὁ θεός μου (nominative used as vocatives), he gave Christ full acceptance of his deity and of the fact of his resurrection (strangely enough, Winer, p. 183, calls this exclamation, rather than address, apparently to avoid the conclusion that Thomas was satisfied as to the deity of Jesus by his appearance to him after the resurrection--R466).
M116 It should be noted that a substantive in the nominative case used in a vocative sense and followed by a possessive could not be anarthrous; the article before θεός may, therefore, not be significant.

29 H469 In this verse, καί occurs in contrast, meaning "but" (cf. 1:10).

30 T337 In this verse, μὲν οὖν has the classical usage of modifying a previous statement by introducing a new one: "nay rather" (cf. M162).

JOHN 21

1   R603 'Επί has the idea of vicinity, thus ἐπι τῆς θαλάσσης seems to mean "on
the sea-shore," and so "by the sea."

3   R882 'Υπάγω and ἐρχόμεθα are used as futuristic present verbs, "I will go . . .
we will come."

5   R155 The diminutive παιδία carries the notion of contempt ("lads"--MT170).

6   R408 Δεξιά is an idiomatic plural, "the right side."
R580 'Από has a causal sense here (cf. H461).

7   R810 The middle verb διεζώσατο means "he girded round himself."

8   R499 The genitive in τὸ δίκτυον τῶν ἰχθύων merely denotes the "net full of fish."
R521 Τῷ πλοιαρίῳ is used as a locative here (or instrumental), "they came in"
or "by boat."
BD161(1) The prepositional phrase with ἀπό denotes how far away (cf. 11:18).

9   BD111(3) John uses ὀψάριον to refer to fish as food (cf. 6:9).

11 R1129 The participle ὄντων has a concessive sense, "although."
H469 The second καί in this verse has an adversative sense. [Ed. Actually,
a concessive notion fits the context more readily. The adversative and concessive ideas occasionally overlap.]

12 R1128 The participle εἰδότες is used with a causal idea.

14 R702 Τοῦτο ἤδη τρίτον simply means "this already a third time" or more commonly "this is now the third time that."

15 T216 Πλέον τούτων may mean "more than these" or "more than these do" (this
phrase is equivalent to ἡ τούτους--BD185[1]). [Ed. If "more than these do"
would have been the desired translation, the pronoun σύ would have been included. The comparison is between μέ and τούτων, with the meaning "more than
these."]

17 R1028 It is not certain whether the first ὅτι in this verse is recitative or
causal. [Ed. Ὅτι appears to be causal since the following clause presents
the reason for Peter's grief.]

18 R969 The notion of repetition is predominant in the imperfect tense of ἤθελες.

21 R736 In the ellipsis here, γενήσεται has been omitted ("what will become of
him," τί is used as the predicate nominative--BD299[2]).

22 B328 The exact meaning of ἕως ἔρχομαι is probably "while I am coming," the
coming being conceived of as in progress from the time of speaking ("until
I come back"--M133; cf. T111 and Luke 19:13). [Ed. In this construction, the
present appears to have a futuristic sense, with the meaning "until I come back"

(cf. 1 Tim. 4:13 and John's tendency to use the futuristic present when recording the words of Christ).]

T37 The pronoun σύ is emphatic here (cf. 18:37).

BD299(3) The verb ἐστιν has been omitted from the phrase τί πρὸς σέ, meaning "what is that to you."

BD373(1) The conditional clause here (ἐάν with the indicative) could conceivably be interpreted "if as is to be expected" (according to Koine Greek, but it is the only possible interpretation according to Attic Greek), but the author includes v. 23 to safeguard against this interpretation.

23 R593 The preposition εἰς has the sense of "among" (cf. Eph. 1:15).

R870 Ἀποθνήσκει is used as a futuristic present, referring to the certainty of expectation (cf. 20:17).

T45 The demonstrative pronouns οὗτος and ἐκεῖνος are not used so much for contrast here as for variety.

24 R416 In this verse, there seems to be the comment of a brother (or several) on the Gospel of John which he has read and approved (the subject of οἴδαμεν is probably in contrast to John, who uses οἴμαι in the following verse to refer to himself--R406).

25 R1205 Notice the hyperbole in the last segment of this verse.

BD305 Καθ' ἕν occurs with the original meaning "in detail."

Acts

1 R663 Luke does not use πρότερος in his writings, so that πρῶτον in this instance
refers to the first of two (not three, cf. MT79; the meaning of πρῶτον is ambiguous: either Luke is guilty of a popular Hellenistic mannerism or he intended
to write three volumes--T32). [Ed. Since Luke never used the comparative of
this adjective and in Hellenistic Greek the superlative is often used for the
comparative, he probably never intended to write three volumes.]
R1193 There seems to be some vehemence or urgency in the use of ὦ here.
M181 The verb ἤρξατο has a sense similar to "from the beginning" (cf. T227).

2 M57 Διὰ πνεύματος ἁγίου perhaps means "by means of the Holy Spirit," or "in contact with the Holy Spirit" (the dividing line between accompaniment and instrumentality is thin; cf. 21:4).

3 M56 Διά with the genitive is used in an expression of time here. Δι' ἡμερῶν
τεσσεράκοντα ὀπτανόμενος is often taken (following Chrysostom) to mean "appearing at intervals during forty days" (cf. T267), but the notion "at intervals"
is derived not from the words but from independent knowledge of the traditions.

4 R618 Notice the idea of "beyond" in the compound verb περιμένω.

5 R389 The dative ὕδατι may have a locative or instrumental sense with βαπτίζω
(instrumental--T240, "baptize with"--BD195; cf. v. 2).
R418 In this verse, the verb comes between the substantive and adjective (ἐν πνεύματι βαπτισθήσεσθε ἁγίῳ) to give unity to the clause.
M60f. It is debated whether οὐ μετὰ πολλὰς ταύτας ἡμέρας is a Latinism, in
which case μετά is used in an absolute, adverbial sense; and if so, whether
it is a "vulgar" Latinism, or (since it is used with a characteristically Lucan
litotes or deliberate understatement -- the only instance in the earlier chap-
ters of Acts) something more deliberate; or, alternatively, is it an Aramaism?
(in οὐ μετὰ πολλὰς ταύτας ἡμέρας, the negative reverses the meaning of πολλάς:
thus the meaning is "after these few days"--T193). [Ed. A characteristic of
Luke's writing is the use of οὐ with an adjective or adverb (cf. Luke 7:6; 15:13;
Acts 20:12; 27:14 and 27), which emphasizes the opposite idea of that portrayed
by the adjective or adverb. In this verse, Luke uses this expression to
dramatize the shortness of time. Luke may have acquired this characteristic
through Aramaic influence.]

6 R916 Εἰ is used to introduce a direct question (consequently, this particle is
not to be translated; cf. Luke 13:23).
R1151 No contrast is intended in the occurrence of οἱ μὲν οὖν here (it may mean
either "now they who had come together" or "now they, when they had come together"--BD251). [Ed. Μὲν οὖν is a formula which frequently occurs in Acts
to introduce a new section of the narrative, meaning "so then." It consistently occurs in a post-positive position; consequently, the word that occurs be-

fore this formula (cf. 8:4, 25; 9:31; 12:53 and 16:5). So in this verse, it is preferable to take the article and participle together, supporting Blass's former suggestion.]

7   M38   Οὐχ ὑμῶν ἐστιν γνῶναι means "it is not for you to know" (the possessive phrase οὐχ ὑμῶν is equivalent to οὐχ ὑμέτερον, "it is not your concern"--BD162 [7]).

8   R787   The two provinces, Ἰουδαίᾳ and Σαμαρείᾳ, are distinct but adjacent (thus the article is not repeated).

10   R904   The pluperfect verb παρειστήκεισαν has the sense of a virtual imperfect (cf. Luke 11:22), "were standing."
      T335   In the καὶ ἰδού construction, at least the καί, if not the ἰδού, is often pleonastic (redundant), as here, with the meaning "behold."

11   M132   Ὂν τρόπον represents a compound adverbial phrase such as ἐκεῖνον τρόπον ὅν, meaning "in that manner in which."

13   R501   The expression Ἰούδας Ἰακώβου probably refers to the brother of Jude, in view of Jude 1, rather than his son (cf. Luke 6:16).

14   R623   Πρός has a perfective idea in the compound verb here, "adhere to."

15   H473   In the New Testament, ἐπὶ τὸ αὐτό has a technical meaning, signifying the union of the Christian body (cf. 2:1 and 47; it has the meaning "all together" --R602).

16   B142   The aorist participles γενόμενου and συλλαβοῦσιν refer to an action which is subsequent to that of the principal verb, although antecedent to the time of speaking. Thus the latter section of this verse should be translated, "which the Holy Spirit spake before by the mouth of David concerning Judas who became guide to them that took Jesus."
      M57   Διά with the genitive means "by means of."

18   M162   Μὲν οὖν has a purely resumptive or transitional sense, "now."
      H440   Τῆς ἀδικίας is an objective genitive (the wages caused the wickedness).

19   T191   Ἰδίᾳ occurs here with the classical meaning "peculiar" or "private."

21   M13n.2   The aorist tense in συνελθόντων, εἰσῆλθεν and ἐξῆλθεν refers to linear action (contrast 9:28; cf. T71; a summary aorist).
      M94f.   For the phrase ἐν παντὶ χρόνῳ, the context strongly suggests the meaning "during the whole time" (generally the noun is articular for this meaning), not "on every occasion."

24   BD390(3)   The infinitive λαβεῖν has the notion of purpose here.

25   R692   There is definite emphasis in the use of ἴδιον here (cf. MT90), "his own place."
      BD442(16)   The co-ordination of two ideas, one of which is dependent on the other, serves in the New Testament to avoid a series of dependent genitives, "this ministry of apostleship."

ACTS 2

1   T145 'Ἐν τῷ with the infinitive here has a causal sense, explaining why they
      gathered together.
      MT233 Blass puts a full stop at the end of this verse. But we may translate
      without the stop; "It came to pass during those days of fulfilment of the day
      of Pentecost, while they were all gathered together, that lo! there was . . ."
      H473 'Ἐπὶ τὸ αὐτό signifies the union of the Christian body (cf. 1:15).

2   R966 Ὥσπερ with the participle is used to portray the astonishment of the
      people (it expresses comparison--T158). [Ed. The latter suggestion is more
      probable, since ὥσπερ has the meaning "just as."]
      R1105 The anarthrous participle φερομένης is used as an attributive. [Ed. It
      may be more accurately considered as a predicative participle, denoting the
      manner in which the sound entered the room.]

4   R748 In this context, ἑτέραις has the sense of "different." [Ed. This seems
      to be implied by the description of the tongues in the following verses.]
      TGr18 Πνεῦμα ἁγίου is considered as a proper name and is anarthrous in the
      first mention of it, but is articular in the following references (vv. 4, 33,
      38, etc.)

6   T161 If this pointless variation (i.e., both the accusative and the genitive
      with a participle and the verb ἀκούω) can occur in a writer like Luke, the
      classical distinction between accusative and genitive has broken down in the
      New Testament (cf. 9:9).

7   M168 Οὐχ ἰδού may not be a semitism, but a koine idiom replacing the classical
      ἆρ' οὐ (introducing a direct question), "are not . . . ?"

8   MT88 'Ιδίᾳ . . . ἡμῶν means "our own."

9   R788 In vv. 9f., note τήν with Μεσοποταμίαν, which stands alone, while Πόντον
      καὶ τὴν 'Ασίαν also occurs, probably because the province of Asia (not Asia
      Minor as a whole) is meant..

12 R747 The idiom ἄλλος πρὸς ἄλλον is almost reciprocal like ἀλλήλων (equivalent
      to πρὸς ἀλλήλους--B287), "to one another."
      BD386(1) Τί θέλει τοῦτο εἶναι occurs as a direct question (but S and E have the
      optative θέλοι, as an indirect question, which after λέγοντες is hardly permis-
      sible), "what does this mean?"

13 R903 The periphrastic perfect construction μεμεστωμένοι εἰσίν expresses an in-
      tensive notion (equivalent to the present tense; of existing state, cf. B84),
      "they are filled."
      R1127 The participle διαχλευάζοντες is used to express the notion of manner,
      "but others mocking said" (cf. B444).

14 BD480(1) Λοιποῖς is implied by the use of the article τοῖς, "with the remaining
      eleven."

17 M95 Πᾶσαν σάρκα means "all flesh" (cf. 1:21).
    T241 Notice the semitic dative ἐνυπνίοις ἐνυπνιασθήσονται, representing the
    Hebrew infinitive absolute (emphasizing the idea of dreaming).

18 T185 The noun δοῦλος assumes the form of an adjective by appearing in the femi-
    nine gender, "my maidservants."
    BD439(2) Καί γε has an emphatic meaning here, "and even" (the classical order
    would be καὶ ἐπί γε).

21 R720 The relative clause becomes a substantive rather than an adjective clause
    (i.e., it has no expressed antecedent), "whoever calls."
    R744 Πᾶς refers to "any one" no matter who.

22 R579 The meaning of ἀπό here is similar to that of ὑπό (showing agency), "by
    God."

23 R1113 The aorist participle προσπήξαντες expresses action which is identical
    with that of the main verb ἀνείλατε, where the slaying was manifestly done
    by the impaling of the cross.

25 R594 Εἰς with the accusative here is like a dative after λέγει. [Ed. Actually
    this prepositional phrase is used with a sense similar to περί with a genitive
    (cf. v. 29), "concerning him."]

27 R593 Εἰς with the accusative has the sense of ἐν with the dative, "in Hades"
    (cf. v. 31 and M68).

30 BD198(6) Notice the semitic dative ὅρκῳ ὤμοσεν (cf. v. 17), "swore with an
    oath ."

32 R714 In this verse, the relative pronoun οὗ most likely means "whereof," although
    "of whom," referring to Ἰησοῦν, is possible. [Ed. The relative pronoun οὗ
    should be considered as neuter, referring to the incident rather than a person.
    This rendering also suits the emphasis of the sentence (cf. 1:22 and 3:15).]

33 R448 The dative τῇ δεξιᾷ may be used with an instrumental sense "exalted by,"
    locative "exalted at," or as a simple dative "exalted to the right hand of God"
    (perhaps instrumental--M20; local rather than instrumental--BD199). [Ed. The
    rendering with "to the right hand of God" denotes the goal aimed at, and is
    usually indicated in the New Testament by πρός or εἰς after verbs of motion.
    Also, both the resurrection and ascension appear to be presented in this con-
    text; cf. vv. 31f. Consequently, τῇ δεξιᾷ seems to refer to the power of God,
    "by the right hand of God," similar to Psa. 118:16 and Isa. 63:12 in the Sep-
    tuagint.]
    R498 The genitive noun τοῦ πνεύματος is used in apposition with (i.e., defining)
    τὴν ἐπαγγελίαν, with the meaning "the promise, that is the Holy Spirit."

36 R772 There is only one house of Israel, so πᾶς οἶκος Ἰσραήλ means "the whole
    house of Israel" (cf. 1:21).

37 R1179 Δέ introduces the whole sentence and τε connects two parts of it (εἶπόν
    τε means "and so they said"--BD443[3]).

38   R389 Εἰς does not of itself express design (cf. Matt. 10:41), but it may be
     used as such here ("with a view to" or "resulting in"--M90).
     T214 Τοῦ ἁγίου πνεύματος is used as an appositional genitive with τὴν δωρεάν
     meaning "the gift, which is the Spirit."

39   M68 It is not certain whether the preposition in εἰς μακράν is used in a local
     sense or as a semitism (local--T15 and BD205; in Isa. 57:19, the Septuagint
     does not have this construction), "afar off."
     T239 Ὑμῖν is used as a dative of possession (cf. BD189[2]; this example is
     an exception to the classical distinction; cf. Luke 12:20), "the promise is
     yours."

40   T30 The comparative adjective in ἑτέροις τε λόγοις πλείοσιν is used as a posi-
     tive; the construction here appears to exclude the meaning "majority" and "more"
     (it must mean "many" or "several").
     BD443(3) In the connection of clauses, τε indicates a rather close connection
     and relationship, meaning "and likewise."

41   M107 The fact that the article followed by δέ or μέν or μὲν οὖν can be used as
     a personal pronoun gives rise to an occasional ambiguity when a participle
     comes into the picture. Thus, in this verse, does οἱ μὲν οὖν ἀποδεξάμενοι
     . . . ἐβαπτίσθησαν mean "so those who had accepted . . . were baptized," or
     "so they having accepted . . . were baptized"? [Ed. The former rendering
     is preferable, cf. 1:6.]

43   BD189 Ἐγίνετο πάσῃ ψυχῇ φόβος is best translated "all became more and more
     afraid" (the imperfect verb occurs with the possessive dative).

45   R581 The compound verb διαμερίζω means "to distribute."
     R967 Καθότι occurs in a comparative sense only twice in the New Testament (here
     and in 4:35). In both instances, ἄν seems to particularize each case, "as any
     has need."
     T67 The imperfect tense of the verbs ἐπίπρασκον and διεμέριζον have an itera-
     tive sense (the action occurs often but spasmodically, cf. R884; the aorist
     tense would have implied that it happened often but was neither universal nor
     completely carried out--BD325).

46   M78 Ἐν ἀγαλλιάσει καὶ ἀφελότητι means "with exultation and sincerity" (an
     adverbial use of the preposition).
     BD444(1) In this verse, the first τε connects the whole new clause, the second
     connects the two participles, "and . . . and."

47   R1116 The notion of repetition (iterative present) occurs in προσετίθει τοὺς
     σῳζομένους, which means "he kept adding those saved from time to time."
     B125 The present participle τοὺς σῳζομένους may be rendered, "those that are
     saved" (in the sense of "those that become saved"), or may be taken as it is
     in the Revised Version translation, as a progressive present of simultaneous
     action. It cannot mean "the saved" in the sense of "those that have been saved"
     (cf. 1 Cor. 1:18).
     BD202 In this context, the verb προσετίθει means "to add to the congregation."
     MT107 Ἐπὶ τὸ αὐτό signifies the union of the Christian body (cf. 1:15).

ACTS 3

1 R602 In the expression of time here, ἐπί indicates a more definite period than
the simple accusative would have expressed, "at the hour of prayer."
T179 Ὥρα is generally anarthrous especially after a preposition, but the article occurs here because further defining words are introduced, "at the hour."

2 R884 Note the iterative imperfect ἐτίθουν (indicating repetition).
R990 Τοῦ with the infinitive expressing the idea of purpose is confined almost
to Matthew, Luke and Acts (τοῦ αἰτεῖν here), "for the purpose of asking."

3 R884 The notion of repetition is clearly present in ἠρώτα ἐλεημοσύνην, "he
repeatedly asked alms."

5 R828 The compound verb ἐπέχω means "to hold on to."
R1127 The participle προσδοκῶν expresses the idea of manner in this picturesque
description.

7 R508 Note αὐτὸν τῆς χειρός, where the whole is referred to by the accusative
and the part is indicated by the genitive, "grasping him by his right hand."

8 R1116 It is not clear why the present participle ἐξαλλόμενος occurs, unless
it is to note that he kept on leaping and walking (alternately; cf. περιπατῶν
καὶ ἁλλόμενος later).

10 R626 The notion of aim or end naturally develops in the use of πρός here, "for
alms."
R885 The imperfect ἐπεγίνωσκον has an inchoative sense (the accent is on the
beginning of the action, cf. Luke 1:64).
R1117 The perfect participle τῷ συμβεβηκότι has the sense of a past perfect.
The action was finished and is now no longer the fact, although the state
represented by the perfect once existed, "at what had happened."
T41 Some degree of emphasis occurs in the use of αὐτός here (cf. BD277[3]).

11 R407 The change in number from ὁ λαός to ἔκθαμβοι is due to the sense (i.e.,
the collective noun λαός refers to several people).

12 R423 Note the position of ἡμῖν here (denoting possible emphasis).
R1140 Ὡς implies a concessive or conditional notion, "as though we had done
this" (subjective motive--T158).
B404 Τοῦ with the infinitive is used to express the object of πεποιηκόσιν (cf.
MT217; the infinitive signifies purpose--M128; consecutive-final--T141). [Ed.
Actually the infinitive is used as the object of the participle πεποιηκόσιν,
to complete the participial idea, "as though we had made him walk."]

13 R707 The contrast is sharp between ὑμεῖς and ἐκείνου (contrasting the Jews with
Pilate).

14 R785 When more than one epithet is applied to the same person, usually only one
article is used (τὸν ἅγιον καὶ δίκαιον).

15 BD458 Both instances of the relative pronoun in this verse are similar to a
        demonstrative pronoun, equivalent to "this very one."

16 R639 Ἀπέναντι merely has the sense of "before," "in the sight" or "presence
        of."
    M58 Does ἡ πίστις ἡ δι' αὐτοῦ mean "faith which is caused by him (Christ)," or
        simply "Christian faith (in him)." [Ed. Moule attempts to make a subjective
        objective distinction, similar to that of the genitive case. But probably
        both concepts should be included here, with the simple rendering, "the faith
        that comes through him."]
    T221 The article ἡ is necessary with the attributive prepositional phrase here
        to avoid ambiguity (showing that the prepositional phrase modifies the noun
        πίστις).
    H473f. Torrey remarks that the ugly repetition of τὸ ὄνομα αὐτοῦ in this verse
        obscures the sense and spoils the sound. Thus, he gives a literal rendering
        in Aramaic concluding that the sentence reads: "and by faith in His name He
        hath made strong this one whom ye see and know, yea, the faith which is through
        Him hath given him this soundness before you all." Dr. Burkitt, however, se-
        cures excellent sense, as well as characteristically Lucan rhetoric, by placing
        a colon before τοῦτον and omitting ἐπί with Aleph and B. The passage now runs:
        "Ye killed the Prince of Life, whom God raised from the dead, whereof we are
        witnesses, even to the faith in His name: This man whom ye see and know His
        name hath made strong, and the faith which is through Him hath given Him this
        perfect soundness before you all."

17 R1128 Κατὰ ἄγνοιαν expresses the notion of manner (Luke prefers the preposi-
        tional phrase to the participle, a koine tendency, cf. 1 Tim. 1:13--T154),
        "you acted in ignorance."

18 B114 The aorist infinitive παθεῖν refers to what is future with reference to
        the principal verb, "God foretold that his Christ would suffer."

20 T27 The plural καιροί refers to the Messianic period of time.

23 TGr89 The genitive occurs with ἀκούω here, with the meaning "every soul which
        will not hear that prophet" (i.e., "which refuses even to let a prophet speak").

25 R625 The use of πρός here denotes the idea of personal conversation.
    T208 The genitives following οἱ υἱοί are used to express a certain quality of
        the sons.

26 R549 Note that ὑμῖν πρῶτον (adverbial) occurs, not ὑμῖν πρώτοις (adjectival).
        Thus, the meaning is not "you as chief," but "the thing is done first for you."
    R891 The present participle εὐλογοῦντα is used as a future in the sense of pur-
        pose, "he sent him to bless you" (cf. B442).
    R1073 The temporal construction ἐν τῷ with the infinitive here has a sense
        which apparently means, "in turning away every one of you from your iniquities"
        ("in turning" is equivalent to "in that you turned"--BD404[3]: instrumental--
        T146). [Ed. The rendering "in turning" is similar to the instrumental trans-
        lation of "by turning."]

ACTS 4

2   R587 The preposition in ἐν τῷ Ἰησοῦ has the sense of "in the case of" (this
       does not differ greatly from the metaphorical use of ἐν with the soul, mind
       etc.; Luke has in mind the Pauline concept of ἐν Χριστῷ, thus life from the
       dead comes through Christ and those who are "in" Christ will rise from physi-
       cal and spiritual death--TGr155f.). [Ed. The issue at hand was Christ's resur-
       rection not the resurrection of the saints. Peter and John appear to be pro-
       claiming (proving) in the case of (or from the fact of) Jesus' resurrection
       the general concept of resurrection.]

7   R678 Notice the emphatic position of ὑμεῖς here.
       R740 Ποῖος seems to retain its qualitative force in this verse, "of what kind."
       BD277(1) The pronouns τοῦτο and ὑμεῖς are used with the resultant meaning "have
       people like you done this miracle" (the pronouns are used together stylistic-
       ally, but it is fanciful to suppose that the meaning is "people like you doing
       a miracle like this," the simple question originated from anger, not subtlety
       --T37). [Ed. It is not definite whether these pronouns portray style or a
       subtlety, but ὑμεῖς certainly is used to emphasize the predominant attitude
       of scorn.]

9   T212 Ἀνθρώπου is an objective genitive referring to "help given to a sick
       man" (cf. R500).

11 R703 Οὗτος is resumptive and takes up the main thread of the story again (the
       antecedent of οὗτος is Ἰησοῦ, although θεός is the nearest noun--T44).

12 R749 In this context the point of ἕτερον is that no other name at all than
       that of Jesus, not that of difference in kind.
       M66 Ὑπό with the accusative portrays the notion of rest beneath, "for neither
       is there any other name under heaven."
       M76 Perhaps ἐν with the dative ἀνθρώποις has the sense of εἰς with the accusa-
       tive (D omits ἐν; the preposition and the dative case are used pleonastically
       for the simple dative, in this instance the sphere of activity is emphasized
       --T264). [Ed. In both of these explanations, εἰς with the accusative is simi-
       lar to the simple dative. But when the recipient is indicated with the verb
       δίδωμι, the simple dative is generally used, rather than including the preposi-
       tion ἐν also, "to men."]
       M77 The prepositions in ἐν ἄλλῳ . . . ἐν ᾧ have an instrumental notion, "by."
       M103 Τὸ δεδομένον is a very odd usage, and some Semitic background has not un-
       reasonably been suspected (possibly a misunderstanding of a semitic participle;
       it is equivalent to ὁ ἐδόθη, "which was given"--T153).

13 R415 In this verse, both Peter and John are called ἀγράμματοι καὶ ἰδιῶται.
       This need not be pushed too far, and yet it is noteworthy that 2 Peter and
       Revelation are just the two books of the New Testament whose Greek jars most
       upon the cultured mind and which show the closest kinship to the koine in
       somewhat illiterate papyri. One of the theories about the relation between
       1 and 2 Peter is that Silvanus was Peter's scribe in writing the first Epistle
       and that thus the Greek is smooth and flowing, while in 2 Peter, Peter's own
       somewhat uncouth, unrevised Greek occurs. So also in Acts, Luke refines Peter's

Greek in the reports of his addresses.

R812   The intensive force of the middle voice is seen in καταλαβόμενοι, denoting mental "comprehending" (this verb doesn't have an active form in the New Testament, but does in early Attic Greek; one expects the active in Acts 4:13, 10:34; 25:25 and Eph. 3:18--T55).

R1421   The imperfect verb ἦσαν carries the idea of "had been."

16   T304   Luke prefers to use a copulative verb whenever necessary, except in set phrases or words such as φανερόν (cf. 2:29), "is manifest."

18   BD399(3)   The article τό should be taken with καθόλου, not with the infinitive, "at all."

19   R1045   Εἰ is used here to introduce an indirect question, "whether."

20   R1094   In οὐ δυνάμεθα . . . μὴ λαλεῖν, the negative is not redundant but both negatives preserve their full force, meaning "for we can not but speak."

21   R766   The article τό is used to introduce a quotation (consequently, the article is not to be translated).
      R1128   The participle εὑρίσκοντες has a causal sense (giving the grounds for the action in the principal verb), "they let them go because they found no way to punish them."

22   M38   Ἐτῶν . . πλειόνων seems to be used as a genitive of definition, meaning "he was of more than forty years."
      BD347(3)   Γεγόνει is used as an aoristic perfect, "was performed."

25   TGr20   Πνεύματος ἀγίου is anarthrous, thus the Psalms are said to have been spoken by God through David's lips by means of a holy inspiration -- literally "holy spirit" (cf. the discussion on Luke 1:15).
      T313   The plural verb is used with the neuter plural ἔθνη, because the noun is used with a personal sense (cf. 11:1).
      H474   Torrey offers an Aramaic rendering for ὁ . . . εἰπών and shows that the common confusion from Aramaic has obscured the true meaning. Consequently, it should be translated, "that which our father David, thy servant, said by the mouth (command) of the Holy Spirit."

27   B92   Because of the ambiguity of English, both συνήχθησαν (v. 27) and συνηγμένοι (v. 31) should be translated "were gathered," even though the former is an aorist and refers to an act, and the latter a perfect and refers to a state.

29   T200   The adjective πάσης with the anarthrous noun here has the sense of "complete" ("with complete candor"--BD275[3]).

30   B417   The infinitive γίνεσθαι, which is taken in the Revised Version translation as the object of δός, is more probably governed by the preposition ἐν. It is however not strictly without the article; the τῷ which precedes ἐκτείνειν in effect belongs also to γίνεσθαι, "while stretching out . . . and performing."
      M77   The preposition in διὰ τοῦ ὀνόματος seems to express an instrumental notion, "through the name."

32   R691   Ἴδιον occurs with the sense of "private."
      R751   Οὐδὲ εἷς is more emphatic than the simple negative οὐδείς.

33 M169 Καὶ . . . ἀπεδίδουν τὸ μαρτύριον οἱ ἀπόστολοι τοῦ κυρίου Ἰησοῦ τῆς ἀναστάσεως is simply extraordinary: one would have expected either καὶ . . . οἱ
ἀπόστολοι τοῦ κυρίου Ἰησοῦ ἀπεδίδουν τὸ μαρτύριον τῆς ἀναστάσεως (i.e.,
"the apostles of the Lord Jesus rendered their witness to the resurrection")
or καὶ . . . οἱ ἀπόστολοι ἀπεδίδουν τὸ μαρτύριον τῆς ἀναστάσεως τοῦ κυρίου
Ἰησοῦ (i.e., "the apostles rendered their witness to the resurrection of the
Lord Jesus"); as it stands, it is both ambiguous and awkward. [Ed. The latter suggestion is preferable since they were witnesses of the resurrection of
the Lord Jesus; cf. v. 2 and 1:22.]
    T350 Interruption of the normal word order to give oratorical effect results
    in ambiguity here (the regular order of words is abandoned because it would
    be too cumbersome and ungraceful--BD473[2]).

34 R1116 The notion of repetition is present in the tenses of πωλοῦντες, ἔφερον
    and ἐτίθουν, meaning "they would from time to time sell and bring and place
    at the feet of the apostles" (cf. BD339[3]).

35 R967 Καθότι has a comparative sense (cf. 2:45).

36 R530 Τῷ γένει expresses the idea of manner (it is used as a dative of reference).
    [Ed. Actually, it is used as a dative of reference but maintains a modal sense,
    "by family" or "by race."]
    R579 The preposition ἀπό has a meaning which is similar to that of ὑπό (cf.
    T258), "by the apostles."
    T208 The genitive following υἱός describes a certain quality of the person
    (cf. 3:25), "son of encouragement."

37 R1116 There is a sharp contrast between the repeated action of v. 34 (imper-
    fect) and the specific instance of Barnabas in v. 37 (aorist).

                                    ACTS 5

2   R627 The verb σύνοιδα seems to refer to the knowing that is shared with another
    (cf. 1 Cor. 4:4).
    R810 Ἐνοσφίσατο is used as an indirect middle, meaning "he kept back for him-
    self."
    R1116 The perfect participle συνειδυίης has lost the notion of completion but
    maintains the linear idea in a present sense, "with his wife's knowledge."

3   B389 Ψεύσασθαι may be regarded as an object infinitive governed by the idea of
    persuading implied in ἐπλήρωσεν τὴν καρδίαν, or as a consecutive infinitive of
    conceived result (the infinitive has a consecutive sense, i.e., Ananias had
    actually lied--R1001; cf. T136 and BD391[4]).

4   R965 Τί ὅτι is actually a shortened form of τί γέγονεν ὅτι (τί has the meaning
    "why" in vv. 4 and 9).
    R1166 Notice the sharp antithesis here with the use of οὐ . . ἀλλά (stressing
    the point that Ananias had lied to God).
    M120f. The dative of possession occurs in the construction οὐχὶ μένον σοὶ ἔμενεν,
    which means "as long as it remained, did it not remain your own?"

8   R810 'Απέδοσθε is used as an indirect middle meaning "you gave away for your
       own interest" (i.e., "sold").

10 M53 The preposition πρός in this verse has a pregnant sense, seemingly combin-
       ing linear motion with punctiliar rest on arrival. Thus the construction has
       the notion, "she fell . . . at his feet . . ., they buried her beside her hus-
       band."

12 M57 Διά with the genitive has the sense of "by means of."

14 R1106 Πλήθη is in apposition to the anarthrous participle πιστεύοντες ("be-
       lieving men"; "believers were added to the Lord, multitudes both of men and
       women"--B423).
       BD465(1) The parenthesis in this verse is harsh, although the connection with
       v. 13 is smooth enough; but the resumption in v. 15 is awkward and ὥστε καί
       εἰς τὰς πλατείας. . . is in reality a consequence of v. 13, not of v. 14.

15 R1091 Ὥστε with the infinitive ἐκφέρειν expresses actual result, "so that they."
       M138 Ἵνα κἄν occurs twice in the New Testament (Mark 6:56 and here), and in
       both instances an implied conditional clause seems to be evident, "even if it
       were no more than the shadow" (as the Authorized Version has).

16 R404 The participle φέροντες is plural, even though the verb συνήρχετο is
       singular like the collective noun πλῆθος (the plural occurs according to the
       actual sense of the collective noun).
       BD474(8) The preposition in τῶν πέριξ πόλεων 'Ιερουσαλήμ is separated from its
       noun (following the texts of S and B; it was first conceived as "the surround-
       ing cities."

17 R1108 'Η οὖσα seems to have a technical sense, "the local school of the Sad-
       ducees" (cf. MT228; this redundant use of the participle is a characteristic
       of the book of Acts, and means little more than "current," or "existent"--
       T151f.). [Ed. Actually, there is not much difference between these two sug-
       gestions, but the former one may be preferable in view of Luke's common use of
       this articular participle; cf. 11:22; 13:1; 14:13 and 28:17.]

19 R581 The preposition in διὰ νυκτός, "at night," adds very little to the genitive
       itself.

20 T57 The passive σταθείς is best translated simply "stand."

21 R635 This verse provides the only example of ὑπό in a temporal expression in
       the New Testament ("about," or "close upon dawn"; cf. M66).

24 R940 The optative and ἄν are used in the indirect question here to express
       doubt and perplexity (the indirect quote has preserved the form of the direct
       --B343), meaning "what would happen," or "how it would turn out."

26 B224 It appears that τὸν λαόν may denote the persons feared, and μὴ λιθασθῶσιν
       the thing feared (cf. The Revised Version), so that the meaning would be ex-
       pressed in English by "for they were afraid that they should be stoned by the
       people." But on the other hand, ἐφοβοῦντο . . . λαόν may be taken as paren-
       thetical, and μὴ λιθασθῶσιν as limiting ἦγεν αὐτούς, οὐ μετὰ βίας (cf. West-

cott and Hort). [Ed. The latter suggestion would have the meaning "they brought without force, lest they (the captain and the officers) be stoned," which is essentially equivalent to the former suggestion.]

BD327 The imperfect tense in ἦγεν is used to portray the manner of the action, that is, a past action is represented as being in progress (with further quali- fication; contrast with the aorist in v. 27 which pictures the action as con- cluded (the imperfect tense indicates action which proceeded until finally they were presented to the Sanhedrin--T66).

28   R697 Τούτῳ occurs here with the notion of reproach (cf. Luke 15:2 and 22:56).
     R878 Βούλομαι is less frequent in the New Testament than θέλω and can hardly be resolved into a mere future. It is purpose that seems to be prevalent here, "you intend."
     R895 The perfect tense in πεπληρώκατε is used to refer to a completed state (an extensive perfect), "you have filled Jerusalem with your teaching."
     M178 The emphatic dative construction παραγγελίᾳ παρηγγείλαμεν ὑμῖν perhaps means "we strictly enjoined upon you."

29   R747 Ἄλλοι is implied before ἀπόστολοι, "Peter and the other apostles."
     BD245a(1) The expression of comparison here has the notion of exclusion.

30   R1127 Κρεμάσαντες is used as a modal participle, "whom you killed by hanging him on a tree" (i.e., the participle indicates the manner or means).

31   R526 Τῇ δεξιᾷ may be used as a simple dative, locative or instrumental. [Ed. The instrumental rendering of this phrase seems to be most probable; cf. 2:33.]
     R1088 The infinitive expresses the notion of purpose, "for the purpose that he may give."

32   T218 The variant reading αὐτοῦ μάρτυρες τῶν ῥημάτων τούτων means "his witnes- ses for these things."

33   M89 The compound verb διαπρίω appears to mean literally, "saw in two."

34   R653 The neuter adjective βραχύ has an adverbial usage here, "a little while."

35   R605 The preposition ἐπί in this verse has the sense of "about," or "in the case of" (with the dative here the resultant idea is "against").
     B72 Μέλλετε is used with an infinitive to portray a future event (cf. Luke 9:44).

36   R581 Διαλύω means "to dissolve."
     R743 Τινα is used as a predicate with an emphatic meaning, "somebody in partic- ular" (cf. 8:9).
     T253 The accusative in ἐγένοντο εἰς οὐδέν is used in place of the predicate nominative (semitic), "came to nothing."

37   R835 Ἀπέστησεν is used as an effective aorist (i.e., emphasis is laid on the end of the action rather than the beginning), "misled the people."

38   R1018 A real distinction is maintained between ἐὰν ᾖ and εἰ . . . ἐστίν (cf. M150). Gamaliel gives the benefit of the doubt to Christianity. He assumes that Christianity is of God and puts the alternative, that it is of men, in the

third class conditional clause. This does not, of course, show that Gamaliel
was a Christian or an inquirer. He was merely willing to score a point against
the Sadducees. Here, indeed, the supposition is about a present situation, but
ἐάν and the subjunctive contemplate the future result ("turn out to be": the
conditional clauses have the meaning, "if, as one may suppose, it be . . , but
if [as these people claim] it really is"--BD372[1a]).
B230 The causal clause (ὅτι . . , καταλυθήσεται) is used as the apodosis to
the conditional clause with ἐὰν ᾖ.

39 R1096 θεομάχοι means "fighting God."
    MT193 The warning in v. 39 may start with either "Perhaps you will be found,"
    or "Do not be found"; the former suggestion suits the meaning of ποτέ better.

41 R632 Ὑπέρ with the genitive here has the resultant meaning "for the sake of."
    R884 The descriptive durative use of the imperfect occurs with the verb
    ἐπορεύοντο (cf. v. 26), "they were going."
    M162 Μὲν οὖν is purely resumptive or transitional here (no contrast is intend-
    ed by the use of μέν--R1151), "and so."

42 B457 The participles διδάσκοντες and εὐαγγελιζόμενοι are used substantivally
    as the subject of the verb, "they ceased not teaching and preaching Jesus as
    the Christ" (there is no need to apply the term "substantive" to these com-
    plementary participles which have purely verbal ideas--R1109). [Ed. Robertson
    is correct because the verb παύομαι generally has a participle complementing
    it, although Burton's translation is sufficient.]

ACTS 6

1   R626 The resultant idea of πρός in this verse is "against."

3   B317 The relative pronoun with the future οὓς καταστήσομεν expresses the idea
    of purpose.

5   TGr20 Since πνεύματος ἁγίου is anarthrous, Stephen is said to be filled with
    spiritual inspiration (cf. the discussion on Lk. 1:15).
    BD214(6) "Pleasing in the eyes of someone" is equivalent to "pleasing to
    someone."
    BD316(1) Ἐκλέγομαι is always middle ("choose"); only in Acts 6:5, 15:22 and
    25 is the force of the middle ("for oneself") not absolutely necessary.

7   T312 Notice the plural verb with the singular subject ὄχλος (A and E correct
    to a singular verb; actually πολύς τε ὄχλος τῶν ἱερέων is equivalent to
    πολλοὶ ἱερεῖς--BD134[1c]).

9   R788 The repeated use of τῶν divides the synagogues into two groups (men from
    Cilicia and Asia on the one hand and men from Alexandria, Cyrene and Libertines
    [?] on the other). The matter is simply geographical except for Λιβερτίνων,
    and it may be so used depending on the meaning of this term.
    T15 Οἱ ἐκ is used to refer to a sect (cf. BD209[2,3]), "the members of the
    synagogue."

11 R594 Εἰς with the accusative has the idea of "against."
    R634 In the compound verb ὑποβάλλω, the notion of suggestion has an evil sense,
    "instigate."

ACTS 7

1   R546 Ἔχει is used with οὕτως in an idiomatic construction, "are these things
    true?"
    R916 Εἰ is used to introduce a direct question (consequently it is not transla-
    ted).

2   R419 Ἄνδρες ἀδελφοὶ καὶ πατέρες is a formal phrase similar to "ladies and gen-
    tlemen."

4   M68 Εἰς has a local notion (perhaps by attraction, at least with the relative
    pronoun), being used in place of ἐν with the dative, "to be resettled in" (cf.
    BD205).

5   R1036 Δοῦναι is used as an infinitive of indirect discourse, "he promised to
    give."
    T285 Οὐ is used with the participle here because Luke has a tendency to use
    classical style (cf. BD430[2]). [Ed. Οὐκ ὄντος αὐτῷ τέκνου is an understood
    expression used occasionally in the Septuagint (cf. 1 Chron. 2:30 and 32), and
    Luke apparently incorporates that phrase into this summary of Old Testament
    history, "although he had no child."]

6   R889 The future verbs in this verse seem to have a progressive sense (rather
    than the usual punctiliar idea of the future).

10 R1100 Ἡγούμενον actually means "governor."

12 T161 The accusative with the participle after ἀκούσας denotes the content of
    what was heard.
    T254 Εἰς is used for ἐν in a local sense, "in" (the Septuagint in Gen. 42:2,
    which is cited, has ἐν; cf. BD205).
    BD62 Πρῶτος here is equivalent to πρότερος (cf. 1:1).

13 BD191(2) The passive verb with the dative means, "Joseph let himself be recog-
    nized by his brothers."

14 R589 The preposition ἐν seems to have the sense of "amounting to" ("consisting
    of"--M79).

16 BD162(3) Identification of the father by the son is impossible, therefore the
    explanation of the variant τῶν υἱῶν Ἐμμὼρ τοῦ Συχέμ (other manuscripts have
    ἐν Συχέμ or τοῦ ἐν Συχέμ) as Ἐμμὼρ πατρὸς Συχέμ (following the Septuagint
    in Gen. 33:19) is not correct.

17 R968 Καθώς seems to have a temporal sense in this verse, "when."
    BD187(4) Ὁμολογέω means "promise" in its usage here (note the variant readings).

18 R639 In this verse, ἄχρι is used both as a preposition and as a conjunction,
    resulting in a temporal phrase (similar to ἕως οὗ--B331), "until there."

19 R1090 Εἰς τό with the infinitive here seems to express a hypothetical result
    (it seems to be final [purposive] or near it--T145), "that these might not be
    kept alive."
    B398 Τοῦ with the infinitive ποιεῖν states conceived result (cf. T141; "so
    that, in that he made," equivalent to ποιῶν--BD400[8]; "so as to make"--R1090).

20 M46 Ἀστεῖος τῷ θεῷ is a possible semitism, meaning "exceedingly fair" (cf.
    BD192 and H443).

21 BD157(5) Εἰς with the accusative pronoun αὐτόν is used for the predicate accu-
    sative (semitic), "as her son."

22 R772 With an abstract noun (πάσῃ σοφίᾳ) "every" and "all" amount practically
    to the same thing ("all wisdom"--M95).

23 M27 The subject of ἀνέβη is ἐπισκέψασθαι, "it occurred to him to visit" (cf.
    Luke 24:38).

24 R805 Ἀμύνομαι means to "assist," not "ward off from one's self," but the force
    of the middle is present (the middle is used in place of the active--BD316[1]).
    [Ed. The middle rendering seems to produce good sense, referring to assistance
    for a friend.]

25 R885 Ἐνόμιζεν is used as a conative imperfect, referring to an action begun
    but interrupted (note the following οὐ συνῆκαν).
    R1049 Two forms of indirect assertion follow ἐνόμιζεν; the infinitive and ὅτι,
    one is dependent upon the other, "he thought that his brothers understood that
    God was giving."

26 R885 Συνήλλασσεν is used as a conative imperfect, "he tried to reconcile them."
    BD191(1) Ὤφθη αὐτοῖς more likely means "appeared to them" than "was seen by
    them."

29 R589 The preposition in ἐν τῷ λόγῳ τούτῳ gives the occasion of the action of
    the main verb ("at these words"--M78f.; actually denoting a causal sense--T253).

30 T213 Πυρός is used as a genitive of quality (cf. 2 Thess. 1:8, ἐν πυρὶ φλογός),
    "burning flame."

31 MT117 A real perfective sense is evident in the compound verb κατανοέω, meaning
    "to master the mystery" (it actually describes the completion of a mental pro-
    cess).

33 T56 Λῦσον occurs in the active voice where we would expect the middle in clas-
    sical Greek (the Septuagint has the middle voice), "take off the shoes from your
    feet."

34 M22 In this verse, an extraordinary subjunctive appears (as it does in the
    Septuagint, Ex. 3:10) where the future would be absolutely natural: for ἀποστεί-
    λω one would expect ἀποστελῶ (a futuristic subjunctive--MT185), "I will send."

T157   The semitic construction ἰδὼν εἶδον is used to strengthen the verbal idea,
"I have surely seen."

35   B82   When the perfect indicative is used of a past event which is thought of as
separated from the moment of speaking by an interval of time, it is impossible
to render it into English adequately. The English idiom forbids the use of the
perfect because of the interval (present in thought as well as existing in fact)
between the act and the time of speaking, while the English past tense fails to
express the idea of existing result which the Greek perfect conveys, "him did
God send (Revised Version has "hath God sent") to be both a ruler and a deliver-
er . . ." (it is a narrative perfect--T70; the abiding results of Moses' mission
formed a thought never absent from the Jewish mind--MT144; it seems to be a
perfect of allegory, which appears several times in the New Testament when the
Old Testament is being expounded, cf. Gal. 3:18--M15). [Ed. In essence Moulton's comment is similar to Moule's suggestion; there is definitely an existing
result portrayed in this verb.]
BD217(2)   Σὺν χειρί is a prepositional circumlocution meaning "through," "by
means of."
BD270(3)   The articular participle here is equivalent to a relative clause, "an
angel, namely, that one who . . ."
BD420(2)   In ὃν ἠρνήσαντο εἰπόντες, the aorist participle occurs because ἠρνήσαντο is not used here as a verb of saying and because the participle is the
first word that introduces the fact of speech, "they refused, saying."

36   B37   In this verse, the aorist verb ἐξήγαγεν seems to refer only to the result,
since the signs wrought in the Red Sea and the wilderness would otherwise have
been represented as accompanying the bringing out, and instead of ποιήσας we
should have had ποιῶν (the aorist of a verb whose present implies effort or intention [ἐξάγω] commonly denotes the success of the effort--B42).

40   R697   Οὗτος occurs here with the idea of reproach (of the Jews against Moses; cf.
5:28).

41   R532   The prepositional phrase ἐν τοῖς ἔργοις expresses a causal sense.

42   BD147(3)   Normally the article occurs with the nominative when it is used as a
vocative, but it is omitted here because in such cases the article does not
appear in Hebrew either (οἶκος ᾽Ισραήλ).

43   R642   The preposition ἐπέκεινα occurs only once in the New Testament (a quotation from Amos 5:27) and with the ablative in the sense of "beyond."

46   T56   Εὑρίσκω occurs in the active voice meaning "obtain" (Attic prose would have
had the middle voice).

48   T287   The position of the negative may be altered to achieve emphasis, as in
this verse the position of οὐχ denotes an emphatic negation (the separation
of the negative from the verb to which it belongs can be ambiguous; as in this
instance, the author probably does not mean to imply that somebody else dwells
there--BD433[1]).

51   T220   Καρδίαις and ὠσίν are used as datives of respect, "uncircumcised in reference to hearts and ears."

52 T209 Notice that the interrogative τίς is used with the partitive genitive,
"which of?"

53 R482 Εἰς διαταγάς is used as a predicate accusative (cf. v. 21; the phrase has
a causal sense--T266; conceivably it may mean "received . . . as . . ."--M204;
the preposition in εἰς διαταγὰς ἀγγέλων is similar to ἐν, "by angelic mediation"
--R596; cf. M70; BD206[1] and H463). [Ed. Εἰς appears to be used for ἐν with
an instrumental sense (causal and intrumental are similar). The mediation of
the Law by angels is referred to in Gal. 3:19 and Heb. 2:2.]
R728 Οὕτινες has a causal sense here (the pronoun has an indefinite reference
--BD293[2]). [Ed. Robertson's suggestion appears to be more accurate since
οὕτινες often has a causal meaning in the New Testament and because the pronoun would have a definite reference to Stephen's audience.]

54 M89 Διαπρίω appears to literally mean "saw in two" (cf. 5:33).

55 T20 Since πνεύματος is anarthrous, it refers to spiritual inspiration (cf. 6:5
and the discussion on Luke 1:15).

56 T25 An exceptional use of οὐρανός in the plural occurs here (generally when
this noun simply has the meaning of "sky," the singular is used).

57 R789 Φωνῇ μεγάλῃ means "with a loud voice" (cf. 26:24).

60 R834 Ἐκοιμήθη is used as an ingressive aorist, representing the point of entrance, "he fell asleep."
T77 The prohibition occasionally occurs in the aorist tense in prayer to the
deity, "do not hold this sin against them."

ACTS 8

1 R581 The compound verb διασπείρω has the meaning of "scatter abroad."
R787 The article is not repeated with Samaria because the two provinces are
adjacent (cf. 1:8).

3 R174 Τὴν ἐκκλησίαν does not have the idea of an assembly, but reference is
made to the body of Christians in a local sense.
T166 Luke introduces Σαῦλος without the article, but refers back to ὁ δὲ
Σαῦλος in an anaphoric sense (9:1).

4 M162 Μὲν οὖν has a purely resumptive or transitional sense (the phrase οἱ
μὲν οὖν is used as a demonstrative--R695), "now those who were scattered."

5 R684 The plural pronoun αὐτοῖς refers to πόλιν, it is not in concord grammatically, but is used according to the sense (the plural masculine is used
to refer to people).

6 T52 The compound verb προσέχω means "listen to."

9 R743 Τινα μέγαν means "a very great man" ("some great man"), in his own esti-
mation, cf. 5:36 (in this context τινα refers to a person of importance, with

μέγαν inserted for emphasis--T195; "somebody extraordinary"--BD301[1]).

11 R533 Ταῖς μαγίαις is used as an instrumental dative, "with his magic."
    R909 The perfect tense of the infinitive ἐξεσακέναι is used as a perfect of
    broken continuity (referring to an action by a series of links, i.e., he had
    amazed them on numerous occasions).

15 TGr20 Since πνεῦμα is anarthrous the believers in Samaria received spiritual
    inspiration by the laying on of the hands of the Apostles Peter and John (vv.
    15, 17 and 19). The strange appearance of τὸ πνεῦμα (v. 18) among several
    references to an anarthrous πνεῦμα can be interpreted only as an instance of
    anaphoric usage. The author wished to add some emphasis: "Simon was aware
    that through the laying on of the Apostles' hand this same spirit was bestowed
    . . ." (cf. the discussion on Luke 1:15).

16 T255 The preposition with the accusative in εἰς τὸ ὄνομα, occurs where the sim-
    ple dative would suffice, "in the name."

18 M57 Διά with the genitive has the sense of "by means of."
    BD257(2) In Luke's writings the anarthrous construction πνεῦμα ἅγιον refers to
    an unknown power. But the article occurs here to show anaphora (cf. v. 15 and
    the discussion on Luke 1:15).

20 T122 Only two instances of an optative in the New Testament are used to express
    an imprecation (i.e., a prayer for evil; Mark 11:14 and here), "may your silver
    perish with you."

21 R541 Σοῦ is used as a dative of possession (cf. "your slave").

22 M158n.1 Εἰ ἄρα means "in the hope that perhaps" (expressing an element of
    doubt).

23 R593 Εἰς seems to be used in a sense similar to ἐν, meaning "in" (cf. BD205;
    it has the sense of "destined for"--T254). [Ed. Εἰς used with a form of εἰμι
    often times expresses destination (cf. v. 20). Consequently, Turner's sugges-
    tion appears to be more probable.]
    R865 Ὁρῶ is used as an aoristic present (i.e., a simple statement).
    R1041 If the idea is merely of intellectual apprehension, an opinion or judg-
    ment, ὁρῶ ὅτι is used (cf. Jas. 2:24). If it is a real experience, the parti-
    ciple occurs (as here).
    B460 A substantive participle forming a part of the object of a verb is some-
    times equivalent to a clause of indirect discourse (as ὄντα is used here), "for
    I see that you are . . ."

24 R706 Ὧν is used for τούτων ἅ, "things of these."
    M65 Ὑπέρ seems to have the sense of "concerning," or "about"; "Do pray for
    (about) me" ("for one's benefit"--R630).

25 M162 Μὲν οὖν is purely resumptive or transitional (no contrast is intended),
    "and so" or "now."

26 T44 The demonstrative pronoun οὖτος may not necessarily refer to the noun which
    is nearest to it, but to the noun which is most vivid in the writer's mind

(αὕτη refers to ἡ ὁδός, not Γάζαν).

27   R877   The participle προσκυνήσων is used to express the notion of purpose or
aim, "who had come to Jerusalem to worship."

30   M158   The construction ἆρα γε is used as an interrogative, although γε perhaps
adds a sense of doubt, and the whole clause possibly should be translated "now,
do you understand . . ?" or "Do you, then, understand . . ?"

31   B178   The optative δυναίμων with ἄν is used to express what would happen on the
fulfillment of some supposed condition (a mixed condition here), "how should
I be able."
B254   Ἐάν with the future indicative should be translated "unless some one shall
guide me."
T65   Where the verb παρακαλέω is found in the aorist, the request is usually
peremptory, demanding obedience (thus "he made Philip come up" [not "invited"]).
BD452(1)   In this verse, γάρ either refers to the reason for an unexpressed denial or refusal, or it may indicate the reason for a reproach (expressed or
unexpressed). [Ed.   The former suggestion is more probable; although the denial
may not be complete, at least there was an understood recognition of the Eunuch's
inability to understand.]

35   T155   Ἀρχόμενος occurs with the meaning "from . . . onwards."

36   R602   Ἐπί with the accusative here has the sense of "as far as."

40   TGr157f.   Εὑρέθη is an idiom meaning "he was found." Luke uses this idiom to
describe how Philip the deacon was guided by the Spirit each step of the journey from the time that he disappeared from the eunuch's sight until the moment
that he walked into Azotus (εὑρέθη εἰς Ἄζωτον means "he came to Azotus, he
appeared suddenly in Azotus"--BD313). [Ed.   The passive verb εὑρέθη does not
imply that Philip did not walk into the city, but simply that Azotus was the
next place where he appeared,   although the verb ἥρπασεν in v. 39 indicates
that a supernatural event did in fact take place.]
BD205   Εἰς is used here instead of ἐν in a local sense, "in" or "at."

ACTS 9

1   M37   Ἐμπνέων takes a genitive object here, with the meaning "whose every breath
was a threat of destruction" ("breathing threats and murder"--BD174).

2   BD416(2)   Εὑρίσκω usually occurs with a participle, "who might be found."

4   TGr87   Much use might be made for the distinction between the genitive and the
accusative with ἀκούω for New Testament interpretation, if only one could be
quite certain that it were still a valid one. The furthest one can go is to
say that when the verb ἀκούω is followed by a participle there is then some
real difference between the accusative and genitive (he heard the sound as well
as the content).

5   BD480(5)   There is an ellipsis of the verb ἔφη in ὁ δέ, "and he said."

6   T330 Sometimes before an imperative, ἀλλά has more of a consecutive sense than
    adversative, and is best translated as an interjection, "I am Jesus . . . Well,
    rise and . . ."

7   M36 It seems to be impossible to find a satisfactory distinction in meaning
    between the genitive and accusative with ἀκούω in 9:7 and 22:9 (there is no
    contradiction between Acts 9:7 and 22:9 since the case alters the meaning of
    the verb. The servants therefore heard a voice (genitive of specification),
    but they did not understand its meaning (accusative of extent) according to
    22:9--TGr88; cf. R449 and MT66).

9   M105 The negative with a participle is usually μή, regardless of how factual
    or confident the denial may be (μὴ βλέπων), "he was without sight."
    BD353(1) In this verse, the participle βλέπων is adjectival and only seemingly
    periphrastic. On occasion periphrasis and an adjectival participle are inter-
    changeable (it is a periphrastic construction--T88). [Ed. Whether we take
    this construction as a periphrastic or consider βλέπων as an adjectival par-
    ticiple, the meaning is essentially the same, "he was without sight for three
    days."]

12 B146 The aorist participle used as an integral part of the object of a verb of
    perception represents the action which it denotes, a simple event without de-
    fining its time, "and he has seen a man named Ananias come in and lay hands
    upon him."

15 R496 Ἐκλογῆς is used as an attributive genitive, "a chosen instrument."
    T239 Ἐστίν μοι οὗτος means "I have in him" (the dative has the idea of credit).

16 BD304 Ὅσα may be understood as introducing an exclamation, although the inter-
    pretation which makes it equivalent to πάντα ἅ seems more obvious, "how much."

17 M75 The local phrase ἐν τῇ ὁδῷ means "on the way."

18 M26 Is there any significance in the comparison between 9:18 and 22:16 (change
    in voice)? Did a Christian in fact generally "baptize himself," "get himself
    baptized," or "submit to baptism"? (the confusion of ἐβαπτίσθη and βάπτισαι
    has long puzzled expositors, but there is no mystery; both the middle and pas-
    sive are [in the New Testament] used in the sense of "to allow oneself to be
    . . .," and both voices become at times virtually an intransitive active [as
    in this instance]--T57).

19 M88 The compound verb ἐνύσχω occurs here and in v. 22 with apparently no idea
    of "inwardness," but only of "intensity."

20 R885 Ἐκήρυσσεν is used as an ingressive aorist, "he began to preach."
    R1034 An epexegetic use of ὅτι occurs here, "that this one is."

21 R905 In this verse, the pluperfect tense of ἐληλύθει is contrasted with the
    present tense of ἐστιν ὁ πορθήσας ("he had come here for this intent"--B89;
    the pluperfect is used here because this purpose is now a thing of the past
    so that the perfect was no longer admissible--BD347[3]).

22 B447 Συμβιβάζων is used as a participle of means, "he confounded . . by proving."

24 T55 Παρατηρέω occurs with the middle voice here, where one expects the active, with the resultant meaning "watch closely."
T235 The temporal genitives ἡμέρας and νυκτός refer to time-within-which.

25 BD223(5) Διά with the genitive has a spatial sense, "along(?)."

26 R1128 The participle πιστεύοντες suggests the ground for the action in the principal verb (i.e., causal; cf. B439).
M153 Ὅτι is used in indirect discourse here, "not believing that he was a disciple."
BD101 Πειράζω has the meaning "to attempt something."

27 R1047 In πῶς . . . καὶ ὅτι . . . , καὶ πῶς there is a change from an indirect question to an indirect assertion and then back again to an indirect question ("he related to them how . . . he had seen the Lord, and that he had spoken to him, and how . . . he had spoken freely"--M153).
T232 Ἐπιλάμβανω, "to take hold of," generally has the genitive object. The accusative αὐτόν occurs here because the pronoun goes with the main verb ἤγαγεν (cf. BD170[2]).

28 M68 The preposition εἰς has a local idea here similar to ἐν, "at Jerusalem."

31 R524 Τῷ φοβῷ is used as a locative with πορευομένη, "walking in the fear of the Lord."
R787 The three sections of Palestine are treated together since the article τῆς is not repeated.
M60 Καθ᾽ ὅλης means "throughout all" (cf. 4:14).
M162 Μὲν οὖν has a purely resumptive or transitional sense, "then" or "so."

32 R1085 The accusative and infinitive occurs with ἐγένετο in the sense of "it befell" or "happened to" one ("and it came to pass, as Peter went throughout all parts, he came down"--B360).

34 B13 The present verb ἰᾶται is used to refer to an action or event coincident in time with the act of speaking, and conceived of as a simple event (aoristic present), "he heals you in this moment in which I proclaim it to you," not "he is healing you" (cf. T64).

38 R538 Ἐγγύς has the dative object twice in the New Testament (here and in Acts 27:8), although the genitive is generally used, "near Joppa."
T171 The article is present with Ἰόππης only because it has an anaphoric reference here and in v. 42 (referring to a previous reference, cf. v. 36).
MT125 The aorist prohibition μὴ ὀκνήσῃς would be answered with "I will avoid doing so."

39 R810 The indirect middle can be seen in ἐπιδεικνύμεναι χιτῶνας where the women were showing garments belonging to themselves (the verb occurs in the middle voice where one expects the active, meaning "display," cf. v. 24--T55; the middle voice with this verb can mean "to show on oneself"--BD316[1]). [Ed. Since a valid meaning can be derived from the middle voice, there is no reason to consider it as active.]
B29 When an action denoted by an imperfect verb precedes an event already mentioned, such an imperfect is sometimes best translated into English by the plu-

perfect (such is the case with ἐποίει here), "which Dorcas had made."

42 R607 Καθ' ὅλης means "throughout all" (cf. v. 31).
T257 'Επί with the accusative after πιστεύω has the meaning "believe in" (this construction possibly retains a sense of movement [towards], metaphorically-- M49).

ACTS 10

3 M206 Εἶδεν . . . ἄγγελον . . . εἰσελθόντα . . . καὶ εἰπόντα presumably means "he saw . . . an angel . . . come in . . . and say" (cf. 9:12).

5 R609 In the compound verb μεταπέμπω the preposition has the meaning "after."

6 T206 Βαρσεῖ is used as a dative of apposition (even though it is anarthrous), "Simon, a tanner."
T273 Παρά with the dative has the meaning "in the house of" (cf. Luke 19:7).

7 R892 By implication the present participle ὁ λαλῶν suggests antecedent time (prior to) in relation to the principal verb (a sort of imperfect participle; cf. 4:34 and B127), "when the angel who spoke to him went away."

9 M62 The prepositional phrase has a temporal sense here, "at about the sixth hour."

14 R1173 Μηδαμῶς is an intensifying compound negative, "by no means."
T196 Οὐδέποτε . . . πᾶν means "nothing" (a peculiarly Biblical Greek phenomenon; cf. Luke 1:37).

15 T37 There is some degree of emphasis in the use of σύ here.
MT125 The present prohibition μὴ κοίνου should be translated "you must stop considering it as common."

17 R940 The context shows doubt and perplexity in the indirect question with ἄν and the optative verb here (cf. 5:24), "as to what the vision might mean."
B154 The perfect participle has the meaning "the men who had been sent."

18 R1104 The articular participle ὁ ἐπικαλούμενος is equivalent to a relative clause (cf. v. 32).
M154 An indirect question possibly may be understood here, "they were inquiring whether Simon was lodging here" (but the fact that εἰ can be used to introduce a direct question and that ἐνθάδε, "here," is strictly incorrect for an indirect question, which requires ἐκεῖ, "there," may point to this verse as not being intended to be indirect at all, but a direct quotation: "they were inquiring, Does Simon . . . lodge here?").

20 T330 'Αλλά is best translated as an interjection before the imperative here (cf. 9:6), "well, arise and go down."

22 R614 Παρά occurs here with an ablative use of the genitive σοῦ, "from you."

B123 The present participle φοβούμενος is used without reference to time or
progress, simply defining its subject as belonging to a certain class, "a
righteous and God-fearing man."

23 B138 The aorist participle ἀναστάς is best translated into English by a finite
verb with "and," with the meaning "he arose and went out."

24 T55 The middle form of συγκαλέω seems to occur in the New Testament with
apparently the same meaning as the active, "call together."

25 R98 Τοῦ εἰσελθεῖν with ἐγένετο is an awkward imitation of the Hebrew infinitive
construct (the infinitive's used as the subject of ἐγένετο, "when Peter's entry
took place"--B404).

28 R967 In this verse, ὡς is used in a declarative sense similar to ὅτι, "how."
R1036 The object infinitive occurs with ἔδειξεν, "that I should not call."

30 R471 In this verse, an interesting example of the accusative occurs where
τὴν ἐνάτην is explanatory of the previous note of time, a point of time, and
yet a whole hour is meant (it may be used as an accusative of respect, unless
it conceivably means "the ninth-hour prayer," and forms a cognate accusative
to προσευχόμενος--M34). [Ed. Moule's final suggestion appears to be the most
accurate, since τὴν ἐνάτην is apparently used to distinguish the ninth-hour
prayer from the third and sixth hours of prayer; cf. the similar usage in 3:1.]

31 T58 The deponent verb μιμνήσκομαι has a passive sense here, "be remembered."

33 R861 The aorist participle παραγενόμενος refers to action which is simultaneous
with that of the principal verb ἐποίησας, "you did well to come."
R990 The infinitive ἀκοῦσαι is used to express the notion of purpose (cf. B366).
MT228 Καλῶς ποιήσεις with the aorist participle is the normal way of saying
"please" in the papyrii, and is classical (the verb occurs in the aorist tense
here).

34 T55 One expects the active verb instead of καταλαμβάνομαι (cf. 4:13), "I
understand."

37 R607 Καθ' ὅλης means "throughout all" (cf. 9:31).
BD137(3) 'Αρξάμενος is an appositional participle in the nominative, further
defining the ῥῆμα (actually, the ending -αμενον is more accurate grammatically and is supported by p⁴⁵, L and P).

38 R533 The datives πνεύματι and δυνάμει have the notion of means.
R1032 'Ως is used here with a declarative sense, although really meaning "how."
TGr20 Since πνεύματι is anarthrous, it implies that Jesus himself was anointed
with a powerful spiritual unction which enabled him to counter the activities
of evil spirits (cf. the discussion on Luke 1:15).
T72 Διῆλθεν is used as a complexive (summary) aorist referring to the action as
a whole without specifying the kind of action (with the present participle
here, it may mean "always," or "time after time" [until his death in Jerusalem,
v. 39]--BD332[1]).
BD209(3) 'Από is used instead of ἐκ to indicate the place of origin.

39   R1113   The aorist participle κρεμάσαντες refers to action which is coincident
with the action of the main verb (i.e., referring to the same event; cf. vv.
29 and 33), "they killed him by hanging him on a tree."

41   R960   There may be a causal sense in the use of οἵτινες here.
       R1095   Notice the sharp contrast denoted by οὐ . . . ἀλλά.

43   R1036   The infinitive of indirect discourse occurs here after μαρτυροῦσιν (the
only instance after this verb in the New Testament), "witness that."

44   BD257(2)   The articular phrase τὸ πνεῦμα τὸ ἅγιον refers to the known fact of
the out-pouring of the Spirit (but the article may also denote personification).

45   R578   Ἐκ is used to denote members of a party (cf. 11:2), "the circumcised believers."
       R1181   The second καί in this verse has an ascensive sense, "even" (the thing
that is added is out of the ordinary and rises to a climax).
       BD345   Verbs of perception may take a following perfect for a pluperfect in the
same way as they do a present for an imperfect (ἐξέστησαν . . . ὅτι . . . ἐκκέχυται), "they were amazed, because the gift of the Holy Spirit had been
poured out."

47   R728   Οἵτινες has a causal sense here, "since they received the Holy Spirit"
(cf. v. 41; this pronoun is more indefinite than a relative pronoun would
have been--M124).
       R1171   In this verse, μήτι is the interrogative particle expecting the answer
"no" while μή is a redundant negative after κωλύω, a verb of hindering.

48   T65   Where the aorist is used, the request is usually dogmatic or emphatic, demanding obedience (προσέταξεν means "to be baptized is essential").
       BD328   The aorist tense of ἠρώτησαν is necessary because the fulfillment of the
request, which did take place, is indicated only by the tense of this verb
(i.e., the request was granted).

ACTS 11

1   T313   The New Testament usually breaks the classical rule with neuter plural
words used in a personal sense; thus the plural verb occurs with ἔθνη (cf.
4:25).
       BD225   In the context here, κατά simply means "in."

2   R885   The imperfect verb διεκρίνοντο is used with an inchoative sense (cf. 3:10),
"they began to . . . "

3   M132   Ὅτι seems to be used as an interrogative, meaning "why did you go in
. . . ?"; although this may also be merely an instance of ὅτι introducing
direct speech, "they said you went in . . ." ("why did you go"--B300[2]).
[Ed. Occasionally in the New Testament this conjunction has the meaning of
"why" (cf. the accusations of the scribes and Pharisees in Mark 2:16 and the
similar construction in Mark 9:11 and 28). In view of this, the interrogative
rendering of ὅτι seems to be more probable in this context as well.]

4   T155 The participle ἀρξάμενος is only slightly pleonastic, since the emphasis
      is on καθεξῆς (cf. BD419[3]), "Peter began . . . in order."

5   M38 Note that in this verse ἐν πόλει Ἰόππῃ occurs, with the meaning of "in the
      city of Joppa."
      M82 Ἄχρι has the meaning "up to" with ἐμοῦ here.

6   R838 Since the imperfect and aorist occur together in this verse a distinct dif-
      ference apparently is present.

13   R1032 Πῶς seems to have a declarative sense similar to ὅτι, with the meaning
      "how" (cf. T137).

14   R402 In this verse, the verb σωθήσῃ agrees grammatically with the first and
      most important member of the group (σύ).
      T37 There appears to be some degree of emphasis in the use of σύ here.

15   B109 In this verse, the action denoted by ἐν τῷ with the aorist infinitive,
      strictly speaking, precedes the action of the principal verb, yet may be thought
      of by the writer as marking more or less exactly the time at which the action
      of the verb takes place (cf. Luke 2:27; "after"--BD404[2]).
      TGr21 For the construction τὸ πνεῦμα τὸ ἅγιον we may safely conclude that what
      came to the assembled company of Cornelius' relatives and friends at Caesarea
      was no mere divine impulse, but the Holy Spirit himself, he who came to the
      Apostles on the day of Pentecost (2:4).

16   M77 Ἐν appears to have an instrumental sense in this verse, "baptized with"
      (some scholars suggest that Luke's consistent use of the plain dative with
      ὕδατι and of ἐν with πνεύματι ἁγίῳ is merely a matter of style and not theo-
      logically significant).
      T240 The dative ὕδατι has an instrumental notion (cf. BD195[1d]).

17   R658 The infinitive κωλῦσαι is used with the adjective here as an accusative
      of general reference, "that I am able to hinder."
      T237 Ἐπὶ with the accusative after πιστεύω has the meaning "believe in" (cf.
      9:42).

18   R1190 Ἄρα has the notion of mere correspondence, "accordingly, so."
      M13 The aorist tense of ἡσύχασαν refers to an extended act or state, however
      prolonged in time, viewed as constituting a single fact without reference
      to its progress (cf. Luke 20:26).

19   T225 Μόνον is used as an adverb here, "only" (but D has μόνοις).
      T271 Ἐπὶ with the dative here has the sense of "on account of," although A
      and E have the genitive meaning "at the time of Stephen's death" (the best
      manuscripts support the rendering "on account of"--BD234[2]).
      H461 Ἀπό here seems to have a causal notion (possibly from semitic influence).

23   R530 The dative τῇ προθέσει is used to express the notion of manner, "to remain
      true, with devotion."

24   TGr20f. It cannot be thought that πνεύματος is anarthrous because it is the first
      mention of the word in the narrative; it has already occurred three times in

this chapter. Consequently, Barnabas is said to be filled with spiritual inspiration (cf. the discussion on Luke 1:15).
BD202 Προστίθημι has the sense of "add to" with τῷ κυρίῳ here (however, B* omits
τῷ κυρίῳ, probably correctly). [Ed. It seems best to retain τῷ κυρίῳ since
the heaviest manuscript support includes it.]

25   R990   The infinitive expresses purpose, "to look for."

26   R659   Πρώτως occurs instead of πρῶτον, meaning "for the first time" (cf. BD102
[5]).
R774   Ἐνιαυτὸν ὅλον means "a whole year."
T72   Συναχθῆναι and διδάξαι are used as complexive aorists, referring to the
action as a whole without specifying the kind of action (cf. 10:38), "they met
and taught."

28   R603   The prepositional phrase ἐπὶ κλαυδίου means "in the time of Claudius" or
"during the reign of Claudius."
R728   The pronoun ὅστις here is equivalent to ὅσπερ, meaning "which very" (cf.
MT92).
R891   Only two future infinitives in the New Testament seem to be durative (in
John 21:25 and here).
R1036   The infinitive of indirect discourse occurs with ἐσήμανεν (the only in-
stance after this verb in the New Testament; cf. 10:43), "he made known that
there would be."
TGr21   Christian prophecy was a gift of the Holy Spirit himself (articular
πνεύματος), and Agabus spoke directly from God (cf. 21:11).

30   R714   The neuter pronoun ὅ refers to the whole previous verbal idea.
R1113   The aorist participle ἀποστείλαντες refers to action which is coincident
with the action of the principal verb (i.e., happening at the same time), "they
did, sending it."
M57   Διά with the genitive here has the sense, "by means of."

ACTS   12

1   R578   Ἀπό here is used to denote members of a party; οἱ ἀπὸ τῆς ἐκκλησίας means
"church folk."
M59   The preposition in κατ' ἐκεῖνον τὸν καιρόν simply means "at."

2   R533   Μαχαίρῃ is used as a dative of means, "with the sword."

3   M177   Προστίθημι with an infinitive here means "do again," or "do further" (semitic; "he also arrested Peter"--T227).
T27   Ἀζύμων is an idiomatic plural referring to a Jewish festival.

4   T56   It is very improbable that ἔθετο in this verse implies that Herod locked
Peter up very carefully, i.e., for himself (as Zerwich holds). The general
lack of nice distinction in the middle verse in the New Testament rules it out.
H176   Τετράδιον has the meaning "a company of four."

5   M162   Μὲν οὖν may be purely resumptive or transitional, or μέν may be distinct
from οὖν, with οὖν having a resumptive sense (the phrase means "nay rather"--

T337).

6 M74 The preposition in πρὸ τῆς θύρας has a local meaning, "before the door."

7 M72 A consistent distinction between ἀπό and ἐκ is not maintained in the New Testament, as seen in this verse where the chains are demonstrably <u>on</u>, not <u>in</u>, one's hands.

8 R807 The verb ζῶσαι is used as a direct middle, meaning "gird yourself."
   T77 Notice the difference in the kind of action between the aorist and present imperative; περιβαλοῦ means "put your cloak on" (punctiliar), whereas ἀκολού-θει means "keep behind me" (linear).

9 R1153 The contrast here is indicated by a simple δέ (it has a strong adversative force of ἀλλά following a negative in vv. 9 and 14--T331).

10 R728 The pronoun ὅστις is equivalent to ὅσπερ, meaning "which very."
    T225 The predicate adjective αὐτομάτη corresponds to an adverb, since it modifies a verb, "it opened by itself."
    BD62 Πρῶτος is used for πρότερος (with a comparative sense, cf. 7:12).

11 M75 The preposition in ἐν ἑαυτῷ γενόμενος seems to have a local sense, Peter came to himself" (the condition opposite to ἐκστάσις as in 11:5; cf. Luke 15:17).
    T200 Πάσης τῆς . . . means "the whole . . ."

12 T206 The proper noun itself is generally anarthrous (especially when another noun is in opposition to it); so the reading τῆς (S, A, B, D) Μαρίας τῆς μη-τρός is probably incorrect (cf. BD268[1]). [Ed. Although Turner's initial premise is correct, on occasion proper nouns occur with the article. Since the greatest manuscript weight supports the inclusion of the article here, it should not be omitted but explained. Τῆς seems to denote possession here.]

14 R580 The preposition in ἀπὸ τῆς χαρᾶς expresses a causal idea.
    R1036 The infinitive is used in indirect discourse in both v. 14 and v. 15, in each instance it is the only time that this construction occurs in the New Testament with ἀπαγγέλω and διϊσχυρίζομαι, "reported that Peter was standing . . . she insisted that it was so."

16 T226 Some verbs are used to express certain adverbial ideas; they are actually principal verbs, but the main verbal idea is presented by the participle, as in "he knocked persistently."

18 M35 Τί is used predicatively, "what had become of Peter" (cf. BD2999[2]).

20 BD119(1) The compound verb θυμομαχέω means "to be very angry."

23 M71 'Ανθ' ὧν means "since" or "because" in this context.

25 R859 Πληρώσαντες is used as an effective aorist (i.e., the emphasis is on the end of the action), "when they had fulfilled", and συνπαραλάβοντες is used as a constative aorist (summary; the whole action is considered as a point), "taking along with them."

R862   There is no problem with the relationship of the participle and the verb
here unless εἰς is included in the text rather than ἐκ or ἀπό. It is true that
S, B and L read εἰς, but this reading is contradicted by the context. In 11:30,
it is plain that Barnabas and Saul were sent from Antioch to Jerusalem, and in
13:3 and 5, they are in Antioch with John Mark (the preposition εἰς seems to
have a local sense, εἰς Ἰερουσαλήμ should be taken with πληρώσαντες τὴν δια-
κονίαν, wth the resultant meaning "after they had delivered the relief offer-
ing in Jerusalem"; Debrunner prefers "after they had [brought the relief offer-
ing] to Jerusalem and delivered it there"--BD205). [Ed. The suggestion to
take εἰς Ἰερουσαλήμ with the following participle produces the most favorable
rendering, but the word order is unusual. Consequently, Robertson's proposal
appears to offer the most probable solution.]

ACTS 13

1   BD268(1) Λούκιος ὁ κυρηναῖος is incorrect (in all the manuscripts except D*)
unless the author perhaps wants to distinguish between this Luke and himself
(Λουκᾶς is equivalent to Λούκιος). [Ed. The latter suggestion seems to be
preferable.]
BD474(5c) The construction ἐν Ἀντιοχείᾳ κατὰ τὴν οὖσαν ἐκκλησίαν means "in
Antioch in the local church" (the articular participle has a technical sense
--R1107).

2   R1149 The use of δή here has a note of urgency (an invitatory particle, "come,
set apart for me"--T333; cf. Luke 2:15).

4   M162 Μὲν οὖν is purely resumptive or transitional (cf. 12:5), "then" or "so."

5   R480 The second accusative ὑπηρέτην is actually sort of in apposition to Ἰω-
άνην ("they had . . . John as an attendant"--M35).
R885 The imperfect tense of κατήγγελλον has as inchoative sense, "they began
to proclaim" (cf. 11:2).

6   M82 Ἄχρι occurs with the idea of place, meaning "up to."

8   R433 Γάρ introduces a clause which is explanatory, "for."

9   M106 Note the use of the article in Σαῦλος δέ, ὁ καὶ Παῦλος, where "who is also
Paul" is expressed by the article joined with the name, without even a participle like ὤν or λεγόμενος.

10   R874 The impatient question οὐ παύσῃ διαστρέφων is almost imperatival, certainly volitive, "will you not stop perverting" (the use of οὐ suggests indigna-
tion--R917; this construction has an imperatival sense, perhaps more of a
reproach than a command--BD387[3]).
T208 The genitive following υἱέ is used to express a certain quality, "of the
Devil."
BD146(1b) Ὦ is usually used to express emotion; in this particular instance it
is the announcement of divine punishment.

11   T51 Περιάγω means "go about, traverse."

T89 The future periphrastic construction occurs in ἔσῃ τυφλὸς μὴ βλέπων (actually it is best not to take this construction as a periphrastic--BD353(1);
cf. T88 and the discussion on 9:9).

13 R766 Οἱ περὶ Παῦλον is a classical idiom, meaning "Paul and his companions"
("the escorts alone" is impossible--T16).

14 T27 The idiomatic plural σαββάτων actually refers to a single day.

16 T153 The articular participle is dependent on the implied personal pronoun
ὑμεῖς, "you that fear God."

18 R528 The temporal accusative χρόνον refers to the extension of time, "for a
period of time."

19 T53 Κατακληρονομέω means "cause to inherit."

20 T243 The dative is used to refer to the duration of time, meaning "for 450
years" (the classical Greek would have used the accusative).

21 BD316(2) The active voice of αἰτέω is usually employed for requests addressed
to God. In ᾐτήσαντο βασιλέα of this verse, the request is probably not directed to God (cf. Septuagint in 1 Kings 8:5).

22 R482 Εἰς βασιλέα is used as a predicate accusative meaning "to be a king for
them."
T28 The plural θελήματα refers to "that which I wish" (cf. Eph. 2:3).

23 BD284(3) The pronoun τούτου occurs in an unusual position here (showing emphasis).

24 R94 Note the use of the circumlocutions πρὸ προσώπου τῆς εἰσόδου αὐτοῦ rather
than the simple πρὸ εἰσόδου αὐτοῦ, "before his coming."

25 M124 In this verse, τί is explained by some as equivalent to a relative pronoun
(not an interrogative): "I am not that which you suppose me to be"; but the
grammar is saved and good sense is made by "What do you suppose me to be? I am
not (the one)."

27 R608 Κατά is used with an expression of time here, "every sabbath."
B137 In the aorist participle ἀγνοήσαντες, only the inception (beginning) of
the action precedes the action of the principal verb (an inceptive aorist),
"because they did not recognize."

28 R1129 The participle εὑρόντες is used to express a concessive idea, "although
they found no . . . "

31 R602 With the expression of time here, ἐπί merely fills out the idea of the
accusative ("for many days").
R728 In this verse, the pronoun οἵτινες has the sense of "which very" (cf.
11:28; it also has this sense in v. 43--BD458).

33 R861 The aorist participle ἀναστήσας refers to action which is coincident with
that of the main verb, "God fulfilled this by raising."

36 BD202 The compound verb προστίθημι with the repeated preposition here has the
    "meaning "to be gathered to one's fathers."

38 M56 The preposition διά in this context seems to be used with an instrumental
    sense, "remission of sins by means of him."

40 R996 The clause following βλέπετε here seems to be paratactic, a co-ordinate
    clause (it seems that in this verse there is not a co-ordinate imperative ex-
    pression, but a dependent object clause [i.e., the object of βλέπετε]--B209).
    [Ed. Burton's suggestion is supported by the usual rendering of μή following
    an imperatival form of βλέπω, and it seems to be more feasible here, "watch
    out lest."]

41 R597 The preposition in the compound verb ἐκδιηγέομαι has a perfective idea,
    with the meaning "declare."

42 R645 Μεταξύ has the sense of "afterwards" here (εἰς τὸ μεταξὺ σάββατον perhaps
    means "on the next sabbath"--M58f.).

44 R990 The simple infinitive ἀκοῦσαι has the notion of purpose here.

46 R810 The middle voice in ἀπωθεῖσθε αὐτόν has the idea "you push it away from
    yourselves" (reject).
    BD420(3) The participle παρρησιασάμενοι seems to be used as a finite verb
    with εἶπαν, "Paul and Barnabas spoke out boldly and said."

47 R482 Εἰς φῶς is used as a predicate accusative, "I have set you to be a light."

50 T259 There is an unusual interchange of ἐκ and ἀπό here (in a local sense), "they
    drove them out."

                                    ACTS 14

1   R502 The genitives here occur before the substantive πλῆθος, because they are
    used to show emphasis (usually the genitive follows the substantive it is used
    with).
    R1000 Ὥστε with the infinitive πιστεῦσαι is used to express actual result.

3   R833 A period of time in this verse is merely regarded as a point (i.e., the
    aorist verb is used in a constative sense; they remained until the end of their
    stay related in vv. 5f., where the limit is indicated--BD332[1]).
    M50 Παρρησιαζόμενοι ἐπὶ τῷ κυρίῳ perhaps means "showing boldness in reliance
    upon the Lord."
    M162 Μὲν οὖν may have an adversative sense here, meaning "however, nay rather"
    or μέν may be distinct from οὖν, with οὖν being resumptive with the relevant
    δέ in v. 5, meaning "so far some time . . . but when . . ." (the phrase seems
    to mean "nay rather"--T337). [Ed. Moule's former suggestion appears to be more
    probable since Paul and Barnabas carried on despite the opposition portrayed
    in v. 2; cf. the similar construction in 25:4 and 28:5.]

4   M81 In this verse, σύν means "with" in the sense of "on the side of."

5   R628 Note the example here where καί could have been used instead of σύν, "with
     their rulers."
     BD393(6) 'Εγένετο ὁρμή with the infinitives here has the meaning "resolved" or
     "intended to."

8   R1096 In this verse, ἀδύνατον means "incapable" (cf. Rom. 15:1), whereas it
     usually means "impossible" (cf. MT221).
     T220 Τοῖς ποσίν is used as a dative of respect with the adjective here, "impo-
     tent in reference to his feet."

9   BD400(3) In πίστιν τοῦ σωθῆναι, the articular infinitive has a consecutive
     sense, "necessary faith for salvation" (cf. T141).

10   R838 In the latter part of this verse, the aorist tense is used to describe the
     beginning of an act and the imperfect is used to describe the continuation.
     T225 The adjective ὁρθός corresponds to an adverb, since it modifies the verb,
     "stand up straight" (cf. 12:10).

12   T41 The pronoun αὐτός has some degree of emphasis in this verse.

15   BD299(1) It seems better to translate τί ταῦτα ποιεῖτε as "why are you doing
     these things?" than "what are you doing?" (cf. R738).
     BD392(3) The infinitive here appears to be complementary to εὐαγγελιζόμενοι,
     "bring you good news, that you should."

17   R1154 Καίτοι seems to have an adversative sense, "and yet."
     BD442(16) The co-ordination of two ideas, one of which is dependent on the
     other, serves in the New Testament to avoid a series of dependent genitives.
     Thus, ἐμπιπλῶν τροφῆς καὶ εὐφροσύνης means "with joy for food" and ὑέτους καὶ
     καιροὺς καρποφόρους means "fruitful seasons through rains" (literally, "rains
     of fruitful seasons").

18   R606 In the compound verb here, κατά has a perfective force, with the meaning
     "restrain."
     R1094 Note the redundant negative here following a verb of hindering (such as
     negative cannot be translated into English--B483), "from offering sacrifice."
     B403 The infinitive with τοῦ μή after verbs of hindering is closely related
     to the infinitives of result (cf. Luke 24:16).

19   R489 The infinitive τεθνηκέναι serves as the object of νομίζοντες, "thinking
     that he was dead."
     R859 The aorist tense in πείσαντες and λιθάσαντες is used with an effective
     sense (i.e., stress is on the end of the action).
     B138 The aorist participles in this verse are best translated into English
     by a finite verb with "and" (cf. 10:23).
     BD327 The variant reading with ἔσυραν (the aorist instead of imperfect) is to
     be preferred, for otherwise the completion of the action, which certainly
     took place, would nowhere be indicated (the imperfect verb was intended to make
     the narrative interesting and continuous until some action is expected in the
     aorist to give point to the whole description; but as is common in the New Test-
     ament, the description is left without climax--T66, cf. Luke 2:47).

21   T53 Μαθητεύω has a causative sense,"make a disciple."
     T80 The present participle ἐπιστηρίζοντες refers to an action which is sub-
     sequent to that of the principal verb, "they returned . . . to strengthen" (cf.
     BD339[3a] and R892).

22   R562 The dative τῇ πίστει occurs with a locative sense, "in faith."

26   R905 The past perfect tense in ἦσαν παραδεδομένοι makes reference to the begin-
     ning of the tour from Antioch.

27   R350 The relative pronoun ὅσα occurs in an indirect question here (the pronoun
     may be understood as introducing an exclamation, although the interpretation
     which makes it equivalent to πάντα ἅ seems more accurate, cf. 9:16--BD304).
     [Ed. This final suggestion is similar to Robertson's suggestion, which has the
     resultant meaning "all that God had done."
     M61 Ὅσα ἐποίησεν ὁ θεὸς μετ' αὐτῶν may well mean "all that God had done in
     fellowship (or "co-operation") with them," in which case the preposition here
     has a plain Greek usage, and no semitism is involved (cf. M184).
     T158 Luke introduces participles quite effectively and thus presents a flowing
     style which is refreshing after the jerky epistolary style of Paul (as here;
     cf. Luke 4:20).
     T212 It is not definite whether πίστεως is an objective genitive, "leading to
     faith," or a subjective genitive, "where faith enters." [Ed. The noun θύραν
     is used as a metaphor with the verb ἀνοίγω (cf. 1 Cor. 16:9; 2 Cor. 2:12 and
     Col. 4:3). In this particular verse, the construction refers to the admission
     of the Gentile to the faith in Christ.]
     BD347(2) The pluperfects of the Vulgate in this verse are translated from the
     aorists; although there is a durative result, it was not necessary to empha-
     size it (as the Vulgate does).

28   BD332(2) The imperfect verb διέτριβον occurs with χρόνον οὐκ ὀλίγον without
     reference to a definite period of time (cf. v. 3), "they remained a long time."

                                   ACTS 15

1   M45 Τῷ ἔθει means "according to the custom" (the more usual way of expressing
     this is with κατὰ τὸ ἔθος; cf. R530 and BD196; τῷ ἔθει may mean "because of
     the Law"; for "according to the Law" we would expect κατά--T242). [Ed. The
     dative is considered as expressing the notion of manner in Moule's rendering.
     This use of the dative occurs frequently in the New Testament, cf. Acts 4:36;
     11:23 and 18:2. Consequently, there is no need to force a causal sense upon
     the text.]

2   T181 The article τούς is not repeated because the two groups are regarded as
     a unified whole (cf. Luke 22:4).

3   M162 Μὲν οὖν has a purely resumptive or transitional sense in vv. 3 and 30,
     with the meaning "so."
     T66 The imperfect tense of the verbs διήρχοντο and ἐποίουν was intended to
     make the narrative interesting and continuous, cf. 14:19 (the imperfect tense
     expresses the manner of the action [everywhere, and every time it was reported];
     the conclusion to the matter is seen in v. 4--BD327).

4   M73 The preposition ἀπό has an instrumental sense, "they were received by the
     Church" (equivalent to ὑπό, cf. v. 3 and T258).

8   R861 The aorist participles δούς and καθαρίσας refer to action which is simul-
     taneous with that of the principal verb (the action denoted by the participle
     occurs at the same time as the action of the main verb).

9   R580 Μεταξύ further explains the διά of the compound verb, "he made no distinc-
     tion between."

10   B375 The infinitive ἐπιθεῖναι is used to define more closely the content of the
     action denoted by the previous verb (closely related to the infinitive of con-
     ceived result and probably from Hebraistic origin), thus the first part of this
     verse means "now therefore why do you tempt God, that you should put (i.e.,
     "by putting," or "in that you put") a yoke upon the neck of the disciples?"
     (cf. Psa. 78:18 in the Masoretic text, M127 and BD392[1a]).
     T37 There is some degree of emphasis in the use of ἡμεῖς here.

11   T137 The infinitive σωθῆναι is used as the direct object of πιστεύομεν, "we
     believe that we are saved."

12   R834 The aorist verb ἐσίγησεν has a constative sense, "kept silence" (an incep-
     tive aorist-B41, cf. 7:60 and "began to be silent"--T71). [Ed. Robertson's
     suggestion appears to be preferable, since the extensive debate seems to have
     ceased in v. 7 when Paul stood up.]

13   B37 The inceptive aorist occurs in this verse, "and after they had become si-
     lent (μετὰ τὸ σιγῆσαι), James answered." It is evident that the infinitive
     must refer to the becoming silent, not to the whole period of silence, since
     in the latter case James must have been silent while the others were silent,
     and must have begun to speak when their silence had ended.

14   R1045 Καθώς is used in an indirect question here, "how."

17   R713 In τὰ ἔθνη ἐφ' οὕς, the relative pronoun has a change in gender from the
     antecedent, according to the actual sense (cf. T40; from the neuter to the mas-
     culine, referring to people).

20   B204 Τοῦ with the infinitive ἀπέχεσθαι is used as the object of the infinitive
     ἐπιστεῖλαι, "we should write to them to abstain."

21   B17 The present verb ἔχει is used to describe an action which beginning in past
     time is still in progress at the time of speaking, "for Moses from generations
     of old has had in every city them that preached him" (cf. M8).

22   B449 The participle ἐκλεξαμένους expresses an attendant circumstance to the
     principal verb, "it seemed good to the apostles and the elders . . . to choose
     men out of their company and send them to Antioch."
     BD401 The participial adjunct here is in the accusative form (ἐκλεξαμένους),
     because it modifies the subject of an infinitive, even though the actual sub-
     ject is initially in the dative.

23   R787 The article τήν is not repeated in this verse; thus Luke groups a city
     with two countries.

R1093 Χαίρειν is used as an absolute infinitive, rather than as an imperatival
infinitive (cf. MT179; it is the wish-infinitive of epistolary style--T78),
"greeting."
R1205 In the New Testament, emphatic words have the constant tendency to become
less so and to need reinforcement. Thus redundant constructions occur, such
as γράψαντες διὰ χειρὸς αὐτῶν.
T24 The noun χειρὸς occurs in the singular in a distributive sense with αὐτῶν.

24   B122 The participle ἀνασκευάζοντες refers to action which is identical to that
of the principal verb, "they have troubled you with words, subverting your
souls."

27   R991 The present participle ἀπαγγέλλοντας expresses purpose (cf. MT230).
T267 Δια λόγου means "openly" (as opposed to "by letter").

28   R1061 In τούτων τῶν ἐπάναγκες, ἀπέχεσθαι, the infinitive is in apposition with
the preceding words, "these necessary things, that you abstain."

29   R808 ᾿Απέχεσθαι is used as a direct middle, "keep yourselves away from."
M41 The genitive of separation occurs in ἀπέχεσθαι εἰδωλοθύτων, meaning "to
abstain from things sacrificed to idols."
T85 The perfect verb ἔρρωσθε has a present meaning, "farewell."
T157 The participle διατηροῦντες expresses a conditional idea, "if you keep."
BD102(3) In the New Testament, εὖ is seldom used for an adverb of manner (but
it occurs here because of the literary language), "you will do well."

32   M57 The preposition in διὰ λόγου πολλοῦ seems to express the idea of attendant
circumstance, meaning "at length (with much talk)."

36   R714 The relative pronoun αἷς occurs in the plural, which differs from the antecedent πόλιν (the plural refers to the people).
T333 Δή is used as a particle of invitation, "come, set apart for me" (cf. 13:2).

37   R857 The aorist infinitive συμπαραλαβεῖν has a constative sense, perfectly natural for the proposed journey. But Paul was keenly conscious of the discomfort
of Mark's previous desertion (v. 38). He was not going to subject himself
again to that continual peril (thus the present infinitive συμπαραλαμβάνειν
occurs).
TGr94f. The imperfect tense of the verbs ἐβούλετο and ἠξίου seems to have a
tentative sense, thus "Barnabas wanted" (had half a mind to initially), and
Paul merely "requested," and not even pressingly (a demand which expects fulfillment requires the aorist tense). Later, he set out in full the reasons
for his hesitant request (the iterative use of the imperfect tense is used in
both instances -- one man opposing the other--R884). [Ed. The initial statements of both requests were probably not expressed forcefully, but both Barnabas and Paul maintained their original propositions.]
     Paul uses the same infinitive as does Barnabas (συμπαραλαβεῖν), but Paul
deliberately alters the tense from aorist to present, because he envisaged that
John Mark might continuously or regularly travel with them, which was the very
thing he wished to avoid. Perhaps it was his intention to give the young man
a rest and take him on a subsequent journey (Paul refuses to have with them
day by day one who had shown himself unreliable--MT130).

39 R1091 Ὥστε with the infinitive in this verse expresses actual result (classical Greek would have used the indicative verb--T136), "so that they separated."

ACTS 16

3   R428 The demonstrative pronoun τοῦτον is used here to reflect the connection
between the two sentences, "this one," or "him."
R1029 In this verse, the imperfect (ὑπῆρχεν) may indicate that Timothy's father
was no longer living, although it is not the necessary meaning (this verb indicates that his father had died--BD330).

4   R562 In διεπορεύοντο τὰς πόλεις, one may either regard the accusative as loosely associated with the preposition (which generally requires the genitive, cf.
διὰ μέσον in Luke 17:11) or consider that the preposition has made an intransitive verb transitive, "they went through the cities."

5   R524 The datives in this verse seem to have a locative sense (τῷ ἀριθμῷ is used
as a dative of respect--T220). [Ed. Turner's suggestion for the second dative
is preferable, since it is somewhat awkward to consider it as "in the area (or
sphere) of numbers." But this dative should be translated "in reference to
numbers."]

6   R863 The participle κωλυθέντες naturally refers to action which is antecedent
to that of the main verb. Paul was headed west for Asia, but, being, forestal-
led by the Spirit, he turned farther north through the Phrygian and Galatic
region. One is not entitled to make κωλυθέντες equivalent to καὶ ἐκωλύθησαν
because of an unproven theory (cf. R788). Besides, the narrative in v. 6 does
not seem to be resumptive, but a new statement of progress (cf. MT133).

7   R1156 Οὐκ εἴασεν means "he forbade."

9   R581 In the phrase διὰ νυκτός, "by night," the preposition adds little to the
genitive itself ("in the night"--M56).

11 R652 The ellipsis of ἡμέρᾳ takes place with τῇ ἐπιούσῃ, "the next day."

12 T210 The geographic genitive (τῆς Μακεδονίας) is actually partitive. It indicates the country within which a town lies, "a city in."
R728f. Ἥτις is used merely as an exclamatory pronoun, agreeing with the gender
of the predicate rather than the antecedent.
M111 Occasionally the article is practically equivalent to a demonstrative pronoun. Τῆς μερίδος Μακεδονίας (if that is the true reading) must mean "of that
division of Macedonia (i.e., the relevant division, the division in question)."
Sir W. Ramsay has demonstrated that μερίς does not mean "province" and we may
not construe Μακεδονίας as in apposition to it -- as though it meant "of the
province Macedonia."

13 T27 The idiomatic plural σαββάτων actually refers to a single day (cf. 13:14).
MT82 According to Ramsay (Paul, p. 195), παρὰ ποταμόν shows familiarity with
the locality. But to accept this involves giving up ἐνομίζομεν προσευχὴν εἶναι,
a step not to be lightly taken (consequently, Ramsay's suggestion is not very
probable).

15   T65   The aorist παρεκάλεσεν means "insisted" (παρεβιάσατο shows how insistent he was; see above 10:48).
      BD442(10)   Καί in the initial part of this verse has the sense of "together with."

16   R728   The pronoun ἥτις has the meaning "which very" (cf. 11:28).
      R810   It is interesting to note the difference between the active verb παρεῖχεν in v. 16 (the damsel who furnished gain for her master) and the middle verb παρείχετο in 19:24 (referring to Demetrius who furnished gain for his craftsmen and himself).
      R1128   The participle μαντευομένη has the notion of means (thus the maid furnished the revenue for her master; cf. B443).
      T22   Sometimes a plural masculine noun includes masculine and feminine subjects. Thus τοῖς κυρίοις may refer to a man and woman owner in vv. 16 and 19.
      BD242   Πύθωνα is used as an adjectival substantive (modifying πνεῦμα), "a spirit of divination."

18   R884   Ἐποίει is used as an iterative imperfect (she did this repeatedly).
      B13   The present tense of παραγγέλλω has an aoristic sense, "I command you" (cf. M7 and T64).
      M49   In the phrase ἐπὶ πολλὰς ἡμέρας, the preposition is used temporally, and of extent, meaning "for many days" (although movement towards may even here be the underlying idea, if the phrase really means "for as much as [i.e., to the extent of] many days").
      M122   Αὐτῇ τῇ ὥρᾳ must mean "in that same hour."

19   T232   Ἐπιλαμβάνω generally has a genitive object. The accusatives τὸν Παῦλον and τὸν Σίλαν occur here because they are the direct objects of the main verb εἵλκυσαν (cf. 9:27 and BD170[2]).

22   R618   The preposition περί in the compound verb here has the idea of "from around."
      TGr96   Whenever the imperfect is used with verbs of asking or commanding, it imparts the idea of incomplete action in the past; there is a feeling of attempt without achievement, of command without confidence of being obeyed. The tense of the verb ἐκέλευον (imperfect) represents a mere pretence at command, satisfying the plaintiff's commercial interests, and yet not constituting a technical breach of Roman law. The magistrates possibly hoped that the gaoler might have the good sense not to carry out what they had diplomatically but halfheartedly commanded. [Ed. This rare instance of the present infinitive following the verb ἐκέλευον seems to support Turner's argument, although the command was carried out thoroughly according to v. 23.]

23   B145   In Acts 16:23; 22:24; 23:35 and 24:23, the aorist participle which is anarthrous and follows the verb is most naturally interpreted as referring to an action subsequent in thought and fact to that of the verb which it follows and equivalent to καί with a co-ordinate verb (perhaps due to Aramaic influence; "they cast . . . and charged").

25   R507   The verb ἐπακροάομαι occurs with αὐτῶν in the sense of "hearken to."

31   R402   In this verse, the verb σωθήσῃ agrees grammatically with the first and most important member of the group, σύ (cf. 11:14).
      T237   Ἐπί with the accusative after πιστεύω has the meaning "believe in" (cf. 9:42 and M49).

33 R576 In the construction ἔλουσεν ἀπὸ τῶν πληγῶν, it seems at first as if the
stripes were washed from Paul and Silas and not Paul and Silas washed from the
stripes (Winer suggests the addition in thought of "and cleansed").

34 T237 Πιστεύω with the dative means "to believe in" (cf. v. 31).

36 M79 The preposition ἐν in this verse may be used with the meaning "go into a
peace in which you may live" (cf. Luke 7:50).

37 R530 The adjective δημοσίᾳ is used as an adverb of manner, "openly."
R1187 One of the most striking instances of ἀλλά occurs in this verse, οὐ γάρ,
ἀλλά, where οὐ γάρ means "not much" with a degree of scorn (cf. καὶ νῦν).
H453 Ἐλθόντες coupled with a finite verb is emphatic in vv. 37 and 39, "let
them come themselves . . . "

39 BD209(1) Ἀπὸ τῆς πόλεως simply means "to leave the city," not "to set out from
the vicinity of the city" (the preposition has a local sense [E corrects to ἐκ,
since they went "out of," not "from" the city]--T259).

ACTS 17

1 R1126 The participle διοδεύσαντες expresses a temporal idea, "when they had
gone through."
T171 There is no apparent reason for the article being used with towns which
are mentioned as halting-places (τὴν . . . τὴν [εἰς Θεσσαλονίκην]; it is peculiar here, but may refer to the fact that these places lie on the well-known
road from Philippi to Thessalonica--BD261[2]).

2 R576 In this verse, ἀπό has the notion of source.
BD327 Διελέξατο is used as a constative (complexive, for three weeks) aorist,
but only as a supplementary description.

3 B30 The imperfect verb ἔδει denotes a past obligation which had already taken
place.

4 R669 Πρῶτων refers to rank in its occurrence here, "leading women."
T282 The negative expression οὐκ ὀλίγαι here forms a single idea (cf. 15:13;
it is a common expression of Luke, meaning "many").

5 R885 Ἐθορύβουν is used as an inchoative imperfect, "began to throw into disorder."

6 R572 The compound verb ἀναστατόω has the sense of "to upset" (Moffatt translates
the construction here as "these upsetters"--R1396).
B16 The present form of πάρειμι means "have arrived" ("have come"--T62).

7 R639 Ἀπέναντι has the hostile idea of "against" ("contrary to"--M82).

10 R728 The pronoun οἵτινες has the meaning "which very" (cf. 11:28).
BD221 The preposition in διὰ νυκτός has a temporal sense meaning "at night."

11   R487   The phrase καθ' ἡμέραν is very close to a pure adverb, "daily."
        T48   One must not read the meaning "because" into the pronoun οὕτινες;   they
        were not more noble "because" they received the message, but simply "who" re-
        ceived the message, whatever the context or theology may demand.
        T127   Εἰ introduces an indirect question here, "to see if."

12   M162   Μὲν οὖν in this verse is purely resumptive or transitional, "then," or "so."

13   B119   The present participles σαλεύοντες and ταράσσοντες refer to an action
        which is subsequent to that of the principal verb (an action following the main
        verb), "they came, stirring up and troubling."

15   R669   Ὡς τάχιστα is used as a true superlative, "as soon as possible" (this is
        a remnant of the rather frequent use of ὡς with superlative adverbs--R974; the
        elative superlative is intensified by the addition of ὡς--T31).

16   R885   Παρωξύνετο is used as a conative imperfect, "became irritated."
        R1204   The pronoun αὐτοῦ points to Christ, who has not been mentioned. [Ed.
        This is highly improbable, since the preceding noun Παύλου appears to be the
        antecedent of αὐτοῦ.]
        BD120(2)   The compound adjective κατείδωλος has the meaning "full of idols."

17   M103   The articular participle τοὺς παρατυγχάνοντας is equivalent to a relative
        clause, meaning "those who happened to be there" (or perhaps "those who, from
        time to time, came"; "casual passers-by"--T151).
        M163   Μὲν οὖν seems to have a purely resumptive or transitional sense (or possi-
        bly it is adversative meaning "however, nay rather"). [Ed. There appears to
        be no basis for taking this phrase with an adversative sense, especially since
        v. 16 presents the reason for Paul's action in v. 17.]

18   R787   The two groups, Epicureans and Stoics, are treated as one group in this
        verse, since the article τῶν is not repeated.
        B385   In the New Testament, the personal construction is regularly employed with
        δοκεῖ, as in this verse, "he seems to be a setter-forth of strange gods" (cf.
        T147).
        M151   The question in this verse seems to mean "what might this cocksparrow be
        trying to say?" (The optative with ἄν is used to express what would happen on
        the fulfillment of some supposed condition, cf. 8:31--B178).
        BD119(1)   The compound noun σπερμολόγος means "one who picks up seeds, a rook,
        a gossip."
        BD290(6)   Οὗτος appears to be used in a contemptuous sense (cf. Luke 18:11).

20   R742   The pronoun τινα may have the meaning "a kind of."
        BD126(2)   The meaning of many words has shifted (usually faded) in the New
        Testament, as with ξενίζω in this verse, which means "to surprise."

21   R665   Καινότερον refers to something newer than what they had recently heard.
        R749   Ἕτερος has the sense of "different" here.

22   R464   Simcox notes that Denosthenes often said ἄνδρες Ἀθηναῖοι, just as did
        Paul in this instance (the noun in apposition, ἀθηναῖοι,   conveys the main
        idea--R399).
        R665   In this verse, δεισιδαιμονεστέρους means "more religious (or superstitious)

than ordinary" or "than I had supposed" (it appears to be used as a popular elative strengthened by ὡς, , meaning "extremely god-fearing," cf. v. 15-- T30). [Ed. Actually the rendering "more religious than ordinary" is similar to "extremely god-fearing."]

T57 Although the passive participle σταθείς is used, no one placed Paul on Mar's Hill, he stood there (intransitive active, cf. Luke 18:11).

T161 The use of ὡς with θεωρῶ here has the sense, "from what I see, it appears as if." [Ed. Actually, ὡς is used with the comparative adjective rather than the verb; cf. the comment above.]

26 R772 Παντός means "every" ("whole"--M95). [Ed. Moule's suggestion appears to be more accurate, since the face of the earth refers to one entity.]

R863 The action referred to by the aorist participle ὁρίσας is not later than that of the principal verb ἐποίησεν (the determination of man's home preceded his creation in the Divine plan--MT133).

M143 The simple infinitives in vv. 26f. (κατοικεῖν and ζητεῖν), are vague, they may be used as final, consecutive or generally descriptive (epexegetic) infinitives (ζητεῖν is used as an epexegetical infinitive--R1086). [Ed. Κατοικεῖν is not epexegetical defining the content of the verb, since πᾶν ἐθνός provides the object of ἐποίησεν. But rather, the infinitive portrays the consecutive-final notion (cf. Rom. 1:20 and 5:20 for the fusion of these two concepts together). The second infinitive ζητεῖν does not appear to be parallel with the former infinitive, since a conjunction such as καί is not used. But this latter infinitive denotes the purpose of the previously mentioned providential arrangement.]

T27 The plural καιρούς means "the allotted span of time."

27 R1129 Καί γε accompanies the participle ὑπάρχοντα to make the concessive idea plain, "although" (cf. B437).

T127 Εἰ with the optative here is closer to a final clause than a real condition (εἰ meaning "whether"--BD386[2]; εἰ ἄρα means "if haply"--R1190; εἰ has the notion of purpose [cf. 20:16]--R1021).

MT230 The negative οὐ occurs with the concessive participle ὑπάρχοντα for emphasis. [Ed. Actually, the negative οὐ negates the adverb μακράν which immediately follows, rather than the participle.]

28 M123 In the quotation from Aratus, τοῦ occurs for τούτου, "of this one."

T221 For the construction (ἐκ) τοῦ γάρ . . . γένος ἐσμέν, the translation is "we are his offspring" (because of v. 29; γένος is used as an adjectival accusative).

T268 The preposition in οἱ καθ᾽ ὑμᾶς ποιηταί is used instead of a possessive genitive, with the whole phrase meaning "your poets."

30 R629 The negative notion of "overlook" appears in the compound verb ὑπεροράω.

M163 Μὲν οὖν may be purely resumptive or μέν may be distinct from οὖν, with οὖν having a resumptive sense. [Ed. The latter suggestion seems preferable, although δέ is not used in the contrast here.]

31 R550 The prepositional phrase ἐν δικαιοσύνῃ has the substantial force of an adverb (with the notion of manner--R589; "justly"--M78).

T262 The prepositional phrase ἐν ἀνδρί may mean "in the person of a man" or it may be instrumental (this phrase was originally instrumental--BD219[1]; it is instrumental here, "by a man"--M77).

ACTS   18

2   R530 The dative τῷ γένει expresses the notion of manner (cf. 4:36), "by race."

4   R885 The imperfect tense of ἔπειθεν has a conative sense (i.e., an action begun,
     but interrupted), "tried to persuade" (cf. T65).

5   R808 In συνείχετο τῷ λόγῳ the middle voice may have the force of a direct mid-
     dle, meaning "he held himself to the word."
     R1036 Εἶναι is used as an object infinitive following διαμαρτυρόμενος, "testi-
     fying that."
     T220 Τῷ λόγῳ is used as a dative of respect, "in reference to the word."

6   R810 The middle participle in ἐκτιναξάμενος τὸ ἱμάτια has the resultant sense
     of "shaking out his clothes from himself."
     T27 The idiomatic plural ἱμάτια refers to "the upper garment."

7   BD353(3) The periphrastic construction here differs very little in meaning from
     the simple verb form, "whose house was next to the synagogue."

8   T67 The iterative use of the imperfect verbs occurs in this verse (repeated in-
     cidents of belief and baptism).
     T237 Πιστεύω with the dative has the meaning "believe in" (D has εἰς with the
     accusative; cf. BD187[6]).

9   R583 Both the notion of means and manner are present in the prepositional phrase
     δι' ὁράματος,"by means of a vision."
     R890 Note the use of the present and aorist tense with the imperatives; μὴ
     φοβοῦ, ἀλλὰ λάλει καὶ μὴ σιωπήσῃς, means "he had been afraid, he was to go on
     speaking, he was not to become silent."

10   R477 Χεῖρας is the implied object of the verb ἐπιθήσεται.
     B398 Τοῦ with the infinitive here appears to express conceived result (it may
     have the idea "so as to"--R1002).
     T318 Subordination indicated by διότι here is so loose that only the feeble
     translation "for" is possible.

11   R833 A period of time here is merely regarded as a point (the aorist tense has
     a constative [summary] use where the limits of the action are being defined
     by eighteen months--T72).

13   R616 The idea of the preposition in παρὰ νόμον is that to go beyond is to go
     against.

14   R1014 In vv. 14f., Gallio neatly justifies his own impatience by the first con-
     ditional clause (second class -- determined as unfulfilled) and shows his own
     opinion by the second conditional clause (first class -- determined as ful-
     filled), "if it were a matter . . . ; but since it is . . ."
     R1193 There apparently is no sense of vehemence or urgency in the use of ὦ here
     (cf. T33). [Ed. Probably the tone of annoyance is expressed.]

B153 The present participle of μέλλω with an infinitive following is not used
to express the purpose of an action (as the future participle is), but is used,
as the future participle is not, to express intention without designating the
intended action as the purpose of another act, "Paul was about to open his
mouth."

15 R686 The pronoun αὐτοί is emphatic, meaning "you by yourselves."
T86 The future indicative ὄψεσθε expresses a command, "see to it yourselves."
T268 The preposition in τοῦ καθ' ὑμᾶς is used instead of a possessive genitive
with the phrase meaning "your law" (cf. 17:28; "your own law"--BD224[1]; notice
the occurrence of the article with the prepositional phrase, but not with the
preceding noun--R766).

18 R1127 The participle κειράμενος has both the temporal and modal sense (an
attendant circumstance, "having shorn his head"--B449).

19 T41 Αὐτός appears to have some degree of emphasis in this verse.
BD103 In the manuscripts B, H, L and P, the pronoun αὐτοῦ is used for ἐκεῖ.

21 BD484 Pleonasm consists in the repetition of an idea which has already been
expressed in the sentence, not for any rhetorical purpose nor because of mere
carelessness, but as a consequence of certain habits of speech. Note πάλιν
ἀνακάμψω ; "I will return again."

22 R1136 There must be a subtle reason for the procedure in this verse, where
the first participle (κατελθών) stands apart in sense from the other two.

23 R788 No absolute conclusions can be drawn as to why the article τήν is not
repeated (cf. 16:6).
BD339(2a) The complexive aorist ἐξῆλθεν is supplemented by the present participle διερχόμενος describing the same action, thus a future nuance is the
result ("he went from Antioch, to go through"--T80).
BD421 Participles are asyndetic (καί omitted) if they do not have equal value
in the sentence, as here (cf. v. 22), "he went . . ., strengthening."

25 R524 Τῷ πνεύματι is used as a locative dative (a dative of respect--T220).
[Ed. It appears to be more feasible to consider this dative as having a locative sense, with the literal meaning of "boiling over in his spirit," i.e.,
"with burning zeal" or "full of enthusiasm."]
T15 Τὰ περί means "things concerning."

26 R665 The comparative adjective ἀκριβέστερον refers to the fact that Apollos
received more accurate information than he had previously had (the comparative
is used for the elative superlative, "very accurately"--T30). [Ed. Since the
comparative adjective may be rendered as such with valid sense in the context,
there is no reason to consider it as an elative superlative.]

28 R582 Διά seems to have a perfective force in the compound verb here, "refute."

ACTS 19

2   R916 The first occurrence of εἰ introduces a direct question here (due to the
    Septuagint rendering of the Hebrew), "Did you receive . . . when you believed?"
    (the aorist participle πιστεύσαντες refers to action which is simultaneous
    with that indicated by the principal verb ἐλάβετε--R861).
    R1045 The second occurrence of εἰ in this verse introduces an indirect question,
    "that there is a Holy Spirit."
    R1186 In ἀλλ' οὐδ', the thought answers the preceding question and is probably
    adversative.
    TGr20 The situation arose in Ephesus on Paul's third journey where he found cer-
    tain disciples who had not received the spiritual unction (since πνεῦμα ἅγιον
    is anarthrous) and who told him that they had not even heard that anyone else
    had received it. The disciples must be understood to deny knowledge of any
    holy spirit; presumably they knew only of evil spirits. Then in v. 6, Luke
    brings back the definite article anaphorically, saying, "When Paul laid on his
    hands, that very holy spirit came upon them" (cf. the discussion on Luke 1:15).

3   R739 Purpose is expressed by εἰς τί.
    T255 The preposition with the accusative in εἰς τὸ . . . βάπτισμα, occurs where
    the simple dative would suffice (cf. 8:16).

5   T255 Εἰς in the baptismal formula here is similar to ἐν, "in the name."

7   R773 Οἱ πάντες ἄνδρες has the meaning "the total number of men" (cf. 27:37 and
    T201).

8   R811 Διαλεγόμενος is used as a reciprocal middle, "discussing together."

9   B119 Subsequent action in reference to the main verb is expressed by the pres-
    ent participle διαλεγόμενος, with the meaning "he separated the disciples,
    reasoning daily in the school of Tyrannus" ("he separated . . . and then used
    to discourse . . ."--M102).

11 M105 Δυνάμεις τε οὐ τὰς τυχούσας refers to the fact that the miracles he worked
    were no ordinary ones.
    MT231 Οὐχ ὁ τυχών is a common vernacular phrase (this οὐ may be explained with
    the participle; οὐ is not used to negate the participle--R1139). [Ed. Οὐ is
    used with the participle rather than with the verb or any other part of the
    sentence, because the point is that these miracles were not the ordinary kind
    (cf. 28:2). The figure of speech in which something is expressed by a nega-
    tion of the contrary is characteristic of Luke's writings; cf. v. 23f.]

15 R736 In interrogative statements, New Testament Greek occasionally distinguishes
    between the essence of a thing (τί) and the classification of a thing (τίς),
    as in this verse.
    M198 The safest principle in reference to synonyms (γινώσκω and ἐπίσταμαι) is
    probably to assume a difference until one is driven to accept identity of mean-
    ing. But the fact remains that sheer variety, and specific verbs with certain
    tenses, have sometimes to be reckoned with among stylistic phenomena.

16 R607 Κατά in the compound verb here has the idea of "down upon."

228

R745 It seems certain that the seven sons of Sceva are alluded to by ἀμφοτέρων.
A corruption of the text is possible (cf. the Bezan text), but it is hardly
necessary to postulate that in view of the undeniable Byzantine use of ἀμφότεροι for more than two (cf. both in old English). The papyri showed undoubted
examples also and the Sahadic and some later versions took ἀμφοτέρων as
"all." But Moulton (MT80) hesitates to admit in Luke a colloquialism of which
early examples are so rare. On the whole, one is safe in this reference (as
well as in Acts 23:8) to admit the free use of ἀμφότεροι.
T158 Ἐφαλόμενος is equivalent to ἐφήλετο καί (cf. 14:27; the variant reading
καὶ κατακυριεύσας [S*, H, L, P] gives the second participle a weaker connection with the first).

19 R828 The compound verb κατακαίω means "to burn up."

20 M169 Note the displacement of τοῦ κυρίου here (τοῦ κυρίου must refer to ὁ
λόγος--T350; the genitive is placed before the noun it modifies probably for
emphasis).

21 R787 The article is not repeated with Ἀχαΐαν because the two Roman provinces
are adjacent, although distinct.
BD392(3) Τίθημι with ἐν τῷ πνεύματι has the meaning "to intend to" (cf. Luke
21:14).

22 R800 Ἐπέχω is an intransitive compound of ἔχω ("tarry"--T52).
M68 The preposition εἰς has a local sense here, "at" (in place of ἐν; cf. BD
205).

24 R810 Note the use of the middle voice in παρείχετο, "he furnished for his
craftsmen and himself" (cf. 16:16).
M105 This verse may mean "Demetrius, . . . a silversmith, a maker . . . brought
the craftsmen no little trade," or "Demetrius, . . . a silversmith, brought
the craftsmen no little trade by making . . ." (the latter seems to be the
more probable rendering of ποιῶν).

25 M62 The preposition in τοὺς περὶ τὰ τοιαῦτα ἐργάτας has a metaphorical sense,
with the meaning "the workmen connected with such things" ("in that line of
business," as one might say; the preposition has the sense of "concerning";
cf. Phil. 2:23--R620).

26 R697 Οὗτος is used with the notion of reproach (expressed by those who had a
commercial interest in idolatry; cf. 7:40).
M39 It is tempting to regard οὐ μόνον Ἐφέσου ἀλλὰ σχεδὸν πάσης τῆς Ἀσίας as
a solitary example of the locative use of the genitive of place names (eg.
"at Ephesus"; cf. R494). But it is possible that the genitives are partitive
and depend on the ἱκανὸν ὄχλον which follows (though at a surprising distance):
"a good crowd out of Ephesus" (cf. BD186[1] and MT73). [Ed. In view of the
word order here, the former suggestion seems more probable.]

27 R518 Τῆς μεγαλειότητος is an ablative use of the genitive, "from her magnificence."
B100 The infinitive μέλλειν with the infinitive καθαιρεῖσθαι dependent on it
has the force of a future infinitive of the latter, "she will suffer the loss
of her magnificence."

B481 It is perhaps as a fixed phrase, unaffected by the infinitive, that εἰς οὐθέν limits λογισθῆναι (generally μή occurs with infinitives), "be regarded as nothing."

29 H369 θέατρον seems to have the sense of "spectacle" in vv. 29 and 31, as in 1 Cor. 4:9.

30 R885 The negative imperfect commonly denotes resistance to pressure or disappointment (undoubtedly the former in οὐκ εἴων).

31 T239 The dative in ὄντες αὐτῷ φίλοι has the idea of credit.

32 R665 Οἱ πλείους means "the majority."
R747 Ἄλλος ἄλλο means "one one thing" or "one another" (classical).
R1029 In this verse, the pluperfect occurs (ᾔδεισαν and συνεληλύθεισαν), where the direct discouse would have the present perfect, "most of them did not know why they were assembled."
M83 Τίνος ἕνεκα means "for what reason."

33 T209 The partitive genitive can be seen in ἐκ δὲ τοῦ ὄχλου, which means "some of the crowd."

35 BD241(7) Ἄγαλμα is to be supplied with the neuter adjective τοῦ διοπετοῦς, "the statue fallen from heaven."

36 R909 Κατεσταλμένους ὑπάρχειν is a periphrastic form of the subject infinitive, "to be restrained."
M102 The participle in ἀναντιρρήτων . . . ὄντων τούτων has a causal idea, with the sense of "as these things cannot be denied" (cf. T157).

37 T157 The participle βλασφημοῦντας has a concessive sense, "although . . ."
MT244 The classical ἡ θεός often appears in Magnesian inscriptions to describe the great goddess of the city, while other peoples' goddesses were θεαί, the usual koine term. The town clerk is accordingly using the technical term, as we might expect.

38 M163 In the construction μὲν οὖν, μέν is distinct from οὖν, with οὖν being resumptive (cf. δέ in v. 39), "if therefore" or "so then."
T26 Ἀνθύπατοι εἰσιν is an idiomatic plural, since there was only one proconsul.

40 M39 The genitive στάσεως may be indicating the accusation with which a defendant is charged, if in this context it means "to be accused of riot concerning this day", as in the Revised Version margin; but this would seem to be the solitary New Testament example (in Acts 23:6 and 29, περί with the genitive is used), and it is very doubtful if it is to be so construed here (the genitive στάσεως appears to denote the ground of accusation. This construction is so rare that one is tempted to take the genitive closely with σήμερον, and thus construe in the usual way περὶ τῆς σήμερον στάσεως--T231). [Ed. Turner's suggestion is appropriate for the construction here, resulting in the translation "charged with riot concerning this day's event."]
H341 Αἴτιον means "cause" in this verse.

ACTS 20

3   B153 In vv. 3 and 7, the present participle of μέλλω with an infinitive is
    used to express intention without designating the intended action as the pur-
    pose of another act (cf. 18:14).
    B400 Τοῦ ὑποστρέφειν is used to limit the noun γνώμης (cf. 14:9; "he decided
    to return"--M129).
    M38 Is the genitive in ἐγένετο γνώμης to be considered as possessive, as though
    it meant "he became possessed of a decision" (equivalent to "he decided"), per-
    haps to be compared with the English phrase "of the opinion"? [Ed. Regardless
    of whether we explain γνώμης as a possessive or not, this construction with
    ἐγένετο has the meaning "he decided"; cf. the similar construction in 2 Pet.
    1:20.]

5   R471 Ἔμενον is used transitively here, with the sense of "wait for" (cf. v. 23).

6   M205 The curious ἄχρι ἡμερῶν πέντε, meaning "within five days," is unique in
    the New Testament (although cf. 3:13).
    T171 The articular εἰς τὴν Τρῳάδα is due to the anaphoric reference (referring
    to a previous mention, cf. v. 5).

7   T187 Μιᾷ has the sense of "first."

9   R579 The preposition in κατενεχθεὶς ἀπὸ . . . is equivalent to ὑπό (causal-
    instrumental, "born down by sleep"--M73).
    H286 The adjective τρίστεγος means "with three stories," or "belonging to the
    third story" (as a noun here).

11 BD425(6) The classical liberty to use οὕτως to summarize the content of a pre-
    ceding participial construction in the New Testament is found only in Acts 20:
    11 and 27:17, "and so departed."

15 R573 In κατηντήσαμεν ἄντικρυς both the verb and preposition have the idea of
    face-to-face (cf. M82).
    R748 Τῇ ἑτέρᾳ has the sense of "next" in this context.

16 B258 Εἰ δυνατὸν εἴη represents the protasis of the sentence ἐὰν δυνατὸν ᾖ γενή-
    σόμεθα which expressed the original thought of Paul, to which the writer here
    refers ("if it were possible for him"); εἰ introduces a parenthetical phrase "if
    possible"--T127; εἰ conveys the notion of purpose; cf. 17:27--R1021). [Ed.
    Actually the idea of purpose is introduced by ὅπως and the subjunctive and not
    by the particle εἰ.]
    BD205 Εἰς has the sense of ἐν after γενέσθαι here, "at Jerusalem."

17 T171 The article in τῆς Μιλήτου is used with an anaphoric sense (referring to
    a previous reference, cf. v. 15).

18 R721 The relative clause points out a sharp distinction from the antecedent,
    when the preposition is repeated with it (cf. 7:4).
    R773 Τὸν πάντα here means "the whole," "the totality." The whole is contrasted
    with a part (cf. Gal. 5:14; "all that time"--T201).

BD434(2) The adverb πῶς is used with ἐγενόμην, with the meaning "how I acted," "behaved."

20   T137 'Ως is used with a sense similar to that of ὅτι (i.e., expressing content; cf. πῶς in v. 18).

22   R523 Τῷ πνεύματι is used as a locative dative, "in the spirit."
R878 The articular future participle here has a futuristic sense (not volitive), "the things that will happen."
T63 The present verb πορεύομαι indicates the continuation of an action during the past and up to the moment of speaking (this is largely rhetorical and poetical in classical Greek; the present verb has a futuristic sense--BD323[3]).
[Ed. Actually, the present verb describes an action that was already in progress, "I am going to Jerusalem."]

23   BD449(1) Πλὴν ὅτι means "except that" (classical).
H122 Certain scholars assert that δεσμά refers to the "actual bonds," whereas δεσμοί refers to bondage. This distinction cannot be pressed for all of the New Testament, although it would suit this context very well and v. 23 gains vividness from it.

24   R499 It is uncertain whether τῆς χάριτος τοῦ θεοῦ is used as a subjective or objective genitive. [Ed. The use of this phrase with τὸ εὐαγγέλιον seems to favor a subjective sense. Paul generally considers the gospel as a tremendous gift from God; cf. Col. 1:6.]
R967 'Ως is used as a final particle (expressing purpose) in this verse (cf. B194), "in order that I may finish."

25   M13 The aorist verb διῆλθον refers to an extended action, however prolonged in time, viewed as constituting a single fact without reference to its progress.

26   M164 Διότι in this context means "and so."

27   R807 'Υπεστειλάμην is used as a direct middle, meaning "withdraw myself."
R1089 Τοῦ with the infinitive is used as the object of the verb of hindering (cf. v. 20), "I did not hesitate from declaring."

28   M121 In this verse, τοῦ ἰδίου is possibly used as a noun meaning "his own Son" (cf. MT90; the latter part of this verse is best translated, "the church of God which he bought for himself by his own blood," i.e., the blood of God! 'Ιδίου is best understood as a possessive adjective rather than as a noun--TGr14f.). [Ed. Since the noun does not occur with τοῦ ἰδίου, the adjective may be used as a noun (cf. 4:23, 21:6 and 24:23).]
T78 The present infinitive ποιμαίνειν means "to shepherd continually" (with the idea of purpose--T135).

29   M41 The simple genitive is used to express the idea of separation with the participle φειδόμενοι, meaning "to spare" (i.e., "refrain from").

30   R689 'Υμῶν αὐτῶν is used as a reflexive pronoun in the second person plural (this phrase coincides with the reflexive pronoun in appearance only--BD288[1]; the pronoun αὐτῶν is intensive not reflexive--R687 and T194). [Ed. The phrase has the meaning "from you yourselves," which appears to be reflexive but is actually emphatic or intensive.]

32 T264 This verse is not simply a general statement that God's grace gives an
inheritance <u>to</u> those who are sanctified, but that he will give to these particular saints at Ephesus, whose pastors Paul is addressing, an inheritance
<u>among</u> all the sanctified, emphasizing the corporate nature of the Church <u>within</u>
which these believers have their place (Luke never uses δίδωμι with ἐν for
"give to").

35 R679 The pronoun in αὐτὸς εἶπεν is emphatic, possibly meaning "the Master said."
B374 The infinitive after ἤ in the New Testament is used as the correlative of
some preceding word or phrase, and usually as a nominative (cf. 18:25), "it
is more blessed to give than to receive."
T31 The positive adjective μακάριον is used for a comparative with the sense,
"happier than."
BD425(6) Ὅτι οὕτως . . . does not mean "thus -- namely by toiling" but with a
forceful gesture, "look, thus must one work and toil."

38 R659 The superlative adjective μάλιστα is used as an adverb, meaning "most of
all."
B72 Μέλλουσιν is used with an infinitive to portray a future event (cf. Luke
9:44), "that they would not see his face again."

ACTS 21

2 R891 In vv. 2f., the present participles διαπερῶν and ἀποφορτιζόμενον are
futuristic (the latter is equivalent to ἔμελλεν ἀποφορτίζεσθαι, literally
meaning "the ship had the characteristic of . . ."--BD339[2b]; it has a prospective notion, "the ship was appointed to unload her cargo"--R1115; "it was
to"--B130).

3 R548 Ἐκεῖσε, meaning "thither," occurs twice in the New Testament (here and
in 22:5). Winer calls this an abuse of language, which is putting it rather
strongly since it is found in the best Greek literature (more elegant--BD103).
R883 The imperfect tense in ἐπλέομεν has a descriptive durative sense ("we
kept on our course to Syria [imperfect] and finally landed at Tyre [aorist]"--
T66).
BD309(1) Ἀναφάναντες means "we made it visible to ourselves" (therefore with
the customary meaning of φαίνειν), that is, by drawing near.

4 R1046 Μὴ ἐπιβαίνειν expresses an indirect command (cf. T149; indicating the
content of ἔλεγον), "they were telling Paul not to go."
M57 The prepositional phrase διὰ τοῦ πνεύματος perhaps means "as a spiritual
insight."
BD103 In this verse, αὐτοῦ is used as an adverb of place, "there."

5 T174 Σὺν γυναιξὶ καὶ τέκνοις means "with their wives and children" (the article
is omitted because it is a formula; cf. 1:14).

6 R691 Τὰ ἴδια means "one's home" in this context.

8 R614 Παρά with the dative has the idea of "at one's house" in vv. 8 and 16.

11 TGr21 Agabus spoke directly from God (cf. 11:28).
    T190 The reflexive pronoun (ἑαυτοῦ) occurs before two nouns (rather than fol-
    lowing) to eliminate repetition (the possessive genitive is emphatic here—
    BD284[2]).

12 M129 Τοῦ μή with the infinitive here seems to have an epexegetic sense (i.e.,
    explanatory or extensive of a preceding idea), meaning "we begged him . . . not
    to go up" (it portrays the object of the finite verb with the notion of purpose
    —R1066 and 1088).

13 R593 Εἰς has a local sense similar to ἐν in this verse, "at Jerusalem."
    R1077 Note that the infinitive occurs with the adverb ἑτοίμως, "I am ready to
    be bound and to die."
    R1181 Καί in ἀλλὰ καί has an ascensive sense, "even."
    T52 Ἔχω in this verse means "to be."

14 R863 The aorist participle εἰπόντες refers to an action which is antecedent
    or coincident with that of the main verb, "this last remark of acquiescence"
    (the aorist participle in such constructions as ἡσυχάσαμεν εἰπόντες, does not
    indicate sequence of time any more than does the equivalent co-ordination with
    καί---BD420[2]; "we ceased with the words"--MT134). [Ed. This construction
    is similar to the common ἀποκριθεὶς εἶπεν which is simply translated by "he
    answered and said."]

16 R502 Notice τῶν μαθητῶν, where the partitive genitive is alone (τινές is im-
    plied--R1202), "some of the disciples."
    R891 There is no idea of purpose in the present participle ἄγοντες, but it is
    merely descriptive (it has a future sense, "in order to bring us"--T80). [Ed.
    Robertson seems to be forcing a specific point here. Ἄγοντες may not portray
    the sole purpose for the disciples accompanying them, but it appears to express
    one of the several reasons for their assistance.]
    R955 The subjunctive verb ξενισθῶμεν has a volitive sense, "we should lodge."
    R989 The relative clause παρ' ᾧ ξενισθῶμεν expresses the notion of purpose
    (this clause is to be distinguished from a true relative clause of purpose in
    that it does not express the purpose with which the action denoted by the prin-
    cipal clause is done, but constitutes a complementary limitation of the princi-
    pal clause--B319).

17 BD205 The preposition εἰς has the sense of ἐν after γενομένων here. [Ed. The
    participle γενομένων has the idea of motion towards. Consequently, the pre-
    position εἰς has its usual sense.]

19 R746 We must not connect ἕν and ἕκαστον in this verse. [Ed. These terms are
    connected, but with the sense of "one by one" rather than meaning "each one";
    cf. 14:27 and 15:4.]

20 T66 The imperfect and aorist tense is used with the meaning "they kept praising
    God and finally said" ("they praised God for some time and in various ways until
    they finally said"--BD327).

21 R524 Τοῖς ἔθεσιν is used as a locative (this dative has the meaning "according
    to our customs"; cf. 15:1--M45). [Ed. Moule's suggestion appears to be more
    accurate within this context, even though κατὰ τὰ ἔθα is the more usual phrase

for this expression (cf. the discussion on 15:1).]
M33 The double accusative with διδάσκεις means "you teach everyone apostasy."

23 R541 'Ημῖν in this context is used as a dative of possession, "we have four
men."
R1127 The participle ἔχοντες has the sense of manner, "with" ("there are men
here . . . who have taken"--BD353[2]).

24 R809 Ξυρήσονται is used as a permissive middle, "so that they may have their
heads shaved."
R816 In ἁγνίσθητι, the passive apparently has the force of "let" or "get" (cf.
the causative middle; "purify oneself"--T57).

25 R476 Φυλάσσω has two accusatives with the sense of "shun" (αὐτούς is the accusative of general reference [so-called subject] of the infinitive--R483).

26 M64 'Υπέρ has the sense of "instead of" (in most cases one who acts on behalf
of another takes his place).

27 BD209(3) 'Από is used for ἐκ to signify the place of origin (cf. 6:9).

28 R894 There is a sharp distinction between the aorist and perfect tense here
(εἰσήγαγεν . . . καὶ κεκοίνωκεν means "he brought in . . . and has defiled"--
T69; the perfect tense shows a continuing effect on the object, the entrance
in the past produced defilement as a lasting effect--BD342[4]).
T26 "Ελληνας may be a plural of species, referring to only Trophimus.
BD103 Πάντας πανταχῇ means "everyone everywhere."

29 T66 The imperfect tense of the verb ἐνόμιζον was intended to make the narrative interesting and continuous (cf. 14:19), "whom they were supposing."

30 T66 A distinction of the tenses can be seen in this verse; they were in the
process of dragging Paul out of the temple (imperfect) when suddenly the gates
were shut (aorist).

31 R1132 In the New Testament, the participle alone (ζητούντων) occasionally
occurs in the genitive absolute (also classical; it can only occur if the noun
is implicit--BD423[6]), "while they sought."

32 R1126 In the aorist participle παραλάβων, there is precedence in order of time,
but it is mere priority with no special accent on the temporal relation (it
possibly merely expresses an attendant circumstance--R1127; "with"--BD418[5]).

33 R736 In this verse, τίς and τί are sharply distinguished, "who . . . and what."
R884 'Επυνθάνετο is used as an iterative imperfect (the imperfect tense of the
verb refers to incomplete action in the past--T65). [Ed. Both of these suggestions are probably correct, since the inquiry extended over some time, deal-
ing with different aspects of Paul, and the answers to the inquiry were not
obtained.]
R1031 In the indirect question τίς εἴη καὶ τί ἐστιν πεποιηκώς, both the optative (representing the indicative in the direct discourse) and the indicative
occur. The variation here (retention of the indicative) gives a certain vividness to this part of the question (Winer states (p. 375) that in this verse the

optative is appropriate in asking about the unknown, while the accompanying
indicative, "what he has done," suits the conviction that the prisoner had
committed some crime--MT199). [Ed. It seems as though Luke would have used
the optative in both instances rather than make such a distinct change, if he
intended to use the optative of indirect discourse (representing the indicative). Consequently, we are compelled to offer a more subtle explanation for
this variation (e.g., Winer's suggestion).]

34 R747 Ἄλλοι δὲ ἄλλο means "some one thing, and some another" (cf. 19:32).
   R884 Ἐπεφώνουν is used as an iterative imperfect (they cried out repeatedly).

35 R1058 The infinitive βαστάζεσθαι is used as the subject of the verb συνέβη,
   "it happened that he was carried."
   H427 The classical word συμβαίνω is used for γίνομαι, possibly because
   has already appeared in the sentence (this is good vernacular Greek).

37 R916 Εἰ is used to introduce a direct question (cf. 19:2), and is not to be
   translated here.

38 R1157 The addition of ἄρα in the question here means "as I supposed, but as I
   now see denied" (indicating surprise--R917; "why, are you not . . ."--BD440[2]).

                              ACTS   22

1 BD473(1) Unemphatic pronouns are placed as near the beginning of the sentence
   as possible, as with μοῦ here.

3 R497 Τῆς Κιλικίας is a descriptive genitive of place (partitive--T210). [Ed.
   The latter suggestion is more accurate since the genitive identifies the province in which the city Ταρσός is located.]
   R615 The preposition in the phrase παρὰ τοὺς πόδας has a local sense (similar
   to ἐν, "at").
   TGr84 As far as this verse is concerned, the evidence does not require that
   "this city" must refer to Jerusalem (cf. 26:4).
   T185 The noun ἀνήρ appears instead of an adjective in an attributive sense (cf.
   3:14), "a Jew.")

4 B122 The present participles in this verse refer to action which is identical
   with that of the prinicipal verb ἐδίωξα.

5 R548 Ἐκεῖσε means "thither" (cf. 21:3).
   R887 The future participle ἄξων expresses the notion of purpose or aim (cf.
   M103; "to bring"--MT149).

6 R539 Μοί is used as a dative of advantage, "for me."

7 R508 The genitive φωνῆς occurs with ἤκουσα, where the content is meant rather
   than just the sound (if this pointless variation can occur in a writer like
   Luke, the classical distinction has broken down for the New Testament--T161;
   the genitive is used here to indicate that Saul heard a voice speaking directly
   to him--TGr87).

9 M36 It seems to be impossible to find a satisfactory distinction in meaning between the genitive and accusative in Acts 9:7 and 22:9 (cf. John 5:28 [genitive] and v. 37 [accusative]; although the servants heard the voice [9:7], they did not understand its meaning—TGr88; cf. R506 and the discussion on 9:7).

10 T75 The present imperative πορεύου occurs where the aorist seems to be intended (it is used here even though the distinction is stated, "go on your way to Damascus"—BD336[1]).

11 R580 The preposition ἀπό expresses a causal idea here.

13 M122 Αὐτῇ τῇ ὥρᾳ means "in that same hour" (cf. 16:18 and T194).

14 R1033 Ὅτι has a causal sense in this sentence.

15 T200 Πάντες ἄνθρωποι means "everybody."
    BD342(2) The effect on the subject is emphasized in the tense of ἑώρακα. The fact that Paul had seen the Lord is what establishes him permanently as an apostle (cf. 1 Cor. 9:1), whereas hearing the voice is far less essential (it is remarkable that ἑώρακα [perfect] occurs so often in the New Testament and ἀκήκοα comparatively seldom; but to explain the aorist of the latter side by side with the perfect of the former by the theory that to have seen the Lord was a more abiding experience than merely to have heard him, is utterly fantastic; cf. John 3:32—T85). [Ed. Since the perfect of ἀκούω occurs infrequently in the New Testament, Blass' precise distinction looses much of its support from the tenses. But Paul himself states that the vision of Christ was the central feature in his conversion experience; cf. 1 Cor. 9:1 and 15:8.]

16 R808 Two causative middle verbs occur in this verse, βάπτισαι is used as a direct middle and ἀπόλυσαι is used as an indirect middle, with the meaning "get yourself baptized and get your sins washed away."

17 B453 The genitive absolute refers to the subject of the sentence, "while I was praying" (cf. 21:34 and Matt. 1:18).

19 R608 The notion of distribution is seen in the preposition κατά here "every synagogue."
    T237 Ἐπί with the accusative after πιστεύω has the meaning "believe in" (cf. 9:42).

22 R920 Οὐ γὰρ καθῆκεν αὐτὸν ζῆν means "he is not fit to live."

24 B145 Following the verb here, the aorist participle εἴπας is equivalent to with a co-ordinate verb, "he commanded . . ., and he ordered" (cf. 16:23).
    MT133 Lysias presumably said in one sentence, "Bring him in and examine him."

25 R916 Εἰ is used to introduce a direct question (cf. 21:37).
    R1181 Καὶ ἀκατάκριτον is an explanatory addition to the previous comment, "and uncondemned."

29 R1033 It is not certain whether ὅτι is causal or declarative. [Ed. The first

ὅτι has a declarative sense denoting the content of ἐπιγνούς, but the second ὅτι has a causal sense portraying the reason for the fear, "he was afraid, because he realized that Paul was a Roman citizen and because he had bound him".]

ACTS 23

1   B137 Only the inception of the action referred to by the aorist participle ἀτενίσας precedes the action of the principal verb.
        T200 The anarthrous πᾶς means "all," or "the whole of."

3   R616 Κατὰ τὸν νόμον and παρανομῶν are in sharp contrast.

5   R874 The volitive future occurs here (ἐρεῖς), "you shall not speak evil."

6   BD442(16) The co-ordination of two ideas, one of which is dependent on the other, serves in the New Testament to avoid a series of dependent genitives. Consequently, περὶ ἐλπίδος καὶ ἀναστάσεως νεκρῶν means "on account of the hope of the resurrection of the dead" (cf. 1:25).

8   R745 It seems certain that three items are referred to by τὰ ἀμφότερα (cf. 19:16).

9   R582 Διά has a perfective sense in the compound verb here, "contend sharply."
        R1203 There appears to be a conscious suppression of part of the sentence under the influence of strong emotion in εἰ δὲ πνεῦμα ἐλάλησεν αὐτῷ ἢ ἄγγελος (supply "what opposition could we make?"--BD482).

10   R564 The compound verb διασπασθῇ expresses the fear that Paul may be drawn in two.

11   R593 Εἰς has a local sense similar to ἐν, "at," twice in this verse (cf. BD205).

12   B330 Ἕως οὗ is in effect a compound conjunction having the same force as the simple ἕως, "until."

14   M178 Ἀναθέματι ἀνεθεματίσαμεν ἑαυτούς perhaps means "we have bound ourselves under a solemn oath" (cf. BD198[6]).

15   R1141 Ὡς is used with a participle to portray an alleged situation (cf. Luke 23:14), "as though you were about to determine his case."
        B200 Ὅπως with the subjunctive here is used in an object clause, "that."
        T30 The comparative ἀκριβέστερον has the sense of an elative superlative, "very accurately." [Ed. The context here seems to support a comparative sense rather than an elative superlative, and consequently should be translated as such, especially since the comparative form is used.]
        T141 Τοῦ ἀνελεῖν with the adjective ἕτοιμοι has sort of an epexegetical sense, "ready to kill."

18   M102 The participle ἔχοντα has a causal sense, with the meaning "for he has something to say to you."

M139 The infinitive here is virtually the object of the participle ἔχοντα,
"he has something to say."
M163 Μὲν οὖν is purely resumptive or transitional in vv. 18 and 31, "so."
T65 When the aorist is used with a verb of asking, the request is usually un-
questioned or emphatic, demanding obedience, "he demanded me to bring this
young man to you" (cf. 10:48 and 16:22).

20 R547 Note the adverbial use of τι and ἀκριβέστερον, "somewhat more closely."
R968 Ὡς with the participle here has the sense of "about."

21 MT125 The aorist prohibition here expects the answer, "I will avoid doing so."

23 R742 Τις with a numeral here is not indefinite ("about two," as in classical
Greek) but definite, "a certain pair."
M126 The infinitive seems to be used as an imperative in vv. 23f., εἶπεν . . .,
παραστῆσαι (here it seems that the preceding εἶπεν is influencing the thought
of the writer), "he said . . ., and provide beasts."
BD119(1) Δεξιολάβος has an uncertain meaning, referring to a certain kind of
troop (δεξιολάβος is supposed to mean "taking [a spear] in the right hand"
[instrumental or locative dependence]. In military phraseology, the spear
was always connected with the right as the shield with the left. It was certainly not a coined word, but as it does not reappear until the seventh cen-
tury A.D., we must suppose it to be a technical term of limited range--H272).

24 R1204 Note the sense of the prepositions in διασώσωσι πρὸς Φήλικα where the
notion is that of taking to Felix and so saving Paul.

27 M100 One fears that in this verse Lysias is represented as deliberately taking
credit for having rescued Paul because he had discovered that he was a Roman
citizen. Ἐξειλάμην, μαθὼν ὅτι Ῥωμαῖός ἐστιν represents a diplomatic adjust-
ment of the facts (cf. Chapter 21) which Lysias is all too likely to have made;
and we are over-refining if we insist that the aorist participle is timeless
in relation to the main verb, and that the sentence may equally well have
meant "I rescued him and (subsequently) discovered that he was a Roman citizen."

30 R1049 In this verse, the future infinitive in indirect discourse is dependent
on the participle in the genitive absolute, "when it was revealed to me that
there would be a plot."
B44 The epistolary aorist occurs with ἔπεμψα (this action would be viewed as
past by the recipient of the letter but present by the author).
M53 Λέγειν πρὸς αὐτόν means "to accuse him."

31 BD223(1) Διὰ νυκτός means "at night."

34 R578 Variety in style accounts for ἐκ . . . ἀπό in this verse (ἀπό occurs for
ἐκ--BD209[3]).
R740 Ποίας does not have a qualitative sense in this verse (it is simply interrogative), "from what province?"

35 B145 The aorist participle κελεύσας is equivalent to καί and a co-ordinate verb,
"and he commanded" (cf. 16:23).
MT133 It is entirely arbitrary to make assumptions as to the order of the items
in this verse. "He said . . ., meanwhile ordering him . . .," may perfectly

well mean that Felix first told his soldiers where they were to take Paul,
and then assured the prisoner of an early hearing, just before the guards led
him away.

ACTS 24

1   R607   Κατά with the genitive here means "against."

2   M57   In both instances here, διά with the genitive has an instrumental sense,
"by means of."

3   R530   Πάντῃ expresses the idea of manner (πάντῃ τε καὶ πανταχοῦ appears   to
mean "in every way and everywhere"--BD103).

4   M45   The dative τῇ σῇ ἐπιεικείᾳ means "with your clemency."

5   BD467   Anacoluthon (a change in sentence structure) occurs in the speech of
Tertullus (vv. 5f.) which is reported by Luke with less care than any other.
Something like εὕρομεν (instead of εὑρόντες) was in the mind of the author
when he introduced the latter part of v. 6 (Luke cruelly reports the orator
verbatim--MT224).

10   R597   In the temporal expression here, ἐκ gives the point of departure.
      R1115   The present participle ὄντα refers to action which is antecedent to that
of the main verb (the present tense refers to past action still in progress--
B131), "for many years you have been judge" (the present tense accents the
vivid reality of the experience--R1103).
      M24   Ἀπολογοῦμαι means "I make _my_ defence" (cf. 26:2).

11   R717   The phrase ἀφ' ἧς is an abbreviation of ἀφ' ἡμέρας ᾗ (a locative attracted
to an ablative), with the meaning "since."
      R877   The future participle προσκυνήσων expresses the notion of purpose or aim
(cf. 22:5 and M103).
      M31   The occurrence of οὐ πλείους εἰσίν μοι ἡμέραι δώδεκα is startling, where
a genitive of comparison would be regular, "it is not more than twelve days."
      BD189(1)   The dative of possession (μοι) occurs here in a temporal construction
(emphasizing the object possessed).

12   BD445(2)   Οὔτε . . . οὔτε . . . οὔτε . . . οὐδέ in vv. 12f., is perfectly
admissible   (the final negative means "not at all," as if a single οὐ had preceded).

15   R1076   The infinitive μέλλειν is used to complement the noun ἐλπίδα, "having a
hope . . . that there will be a resurrection."

16   M79   Ἐν τούτῳ perhaps means "that being so" (causal--T253; "for that reason"
--BD219[3]).   [Ed.   All of these suggestions portray a causal notion.   The
preposition ἐν is often used in the New Testament, with this sense, cf. 7:29.]

17   R535   Εἰς with the accusative occurs here instead of a simple dative (with the
meaning "for the benefit of"--T236).

R581 In the context here, the preposition διά has the meaning "after" (cf. M56).
R877 The future participle ποιήσων expresses the notion of purpose or aim (cf. 22:5), "I came to bring."

19 R920 The imperfect tense of ἔδει implies that they ought to be here, but they are not.
M150 Εἴ τι ἔχοιεν πρὸς ἐμέ means "if they (really) had any complaint (which they have not)."
BD209(3) The preposition ἀπό is used for ἐκ to signify the place of origin (cf. 21:27 and R578).

21 R702 It is difficult to understand περὶ μιᾶς ταύτης φωνῆς ἧς ἐκέκραξα. Here, "concerning this one voice which I cried" makes perfectly obvious sense. But if this is how it is to be understood, it is the only New Testament example of such an attributive usage (of οὗτος) without the article. (This pronoun is attributive, "this single utterance." The definite article was being carelessly used, as times went on, in this type of construction--T193; this construction is equivalent to ἡ φωνὴ ἦν μιᾷ αὕτη [predicate]--BD292). [Ed. The preposition and adjective περὶ μιᾶς makes φωνῆς definite enough without the article. Then, from a desire to make φωνῆς more certain, the adjective ταύτης was included between the noun and the preceding adjective. Consequently, ταύτης is used as an attributive adjective.]

22 R665 Ἀκριβέστερον εἰδώς means that Felix knew more accurately than one would suppose (the comparative adverb is used as an elative superlative, meaning "very accurately"--T30; it is equivalent to ἀκριβέστατα--BD244[2]). [Ed. Although the object of comparison is not stated, it is implied in the context as the knowledge expressed in the present discussion. Felix knew more about Christianity than that which had been immediately set before him. When it is possible for a comparative adjective (adverb) to be translated as such with a valid meaning in the context, there is no reason to give it an alternate rendering; cf. 23:15.]
R1128 The participle εἰδώς seems to have a causal sense, although εἰδώς may mean "wishing to know." [Ed. The latter suggestion is less feasible since that is a very unusual rendering of εἰδώς. It seems quite probable that Felix may have learned about Christianity from his wife Drusilla.]

23 R828 Τηρέω means "to watch."
R863 Ἀνεβάλετο is expanded by three coincident aorist participles (i.e., three aspects of the same action), εἰδώς . . . εἴπας . . . διαταξάμενος (cf. MT133).

24 R692 It is possible that ἰδίᾳ may have a covert hint at the character of Drusilla. For the present she was with Felix (by using ἰδίᾳ, Luke is not ironically suggesting the poverty of Felix's title--MT88; actually it is difficult to determine--MT90). [Ed. Ἰδίᾳ may only indicate possession with no special nuance (this usage occurs elsewhere in the New Testament), but the simple article τῇ would have been sufficient.]

25 R1126 In vv. 25f., there are several examples of the participle. In διαλεγομένου αὐτοῦ, we see the temporal notion of "while" with the genitive absolute. In τοῦ μέλλοντος, the temporal notion in this attributive participle is due to the root meaning of μέλλω. In γενόμενος it is mere antecedence with ἀπεκρίθη (almost simultaneous, in fact). In τὸ νῦν ἔχον, the attributive participle

again has the temporal idea due to the words themselves. In μεταλάβων, we
have antecedence emphasized by καιρόν. In ἅμα καὶ ἐλπίζων, we have the
linear notion stressed by ἅμα. In πυκνότερον . . . αὐτῷ, the note of repetition in πυκνότερον reappears in participle and verb.

M160 Τὸ νῦν ἔχον means "for the time being" (ἔχον is not very easy to explain;
ἔχω is intransitive when used with adverbs--R800).

BD169(1) Μεταλαμβάνω always takes the genitive, except in this verse, καιρόν
occurs with the meaning "to find time later."

26   R529 Αὐτῷ is used as a dative of association with ὡμίλει, "talk with him."
TGr90 Felix, hoping for a bribe, <u>repeatedly</u> sent for Paul to parley with him,
the comparative must have the elative meaning, "very often" (it may also be
used as a comparative, "so much the more often"--T30; it has a comparative
sense, showing that he sent for Paul more frequently than he had been doing
before--R665; cf. the discussion on v. 22).

BD425(2) Ἅμα καὶ ἐλπίζων means "at the same time also in the expectation."

ACTS   25

4   M68 The preposition εἰς has a local sense, used in place of ἐν, "at."
M78 Ἐν τάχει means "shortly."
M153 An accusative with the infinitive is used in indirect discourse here,
meaning "Festus however answered that Paul was to be kept . . . and that he
himself was going to leave."
M163 Μὲν οὖν has an adversative sense in this context, "however."

5   R742 In vv. 5, 8 and 11, τι means "anything."

6   R666 In this context, ἤ does not go with πλείους (i.e., a comparative), but
instead it is used as a connective, "or."

7   R655 When two or more adjectives occur together the conjunction may be used
as in πολλὰ καὶ βαρέα αἰτιώματα, "many serious charges."

9   R603 Ἐπ' ἐμοῦ means "before me" or "in my presence."
R878 θέλεις seems to be used as a volitive future here. [Ed. It seems more
probable that this verb is to be rendered as a simple present, rather than to
impose a volitive sense on it, especially since this verb occurs in an interrogative sentence.]

10   R603 Ἐπί with the genitive in this verse has the meaning "before" while in
v. 17, the usual idea "upon" is present.
R1116 The perfect periphrastic construction ἑστώς . . . εἰμι has the linear
notion in the present sense (cf. B84 and M18; the periphrasis provides a rhetorically more forceful expression--BD352), "I am standing."
T30 Κάλλιον is used as an elative superlative, "very well."

11   R809 Καίσαρα ἐπικαλοῦμαι means "I call upon Caesar in my behalf" (an indirect
middle).
R881 Ἀδικῶ approaches a perfect sense in this verse (cf. πέπραχα; it is almost
equivalent to "be in the wrong"--T62).

R896 Perhaps πέπραχά τι is to be understood as a perfect of broken continuity (i.e., referring to a series of events).
R1059 The infinitive το ἀποθανεῖν is used as the object of the verb παραιτοῦμαι ("I refuse not to die"--B394).

13 R580 Ἡμερῶν διαγενομένων τινῶν actually means "some days came in between" (διά).
M100 The latter section of this verse means "they went down . . . and greeted Festus"; an abnormal use of the aorist participle (the aorist participle may refer to coincident action, with the arrival and greeting being timed together --T80; cf. B145).

14 R608 Κατά with the accusative is more than a mere substitute for the genitive ("Paul's case"--M58 and T15).

15 R787 The two distinct groups, the chief priests and the elders, are treated separately (the article οἱ is repeated).
BD205 Εἰς is used in a local sense for ἐν here, "at" (cf. v. 4).

16 B333 There are only two instances of a finite verb after πρίν in the New Testament, Luke 2:26 and here. In both cases the clause is in indirect discourse and expresses what was from the point of view of the original statement a future possibility.
T58 Κατηγορέομαι with the genitive means "to be accused."
BD458 The relative pronoun οὕς is similar to a demonstrative pronoun in vv. 16 and 18, equivalent to "and them" (cf. 3:15).

20 R1021 Εἰ introduces an indirect question, "whether."
M154 The optative is used to give a more tentative and cautious tone, meaning "I asked whether he would like . . ."; more loosely and idiomatically, "I said, would he like . . .?" (the optative occurs in indirect discourse where the indicative was used in the direct discourse--R1031). [Ed. The indicative verb θέλεις was used in the direct discourse in v. 9. So, both the verb and the mood are altered in the account in v. 20. Festus makes this change, in his report to Agrippa, in order to soften the force of the actual command, and consequently to conceal the original motive for this question.]

21 M139 The infinitive τηρηθῆναι (with αὐτόν) is used as the object of the preceding participle, meaning "when Paul appealed that he might be kept" (or "to be kept").

22 R919 In this verse, Agrippa does not bluntly use βούλομαι (cf. 1 Tim. 2:8 and 5:14) nor ἐβουλόμην ἄν, which would suggest unreality, a thing not true. He does wish this (the use of the imperfect rather than the present tense softens the request for politeness' sake, and may well be rendered "I should like"-- B33).
BD480(5) The repetition of "he said" can be omitted as superfluous and cumbersome in reports of conversations, as in this verse (εἶπεν is omitted here).

23 R405 Notice in this verse that one participle is singular and the other is plural with the compound subject. [Ed. Ἐλθόντος agrees in number, gender and case with τοῦ Ἀγρίππα. Whereas Βερνίκης seems to be added as an afterthought. The plural masculine participle occurs later, taking in to account both individuals.]

M59 Ἀνδράσιν τοῖς κατ᾽ ἐξοχήν means "with the eminent men" (literally, "the men at prominence," "in positions of eminence"); κατ᾽ ἐξοχήν commonly means "par excellence."

24 R1047 The infinitive δεῖν is used in an indirect command here, "shouting that he ought not to live any longer."
R1173 The use of the compound negative as a second negative is simply to strengthen the negation.

25 T55 For the verb κατελαβόμην, one would expect the active voice (cf. 4:13).

26 R743 Τι intensifies the adjective ἀσφαλές, "anything definite."
R1045 The use of τί with γράφω here may be compared with ποῦ after ἔχω in Luke 9:58, "anything to write."
B368 The infinitive γράψαι is used as an indirect object of ἔχω, "I do not have . . . to write."

ACTS 26

1 R885 Ἀπελογεῖτο is used as an inchoative imperfect, "he began to defend himself."
B13 The present tense in ἐπιτρέπεται has an aoristic sense ("it is now permissible," a simple [punctiliar] present--M7).
T58 The passive verb occurs with the dative here, "be permitted" (almost equivalent to "herewith receive permission"--T64).
BD229(1) Περί with the genitive has the meaning "on account of," "because of" (instead of ὑπέρ, cf. the variants).

2 R690 Usually when the reflexive pronoun occurs with the middle voice, the force of the middle is practically lost, as· in ἥγημαι ἐμαυτόν (this verb does not occur in the active in the New Testament--R811; consequently, the pronoun may be necessary to portray a reflexive idea), "I consider myself."
M24 Ἀπολογεῖσθαι means "to make _my_ defense" (middle voice).
BD341 The perfect tense in ἥγημαι has the sense of a present, meaning "consider" or "regard" (classical).

3 T316 The dangling participle ὄντα σε shows that a lack of congruence in participles is not confined to the least educated writers of the New Testament (its antecedent is ἐπί σοῦ).

4 R1152 In vv. 4ff., μέν is followed by καί νῦν by way of contrast (cf. 17:30).
TGr84f. On this occasion, Paul apparently meant by "my notion" something different from his meaning on a future occasion (22:3). He is referring not to his present position but to the situation of childhood days before he went for his education to Jerusalem. Before that, he would naturally have thought of his notion as being the people in the home town of which he was so proud, Tarsus, "no mean city."

5 R670 Ἀκριβεστάτην is used as a true superlative here (cf. MT78; an elative superlative--T31). [Ed. This adjective seems to have a true superlative force,

244

since the Pharisees were actually the strictest party of the Jewish religion.]

7 R550 'Εν ἐκτενείᾳ has the substantial force of an adverb, "earnestly."
BD458 The relative pronoun ἧς in this verse,and ὅ in v. 10, is similar to a demonstrative pronoun, "for this hope" (cf. 3:15).

8 B277 After expressions of wonder, a clause introduced by εἰ has nearly the force of a clause introduced by ὅτι.
M52 The preposition παρά with the dative has a metaphorical sense here, with the resultant meaning "why is it judged incredible in your eyes . . . ?"

10 R714 The relative pronoun ὅ refers to a verbal idea or to the whole previous sentence.
R1113 The aorist participle λαβών refers to action which is coincident with that of the main verb (i.e., referring to the same event; cf. 10:39).

11 R885 The conative imperfect ἠνάγκαζον refers to an action begun, but interrupted (with due modesty Paul actually said, "I tried to make them blaspheme," and one must not infer that his vicious onslaught achieved anything beyond the further spread of the new faith--TGr86f; in itself, ἠνάγκαζον might of course be "I repeatedly forced," the iterative imperfect. But the sudden abandonment of the aorist, used up to this point, gives strong grammatical argument for the alternative "I tried to force," which is made certain by the whole tone of the apostle in his retrospect: we cannot imagine him telling of such a success so calmly--MT129).
BD60(3) Περισσῶς means "very" in this context.

12 M131 It is not certain in this verse whether the relative pronoun οἷς refers strictly to what precedes, as though it meant "in the course of which activity . . .," or whether it is a vague resumptive phrase, corresponding to our "and so, well then." [Ed. Since Paul makes a specific point of laying out the historical setting of his journey to Damascus, the prepositional phrase ἐν οἷς is used as a connective with a meaning such as "under these circumstances."]

13 R550 'Ημέρας μέσης means "middle of the day" (the genitive refers to a point of time).

14 T27 Κέντρα is perhaps plural because the goad was double-pointed.

16 R871 'Οφθήσομαι has an ingressive sense, "I will begin to appear."
R1078 The infinitive here is in apposition to τοῦτο, "for this purpose, to appoint."
T330 Before the imperative here, ἀλλά has a consecutive sense and is best translated as an interjection, "well" (cf. 9:6).

17 R713 The change of gender in τῶν ἐθνῶν . . . οὕς, is according to the sense (the masculine gender is used to refer to people).
T142 In ἀποστέλλω σε, ἀνοῖξαι . . . , τοῦ ἐπιστρέψαι . . . , τοῦ λαβεῖν, the simple infinitive has a purpose sense, but for the sake of clarity τοῦ is added to the following purpose infinitives (this occurs only in writings with a pretense to style).

19 R962 Ὅθεν is used to introduce a co-ordinate causal sentence (the relative ὅθεν is similar to a demonstrative pronoun [cf. v. 7]--BD458), "because of this."

20 R1047 The infinitive μετανοεῖν occurs in an indirect command, "I proclaimed . . . that they should repent."
BD161(1) The accusative of the extent of space occurs here (πᾶσάν τε τὴν χώραν; answering the question "how far?").

21 BD35(3) The Attic form ἕνεκα is not to be tolerated in the New Testament, except in this verse (ἕνεκα here is regarded by Blass as in keeping with a speech in the presence of royalty--H67), "because of."
BD101 Πειρᾶσθαι means "to attempt something" (Attic).

22 R1138f. Οὐ occurs with the participle here (cf. B485 and MT231). [Ed. Actually the negative does not negate the participle (Paul is not saying that he didn't speak) but the negation refers to the adjective itself (οὐδέν) which is used as a substantive, i.e., when Paul spoke, he did not say things that were inconsistent with the scriptures.]

23 R372 Παθητός has a verbal idea, "liable to suffering" ("capable of . . ."--R1097).
R1024 In this verse, εἰ has the sense of a declarative ὅτι, "that."
M73n.2 Εἰ πρῶτος ἐξ ἀναστάσεως νεκρῶν φῶς μέλλει καταγγέλειν . . . invites comparison; but here it is just possible that ἐξ is not instrumental but quasi-local, "if he was destined to be first (to come from) a rising from the dead and announce . . ." -- as though Christ were pictured as coming from his act of resurrection. But some scholars translate it as instrumental. [Ed. The instrumental sense of ἐκ doesn't appear to be required here, since Luke is simply listing the necessary things for Christ to accomplish, according to the Old Testament, as relayed by Paul (cf. 17:2ff).]

24 R420 The tendency to draw the pronouns toward the initial part of the sentence may account for the position of σε here (cf. BD473[1]).
R656 In μεγάλῃ τῇ φωνῇ, the adjective is used predicatively (when the article occurs with the substantive, but not with the adjective, the result is the equivalent of a relative clause, "with the voice elevated"--R789).

25 T31 Κράτιστε is used as an elative superlative, "most excellent" (as a title, cf. Luke 1:3).

26 R903 In the periphrastic perfect construction ἐστιν . . . πεπραγμένον, the main stress is on the punctiliar aspect (at the beginning; cf. John 6:31), "this has not been done."
B482 A compound form of οὐ may occur with an infinitive dependent on a principal verb limited by οὐ. Consequently, this verse should be translated "I am not persuaded (i.e., I cannot believe) that any of these things was hidden from him" (οὐ belongs not with πείθομαι but, as a double negative, with λανθάνειν--M167f.).

28 R880 Πείθεις is used as a conative present, referring to an act begun but interrupted ("you try to persuade me"--T63).

TGr97f. This verse is best translated, "you think it will not take much to win me over and make a Christian of me" (N.E.B.).

T147 If the object of the verb is identical with that of the infinitive, there need be no repetition of the object. Thus this verse means "you seek to convince me that you have made me in a moment a Christian" (cf. BD405[1]).

T262 'Εν ὀλίγῳ may mean "in a short time" (although "by a short argument" [supply λόγῳ] is not impossible; it probably has the meaning of "quickly" or "hastily"--M78).

29 R938 Εὐξαίμην ἄν is the only instance of a softened assertion ("I could pray" --MT198; strictly speaking, a protasis is implied, such as "if only it were possible"--M151).

BD195 The preposition in καὶ ἐν ὀλίγῳ καὶ ἐν μεγάλῳ has an instrumental usage here, meaning either "easily, with difficulty" or "concerning both small and great," that is, persons with and without rank -- a play on Agrippa's words in v. 28.

BD442(13) In ὁποῖος καὶ ἐγώ the conjunction means "as."

30 T182 The repetition of the article in ὁ βασιλεὺς καὶ ὁ ἡγεμών prevents misunderstanding (to specify different persons here).

31 T62 The present verb πράσσει refers to the continuation of a past action up to the moment of speaking (his manner of life still continues).

32 R886 'Απολελύσθαι ἐδύνατο expresses a past possibility (note the perfect infinitive; the object infinitive occurs with implied antecedence--R909), "this man could have been released."

ACTS 27

1 R1424 Τοῦ with the infinitive is used as the subject of ἐκρίθη ("it was determined that we should sail for Italy"--B404).

BD327 The imperfect tense with παρεδίδουν is used to portray the manner of the action (cf. the aorist participle ἐπιβάντες in v. 2).

3 R861 The aorist participle χρησάμενος refers to action which is simultaneous to that of the following verb (i.e., occuring at the same time).

4 R634 The compound verb ὑποπλέω means "sail close by."

BD443(3) In vv. 4f., the particle τέ is used to connect clauses, with the meaning "and likewise" (cf. 2:40).

5 R787 The two provinces are treated as one since the article τήν is not repeated (cf. 9:31).

6 BD104(1) Κἀκεῖ (p[47] and A have κἀκεῖθεν) means "from there" (referring to the continuation of a journey).

7 M101 The present participle βραδυπλοοῦντες may refer to the whole episode, meaning "in the course of" rather than "after" (i.e., a simultaneous instead of antecedent sense).

9   BD328 The imperfect tense of παρῄνει implies that the completion of this
    advice was not carried out.

10 M154 The mixed construction of a ὅτι clause and an infinitive here is an under-
    standable confusion paralleled in the papyri and even in classical Greek (this
    is an irregular mixture, ὅτι was required to avoid ambiguity and the infinitive
    is due to a lapse of memory [a long phrase intervenes]), "I perceive that there
    will be much loss."

12 R1021 Εἴ πως expresses purpose and implies indirect discourse.
    B258 The optative of indirect discourse represents the subjunctive of the
    direct. The omitted apodosis is virtually contained in the protasis (cf.
    8:22; it occurs with the meaning "if by any means they could reach Phoenix,
    and winter there"--B276).
    M95 The comparative adjective οἱ πλείονες is used pronominally, meaning "the
    majority."

13 R634 In the compound verb ὑποπνέω the preposition minimizes the force of the
    verb, with the resultant meaning "blow softly."
    R665 The comparative even without the expressed object of comparison is not
    just the positive. So in this verse, ἆσσον παρελέγοντο clearly means "nearer
    than they could do before" (the comparative is used as an elative superlative,
    meaning "as near as possible"--T30 and BD244[2]). [Ed. The comparative adverb
    seems to have a comparative sense in reference to vv. 7f.; they sailed closer
    to the coast of Crete than could previously be done (cf. 18:26).]
    B137 In the aorist participle ὑποπνεύσαντος, only the inception of the action
    precedes the action of the main verb (cf. 13:27).
    B138 The aorist participle ἄραντες is best translated into English by a finite
    verb with καί (cf. R.S.V. and 10:23), "they weighed the anchor and sailed."
    T232 The more literary writers use the genitive with κρατέω when it means "to
    hold fast," as in this instance.

14 R834 Ἔβαλεν is used as an effective aorist, meaning "beat."
    M60 The prepositional phrase κατ᾽ αὐτῆς in this context, has the sense "a tor-
    nado struck down from it." It is topography which here decides in favor of
    "down from Crete," rather than the Authorized Version rendering "against (i.e.,
    down upon) it" (αὐτῆς refers to Κρήτην, "down from Crete"--R606).

15 R572 In the compound verb ἀντοφθαλμέω, the preposition merely carries on the
    idea of the ὀφθαλμός. The boat could not look at (eye, face to face) or face
    the wind.

16 R634 The compound verb ὑποτρέχω means "run under" or "past."
    R834 Ἰσχύσαμεν is used as an ingressive aorist, "we were barely able."

17 R802 In vv. 17, 26 and 29, ἐκπίπτω occurs with the meaning of the passive of
    ἐκβάλλω (cf. T53).
    R995 Μή with the subjunctive introduces an object clause following φοβούμενοι,
    "fearing that."
    BD425(6) Οὕτως is used to summarize the content of a preceding participial
    construction (cf. 20:11), "and so."

18 R885 Ἐποιοῦντο is used as an inchoative imperfect, "began to lighten."

T56 The middle voice of ποιέω is very rare in the New Testament, but ἐκβολὴν ἐποιοῦντο is a technical construction.

20 R1076 The articular infinitive τοῦ σώζεσθαι is used with the noun ἐλπίς in a complementary way, "hope of our being saved."
R1179 In this verse, μήτε . . . μήτε stand together and both are parallel to the τε which follows (τε is connective rather than correlative--BD445[3]), "neither . . . nor . . . , and no."
M161 Λοιπόν is an adverbial expression, with the meaning "at last all hope began to disappear."
T52 Ἐπιφαίνω means "to show oneself" (of stars, cf. Luke 1:79).

21 R1152 There is practically no contrast evident in μέν -- τέ (τέ is simply continuative, "and").

22 T138 The accusative of the object ὑμᾶς with an infinitive after παραινέω is a mark of literary style (this is the only instance in the New Testament).
MT241 The particle πλήν has the sense "but only."

23 R758 In τοῦ θεοῦ, the article points out the special God to whom Paul belongs and is to be preserved in English. But in the very next verse, the article is not necessary with ὁ θεός in English, even if, as is unlikely, the angel has the notion of "the special God."

27 T51 Προσάγω means "draw near."
T137 The infinitive with the accusative in this verse is used as the direct object of ὑπενόουν, "the sailors thought that they."

29 R995 Μή introduces an object clause, "fearing that we might run on the rocks" (cf. v. 17).
R886 The imperfect tense in ηὔχοντο has a tentative force, "they wished" (cf. Rom. 9:3).

30 R966 Ὡς occurs with the genitive absolute participle to express an alleged reason ("under pretense of"--T158; cf. Luke 23:14).

33 BD161(3) The use of the accusative in τεσσαρεσκαιδεκάτην σήμερον ἡμέραν προσδοκῶντες is a special idiom, with the resultant meaning "having been in suspense now already fourteen days" (cf. R1102; διατελέω occurs here with the adjective but without ὤν, with the meaning "to be continuously" (classical), unless we should construe προσκοκῶντες and διατελεῖτε together: "you have been waiting uninterruptedly"--BD414[1]). [Ed. Apparently this clause is a unique idiom, not to be taken directly with the principal verb, with the resultant meaning "having been in suspense now already fourteen days, you have continued without food."]

34 M54 Τοῦτο πρὸς . . . ὑπάρχει means "this is in the interests of your safety" (cf. BD240[1]).

37 R773 Ἤμεθα αἱ πᾶσαι ψυχαί has the meaning "we were in all" (cf. T201 and 19:7).

39 M151 The use of εἰ here is not absolutely clear. Does this context mean "they
    were planning <u>whether</u> they could," or "they were planning (<u>if</u> they could), to"?
    (εἰ means "if" or "as it were"--T127; "whether," cf. v. 12--BD386[2]; cf. R1021;
    "if"--MT196). [Ed. Εἰ δύναιντο appears to refer to the content of the verb
    ἐβουλεύοντο (the particle would then have the meaning "whether"), since it
    occurs immediately after the verb; cf. the similar construction in Luke 14:31.]
    MT117 Κατενόουν appears to mean "noticed one after another."

40 BD425(2) Ἅμα with the participle here means "while they at the same time also"
    (cf. 24:26).

41 R580 Διθάλασσος originally meant "resembling two seas," but in the New Testa-
    ment it apparently means "lying between two seas."
    R885 Ἐλύετο is used as an inchoative imperfect, "began" (cf. v. 18; it may
    have this sense, or it may refer to an interrupted action, "the surf seemed to
    be trying to break up the prow"--T65). [Ed. The action taken by the crew mem-
    bers and passengers in the following verses seems to support Robertson's sug-
    gestion. This drastic action seems to indicate that the stern was definitely
    being destroyed.]

43 B42 The aorist verb ἐκώλυσεν denotes the success of the effort, "but the cen-
    turion . . . prevented them from their purpose" ("succeeded in preventing"--
    T72).
    M41 The genitive of separation (ablative) occurs after ἐκώλυσεν, meaning "he
    hindered them from their plan" (cf. Luke 6:29).

                                ACTS 28

2   T56 The active verb παρεῖχον occurs where we would expect the middle. [Ed.
    The active rendering of this verb, "grant" or "show," has a valid sense within
    this context. Consequently, there is no need to expect the middle voice.]
    MT231 Οὐ τὴν τυχοῦσαν is a common vernacular phrase (cf. 19:11; this explains
    the occurrence of οὐ with the participle), "unusual kindness."

4   R697 There is a sense of reproach in the use of οὗτος here (cf. 19:26).

5   M163 Μὲν οὖν has an adversative sense, meaning "however, nay rather."

6   B100 The infinitive construction μέλλειν πίμπρασθαι is equivalent to the future
    of the latter, "but they expected that he would swell or fall down suddenly."
    M101 The present participles προσδοκώντων and θεωρούντων refer to action which
    is antecedent to that of the main verb ἔλεγον (i.e., action taking place before
    the action of the verb), "after they were waiting and observing . . ., they
    began to say."
    M153 The accusative and infinitive εἶναι are used in indirect discourse, "they
    began to say that he was a god."

7   M62 Περὶ with the accusative has a spatial sense, meaning "now in the neighbor-
    hood of that place."

10 M134 The participle ἀναγομένοις is used in a temporal clause, meaning "when we
    put to sea."

11 BD198(7) Παρασήμῳ Διοσκούροις does not mean "marked by the Dioscuri," but
    either it is used as a dative absolute, meaning "with the Dioscuri as the ships
    insignia" or better a mechanical declension of a registry-like (πλοῖον) παρά-
    σημον Διοσκούροι, meaning "a ship, insignia the Dioscuri."
    H271 Διοσκούροι actually means "sons of Heaven."

13 R550 The ancient Greek idiom of the adjective rather than the locative of time
    appears in this verse (δευτεραῖοι ἤλθομεν literally means "we came second-day
    men" [i.e., on the second day]--R657).

14 T72 Παρεκλήθημεν is used as a perfective aorist, "we were prevailed upon."
    T171 In this verse, the article denotes Rome as the goal of the journey (simi-
    lar to a demonstrative pronoun; cf. BD261[1]).

16 T58 Ἐπιτρέπομαι with the dative means "be permitted" (cf. 26:1).

17 R1108 In τοὺς ὄντας . . . πρώτους the articular participle has a technical
    sense (cf. 5:17 and MT228), "the local leaders of the Jews."
    R1138f. The negative οὐ is used with the participle here (cf. MT231). [Ed.
    Οὐδέν is a negative adjective used as a substantive in this context. Conse-
    quently, οὐδέν is used as the direct object of the participle rather than
    actually negating the participle, thus indicating what Paul did against the
    people; cf. 26:22.]
    T55 In the New Testament, the middle form of συγκαλέω seems to occur with the
    same meaning as the active, "call together" (cf. 10:24).

19 R1140 The phrase οὐχ ὡς means "not as if" (cf. 2 John 5).
    BD430(2) The negative οὐ occurs with the participle here because ὡς is included,
    thus this construction means "I did not do this as one who . . ." (cf. 1 Thess.
    2:4). [Ed. The distance between the negative and the participle seems to
    account for the use of οὐ here.]

20 R562 In τὴν ἅλυσιν ταύτην περίκειμαι, a change of standpoint takes place,
    since the chain is around Paul (the use of περίκειμαι as the transitive passive
    of περιτίθημι is somewhat unusual).
    H319 The compound verb παρακαλέω means "call to one."

22 BD447(4) Μέν occurs in this context with the notion "this much we do know."

23 R1116 The present participle πείθων has a conative sense, "trying to convince
    them" (cf. B129).

26 B167 Οὐ μή with the aorist subjunctive in this passage from the Septuagint, is
    probably to be understood as prohibitory (as in the Hebrew of the passage in
    Isa. 6:9), rather than emphatically predictive (as in the Revised Version
    translation).

27 B197   Μήποτε with the subjunctive is used in a pure final (purpose) clause,
        meaning "lest haply they should perceive with their eyes" (the future indica-
        tive occurs along with the subjunctive here--B199).

30 R833   The aorist verb ἐνέμεινεν refers to a period of time as a point (viewed as
        constituting a single fact without reference to its progress--B39).

Romans

1 T211 θεοῦ is a subjective genitive (since the object is περὶ τοῦ υἱοῦ αὐτοῦ in v. 3), "proceeding from God."

3 M58 Κατὰ σάρκα (i.e., physical) is contrasted with κατὰ πνεῦμα ἁγιωσύνης in v. 4.

4 M73 Is ἐξ ἀναστάσεως temporal ("from the time of resurrection . . .") or causal ("on the ground of resurrection . . .")? [Ed. It is difficult to determine how ἐκ is used here. Generally when ἐκ is to be taken with a temporal sense, there are other time-designating words in the context; cf. Mk. 10:20; Lk. 23:8; and the idiom in Mt. 19:12. But such words do not occur here. Consequently, the alternate rendering is preferable.]

5 R500 Πίστεως is a subjective genitive ("obedience that comes from faith").
BD280 'Αποστολήν evidently applies to Paul himself, but the addressees and all Christians are included in χάριν. (The coordination of two ideas, one of which is dependent on the other [hendiadys], serves in the New Testament to avoid a series of dependent genitives, i.e., "the gift of apostleship"--BD442 [16]; is καί epexegetical, "that is, apostleship," or is this a case of hendiadys, "grace of apostleship"?--T335). [Ed. In essence the statement of BD442 contradicts the statement in BD280. The way in which χάριν and ἀποστολήν are interpreted depends upon the use of καί. Are these two nouns to be considered as independent of each other, or is one dependent upon the other? The use of καί in hendiadys is an unusual usage of this conjunction. Consequently, the context has to necessitate this type of rendering for καί to be translated in such a way. Καί apparently should be taken in its more common sense as connecting two distinct aspects, although these aspects are not completely parallel. Χάριν represents a general category, whereas ἀποστολήν represents a more specific category.]
MT136 Paul clearly means (in the aorist verb ἐλάβομεν) that when he did receive a gift of grace and a commission from God, it was through Christ he received it. This is not an indefinite aorist at all.

6 BD183 Κλητοὶ 'Ιησοῦ is not used to designate the agent with an implied passive, but the genitive is a possessive genitive (the one calling is God).

7 T234 The substantivized verbal adjective ἀγαπητοῖς (an adjective made into a noun), as a passive, has the genitive θεοῦ to designate agency, "beloved of God."

8 R1152 In πρῶτον . . ., there is no hint of other grounds for thanksgiving (a comparison is lacking).
BD447(4) The use of μέν here perhaps means "from the very outset."

9 R589 The second ἐν in this verse suggests the sense of "in the sphere of."
R1032 'Ως used with μάρτυς should be considered as a declarative here, although

it really means "how" (ὡς is equivalent to ὁτί--T137).

10 R603 The period of prayer is denoted simply by ἐπί ("in" or "during").
R1090 The infinitive ἐλθεῖν is used to show the notion of result (hypothetical rather than actual, "that I come").
R1147 The notion in ἤδη ποτέ is more that of culmination than of time, "now at last."
B276 An omitted apodosis is sometimes virtually contained in the protasis, and the latter expresses a possibility which is an object of hope or desire, and hence has nearly the force of a final clause (as here: εἰ means "to see if"-- MT194).

11 R983 Ἵνα with the subjunctive here expresses a pure final meaning (purpose).
R1071 Εἰς τό with the infinitive carries the notion of purpose (that is true here, but there is no doubt that in the N.T. this idiom has broken away to some extent from the classic notion of purpose: cf. B409 and T143; it may be consecutive-- M140; εἰς τό with an infinitive is a construction which does not necessarily express the result of strict causality in the theme of the epistle to the Romans. It may be translated, "and so"--TGr12). [Ed. Paul employs a similar construction in I Thess. 3:2 with the notion of purpose, and in I Thess. 3:13 with the notion of result. Possibly the notions of purpose and result cannot be separated in this example in Romans, in which case Turner's latter suggestion is more probable; cf. 5:20.]
BD473(1) Elements belonging together in a sentence are often separated because unemphatic pronouns are placed as near the beginning of the sentence as possible (ὑμῖν is so used here).

12 R682 There is some emphasis indicated here in the use of the long form of the possessive ἐμοῦ.
R1059 Note the substantival aspect of the infinitive συμπαρακληθῆναι used as a predicate nominative ("that we may be mutually encouraged").

13 R1181 Καί meaning ("also") occurs in both parts of the comparison, displaying a studied balancing of the two members of the sentence (καί ἐν ὑμῖν καθὼς καί...).

14 T239 Where a stative verb with a dative forms part of the predicate it usually carries the idea of credit (or discredit) in the person's eyes (in this verse the idea of credit is portrayed, "both to the wise and the foolish...").

15 M58 Τὸ κατ' ἐμὲ πρόθυμον may simply mean "my eagerness"; but more probably is a self-contained adverbial phrase, meaning "as far as I am concerned," (cf. Rom. 12:18; the adjective πρόθυμον is used as a noun--M96; τὸ κατ' ἐμέ is not adverbial but nominal, which means that it may stand in place of a noun and form the object of the verb, "preach...." The verb may be translated simply "announce." Paul had heard of their Christian life and beliefs; they too would have heard of his. He wanted to exchange experiences and teachings with them, and so he writes, "I owe much both to Greeks and barbarians...and therefore I am anxious to tell you in Rome also my own point of view"--TGr92; τὸ κατ' ἐμὲ πρόθυμον is equivalent to ἡ ἐμη προθυμία--BD224[1]). [Ed. It appears as though τὸ κατ' ἐμέ should not be taken as a separate phrase. When such a phrase is used as a self-contained phrase in Paul's writings it occurs without a noun or substantive word, other than the object of the preposition, cf. Rom. 9:5 and 12:18. Generally when a phrase similar to that in Romans 1:15 occurs in the N.T., the article is

taken with the following noun and the prepositional phrase is considered as attributive to the same noun, cf. Rom. 11:21, 27 and 16:15. In the particular instance in Romans 1:15, the prepositional phrase appears to be used with a possessive sense, cf. Acts 18:15; Eph. 1:15, 6:5 and I Tim. 6:3. Consequently, the whole phrase seems to mean "my desire" or "wish." Furthermore, in Paul's vocabulary εὐαγγελίζω refers to preaching the gospel. Turner's evidence contrary to that is not completely convincing.]

16 R1152 Πρῶτον refers to what precedes temporally ('Ιουδαίῳ).

17 R499 Δικαιοσύνη θεοῦ (subjective genitive) means "the righteousness which God has and wishes to bestow on us" (cf. T211).
   R599 With the verb ζάω here, ἐκ has the notion of cause or occasion, "because of faith."
   M68 The prepositional phrase εἰς πίστιν means "leading to faith."

18 R606 A perfective sense of κατά is present in the compound verb ("suppress").

19 BD220(1) Probably the preposition in ἐν αὐτοῖς means "for" or "to" rather than "among."
   BD263(2) Τό...αὐτοῖς is interpreted by Origen as "what is known (knowable) of (or about) God is manifest to them," for which the continuation of ὁ θεὸς γὰρ ἐφανέρωσεν is suitable; therefore comparable to τὰ ἀόρατα αὐτοῦ in v. 20. Bultmann considers the conception "God in his knowableness."

20 R1002 Meyer insists that εἰς τό with the infinitive always shows purpose. In this particular instance divine purpose may be the idea, although result is the probable idea (cf. B411; εἰς τό with the infinitive means "and so"--TGr12). (Cf. 1:11; near-final--T143). [Ed. This clause seems to indicate some degree of result, especially in view of the following verse.]
   M44 Τὰ ἀόρατα αὐτοῦ...τοῖς ποιήμασιν νοούμενα means "his invisible qualities... perceived by means of his work" (an instrumental dative--T240).
   M73 Does ἀπὸ κτίσεως κόσμου mean "from the created universe" (as the source of knowledge--the basis of a deduction), or "ever since...?" (temporal). [Ed. The parallel phrases, ἀπ' ἀρχῆς κτίσεως (cf. Mark 10:6) and ἀπὸ καταβολῆς κόσμου (cf. Matt. 25:34) seem to indicate that the force of the prepositional phrase is temporal. Nevertheless, the context portrays the notion that knowledge about God may be derived from the created world.]

21 R1129 The participle γνόντες presents a concessive idea, "although...."
   T23 The distributive singular of καρδία is used with a plural pronoun (something belonging to each person in a group of people is placed in the singular).
   H463 There is a possibility in which the Septuagint rendering of ל has probably left its influence upon the use of ἐν with the meaning "because of, by reason of, for the sake of" (which sense it has here).

22 R457 The infinitive εἶναι has a predicate in the nominative (σοφοί) because the subject of the principal verb is referred to.
   H402 Μωραίνομαι means "to become foolish."

23 BD179(2) "Ηλλαξαν τὴν...ἐν means "to exchange for."

24 R585 The first ἐν in this verse appears to be used for εἰς (it has a causal

sense--H463 and T262; cf. v. 21). [Ed. Since a phrase with εἰς immediately follows, there is no reason to take ἐν as used for εἰς. A causal sense seems to
fit the context more readily, "because of the lusts of their hearts."]
R1002 Τοῦ with the infinitive is probably used in an epexegetic sense ("so as
to") after παρέδωκεν (cf. MT217; consecutive--T141; a loose relationship between
the infinitive and verb tends toward a consecutive sense--BD400[2]).

25 R585 Ἐν is used after a verb of motion where εἰς may at first seem more natural
("for").
R616 Παρά has the idea of "rather than" (cf. M51 and Luke 3:13; "instead of"--
BD236[3]).
R960 Οἵτινες has the notion of ground or reason, "because."

27 H309 The compound verb ἐκκαίω has a perfective force (of fire "blazing out"--
metaphorical here; cf. I Cor. 7:9 for the simplex idea).
R968 Καθώς has a causal sense (cf. BD453[2]).
R1087 The infinitive ποιεῖν is epexegetical after παρέδωκεν, "so as to do" (in v.
28).

30 M40 The composite adjective θεοστυγεῖς presents a problem of interpretation.
Does the θεο represent a subjective θεοῦ ("hated by God") or an objective θεοῦ
("haters of God")? ("Out of favor with God"--T234; "God hated"--H273). [Ed.
In classical literature this adjective had a passive sense, "hated by God." But
it occurs in the writings of the apostolic fathers in an active sense. This
instance, which is the only occurrence in the N.T., probably has an active
sense which would be in line with the remainder of the list of vices, "haters of
God."]

ROMANS 2

1 R402 Paul is fond of arguing with an imaginary antagonist. In vv. 1 and 3 he
calls him ὦ ἄνθρωπε πᾶς ὁ κρίνων.
R748 Τὸν ἕτερον is equivalent to "neighbor."
M103 The last segment of this verse should be translated, "for you who judge do
the same yourself" ("you the judge"--T151).
T253 Ἐν ᾧ here means "because."
BD281 The second person is used to represent the third person (direct address).

3 R464 The tone in the use of ὦ here may be one of censure (there is no great emotion expressed by the use of ὦ in this verse--T33; cf. BD146[16]).
R678 The singular pronoun σύ is used in a representative sense.

4 R880 The present verb ἄγει refers to an act just beginning (cf. T63; "such is its
tendency"--B11; "is trying" or "tending to lead"--M8).
T14 Τὸ χρηστὸν τοῦ θεοῦ means "God in his kindness."

7 M58 Καθ'...ἀγαθοῦ, means "by patiently doing good" (cf. BD163; "perseverance in"
--T212).

8 M58 Ἐξ ἐριθείας means "in a spirit of self-interest."

T317 The nominatives ὀργή and θυμός are used as accusatives (a slip! - objects of ἀποδώσει). These nouns are parallel to ζωὴν αἰώνιον.

9 R549 Πρῶτον is used as an adverb of time here and means "the thing is done first of the Jew," not "to the Jew as chief."

11 M52 The preposition παρά with the dative means "in the sight of."

12 R589 Ἐν with the dative has the sense of "in the sphere of."
   B54 The aorist tense of ἥμαρτον is used in an historical comprehensive sense (i.e., best translated by an English perfect).

13 R757 The article is used here to specifically designate different classes, οἱ... οἱ.
   R796 There is a problem here as to whether νόμου (note the article with the other nouns) refers to the Mosaic law and so really definite or to law as law ("the hearers of law, the doers of law"). [Ed. This verse portrays a general principle. One cannot make a definite rule regarding the articular and anarthrous νόμος, only the context can be the final guide. Although νόμου is anarthrous it refers to law in general and not to the Mosaic law specifically (cf. T177 and v. 17).]

14 R704 In οὗτοι the gender changes according to the sense (from ἔθνη; the masculine is used to refer to people).
   R796 In ἔθνη τὰ μὴ νόμον ἔχοντα, the Mosaic law is meant, but not in ἑαυτοῖς εἰσιν νόμος.
   BD188(2) Ἑαυτοῖς means "for themselves."

15 R728 Οἵτινες is used with a causal sense.
   BD465(1) In vv. 15f. there appears to be a gap in thought between ἀπολογουμένων and ἐν ᾗ ἡμέρᾳ so that a parenthesis may be supposed; but a logical connection for ἐν ᾗ ἡμέρᾳ is to be found only some distance back, so that the simplest solution would be the deletion of ἐν ᾗ ἡμέρᾳ. Thus we have the omission of a connective--ἢ καὶ ἀπολογουμένων, κρίνει ὁ θεός... (cf. BD382[3]). [Ed. If a phrase has very strong textual support it is best not to eliminate it. Even the remaining text with this phrase excluded is not without difficulty in interpretation. This verse is actually a conclusion to the whole paragraph which deals with divine judgment. Verses 14 and 15 contain a brief explanation describing why the Gentiles will be judged although they have not received a written law.]

16 M130 The antecedent of a relative pronoun is often omitted. But where necessary, the relevant noun is placed after the pronoun (ᾗ ἡμέρᾳ).

17 R796 In general when νόμος is anarthrous in Paul, it refers to the Mosaic law, as in νόμῳ here; cf. v. 13.
   T39 Paul instances both himself and his reader in a vivid way (by employing σύ here) to illustrate a point, not intending to apply what is said literally to himself or his reader.
   T115 The conditional clause here refers to something actually happening, "since.. .."
   T253 Ἐν with the dative here has a causal sense.

BD467 In vv. 17ff. it is possible to transform what appear to be protases without
a correct apodosis (cf. v. 21?) into independent clauses by adopting the reading ἴδε instead of εἰ δέ (ΕΙΔΕ - ΙΔΕ, both are equivalent and it is hardly
therefore a variant!).

18 T151 Τὰ διαφέροντα is ambiguous; it means either "different values" ("moral
distinctions"--NEB) or "superior things" (RV, RSV; cf. Phil. 1:10). [Ed. The
latter suggestion seems more probable, since the following verse portrays the
one who has received special revelation from God as leading the one who hasn't.]

19 M153 The accusative and infinitive are used to show indirect speech here. Thus,
the first part of this verse should be translated, "and you are confident that
you are a guide to the blind."

21 M106 Notice the exact parallel between the articular participles and a relative
clause in vv. 21ff. (cf. BD490).

23 R796 The anarthrous νόμος refers to the Mosaic law in vv. 23 and 25 (cf. 2:13).
T253 Ἐν is used with a causal sense (cf. v. 17).

26 R481 Εἰς is used with the accusative instead of a predicate nominative ("as circumcision").
R819 The verb λογισθήσεται is passive in sense (even though it is deponent), "be
considered."
T40 The pronoun αὐτου has no expressed antecedent and is vague in reference. [Ed.
The pronoun apparently refers to the implied substantive ("one") of the first
ἡ ἀκροβυστία in this verse.]

27 R1022 In v. 27 the participle τελοῦσα has a conditional sense ("if...," the
participle is adverbial; cf. T187).
B427 The participle τελοῦσα is attributive. Thus, the whole clause means, "the
uncircumcision which by nature fulfills the law" (cf. v. 14). [Ed. This suggestion apparently has two difficulties. In its position here the prepositional
phrase ἐκ φύσεως modifies the noun ἡ ἀκροβυστία. Also, the participle τελοῦσα
is anarthrous and is separated from the noun which it is in concord with. These
criteria tend to indicate that it is not attributive but adverbial. Consequently, the clause should be translated, "if the natural uncircumcised one fulfills
the law."]
M57 Διά expresses the idea of environment or attendant circumstance. Therefore
the second part of this verse should be translated, "you, who with all your
observances of the letter and your circumcision, still transgress the law" (cf.
T267; the preposition διά is used in this context with the resultant meaning "in
spite of"--TGr105 [cf. Rom. 4:11]; designating means--R583; causal, "because" or
"while"?--BD223[3]). [Ed. The most probable sense of διά here is that of attendant circumstance (cf. 4:11 and Eph. 6:18). But even with this usage it
carries a concessive sense, as Turner suggests, although it appears to be
slightly forced to gain a causal or instrumental sense from this preposition in
this context.]

28 R962 The common inferential particle γάρ introduces an independent, not a dependent, sentence. Paul usually employs this particle to introduce a separate
sentence.

1 R408 The article is used with the singular noun Ἰουδαίου to signify the whole
  class, "the Jew" (generic).
  R1198 The rhetorical questions in this verse show dialectical liveliness and
  perspicuity (cf. BD496; Paul is fond of the rhetorical τί--R739).

2 R816 The accusative of thing is retained with the passive of πιστεύω, "be entrusted with" (cf. I Thess. 2:4).
  R1152 The occurrence of πρῶτον μέν may be due to a change of thought on Paul's
  part (anacoluthon) or it may be the original use of μέν, with the phrase meaning "first of all in truth." [Ed. The latter suggestion is more probable,
  especially since Paul occasionally uses πρῶτος in this way with no further
  enumeration (cf. Rom. 1:8 and I Cor. 11:18).]

3 R1190 The explanation denoted by the use of γάρ comes in by way of appendix to
  the train of thought.
  TGr111 "The faith of God," gives better sense in its context if it is understood
  as "God's faithfulness" (subjective genitive), for it is contrasted with man's
  lack of it.
  BD299(3) Τί γάρ means "what does it matter?" or "what difference does it make?"

4 R986 This verse provides the only instance of ὅπως with the future indicative in
  a purpose clause in the N.T. (it is a quotation from the Septuagint Psalm 51:6,
  but changed from the subjunctive there).
  R1170 The optative of wish with μή occurs in vv. 4, 6, 31 of this chapter (it
  strongly deprecates something suggested--B176f; "let it not be").
  T145 Ἐν τῷ with the infinitive here is used in a causal sense, "when you are
  judged."
  B98 Γενέσθω is equivalent to ἔστω ("let God be").

5 B428 An attributive participle equivalent to a relative clause, may like a relative clause convey a subsidiary idea, such as cause. It then partakes of the
  nature of both the adjective participle and the adverbial participle. The
  whole clause should thus be translated, "is God unrighteous, who (because He)
  visiteth with wrath?" (Cf. R1108; temporal, "when He"--M103). [Ed. In essence
  these interpretations are similar. If we include a temporal translation, a
  causal sense (i.e., the reason) is still implied by Paul's argument in the
  context here.]
  T211 θεοῦ is like a possessive genitive meaning, "the justice which God dispenses."
  [Ed. This translation actually indicates that θεοῦ has been taken as a subjective genitive.]
  BD495(3) Paul knows how to change his tone in an astonishing way and use epi-
  diorthosis (a subsequent correction of a previous impression) when he feels that
  he has offended someone (κατὰ ἄνθρωπον λέγω), always maintaining the most sen-
  sitive contact with his readers.

6 T318 Ἐπεί is weakened in Biblical Greek from a causal sense to mean "for otherwise," as here (cf. BD456[3]).

7 R678 The first person singular is used here in a representative manner as one of
  a class (all of humanity).

M167 Characteristic, it would seem, of Paul is the displacement of a καί which ought logically to cohere closely with the verb. Thus, τί ἔτι κἀγὼ... κρίνομαι... does not mean "why am I also...," but "why am I <u>actually judged</u>...?"

8 BD427(4) The use of μή in the first segment of this verse appears to be due to the fact that the parenthetical clause (καθώς) is mixed up with the indirect discourse somehow: perhaps from the original comment μὴ λέγομεν (λέγωμεν) ὅτι, "do we say perhaps" ("should we perhaps say"), or from τί (v. 7) οὐ ποιοῦμεν or μὴ ποιήσωμεν, "we surely do not want to do evil."

9 R621 The compound verb προέχω has the meaning, "to surpass."
M168 If οὐ πάντως is the correct reading here, then it must mean what would logically be expressed by πάντως οὐ ("certainly not!," rather than "not absolutely"; cf. T287).
TGr106 It is debated among scholars as to whether the verb προεχόμεθα has an active or passive sense. In view of the evidence it most probably has an active sense, "are we better than they?"

10 R751 Οὐδὲ εἷς is particularly an emphatic negative, even more so than οὐδείς.

11 B413(1) The article ὁ is used with the substantival participles here, resulting in the meaning, "one who...."

12 R751 Notice the emphatic negation in the last part of this verse (B omits the second οὐκ ἔστιν).

13 M66 Ὑπό with the accusative is used to designate rest beneath ("the poison of asps is under their lips").

15 R1062 Ὀξεῖς ἐκχέαι αἷμα means "swift for shedding blood."

18 R500 θεοῦ is used as an objective genitive (i.e., "fear" or "reverence for God"). M82 Ἀπέναντι has the sense of, "in the presence of, before."

20 R752 Οὐ...πᾶσα has the idea of "no flesh," rather than "not all flesh." R962 Διότι is used as a paratactic (co-ordinate) causal particle. T177 The anarthrous νόμου is used to designate any law ("to know any sin there must be some law;" cf. BD258[2] and 2:17).

21 R781 Δικαιοσύνη θεοῦ probably means, "a righteousness of God," not "the righteousness of God."

22 R567 Paul is especially fond of varying the prepositions, thus in a skillful way condensing thought with each preposition adding a new idea (such as the construction here; cf. vv. 25f.).
R1184 Sometimes a word is repeated with δέ for special emphasis, as δικαιοσύνη δέ in v. 22 (cf. 9:30).
TGr122 The controversial phrase, "the faith of Jesus Christ," is an instance where careful interpretation of the genitive proves to be rewarding; it is difficult to comprehend it within the limits of either the subjective or objective genitive exclusively, but it shares in the qualities of both (one of Paul's "mystical" genitives?). It is best to understand it as "faith exercised within the Body of Christ" (vv. 22-26).

23 R518 **The** verb ὁστερέω takes a genitive object, "to fall short."
B54 ʽΗμαρτον is evidently intended to sum up the aggregate of the evil deeds of
men, of which the apostle has been speaking in the preceding paragraphs (1:18-
3:20). It is therefore a collective historical aorist (best expressed in
English by the perfect tense).

25 R589 The prepositional phrase with ἐν here seems to indicate price ("at the cost
of his blood"--T253).
R595 The preposition in εἰς ἔνδειξιν appears in an atmosphere where aim or purpose
is manifestly the resultant idea.
R781 In v. 25 it is possible to take εἰς...αὐτοῦ to mean, "for a showing of his
righteousness," while in v. 26 πρός...αὐτοῦ may refer to the previous mention of
it as a more definite conception.
M35 The accusative ἱλαστήριον is used predicatively, "whom God set forth as
expiation" or perhaps "with expiatory effect" (cf. R480).
M54f. Of particular interest is the use of διά with the accusative where it makes
a difference whether the preposition is taken strictly as meaning "because of,"
or more loosely as almost equivalent to "by way of, involving," or even "with
a view to" ("with a view to"--T268). [Ed. The preposition seems to have a
causal sense, giving the reason why it was necessary to prove God's righteousness. Throughout this paragraph Paul supports the fact that God is just.]
M56f. Διά with the genitive here is used in an instrumental sense ("by means of
faith").
T190 Αὐτοῦ occurs in an emphatic position (cf. BD284[3]).

26 TGr12 Εἰς τό with the infinitive means "and so" (cf. 1:11).
T15 ʼΕκ is used very frequently in Paul's writings for members of a sect or
persuasion ("believers in").

27 R498 Πίστεως is used as the genitive of definition ("the faith law").

28 T137 The infinitive clause is used as a direct object, after λογιζόμεθα ("we
consider that").
T240 The instrumental dative πίστει is used here with the resultant meaning "to
vindicate by faith."

30 M195 It should be noted that in v. 30 one's credulity is strained by the attempt
of Sanday and Headlam (I.C.C. in location) to draw a fine distinction between
ἐκ πίστεως and διὰ πίστεως, as though it meant that the Gentile is justified
ἐκ πίστεως, while the Jew is justified ἐκ πίστεως διὰ περιτομῆς.
TGr107ff. What significance is there in the change from ἐκ πίστεως to διὰ τῆς
πίστεως? The basic difference between these two phrases is that the latter is
articular. This occurrence of the article is no more than the normal use in
anaphora (i.e., the article on the second occasion refers back, like a demonstrative adjective, to the immediately previous mention of the word "faith").
In view of this, we ought to translate the phrase, "God will justify the Jews as
a direct result of their faith and then will justify the Gentiles by means of
that same faith." This brings out the important point that the faith of which
Paul is speaking is not the faith of the Gentiles, not even the faith of both
Jews and Gentiles, but unexpectedly enough the faith of Jews alone. The Gentiles
are saved by means of the faith of the Jews! In the following verse (v. 31) the
word νόμος, meaning either "law" or "principle," occurs twice, without the
article, and this would suggest that as there is now no anaphora, νόμος in each

instance does not refer to the same thing (i.e., the second νόμος cannot mean
"the same law"). It is difficult to bring this out in English, but our translation must be: "are we then (by our argument that Jews are saved by faith, not
the Torah) setting the Torah at nought? Oh, no! At least we have established
a principle. The principle is that Israel's faith will be the means of the
world's salvation." He avoided all suspicion of disrespect for the ancient Law
of Moses, but asserted that if his reasoning did after all involve the end of
that Law (sad thought for a proud Jew!), yet he exalted a far more important
principle: Israel's faith will save the world. [Ed. The anaphoric article
apparently refers to the same faith denoted previously, but probably not in
the same sense as Turner suggests. This construction may indicate that the
Gentile gains salvation through the same faith that is required for the Jew.]

ROMANS 4

2 B242 In the conditional clause here, the protasis simply states a supposition
  which refers to a particular case in the present or past, implying nothing as
  to its fulfillment ("if Abraham was justified by works").

3 R458 Εἰς with the accusative seems to take the place of a predicate nominative
  (from semitic influence), "it was reckoned to him as righteousness" (cf. R481).
  T253 The deponent verb ἐλογίσθη is used with a passive sense, "be reckoned."

4 R609 Κατά is used to denote a standard or rule of measure.
  R757 The article in ὁ μισθός refers to the particular wage due to each one.

7 T296 The pure nominal phrases μακάριοι and μακάριος are in the form of exclama-
  tions.

8 BD365(3) The double negation οὐ μή with the aorist subjunctive or future indicative is more common in the N.T. and for the most part less emphatic than in the
  classical literature, but it is virtually limited to quotations from the
  Septuagint and sayings of Jesus. In v. 8 this construction is equivalent to a
  simple negation.

10 R1198 The rhetorical questions here portray dialectical liveliness and perspicuity (cf. 3:1; especially often in Romans--BD496).

11 R781 The anarthrous noun σφραγῖδα does not mean "the seal," but "a seal."
   M38 The defining genitive (περιτομῆς) represents more than an adjective; it represents nothing less than a second noun in apposition to the first. So the first
   part of this verse should be translated, "he received the sign of circumcision"
   (i.e., "received circumcision as a sign," or "received a sign consisting of
   circumcision").
   M57 Διά is used with the genitive to express an attendant circumstance, "who, in
   a state of uncircumcision, are yet believers" (cf. v. 13 διὰ νόμου; the preposition has a concessive idea, "though they be not circumcised"--TGr105). [Ed.
   These suggestions have resultant renderings which are similar in meaning, cf.
   2:27.]
   TGr12 The first occurrence of εἰς τό with the infinitive here has the meaning
   "and so" (cf. 1:11).

T211 Τῆς πίστεως indicates the source of δικαιοσύνης (cf. v. 13), and is therefore subjective (cf. Romans 9:30 and Philippians 3:9), "the righteousness which
he had by faith."

12 R423 Generally the negative immediately precedes that which it negates. But in
vv. 12 and 16 the negative οὐ is separated from μόνον and the repetition of the
article τοῖς (v. 12) would make οὐ μόνον seem quite misplaced.

13 B395 In view of the appositional infinitive, the first part of this verse should
be translated, "for not through the law was the promise to Abraham or to his
seed, that he should be heir of the world."

14 B273 The verb of the protasis or apodosis of a conditional clause may be omitted.
So in v. 14 we have, "for if they which are of the law (are) heirs."
T15 Ἐκ is used of members of a sect or a persuasion--"who live by the law" (also
v. 16, "who share Abraham's faith").

16 TGr12 Εἰς τό with the infinitive has the meaning "and so" (cf. 4:11).

17 R717 In κατέναντι οὗ ἐπίστευσεν θεοῦ a dative relative pronoun has been attracted
into the genitive along with incorporation, "in the presence of God in whom he
believed."

18 R616 In παρ' ἐλπίδα ἐπ' ἐλπίδι the two prepositions answer over to each other,
"beyond-upon."

19 R1146 Πού means "somewhat," ("approximately"--BD103).
B145 The participle ἀσθενήσας, though preceding the verb, is naturally interpreted as referring to a (conceived) result of the action denoted by κατενόησεν.
It is in that case an inceptive aorist participle denoting a subsequent action.
Its position is doubtless due to the emphasis laid upon it ("without weakening
in faith, he considered his own body.").
M105 The negative with a participle is usually μή, no matter how factual or confident the denial may be, "with no weakness in his faith" (μή belongs to the
participle [where it is correct] and to the finite verb [where οὐ should have
been used; see variant readings] and should be translated "did he become weak in
the faith and did he not consider...?"--BD427[1]). [Ed. Actually the negative
appears to be used only with the participle, as Moule states.]

20 R532 The datives τη ἀπιστίᾳ and τη πίστει are used to express the notion of cause,
motive or occasion, this idea of ground wavers between the idea of association
and means (i.e., causal--T242).
R861 The aorist participle δούς is used to show action which is simultaneous to
the action of the main verb (in vv. 20f. the participles δούς and πληροφορηθείς
may be understood as together defining ἐνεδυναμώθη τῇ πίστει, although δούς is
strictly subsequent to ἐνεδυναμώθη--B145). [Ed. The final comment here appears
to be incorrect. The aorist participle is seldom used to refer to an action
which is subsequent to that of the main verb. Consequently, the context must
require a subsequent sense from an aorist participle before that sense can be
maintained. The context here appears to favor a simultaneous sense; one generally gives glory to God while growing strong in faith.]
M204 Εἰς...τὴν ἐπαγγελίαν means "at (or "in view of") the promise" (the preposition εἰς may have a causal sense; thus, "on account of [but "looking to" is

sufficient] the promises of God, Abraham did not waver"--T266). [Ed. In essence
these explanations are similar in meaning.]

21 R1035 Ὅτι has a declarative sense after πληροφορηθείς here, "being fully convinced that."

24 T237 Πιστεύω with ἐπί and the accusative has the meaning, "believe in" (the
   preposition possibly retains a sense of movement, metaphorically--M49).

25 M194f. There are passages which, judged by their words rather than their ideas,
   contain antitheses or parallelisms, but which, judged by their ideas, appear
   less obviously balanced in structure; and it is possible that, in such cases,
   the antitheses or parallelisms may be for nothing more than rhetorical effect.
   Thus, in v. 25, are we to understand a real distinction between the cause of the
   death and the cause of the resurrection:
        "it was owing to our sins that he was handed over,
         it was owing to our acquittal that he was raised?"
   Or is it a rhetorical way of saying that the "death-and-resurrection" (together)
   are connected inseparably with our "guilt-and acquittal," without any intention
   of separating the two pairs in thought? The latter is now fashionable exegesis
   --especially because of the difficulty of finding any logic in the separation
   of the terms and of squeezing the second διά into significance (cf. the comment
   on 5:10).
   T268 The second διά in this verse has a prospective sense, "with a view to" (cf.
   M55).

                                ROMANS 5

1 R598 Ἐκ conveys the notion of cause.
   R850 In εἰρήνην ἔχωμεν the durative present occurs with the resultant meaning,
   "keep on enjoying peace with God"--the peace already made.
   M15 The initial part of this verse should be translated, "let us enjoy the
   possession of peace": (δικαιωθέντες) ἔχομεν εἰρήνην is the unexpressed antecedent premise (cf. MT110). [Ed. In view of textual considerations it is
   difficult to determine whether the subjunctive ἔχωμεν or the indicative ἔχομεν
   is the correct reading.]

2 T70 Ἐσχήκαμεν is probably a true perfect, "as we still possess it?" (cf. BD343
   [2]).
   T262 Ἐν may be used here to denote the meaning "in the sphere of."

3 R394 The verb καυχώμεθα is to be supplied with οὐ μόνον δέ.
   R1200 In the list of virtues (vv. 3-5), there is a cumulative force in the
   repetition, building up to a climax (cf. BD493[3]).
   M117 The formula of renewed mention is spoken of again, the article is inserted
   when the mention is renewed (vv. 3-5).
   T253 The preposition ἐν seems to have a causal sense (cf. H463).

5 R896 The perfect tense is used here (ἐκκέχυται) to show punctiliar-durative action,
   "has poured out" (cf. B74).

6 R632 Ὑπέρ is used in the sense of "instead of" (similar to ἀντί).
   M166 This verse gives an impressive example of bringing the emphatic words near
   the beginning of the sentence.
   BD255(3) Does κατὰ καιρόν mean, "at the right time, in his own good time," or is
   it to be attached to the preceding clause (i.e., "while we were yet in the
   period of weakness?") [Ed. This prepositional phrase apparently is used in a
   way similar to the following phrase to modify the verb ἀπέθανεν (supporting
   Blass' first suggestion); cf. the similar idea in Gal. 4:4.]

7 R876 In the gnomic future ἀποθανεῖται the act is true of any time, with the
   meaning "is willing to die" (cf. B69; T86; BD349[1]).
   M64 Ὑπέρ is used in a sense similar to ἀντί, "instead of" (cf. v. 6).
   M111 The article is used to point out some familiar type or genus, "for the good
   type of man," or as colloquial English might put it, "for your good man"
   (generic--T180).

8 R594 Εἰς ἡμᾶς takes the place of a dative, "to us" (the prepositional phrase
   modifies the verb συνίστησιν, not ἀγάπην--R784).
   R1034 Ὅτι seems to imply ἐν τούτῳ (meaning "in that"--BD394).

9 M77 The instrumental use of the dative case can be seen in ἐν τῷ αἵματι--"acquit-
   ted now by his blood" (cf. BD219[3]; an instrumental dative of price--T253).

10 M195 This verse seems to confirm (curiously) the presence of an antithesis latent
   in Paul's actual thinking (cf. 4:25).

11 R1134 It is somewhat forced to take οὐ μόνον δέ, ἀλλὰ καὶ καυχώμενοι other than
   independent (i.e., taking the participle as a verb). If we once admit the fact
   of this idiom, this is certainly the most natural way to take it here (the
   participle is used for the indicative verb--M224), "not only is this so, but we
   also rejoice in God" (cf. v. 3).
   T253 Ἐν is used with a causal sense.

12 R438 One of the most striking examples of anacoluthon (a change in sentence
   structure) is found at the end of v. 12 where the apodosis to the ὥσπερ clause
   is lacking. The next sentence (ἄχρι γάρ) takes up the subordinate clause ἐφ'
   ᾧ ἥμαρτον and the comparison is never completed. In v. 18 a new comparison is
   drawn in complete form.
   R684 The antithesis here is better sustained by the repetition of the substantive
   rather than a mere pronoun (ἁμαρτία - ἁμαρτίας).
   R833 Ἥμαρτον is a striking example of the constative (summary) use of the aorist
   (i.e., a series of events referred to by the aorist).
   M132 The "in quo" interpretation of v. 12, closely connected with theories of
   Original Sin, is almost certainly wrong (ἐφ' ᾧ almost certainly means "inasmuch
   as," cf. II Cor. 5:4).
   TGrl16ff. There is no doubt that ἐφ' ᾧ is not a conjunction meaning "because,"
   but the ᾧ is a relative pronoun referring the reader back to Adam, the "one
   man" by whom sin entered the world (ground or occasion is conveyed by ἐπί here,
   "because"; cf. T272; MT107; the resultant meaning is "inasmuch as," "because"--
   M50). [Ed. Turner's initial statement does not negate the probability that the
   preposition itself expresses a causal idea.]

13 T177 The initial part of this verse should be translated, "till a law came," be-

cause of the anarthrous νόμος (ἄχρι has the resultant meaning of "before"--BD258 [2]).

14 R833 In ἐβασίλευσεν a period of time is summed up by the constative aorist (cf. v. 12).

15 M44 Παραπτώματι is used as an instrumental dative meaning, "by the transgression" (cf. v. 17 and T240).

18 R500 Ζωῆς is used as an objective genitive, "to life" (it is an appositional genitive, "justification which is life"--T214). [Ed. In this verse εἰς δικαίωσιν is parallel to εἰς κατάκριμα; to maintain this parallel structure ζωῆς probably should be considered as an objective genitive. Thus, this phrase refers to justification which issues in life, just as condemnation issues in death.]
M70 In εἰς κατάκριμα the preposition has the sense of "with a view to," or "resulting in" (i.e., the circumstances "led to condemnation, the result was condemnation"). [Ed. Moule unifies the purpose and result ideas.]
BD481 Paul emphasizes the correspondence between the two contrasting causes (διὰ) and ultimate ends (εἰς) and in between their equivalent extension (εἰς).

20 R722 The pronoun οὗ does not have an antecedent here (it has a local sense, "where"--T344).
R998 Ἵνα possibly may be used in a consecutive sense (cf. MT207: vv. 20, 21 and 6:1 all seem to contain genuinely final ἵνα-clauses, i.e., purpose--M143). [Ed. Occasionally in the N.T. purpose and result cannot be clearly differentiated, in which case ἵνα is used for the result which follows according to the purpose of the subject. In the mind of a Jew, purpose and result were identical in declarations of the divine will (cf. Rom. 3:19; 7:13 and 8:17). In vv. 20, 21 and 6:1 there is a definite notion of purpose (cf. the development of thought in Rom. 7:7ff. and Gal. 3:19ff.) as well as result; cf. also Rom. 1:11.]

ROMANS 6

2 R728 Οἵτινες appears to be used in a causal sense (cf. B294).
R940 The optative of wish strongly deprecates something suggested (cf. 3:4), "let it not be."
B60 Notice the progressive use of the future tense in this verse (cf. M10), "how can we still live?"

3 R592 In both instances of εἰς with the accusative here, the notion of sphere is evident (i.e., εἰς is used for ἐν), "in."

4 R493 Although the function of the genitive case is largely adjectival, the adjective and the genitive are not exactly parallel, for with two substantives each idea stands out with more sharpness, as in ἐν καινότητι ζωῆς ("new life"--T213).
R784 Phrases that are consciously verbal in origin readily do without the repeated article. It is plain, therefore, that here εἰς τὸν θάνατον is to be construed with βαπτίσματος, not with συνετάφημεν (especially since εἰς τὸν θάνατον... occurs in the preceding verse; cf. BD272 and MT83), "baptism into death."
R850 The aorist tense in περιπατήσωμεν has an ingressive usage "begin to walk" (cf. 13:13 and BD337[1]).

5 T220 Τῷ ὁμοιώματι seems to be used as an adjectival dative, unless it is an instrumental dative, in which case the genitive goes with σύμφυτοι, but this is unnatural (cf. BD194[2]), "in the likeness of his death."

6 R990 Τοῦ with the infinitive here is probably used to show purpose (generally Paul doesn't use this construction to express the idea of purpose--R1088 and MT217; it is used as a weak consecutive here--T141). [Ed. In essence a weak consecutive sense is similar to that of purpose.]
  R1128 The participle γινώσκοντες suggests the ground of action for the principal verb (causal).
  M38 Ἁμαρτίας is used as a genitive of definition, meaning "the sin-possessed body" (cf. a genitive of quality).

9 R1128 The participle εἰδότες has a causal meaning.

10 M46 The dative nouns in this verse have the sense of "in regard to" (i.e., dative of reference).
  M131 ὅ seems to be used as an adverbial relative. Presumably it is best rendered, "whereas he died, he died...", rather than making ὅ a strictly cognate relative, as though it stood for τὸν θάνατον ὅν (or ᾧ) ἀπέθανεν... (ὅ is used as a cognate accusative--R478; it may be adverbial--R715; as a cognate accusative--BD154). [Ed. Grammatically, the evidence is not conclusive which way the relative pronoun is to be translated; cf. Gal. 2:20. In either case a similar concept of Christ dying is presented.]
  BD188(2) The dative of advantage and disadvantage occurs here, but the dative θεῷ seems to express more the idea of possessor (the datives are used to denote advantage and disadvantage, cf. v. 2--R539). [Ed. It appears that these datives may be translated specifically as denoting advantage and disadvantage, rather than with the general idea of reference. It is certainly true that because of this event it was to God's advantage and to sin's disadvantage.]

11 R587f. Paul frequently uses ἐν χριστῷ with a mystical notion. This mystical indwelling is Christ's own idea adopted by Paul (cf. John 15:4).
  T264 When Paul wishes to express the idea "to live to," and not "in the sphere of," he employs the simple dative with a form of ζάω (as here).

12 R1090 Εἰς seems to be used with the infinitive to show a hypothetical result ("so that you obey").
  R1097 θνητός means "liable to death" not "dying."
  T76 The present and aorist imperatives in vv. 12f. should be translated as follows: "let not sin continue...," "do not continue yielding your members to sin...," "but start yielding yourselves to God" (a marked antithesis is presented--MT139).

14 R635 The concept of ὑπό is that of rest in vv. 14f. ("beneath law").
  R796 Anarthrous νόμου refers to the Mosaic law (cf. 2:13 and 17).
  T177 Ἁμαρτία here does not carry the idea, "no sin," but "no sin as power" (as usual in Paul; cf. BD258[2]).

15 R850 The punctiliar force of the aorist tense is brought out in the subjunctive verb ἁμαρτήσωμεν ("should we sin?").
  B176 The optative of wish is used to strongly deprecate something suggested (cf. 6:2).

BD299(3) In the first segment of this verse ἐροῦμεν is implied (cf. v. 1).

16 T334 The disjunctive particles ἤτοι and ἤ denote a correlation here and mean "either...or."

17 R719 The resolved form of εἰς...διδαχῆς would probably be τύπῳ διδαχῆς εἰς ὅν παρεδόθητε (cf. BD294[5]), "obedient to the pattern of teaching unto which you were given."
BD327 The imperfect tense of ἦτε is used to show past descriptive (durative) action in sharp contrast to the present.

19 M97 Δοῦλος is commonly a normal noun like λόγος, but also appears as an adjective (the neuter plural here, "for as you have yielded your members as servants").

20 M46 The dative τῃ δικαιοσυνῃ has the concept of, "with regard to" (probably not "from," although it might be argued that the dative here is an ablatival one; τῃ... is used as a dative of advantage--T238; a locative dative--R523). [Ed. Generally when an ablatival sense follows ἐλεύθερος, the genitive case is used rather than the dative. A dative of advantage doesn't appear to have much meaning in this context. The point that Paul makes here seems to be most precisely expressed by a dative of reference, cf. Moule's suggestion.]

21 M132 Does ἐφ' οἷς mean "at which things"? [Ed. This instance is the only example of ἐπί and a dative with ἐπαισχύνομαι in the N.T. The preposition appears to have the meaning "at".]

ROMANS 7

2 R500 Νόμου τοῦ ἀνδρός means, "the law about the husband" (objective genitive). R1190 Γάρ introduces an explanation by way of appendix to the train of thought (cf. 3:3).

3 B398 The idea of conceived result is expressed by τοῦ with the infinitive here (cf. T141; τοῦ with the infinitive has an epexegetic sense--R996; it is equivalent to ὥστε μὴ εἶναι--M128; very little of the consecutive force is present--BD400[8]). [Ed. The clause with the infinitive apparently makes reference to the previous clause rather than explain the following participle. Thus, it portrays a remote result of the former clause depending upon the action described by the following participle.]
T215 Ἐλευθέρα...ἀπὸ... means "independent of..." (cf. BD182[3]).

4 R539 Τῷ θεῷ is used as a dative of advantage, "for God."
R1071 Εἰς τό with the infinitive presents the notion of purpose (cf. B409 and T143; it has the meaning "and so"--TGr112). [Ed. On occasion the notion of purpose and result are difficult to distinguish (cf. 1:11 and 5:20). But in this context Paul apparently stresses that the Christian died to the law for the purpose of uniting with Christ.]
M144 Ὥστε is used simply as an inferential particle meaning "and so, accordingly."

5 TGr112 Ἐνηργεῖτο has the sense of "operated."
T187 The article τά is repeated to avoid ambiguity here.

6 T213 The genitive of quality occurs here making the translation, "in a new spirit
    and not according to an out-of-date literalness."

7 R874 The volitive future occurs in this verse (ἐπιθυμήσεις), "Do not lust."
    TGr86 Paul speaks of lust as a personal experience (v. 7), and apparently makes
    his own confession, "Sin wrought in me all manner of concupiscence" (v. 8;
    cf. BD281; vv. 7-25 are not clear, but the vehemence of passion argues for
    Paul's own experience--R402).
    T39 Paul instances both himself and his reader in a vivid way to illustrate
    a point, not intending to apply what is said literally to himself or his reader
    (vv. 7ff.). [Ed. Compare Turner's two statements. The emphatic αὐτὸς ἐγώ with
    δουλεύω in v. 25 seems to indicate that this passage is applied to Paul himself.]

10 R539 Μοῦ appears to be used as a dative of disadvantage, "against me."

12 M144 Ὥστε is used simply as an inferential particle (cf. v. 4), "and so."

13 R609 Κατά introduces a standard or rule of measure.
    B176 The volitive optative occurs here (cf. 3:4; "let it not be" is similar to
    "God forbid").

14 R158 Σάρκινος must mean more than "made of flesh" or "consisting in flesh,"
    perhaps "rooted in the flesh" (cf. I Cor. 3:1).

16 T115 In vv. 16 and 20 the conditional clause refers to something actually happen-
    ing ("since").

17 T37 In the use of ἐγώ here there is at least some emphasis or antithesis.

18 R1059 The subject of παράκειται is expressed by τό with an infinitive (cf. T140;
    "for I am ready to will what is good for me").

23 R748 Ἕτερον carries the idea of difference of kind.
    R796 νόμος means "principle," and is indeterminate as to any specific law in
    ἕτερον νόμον.

24 R497 θανάτου is an attributive genitive ("the body of this death"--T214).

25 R540 In τῷ νοΐ...νόμῳ both the instrumental dative and simple dative occurs, "in
    (or by) my mind...to God's law."
    BD281 In αὐτὸς ἐγώ, Paul certainly applies the words to himself (cf. v. 7).

ROMANS 8

2 R784 It is reasonably clear that ἐν Χριστῷ is predicate with ἠλευθέρωσεν ("through
    Christ the law has set me free").
    T39 Μέ is representative here (it has a universal sense--BD281).

3 R784 There is some ambiguity in the use of ἐν τῇ σαρκί. If it is attributive with
    ἁμαρτίαν, there is a definite assertion of sin in the flesh of Jesus. But if
    the phrase is predicate, and is construed with κατέκρινε, no such statement is
    made.... One conversant with Paul's theology will feel sure that ἐν τῇ σαρκί

is here meant to be taken as predicate.

M35 When a word or phrase is flung loosely into apposition with a whole sentence it is (or, where the form is ambiguous, may be assumed to be) in the accusative. Thus τὸ γὰρ ἀδύνατον τοῦ νόμου...ὁ θεὸς τὸν ἑαυτοῦ υἱὸν πέμψας...κατέκρινεν τὴν ἁμαρτίαν..., means "God, by sending his own Son...condemned sin...--a thing impossible for the law."

M63 It is not certain whether περὶ ἁμαρτίας here is the technical Septuagint term equivalent to "sin-offering" (as in Heb. 10:6, cf. 5:26), or whether it is meant more generally as "to deal with sin, in connection with sin"; but in any case, even the technical sense is clearly derived from the more general one, the general sense is preferable,--"from sin" (i.e., "from around sin"--R618).

M131 Ἐν ᾧ is used to mean "since (or in that) it is weak..." (causal; cf. R978; T253 and BD219[3]).

BD263(2) Peculiar to Paul (and Hebrews) is the use of a neuter singular adjective, with a dependent genitive (cf. 2:4). τὸ ἀδύνατον τοῦ νόμου means "the one thing the law could not do," (not abstract).

MT221 It is uncertain what ἀδύνατον means in this verse. Does it mean "incapable," as in Acts 14:8 and Romans 15:1, or "impossible," as in the other N.T. occurrences? [Ed. This adjective seems to have the more usual sense of "impossible." The law was never intended to condemn sin.]

4 T285 Since μή is generally used with participles, that is what we expect here. In classical Greek τοῖς μὴ... would be "If we do not walk...", but Paul probably means "us who do not walk...".

7 R962 Διότι is used as a co-ordinate causal particle (cf. 3:20). The corresponding negative form is οὐδὲ γάρ, "for it cannot either" (cf. BD452[3]).

9 R1186 Notice the adversative use of δέ in vv. 9ff ("but").

M38 In N.T. Greek there is no third person singular possessive adjective, his, etc.; thus the genitive pronoun may occur alone--οὐκ ἔστιν αὐτου means "he is not his."

TGrl19 The mystical union with Christ, described as ἐν Χριστῷ, is explained in complementary terms as Christ or the Spirit existing in the believer. It is a reciprocal indwelling. "You are not in the flesh but in the Spirit, if the Spirit of God dwells in you." The idea of mutual indwelling is real enough to those who actually live inside this new sphere of spiritual existence.

10 M195 The second occurrence of διά with the accusative probably means "because of (the survival-force of Christ's) righteousness."

11 T115 Εἰ with the indicative here has the meaning "since."

12 R996 Τοῦ with the infinitive here is epexegetical (cf. MT217; it tends towards a consecutive sense--BD400[2]; cf. T141). [Ed. If τοῦ ζῆν is taken as epexegetical, it would express the content of the debt "to live according to the demands of the flesh." Whereas if it is consecutive it expresses the result of not being bound to the flesh, "that we should live according to the flesh" (but by the Spirit). The latter suggestion seems to be more probable, since Paul's main point in this context is to contrast walking by the flesh with walking by the Spirit (cf. v. 4).]

R1095 Οὐ negates τῇ σαρκί rather than the infinitive.

T238 Τῇ σαρκί is used as a dative of advantage, "for the flesh."

13 M44 The dative is used to designate an instrumental idea; "if by the Spirit you put to death sensual activities, you shall live" (cf. T240 and v. 14).

15 R595 Εἰς with the accusative φόβον portrays the resultant idea of aim or purpose (cf. 3:25), "to fear."
M131 Ἐν ᾧ should be translated, "in (or by) which."
MT10 It is highly precarious to argue with Zahn from "Abba Father" (here and Gal. 4:6), that Aramaic was the language of Paul's prayers.

18 R535 Εἰς is used for ἐν. [Ed. A simple dative would have been sufficient.]
R626 The preposition πρός may be used in a technical comparison, as here (cf. M53), "in comparison with."
R1191 Notice that Paul begins every sentence with γάρ in vv. 18-24.
M169f. Both Rom. 8:18 and Gal. 3:23 show a curious order of words in nearly identical clauses (where one would expect πρὸς τὴν δόξαν τὴν μέλλουσαν; possibly a stereotyped phrase may account for the order—T350).

20 BD222 Διά is used with the accusative in a local sense "through" ("by someone's merit"; it has the usual meaning, "because of"—MT105). [Ed. Grammatically, the usual causal sense appears to be more probable. Many exegetes have a problem with this rendering because the verse states that creation was subjected to futility because of God. This was an action carried out by God because of sin. Actually this sense can be gained by taking διά as causal.]

21 R964 If the true text reads διότι, then this would be the only time that this conjunction is used in the sense of an objective ὅτι ("that") in the N.T.
M175 It is a mistake to claim a semitic genitive where a good Greek genitive makes better sense: it would be a misplaced subtlety to translate τῆς δουλείας τῆς φθορᾶς, as "corrupting bondage," when it obviously means "bondage to corruption" (or "mortality"); although in the same verse it seems more natural to translate τὴν ἐλευθερίαν τῆς δόξης semitically as, "glorious freedom" (rather than, for example, "freedom consisting in the glory...").

23 T41 The pronoun αὐτοί has some emphasis in this verse.

24 R533 Τῇ ἐλπίδι is used either as the modal instrumental or the instrumental of means (it is used to denote manner, "in hope" but not actually—T241; "in hope though not in actuality," proleptically—M45). [Ed. The dative seems to portray a notion of manner. The question is whether it is actual or proleptical. In view of the previous verse it appears to be proleptical, meaning "we have been saved, though only in hope."]
B290 In "who hopeth for that which he seeth," the relative clause apparently does not refer to a definite thing seen and an actual act of seeing, but is equivalent to a conditional clause, "if he sees anything."

25 M58 Δι᾽ ὑπομονῆς means "with fortitude" (cf. T267).

26 R573 In the double compound verb συναντιλαμβάνεται the fundamental meaning is obvious. The Holy Spirit lays hold of our weakness along with us (σύν) and carries His part of the burden facing us (ἀντί) as if two men were carrying a log, one at each end.

R629   The idea of "defence," "in behalf of," "bending over to protect," occurs in
ὑπερεντυγχάνω.
R766   The article τό makes clearer the substantival idea of the indirect question
and its relation to the principal clause (it is possibly a sheer idiosyncrasy of
Paul's--M111).
T268   In vv. 26f., κατά has the sense of "in accordance with" (cf. M59).

29 R1071 Εἰς τό is used with the infinitive to express purpose (cf. B409 and T143).
T215   The adjective σύμμορφος takes the ablatival genitive, "participating in the
form of his image."
BD493(3)   The repetition in vv. 29f. portrays a sense of climax (cf. 5:3).

30 R837   The gnomic aorist is used in ἐκάλεσεν and ἐδόξασεν (i.e., describing
a general truth).

31 R630   The notion of "in behalf of," "for one's benefit" (for ὑπέρ) comes out with
special force in instances where κατά is contrasted with ὑπέρ.
M53   Πρός is used in a transferred sense meaning "in view of."
BD496(2)   The rhetorical question is used to express joyous elation in v. 31; to
which are subjoined pairs of questions with their pretended answers.

32 R632   Ὑπέρ is used for ἀντί ("instead").
R725   Ὅς introduces a causal clause (it is a relative clause indicating a
causal relationship).
R773   Τὰ πάντα means "the sum of things," "the all."
R1148 The particle γέ has climactic force here. All of the examples of γέ in the
New Testament occur with the conjunctions or other particles except the instance
here and in Lk. 11:8 and 18:5 (within the context here it should be translated
"he who even"--T331).

34 M103   In τίς ὁ κατακρινῶν the articular participle has a sense similar to a relative clause, "who is there to condemn (us)."

35 T211   Τοῦ Χριστοῦ may be subjective, objective or both. [Ed. This genitive
appears to be subjective, because it is Christ's love for us that is unchange-
able not our love for him.]

36 R501   Σφαγῆς is used as an objective genitive, "doomed to slaughter."

37 M78   Perhaps ἐν τούτοις πᾶσιν means "in the midst," or "in spite of all these
things" ("in regard to"--T265). [Ed. Moule's former suggestion appears to be
more probable since Paul's main point in this context is that the Christian can
be victorious because God will not forsake him. In the midst of the circumstances that may occur, God's love will not be separated from the Christian.
Consequently, glorious victory is possible for the Christian.]
M87   In ὑπερνικάω, the preposition means "exceedingly" (cf. R629).

39 T187   The article τῆς is repeated with the prepositional phrase to avoid
ambiguity (for emphasis--BD269[2]).

ROMANS 9

1 BD463   The lack of connection between the two major divisions of the letter (9:1),

which are so different, may appear odd, but a mere conjunction here would still
be a far cry from a real connection.

3 **B**33   Paul may have chosen the imperfect with ηὐχόμην because he shrank from
expressing a deliberate choice in regard to so solemn a matter, or because he
thought of it as beyond the control or influence of his wish (cf. T65; Paul
uses the potential imperfect where he almost expresses a moral wrong--R886; for
the sake of courtesy--R919; "I could almost pray to be accursed"-M9).
M64 ῾Υπέρ is used with the meaning "instead of" (cf. 8:32).
BD211 ᾿Από denotes alienation in some expressions, especially in Paul (as in this
verse) which cannot be directly paralleled from the classical language (ἀπό con-
forms with ἐκ--M72).

4 R427 In enumerations the repetition of καί gives a kind of solemn dignity (it is
rhetorically effective--BD460[3]).
BD141(8) Διαθῆκαι is doubtless a literal plural; for the singular elsewhere
always ends with -η (note the variant), "covenants."

5 R1108 As is well known, the difficulty here is a matter of exegesis, and the
punctuation of the editor will be made according to his theology. But it may be
said in brief that the natural way to take ὁ ὤν and θεός is in apposition to
ὁ Χριστός. It is a very common thing in the N.T. to have ὁ and the participle
where a relative clause is possible (cf. MT228; "the Messiah is God"--TGr15).
M58 Τὸ κατὰ σάρκα means "as far as physical descent is concerned" (cf. T15; the
article strongly emphasizes the limitation--BD266[2]).

7 H463 The causal use of ἐν occurs here (semitic).

8 R701 The copula ἔστιν should be supplied between the words ταῦτα and τέκνα.
H463 Εἰς with the accusative is used in place of a predicate nominative (semitic),
"considered as descendants."

11 R425 The final clause with ἵνα seems to interrupt the flow of the sentence (the
final clause has been shifted forward--BD478).
B454 A participle in the genitive absolute construction occasionally stands alone
without an accompanying noun or pronoun, when the person or thing referred to is
easily perceived from the context, as with γεννηθέντων and πραξάντων here ("having not yet been born, done anything").
T268 ῾Η...θεοῦ means "God's purpose of choosing."

17 BD290(4) Εἰς αὐτὸ τοῦτο means "for this very reason" (referring to the following
ὅπως; cf. B197; "just this reason"--T45).

20 R402 Paul is very earnest when he uses the combined particles μενοῦνγε here.
R678 The pronoun σύ has a very emphatic position. This pronoun also occurs in a
representative sense.
R1148 There is a keen touch of irony in the first sentence of this verse.
T226 Οὕτως appears to be used as a predicate accusative (cf. BD434[2]), "why did
you make me thus (or like this)?"

21 R1062 ᾿Εξουσίαν ποιῆσαι means "power for making."

273

22 R1129 The participle θέλων is used with a concessive idea ("although...").
T14 Τὸ δυνατὸν αὐτοῦ means "how powerful he is."
BD165 Ὀργῆς and ἐλέους (vv. 22f1) are used as genitives of quality with a figur-
ative sense, as if they mean "bearers of wrath...of mercy" (cf. T213).
BD467 Anacoluthon (a shift in sentence structure) is not involved in v. 22 if
καί in v. 23 is dropped with B and other manuscripts (cf. R438 and M151).

24 R713 The relative pronoun οὕς changes to the real gender (it changes to the
masculine because people are referred to) rather than maintaining the grammatical
gender.
M168 Notice the word order of οὕς, which precedes ἡμᾶς (the antecedent).

25 M105 It is difficult to account for the uses of οὐ with a participle, but the
negative οὐ seems to coalesce very closely with the participle here, almost as
though it were an alpha privative (a sort of title; also the Hosea passage is
behind it; οὐ is used because it is a quote from the Septuagint--BD430[3]).
T282 Οὐ is used with the noun λαόν to express a single idea (a proper name--BD426).

27 R632 Ὑπέρ has the sense of "concerning" with the verb κράζω (cf. M65).
B285 Ἐάν introduces a concessive clause, "although."

30 R1184 Sometimes a word is repeated with δέ for special emphasis, as here (cf.
3:22 and BD447[8]).

33 T237 Ἐπί is used with πιστεύω in the sense of "believe in" (cf. BD187[6]).

ROMANS 10

1 M70 Perhaps the preposition εἰς is used in a final sense in this verse, "my
heart's desire...has their salvation as its purpose."
T191 There is no emphasis in the possessive adjective ἐμῆς (it is equivalent to
μοῦ in this verse), "of my heart."
BD463 The omission of a connective for this verse makes the emotional appeal more
distinct.

2 M40 Ζῆλον θεοῦ, literally "zeal of God," is an objective genitive, because it
represents the idea ζηλοῦσιν θεόν, "they are zealous after God," in which God
is the object (cf. R500).

3 R818 In modern Greek the passive aorist form is almost invariably used for both
the middle and passive ideas. This tendency seen in the N.T. (and the rest of
Koine) has triumphed over the aorist middle. In v. 3 the R.V. has the preferred
translation "they did not subject themselves to the righteousness of God."

4 M70 Τέλος...δικαιοσύνην probably means "Christ is an end to legalism for the
attainment of righteousness, as a means to righteousness."

6 T135 The infinitive καταγαγεῖν is used to express purpose.

8 R505 Notice that the genitive σοῦ is used with the adverb ἐγγύς, "near you."

9 R1123 In the double accusative here κύριον is used as a predicate to Ἰησοῦν, "that Jesus is Lord."

10 M70 The preposition εἰς seems to be used in a consecutive sense, "for with the heart one believes, and it results in righteousness."

11 T237 Ἐπί is used with πιστεύω to mean "believe in" (cf. 9:33).

12 R594 Εἰς with the accusative is used in place of a dative, "upon all."

13 M151 There is a conditional clause latent in ἄν...; "whoever invokes" is close in sense to "if anyone invokes."

14 R706 The implied antecedent of the pronoun οὗ is probably εἰς τοῦτον.
   R1106 The idea in χωρὶς κηρύσσοντος is not "without preaching," but "without one preaching," "without a preacher." For "without preaching" the text must read χωρὶς τοῦ κηρύσσειν.
   R1200 The repetition of the verb here gives a cumulative force building up to a climax (cf. 5:3).

15 R302 Ὡς is used to indicate exclamation in ὡς ὡραῖοι, "How beautiful...."

16 R752 Οὐ πάντες merely means "not everyone" instead of "none."

18 R506 Ἀκούω means "to understand" in this context.
   R1159 When μὴ οὐ occurs in questions, μή is the interrogative particle while οὐ is the negative of the verb (vv. 18f.; "did they fail to hear?"; cf. B468; "surely they haven't not – heard it [missed hearing it]"--T283).
   M163 The particle μενοῦνγε seems to be adversative, μενοῦνγε εἰς πᾶσαν τὴν γῆν means "on the contrary, into all the earth."

19 R657 Πρῶτος is used as an adjective rather than an adverb here, "Moses is the first who says..." (cf. T225).
   T282 The negative οὐκ is used with the noun ἔθνει to express a single idea (cf. 9:25).

20 T58 The passive of εὑρίσκω may attach the person concerned by means of the dative, rather than ὑπό with the genitive, with a resultant intransitive meaning, "I was found."
   T264 The meaning "among" is possible in v. 20, where the presence of the preposition (ἐν) depends on the variant readings (the preposition ἐν is used for the customary dative, similar to "appeared to...," the Septuagint omits ἐν--BD220[1]. [Ed. The manuscript support for ἐν is divided. But if the preposition is to be included, the clause appears to have a sense parallel to the following clause, i.e., similar to the latter suggestion.]

ROMANS 11

1 R810 The middle voice in ἀπώσατο expresses an indirect idea, "Did God push his people away from himself?"

2 T261 The local use of ἐν with the dative has the resultant meaning "in the story of Elijah" (a quotation formula).

3 R634 The perfective idea appears in the compound verb ὑπολείπω, meaning "to leave behind" or "over."

4 M183 The curious τῇ βάαλ (rather than the masculine) in this verse is usually (and plausibly) accounted for by the Hebrew habit of reading a word meaning "shame" or "abomination" where the name of an alien deity (or some other abominable word) was written; hence, for "Baal" one might read "bosheth," "shameful thing"; and this, being a feminine (or neuter) word, would suggest a feminine article in the Greek (if not an actual feminine Greek word such as αἰσχύνη as in the Septuagint; cf. MT59).

5 TGr49 Mark's view of the Messianic "secret" agrees with a similar view in the writings of Paul, especially in Romans 11:5-8.

6 T318 Ἐπεί has a causal sense, but it is weakened in Biblical Greek to "for otherwise" (as here and in v. 22; cf. BD456[3]).

7 M37 The genitive usually occurs with ἐπιτυγχάνω, which means "to attain to" (but v. 7 has the accusative).

8 R1061 The infinitives in this verse are parallel with κατανύξεως (the quotation here differs significantly from the Septuagint text of Deut. 29:4).
  B400 The infinitives here with the article τοῦ are used to limit nouns. Thus the initial part of this quotation means "God gave them a spirit of stupor, eyes that see not, and ears that hear not" (its usage in this context tends towards a consecutive sense--BD400[2]).
  BD109(4) The substantive κατανύξεως originally was derived from the verb meaning "to stun."

10 BD400(2,4) As in v. 8 this passage exhibits a very loose relationship between the substantive and infinitive and tends toward the consecutive sense (the Septuagint style is responsible for this construction--H450), "so that they cannot see."

11 T190 Regardless of its position αὐτῶν is unemphatic here.
   MT207 Ἵνα is used to introduce the contemplated result, "so as to fall."

13 R602 Ἐπί is used with the idea of degree or measure here, "in so far as."
   BD474(4) The attributive genitive ἐθνῶν comes before the noun it modifies (indicating possible emphasis).

14 B276 Εἰ with the verb here has the force of a final clause (cf. 1:10), "in order that" (the verbs may be aorist subjunctives--R1017).

15 TGr109 Paul states in this verse that God's temporary rejection of Israel has brought about the reconciliation of the whole world to him, and the blessings to the world will be correspondingly greater when Israel's own faith brings her back to God.

17 R418 The position of σύ shows rhetorical emphasis ("you" as opposed to those

previously mentioned; this singular pronoun has a representative sense--R678).
T115 The conditional clause here refers to something actually happening
("since...").

18 BD483 This verse contains an example of brachylogy, that is an omission (for the
sake of brevity) of an element which is not necessary for the grammatical
structure but for the thought (εἰ δὲ κατακαυχᾶσαι, supply "you should know
that" or "remember that," οὐ σύ...).

20 R532 The dative τῇ ἀπιστίᾳ is used to express a causal sense ("because of unbelief"
--M44; cf. v. 30).
R1199 There is more irony in Paul's writings than in the rest of the N.T. litera-
ture (as this verse seems to portray an example).

21 R609 Κατά is used to denote a standard or rule of measure (the phrase means
"natural, in accordance with nature"--M59).
R1012 It is hardly possible to translate εἰ οὐ as meaning "unless."

22 R524 The datives in vv. 22ff. are used as locatives ("in kindness...in unbelief").
R965 Ἐπεὶ καί is equivalent to "else" ("for otherwise"--T318; cf. v. 6).

23 R418 The position of κἀκεῖνοι displays rhetorical emphasis (cf. v. 17).

24 R616 Παρά with the accusative has the idea of "beyond" and so "contrary to."

25 T238 Ἑαυτοῖς is used as a dative of disadvantage (hence "of his own accord"--
BD188[2]).

26 BD275(4) Πᾶς Ἰσραήλ means "the whole of Israel" (because the proper name is
considered as articular--R772).

27 R616 The preposition παρά in this verse carries the notion of authorship, "the
from me covenant."

30 M44 In vv. 30f. it would certainly make good sense if τῇ τούτων ἀπειθείᾳ and
τῷ ὑμετέρῳ ἐλέει were translated in a temporal sense, "at the time of their
disbelief," and "at the time when pity is shown to you" (cf. T243); the dative
τῇ ἀπιστίᾳ in v. 20, on the other hand seems to be virtually instrumental. (The
dative τῇ ἀπειθείᾳ is used with a causal sense--R532 and BD196). [Ed. Verse 30
is a sort of repetition of the concept expressed in vv. 11, 12, 15, and 28 that
the Gentiles had become the recipients of God's mercy by (because of) the disobedience of Israel. Consequently, the more specific causal rendering seems
preferable.]

31 BD196 The dative here portrays a causal idea "because God desired to show you
mercy" (cf. R532).
BD284 (2) The possessive adjective expresses the idea of the objective genitive
here, "to the mercy shown to you."

32 T266 The preposition εἰς is used here to portray a causal idea, "God has impris-
oned all because of disobedience."

33 R302 The relative adverb ὡς is used as an exclamation (cf. Rom. 10:15; both
     references show the absence of the connecting verb), "How unsearchable...!"
     BD146(2) ὦ βάθος πλούτου..., introduces an act of adoration, thus excluding the
     possibility that an abstract quantity is being addressed.

36 R583 In this noble doxology Paul regards God as source, mediate agent, and ultimate
     object or end (cf. Paul's use of prepositions in 3:22).
     R595 Εἰς does not mean "for" although that is the resultant idea here.
     R773 Τὰ πάντα means "the sum of things" ("the universe"--BD275[7]).

                              ROMANS 12

                                    "added to"
1 R1205 Τὴν λογικὴν λατρείαν ὑμων is (in apposition to) the infinitive clause
     παραστῆσαι... (it has the meaning "I beg you therefore...to present yourselves...
     --which is your spiritual service"--M35f.; cf. Rom. 8:3).
     M58 The prepositional phrase διὰ τῶν... means "in (accompaniment is similar to
        instrumentality) God's mercies' name" ("by"--T267).
     T28 The plural οἰκτρμῶν is used for an abstract idea, "mercy."

2 M44 The dative τῇ ἀνακαινώσει is used with an instrumental sense (cf. T240), "by
     the renewal."

3 R629 The notion of "excess" or "more than" appears in the compound verb with ὑπέρ.
     R1072 Εἰς τό with the infinitive seems to express conceived or actual result (cf.
        B411; MT219; perhaps it means "to adopt an outlook which tends to sobriety"--
        M70).
     M58 The preposition διά here perhaps means "in virtue of."
     BD488(16) Paul's choice of similar words here may almost be called flowery (i.e.,
        with the variation of φρονέω).

5 R487 The phrase τὸ καθ' εἷς is accusative, even though εἷς itself is nominative
     in form.
     R606 Κατά is used in the distributive sense with the nominative (τὸ καθ' εἷς is a
        stereotyped adverb--T15; it has the meaning "individually," "with relation to
        each individual"--BD305).

6 R946 Ἔχοντες appears as a practical indicative (either the participle is impera-
     tival or indicative, or Ἐσμέν or ὦμεν must be supplied--R1134; the subjunctive
     verb ὦσιν may be supplied before ἐν τῇ διακονίᾳ--T302).
     MT183 There is a case of heaped-up ellipses in vv. 6ff. There is much to attract
     the treatment of ἔχοντες as virtually equivalent to ἔχομεν: "but we have grace-
     gifts which differ according to the grace that was given us, whether that of
     prophecy (differing) according to the measure of our faith, or that of service
     (differing) in the sphere of the service, or he that teaches (exercising--ἔχων--
     his gift) in his teaching, or he that exhorts in his exhorting, he who gives
     (exercising this charism) in singleness of purpose, he who holds office in a deep
     sense of responsibility, he who shows compassion in cheerfulness." In this way
     διάφορον is supplied with προφετείαν and διακονίαν, and then the ἔχοντες χαρίσματα
     is taken up in each successive clause, in nearly the same sense throughout: the
     durative sense of ἔχω, "hold" and so "exercise," must be maintained. On the
     other hand, the imperatival idea, which in the usual view

is understood here, must be derived from the fact that the prepositional phrases are successively thrown out as interjections (which is less probable).

8 M114 The omission of the article in this verse is perhaps due to the adverbial usage of the prepositional phrase.

9 R439 Participles are scattered along in this chapter in an unending series mingled with infinitives and imperatives. Thus in vv. 9-13 participles occur, in v. 14 the imperative, in v. 15 an infinitive, in v. 16a participles, in v. 16b an imperative, and in v. 17 participles. Here the participle seems to be practically equivalent to the imperative; the infinitives also seem to be imperatival (cf. MT180; TGr166 and BD468[2]).
T177 The article is used with the nouns in vv. 9f. because they refer to virtues assumed to be well known.

10 M46 Τῇ φιλαδελφίᾳ...φιλόστοργοι seems to be an adverbial usage of the dative (cf. T239), "love one another with brotherly love."
M180 The simple adjectives φιλόστοργοι and ὀκνηροί are used imperativally (cf. R1172).
BD150 Προηγούμενοι means "preferring" (not "outdoing"), construed like προκρίνειν.

15 R944 In this verse χαίρειν and κλαίειν are clearly parallel with εὐλογεῖτε καὶ μὴ καταρᾶσθε (infinitives used as imperatives; cf. B365; M126; MT179; BD389; χρή δεῖ may perhaps be assumed--T78).

16 R594 Εἰς with the accusative is used in place of a dative, "to," or "with one another."
M52 Παρά with the dative gives the resultant meaning "wise in their own eyes."
TGr166 The participles here are imperatival (cf. v. 9); "live in harmony...").

17 R573 In ἀντί the idea of "in the place of" or "instead of" is present where two substantives placed opposite each other are equivalent and so may be exchanged.

18 R611 The preposition μετά expresses the idea of "general fellowship" with the participle in this verse.
M33f. Τὸ ἐξ ὑμῶν means "for your part," "so far as it is in your power" (accusative of respect; the whole phrase becomes adverbial; "so far as it originates from you"--T14).

19 T173 The article τῇ is used here because the well-known wrath is referred to.
MT180 The participle ἐκδικοῦντες means either "do not avenge yourselves (whenever wronged)," an iterative sense, or "do not (as your tendency is)...". [Ed. Possibly both ideas are prevalent.] This present participle is strongly contrasted with the decisive aorist δότε, "once and for all make room for the Wrath (which alone can do justice or wrong)".

21 R881 The present tense of νικάω is used as a perfect. The action is durative only in the sense of state, not of linear action (cf. T62), "be overcome."

ROMANS 13

2 R807 Ἀντιτασσόμενος means "line one's self up against" (a direct middle).

M144 "Ὥστε is simply an inferential particle meaning "and so," "accordingly."
BD188(2) The dative ἑαυτοῖς is used to show disadvantage ("for themselves").

3 T319 θέλεις δὲ μὴ φοβεῖσθαι... should be translated, "if you wish to be fearless
of...."

4 M70 The first εἰς in this verse is used in a final sense (indicating purpose),
"for your good."

5 R1181 The notion of "even" from καί is an advance on that of mere addition which
is due to the context, not to καί. The thing that is added is out of the ordinary and rises to a climax.

7 R758 In this verse the article is used with each thing and quality (particular-
izing each quality).

8 R748 Τὸν ἕτερον means "neighbor."
R897 The verb πεπλήρωκεν seems to be used as a gnomic perfect (referring to a
customary truth, well known by the recipients).
R1173 The use of the compound negative as a second negative is simply to strengthen the negation ("owe no man anything"--B489).
BD399(1) The articular infinitive is anaphoric, in that this is a well-known
command.

9 R766 The articles τό and τῷ introduce the quotations.

11 R1059 The infinitive is in predicate apposition with ὥρα, "time for arising"
(cf. T139).
R1181 Καὶ τοῦτο denotes an explanatory addition ("and indeed"--T45).
MT182 An imperative should be supplied, "and this (do) with knowledge" (the participle being rather the complement of an understood imperative than an imperative itself).

12 R901 The use of the aorist and perfect together in this context does not prove
confusion of the tenses, but supports their distinction.

13 M155 Μή is used here because of the close association of the previous subjunctive
verb.
T76 The aorist subjunctive has the concept "now let us walk" (denoting the
commencement of this way of life--BD337[1]).

ROMANS 14

1 M44 Τῇ πίστει is probably used in a metaphorical locative sense ("weak in faith").
T22 Τὸν ἀσθενοῦντα is a generic singular (representing a whole class).

2 B387 The infinitive here is used as the object of πιστεύει, "has conficence."
BD397(2) Πιστεύει does not mean "believe" here, but "have the confidence to risk,"
"feel equal to...."

4 R539 The dative τῷ ἰδίῳ κυρίῳ is used as a dative of advantage or disadvantage

(cf. 6:2), "to the advantage" or "disadvantage of his own master."
R678 The pronoun σύ has a very emphatic position.

5 R692 This verse shows ἴδιος as the equivalent of ἑαυτοῦ. Although the N.T. passages may be assumed to show emphasis when ἴδιος is used ("for himself" emphasizing the pronoun--MT89).
   M51 The preposition παρά is used in the sense of "more than" or "beyond."
   M125 The relative pronouns ὅς and ὅς are used as demonstratives ("one man...,
   another man").

6 R539 Κυρίῳ is used as a dative of advantage (cf. BD188[2]; "in honor of the Lord"
   --T238).

7 BD188(2) The datives in vv. 7f. express more the idea of possession than advantage
   and disadvantage (it ends with τοῦ κυρίου ἐσμέν). [Ed. These datives are most
   probably used to show advantage and disadvantage ("lives for himself"). A dative
   of possession is actually a predicative dative and generally occurs with εἰμί,
   γίνομαι, or ὑπάρχω. The construction τοῦ κυρίου ἐσμέν is not exactly parallel
   with any of the preceding dative constructions, especially since there is a
   change in the verb.]

9 R834 ῎Εζησεν has the meaning "became alive." (Inceptive aorist; cf. ἀπέθανεν
   just before; B41; M10 and T71).
   M195 Possibly there is something more than mere rhetoric in the parallelism of
   this verse; as though his death was for the dead and his life for the living.

10 R678 Σύ has an emphatic position here.

11 BD188(2) Ἐμοί is used in a sense similar to a dative of advantage ("for me").

13 R1059 The articular infinitive is in apposition with τοῦτο (the infinitival
   clause describes the decision to be made).

14 T137 The infinitive εἶναι is the object (expressing the content) of λογιζομένῳ.

15 M44 The dative Βρώματι is used in an instrumental sense, "do not by your food
   destroy him..." (it is causal--T242). [Ed. A causal notion seems to be included
   in the instrumental rendering; "because of your food" is similar to "by your
   food."]

16 T189 The possessive pronoun does not commonly occur in first position as ὑμῶν
   does here (there is possible emphasis here).

17 R784 The prepositional phrase ἐν πνεύματι ἁγίῳ is understood as attributive without the article (cf. T221; modifying the noun χαρά, "joy in the Holy Spirit").

19 BD266(3) Τὰ τῆς εἰρήνης means "what makes for Peace."

20 R1153 Paul expresses sharp contrast by using μέν-ἀλλά.
   M58 Διά with the genitive here is used almost as an adverb, meaning "he who eats
   in a way which causes stumbling" (the notion of means and manner shade into one
   concept--R583; "with offence"--T267).

21 R978 Ἐν ᾧ seems to express an instrumental idea (causal--T253). [Ed. Compare
   these suggestions with the observation on v. 15. Actually a causal rendering
   seems to portray Paul's argument more precisely.]
   BD338(1) In καλὸν...προσκόπτει the aorist infinitive is to be taken strictly:
   "it is good not to eat meat for once (in a specific instance)...if it might cause
   offence"; it is not a question of continuous abstention.
   BD480(1) In this verse "or to do anything else" is implied.

22 R716 Ἐν ᾧ implies ἐν τούτῳ ("with regard to"--T265).

23 R897 Κατακέκριται seems to be used as a gnomic present perfect (for a customary
   truth), "is condemned."

                                     ROMANS 15

1 R1096 Ἀδύνατος means "incapable" here, whereas usually it means "impossible"
  (cf. MT221).

2 M53 Πρός with the accusative is used in a transferred sense, meaning "making for
  up-building."

3 BD332(1) The aorist tense of ἤρεσεν is used for a linear action which (having been
  completed) is regarded as a whole (in Christ's whole earthly life; a complexive
  aorist; "Christ did not please himself").

4 R563 The preposition πρό is used with the first verb and dropped from the second,
  although retained in sense (cf. MT115).

5 B176 Δῴη is used as an optative of wishing (expressing a prayer).

7 R809 Προσλαμβάνεσθε means "take to yourselves" (an indirect middle).

13 B176 The optative of wishing πληρῶσαι occurs here (cf. v. 5).
   T145 Ἐν τῳ πιστεύειν has a causal sense here, "because you believe" (it is tem-
   poral--BD404). [Ed. Ἐν τῷ with an infinitive is generally considered as a temporal expression in the N.T. But if the temporal rendering is included here,
   the notion of basis or reason (i.e., cause) is still implied; faith is the basis
   for the blessing of joy and peace.]
   T265 Ἐν τῇ ἐλπίδι is used to denote the concept "with regard to hope."

14 R686 In this verse αὐτός occurs with the first person and αὐτοί with the second
   person designating a sharp contrast.
   B154 The perfect participle (πεπληρωμένοι) is used to refer to completed action,
   "filled with all knowledge."

15 R846 In v. 15 the reference may be to another portion of the same epistle or to
   the epistle as a whole (ἔγραψα; an earlier part is indicated--T73). [Ed. The
   latter suggestion appears to be more probable. But actually reference is made
   to former parts (plural) by the phrase ἀπὸ μέρους.]
   T30 The comparative adjective is used simply as a positive, "boldly" (the comparative adjective is not just the positive in sense, even without the expressed

                                        282

object of comparison--R655). [Ed. Turner's observation is questionable, since
it is not necessary to include the object of comparison in a comparative sentence.]

16 R594 Εἰς with the accusative is used here where one expects a simple dative, "to
the Gentiles."
T211 Τοῦ θεοῦ is a subjective genitive since the object is said to be περὶ τοῦ
υἱοῦ αὐτοῦ ("the gospel from God").

17 BD160 The phrase τὰ πρὸς τὸν θεόν is used as an adverbial accusative ("the things
for God.").

19 M85 Μέχρι means "as far as."

20 R748 Ἀλλότριον, means "belonging to another."

22 R1061 Τοῦ with the infinitive is used as an ablative with the verb of "hindering"
(cf. B401), "I have been hindered from coming."
B28 When an imperfect refers to an action not separated from the time of speaking
by a recognized interval, it is best translated into English by the perfect.
M108 Does τὰ πολλά in v. 22 mean "those many times" (of which you are all aware),
or "the majority of occasions, more often than not"? [Ed. The former suggestion
more readily brings out the usual meaning of πολύς. This rendering also seems
to explain the inclusion of the variant πολλάκις by some manuscripts.]
BD400(4) Paul omits μή after "to hinder" so that the dependence on the verb is
clear (actually τοῦ μή with an infinitive after such verbs means "so that...not").

23 T141 Τοῦ ἐλθεῖν is epexegetical after the noun ἐπιποθία, "a longing to see you."

24 M133 Ὡς ἄν with the subjunctive verb refers to a time with a degree of indefiniteness ("on my imminent journey to Spain"--ED445 (2); it refers to a definite
action in the future--T112). [Ed. In essence, Turner implies that the degree of
indefiniteness is in the futuristic aspect.]

25 R891 The present participle διακονῶν is used like a future in the sense of purpose (by implication only, however), "for the purpose of helping."

26 R502 Τῶν ἁγίων is used as a partitive genitive ("the poor among God's people"--
M43).
R528 The preposition εἰς with the accusative is used for the simple dative here
("for the poor").

27 BD113(2) Σαρκικός means "belonging to σάρξ," "of the nature of σάρξ."

28 R582 Winer takes δι' ὑμῶν to mean "through you," that is "through your city,"
"through the midst of you" (the preposition is equivalent to via--M55).

29 R589 The dative ἐν πληρώματι is used to portray an idea of accompanying circumstance, "in the fullness."
M134 The notion in the participle ἐρχόμενος may be "when" or "if I come" (this
example shows how conditional and temporal clauses overlap).

30 BD223(4) Διά with the genitive is used here idiomatically (in an urgent appeal),
   "by our Lord."

31 R783 The article τῶν was not repeated with the prepositional phrase ἐν τῇ Ἰουδαίᾳ
   simply because the need of another article was not felt (the prepositional phrase
   modifies τῶν ἀπειθούντων).
   M204 Εἰς with the accusative, following διακονία, probably should be taken in a
   local sense replacing ἐν with the dative, "in Jerusalem."

                              ROMANS 16

 2 R505 The adverb ἀξίως is used with the genitive similar to a preposition, (cf.
   Phil. 1:27), "worthy of saints."
   M145 The ἵνα clause here denotes the content of συνίστημι, rather than being
   imperatival.
   T41 Αὐτή means "she herself."
   T265 The preposition in ἐν ᾧ is used in the sense of "with regard to."

 4 R633 The preposition in the compound verb ὑπέθηκαν has the idea of "put under."
   BD293(4) The definite relative pronoun ὅς and the indefinite ὅστις are not clearly
   distinguished in the N.T. In vv. 4ff. a simple assertion is made by using ὅς,
   whereas a characteristic is presented in the usage of ὅστις (cf. T47).

 6 H446 The adjective πολλά has an adverbial sense, "very" (in vv. 6 and 12), may be
   due to semitic influence.

 7 B82 The perfect indicative γέγοναν is used of a past event which is by reason of
   the context necessarily thought of as separated from the moment of speaking by
   an interval of time. It is impossible to render it into English adequately.
   The last clause of this verse is best translated "who also were (R.V. "have been")
   in Christ before me" ("who have been in Christ longer than I"--MT141).

10 R783 The prepositional phrase ἐν Χριστῷ is attributive, even though the article
   τόν is not repeated ("the approved one in Christ").
   T169 The possession of slaves by a family seems to be indicated by the construction τοὺς (supply "brothers, Christians") ἐκ τῶν (supply "slaves") Ἀριστοβούλου,
   ...Ναρκίσσου (cf. BD162[5] and M38).

15 M93n.1 When πᾶς means "all" or "every" it is not enclosed within the article-noun
   unit. Verse 15 is a striking exception. Surely τοὺς σὺν αὐτοῖς πάντας ἁγίους
   means "all the saints with them."
   H350 Νηρεύς is a personal name, possibly referring to one of Nero's freedmen.

16 T212 Τοῦ Χριστοῦ is used as a genitive of relationship with ἐκκλησίαι, with a
   mystical concept similar to the ἐν Χριστῷ formula ("the churches of Christ").

17 R616 Παρά with the accusative here has the idea of "beyond" and so "contrary to"
   (cf. Rom. 11:24 and 12:3).
   R954 In σκοπεῖν τοὺς...ποιοῦντας the relative clause is adjectival, but in itself
   a mere incident between τοὺς and the participle ποιοῦντας (note also the neat
   classic idiom of τοὺς being separated from ποιοῦντας).

19 BD447(5) It is to be noted in cases of an uncertain reading involving μέν that the inclusion of μέν throws the emphasis on the second member (indicated by δέ); therefore, where the emphasis is on the first part, the second is only an appendage, and μέν is not to be read (as in σοφοὺς [μέν]).

21 R173 Σωσίπατρος is from Corinth and Σώπατρος is from Beraea (Acts 20:4), although it is possible that they represent the same man (note the textual variants in the reference in Acts).
BD268(1) The articular expression ὁ συνεργός means "my well-known co-laborer."

25 R609 The preposition in κατὰ τὸ εὐαγγέλιον, is used to introduce a standard or rule of measure.

26 R1117 Notice the sharp contrast between the aorist (with νῦν) and a perfect participle.

27 BD467 ᾯ is to be deleted with B, not only because of anacoluthon, (a shift in sentence structure), but especially in order to connect the phrase διὰ Ἰησοῦ Χριστοῦ to the rest of the sentence (B improves the text--T343)

I Corinthians

1 M958 Κλητός in vv. 1 and 2 means "a called (person)," and is simply noun-like to stand in precisely the same place as a participle.

5 T265 'Εν παντί is used as a dative of reference, meaning "with reference to all."

6 R500 Μαρτύριον τοῦ Χριστοῦ means "witness concerning Christ" (an objective genitive).

9 R583 Διά with the genitive is used to refer to God as the intervening cause or agent (cf. M204 and T267; it denotes the originator--BD223[3]).

10 R1186 In the μή...δέ contrast, δέ is clearly adversative (similar to the οὐ. . . ἀλλά construction), "that there be no divisions . . ., but."
R1413 When the construction with ἵνα is continued in a further clause by μή, μή alone is repeated, but with the continued sense of ἵνα μή (ἵνα is used to introduce an object clause after a verb of exhorting, "I appeal to you that"--B200)
BD223(4) Διά with the genitive here is used idiomatically with an urgent request, meaning "by."

11 R502 The article τῶν used with Χλόης refers to the family in general ("by them of Chloe's house"--T16).

16 M161 Λοιπόν is used as an adverbial expression. Thus, the whole clause should be translated, "I do not know that I baptized anybody else besides."

17 B481 Οὐ is used to negate the limitation of the infinitive rather than the infinitive itself (i.e., οὐ negates the verb), "Christ did not send me to baptize."

18 R827 In οἱ ἀπολλύμενοι, "the perishing," the destiny is accented by ἀπό, and the process is depicted by the tense.
B125 The participle, σῳζομένοις may be rendered, "we that are (in the sense "we that become") saved," or may be taken as in the R.V. translation as a progressive present as simultaneous action. It cannot mean "the saved" in the sense of "those that have been saved."
BD190(1) Μωρία ἐστίν means "is considered as folly."
M114 The participle ἀπολλύμενοι is strongly durative, although the verb itself (ἀπολλύω) is perfective in the fact that the goal is ideally reached: a complete transformation of its subjects is required to bring them out of the ruin implicit in their state.

20 H402 Μωραίνω in classical usage means "to be foolish," but here it means "to make foolish."

21 B231 'Επειδή introduces a subordinate clause in v. 21, but a co-ordinate one in

286

v. 22 (cf. Luke 11:32).

M40 Τῇ σοφίᾳ τοῦ θεοῦ might be classed as a subjective genitive (parallel to
ὁ θεός σοφός ἐστίν); but it may equally well (or better) be called possessive,
"the wisdom which belongs to God."

25 R962 ῞Οτι in v. 25 and γάρ in v. 26 both seem to introduce co-ordinate clauses.
M98 Τῶν ἀνθρώπων is probably used loosely for τῆς σοφίας τῶν ἀνθρώπων ("wiser
than the wisdom of men").
T14 Τὸ μωρὸν τοῦ θεοῦ is equivalent to μωρία (which precedes) or "God seeming
to be foolish."

26 T282 The negative expressions with οὐ form a single idea (οὐ πολλοί is similar
to "very few").

27 R411 The neuter plural is used in a collective sense to represent persons
(stressing the quality rather than the individuals--T21).
BD138(1) The plural is used here because the singular would be understood in
view of v. 25, as "the foolishness, . . . weakness of the world" (consequently
the plural is used to refer to people).

29 R752 Μή . . πᾶσα means "no flesh."
T105 ῞Οπως is used for the sake of variety here (cf. v. 28), consequently it has
the same sense as the preceding ἵνα.

30 BD444(4) In the enumeration here τε is merely a connective and not correlated
with καί (simply meaning "and").

31 R949 There is probably an ellipsis of γένηται after ἵνα (thus meaning "in order
that it may come to pass, work out just as . . .," the adoption of a literal
quotation in place of a paraphrase would have required the subjunctive [instead
of γέγραπται]--BD481; cf. M139).

I CORINTHIANS 2

1 R85 One should not stress Paul's language in I Cor. 2:1-4 into a denial that he
could use the literary style. It is rather a rejection of the bombastic art
that was so common from Thucydides to Chrysostom. It is with this comparison
in mind that Origen (Celsus, VII, 59) speaks of Paul's literary inferiority.
M105 The reason that οὐ occurs with the participle here is that the distance of
the negative from the participle would make μή sound strange, with the resultant
meaning "not proclaiming."

2 R1181 The last clause in this verse introduced by καί is an explanatory addition
to Χριστόν (epexegetical καί; cf. T335; the conjunction with the demonstrative
pronoun is emphatic--BD442[9]0, "and him crucified."
M156 Οὐ γὰρ ἔκρινά τι εἰδέναι evidently means what would normally have been expressed by ἔκρινα γὰρ μηδὲν εἰδέναι, and the use of οὐ instead of μή appears
to be due to the displacement of the negative preceding the indicative (but
J. B. Lightfoot [in location] argues on the contrary, that "I had no intent,
no mind to know anything . . ." is the meaning). [Ed. It appears that Lightfoot

is correct since he offers a more simple explanation of the text as it is recorded. Οὐ is the negative one would expect with an indicative verb (ἔκρινα).
Also it is best not to change the order of words if a satisfactory translation
can be obtained without alterations.]

4   R1206 The Judaizers at Corinth did not discuss the rhetorical niceties of
    these letters. They felt the power of the ideas in them even when they re-
    sisted Paul's authority. Paul used tropes (figurative language), but he smote
    hearts with them and did not merely tickle the fancy of the lovers of sophistry
    (subtle argument and reasoning). Paul denied that he spoke ἐν πιθοῖς (πειθοῖς)
    σοφίας λόγοις, though his words seem to the lover of Christ to be full of the
    highest appeal to the soul of man. One must discount this disclaimer, not
    merely by Paul's natural modesty, but by contrast with the Corinthians' con-
    ception of πιθός. They loved the rhetorical flights of the artificial orators
    of the time.
    M78, 79 Ἐν with the dative πειθοῖς is probably used in the sense of accompani-
    ment (cf. 1 Thess. 2:5), "with persuasive words of wisdom."

5   T253 In both occurrences here ἐν with the dative is used in the sense of "be-
    cause of."

6   T264 Ἐν is used with the dative pleonastically for the normal dative here mean-
    ing "we speak to the perfect . . ." (for their advantage).
    BD447(8) The second δέ in this verse is used to introduce an explanation, "yet
    (or "although") not the wisdom."

7   R418 The order of the words in θεοῦ σοφίαν, throws proper emphasis upon θεοῦ
    (God's wisdom).
    R589 The preposition ἐν has the idea, "in the form of" (cf. BD220[2]; perhaps
    descriptive, "consisting of"--M78).
    R1117 The use of the perfect tense of the participle here indicates that the
    wisdom of God is no longer hidden. (The perfect participle here is used as a
    pluperfect to denote a state existing which is antecedent to the time of the
    principle verb. The action, of which it is the result, is still earlier. Cf.
    v. 10-B156).
    M74 The preposition πρό is used temporally here, meaning "before the ages,
    before time."

9   M183 Ἐπὶ τὴν καρδίαν (for ἐν τῇ καρδίᾳ) may be good Greek, but it looks like
    a literal translation from the Septuagint (it has the resultant meaning "no
    thought came to man"--BDp.3 n.4).

13 R654 An ambiguity exists in πνευματικοῖς πνευματικὰ συγκρίνοντες, but the pres-
    ence of λόγοις inclines one to think that Paul is here combining spiritual
    ideas with spiritual words.
    M40 The adjective διδακτοῖς occurs with a subjective genitive twice in this
    verse, meaning "not in words taught by human wisdom, but in words taught by the
    Spirit" (cf. T211).

14 R159 Ψυχικός refers to the man possessed of mere natural life (v. 14) as op-
    posed to the regenerate life (πνευματικός in v. 15).
    BD190(1) Μωρία ἐστίν means "is considered as folly" (cf. 1:18).

16 R724 Ὅς is used to denote a consecutive idea, "that," or "so as to."

I CORINTHIANS 3

1   BD113(2) Σαρκικός ("belonging to" σάρξ, of the nature of σάρξ [in contrast to
    πνευματικός]) is sometimes confused with σάρκινος ("made of flesh") in the
    manuscripts. (The adjectives in -ικός generally denote "like" and those in
    -ινος generally portray the notion "made of." The termination -ινος denotes a
    material relation, while -ικός denotes an ethical or dynamic relation, to the
    idea involved in the root. In this verse, σαρκίνοις is deliberately chosen in
    distinction from σαρκικού in v. 3. The inclusion of σαρκικοῖς by some later
    manuscripts is an obvious correction--H378; cf. R158 and 1 Pet. 2:11).

2   T330 Introducing a strong addition, ἀλλά means "yes, indeed" (emphatic--BD448[6]).
    BD479(2) Ἐψώμισα probably should be supplied with βρῶμα, "I did not feed you
    solid food."

3   BD456(3) Ὅπου means "insofar as."

5   R583 The intermediate idea (agency) of διά is seen clearly here ("through whom").
    BD442(9) Καί has an epexegetical sense here ("that is to say").

6   BD448(2) The sense of this verse is, "but he who caused it to grow was not
    Apollos or I, but God" (ἀλλά shows distinct contrast).

7   M144 Ὥστε is used simply as an inferential particle meaning "and so, accordingly".

8   R691 The adjective ἴδιον here implies what is peculiar to one, his particularity
    or idiosyncrasy (cf. T191, MT90 and 1 Cor. 7:7).

9   H341 The noun γεώργιον here seems to mean "husbandry, tilth."

11 R616 The preposition παρά in this verse has the notion of "beyond" or "above"
    (sort of comparative, "other than"; cf. M51).

12 B240 In v. 12, it is probable that we ought to read, "if any man is destroying,"
    and take the clause as referring to what was then hypothetically going on, ra-
    ther than referring to what might at any time occur.
    BD460 The asyndeton (the omission of a connecting word) in the verse is rhetori-
    cally effective, and should be read with animation (vivacity) emphasizing the
    studied scale of descending value.

13 M77 Ἐν πυρί may go with ἔργον as instrumental, or with ἡμέρα to express accom-
    paniment (the prepositional phrase has an instrumental sense--R590). [Ed. The
    most appropriate subject of ἀποκαλύπτεται is the previous τὸ ἔργον. Consequent-
    ly, the prepositional phrase presents an instrumental sense.]

14 BD372(2a) In vv. 14 and 15, εἰ with the future indicative (of reality) is used
    to express a deduction (presenting a logical deduction of the previous state-
    ment, cf. 11:16).

15 R582 The preposition διά here carries the root idea of "passing between, through."

17 M131 The relative clause here (οἵτινες . .) is clearly added to give additional
    sense to the previous statement (explanatory, "and that is what you are").

19   M52   Παρά with the dative is used in a metaphorical sense with the meaning "in the sight of God."

21   M144   Ὥστε is used simply as an inferential particle meaning "and so, accordingly" (cf. v. 7; it has the meaning "therefore"--R1000). [Ed. In essence, these translations are similar. The particle introduces an inference which arises from the previous discussion.]
      T265   Ἐν with the dative has the meaning "with reference to."

I CORINTHIANS 4

1   H433   Ἄνθρωπος is used in an indefinite sense (possibly Semitic), "one."

2   R992   Ἵνα of content (a subject clause) follows ζητεῖται (the clause should be rendered "it is required in stewards that a man be found faithful"--B212).
      M161   Ὧδε . . . ἵνα should be translated, "on that showing (ὧδε referring back to the preceding verse where the apostles have been called stewards) it follows that (λοιπόν) what is looked for in stewards is that . . ."(cf. BD451[6]).
      T265   Ἐν with the dative means "with reference to" (cf. 3:21).

3   T31   Ἐλάχιστος means "very small," an elative superlative (cf. MT236).
      T139   The ἵνα clause explains the content of the adjective ἐλάχιστον (a subject clause; cf. R992), "it is a very small thing, that I should" (cf. v. 2).

4   M51   Ἐν τούτῳ means "on that score, for that reason" (i.e., causal; cf. T253).

5   R757   Ὁ ἔπαινος means "the praise due to each one" (the article brings out that connotation).
      M144   Ὥστε is used simply as an inferential particle meaning, "and so, **accordingly**".
      TGr131f   What exactly did Paul conceive that God would one day bring to light? Was it the things which darkness hides, or was it not rather the concealing darkness itself? His reasoning closely followed is this. In a world where decisions are reached by biased judgment, and where motives are mixed, it may be impossible to judge fairly because of an ignorance and prejudice which amounts to blindness. It is not simply that man falls short of omniscience or some facts are hidden from him when he makes a decision, but the situation is far worse. there is a positive darkness which poisons and misdirects the mind, to be removed only by the brightness of the Lord's "parousia" not by the mere acquisition of further knowledge. So Paul was suggesting that Christ will dispel "the darkness itself which hides." At Corinth he was on trial for his stewardship and if it were only a matter of revealing facts of which his accusers were ignorant, that could soon be put right. It did not need the "parousia" to bring new facts to light; yet only the "parousia," nothing less, could dispel the prejudice which is "the darkness which hides" the truth deliberately (v. 6).

6   R675   Εἷς is used as an indefinite pronoun ("each"--BD305).
      B198   Ἵνα occurs with a future indicative in a pure final clause here (unless θυσιοῦσθε is regarded as subjunctive; it is a subjunctive--H75). [Ed. It appears that this contract verb is best taken as a subjunctive (cf. BD91), especially since it follows ἵνα .]
      M64   Τὸ μὴ ὑπὲρ ἃ γέγραπται means "not beyond what is written." But it may be a

marginal gloss, in which the ὑπέρ was used in its rare local sense by a scribe, in reference to a manuscript he had seen: the μή is written over the α. (But if an emendation is not resorted to, it is best taken as the quotation of some slogan known to Paul and his readers—M111; cf. T182). [Ed. The text as it stands has weighty manuscript support. Consequently, it would be a poor method of exegesis to alter the text if a valid rendering may be obtained without resorting to such a practice.]

M77 An extension of the instrumental use of ἐν might be called exemplary. ῞Ινα ἐν ἡμῖν μάθητε, perhaps means "that, by considering our case, you might learn" (cf. R587; it has a causal sense—H463). [Ed. Actually, a resultant causal sense is apparent in Moule's suggestion.]

BD247(4) The last section of this verse means "each one on behalf of one against the other (none . . . in favor of one against the other)."

7   R1184 The first δέ in this verse is properly translated "yes" and the second "but" (adversative).

     B282 In the conditional clause, καί is simply intensive, emphasizing the following word and suggesting a supposition in some sense extreme, "but if you have indeed received it" (cf. 7:11).

8   R841 In wishes about the past (unattainable wishes) the N.T. uses ὄφελον (a shortened form of ὤφελον) with the aorist indicative (cf. BD359[1]; expressed as a regret—T91; "I even wish that you would have become kings").

     B27 The wish expressed here seems to refer to present time. The aorist tense was used to represent the action indefinitely as a simple event. [Ed. If Paul would have desired to express a present wish, the usual method would be to employ an imperfect verb with ὄφελον rather than an aorist.]

     B54 The aorist tense of ἐπλουτήσατε is inceptive representing the point of entrance; ἐβασιλεύσατε is also inceptive, meaning "you have become kings"—M11).

     BD439(2) The particle γε is emphatic here, "and I even wish that you . . ."

     BD495(2) The first three statements in this verse provide an example of Paul's use of irony (cf. R1148).

9   R481 Notice the double accusative that occurs with ἀπέδειξεν (a predicate accusative), "God has exhibited us as the apostles as the last ones."

     R788 The anarthrous nouns ἀγγέλοις and ἀνθρώποις particularize τῷ κόσμῳ, "to the world, both to angels and men."

10   H307 ῎Ενδοξος means "with glory."

12   M150 The participle λοιδορούμενοι has a meaning similar to a conditional clause (in a concessive sense), "although being reviled."

13   R618 Περικάθαρμα means "off-scouring" and περίψημα means "off-scraping."

     M13 ῾Ως . . . ἕως ἄρτι (with the aorist) literally means "we became the filth of the world . . . until now"; but the "until now" (obliterating the interval between the fact and the time of speaking) demands an English perfect, "we have become. . ."

14   R1138, 1139 The negative οὐκ is negating the participle εντρέπων. [Ed. Οὐκ is used here to negate the participle because of the formal contrast indicated by οὐ . . . ἀλλά.]

15   R283   Μυρίοι literally means "many thousands."
      R582   Διά with the genitive is used in an instrumental sense, "by means of."
      R1018   Ἐάν with the subjunctive here contemplates the future result (turn out
      to be).
      T330   After the conditional clause, ἀλλά should be translated "at least" (cf.
      BD448[5]).

17   R960   The relative clause ὅς ὑμᾶς ἀναμνήσει is used to portray purpose (it may
      be contrasted with the merely explanatory relative ὅς ἐστίν μου τέκνον in the
      same sentence (cf. BD351[1]).
      M33   The double accusative here should be translated, "he will remind you of my
      ways."

18   B440   Ὡς . . . τινες should be translated, "but some are puffed up, as though
      I were not coming to you (i.e., "because [as they suppose] I am not coming";
      ὡς with the participle expresses a subjective motive--T158).

20   M79   Ἐν is used in a descriptive sense, "the kingdom of God is not a matter of
      words, but of power" (cf. T265).

21   R534   The preposition in ἐν ῥάβδῳ shows instrumentality (cf. MT12; there is also
      a possibility that the accompanying circumstance is designated--R589; associa-
      tive--T241; "armed with"--H23). [Ed. Ἐν seems to have an associative sense
      (i.e., accompanying circumstance), describing the manner of ἔλθω. If Paul would
      come with a rod, the implication is that it would be the means to punish them.]
      BD443(3)   Τε is used to combine single ideas (this is not common in the N.T.).

I CORINTHIANS 5

1   R803   The passive ἀκούεται occurs with the sense "it is reported" (iterative).
      M140   In πορνεία . . τοιαύτη . . ὥστε, the particle ὥστε seems to be more epex-
      egetic than either consecutive or final, although the τοιαύτη may well have in-
      fluenced the choice of ὥστε by casting the sentence into a consecutive form,
      "that is a man has his father's wife."
      BD473(1)   The pronoun (τινα) is usually placed as near the beginning of the sen-
      tense as possible. The position in which it occurs here seems to emphasize
      γυναικά as well as πατρός.

2   T95   The ἵνα in this verse is usually taken as final, but only the imperatival
      ἵνα will make good sense, "let him . . . be removed."

4   R628   The preposition σύν has a technical sense, "together with."

7   R399   The word in apposition, τὸ πάσχα, precedes the noun Χριστός (unusual,
      denoting possible emphasis on the concept of suffering).
      BD452(3)   The well-known use of καὶ γάρ meaning "for," in which καί has complete-
      ly lost its force, is sometimes suggested in this verse; but here, καί is equiva-
      lent to "also," although it refers to the whole sentence and not to a lone idea.

8   R931   In ὥστε ἑορτάζωμεν, the subjunctive is hortatory and ὥστε is an inferential
      particle ("and so let us celebrate"; cf. M144).

9 R1047 In vv. 9 and 11 the infinitive is used for an indirect command (imperatival; "not to associate").
T93 The meaning in ἔγραψα is clearly that in the past he had written a previous letter, which had given rise to questions which he now was preparing to answer (cf. Rom. 15:15, R757 and BD334).

10 B249 The contrary to fact conditional clause occurs in this verse, but ἄν is omitted from the apodosis ("you would have in that case to go . . ." ["but do not go"]--BD358[1]).
T318 Ἐπεί has a causal sense in the N.T., but it is weakened to mean "for otherwise" on occasion, as in this verse (cf. BD456[3]).
BD433(2) Οὐ πάντως appears to have the sense "not meaning the immoral in general".

11 R1185 Μηδέ is used with the meaning "not even."
B44 Ἔγραψα is an epistolary aorist (thus the writer puts himself in the place of his readers; notice the contrast in meaning with the identical word in v. 11).

12 T240 Εἰμί (even though omitted) with the dative has the meaning "happen to."

13 BD288(1) In the quotation from Deut. 17:7, the reflexive pronoun ἑαυτῶν has been replaced by ὑμῶν αὐτῶν, "out from yourselves."

I CORINTHIANS 6

1 R603 Ἐπί with the genitive here has the meaning "before, in the presence of."
R811 The middle κρίνεσθαι is used with a reciprocal idea (i.e., as if ἀλλήλων occurred in the context), "to judge one another."
M53 Πρᾶγμα ἔχων πρὸς τὸν ἕτερον should be translated, "having a suit against his neighbor" (cf. T274).

2 BD219(1) Ἐν ὑμῖν is used in an instrumental sense (this prepositional phrase has a unique use here, "in your judgment"--T253). [Ed. The passive of κρίνω with ἐν and the dative may have the meaning "to judge before." In essence this is similar to an instrumental rendering.]
MT236 Ἐλαχίστων is used as an elative superlative, "very small," cf. 4:3.
H343 The noun κριτήριον has the meaning "law-suit," in vv. 2 and 4.

3 BD427(3) Elliptical μήτιγε is equivalent to πόσῳ γεμᾶλλον, meaning "not to speak of" ("not to speak of mere affairs of daily life"--MT240).

4 BD450(4) Μὲν οὖν is used in replies either to heighten or correct (with compound force--Classical), "therefore."

5 R409 A difficulty exists in the use of the singular ἀδελφοῦ. The fuller form would have been the plural or the repetition of the word; ἀδελφοῦ καὶ ἀδελφοῦ. It seems that Paul (with other N.T. writers) follows normal Greek usage with proper freedom and individuality. This phrase means "between his brothers."

6 R610 In v. 6, μετά is used in a hostile sense (in the context of legal trials, "brother goes to law with brother").

T45 Καὶ τοῦτο in vv. 6 and 8 means "and indeed" (the epexegetical καί is used with the demonstrative emphatically to particularize the point--BD442[9]).

7   R690 Ἑαυτῶν is used in a reciprocal sense, "with one another" (i.e., for ἀλλήλων, cf. T43).
    R808 The verbs ἀδικεῖσθε and ἀποστερεῖσθε may be in the middle voice, meaning, "let yourselves be wronged and robbed." This permissive sense of the middle is closely allied to the causative and approaches the passive (these two verbs are active in idea rather than passive or middle; "submit to fraud" and "submit to loss"--T57; "allow"--BD314). [Ed. There is no apparent reason to force an active sense from the middle voice of these verbs.]

11 R411 The neuter pronoun ταῦτα is used to refer to people (the pronoun is used in a way similar to τοιοῦτοι, but more definite and emphatic--R704).
    R807 Ἀπελούσασθε means "you washed yourselves" (the correct translation occurs in the margin of the R.V. translation).
    BD448(2) Ἀλλά occurs without a negative preceding or following in the context, where "but you are so no longer" may be easily supplied, followed by "on the contrary."
    H397 Δικαιόω has a factitive meaning and should be translated "to regard as . ." or "to treat as . . ." not "to make righteous."

12 M196f. It is conceivable that a crux in 1 Cor. 6 is to be met by the dialogue expedient (stylistic). Many commentators recognize that v. 12 may represent a "libertine" antinomian slogan quoted by Paul in order to be met by (his own) v. 12b, and that the case is similar with the two parts of v. 13; but it seems not to have been suggested that v. 18 may also be essentially a "dialogue." If it is not, we are faced with the perplexity that Paul pronounces fornication to be essentially different (and not merely different in degree) from any other sort of sin--a position with which few modern Christians would agree. But if it is in dialogue form, we have:
       18a (Corinthian "libertine" slogan): πᾶν . . . ἐστιν (i.e., no sin can effect a man's true "body": physical lust cannot touch the secure "personality" of the initiated).
       18b (Paul's retort): ὁ δὲ . . ἁμαρτάνει (i.e., on the contrary, anyone who commits fornication, commits an offence against his very "personality").
    This more than corporeal sense for σῶμα is clearly required in some contexts; and although it may be thought improbable here (especially in view of 2 Cor. 12:13, where it is demonstrably "corporeal"), the logic of the passage is so difficult on the ordinary showing that this alternative is worth considering.

14 R582 Διά with the genitive is used to portray agency, "by means of."

15 B176 The optative of wishing occurs here (μὴ γένοιτο), strongly deprecating something suggested.

16 T253 Εἰς with the accusative is used for the predicate nominative (Semitic), "the two shall become one flesh."

19 T23 Τὸ σῶμα ὑμῶν is an instance of the distributive singular with a plural pronoun (i.e., something belonging to each person in a group of people is placed in the singular).

20   R1149 Δή is used with the imperative to show a note of urgency,"so glorify God."
      M39 Τιμῆς is used as a genitive of quantity, "you were bought for a price."

                              I CORINTHIANS 7

1   M63 The preposition περί is used in an absolute sense. The translation of the
      first section of this verse should be "as for the things you wrote about."

2   M121 Ἴδιον and ἑαυτοῦ seem to be practically equivalent here (cf. T191 and
      MT89), "own."

5   M53 Πρὸς καιρόν means "for a time," denoting duration.
      M145 The first ἵνα clause in this verse seems to have an imperatival sense (the
      imperatival sense is doubtful--T95). [Ed. The clause introduced by ἵνα is
      dependent upon the imperative ἀποστερεῖτε. Consequently, ἵνα has an impera-
      tival sense, although that idea is not inherent within the particle itself
      ("do not deprive each other . . . except . . . that you may").]
      BD376 In εἰ μήτι ἂν ἐκ συμφώνου, the particle ἂν is added for a hypothetical
      modification of that phrase with the resultant meaning,"except by agreement."

6   R609 Κατά with the accusative is used to express a standard (the phrase means
      "by way of concession"--M59).

7   R691 Ἴδιον implies what is peculiar to one, his own particularity or idiosyn-
      crasy ("his own private gift"--T191).

9   T79 Note the subtle nuance in γαμεῖν (the use of the tense), which means "to
      be in a married state" (not "to marry"; Turner follows an alternative text).

10   TGr101ff. In vv. 10-16 Paul presents the teaching that in general no man was
      to divorce his wife, nor a wife her husband.

11   B282 The first καί in this verse is intensive, emphasizing the following word
      and suggesting a supposition in some sense extreme (cf. 4:7), "but if she does
      indeed separate."

12   TGr101 In this verse, Paul declares that our Lord's words about the indissolu-
      bility of marriage do not apply to instances such as these.
      T37 There is a certain degree of emphasis or antithesis in the use of ἐγώ,
      "I say" (in contrast to κύριος).

14   T262 Ἐν with the dative may be used with a local sense meaning "in the sphere
      of" the Christian wife or husband. (Ἐν with the dative used in a causal sense
      --H463). [Ed. The preposition in this verse appears to have a causal sense;
      the husband (or wife) is sanctified because of the influence of his or her
      marriage partner. But the local idea would be implied as well (as opposed to
      separation). Paul specifically points out the logical reason for conversion
      rather than simply presenting the situation in which it occurs.]
      T318 Ἐπεί means "for otherwise" (cf. 5:10).

15   R948 Note the permissive use of the imperative in χωριζέσθω, meaning "let him

separate."
M79 The preposition ἐν (in ἐν εἰρήνῃ) may be used for εἰς with the resultant
meaning, "God has called you into a peace in which he wishes you to live"(cf.
T263).

16 M154 It is uncertain whether the direct question implied is intended to expect
    the answer "yes" or "no" (the question is purposely left indefinite).

17 R1025 In this verse εἰ μή has the sense of "only" and is not to be construed with
    περιπατείτω (it has the meaning "but," equivalent to πλήν--BD376). [Ed. Both of
    these renderings are similar in that they are adversative.]
    T75 The present imperative of περιπατέω here has the meaning "go on walking."
    T262 'Εν with the dative in this verse may mean "in" or "to the churches."
    [Ed. The usual sense of ἐν provides a valid translation. If Paul desired to
    express the notion "to," he could have employed the simple dative.]

18 T264 With καλέω in v. 18, the phrase does not mean "to uncircumcision" but
    "while he was uncircumcised."
    BD494 The resolution of a sentence into unconnected component parts (as occurs
    in this verse), produces a more powerful effect than would the regular form.

21 M21 A passage where the aktionsart of an imperative might, if it could be cer-
    tainly depended on, carry exegetical importance is the much debated v. 21. Does
    this mean "but choose to use it (the opportunity to do so)?" Or does it mean
    "but even if you can . ., choose instead to continue in your present employ?"
    In the latter case one would have expected a linear (present) imperative; and
    in fact the former interpretation is preferable (in the context esp.; cf. M167).
    TGr103 Paul selected the aorist imperative, "seize your opportunity to be free!"
    The question of the precise meaning of the conditional particle (εἰ καί), whether
    it is "if" or "even if," is not actually relevant to the discussion, since εἰ
    καί is capable of either meaning ("once and for all;" only with a present im-
    perative ought the interpretation to be "use your present state to the glory of
    God"--T76; cf. MT247).
    H165 Μᾶλλον is used in an elative sense, meaning "by all means."

25 R1128 'Ως ἠλεημένος is used with a causal idea (i.e., the ground of action in
    the principal verb is suggested by the participle; it shows the notion of manner
    --B446; it expresses a subjective motive, "in the conviction that"--T158; cf.
    "as one who"--BD425[3]). [Ed. 'Ως appears to point out a characteristic quality
    of Paul, with the sense "as one who;" cf. 2 Cor. 6:4; Eph. 5:1 and 1 Thess. 2:4]
    M63 The preposition περί has an absolute sense (cf. v. 1), "about the unmarried."
    M127 The infinitive is used in an epexegetic way, thus ἠλεημενος . . . πιστὸς
    εἶναι means "pitied . . . enough to be trustworthy."

26 R1059 The articular infinitive is used as the subject of the implied stative
    verb ("it is good to be").
    R1205 "Οτι καλὸν is an expansion of τοῦτο καλόν, meaning, "that it is good."

27 MT125 The prohibition here in the present tense means "stop seeking."

28 R1027 'Εὰν καί has the notion "if even" rather than "if also."
    B50 The aorist tense is used proleptically, but this is a rhetorical figure
    rather than a grammatical idiom. The conditional sentence has the meaning
    "but even if thou shalt marry, thou hast not sinned."

29 R1140 The participle with ὡς here has a concessive or conditional notion. [Ed.
This context seems to favor a concessive sense, "as though."]
M34 Τὸ λοιπόν means "finally" or "henceforward" ("so that, for what remains"--
M161).
M145 The ἵνα clause is used as an imperative (cf. T95; BD387[3] and MT179),
"Let those who have wives live as though they had none."

31 T51 Παράγω in this verse means "disappear."

34 T220 The dative of respect occurs here, "in reference to body and spirit."

35 R689 Ὑμῶν αὐτῶν is used as a reflexive pronoun, "your own."
BD117(1) Εὐπάρεδρον means "constant" in v. 35 (peculiar because the adjective
is used instead of the noun).

36 R1204 For the verb γαμείτωσαν the subject is implied in the context (i.e., the
two young people), "let them marry."
B182 The imperative verbs are used to express consent, or merely to propose an
hypothesis; thus, the last half of this verse should be translated "and if need
so require, let him do what he will; he sinneth not; let them marry."
T75 The present imperative ποιείτω means "let him go on doing what he wants"
(the quality of behavior is denoted by the present tense--BD336[2]).
T115 Εἰ with the indicative νομίζει seems to indicate that Paul knows this is
actually happening (the following ἐὰν ᾖ refers to the future--BD372[1a]).
H352 The comparative force of the adjective ὑπέρακμος may be taken as modal rather than temporal (i.e., "exceedingly lusty," not "past the flower of youth").

37 BD468(3) The participle ἔχων is continued by a finite verb, "having no necessity
but having his desire under control."

38 M120 In τὴν ἑαυτοῦ παρθένον, the reflexive ἑαυτοῦ appears to have lost its reflexive force. Τὴν παρθένον αὐτοῦ would appear to mean exactly the same (cf.
v. 36), whether the context is interpreted as referring to spiritual marriage
or to a father's dealings with his daughter ("his virgin").
M144 Ὥστε is used as an inferential particle, meaning "and so, accordingly."
H409 Γαμίζω may mean no more than γαμέω (cf. Mk. 12:25; Lk. 17:27); i.e., it
may mean either "to marry" or "to give in marriage."

39 R897 The perfect δέδεται is used as a gnomic perfect (denoting a customary
truth; cf. B79), "a wife is bound."

I CORINTHIANS 8

1 M63 The preposition περί means "as for" (cf. 7:1).

3 R845 The perfect tense does not lay the same stress on what is recently completed as does the English "have" (ἔγνωσται means "this one is known").

5 R1026 With καὶ εἴπερ the supposition is considered improbable. The truth of
the principal sentence is stoutly affirmed in the face of this one objection.
Rhetorically, it is an extreme case (the introductory particles have the meaning, "even if"--R1181).

6   R583 In this verse ἐξ οὖ refers to God the Father as the source of all things
    and δι' οὖ refers to Jesus as the mediate agent by whom all things come into
    existence (cf. BD223[2] and MT106).

7   R532 Τῇ συνηθείᾳ has a causal notion, "because of habit."

10 B411 Εἰς τὸ ἐσθίειν in v. 10 either expresses a measure of effect or is the
    indirect object of οἰκοδομηθήσεται (it expresses a measure of effect, "leading
    him to eat"--T143).

12 BD442(9) Καί is used here with an explicative sense to particularize and further
    explain ("sinning against your brothers and wounding their conscience").

13 M164 Διόπερ apparently has much the same meaning as διό, but perhaps with a
    greater stress upon the logical connection between the clauses it connects
    (cf. 10:14), "for this very reason."

                              I CORINTHIANS 9

1   R587 The use of the preposition seems to have a mystical sense in ἐν κυρίῳ (cf.
    ἐν Χριστῷ).
    R1157 The form οὐχί of the negative is a bit sharper in tone than the simple οὐ
    (indicating some emphasis on the third question).

2   R1148 Ἀλλά γε ὑμῖν (the earlier Greek would prefer ὑμῖν γε) means "to you at
    least (if not to others)."

4   R1169 When μὴ οὐ occurs in questions μή is the interrogative particle while οὐ
    is the negative of the verb (i.e., a negative answer is expected from a nega-
    tive statement; "are we without-the-right . . .?--M156).

5   T246 Ἀδελφὴν γυναῖκα does not mean "a wife who is a sister," but "a sister as
    a wife" (i.e., a predicative accusative, not attributive).

6   BD431(1) The negatives in this verse have a tendency to cancel each other out
    (because both still have their full force--for emphasis), "have no right to
    refrain from."

7   R532 The dative ἰδίοις ὀψωνίοις is used with a causal sense ("at [or because of]
    his own wages").
    R1147 Ποτέ has the notion of "ever" rather than "once upon a time."

9   M28 The verb μέλει is constructed impersonally with a plain genitive of refer-
    ence (without περί), "concerning the oxen," "for the oxen."

10 B400 The infinitive with τοῦ is used after a noun here to limit (define) it.
    It is used similar to another substantive, "in the hope of sharing."
    BD452(2) Γάρ is used in a reply (to the rhetorical question ἢ . . λέγει) to
    affirm what is asked (giving the reason for a tacit "yes"), "to be sure."

11 R681 The position of ὑμῶν here seems to show emphasis, "your material goods."

                                    298

BD113(2) Σαρκικός means "belonging to, of the nature of σάρξ" (i.e., material things).

BD372(1c) Εἰ with the aorist has the notion "since we, as everyone admits . . ," and εἰ with the future means "if subsequently, as actually happened, we . . ."

12 R500 The genitive with ἐξουσίας has the idea of "over" with the resultant meaning of "authority" or "right over you."
T211 Τοῦ Χριστοῦ is an objective genitive, meaning "the gospel about Christ."

13 R521 The dative τῷ θυσιαστηρίῳ seems to be used as a locative, meaning "at the altar."

14 R598 'Ἐκ with the genitive conveys the notion of cause or occasion (the idea of cause is similar to that of means).

15 R587 'Ἐν with ἐμοί has the resultant notion of "in the case of" (i.e., "in my case"; cf. M77).
R845 The aorist verb ἔγραψα is an epistolary aorist (the author views the literature from the perspective of the readers).
BD369(2) "Ἵνα τις (rather than οὐδείς) with the future indicative is the correct text expressing purpose. [Ed. It seems unlikely that the text with ἵνα τις and the future indicative is to be included, since it has very weak manuscript support and ἵνα is seldom used with a future indicative in the N.T.]

16 B285 In the conditional clause of this verse the protasis is concessive (i.e., "although I . . .") and the apodosis is affirming what is true and will still be true.

17 M32 The accusative is retained with the passive verb πεπίστευμαι, meaning "I have been entrusted with a stewardship," where the active word would be πιστεύω οἰκονομίαν τινί. (The person which appears in the dative with the active voice may become the subject with the passive, and therefore such a passive will have the accusative of the thing--T247).

18 R1079 "Ἵνα is used to introduce a clause in opposition to the previous statement (describing it further; cf. B213), "that when I preach."
T143 Εἰς τό with the infinitve καταχρήσασθαι seems to express purpose.

19 R595 'Ἐκ is used with the genitive πάντων to express an ablative idea, "independent of, free from."
R665 Τοὺς πλείονας means "the majority."
R1129 The participle ὤν has a concessive sense (i.e., "for though I . . ."; cf. M102, it is used in this same way in v. 21).

20 M66 'Ὑπὸ νόμον means "beneath the law."
T169 'Ἰουδαῖοι does not require the article any more than personal names. Thus, when Paul uses the article here he must have some special occasion in mind like Timothy's circumcision. Τοῖς in the following clauses is virtually demonstrative; (τοῖς ἀνόμοις may refer to the Galatians; articular 'Ἰουδαῖοι refers to "those with whom I had to deal on each occasion"--BD262[1]).

21 H307 "Ἄνομος meaning "without law" is contrasted with ἔννομος "under law."

22 R742 The plural τινας means "some."
    BD275(7) The articular expression τοῖς πᾶσιν refers to the individual groups
    named in vv. 20ff. (treated as a whole).

25 M163 Μεν οὖν is used here as antithetic, practically identical with a simple:
    "those on the one hand . . ., but we . . ."
    BD154 The adjective πάντα is used as an accusative of general reference: "in
    reference to all things."

26 R1127 The participle with ὡς here has the idea of manner (cf. B445; "as one
    beating the air").
    R1163 Οὐ is used with the participle here to show some degree of emphasis.
    [Ed. Οὐ is used with the participle δέρων because of the formal contrast
    indicated by οὐ . . . ἀλλα. Consequently, there is no particular emphasis
    shown by the use of οὐ here.]

I CORINTHIANS 10

1 R419 In the construction οἱ πατέρες ἡμῶν πάντες the noun πατέρες carries
   the emphasis rather than the adjective (because of the word order: "our fathers were all . . .")

2 R808 The middle voice of ἐβαπτίσαντο is used in a causative sense, "all got
   themselves baptized."

3 R883 In vv. 3f. the aorist verbs ἔφαγον and ἔπιον give the summary record (constative), while the imperfect verb ἔπινον portrays an explanatory description.

4 T67 The change from the aorist to the imperfect (cf. also vv. 6 and 11) may be
   nothing more than a variation for the sake of variety. The most that can be
   said is that the aorist records the action without stressing its execution
   (the aorist protrays the fact whereas the imperfect describes the manner of
   the action--BD327).

5 M108 Τοῖς πλείοσιν seems to mean "the majority" (but would Paul use ἐν with
   this adjective for this meaning? It has the sense of "many"--T30). [Ed.
   Moule's suggestion appears to be more probable, since it brings out the
   comparative idea and it more accurately describes the account in Numbers 14,
   cf. 1 Cor. 9:19.]
   T253 The second ἐν here is used with a causal sense. [Ed. Actually the reason for the preceding clause is expressed by the previous particle γάρ. Thus
   the preposition ἐν appears to have a local sense.]

6 R500 Τύποι ἡμῶν has the sense of "types for us" (an objective genitive).
   T143 Εἰς τὸ with the infinitive is used to express the idea of purpose.

7 R931 In vv. 7ff. Paul changes from the second to first person.
   R1185 The continuative μηδὲ is repeated several times in vv. 7-10.

8 T262 The preposition ἐν reinforces the dative of time, "in one day."

10 R967 Καθάπερ occurs only in Paul's writings except Hebrews 4:2 (without a verb).
It is thoroughly Attic and has a slight literary touch (as here).

11 R626 Πρός is used with the accusative here to express the notion of aim or end,
"for our instruction."
T114f. The plurals τέλη and αἰώνων are idiomatic here and it is best to translate them as singulars. Thus the latter section of this verse means, "they are
written for our admonition, upon whom the End of the World is come." Paul
shared a vivid expectation of the Parousia with all his early converts. There
is no great division of dispensations implied here.

12 R430 Μή clearly functions as a conjunction here, "lest he fall" (after the verb
"to take heed"--B206).
R1000 Ὥστε used in a co-ordinate construction here, with the sense of "therefore."

13 R996 Τοῦ with the infinitive is used in an epexegetical sense (cf. MT217; the
construction here exhibits a very loose relationship between the substantive
and infinitive and tends toward a consecutive sense). [Ed. This construction
appears to express the idea of purpose, or conceived result. God provides the
ἔκβασις for the purpose that the Christian may be able to endure the temptation.]
R471 See above 6:18

14 M164 Διόπερ apparently has the same meaning as διό, but with perhaps a greater
stress upon the logical connection between the clauses it connects (cf. 8:13),
"for this very reason."
T173 The noun εἰδωλολατρίας has the article (even though the preposition is used
with it) because it refers to the "worship of idols which you know so well."

16 R880 The present verbs εὐλογοῦμεν and κλῶμεν have an iterative sense (i.e.,
repeated action).
BD490 An example of parallelism occurs here (cf. 1:25).

17 M62 See above 9:12 (cf. 10:21, 30).
TGr104 Paul omits a verb which is more than a mere copula (this appears in
Paul's writings about thirty times--T303; supply ἐστιν). Thus the first part
of this verse should be translated, "Because there is one bread, we the many
are one body" (cf. the marginal reading in the R.V. translation), instead of
the usual rendering which is less intelligible.

19 R233 The pronoun in τί ἐστιν is not interrogative, but it is the enclitic **indefinite** pronoun with the accent of ἐστιν (i.e., it is used as a predicate nominative meaning "anything").

20 T313 Generally a neuter plural subject has a singular verb, but that classical
rule is broken here and in a few other passages in the N.T. (because the neuter
noun ἔθνη is taken in a personal sense).

21 R509 The verb of sharing here μετέχειν takes the partitive genitive.
R1183 In v. 21, οὐ καί occurs in contrast.
BD259(2) Generally an article would have been used with the governing noun
τραπέζης that has a definite genitive (κυρίου--δαιμονίων). But here the em-

phasis lies on the characteristic quality (the one is a table of the Lord, the other a ţable of the devil).

22 R923 In ἤ παραζηλοῦμεν τὸν κύριον the indicative notes the fact, while the surprise and indignation are denoted by the interrogative form ("shall we make the Lord jealous?").

29 R688 In v. 29, ἑαυτοῦ means "one's own" (cf. M120).

30 TGr86 "Why am I evil spoken of?" means "Why is such a Christian evil spoken of?" (The first person has a representative sense; cf. R402 and BD281.)
   T241 Χάριτι is loosely connected with the verb to describe accompanying circumstances or manner, "with thankfulness."
   BD372(2c) Εἰ with the indicative here may mean "if, as of course I do, I partake . . ." (possibly equivalent to "inasmuch as").

31 BD454(3) The correlatives εἴτε . . . εἴτε appear only in Paul's writings and I Peter and mean "whether . . . or."
   BD480(1) "Αλλο meaning "whatever else" is omitted after τι.

33 M35 The accusative πάντα is used as an accusative of respect denoting number, "in all respects."
   TGr86 When Paul says that he pleases all men in all things, this is a precept for Christians in general, rather than a private technique of evangelism.
   T190 Only here does ἐμαυτοῦ occur in the New Testament as a possessive genitive with a noun (emphatic; "my own advantage," as opposed to the advantage of others; cf. BD283[3]).
   BD245(1) Τῶν πολλῶν is contrasted with ἐμαυτοῦ, therefore similar to πλείονες, with the resulting meaning "the majority" (cf. R660).

I CORINTHIANS 11

2 R881 The perfect verb μέμνημαι is used as a durative present (the attention is directed wholly to the present resulting state--B75), "that you remember me."
   M35 The accusative πάντα is used to denote respect ("in all respects," cf. 10:33).

3 R769 When an article occurs with the subject and predicate nominative, both are definite, treated as identical, one and the same, and interchangeable (ἡ κεφαλὴ ὁ Χριστός ἐστιν; compare this with κεφαλὴ γυναικὸς ὁ ἀνήρ and notice that man is not affirmed to be woman's head in quite the same sense that Christ is man's head--R781).

4 R606 The preposition κατά portrays the notion "down from" (i.e., "the veil hanging down from the head"; "with a covering on the head"--M60).

5 R530 The dative τῇ ἐξυρημένῃ is used with a word of identity (τὸ αὐτό), whereas ἀκατακαλύπτῳ τῇ κεφαλῇ is used as a dative of manner (meaning "with the head unveiled"--R789).
   T21 The neuter pronoun here refers to a person, with the meaning "she is one and the same as if . . ."

BD131 Τὸ αὐτό is identical with the unveiled woman in meaning but not in person, hence the feminine gender is inconceivable. [Ed. It appears that the
neuter is used because the general concept is referred to.]

6   T57 Κείρασθαι and ξυρᾶσθαι have an intransitive active idea rather than passive
or middle, "cut her hair" (they are used as permissive middles--R809).
[Ed. If the middle voice may be translated as such with valid sense, an active
sense should not be forced upon it. Consequently, the preferable rendering
seems to be "she should allow her hair to be cut off . . ."]
BD372(2a) Εἰ with the indicative is used in a deduction (indicating the logical deduction; this phenomenon occurs predominantly in Paul's writings, cf.
3:14).

9   BD452(3) In the construction καὶ γάρ, the conjunction καί means "also," although it refers to the whole sentence and not to a single idea (cf. 5:7).

11 R1187 Paul uses πλήν, at the end of an argument to single out the main point.

12 R582 Note διὰ τῆς γυναικός . . ἐκ τοῦ θεοῦ, where source (ἐκ) and mediate
agent (διά) are distinguished.
R773 Τὰ πάντα refers to "the sum of things, the all."

13 R687 Ὑμῖν αὐτοῖς is used as a reflexive pronoun (σεαυτοῖς, "judge for yourselves;" cf. 7:35).
T253 Ἐν is used here with a semi-forensic sense, meaning "in your judgment"
(cf. 6:2).

14 R686 Ἡ φύσις αὐτή means "nature of itself."

15 M71 Ἀντί is used in its original sense here, "her hair has been given her as
(i.e., instead of) a wrap."

17 BD244(2) The comparatives here have a positive sense ("in a good . . .bad
way . .").

18 R174 Ἐκκλησίᾳ has the sense of "assembly."
R803 In this verse ἀκούω has the classic sense of "I am told."
R893 The present tense of ἀκούω is used as an effective aoristic present (similar to the perfect tense). The action is durative only in the sense of state,
not of linear action ("have heard"--BD322).
R1152 In πρῶτον μὲν γάρ there is am implied contrast with vv. 20ff. (δέ is
omitted, thus the meaning is "from the very outset"--BD447[4].)
H473 A comparison of v. 18 with v. 20 shows clearly that ἐπὶ τὸ αὐτό and ἐν
ἐκκλησίᾳ are synonymous phrases. They have a technical meaning signifying
the union of the Christian body.

21 R880 Προλαμβάνει is used as an iterative or customary present (this is repeatedly done).

22 R918 Μή is the interrogative particle while οὐ is the negative of the verb
(cf. 9:4), "Don't you have houses?'
R1090 The purpose idea of εἰς τό with the infinitive here changes into the notion of hypothetical result. The infinitives here are used, like the simple

infinitive, to represent an indirect object ("What? Have you not houses to eat and to drink in?"--B410; cf. R1072). [Ed. The infinitives here appear to be used as indirect objects denoting the idea of purpose-result.]
H226 Ἐπαινέσω is probably aorist subjunctive rather than future indicative.

23   R579   There doesn't seem to be any radical distinction between ἀπὸ τοῦ κυρίου and ἀπὸ τοῦ πατρός (which occurs in John 10:18; ἀπό has the sense of παρά with the genitive after παραλαμβάνω--T259), "from the Lord."

24   R595   The preposition εἰς with the accusative has the notion of purpose, "in order to remember me."
M64   Ὑπέρ with the genitive has the sense of "instead of" (cf. Rom. 5:7f).

25   R974   Ὁσάκις is only used with the notion of indefinite repetition, "whenever."

26   B312   Ὁσάκις γὰρ ἐάν with the present subjunctive expresses a general supposition, "for as often as . . ." (cf. v. 25).

27   M144   Ὥστε is used simply as an inferential particle meaning "and so, accordingly."

28   R519   Ἐκ with the genitive expresses the partitive idea here (i.e., "let him eat a part of the bread . . .").

29   B436   The adverbial participle διακρίνων is equivalent to a conditional clause (cf. MT230), meaning "if he is not discerning."
BD488(1b)   The repetition of the root in κρίμα . . . διακρίνων . . . διεκρίνομεν . . . ἐκρίνομεθα . . . κρινόμενοι . . . κατακριθῶμεν (in vv. 29ff.) seems to present a certain subtlety (i.e., each term designating a specific sense).

31   R1015   This verse has a contrary to fact conditional sentence (the imperfect tense of this type of sentence designates the present time, "if we judge ourselves we would not be judged").
T42   The third person reflexive pronoun ἑαυτούς is used for the first person reflexive, "ourselves" (a development that occurs in the Septuagint, N.T., and illiterate papyri; the first person reflexive plural pronoun does not occur in the N.T.).

33   R1000   Ὥστε here is used as an inferential particle similar to οὖν , meaning "therefore" (as a co-ordinating particle).

34   BD455(2)   Ὡς ἄν with the subjunctive is equivalent to ὅταν with the subjunctive meaning "when I come" (with an indefinite sense--MT167).

I CORINTHIANS 12

1   M63   The preposition περί is used in an absolute sense, "as for" or "now about."

2   R974   The imperfect indicative verb with ἄν has the notion of repetition (cf. ὅταν; "as you would be led [from day to day]" is an iterative construction which coincides with the conditional clause--MT167).

6   T265 'Εν πᾶσιν is used as a dative of reference (i.e., "with respect to").

7   M53 Πρός with the accusative here has the sense of "leading to" ("for the com-
    mon good").

8   R746, 749 Both pronouns ἄλλος and ἕτερος simply mean "another" in vv. 8-12
    (the change occurs for variety in style; cf. T197 and BD306[2]).
    T267 Διά with the genitive has the sense of agency, "through the Spirit."

9   R758 The gifts mentioned in vv. 9ff. are anarthrous because the article is
    not necessary with qualities, "to another faith . . ."

11 T191 'Ιδίᾳ has the classical sense here, "his own private gift" (the dative
    portrays the notion of manner--R530).

12 R419 In the construction πάντα τὰ μέλη τοῦ σώματος the first word (the adjec-
    tive πάντα) carries the emphasis, "all the members of the body" (cf. 10:1).

13 BD452(3) Καὶ γάρ means "for even" (both particles retain their complete sense).

15 R1164 The repetition of the negative οὐ does not constitute a double negative,
    but the full force of each negative is retained (cf. B486, "because I am not
    . . I am not . . .").
    M51 In vv. 15f, παρὰ τοῦτο means "on that score, for that reason" (i.e., "it is
    not for that reason any the less . . , nevertheless it still belongs . . .";
    cf. ἐν τούτῳ in 4:4 and cf. R550).

22 T31 The positive is used for the comparative, thus πολλῷ μᾶλλον . . . ἀναγκαῖα
    means "much more necessary."

23 TGr59 Paul refers to the least honorable parts of the body by means of the
    comparative degree (i.e., using the comparative adjective for the superlative).

24 T56 'Υστερέομαι means "to be inferior."

25 R1413 When the ἵνα μή construction is continued by ἀλλά (meaning "but on the
    contrary"), ἵνα is not repeated (but with the idea of purpose still maintained).

27 BD212 In this verse, ἐκ μέρους means "(each) for his part."
    BD442(9) Καί is used with an explicative sense to particularize and further
    explain (cf. 8:12).

28 T55 The verb ἔθετο is used in the middle voice here, where the active is expect-
    ed since it has a transitive sense. [Ed. The middle voice may indicate that
    God appointed for his own use (i.e., an indirect middle).]

31 R777 In τὰ χαρίσματα τὰ μείζονα both the substantive and adjective receive
    emphasis and the adjective is added as a sort of climax in apposition with a
    separate article ("the spiritual gifts, the more important ones").
    T221 A prepositional clause is rarely used as an attributive to an anarthrous
    noun; in v. 31, εἴ τι occurs for ἔτι in p[46], D* and F, by making καθ' ὑπερβολήν
    no longer an attribute of the anarthrous noun (i.e., supply ζηλοῦτε; cf. BD272;

the prepositional clause is attributive--R784). [Ed. An attributive prepositional phrase occurs much less frequently in the N.T. than an adverbial prepositional phrase, nevertheless it is used (cf. Mark 1:23; Rom. 14:17 and II Cor.
12:2). It is better to render this verse as having a somewhat less common construction than to emend the text. Consequently, this phrase should be translated "a more excellent way.")

I CORINTHIANS 13

1   R758 It is not necessary to have the article with qualities, as with ἀγάπην
here (Paul does not desire to particularize the love, but he simply states it
as a quality; cf. 12:9-11).
R1105 The anarthrous participle ἠχῶν is attributive to χαλκός, "a noisy gong."

2   R772 There is very little difference in idea between πάσῃ γνώσει (in 1:5) and
πᾶσαν τὴν γνῶσιν (here). With this abstract word the adjectives "every" and
"all" amount practically to the same thing.
R1090 Ὥστε is used with the infinitive to express a hypothetical result, "so
as to" (cf. B371).
T116 Ἐάν with the indicative (ἔχω . . . εἰδῶ) may be partially an actual
statement between "I may have" (ἐάν with the subjunctive) and "since I have"
(εἰ with the indicative; this construction portrays an indefinite relation to
a definite reality--BD372[1a]).

3   R764 Τὰ ὑπάρχοντα is used as a substantive followed by a genitive, "my belongings."
R984 A development in Greek can be seen in the use of ἵνα. In classical Greek
ἵνα was not used with the future indicative (the future was not common even with
ὅπως, ὡς and μή). But the similarity in form and sense (between the subjunctive and future indicative) made the change very easy in later Greek. Thus in
this verse ἵνα with the subjunctive is supported by the earliest manuscripts
(καυχήσωμαι), but the future is included by the late documents.

4   R1178 In vv. 4ff. the verbs follow one another in solemn emphasis with no connective except one occurrence of δέ.
BD108(5) The verb περπερεύομαι means to "conduct oneself like a πέρπερος"
(i.e., a "braggart, windbag").

8   BD454(3) The correlatives εἴτε . . . εἴτε mean "whether . . or" (cf. 10:31).

11   R900 The perfect verb γέγονα is used in the sense of a present, "when I became"
(the present state is the primary idea in mind; cf. BD382[1]).

12   R600 The preposition ἐπί has a perfective idea in the compound verb here (the
last segment of this verse means "Now I am acquiring knowledge which is only
partial at best: then I shall have learnt my lesson, shall <u>know</u>, as God in my
mortal life knew me"--MT113).

13   R405 The singular verb is used here with a compound subject because the author
initially had only the first subject in mind ("there abideth . . .").

T177 'Αγάπη is articular because reference is made to the previous mention of it in the same verse.

BD244 The comparative μείζων is used as a superlative, "the greatest."

I CORINTHIANS 14

1 R993 "Ινα expresses the content of the verb ζηλοῦτε (equivalent to ὅτι), "that you may" (cf. v. 12).

4 T176 It is not certain whether ἐκκλησίαν refers to a "a congregation" or "the Church." [Ed. The former suggestion appears to be more probable since ἐκκλησία generally has the article in the N.T. when it is specifically definite. Furthermore, this noun is frequently articular even when it is the object of a preposition (cf. 6:4; 7:17; 12:28; II Cor. 8:1 and 19).]

5 R640 'Εκτός is a combination of ἐκ and the adverbial ending -τος with just a fuller expression of the original preposition, meaning "without."

B253 In this verse a preference for the more common εἰ μή over the somewhat un- usual ἐὰν μή may have led to the use of the former inspite of the fact that the meaning called for a subjunctive particle, "unless someone interprets."

M83 In the use of ἐκτός εἰ μή, there is obviously a redundancy, but it may be presumed that, without the εἰ μή, ἐκτός would have been virtually a preposition (cf. the illiterate "without he interpret"; in this context it has the sense "except if"--T321).

T135 The infinitive and ἵνα clause are parallel in this verse (denoting the con- tent of θέλω), "I wish . . ., that you would speak . . ., and especially that you may prophesy."

6 M79 'Εν with the dative is used to portray the idea "consists of."

7 R871 The future of γινώσκω (in vv. 7 and 9) expresses an ingressive punctiliar idea, "How shall anyone come to know . . ?"

T337 "Ομως is displaced in this verse, where in sense it should be transferred after διδόντα, "lifeless things may give a sound, nevertheless if." (Usually this verse and Gal. 3:15 are explained as cases of displaced ὅμως. Since in both instances, however, a comparison is introduced and in I Cor. 14:7 οὕτως also follows, the earlier sense of ὅμως is present ["equally"] and it is there- fore to be translated "also, likewise" [rather than explaining this as displace- ment]--BD450[2].) [Ed. In both instances in which ὅμως occurs in Paul's writ- ings, it is used to introduce a comparison. Consequently, the latter sugges- tion seems preferable.

8 R807 The middle voice in παρασκευάσεται is used with a direct sense, meaning "prepare himself" (cf. MT156).

9 R353 The linear aspect of the action is stressed by the periphrastic construc- tion ἔσεθε λαλοῦντες ("you will be speaking").

10 R1021 Paul uses the stereotyped phrase εἰ τύχοι here (and in 15:37), which is an example of the protasis, "if it should happen" (εἰ introduces a

parenthetical phrase, "if possible" or "as it were"--T127; "it may be, for example"--BD385[2].)

11　M46　The expression τῷ λαλοῦντι is used as a dative of respect, "I shall be, in the eyes of the speaker, a barbarian."
　　　　M76　'Εν with the dative takes the place of the simple dative. (cf. BD220[1]; ἐν ἐμοί means "in my judgment"--MT103.)

12　B229　The causal clause should be translated "since you are jealous of spiritual gifts, seek that you may abound unto the edifying of the church" (the clause designates the content of ζητεῖτε--B210; cf. v. 1).

13　M164　Διό means "and so."

15　R533　Either the datives here are used as modal instrumentals or instrumental of means (modal--T241). [Ed. The modal interpretation appears to be the most probable since the major point that Paul makes in this paragraph is the manner in which one is to express himself rather than the means by which he is enabled to speak.]
　　　　R874　The volitive future here expresses purpose, not mere futurity, "I will pray, I will sing."

17　R1153　Μέν . . ἀλλά is used here to express a sharp contrast, "for you . . . but the other . . ."

19　R792　'Εν ἐκκλησίᾳ means "at church."
　　　　T32　"Η takes the place of μᾶλλον -- ἤ here (portraying a comparison; cf. BD480[4].)

20　R524　The datives are used in a locative sense (they seem to be datives of respect--T220.) [Ed. In this context "in the sphere of" is similar to "in reference to."]
　　　　R1383　Note the use of ἀλλά . . . δέ side by side where the main contrast is presented by δέ and the minor one by ἀλλά.
　　　　T177　The article is used with κακίᾳ because of the attraction to the concrete ταῖς θρεσίν, "your minds."

21　R591　Εἰς is not used much in compound verbs in the N.T. and always where motion is involved except in the case of εἰσ-ακούω where there seems to be little difference between εἰς and ἐν(cf. Matt. 6:7, "listen to.")

22　M70　Εἰς with the accusative here has the resultant meaning "intended as a sign" (indicating the purpose; or "to serve for"--BD145[1].)
　　　　M144　"Ωστε is used simply as an inferential particle, meaning "and so, accordingly."

24　R427　Asyndeton (the omission of a connective) occurs in this verse to portray emphasis (on the separate segments of the verse).

26　R626　Πρός with the accusative here expresses the notion of aim or end, "for edification."

27 R571 'Ανὰ μέρος usually has a distributive sense, but here it means "in turn"
    (although it may be distributive--M67). [Ed. The best rendering is "in turn"
    since Paul's major concern in this context is that there must be order in the
    assembly; cf. vv. 30f.]
    R670 Τὸ πλεῖστον is a true superlative, meaning "at the most" (cf. M98).
    BD442(9) The explicative use of καί occurs in this verse (to particularize
    and further explain the previous statement).

28 BD188(2) 'Εαυτῷ is used as a dative of advantage, "for himself."

31 M60 Καθ' ἕνα means "one by one" (the preposition has a distributive sense).

34 T58 The dative pronoun αὐταῖς is used as the subject of the passive verb ἐπι-
    τρέπεται (this verb becomes impersonal in the passive), "they are not per-
    mitted to . . ."

39 R1059 Both articular infinitives here are used as objects of the imperative
    verbs, "strive for prophesying and do not hinder speaking."
    MT125 How are we to imagine Paul bidding the Corinthians to "stop forbidding"
    (the present imperative) the exercise of their darling charism? His μὴ κωλύετε
    means "do not discourage glossolalia, as after my former words you might be
    inclined to do."

I CORINTHIANS 15

1 R427 The occurrence of asyndeton (the omission of a connective) in vv. 1f.
   shows emphasis (cf. 14:24).

2 R530 Εἰκῇ is used as a dative of manner, "in vain."
   R954 Τίνι λόγῳ is used almost like a relative pronoun among the numerous relatives in vv. 1ff., "what I preached to you."
   BD478 It would be forced to make τίνι λόγῳ εὐηγγελισάμην ὑμῖν dependent on the
   following εἰ κατέχετε; it is more likely that εἰ as well as the reading of
   D*, F, G, i.e., ὀθείλετε κατέχειν (for εἰ κατέχετε), is an explanatory gloss
   (p⁴⁶ has a dash, then κατέχειν deleted by dots, then εἰ κατέχετε) so that it is
   only a question of a subordinate clause preceding a main clause (κατέχετε ;
   therefore a full stop after σῴζεσθε and a new, independent sentence following),
   "what I preached to you, hold fast to it." [Ed. There are no manuscripts to
   support the text that Blass proposes. It is better to explain the preferred
   text than to emend that text. Consequently, the most probable translation of
   this part of the verse is "if you hold fast what I preached to you."]

3 M59 The preposition κατά with the accusative here has the resultant meaning
   "in accordance with the scriptures."

4 R846 The perfect tense is used between two aorists because Paul wishes to
   emphasize the idea that Jesus is still risen. (It is difficult to find an
   idiomatic English translation that will do it justice--M15; cf. T69. It seems
   most fitting to translate this perfect as follows: "that he hath been raised
   -- raised on the third day, according to the scriptures"--M137.)

6   MT136 The aorist verb ἐκοιμήθησαν means "fell asleep (at various times),"
    and so, "have fallen asleep."

7   T200 If πᾶς is placed after a noun with the article (as here), special stress
    is laid upon the noun (i.e., "to the apostles, indeed to all the apostles,"
    because James, who never left Jerusalem, was not an emissary"; cf. BD275[5]).

8   R757 In τῷ ἐκτρώματι Paul speaks thus of himself because he alone of the apos-
    tles saw Jesus after His ascension (i.e., the reason for the article; cf. M111).
    BD433(3) ʽΩσπερεὶ τῷ ἐκτρώματι is equivalent to τῷ ὡσπερεὶ ἐκτρώματι ὄντι mean-
    ing "to me who am, so to speak, one untimely born."

9   R279 ʽΟ ἐλάχιστος is a true superlative (cf. MT79), a thing so rare in the
    New Testament that Blass (60[2]) attributes this example either to the liter-
    ary language or to corruption in the text; "the least of the apostles."

10 R713 ʽΟ means "what I am," not "who I am." [Ed. The gender of the pronoun
    is the primary factor for the difference in meaning.]

12 T210 The partitive use of ἐν occurs here with τινες ("some of you").

13 BD372(2b) Εἰ with the indicative of reality is not used in vv. 13ff. to express
    a causal or restrictive idea but for Paul's logical reasoning (to denote a
    logical deduction).

15 R607 Κατά with the genitive here may have the meaning "against God," or it may
    carry the idea of taking an oath (perhaps that the hand is placed down on the
    thing by which the oath is taken). [Ed. The former suggestion brings out the
    root idea of κατά more appropriately. This rendering also fits very well
    into the context in which Paul tends to use a reversed reasoning.]
    R817 The true passive emphasizes the action of God in vv. 15f. (ἐγείρονται).
    R1154 Πέρ in the compound conditional particle εἴπερ adds a note of urgency
    (i.e., "if, as they say, it is true that . . ."; cf. BD454[2]).
    BD254(2) In vv. 15, 16, and 32, the article is omitted with νεκροί because
    the concept, not the collective dead, is under discussion (otherwise it
    would be equivalent to v. 52).

18 B139 The aorist participle here is used to express identical action with the
    main verb (they perished when they died).

19 M170 Εἰ ἐν . . . μόνον should, strictly, mean "if in this life we only have our
    hopes fixed in Christ" (as opposed to something securer than hope); but the
    New Testament use of ἐλπίζω and the context both call rather for the translation
    "if it is only in this life . . ." (equivalent to εἰ μόνον . . .)
    TGr113 In Greek word order an adverb tends to follow very closely upon the verb
    or adjective or another adverb which it is intended to qualify. In this sen-
    tence the adverb μόνον occurs, not after the words "in this life," but after
    the verb, indeed after the whole sentence. There is no contrast intended
    between having faith while we are in this world and having it in some other.
    The contrast is rather between having faith only and having faith supported
    by the reality of Christ's present risen life.

20 TGr113 The last part of this verse means "Christ is the first fruits of those
    who have been sleeping" (the perfect participle is deliberately used).

22 T262 'Εν with the dative is used to denote "in the sphere" here. Adam is a
    representative man in whom all mankind is viewed (not instrumental; it is used,
    with the sense of "in the case of"--R587; ἐν τῷ 'Αδάμ is parallel to ἐν τῷ
    Χριστῷ, the preposition refers to spiritual incorporation--M80). [Ed. Actually
    Moule's suggestion is similar to the one presented by Turner. A representative
    sense appears to be portrayed in the context; cf. v. 21.]
    MT114 The present verb ἀποθνήσκω (the verb itself has a perfect sense) is used
    with a frequentative sense in v. 22 and with an iterative sense in v. 31, with
    the resultant meaning "all die" and "I die every day."

23 M38 The genitive is used with a possessive or adjectival phrase here, meaning
    "those who belong to Christ" (possibly μαθηταί should be supplied with the
    article οἱ--R767).

24 T112 "Οταν with the subjunctive here refers to a definite action occurring in
    the future ("when").

26 T63 The futuristic use of the present tense (καταργεῖται) occurs in this verse.
    This differs from the simple future sense mainly in the tone of assurance which
    is imparted, "will be abolished."

27 BD275(7) Πάντα means "the universe" and also has reference to πάντας in v. 25.

28 M70 'Εν πᾶσιν may be used in a local sense (as though the meaning were "in all
    persons" or "permeating the whole of things"), or πάντα ἐν πᾶσιν may be a mere
    phrase of emphasis such as "all in all" ("that God may be absolutely everything;"
    cf. Eph. 1:23; ἐν means "with regard to"--T265). [Ed. Πάντα ἐν πᾶσιν appears
    to be a set phrase meaning "absolutely," cf. Eph. 1:23.]
    M149 'Υποταγήσεται may be used as an ingressive future: the τότε seems to show
    that the Parousia is thought of as initiating a new kind of subordination of the
    Son to the Father, and not the perpetuation of that which had been conspicuous
    in the whole of the mediatorial aeon.

29 R1012 Εἰ . . . οὐ should not be translated by "unless" but by "if . . . not."
    B230 The first sentence of this verse should be translated "else what shall they
    do which are baptized for the dead (i.e., "since [if the dead are not raised]
    they that are baptized for the dead are baptized to no purpose")?"
    M64 'Υπέρ is used with the sense of ἀντί, "instead of" (which is similar to the
    usual meaning of ὑπέρ, "on behalf of"; perhaps ὑπέρ is used with the sense of
    περί, "about" or "concerning"--R632). [Ed. It appears that the more usual
    meaning, "on behalf of" or "instead of" is the most probable rendering here.]
    BD442(14) Τί καί in this verse means "why at all, still?"

30 R470 In Πᾶσαν ὥραν, the noun ὥραν may not have been regarded as essentially
    different from the idea of extension. Either the action was regarded as going
    over the hour or ὥραν was looked at more as an adverbial accusative (similar to
    the adverbial use of τὸ λοιπόν). [Ed. The resultant sense of πᾶσαν ὥραν is
    an adverbial notion, "constantly," cf. Rom. 8:36 and II Cor. 4:11.]

31 R1150 The only time that νή occurs in the N.T. is here. This particle is a
    peculiarity of the Attic dialect and is used in solemn emphatic statements

(oaths, etc.) and means "truly, yes." It is probably the same word as ναί, the affirmative adverb (cf. BD107).

32 M7 Ἀποθνῄσκομεν is used as a futuristic present, "we shall die" (cf. v. 26).

34 R626 Πρός with the accusative has the notion of aim or end, "to" or "for your shame."

35 R740 Ποίῳ has its original qualitative sense here, "with what kind."

36 BD475(1) When an element belonging to a subordinate clause precedes the subordinating conjunction, that element is emphasized (the pronoun σύ here).

37 R892 The future participle γενησόμενον refers to an ingressive punctiliar action, "the body that shall be."
    T127 Εἰ introduces a parenthetical phrase, meaning "if possible," "as it were" (cf. 14:10).

38 T191 Ἑκάστῳ . . . ἴδιον means "its own peculiar body."
    ΒD442(9) Καί is used in an epexegetical sense, "that is, to each."

39 R748 In vv. 39ff. ἄλλη is used in the sense of "different" (similar to ἕτερος).
    R752 Οὐ may negate either the whole sentence (because of the following ἀλλά, meaning "no flesh") or just πᾶσα ("not all"). In view of the context the latter sense seems preferable ("not every kind of flesh"--R1163).

40 BD127(5) The verb ἐστίν is omitted here, with the sense of "there are".

41 T265 Ἐν has the meaning of "with reference to."

42 R424 In vv. 42ff., the connective between the verbs is omitted to portray distinct contrast.

45 M204 Εἰς with the accusative follows ἐγένετο in the sense of a predicate nominative, "became a living being" (due to the Hellenistic tendency towards greater expressiveness and the Semitic εἰς).

47 BD253(3) Ἐκ γῆς is equivalent to "earthly"; the essential thing is the earth's specific quality in contrast to ἐξ οὐρανοῦ.

50 R405 The singular verb occurs with a compound subject because the author initially had only the first subject in mind (cf. 13:13), "flesh and blood are not able to inherit."

51 M168 Πάντες οὐ seems to mean οὐ πάντες (i.e., "all of us shall not"), and the irregular order is possibly due to the desire to align it with the πάντες δέ which follows (cf. T287; R423; and BD433[2]).

55 H22 Paul deliberately mars the rhetorical effect of the quotation from Hosea here by substituting θάνατε for ᾅδη. For Hades was a Greek divinity, not a place, and the name, though common enough in literature, had dropped out of the ordinary vernacular.

57   R1116   The present participle (διδόντι) is used to describe action which takes
     place during the implied verb and beyond (i.e., future from the verb), "who
     gives."

I CORINTHIANS 16

1   R594   Εἰς with the accusative is used here where the simple dative would be
     sufficient, "for the saints."
     M63   Περί is used in a virtually absolute sense, "as for the contribution."

2   M155   Ἵνα μή means "that . . . not."
     H238   Εὐοδόω means "give a fair way."
     H439   The use of μίαν for "first" seems to show semitic influence.

3   B310   In οὓς ἐάν the supposition is particular, referring to a specific occasion
     and event (the indefinite element is necessitated by the previous indefinite
     clause).
     M57   Διά with the genitive expresses the idea of attendant circumstances, "I
     will send them with letters" (or perhaps "a letter," an idiomatic plural).
     M133   Ὅταν with the subjunctive is indefinite (Paul is not certain as to when
     he will arrive at Corinth).
     T135   The simple infinitive is used here to express purpose, "to bring."

4   R1061   The infinitive with τοῦ is used as a subject, with the resultant meaning
     "if my going too is worth while" or "fitting" (cf. B405 and M129).

5   R869   The present verb διέρχομαι (in contrast with διέλθω) means "I am going
     through (Macedonia)."
     M7   The present verb διέρχομαι is equivalent to a future "I shall go through"
     (cf. 15:32; cf. BD323[1] and MT120). [Ed. Actually a futuristic sense is
     implied in Robertson's rendering.]

6   R490   The participle τυχόν is really the accusative absolute though used as an
     adverb (i.e., with the notion of manner, "perhaps, possibly"; cf. BD424).
     M52   Πρός with the accusative is used in vv. 6f. to denote position, "with."

10   B210   Ἵνα introduces an object clause after βλέπω (denoting content), "see that."

11   R943   The third person aorist subjunctive ἐξουθενήσῃ with μή is used to express
     a prohibition ("let no one despise him"; this rarely occurs in the New
     Testament).

12   R423   Πάντως οὐκ means "wholly not."
     H446   Πολλά is used in an adverbial sense (this possibly shows some semitic
     influence), with the meaning "greatly" or "strongly."

15   BD134(1a)   The plural verb ἔταξαν is used according to sense (rather than gram-
     matically accurate -- a singular subject οἰκίαν occurs in the main clause;
     there would have been several people in the household of Stephanas).

21   R416   Παύλου is in apposition to the possessive pronoun ἐμῇ, "with my own hand,
     Paul."

TGr86 According to this verse, Paul apparently dictated all of I Corinthians
except the salutation (which he wrote himself). Rhetorical devices would come
naturally to one who was dictating.

22 R939 ῎Ητω expresses an imprecation (prayer for evil) and is used as an optative,
"let him be accursed."

H154 Μαραναθά is of special interest -- a semitic term found only in a letter
to Greeks (it appears to mean "our Lord, come!"). It apparently was a password
in a foreign language, which embodied the Christian hope so as to be unintel-
ligible to the uninitiated.

II Corinthians

3   T296   The omission of a verb in εὐλογητὸς ὁ θεός portrays the liveliness of the
exclamation.

4   T200   Sometimes a distinction of content can be traced between πᾶς with and
without the article (actually with the noun) in the same passage. In this
verse the sense seems to be "in all our affliction . . . in any affliction"
(i.e., in any affliction which may be encountered; cf. R772 and BD275[3]).

6   R632   In this verse ὑπέρ suggests the object at which one is aiming, "(it is)
with a view to your encouragement and salvation" ("for" that which one wants to
attain--BD231[2]).
    T190   The attributive position of ὑμῶν is emphatic (it takes the place of
ὑμέτερος), "your comfort."

8   R632   Ὑπέρ with the accusative has the notion of "beyond."
    B371   Ὥστε with the infinitive is used to express a tendency realized in actual
result by implication ("insomuch that we despaired . . .").
    B401   Τοῦ with the infinitive is used after an infinitive of hindering with an
ablative sense ("even of life"; it is epexegetical to the previous infinitive
clause--T141).
    M65   The preposition in ὑπέρ τῆς θλίψεως is used with the sense of "concerning"
or "about" (equivalent to περί).

9   R498   θανάτου is used as a genitive of apposition or definition ("the death
sentence").
    R897   Ἐσχήκαμεν is used as a vivid perfect (he still had the sentence), which
is a dreadful memory to Paul (the perfect indicative is used to express a simple past fact where it is scarcely possible to suppose that the thought of existing result was in the writer's mind--B80; aoristic perfect--T70; it may be
taken as a correct perfect, cf. 7:5--BD343[2]). [Ed. This verb seems to have
the usual sense of a perfect, whereas the existing result appears to be Paul's
reliance upon God.]
    B103   The periphrastic perfect here is used for showing the existing state, "we
should not trust."
    BD283(4)   The reflexive pronoun is strengthened by the use of the pronoun αὐτοί,
"we had . . . in ourselves."

10   R710   The correlative of age τηλικοῦτος always refers to size in the N.T.
    B77   The perfect verb ἠλπίκαμεν has the sense of an emphatic or intensive present,
"on him we have set our hope."
    T28   The plural noun θανάτων may imply ways of dying, i.e., "deadly perils."

11   R474   In this verse εὐχαριστέω occurs in the passive in a construction that shows
that the active would have had an accusative of the thing and a dative of the

315

person (i.e., thanks was given for the gift).

M108 If διὰ πολλῶν goes with εὐχαριστηθῇ as equivalent to "May be thanked for
by many," then ἐκ πολλῶν is redundant; but if διὰ πολλῶν goes with το εἰς ἡμᾶς
χάρισμα as equivalent to "the gift which reached us by the agency of many,"
then strict grammar requires a second article (i.e., τὸ διὰ πολλῶν). [Ed. The
former suggestion appears to be more probable, since an anarthrous prepositional phrase generally modifies a verb rather than a noun. In addition, repetition
occurs frequently in the N.T.]

12 H378 The adjective with the termination -ικος denotes an ethical or dynamic relation to the idea involved in the root (cf. I Cor. 3:1), "fleshly."

13 M89 Ἀναγινώσκω is usually taken to mean "read," presumably in the sense that
the reader discerns "again" (ἀνά) what the writer originally had in mind. But
J.H. Kennedy (in loc.) argued interestingly, if not convincingly, for interpreting this verb in v. 13 and in 3:2 as an intensive, making the verb mean "admit"
or "acknowledge."   [Ed. In view of the usual use of ἀναγινώσκω in Paul's writings (cf. 3:15) and the meaning of the following ἐπιγινώσκω, the former suggestion is preferable.]

15 M68 There is a tendency in N.T. Greek for πρός to be used with a personal object and εἰς with an impersonal one (as here and in v. 16, although this is not
a rigid rule).
M119 In vv. 15-24 there appears to be a very careful distinction between the
singular and the plural (i.e., of personal references).

17 R614 In παρ' ἐμοί the preposition is used in an ethical relation ("with me").
B218 Ἵνα is used to introduce a clause which expresses the concerned result of
an action (cf. BD391[5]; The ἵνα in this verse should be treated as final;
Paul is disclaiming the mundane virtue of unsettled convictions, which aims at
saying yes and no in one breath--MT210). [Ed. Occasionally in the N.T., result
and purpose are not to be distinguished, which may be the case here (cf. Rom.
5:20).]

19 BD475(2) Emphasis is given to τοῦ θεοῦ here since the conjunction γάρ follows
rather than precedes (it is rare for γάρ to occur in this position; τοῦ θεοῦ
also precedes the noun υἱός).

22 M76 Ἐν with the dative is used with the sense of εἰς and the accusative, "put
into our hearts" (cf. 8:16 and Rev. 17:17).

23 M185 Ἐπὶ τὴν ἐμὴν ψυχήν seems to mean "on my life."

24 T303 There is an ellipsis of a verb which has a stronger meaning than the simple
ἐστίν in οὐχ ὅτι, "it is not that."

                             II CORINTHIANS 2

1 R401 Τό with the infinitive is in apposition to τοῦτο, "for I determined this
for myself, that I would not come again to you with sorrow."
T238 Ἐμαυτῷ is used as a dative of advantage, "for myself" (cf. R539).

2   BD442(8) Καί is to be understood in a special sense when the apodosis is a
    question, "who then?"

3   R705 Τοῦτο αὐτό means "for this very reason."
    R846 Ἔγραφα in vv. 3ff and in v. 9 seems to refer to a previous letter.

4   M57 Διά with the genitive here expresses the notion of attendant circumstance,
    "with many tears."

5   B240 The occurrence of an indefinite pronoun in the protasis of a conditional
    clause does not necessarily make the supposition general. In v. 5, "but if
    anyone has caused sorrow, he has caused sorrow not to me, but . . . to you all,"
    the supposition refers to a specific case, and is particular.

6   M108 Τῶν πλειόνων perhaps means "the majority" (though not all).

7   M144 Occasionally in the use of ὥστε, there is an ellipsis that occurs (as here,
    supply δεῖν before the infinitive; the sense is tendency or conceived result;
    cf. 1 Cor. 13:2), "so as to."
    T242 The dative λύπῃ is used to express a causal sense (cf. R532).
    MT193 The fineness of the distinction between the latent prohibition (with μή)
    and purpose clause may be illustrated by this verse, where the original may
    equally well be "perhaps he will be overwhelmed" or "let him not be overwhelmed."

10 M184 In this verse ἐν προσώπῳ seems only to mean "in the presence of."

11 T282 Οὐ . . . ἀγνοοῦμεν has the resultant meaning "know well."

12 R595 The second εἰς in this verse suggests the purpose of his coming to Troas.
    T171 Τρῳάς is articular because it refers to 1:23 where Troas was in mind (or
    "to the Troas where we had agreed to meet"; cf. BD261[1]).

13 R532 The dative with the infinitive, τῷ μή εὑρεῖν, is used in a causal sense
    (the only instance in the N.T. without a preposition; virtually instrumental,
    "because I failed to find," cf. B396 and M44).
    R539 Τῷ πνεύματι is used as a dative of advantage, "rest for my spirit."
    B80 The perfect indicative ἔσχηκα is used to refer to a simple past fact (an
    aoristic perfect, cf. 1:9, 7:5; cf. M14 and BD343[2]), "I did not have rest."

14 R407 Paul has in mind only himself but he uses the plural in vv. 14ff (the
    idiomatic plural).
    BD148(1) Θριαμβεύειν means "to lead in triumphal procession; to mock, deride"
    (cf. T53 and H400; for "celebrate a triumph," see Col. 2:15. But can this verb
    mean "cause to triumph" in 2 Cor? Col. and 2 Cor. have a different sense of
    the same verb--R474).

15 B125 The participle σωζομένοις may be rendered "those that are (in the sense
    "we that become") saved" or as in the R.V. translation as a progressive present
    of simultaneous action.
    T239 Where a stative verb with the dative forms part of the predicate, it usually
    carries the idea of credit (or discredit) in the persons eyes, "for God."

16 R626 Πρός occurs here in a general sense of fitness in connection with the ad-
    jective ἱκανός(i.e., "who is sufficient for these things").

17 M17 The present periphrastic construction occurs here (rare in the N.T.), οὐ
     γάρ ἐσμεν . . . καπηλεύοντες . . ., meaning "for we are not, like the majority,
     merely making merchandise of God's message" (generally this construction stres-
     ses the linear action, although it is difficult to see exactly how the sense
     would have been altered by the use of the simple present here).
     T158 The participle has been omitted with ὡς here, with the resultant meaning
     "as being of God" (i.e., "commissioned by Him").

                              II CORINTHIANS 3

1   M158 The form of the initial question in this verse does not make it clear what
     answer is expected, but the context does.
     H379 Συστατικῶν means "commendatory."

3   R1034 Ὅτι is used in a declarative sense, "that."
     T287 Οὐ negates the noun μέλανι, not the participle, "written not with ink."
     BD113(2) Σάρκινος has the meaning "made of flesh" (cf. I Cor. 3:1).

5   T303 Οὐχ ὅτι has the resultant sense of "it is not that" (cf. 1:24; ellipsis of
     a verb).

7   M15 The aorist verb ἐγενήθη is strictly appropriate, referring to a glory which
     is past.

8   R1136 When Paul's heart was all ablaze with passion, in this book, he piled up
     participles like boulders on the mountain side, a sort of volcanic eruption
     (as in vv. 8-10).

10 M15 The perfect verb δεδόξασται is the strictly correct correlative of the
     aorist verb in v. 7. The perfect here refers to a glory which "no longer
     exists" because it is superseded.

11 T267 Διά with the genitive δόξης has the sense of accompaniment, "with glory"
     (this is practically equivalent to "glorious," cf. the following ἐν δόξῃ).

13 B414 Πρὸς τό with the infinitive ἀτενίσαι is used to express purpose ("so that
     the sons of Israel might not see . . ."; cf. T144).
     BD482 The concept "we do not do" should be supplied after οὐ.

14 BD424 Μὴ ἀνακαλυπτόμενον ὅτι may mean "because it has not been revealed (to
     them) that," or does the participle refer to κάλυμμα, "the same veil remains
     unlifted"? [Ed. In the former rendering, the participle is taken as a nomina-
     tive absolute referring to what follows. In the N.T., the participle is sel-
     dom used in this way. Since the noun κάλυμμα is in concord with this participle
     it is best to take them together.]

15 T23 Contrary to normal Greek practice, the N.T. sometimes follows the Aramaic
     and Hebrew preference for a distributive singular. Something belonging to each
     person in a group of people is placed in the singular (τὴν καρδίαν αὐτῶν).
     BD455(1) Ἡνίκα (occurring only twice in the N.T., vv. 15f.) strictly refers to
     an hour or season of the year, but in Attic Greek it is used interchangeably
     with ὅτε.

                                   318

16 R617 The compound verb περιαιρεῖται means "the veil is removed from around
the head" (it is better to take this compound verb as intensive rather than
gaining the idea of something "enveloping" or "lying on both sides"--H321).
[Ed. The preposition in the compound verb here apparently maintains a local
sense, since that is the idea portrayed in the O.T. quotation and it is the
usual meaning in the N.T.]

17 TGr126ff. Normally in Paul's writings articular κύριος refers to Christ but
anarthrous κύριος refers to Yahweh, the God of Israel revealed through most of
the Old Testament. But in this verse the article ὁ is likely to have an anaphoric sense (i.e., taking up an immediately previous reference). Thereby the
article becomes virtually demonstrative. The immediately previous reference to
κύριος is in v. 16, and it refers to Yahweh (it has no article and the discussion is centered around Ex. 34:34). Thus the first part of this verse should
be translated "Yahweh is the Spirit." Yahweh is sometimes the pre-existent
Lord Jesus, and sometimes the Holy Spirit, in the interpretation of these O.T.
theophanies. [Ed. Κύριος is almost like a personal name in the N.T. and it is
impossible to form a rigid rule with reference to the article. Paul uses the
articular κύριος to refer to the Father in 2 Tim. 1:16 and 18 and the anarthrous
κύριος to refer to Christ in Rom. 10:13, 1 Cor. 4:4 and 7:22. It is very probable that Paul refers to Christ in 2 Cor. 3:17. This whole context presents
the contrast between the letter and the spirit (cf. v. 6).]

18 R789 Ἀνακεκαλυμμένῳ προσώπῳ means "unveiled face."
R810 Κατοπτριζόμενοι probably has the sense "beholding for ourselves in a mirror"
(an indirect middle).
R820 The preposition in ἀπὸ κυρίου πνεύματος expresses agency.
TGr126 In this verse Paul promised the Corinthians that if Jew and Gentile
turned to Yahweh with face unveiled, the resulting vision would be glorious;
yet it would be the glory of a looking-glass rather than reality, and man has
to be transformed from this glory to another which is final, involving the whole
race in one united Body of Christ, the Church, the perfect icon (image) of God.
BD474(4) Ἀπὸ κυρίου πνεύματος means "from the spirit of the Lord" (cf. T218).

II CORINTHIANS 4

2 R810 Ἀπειπάμεθα carries the sense of an indirect middle, "we renounced such
things from ourselves."

3 B84 The periphrastic perfect construction (a perfect participle with a present
stative verb) denotes the existing state here, "if our gospel is hidden" (unknown).
T264 Ἐν with the dative here stands for the normal dative of disadvantage,
"veiled to those" ("for" or "to" is better than "among"--BD220[1]).

4 M143(n.2) Εἰς τὸ μὴ αὐγάσαι may be used to express the idea of purpose (the purpose of the blinding effort "to keep them from seeing the light of the gospel")
or consecutive notion (the result of the blinding). [Ed. The former suggestion appears to be more probable, since this is Satan's goal, but compare Rom.
1:11.]
T218 When several genitives are joined together, usually the governing genitive
will precede the dependent one as here, τὸν φωτισμον τοῦ εὐαγγελίου (genitive

of origin; means "light emanating from the Gospel") τῆς δόξης τοῦ Χριστοῦ.
Both δόξης and Χριστοῦ modify εὐαγγελίου (δόξης is a genitive of content and
Χριστοῦ an objective genitive).

6   R962 Ὅτι is used to introduce a co-ordinate causal sentence (cf. I Cor. 1:25).
     M184 Ἐν προσώπῳ may mean "in the face (countenance)" or "person." [Ed. The
     former suggestion portrays the more literal sense of προσώπον and has a legi-
     timate meaning here.]

7   R1413 When the construction with ἵνα is continued in a further clause by μή,
     μή alone is repeated, but with the sense of ἵνα maintained (cf. I Cor. 1:10).

8   R596 The perfective idea of ἐκ in a compound verb can be seen here in contrast
     to the simple verb ἀπορέω ("despair"--MT237).
     T56 The middle participles ἀπορούμενοι and ἐξαπορούμενοι are used as actives
     with an intransitive sense, "in perplexity, but not in despair."
     BD430(3) Οὐ occurs with the participles in vv. 8f. because it negates the single
     idea (οὐ rarely occurs with the participle in the N.T.) [Ed. Actually, οὐ is
     the negative to be expected since there is a subtle contrast in each instance
     here (ἀλλ' οὐ). The usual negative employed to denote a contrast with ἀλλά (or
     δέ) is οὐ.]
     BD488(16) The repetition of the same word stem occurs in the contrast here,
     presenting a certain subtlety.

10   T167 In the epistles and Revelation, Ἰησοῦς occurs without the article except
     in four references; and then there is strong anaphora (as here, τοῦ Ἰησοῦς re-
     fers to a previous mention, cf. vv. 5f.).

12   M144 Ὥστε is used simply as an inferential particle (equivalent to ὡς τε),
     meaning "and so, accordingly" (cf. 1 Cor. 3:7, 21).

13   R1134 It is probable to take ἔχοντες with πιστεύομεν (though awkward), "having
     . . . we believed."

15   M108 The use of πλεονάσασα and περισσεύσῃ here suggest that τῶν πλειόνων means
     "the increasing numbers."

16   B284 Ἀλλ' εἰ καί, introduces a concessive clause, "although . . ."
     T243 Ἡμέρᾳ καὶ ἡμέρᾳ means "every day" (semitic, cf. BD200[1]).
     BD448(5) The repeated ἀλλά after ἀλλ' εἰ, means "yet, certainly, at least."

17   M186 The association of βάρος and δόξα in this verse may have been suggested
     by the fact that both "weight" and "glory" are expressed in Hebrew by the same
     consonants.

II CORINTHIANS 5

1   R882 Ἔχομεν is used in a durative futuristic sense (the condition introduced
     by ἐάν is future in conception, but the conclusion is a present reality, so
     confident is Paul of the bliss of heaven).

2   R600 The prepositions retain their root idea in ἐπ-ἐν-δύω , "to put on."
TGr128ff Verses 1f. should be translated as follows: "For we know that if our
earthly house of this tent were dissolved, we have a building of God, an house
not made with hands, eternal in heaven (plural οὐρανοῖς). For in this tent we
groan, earnestly desiring to put on (as an extra garment) our house which we
will receive from the sky (singular οὐρανοῦ)."

3   MT115 The preposition in a compound verb may be omitted without weakening the
sense, when the verb is repeated (a classical idiom; as with ἐνδυσάμενοι here;
Robertson is not certain whether or not this is an example of that idiom--R563).

4   R762 The article with σκῆνει is used in an anaphoric sense (referring to v. 1).
R963 In this verse, ἐφ' ᾧ means "because." Thus the Corinthian Christians (not
necessarily Paul) were anxious; they did not want to remain "unclothed" in
some intermediate state between death and resurrection, but hoped for the resurrection of the body (cf. TGR131; "in view of the fact"--MT107; "inasmuch as"
--M132).

5   R595 The preposition εἰς expresses the notion of purpose.
T214 The genitive τοῦ πνεύματος is used in apposition to the preceding noun,
"the guarantee consisting of the Spirit" (cf. v. 1).

6   R440 The participle θαρροῦντες is not used as an indicative verb, but an indicative verb has been omitted. Paul, after using the participle, repeats it in
the form of θαρροῦμεν, because in the intermediate clauses, he expresses εὐδο-
κοῦμεν ("therefore we are always confident").

7   T267 Διά with the genitive means "with" here (indicating the manner in which one
walks).

8   R625 In πρὸς τὸν κύριον Paul has in mind the face-to-face converse with the
Lord.

10 R582 Διά with the genitive here is used to express means, "through the agency
of the body."
M53 Πρός is used in a transferred sense, meaning "in proportion to his deeds."
T201 In essence, τοὺς πάντας ἡμᾶς means "the sum total of us."
T303 Probably a subjunctive verb should be supplied with εἴτε . . . εἴτε,
"whether it may be."

11 R500 Κυρίου is used as an objective genitive in τὸν φόβον τοῦ κυρίου, "the fear
directed towards the Lord."
R880 The conative present πείθομεν refers to an action begun but interrupted
(with the notion of incompleteness, "we try to persuade"; cf. T63).
BD350 Ἐλπίζω with the perfect infinitive here shows a deviation of the conception "hope" in the direction of "think."

12 R626 Πρός has the resultant meaning of "against."
T343 Paul makes the participle διδόντες co-ordinate with a finite verb thus
intending the participle to be used as indicative verb (cf. M179), "we are not
commending . . . , but giving."

13 B47 The aorist indicative ἐξέστημεν is used to denote a present state, the result of a past act, hence with the proper force of a Greek perfect ("we yielded

to ecstasy"--BD342[1]).

M195 It is difficult to detect a more than rhetorical antithesis in this verse:

Εἴτε γὰρ ἐξέστημεν, θεῷ·
εἴτε σωφρονοῦμεν, ὑμῖν,

For what logic is there in saying that ecstasy is for God's sake, sanity for
the sake of the Corinthians? [Ed. This may refer to a similar concept expressed in 1 Cor. 14:2.]

T238 Ὑμῖν is used as a dative of reference, thus the datives should be translated, "for God's sake . . . in your interest." This is aptly named a dative of
reference, in so far as the idea of personal interest (advantage) is so dimin-
ished as to be no more than a vague reference (advantage--R539; cf. BD188[2]).

14 R499 Χριστοῦ is a subjective genitive (i.e.,"the love proceeding from Christ";
cf. T211).

15 R539 Ἐαυτοῖς has the sense of a dative of advantage, "that they may live no
longer for themselves but for him who . . . ."
M64 In this verse ὑπέρ has the idea of "instead of" (substitution, equivalent
to ἀντί; cf R631).
BD442(9) The initial καί in this verse has an explicative sense (i.e., introducing a further explanation of the previous statement).

16 M144 Ὥστε has the meaning "and so, accordingly" (cf. 4:12).

19 R683 The plural pronoun αὐτοῖς is used according to the sense rather than the
grammar (its antecedent is κόσμον; the individuals in the world are referred to).
R964 Ὡς has a causal force here with ὅτι, similar to "since that" ("to the
effect that"--T137).
M17 In v. 19, it is debatable whether ἦν . . . καταλάσσων is periphrastic or
not. [Ed. It seems preferable not to take this as a periphrastic construction
but rather to take the participle as an adjective, especially in view of the
word order, "God was in Christ, reconciling the world to himself."]

20 B445 Ὡς with the participles is used with the notion of manner, "we are ambas-
sadors therefore on behalf of Christ, as though God were entreating by us."

II CORINTHIANS 6

3 T343 The participle διδόντες is used as a finite verb, "we give no offence"
(cf. 5:12).

4 R454 The nominative διάκονοι (literal plural) has the meaning "as a minister of
God I commend myself," whereas the accusative would be "I commend myself as a
minister of God."
M78 Ἐν παντί may be used adverbially, "in every respect," or temporally, "on
every occasion." [Ed. This prepositional phrase seems to be used adverbially
since it has this meaning in other similar constructions (cf. 1 Cor. 7:11 and
11:9) and it is in direct contrast with ἐν μηδενί of the previous verse (cf.
also the various aspects portrayed in the following list).]

M196 Verses 4-10 make up an impassioned and almost lyrical passage, where precision in the interpretations of the prepositions is probably impossible because the catalogue has lured the writer into repeating a preposition in some instances where in sober prose it might have been unnatural.
T28 The plurals here imply cases of "in tribulation . . ."

7   R582 Διά with the genitive here has an instrumental sense, "by means of the weapons" (cf. M58).
T207 "The armour of righteousness" is probably that which the divine righteousness provides (adjectival genitive).

8   M58 Διὰ δόξης may express a local idea, "passing through glory" (the preposition carries the notion of "with" [attendant circumstances]--T267). [Ed. In essence these suggestions are similar but the former one more readily fits the context since this verse describes the conditions or circumstances in which Paul commends himself.]

9   B446 Ὡς is used with adjectival participles in vv. 9f. to express the notion of manner (indicating the way in which they are treated).

10 R828 The preposition in the compound κατέχοντες has a perfective force, "keep in one's possession."

11 R895 Ἀνέῳγεν is used as a durative perfect, "is open."

13 M160f. Τὴν δὲ αὐτὴν ἀντιμισθίαν may be an instance of an adverbial phrase constructed from a basis other than that of a neuter noun: it looks like a subtle blend of τὸ δὲ αὐτό, "in the same way," and κατ' ἀντιμισθίαν, "by way of recompense," and, on this showing, might be rendered "and accordingly, by way of response on your part." But it may be rather an accusative in apposition to the whole sentence which follows it (excluding the parenthesis ὡς τέκνοις λέγω) "widen your hearts in the same way in exchange" (cf. R486; it is perhaps the equivalent to τὸν αὐτὸν πλαστυσμὸν ὡς ἀντιμισθίαν-BD154). [Ed. All of these renderings have the resultant idea that the Corinthian believers are to have an adequate response to Paul's appeal. However, Moule's second suggestion seems to be most probable; cf. the similar construction in 3:18.]

14 R625 Πρός following κοινωνία refers to a living relationship or intimate converse.
BD189 The dative of possession tends to emphasize the object possessed more than the possessor, "for what partnership has righteousness . . ." (without the verb here).
BD345 Γίνομαι with a present participle is used to denote the beginning of a state or condition, "do not lend yourselves to . . . "

15 R217 Βελιάρ is from two Hebrew words meaning "lord of the forest."

17 R853 In using the present imperative μὴ ἅπτεσθε, the prophet (Isa. 52:11) assumes that the people were guilty (they were to stop).

18 T253 Occasionally εἰς with the accusative appears in place of the predicate nominative owing to the Hellenistic tendency towards greater expressiveness and the Semitic influence, ."and I will be a father to you."

II CORINTHIANS 7

3   BD494(3) Paul knows how to change his tone in an astonishing way and uses a
    subsequent correction of a previous impression when he feels that he has of-
    fended, still maintaining the most sensitive contact with his readers (cf.
    12:11).

4   BD195(2) The instrumental dative τῇ χαρᾷ is used where a genitive would have
    been used in classical Greek, "with joy."

5   T28 The plurals μάχαι and φόβοι imply "cases of . . ." (cf. 1:10 and 6:4).
    BD468(1) θλιβόμενοι is used as co-ordinate with a finite verb (it is equivalent
    to an indicative verb; cf. 4:12), "we were afflicted."

7   R1091 Ὥστε with the infinitive χαρῆναι is used to express actual result, "so
    that I rejoiced still more."

8   M167 Εἰ καί is concessive, meaning "even if," or "for, though I made you sorry"
    (cf. B284).

9   R599 The notion of cause or occasion is conveyed by ἐκ (cf. T260).
    R834 The aorist ἐλυπήθητε has an inceptive sense ("became grieved"; cf. T72).
    M59 In vv. 9ff., the preposition κατά, in the repeated phrase κατὰ θεόν, means
    "in a godly way . . . godly grief . . . in a godly way" (cf. T268).

11 R523 The dative ὑμῖν (without the preposition) seems to be used in a locative
    sense, "in you."
    R741 Πόσος has an exclamatory sense here, "how much zeal."
    T330 Introducing a strong addition ἀλλά means "yes, indeed" (emphatic).
    BD197 Τῷ πράγματι is used as a dative of respect, "in reference to the matter"
    (the use of ἐν with the dative would seem more accurate).
    BD399(1) Τό with the infinitive is in apposition to the pronoun τοῦτο(cf. 2:1),
    "that you sorrowed."
    BD406 Συνεστήσατε means "you have demonstrated."

12 R846 Ἔγραψα refers to a previous letter (cf. 2:3, 4, and 9).
    R1073 Usually ἕνεκεν τοῦ with an infinitive occurs in a final sense, i.e., pur-
    pose , but in this verse it is causal (as well as the two preceding participles
    (it expresses purpose--M140). [Ed. The usual notion of purpose for ἕνεκεν
    with the infinitive more readily fits the context than does the causal idea.]

13 T29 The double comparative here is used to heighten the comparison with the re-
    sultant meaning "still much more" (cf. BD246).
    T258 Ἀπό is used for ὑπό with an agent after a passive verb ("prepared and de-
    rived from").

14 R603 Ἐπί with the genitive Τίτου has the meaning "before" or "in the presence
    of."
    R632 Ὑπέρ has the sense of "concerning" with the verb κεκαύχημαι here.

15 R612 Μετά carries the idea of accompaniment, "you were accompanied with fear
    and trembling."

BD60(3) Περρισοτέρως appears to have a strong force equivalent to ὑπερβαλλόντως, "especially," or "all the more."

II CORINTHIANS 8

1 T264 For the prepositional phrase ἐν ταῖς ἐκκλησίαις the meaning "to the churches" (i.e., used for a simple dative) is possible, although "within" is not impossible (it is used for the simple dative, see above 4:3--BD220[1]; ἐν means "among"--R587; the preposition is used instead of εἰς, cf. 1:22-- M76). [Ed. Following the transitive verb δίδωμι the preposition ἐν with a dative seems to have a sense which is equivalent to a simple dative, cf. Acts 4:12. In essence this is similar to Moule's suggestion.]

2 R607 In κατὰ βάθους the idea is "down to the depth" (i.e., "their profound poverty"; "extreme, radical poverty"--BD225).

3 M59 The preposition in κατὰ δύναμιν is used in a transferred sense ("according to, in respect to"), with the resultant meaning "to the utmost of their power," which is contrasted with παρὰ δύναμιν, meaning "beyond their power."

6 R1003 Εἰς τό with the infinitive is used with a consecutive notion, "so that we besought Titus." This idiom is not present in the Johannine writings, although it is very frequent in Paul's literature (especially in Romans and 1 Thess.) and in Hebrews (cf. M141; "to such a degree that"--T143).
B200 Ἵνα introduces an object clause after an infinitive of exhorting (ἵνα of content), "that as he . . ."

7 TGr147 In the words of Paul to the Corinthian Christians here, he solicits their affectionate understanding: "See that (ἵνα) you abound in this grace also" (A.V.). The addition of "see that" in the A.V. and R.S.V. translations implies that something more than simple imperatival force is intended (cf. N.E.B.; ἵνα with the subjunctive has an imperatival sense--M144; cf. R994).

8 T14 The neuter articular adjective (with a genitive) is used as an abstract substantive here, "what is genuine with respect to your love" (cf. BD263[2]).

9 R834 Ἐπτώχευσεν is used as an ingressive aorist, "he became poor" (cf. B37 and 1 Cor. 4:8).
B438 The participle ὤν is used in a concessive sense, "although he was rich."

10 R1059 The articular infinitives are objects of the verb προενήρξασθε ("you began a year ago not only to do but also to desire"). M124 Οἵτινες in this context seems to be distinctly different than the relative pronoun (more indefinite), "whatever."

11 R395 The ellipsis of the subjunctive verb ᾖ occurs after ὅπως , "that it may be."
R600 The perfective force of ἐπί is present in the compound verb here, "completely fulfilled."
R1073 Ἐκ τοῦ ἔχειν (the only occurrence of ἐκ τοῦ with an infinitive in the N.T.) most likely is meant to accent the ability growing "out of" the possession of property, whatever it may be; "according to your means."

BD400(2) The relationship between the substantive and infinitive in ἡ προθυμία τοῦ θέλειν is loose and tends toward a consecutive sense, "zeal in willing so that one really will" (cf. T141).

12 M59 Καθὸ ἐὰν ἔχῃ equivalent to καθ' ὃ ἐὰν ἔχῃ means "in proportion to what one has" (cf. v. 3).

13 M145 Ἵνα with the omitted subjunctive verb (ᾖ) may possibly be used in an imperatival sense (it is doubtful--T95). [Ed. Ἵνα is not used as an imperative but it seems to introduce the content of the ellipsis that occurs in οὐ γάρ, with the resultant meaning "it is not that there may be rest for others."]

14 R707 The contrast is sharp between ὑμῶν and ἐκείνων.
    R986 Ὅπως is used here for the sake of variety (since ἵνα occurs previously; cf. BD369[9]).

15 BD263(1) The neuter singular adjective (τὸ πολύ . . ., τὸ ὀλίγον)is used in an individual sense of a particular definite thing or act, "much . . ., little."

16 R585 The preposition ἐν here is used in the sense of εἰς, "into the heart" (cf. 1:22 and M76).

17 M12 In vv. 17, 18, 22; 9:3, and 5, the aorist tense seems to be used in an epistolary sense, whereby the writer courteously projects himself in imagination into the position of the reader, for whom actions contemporaneous with the time of writing will be past (cf. T73).
    T30 The comparative σπουδαιότερος is used for an elative superlative, meaning "very jealous" (cf. BD244[2]0.

18 MT68 Ἐν τῷ εὐαγγελίῳ appears to mean "in the sphere of the Gospel."

21 BD176(2) Προνοοῦμεν καλά means "we are intent on the good."

22 R530 An associative instrumental idea appears in the use of αὐτοῖς, "with them."
    R659 The accusative adjective πολύ is used as an adverb ("much more diligent").

23 R632 Ὑπέρ here has the general idea of "about" or "concerning" (cf. MT105 and 7:14).

24 TGr166 The participle ἐνδεικνύμενοι is used as an imperative, "you must be showing them a proof of your love" (note that it is changed to an imperative in form in some manuscripts).

II CORINTHIANS 9

2 M108 Τοὺς πλείονας perhaps means "the majority" (though not all; cf. 2:6).
    T190 Notice the attributive pronoun τὸ ὑμῶν (variant readings have ἐξ ὑμῶν ; cf. 1:6). In Paul's writings when the personal pronoun takes this position, it is emphatic (cf. BD284[2]).

3 T187 The article τό is used with the prepositional phrase in this verse to avoid confusion (to show that it is attributive, "our boasting concerning you").

4   M139 Μή πως means "lest perhaps" (it is used as a co-ordinate conjunction--
     BD471[3]).
     BD495(1) "Ἵνα μὴ λέγωμεν ὑμεῖς is far from a simple and straightforward state-
     ment; the simple expression of the thought would be ἵνα μὴ καταισχυνθῆτε , but
     since that would be painful to his readers, he turns the reproach ostensibly
     against himself while making it clear that he is doing so.

5   R996 The infinitive clause (ταύτην ἑτοίμην εἶναι) is used after the ἵνα clause
     to express an epexegetic or complementary purpose (susidiary to the ἵνα clause;
     it may be consecutive or final--M141). [Ed. Probably both the notion of pur-
     pose and result are involved in the infinitive here, cf. Rom. 1:11 and 5:20.]

6   BD481 The verb θήμι should be understood to go with τοῦτο δέ following the same
     construction in 1 Cor. 7:29 and 15:50 ("but this I say").

7   B12 Ἀγαπᾷ is used as a gnomic present (for generalizations or proverbs), "God
     loves a cheerful giver" (cf. M8).

10 TGr166 In vv. 10f, the participle πλουτιζόμενοι is used with an imperatival sense,
     "he shall increase the fruits of your righteousness; (be ye) enriched in every-
     thing" (cf. M179).
     BD101 Αὐξάνω has a transitive use here, meaning "cause to increase."

12 M17 The clause with the present periphrastic construction should be translated,
     "the ministry of this service is not merely supplying . . . " (cf. 2:17).
     TGr166 The participle δοξάζοντες has an imperatival sense (cf. M179). Thus,
     vv. 12f. should be translated, "the carrying out of this service not only supplies
     the needs of the saints, but causes them to thank God. (They ought to be)
     praising God because of this testing of you."

13 R783 The prepositional phrase εἰς αὐτούς is attributive to τῆς κοινωνίας, "the
     generosity of your distribution unto them."

14 R605 Ἐφ' ὑμῖν seems to be a simple use of the dative case with ἐπί supplementing
     it, "in you."

15 R605 In this verse ἐπί conveys the notion of ground or occasion, "for" or "be-
     cause of."

II CORINTHIANS 10

1   R407 Paul defends his own apostolic authority in 10:1 - 11:6, where the whole
     point turns on his own personality. But he uses the plural as well as the
     singular. Thus even in the use of the plural he refers to himself (cf. vv. 3,
     7, 11, and 13).
     M58 Διά has the notion of accompaniment here, "I appeal to you in Christ's
     meekness and gentleness."
     M205 Possibly ἐν is used for εἰς in this verse, "unto you."
     H466 Κατὰ πρόσωπου is used adverbially, "humble when personally present."

2   T146 The nominative with the infinitive should be translated "I beg that when
     I am present I may not be bold." (Τὸ μή here is the equivalent of a ἵνα μή

327

clause and is to be compared with the classical τὸ μή, after verbs of hindering; δέδμαι τὸ θαρρῆσαι without μή would obviously be impossible even in Paul--
BD399).
BD488(1b) The repetition of a word in close proximity is used in a contrast,
so that a certain subtlety is present (κατὰ σάρκα . . . ἐν σαρκὶ . . . κατὰ
σάρκα).

3   M59 The prepositional phrase κατὰ σάρκα means "in accordance with material
    standards" (to be distinguished in meaning from κατὰ σάρκα in Rom. 1:3 and τὸ
    κατὰ σάρκα in Rom. 9:5).
    M102 The participle περιπατοῦντες is used with a concessive sense, "although
    we (I) are walking" (cf. T157).

4   R626 Πρός occurs here in the general sense of fitness in connection with the
    adjective δυνατά (cf. 2:16; it has the idea of purpose, cf. Eph. 4:29--T247).
    [Ed. The adjective seems to contain an idea of fitness, but the preposition
    with the accusative has the notion of purpose, cf. Acts 27:12; 2 Cor. 1:20;
    1 Tim. 4:8; 2 Tim. 3:16 and Tit. 1:16.]
    M184(cf. 46) Τῷ θεῷ after δυνατά here may be used in an intensive sense (it is
    Semitic, "great power" or "divine power in honor of," or "in favor of God"--
    H443).
    T343 The participle καθαιροῦντες seems to be co-ordinate with a finite verb,
    "we destroy arguments."

5   R500 Τὴν ὑπακοὴν τοῦ Χριστοῦ means "obedience to Christ" (an objective geni-
    tive).

7   M58 The phrase τὰ κατὰ πρόσωπον means "what is in front of you" (cf. T15).
    M137 The infinitive εἶναι is used as the direct object of the verb πέποιθεν,
    "if anyone is confident that."

8   R716 The accusative relative pronoun has been assimilated into the genitive
    ἧς, because of the antecedent which is in the genitive case (thus ἧς can act
    as the direct object of ἔδωκεν).
    T339 Τε appears before γάρ here as a superfluous pretension (i.e., τε γάρ is
    equivalent to γάρ or καὶ γάρ, cf. BD443[2]), with the resultant meaning "for
    even if."

9   R597 Ἐκ has a causative force in the compound verb in this verse, "cause to
    fear."
    R959 In its occurrence here, ἄν is probably the same as ἐάν and ὡς ἄν and means
    "and if" (cf. M152; "so to speak"--BD453[3]).
    M145 Ἵνα seems to introduce a content clause, "that."
    T267 Διὰ τῶν ἐπιστολῶν means "with the letters" (διά with the genitive expres-
    ses the medium; cf. BD223[3]).

10 R392 Paul uses φησίν to refer to his opponent in an indefinite sense, "says my
    opponent" ("the [imaginary] opponent says"--BD130[2]).

12 T160 The last segment of this verse should be translated "they do not realize
    that they are measuring and comparing themselves by their own standards."
    BD283(4) The strengthening of the reflexive with αὐτός appears only in scattered
    instances in the N.T. (a characteristic of literary language; it occurs fre-
    quently in Attic Greek).

13 M71 Does the prepositional phrase εἰς τὰ ἄμετρα with the verb καυχησόμεθα mean
      "by reference to a standard which we have no right to use?" Or does it simply
      mean "with reference to what is outside our scope?" [Ed. The former suggestion
      is preferable, since it would not be necessary for Paul to convince the Corin-
      thian Church that he was not boasting about things beyond which he actually
      knew. This context portrays the fact that Paul did not want to boast about an-
      other man's labor (thus taking the credit for it, cf. v. 15).]

14 R629 The preposition ὑπέρ presents the idea of "beyond" in the compound verb.
      T285 Ὡς μή is used with a participle to express a conception only and not a
      fact ("as though we did not reach you").
      MT68 Ἐν τῷ εὐαγγελίῳ appears to mean "in the sphere of the Gospel."

15 B378 The infinitive μεγαλυνθῆναι modifies the noun κανόνα, "our sphere of action
      among you may be enlarged."
      T343 The first two participles in this verse are co-ordinate with a finite verb,
      "we do not boast . . ., but our hope is" (cf. v. 4).

16 R647 Ὑπερέκεινα is merely the composition of the preposition ὑπέρ and the pro-
      noun ἐκεῖνα. It occurs only once in the N.T. and with the ablatival genitive
      in the sense of "beyond." Thus the resultant meaning is "into the regions be-
      yond you."

II CORINTHIANS 11

1 R1186 In ἀλλὰ καὶ ἀνέχεσθε, the tone of irony makes it doubtful whether to take
      ἀλλά as copulative or adversative (it is introducing a strong addition, "yes,
      indeed"--T330).
      M137 Ὄφελον is used as a particle introducing an unfulfilled wish, and is fol-
      lowed by an imperfect verb to refer to the present time, "I wish."
      BD448(6) Ἀλλὰ καί is used in an emphatic way, "I will not only express the
      wish, but I forthwith entreat you" (ἀνέχεσθε taken as an imperative), or it may
      translated "but you have already done it" (ἀνέχεσθε taken as an indicative verb).
      [Ed. It is difficult to determine which rendering of this verb is correct. It
      may be preferable to take it as an indicative, since Paul changes the point of
      stress in a train of thought; cf. the similar use of ἀλλὰ καί in Phil. 1:18.]

2 R1088 The simple infinitive is used to express the notion of purpose here ("that
      I may present you").
      M184 Should θεοῦ ζήλῳ be interpreted as "a divine (i.e., "supernaturally great")
      eagerness" or is it nearer to the meaning "an eagerness which is God's own
      eagerness" (or "which springs from God Himself"; cf. 10:4)? [Ed. The genitive
      θεοῦ may be used in the N.T. with the meaning represented by Moule's first sug-
      gestion (cf. τοῦ θεοῦ in 2 Cor. 1:12), however this occurs infrequently. In
      view of this infrequency and the position of θεοῦ here, Moule's last suggestion
      seems preferable.]
      M160 The middle voice is justified in Paul's use of ἡρμοσάμην by the profound
      personal interest that he took in this art of spiritual match-making.

3 BD211 Ἀπό denotes alienation in some expressions, especially in Paul (as in
      this verse), which can not be directly paralleled from the classical language,
      "be led astray from."

4   R747 The change from ἄλλον to ἕτερον may be only for the sake of variety. But
        it is also possible that Paul stigmatizes the gospel of the Judaizers as ἕτερον
        (cf. Gal. 1:6) and the Spirit preached by them, while he is unwilling to admit
        another (ἄλλον) Jesus even of the same type as the one preached by him (the
        change occurs only for the sake of variety--T197 and BD306[4]). [Ed. Robert-
        son's distinction seems slightly forced, although there seems to be more in the
        change than just stylistic variety.]

6   R129 Paul disclaims classic elegance and calls himself ἰδιώτης τῷ λόγῳ, yet
        this was in contrast to the false taste of the Corinthians.
    M119 There appears to be an obvious epistolary plural participle in this verse
        (Paul refers to himself).
    M180 The participle is used as a finite verb (co-ordinate with a verb--T343),
        "I made this plain."
    BD448(5) Ἀλλά in an apodosis after εἰ means "yet," "certainly," "at least."

9   M53 Πρός denotes the idea of position, "with."
    M206 The present participle πάρων seems to refer to what preceded the main verb
        (with a durative sense).

10 M112 Ἔστιν ἀλήθεια Χριστοῦ ἐν ἐμοί, ὅτι . . . presumably means "I am speaking
        Christian truth when I say that . . ."; if so, it is a very small and particu-
        larized sense of ἀλήθεια as associated with Christ (ὅτι is used to introduce
        the content of a solemn oath).

14 M175 The genitive φωτός is used in an adjectival sense equivalent to φωτεινόν,
        "a bright," or "shining angel."

15 B282 Εἰ καί should not be taken together, εἰ is the conditional particle and
        καί means "also" (cf. T321).

16 R743 The indefinite pronoun is used with the adjective μικρόν to soften the
        statement, "I may boast a little."
    M151 Κἂν ὡς ἄφρονα δέξασθε με is best translated "receive me, even if it be only
        as a fool."
    T137 The infinitive is used as a direct object of the verb δόξῃ, "that I am a
        fool."
    BD336(3) The hortatory aorist subjunctive δόξῃ (note the third person singular
        here, cf. 1 Cor. 16:11) should be translated "let no one get the idea . . .,"
        with the connotation that no one did, of course, think of Paul as a fool (cf.
        R853; less peremtory than the imperative--MT178).
    BD473(1) Generally an unemphatic pronoun is placed near the beginning of a
        sentence. However, δέξασθε is placed before the pronoun με (probably for em-
        phasis).

18 T177 The anarthrous noun σάρκα means, "the natural state of man" (with an ab-
        stract sense).

20 R606 Κατά has a perfective force in the verb καταδουλοῖ (i.e., stressing the
        enslaving).
    T256 The preposition εἰς is used with a part of the body which an act is directed
        to or on, "strikes you on the face."

21 T170 The perfect tense is used here as an aoristic perfect (cf. 2:13), "we
      were too weak."
      T268 Κατὰ φύσιν means "in accordance with nature."
      BD396 Ὡς ὅτι has the sense of "to the effect that" (cf. 5:19).

23 R293 In ὑπὲρ ἐγώ the preposition is used as an adverb, and should be taken with
      the implied verb rather than the pronoun, "I am even more so" (cf. M64 and T250).
      T28 The plural noun θανάτοις may imply ways of dying (cf. 1:10).

24 R615 Παρά is used with the accusative here for the notion of "minus" ("short
      of . . .").
      TGr94 The famous "stake in the flesh" which has given rise to so much contro-
      versy in vv. 24f., is consistent with the theory of crucifixion.

25 B39 The aorist is used to refer to a series or aggregate of acts viewed as con-
      stituting a single fact, "three times I suffered shipwreck."
      MT144 The perfect tense of πεποίηκα can be translated quite naturally into
      English. But it does not follow that we have here a mere equivalent for ἐποίησα.
      That would only place the experience on a level with the others: the perfect
      tense recalls it as a memory especially vivid now (the perfect of broken con-
      tinuity; the perfect tense is used as an aoristic perfect [cf. v. 21; 1:9 and
      2:13]; apparently there is no reason for the change to the perfect tense--BD343
      [2]). [Ed. Moulton's suggestion seems to be the most plausible, since the
      close proximity of different tenses does not necessarily prove their identity.]

26 T212 The genitives ποτάμων and ληστῶν mean "in rivers" and "among robbers" (in
      spite of ἐν θαλάσσῃ which follows, the dangers are those which "spring from . ."
      [not "in," cf. ἐξ ἐθνῶν]--BD166).

28 R547 Παρεκτός is an adverb used as a substantive (with the article τῶν), "what
      is external."

29 T38 The sudden insertion of ἐγώ in the second sentence of this verse is without
      cause and meaningless.

32 R498 In τὴν πόλιν Δαμασκηνῶν, the genitive is used in an adjectival sense (des-
      cribing the city).

33 BD223(5) The phrase διὰ τοῦ τείχους means "along the wall."

II CORINTHIANS 12

1   BD353(5) Supply ἐστίν with the participle συμφέρον (i.e., the periphrastic con-
      struction is understood), or the participle may be taken as an accusative abso-
      lute (it is to be taken as a periphrastic construction--T88). [Ed. Generally
      οὐ is not the negative used with a participle in N.T. Greek. But it occurs here
      because of the understood periphrastic construction. Thus there is no emphasis
      indicated by the use of οὐ.]

2   R408 Paul's allusion to "third heaven" is an apparent reflection of the Jewish
      idea of seven heavens (cf. Eph. 4:10). [Ed. Robertson disagrees with this as-
      sumption in Word Pictures in the N.T. (v. IV, p. 264).]

331

M74 Πρὸ ἐτῶν δεκατεσσάρων evidently means "fourteen years ago" (cf. Jn. 12:1);
but what is the construction? Is ἐτῶν δεκατεσσάρων a genitive of time, leaving
πρό to stand absolutely? It is difficult to see why the genitive rather than
an accusative is used to denote a period of time, unless it be a genitive to
define quantity simply (cf. Amos 1:1), comparable to a genitive of price, with
the linear idea of extent scarcely visible.

T46 The articular pronoun τὸν τοιοῦτον in vv. 2, 3, and 5 is merely used for
the simple τοῦτον(i.e., simple reference is made to the previous ἄνθρωπον),
"this man."

T221 The prepositional phrase ἐν Χριστῷ is attributive to the anarthrous noun
ἄνθρωπον (this seldom occurs in N.T. Greek), "a man in Christ."

3   M197 Σώματι here definitely refers to a material nature (i.e., physical; cf.
     1 Cor. 6:12).

4   T88 The verb ἐστίν, is understood to go with the impersonal participle ἐξόν
     (actually making this a periphrastic construction; cf. v. 1 for the use of the
     negative οὐ with such a construction).

5   H463 The preposition ἐν is used in a causal sense here (possibly because of
     Semitic influences).

6   R988 Μή τις is used with the subjunctive here in a final sense, "so that no one
     may think more."
     BD145(2) Εἰς ἐμέ with λογίσηται may literally mean "to charge to my account."

7   R532 The dative τῇ ὑπερβολῇ expresses the idea of cause.
     R538 Τῇ σαρκί is used either as a dative of advantage, "for the flesh," or
     locative, "in the flesh." [Ed. Paul probably would have included the prepo-
     sition ἐν for the latter rendering. In addition, when a dative is used with
     a substantive such as σκόλοψ, it frequently has the notion of advantage or dis-
     advantage, cf. 2:13.]
     R629 The preposition ὑπέρ in the compound verb ὑπεραίρω has the notion of "ex-
     cess," "more than."

8   M65 The preposition in ὑπὲρ τούτου has the sense "concerning" or "about" with
     the resultant meaning "about this I three times begged the Lord" ("because of
     that"--BD231[1]). [Ed. The former suggestion appears to be more compatible
     with the finite verb παρεκάλεσα. But even in that rendering a causal notion is
     present.]

9   R602 Ἐπί with the accusative here is used in a metaphorical sense, "the power
     of Christ may rest upon me."
     R664 Ἥδιστα and μᾶλλον are not to be taken together; "gladly (a stereotyped
     elative superlative, "very gladly"--BD60[2]) will I boast rather . . ." (cf.
     BD246).
     M15 Εἴρηκεν is probably a true Greek perfect, "his answer to me has been."
     M79 Καυχήσομαι ἐν probably means "I will boast about" (ἐν is causal--H463).
     [Ed. Generally when ἐν is used with καυχάομαι it has the resultant meaning of
     "in" or "about"; cf. 10:15, and the similar statement in 11:30.]
     MT130 The present verb τελεῖται means "my power is perfected in weakness."

10   T28 The plural nouns here imply "cases of."

11 B284 Εἰ καί introduces a concessive clause (cf. 7:8), "although."
T90 It is not suggested by ὤφειλον that the past obligation was not lived up
to; it is simply a present obligation expressed for some reason in the imperfect
(the imperfect is used to express an obligation which does not or did not take
place--BD358[1]). [Ed. The obligation was one that was not in fact being
carried out. That is the very reason why Paul was forced to present his creden-
tials.]
BD495(3) Paul changes his tone in an astonishing way (cf. 7:3).

12 R408 The articular noun ἀποστόλου refers to the whole class of apostles.
T58 The transitive deponent verb κατειργάσθη is used with a passive sense here,
"were performed."

13 R1199 Notice Paul's use of irony in this verse (cf. 11:19).
M131 In τί γάρ ἐστιν ὅ ἡσσώθητε, the meaning must be "what is there in regard
to which you came off worse" (i.e., ὅ is a genuine accusative of respect).

14 M161 Notice the use of ἔχω with ἑτοίμως to express a state or condition, "I am
ready."
BD154 Τρίτον τοῦτο means "for the third time."

15 BD60(2) Ἥδιστα means "very gladly" (elative superlative, cf. v. 9).
BD60(3) The comparative περισσοτέρως has strong force here equivalent to
ὑπερβαλλόντως (cf. 7:15), "especially."
BD61(1) Ἧσσον is used as an adverb meaning "less" (of degree).

16 R392 The verb ἔστω has the meaning "let it be so," or "granted" (the sentence
is the subject).
M103 The participle ὑπάρχων is used in a causal sense, "villain as I was . . ."
(cf. T157).

17 R896 Paul uses the perfect verb ἀπέσταλκα to refer to various missions to the
Corinthians (cf. MT144; the perfect tense appears to be used in an aoristic
sense, although it is possible that the thought of an existing result is more
or less clearly in mind--B88; aoristic--T70 and BD343[2]). [Ed. Paul uses
the perfect tense here to refer to various mission to Corinth but he implies
that there is no present harm or burden placed upon them as a result of those
endeavors (the existing result).]

18 R684 The article is used with ἀδελφόν with the meaning "his brother" (cf. T173).
M156 Notice the different answers anticipated by the questions in this verse;
first "no", then "yes" (denoted by the negative used, μήτι . . . οὐ . . . οὐ).

19 T62 The present tense of δοκεῖτε has a definite progressive sense, "have been
thinking all this time . . .?"
T190 The pronoun ὑμῶν has an emphatic position (cf. 9:2), "your edification."

20 B475 Οὐ is used with a subjunctive verb (εὕρω) in clauses introduced by the
conjunction μή (i.e., "lest"), with the resultant meaning "for I fear that
perhaps I may come and find you not what I wish" (cf. R1159 and BD428[6]).

21 R1117 Notice the sharp difference between the perfect and aorist participles
here (to emphasize the continuation of their sinful state).

II CORINTHIANS 13

1 BD154 Τρίτον τοῦτο means "for the third time" (cf. 12:14).
BD234(4) Ἐπί with the genitive means "before."

2 M69 Εἰς τὸ πάλιν means "again, for another visit" (the preposition is used in a metaphorical-temporal sense).

4 R598 The preposition in ἐξ ἀσθενείας has a causal notion.

5 R1045 Εἰ introduces an indirect question, "to see if."
T321 For the sense of "except if" ("unless") Hellenistic Greek tends to have ἐκτός, whereas Classical has εἰ μή (as here).

7 R919 Paul does not use εὔχομαι but εὐχόμεθα; he does not dare to pray such a prayer, nor did he (cf. Acts 27:29).
R1173 μηδέν is used to strengthen the force of the previous negation, "no evil at all."

9 R698 Τὴν ὑμῶν κατάρτισιν is in apposition to τοῦτο (further explanation), although it does not agree in gender, "we pray that you may be made complete."

11 M161 Λοιπόν, ἀδελφοί, χαίρετε means "finally (or "and so"), brothers, rejoice" (or perhaps "farewell").

12 M21 Does ἀσπάσασθε have any significance in contrast to the present imperatives which precede it and the present indicative which follows it (there is no apparent significant change in the sense--T75)?

13 T211 It is difficult to decide whether the genitive is subjective or objective in ἡ κοινωνία τοῦ ἁγίου πνεύματος. [Ed. To maintain parallelism with the previous two phrases, it is best to consider this genitive as subjective, "the fellowship from the Holy Spirit."]

Galatians

1   R567 Paul covers source and agency in the denial of man's control over his apostleship by the use of ἀπό and διά.

5   MT183 In view of the context an imperative needs to be supplied, "be glory."

6   R879 In θαυμάζω, "I wonder" brings out the durative idea, although "you are changing" is necessary for μετατίθεστε.
BD308(4) The adjectives ἄλλος and ἕτερος are sometimes used together it seems, only for the sake of variety. In Gal. 1:6f, they appear to be used without distinction; ἄλλο is used pleonastically to a certain extent in order to introduce εἰ μή . . ., "not that there is any other, except that . . ." (cf. T197; Blass's position seems to be supported by 1 Cor. 12:9f, where certainly no real distinction can be found. But I am bound to insist on a real difference in Gal. 1:6f. The change is made from ἕτερον to ἄλλον for the very reason that Paul is not willing to admit that it is a gospel on the same plane[ἄλλο] as that preached by him. He admits ἕτερον, but refuses ἄλλο. The use of εἰ μή by Paul stigmatizes the gospel of the Judaizers as ἕτερον [v. 6] and the Spirit preached by them, while he is unwilling to admit another [ἄλλον] Jesus even of the same type as the one preached by him--R747; Ramsay [on Gal. 1:6] argues that, when ἕτερος occurs in contrast with ἄλλος, it means not "different" [as Lightfoot, in location], but "another of the same kind"). [Ed. Since the positive statement with ἕτερον changes to a negative clause with ἄλλον, there is an indication that some distinction occurs between the two adjectives; "not that there is another," i.e., true gospel. But one should not make more of the distinction than is actually there.]

7   B274 Εἰ μή does not state a condition on fulfillment of which the apodosis is true or its action that takes place, but a limitation of the principal statement. It is, however, never in the N.T. purely adversative (εἰ μή means "except that," cf. Acts 20:23--BD376).
M106n.1 A rather curious use of the article occurs in v. 7, οἱ ταράσσοντες, where what is really required seems to be οἳ ταράσσουσιν.

8   R402 When the subject comprises two or even all three persons, the first prevails over both the second and third (in agreement with the verb). But in Gal. 1:8, the reverse is true either because Paul follows the nearest in both person and number or because he acknowledges thus the superior exaltation of the angel (it is impossible to embrace both subjects by εὐαγγελιζώμεθα--BD135 [4]), "we or an angel from heaven should preach."
R616 In vv. 8f, παρ' ὅ has the idea of "beyond" and so "contrary to" ("other than"--M51).
R939 There is a strong inclination to use the imperative instead of the optative in the N.T., not only in requests, where the imperative has a legitimate place in Classical Greek as well, but also in imprecations, where it takes the

place of the classical optative, as with ἀνάθεμα ἔστω, "let him be accursed."
B278   In Gal. 1:8, the fulfillment of the element of the protasis expressed in
παρ' ὃ εὐηγγελισάμεθα is favorable to the fulfillment of the apodosis ἀνάθεμα
ἔστω, and the clause is so far fourth conditional. But the element expressed
in ἡμεῖς ἢ ἄγγελος ἐξ οὐρανοῦ which is emphasized by the καί, is unfavorable
to the fulfillment of the apodosis, and the clause is concessive. It might
be resolved into two clauses, thus, "if any one shall preach unto you any gospel other than that we preached unto you, let him be anathema; yea, though we
or an angel from heaven so preach, let him be anathema."
B285   Καὶ ἐάν introduces an extreme case (of a concessive clause), usually one
which is represented as highly improbable.

11   B13   The verb γνωρίζω is used as an aoristic present (cf. M7), "I want you to
know."

13   R885   Ἐδίωκον is not a conative imperfect (i.e., action begun, but interrupted). [Ed. It more probably has a progressive or iterative sense, such as
"I was persecuting."]
T191   There is no emphasis in the use of the possessive adjective here (ἐμήν is
equivalent to μοῦ, "my former conduct").

14   R633   Ὑπέρ carries the concept of "beyond" in harmony with the accusative case.
BD60(3)   In Paul's writings, περισσοτέρως seems to have a strong force equivalent to ὑπερβαλλόντως, "more exceedingly."

15   M73   The prepositional phrase ἐκ κοιλίας μητρός μου is used with a temporal
sense, "before I was born."

16   R587   The preposition ἐν with ἐμοί is used here with the resultant meaning
"in the case of." (The preposition ἐν with ἐμοί perhaps is used instead of
the simple dative. The use of ἐν may be due to the desire to make the phrase
parallel with ἐν τοῖς ἔθνεσιν—M76; it means "to me" or "in my case" ["in me"
i.e., "in my spirit" would be unnatural]—BD220[1]; "to me" denoting advantage
[perhaps "through me"]—T264). [Ed. In the N.T., ἐν may be used with a dative with the sense of a simple dative, as it appears to be used here, with the
meaning "to me." cf. 1 Cor. 14:11.]

18   M53   Πρός denotes position, "with."

22   R487   The dative τῷ προσώπῳ is used as an instrumental dative (the notion of
manner is expressed by the instrumental case—R530), "by face" or "by sight."
R888   Notice the periphrastic imperfects in vv. 22f., stressing durative action
(cf. M17 and B34; "I was still unknown . . ., they were only hearing").

23   R659   Only the context can determine whether μόνον is used as an adjective or
as an adverb (here it is an adverb, "only").
R892   The present participle διώκων is used to refer to action which is antecedent to the finite verb (a sort of imperfect participle). Both the participle and the verb have adverbs of time by way of contrast, "the one who former-
ly persecuted us."
R1147   The adverb ποτέ has the notion of "once upon a time."
BD134(2)   Feminine or neuter personal collective nouns standing in the plural

336

may be continued by a masculine plural: ἀκούοντες ἦσαν refers to ταῖς
ἐκκλησίαις in v. 22.

GALATIANS 2

1   R581 The preposition διά is used with the genitive here to refer to an inter-
    val of time ("fourteen years later"; διά seems to mean "after"--M56).

2   R988 Μή πως . . . ἔδραμον is a difficult construction (cf. 1 Thess. 3:5). One
    view is to take it as an indirect question. This is possible here, but not in
    1 Thess. 3:5. Even here there would be an ellipsis of a participle (ἔδραμον
    as an after thought in v. 2 has plenty of classical parallels--MT201), "or had
    run in vain").
    B227 Μή πως introduces an object clause of apprehension that is conceived of
    as already present or past (i.e., as a thing already decided, although the is-
    sue is at the time of speaking unknown, the indicative is used; τρέχω is a sub-
    junctive--BD370). [Ed. It appears more correct to consider τρέχω as indica-
    tive, thus making it parallel with the aorist indicative ἔδραμον; cf. 4:11
    and 1 Thess. 3:5.]
    M70 The prepositional phrase εἰς κενόν with the negative preceding means "to
    no purpose."
    MT193 In the purpose clause (if such it be) the desired response seems to be
    negative (μή), having the resultant meaning "can it be that I am running, or
    ran in vain?" Τρέχω would be subjunctive, since the sentence as it stands is
    felt as final. This interpretation as a whole has to reckon with the alterna-
    tive rendering "Am I running (said I), or have I run in vain?"--a decidedly
    simpler and more probable view. [Ed. Actually a final sense may be inherent
    in the object clause of apprehension here, which is similar to an indirect
    question.]

3   M102 The participle ὤν is ambiguous, as to whether it is used in a concessive
    or causal sense. Is it "although" or "because he was a Greek"? [Ed. The
    meaning of this participle cannot be determined on purely grammatical consid-
    erations, since Paul uses it for both a concessive and causal sense; cf. 1 Cor.
    9:19 and 1 Thess. 5:8. But here it has a causal meaning, since circumcision
    was a Jewish custom and Gentiles were not required to be circumcised (cf. Acts
    15:1 and 23ff).]
    BD448(6) Ἀλλ' οὐδὲ Τίτος is probably an afterthought -- "moreover even Titus
    was not . . ."; v. 3 fits better between vv. 6 and 7.

4   B199 The future indicative occurs in a pure final clause with ἵνα, "in order
    that they might enslave us."

5   M45 The use of the dative in τῇ ὑποταγῇ is difficult to determine; perhaps it
    means "yielded in subjection," i.e., "submissively" (cf. T220).
    M53 The prepositional phrase πρὸς ὥραν means "for an hour", denoting duration.

6   R438 The anacoluthon in Gal. 2:6 is noteworthy for the complete change of con-
    struction as shown by the repetition of οἱ δοκοῦντες in the nominative and
    followed by the middle instead of the passive voice. Observe the two parenthe-
    ses that led to the variation. It is easier in such a case to make a new start,

as Paul does here. In Gal. 2:5, Blass follows the manuscript of D in omitting οἷς in order to get rid of the anacoluthon, as he does also in Rom. 16:27
(ᾧ), but it is more than likely that the difficulty of the anacoluthon with
οἷς led to the omission in D (as an attempt to clarify the text).
R731 Ὁποῖος is used in an indirect question. Together with ποτε this pronoun
presents an indefinite concept, "whatever kind" (ποτε is not a separate word).
R743 As a predicate the pronoun τις may be emphatic (here it means "something
in particular").

7   R540 Πιστεύω means "entrust." [Ed. The retained accusative occurs here with
a passive verb, "entrusted with the gospel," cf. 1 Thess. 2:4.]
R546 Τουναντίον has a loose relation to the main verb and to every other part
of the sentence, "on the other hand."
TGr86 Τῆς ἀκροβυστίας is used as an indirect objective genitive. The complete
phrase then means, "the good news for the uncircumcision."

9   B217 The ἵνα clause defines the content of the agreement mentioned in the preceding portion of the sentence (it practically has the idea of "on condition
that"--R1000).
T37 There is some sort of emphasis in the use of ἡμεῖς here. [Ed. There is
am emphatic contrast between ἡμεῖς and αὐτοί.]

10   R723 Here there is the intensive use of αὐτό, but τοῦτο is pleonastic (i.e.,
a repetition after the relative; together they mean "which very thing").
R933 Ἵνα seems to be merely an introductory expletive with the volitive subjunctive (it appears to be imperatival, "only, we were to remember"--M144; cf.
T95; indirectly imperatival--M179). [Ed. In essence a similar conclusion is
arrived at whether ἵνα is considered imperatival or the subjunctive taken as
a volitive; ἵνα as imperatival is the more likely explanation.]
R960 The sense of the relative clause glides from mere explanation to ground or
reason (i.e., causal). [Ed. It is unnecessary to force unusual meaning from
a relative clause, when it may easily be taken as a mere explanation, "which
very thing."]

11   R608 The preposition is used in a local expression in κατὰ πρόσωπον, "to his
face."
T58 Καταγινώσκω means "stand condemned."

12   R579 One must not read too much into the preposition ἀπό; τινας ἀπὸ Ιακώβου
does not mean "with the authority of James," although they undoubtedly claimed
it (simply "from James").

13   R533 Τῇ ὑποκρίσει is used as a dative of means, "by their hypocrisy."
R1000 In the N.T. there are only two instances of the indicative with ὥστε as
a subordinate conjunction--here and in Jn. 3:16. This construction distinctly
accents the actual result. Blass on the flimsiest ground seeks to replace ὥστε
with ὅτι in John and include an infinitive here, so as to get rid of this construction entirely in the N.T. [Ed. In the revised edition (BD391[2]) it is
made clear that the infinitive variant has very little manuscript support.]
R1181 The second καί in this verse has the sense of "even" (climatic).
TGr144 The resultant idea is seen in the use of ὥστε with the indicative here.
St. Paul writes, "the other Jews dissembled likewise with Peter, so that even
Barnabas was carried away." Of most concern to him was a colleague's failure

to resist the Judaizers' deception. Quite subordinate to this is the cause,
which is stated by the main verb: "the other Jews dissembled likewise with
Peter."

14 R880 Ἀναγκάζεις is used as a conative present (an act begun but interrupted),
"how can you compel."
M53 Πρός is used in a transferred sense, thus the whole clause has the meaning,
"their conduct does not square with the truth" (alternatively, "they do not advance towards the truth").

15 R598 Ἐκ is used here for the idea of origin or source.
T220 Φύσει is used as a dative of respect (almost an adverb), especially since
there is contrast here (it is used as a dative of manner--R530). [Ed. The noun
φύσει has an adverbial sense denoting the manner by which they were Jews "by nature," i.e., "by birth."]

16 R752 When the οὐ . . . πᾶς construction occurs, the negative goes with the verb.
A negative statement is made as to πᾶς. the result is the same as if οὐδείς had
been used with an affirmative verb. The idea is "no flesh," not "not all flesh."
R796 In general when νόμος is anarthrous in Paul's writings, it refers to the
Mosaic Law, as in this verse.
R1025 The use of ἐὰν μή seems to be adversative instead of exceptive ("but only"
--MT241).

17 B177 The phrase μὴ γένοιτο is an optative of wishing which strongly deprecates
something suggested by a previous question or assertion. Here, as many times
elsewhere, it expresses the apostle's abhorrence of an inference which he fears
may be (falsely) drawn from his argument.
B242 The protasis here introduced by εἰ simply states a supposition which refers
to a particular case in the present, implying nothing as to its fulfillment,
"but if you are led by the Spirit, you are not under the Law."
M196 In vv. 17f., it is best to read ἄρα (not ἆρα) and a full stop (not a question mark), and to assign μὴ γένοιτο to the (imagined) St. Peter; St. Paul
will then continue to the effect: "You may repudiate the position with a μὴ
γένοιτο, but that is the position you logically place yourself in by your action; for . . ." (ἄρα is probably correct--R1176).
T330 The accent would be ἆρα here, since μὴ γένοιτο in Paul always answers a
question; it may, however, be ἄρα if the clause is not interrogative but an argu-
mentative statement posed for an imaginary opponent to answer, "then, consequently." [Ed. There appears to be no decisive reason to determine whether
ἄρα or ἆρα is to be read. Ἆρα, which is an interrogative particle, may imply
an illative notion, while ἄρα, an illative particle, may imply an element of
interrogation. But the fact that Paul uses ἆρα 27 times and ἄρα only in this
instance may indicate that even in this instance ἄρα should be read.]

18 M35 The accusative παραβάτην is used predicatively (i.e., to predicate something of a noun already in the accusative). Thus the last part of this verse
should be translated, "I constitute myself a transgressor."
T115 Εἰ is used with the present indicative here to refer to an actual incident.

19 R539 θεῷ is used as a dative of advantage, "for God."
R796 Anarthrous νόμος apparently refers to the Mosaic Law (cf. v. 16).

20 R632 The preposition ὑπέρ conveys the notion "instead of."
    M131 Adverbial relative clauses are difficult to analyze or define with pre-
    cision. In Gal. 2:20, the interpretation is not very obvious: the A.V. and
    the R.V. translations take it as cognate--"the (that) life which I now live";
    but it could be "whereas I now live, I live . ."(ὅ νῦν may be equal to "in
    that" [adverbial accusative]--R479).
    TGr120 When Paul claims no longer to "live independently" but that Christ lives
    in him (Gal. 2:20), this is strangely like what the accredited mystic asserts
    when he becomes God and God is identified with him.

GALATIANS 3

1   R608 Κατά is used in a local expression "before" (cf. the phrase κατὰ πρόσωπον
    in Acts 25:16 and 2 Cor. 10:1).
    R1193 There is usually some vehemence or urgency when ὧ is used (anger is in-
    dicated here--T33).

2   M158 The second part of this verse should be translated "was it by performing
    the law that you received the Spirit, or by hearing and trusting?" (Here the
    context makes it clear enough what answer is expected, but not the form of the
    sentence itself.)
    M175 Ἐξ ἀκοῆς πίστεως (in vv. 2 and 5) evidently means "hearing and believing"
    (i.e., a sort of hearing which issues in belief).
    MT117 Μανθάνω here simply has the meaning "ascertain."

3   M90 In ἐναρξάμενοι πνεύματι the force of ἐν is sufficiently strong to be fol-
    lowed by another simple dative in conjunction with a fresh verb without a rele-
    vant preposition repeated, "having begun with the Spirit, are you now ending
    with the flesh."

7   T208 The genitive of quality is understood here, "children of Abraham."
    T260 The articular phrase οἱ ἐκ πίστεως means "those who share Abraham's faith."

8   M24 n.2 There is some ambiguity in the use of the passive voice here (ἐνευλογη-
    θήσονται). The Septuagint has the passive, but the original probably meant not
    "shall be blessed" but "shall bless themselves."
    T260 The use of ἐκ may be instrumental, meaning "by means of faith."

9   M144 Ὥστε seems to be simply an inferential particle meaning "and so, accord-
    ingly."

10 R720 Πᾶς ὅς becomes a substantive rather than an adjective clause ("anyone" no
    matter who--R744).
    R1088 Τοῦ with the infinitive ποιῆσαι is used to show purpose. This idiom is
    used frequently in the O.T. (note the quotation here) but seldom in Paul's writ-
    ings.
    T260 The concept of "by" works is used here (ἐκ; the preposition conveys the
    notion of cause or occasion--R598).

13 R631 In v. 10, Paul said that those under the law were under a curse (ὑπὸ
    κατάραν). In v. 13, he carries on the same image. Christ bought us "out from

under" (ἐκ . . .) the curse of the law by becoming a curse "over" (ὑπέρ) us.
In a word, we were under the curse; Christ took the curse on Himself and thus
over us (between the suspended curse and us) and thus rescued us out from under
the curse. We went free while He was considered accursed (v. 13). In this
passage ὑπέρ has the resultant meaning of "instead" (generally one who acts on
behalf of [ὑπέρ] another, takes his place [equivalent to ἀντί]--M64).

14 M176 Τὴν ἐπαγγελίαν τοῦ πνεύματος is equivalent to "the promised spirit" (and
so, curiously enough, equivalent to the reverse phrase in Eph. 1:13).
T253 The preposition εἰς may occur here as a substitute for the dative (or genitive), unless εἰς means "among." [Ed. Generally when εἰς has the sense of
"among," it occurs with verbs of motion, which result in movement or include
a movement of the body. Here, it seems to have the meaning "upon, on" or "to."
The preposition εἰς may have been used to portray the idea of goal.]

15 M59 Κατά is used in a transferred sense (i.e., "according to, by virtue of,
in respect of"); κατὰ ἄνθρωπον λέγω means "I am using a human analogy, I am
speaking like a man."
T337 Ὅμως . . . οὐδείς means "it may be only a man's will, nevertheless no
one" (a transfer occurs before οὐδείς; ὅμως means "even though only"--BD450[2]).

16 R604 The idea of basis naturally results from ἐπὶ πολλῶν. [Ed. Actually this
preposition has the notion of "in respect to."]
T158 Ὡς with the understood adverbial participle here expresses a subjective
motive (cf. BD425[4]), "as referring to many."

17 R580 A διαθήκη is an arrangement or covenant between two individuals (note the
root idea of διά).
R1072 Εἰς τό with the infinitive καταργῆσαι seems to express conceived or actual
result ("to such a degree that"--T143).

18 R583 In the use of διά here, both the notion of means and that of manner merge
into one concept, "by promise."
M15 An interesting use of the perfect tense is a perfect of allegory, which
appears several times in the N.T. when the O.T. is being expounded. It was as
though this type of Christian interpretation viewed the O.T. narrative as contemporary, and could therefore say "such-and-such an incident has happened"
(as with κεχάρισται here).

19 M57 Διά with the genitive here portrays an instrumental sense, "by means of."
M184 The phrase ἐν χειρί is a pure Hebraism for "by means of, by the agency of,"
and should not be translated into English by any phrase containing the word
"hand."
T58 Many transitive deponent verbs may be used with a passive sense, as ἐπήγγελ-
ται here, "for whom the promise was intended."

22 T21 The neuter gender (τὰ πάντα) may refer to a person, provided that the emphasis is less on the individual than on some outstanding general quality (the
reference here is more general than that in τοὺς πάντας of Rom. 11:32--BD138[1]).
[Ed. The neuter adjective τὰ πάντα refers to people because of Paul's argument
in the context (cf. v. 10) and the following verse.]

23 M169f. Both Rom. 8:18 and Gal. 3:23 show a curious order of words in nearly i-
dentical clauses (where one would expect εἰς τὴν πίστιν τὴν μέλλουσαν; "unto the

faith that is about to be revealed").

24 M144 "Ωστε seems to be simply an inferential particle meaning "and so, accord-
       ingly" (cf. 3:9).

25 M66 'Υπό is used with the accusative to denote rest beneath. Thus the second
       segment of this verse means "we are no longer subject to a tutor-slave."

                                    GALATIANS 4

4   R820 The agent is expressed by ἐκ, "by a woman."
    M66 In both v. 4 and v. 5, ὑπὸ νόμον means "beneath law."

5   R960 "Ινα appears to occur where a relative pronoun may have been used. [Ed.
       The usual purpose sense of ἵνα seems to fit quite well in both clauses of this
       verse.]

6   R441 In vv. 6f, Paul changes from the plural ἐστέ to the singular εἶ for the
       sake of variety.
    M147 The ὅτι clause does not mean "because you are sons, God sent . . .," but
       (proof) "that you are sons (is the fact that) God sent . . ." The context
       clearly favors this sense (ὅτι means "that" rather than "because").

7   M144 "Ωστε appears to be used as a simple inferential particle meaning "and so,
       accordingly" (cf. 3:9).

8   BD430(3) The use of οὐ with the participle εἰδότες is classical in style (a
       distinction is drawn between the use of οὐ and μή with the participle--R1172;
       a participle not conditional in force occasionally takes οὐ--B485). [Ed. The
       fact that this verse is in sharp contrast to the following verse may account
       for the use of οὐ here (i.e., similar to the formal contrast pattern οὐ . . .
       ἀλλά, thus there may not be any exegetical significance in the use of οὐ). But
       it seems quite probable that Paul is emphasizing that previously the Galatians
       were not at all personally acquainted with the only true God. Paul changes
       from οὐ with the participle to μή with the participle not to indicate some spe-
       cial nuance, but for reasons of usage (i.e., μή is used with articular partici-
       ples in N.T. Greek, and μή is the more common negative used with participles in
       the N.T. regardless of how definite the negation is).]

9   R879 The present tense of ἐπιστρέφετε portrays a descriptive sense (i.e., con-
       tinuous), "how can you turn."
    BD495(3) The correction intensifies what has been said in γνόντες . . . γνωσθέν-
       τες.

10 R613 Παρά in the compound verb παρατηρέω has a perfective sense, "watch care-
       fully."
    R810 The indirect middle is used with παρατήρεισθε, "observe for yourselves"
       (the middle occurs where one expects the active ["observe scrupulously"]--
       T55). [Ed. When a middle verb may be translated with valid meaning as such
       (as in this instance), it is best not to translate it by using another voice.]

                                        342

11 B227 This verse should be translated "I am afraid I have perhaps bestowed labor
     upon you in vain" (μὴ πως introduces an object clause of apprehension, cf. 2:2).
     T325 The object is brought forward in the sentence (prolepsis--the anticipation
     of the object of the subordinate clause by making it the object of the main
     clause; ὑμᾶς has the sense "for you"--BD476[3]).

13 TGr90 The expression τὸ πρότερον was more likely to have been intended by the
     apostle as an elative superlative rather than a true comparative, thus it has
     the resultant meaning "originally," "at the very first" (but the true compara-
     tive sense is possible, "the first time"--T30; it has the meaning "formerly"--
     M98). [Ed. Τὸ πρότερον appears to have an adverbial sense, "formerly"; cf.
     1 Tim. 1:13.]
     M106 The prepositional phrase with διά means "because of an illness."

16 M144 Ὥστε is used as an inferential particle meaning "and so, accordingly"
     (cf. 3:9).

17 T194 In the last clause of this verse, αὐτούς is equivalent to αὐτοὺς αὐτούς
     meaning "the men themselves" (cf. 1 Cor. 5:13; but the pronoun αὐτός is not
     repeated in the N.T.).

18 R1162 Οὐ is the negative always used with μόνον except here (the negative
     actually negates the infinitive--B481), "not only when I am present."
     M25 Amid much uncertainty in vv. 17f., the folowing paraphrastic interpretation
     may be suggested, making ζηλοῦσθαι passive. "The Judaizers are zealously cul-
     tivating you (showing solicitous concern for you as evangelists over converts),
     but their motives are unworthy: they want to make you feel excluded whenever
     you do not come into their circle of elite ritualists, so that you may emulate
     them (a slightly different sense of ζηλόω from the first). But (returning to
     the first sense, but in the passive) what is really good is to be zealously
     cultivated in a worthy cause; and that is the condition I want you to be in
     always, and not only while I am with you to keep you on the right lines . . ."
     T145 Ἐν τῷ with the infinitive is used in a causal sense (semitic--H450; the
     temporal and causal sense are similiar here, "while," or "because I am with you").

19 R713 The relative pronoun οὕς has the gender according to sense rather than
     grammatical (it is preceded by both ὑμᾶς and τεκνία; i.e., the masculine gender
     is used to refer to persons).

20 R886 The imperfect is used with θέλω portraying the meaning, "I was just on the
     point of wishing." Paul uses this particular expression to refer to the present,
     making the statement a polite idiom. (Paul could change his tone because he
     loved the Galatians even when they had been led astray--R1199; the impossibili-
     ty of realizing the wish is denoted--B33).
     T56 The middle ἀπορούμαι is active with an intransitive sense "be in doubt."

23 M15 Γεγέννηται is used as a perfect of allegory (cf. 3:18; this event still re-
     tains its exemplary meaning--BD342[5]).

24 T187 Μία μέν means "the first."

25 R411 The neuter article τό with Ἀγάρ agrees with the word Hagar, not the gen-
     der of the person.

R760 Ἰερουσαλήμ does not have the article, except when an adjective is used (vv. 25f.; actually an adverb [νῦν] is used as an adjective).

27 BD43(3) The use of οὐ with the participles is a Hebraism (Septuagintalism here, note the quotation) consequently there is no special significance in meaning with the use of οὐ here.
MT127 Ἡ τίκτουσα is common in tragedy as a practical synonym of ἡ μήτηρ ("the mother"), the title of a continuous relationship.

28 R1379 Κατά with the accusative is used in the sense of "like" (standard).

GALATIANS 5

1 M44n.2 Τῇ ἐλευθερίᾳ . . . ἠλευθέρωσεν seems to be an emphatic use of the dative (if this is the correct reading), not strictly instrumental (a semitism; this construction is derived from the Hebrew infinitive absolute--T242), "Christ completely freed us."
MT125 The present tense of the prohibition here is used in a conative sense (i.e., an action which implies the possibility of its failure to reach an end), "try not to be loaded down again with the yoke of slavery."

2 MT162 The passive idea in περιτέμνησθε is "allow," or "let oneself be."

3 R1062 The infinitive construction ὀφειλέτης . . . ποιῆσαι means "debtor for doing" ("a debtor to do"--B379).
B124 Παντὶ ἀνθρώπῳ περιτεμνομένῳ (cf. 6:13) does not mean, "to every man that desires to be circumcised" (nor is it equivalent to a perfect "every circumcised man"), but, "to every man that is circumcised," that is, "that receives circumcision" (R.V. correctly translates although not literally). The apostle is not speaking of circumcision as an accomplished fact, but of becoming circumcised.

4 R880 Δικαιοῦσθε is used as a conative present (cf. 2:14; "try to get justified" --M8).
R960 Οἵτινες introduces an argument (the notion of ground or reason is present).
T74 The proleptic aorist looks like a future, taking place after some actual or implied condition. In this verse the construction means "if you are going to be justified by the law," κατηργήθητε ἀπὸ Χριστοῦ, "you will be severed from Christ" (cf. 1 Cor. 7:28; cf. BD333[2]).

5 M44 The dative πνεύματι is used in an instrumental sense, "through the Spirit."
T214 Δικαιοσύνης may be either an appositional genitive ("the thing hoped for, which is righteousness") or a subjective genitive ("the thing which the righteous hope for"). [Ed. The latter suggestion forces an unusual sense from δικαιοσύνης. It appears that this noun is used as an appositional (or possibly objective) genitive, portraying the righteousness as the object of both hope and expectation.]

6 R583 Διά is used here with both the notion of means and of manner merging into one concept, "by love."
M26 It seems most probable to translate the participle ἐνεργουμένη not as a passive ("faith operated by love") but as an active ("operating") or with some mid-

dle nuance of the same ("faith now operates showing love"--TGr111; cf. Rom. 7:5).

7   R1094 With verbs of hindering and denying the negative μή is not necessary (i.e., with the following infinitive), but it may be used as a redundant negative repeating the negative notion of the verb, just as double negatives carried on the force of the first negative, "who hindered you from obeying the truth?"
    BD488 The last part of v. 7 and all of v. 8 should be translated as follows: "obey no one in such a way as to disobey the truth; that (sort of) obedience is not from him who calls you" (πεισμονή here means "obedience, acquiescence", and takes up πείθεσθαι again--which would correspond well to the Pauline style).

10 R746   Oὐδὲν ἄλλο means "nothing else."

11 BD372(3) Eἰ is encroaching upon the sphere of ἐάν in the N.T., "assuming that I preach."

12 R809 The middle verb ἀποκόψονται is causative, "have themselves castrated" (the middle voice here is used in the sense of "to let oneself be . . ;" "get themselves emasculated"--BD317).
    R940 Ὄφελον with the future indicative occurs for a future wish (cf. B27; BD 384), "wish that."
    MT201 There is one example of ὄφελον with the future in the N.T. (Gal. 5:12); the associations of the particle help to mark an expression never meant to be taken seriously. [Ed. Καί is used in the wish clause with ὄφελον meaning "I would that." There is no indication here that the wish is not to be taken seriously.]

13 M50 Ἐπ' ἐλευθερίᾳ ἐκλήθητε should be translated "you were called to (or "with a view to") freedom," cf. 1 Thess. 4:7; Eph. 2:10 (denoting aim or purpose--R605; purpose, result--BD235[4]).

14 R419 In ὁ πᾶσ νόμος the first word carries the emphasis, "the totality of the law."
    R766 The article τῷ introduces the quotation (and should not be translated).
    R874 Ἀγαπήσεις is used as a volitive future (chiefly found in quotations from the O.T.), "you shall love."

15 M152 There are two instances in the N.T. of conditional clauses which are perfectly correct in grammatical form, but which are logically inconsequent, as it would seem (Gal. 5:15; Jas. 3:14). In both instances the imperative clause remains valid whether or not the condition in the protasis is fulfilled. Logically, the imperative clauses should be future indicative clauses, "if you go on like this, you will . . ."
    MT124 In v. 15, "take heed lest" can hardly be considered as a prohibition.

16 R834 Τελέσητε is used as a constative aorist (the constative aorist treats an act as punctiliar which is not in itself point-action; cf. MT118 and 130), "do not fulfill."
    M44 Πνεύματι is used as an instrumental dative, "by the Spirit."
    T75 The present imperative has the meaning, "go on walking."

17 R998 Ἵνα is used with consecutive force (cf. M142; MT249; ἵνα expresses the
        purpose of the hostility of the flesh and the Spirit--B222). [Ed. Perhaps
        ἵνα is used to portray a potential result. Many times in the New Testament,
        purpose and result cannot be differentiated (cf. Rom. 5:20), "that you can not."]

18 M44 Πνεύματι is used as an instrumental dative here and in v. 25 (it denotes
        the agent--T240), "led by the Spirit."

                                    GALATIANS 6

1   R439 The variation from καταρτίζετε to σκοπῶν is a natural singling out of the
        individual in the application.
        B206 Μή is used to introduce an object clause after σκοπῶν, "look to yourself,
        that you not . . ."
        B285 Καὶ ἐάν introduces an extreme concessive clause, one which is represented
        as highly improbable, "even if" (cf. 1:2).

3   R1127 It is difficult to classify the participle ὤν. It makes sense either as
        temporal, causal or modal. [Ed. Actually the participle appears to have a
        concessive sense. Μηδὲν ὤν portrays a situation which is contrary to the con-
        dition expressed in the previous clause, "although he is nothing."]
        R1173 In this verse there is a sharp contrast between τι and μηδέν (both neuter
        abstracts referring to a person; "something . . . nothing").
        BD131 The use of the pronominal predicate gives the sense of "he gives the
        appearance of being something" (εἶναί τι means "something special"--BD301[1]).

4   M70 Note the use of εἰς in this verse (Moffatt translates it as "on his own
        account . . . in comparison with"; cf. the use of πρός as meaning "compared
        with").
        T190 The reflexive pronoun ἑαυτοῦ is used as an emphatic possessive pronoun
        in vv. 4 and 8, "his own work."

5   R692 Ἴδιον is used with an emphatic sense, "his own" (cf. MT90).

9   M110f. It is possible that the neuter article introduces a familiar proverbial
        phrase, and that the sentence means something like this: "And (there is) the
        saying: Let us not grow tired . . ."; alternatively, the article simply goes
        with καλόν, a generic sense--"what is good." However, it must be admitted
        that it may have been a sheer idiosyncrasy of Paul's to use the neuter article
        in that way (cf. Rom. 8:26).
        T285 In classical Greek μὴ ἐκλυόμενοι would have been conditional ("if we do
        not faint"), but in the Pauline Corpus it is intended as a fact, "since . . ."
        (the participle has a conditional sense--R1023 and B436). [Ed. The conditional
        clause seems to be the most appropriate rendering of μὴ ἐκλυόμενοι. Conse-
        quently, the rewards of a Christian are conditional upon his persistence in
        doing good (cf. Lk. 6:35, 1 Cor. 3:8). In response to Nigel Turner, μή can
        be used with a participle that expresses a conditional clause (in Paul's
        writings--2 Cor. 4:18; in Peter's writings--1 Pet. 3:6).]

10 R968 Ὡς is used in a temporal sense ("now while"--BD455[2]).
        T14 Τὸ ἀγαθόν means "good works" (generic use of the article).

11 R741 Πηλικοις represents the size of the letters, "how large."

M12n.1 The epistolary aorist makes a difference in exegesis; the ἔγραψα the
R.V. translation renders "See how large letters I have written . . .," but the
R.V. margin substitutes "write" for "have written," which means that the apostle here takes the pen from the amanuensis, writing the closing paragraph himself in a notably larger hand.

TGr94 Ἔγραψα is not an epistolary aorist but a true past tense. Thus, it
should be seriously questioned whether Paul did use any kind of secretary at
all when he wrote to the Galatians (it is used as an epistolary aorist--R846;
it may be either--T73). [Ed. Ἔγραψα appears to be used as an epistolary
aorist. The paragraph contained within vv. 11-16 reiterates certain of the
main points of the letter, signifying that Paul takes the pen himself to emphasize certain points; cf. Rom. 16:22; 1 Cor. 16:21; Col. 4:18 and 2 Thess.
3:17.]

H8 Professor Deissmann's brilliant work, St. Paul, seems to miss the mark altogether in describing Paul as a working man, largely on the strength of his big
clumsy handwriting inferred from Gal. 6:11. If this interpretation of πηλικοις
γράμμασιν be conceded, such writing does not nowadays imply illiteracy, and we
have no evidence that it did in Paul's day.

12 R532 The dative σταυρῷ may be used to express the idea of cause, motive or
occasion. This notion of ground wavers between the idea of association and
means ("to avoid persecution for the cross"--M45).

R880 The present tense in ἀωαγκάζουσιν has a conative sense (cf. 2:14; "try to
compel"--T63).

13 M107 The articular participle οἱ περιτεμνόμενοι is used as a noun and means
"for not even the very ones who get circumcised keep the law," whereas, if the
article had been omitted, it would have been adverbial, and the sense would
have been "for not even when they get circumcised do they keep the law themselves."

14 R1003 The use of the optative for a future wish like μη γένοιτο is not a subordinate construction, but a co-ordinate one (it strongly deprecates something
suggested--B177), "may I never."

16 R1381 The future verb στοιχήσουσιν has a continuous sense, "all who walk."

17 R495 The temporal use of the genitive τοῦ λοιποῦ implies nothing as to the duration of time, but has the meaning "henceforth, finally, for the rest" (cf.
T235).

Ephesians

1   R582 Διά is used with the sense of agency, "by the will of God" (διά is also used in this way in v. 5).
M108 Τοῖς . . . πιστοῖς ἐν Χριστῷ means "those believing in Christ" rather than simply "believing Christ."

6   T218 Εἰς ἔπαινον δόξης is to be taken very closely together, as in Ph. 1:11, "for the praise of his glory" (it is cumbersome--BD168[2]).

9   B139 The aorist participle γνωρίσας is used to refer to action identical with that of the main verb ἐπερίσσευσεν, "which he granted to you richly . . ., making known . . ."

10   T271 Ἐπί with the dative as local is not easy to distinguish from ἐπί with the accusative meaning "before" or "upon" (cf. MT107; the change of case here is merely a stylistic variation--M49).

13   M175 Τῷ πνεύματι τῆς ἐπαγγελίας means "the promised Spirit."
MT67n.2 In Eph. 1:13 the second ἐν ᾧ is assimilated to the first, and its sense is determined by ἐσφραγίσθητε (cf. R453), "in whom you also . . . were sealed."

14   T215 The genitive here (εἰς . . . περιποιήσεως) is either appositional, with the meaning "till our redemption which is our possession," or objective, with the meaning "till the redemption of those whom God has acquired" (interpreting the abstract noun by a concrete noun). [Ed. It is unusual for περιποίησις to have this concrete sense. Consequently, the former suggestion seems preferable.]

15   T263 The preposition in πίστιν ἐν means "in the sphere of."
BD224(1) The use of κατά as a circumlocution for the possessive or subjective genitive is generally Hellenistic. It is virtually limited to pronouns in the N.T. (Καθ' ὑμᾶς πίστιν is more than a mere circumlocution for the genitive here--R608). [Ed. The preposition κατά appears to be used as a possessive genitive, the possessive article in the following parallel phrase tends to support this, "your faith."]

17   MT196 If ἵνα δώῃ is to be read, it will have to be a virtual wish clause, ἵνα serving merely to link it to the previous verb, but δώῃ is preferable (a subjunctive purpose clause; cf. T128), "that God . . . may give."

22   R1206 The greatest metaphor in the N.T. is Paul's use of σῶμα for the church (as in this verse).

23   M25 The A.V. and R.V. translations both take πληρουμένου in this verse as mid-

dle with an active sense: "him that filleth all in all." J. Robinson takes
it as passive: "him that all in all is being fulfilled (to St. Paul's mind
the Christ in a true sense still waited for completion, and would find that
completion only in the Church). W. L. Knox also takes it as passive, but refers it to the "filling of Christ, not by the growth of his body, the Church,
but by God: "him who is always being filled by God." Dibelius questions whether the phrase may not imply both these latter senses. It is possible, though
this is strenuously denied, eg. by T. K. Abott (I.C.C. in location), that το
πλήρωμα itself may be in apposition, not with the Church, but with Christ. It
will then be right to take πληρουμένου as active in sense and as designating
God, of whom Christ (as elsewhere in the Epistles) is spoken of as the πλήρωμα
(cf. R806).

M160   Τὰ πάντα ἐν πᾶσιν appears to be simply an adverbial elative, meaning
"wholly and entirely," "absolutely" like παντάπασι in Classical Greek.

EPHESIANS 2

3   R530   The dative φύσει has the notion of manner, "by nature."
    M174   The semitic adjectival genitive τέκνα φύσει οργῆς perhaps means "left to
    ourselves (φύσει) we are destined to suffer the consequences of sin."
    T28   θελήματα is the poetical plural for an abstract subject used in a classic-
    al way, "that which is wished."

4   R833   The constative aorist ἠγάπησεν is used to simply portray an action which
    in reality may not be punctiliar, "with which he loved us."

5   M44   Χάριτι is used as an instrumental dative, with the meaning "for by favor
    you are saved."
    T176   Translators do not trouble to distinguish τῇ χάριτι in Eph. 2:8 from
    χάριτι in 2:5 (the N. E. B. has "by his grace" both times): it may be that
    τῇ is merely anaphoric, looking back to v. 5, but there is another point of
    view: omission of the article tends to emphasize the inherent qualities of ab-
    stract nouns while the article makes them more concrete, unified and individual.
    In v. 8, then, the reference is to God's historical act of saving grace; in v.
    5, to grace as such, in contrast to other means of redemption.   The difficulty
    therefore is not to account for the presence of the article, just as with con-
    crete nouns, the problem is rather to account for its absence. [Ed. Turner
    cites Zerwick for support, but actually Zerwick states that the presence of
    the article requires special attention rather than the omission of the article.
    The most simplistic explanation appears to be that the article points to pre-
    vious reference (that of v. 5).]
    BD258(2)   The article is often lacking with abstract nouns. The more abstract
    the sense in which the noun is used, the less likely it is to take any other
    than the generic article: hence in some instances the problem is rather to
    account for the presence of the article than its absence. In v. 5 it is "grace
    which has saved you," but in v. 8 it means "the grace previously mentioned
    (well known?) has delivered you to faith's way."
    MT127   Ἐστε σεσωμένοι refers to a work which is finished by its author's per-
    spective, but progressively realized by its objects.

8   R704   In this verse, there is no reference to πίστεως in the pronoun τοῦτο,

349

but rather to the idea of salvation in the clause before.

M18f. It is not always easy to see the force of the distinction between the simple and the periphrastic perfect. For example, would the sense be altered if, for χάριτί ἐστε σεσωσμένοι, χάριτί σέσωσθε had been written? Perhaps the answer is that this too is an instance where the participle has little or no time significance and is practically adjectival--"as a result of free favor you are safe;" but nevertheless, "you have been saved and therefore enjoy your present status" makes good sense (cf. the comment in v. 5).

T45 Καὶ τοῦτο means "and indeed" (καί is emphatic with the demonstrative pronoun here--BD442[9]).

10 R505 The preposition ἐπί has the idea of aim or purpose in this verse, "for good works."

R681 The position of αὐτοῦ is emphatic, "we are his workmanship" (not our own).

12 M41 The genitive of separation occurs in ἀπηλλοτριωμένοι . . . meaning "estranged from the citizenship of Israel."

13 M206 The present participle ὄντες refers to what precedes the main verb, with a durative sense, "you who once were."

14 R498 Τοῦ φραγμοῦ is used as a genitive of apposition or definition, "the barrier formed by the dividing wall."

T242 Ἐν with the dative is used as a dative of attendant circumstance, or even instrumental, i.e., take the phrase closely with the verb implied in χειρόγραφον, "written in."

15 T265 Ἐν δόγμασιν means "consisting in ordinances."

16 T43 Ἐν αὐτῷ means either "by himself" or "by it," i.e., the cross. [Ed. The nearest in proximity and the most probable antecedent of αὐτῷ is τοῦ σταυροῦ, thus making διά parallel with ἐν, "by it."]

20 M110 In ἐπὶ . . . προφητῶν, interpretations include: (1) the apostles and the (O.T.) prophets (two separate groups); (2) the (N.T.) apostles and prophets (two separate groups); (3) the apostles who are also prophets (the one in apposition with the other). The latter (cf. Hort's suggestion in The Christian Ecclesia, p. 165) seems unlikely, considering the ambiguity of the Greek which it implies and the question whether the two were in fact identified. The other two are both possible, and I doubt if T.K. Abbott (I.C.C., in location) is right in saying that the absence of the article before προφητῶν is against their being O.T. prophets (the two groups are treated as one--R787). [Ed. When an article is not repeated in a series, the groups connected are not necessarily one but they may be treated as one. Consequently, in this verse the two groups are distinct but both are considered as N.T. people; cf. the similar formula in 3:5.]

21 M94 Lightfoot thinks that πᾶσα οἰκοδομή does not mean "the whole building" but "every building," adducing συνοικοδομεῖσθε to show that many οἰκοδομαί are required to make up one temple (anarthrous πᾶς [S[a], A, C, and P have the article] probably does not mean as in classical Greek "whatever is built," but [under semitic influence] "the whole building"--T200; it probably means "every build-

ing" because of the following εἰς ναόν--R772). [Ed. Generally the sense of
the anarthrous πᾶς is "every," which is very probable here.]

EPHESIANS 3

1   M198 Does τούτου χάριν refer forward or backward? A study of the author's
    style may be the only clue. [Ed. Paul uses this construction three times in
    the N.T.; Eph. 3:1, 14 and Tit. 1:5. Here it seems to refer to the preceding
    argument.]

3   R845 In καθὼς προέγραψα ἐν ὀλίγῳ the allusion may be to what Paul has just
    written or to the whole epistle. [Ed. In this context it appears to refer
    to what has just been written, especially since he has explained at some
    length the mystery that was made known to him.]

4   M117 Νοῆσαι may be a constative aorist, "understand," or it may be ingressive,
    "realize." [Ed. The former may be the most probable, because Paul did not
    write so that the recipients would realize the burdensome revelation made known
    to him, but so that they might understand the mystery.]

5   R787 The two groups ἀποστόλοις and προφήταις are treated as one, since the ar-
    ticle is not repeated (cf. 2:20).

6   M61n.3 Συμμέτοχος occurs with the sense of "co-participant."

8   R663 The occurrence of ἐλαχιστοτέρῳ is due to the fading of the force of the
    comparative suffix and the desire for emphasis (this adjective means "less
    than the least"--M98). [Ed. Moule's suggestion seems more probable because
    it portrays a simple, literal sense of the adjective.]

12 R784 Ἐν πεποιθήσει is predicative rather than attributive (i.e., to be taken
    with ἔχομεν rather than with προσαγωγήν), "in whom we have . . . with confi-
    dence."
    T263 Αὐτοῦ is used as an objective genitive, with the resultant meaning "through
    faith in him."

13 R728 Ἥτις is used with a causal sense.

14 R435 Τούτου χάριν shows the resumption after the long digression in vv. 1-13.
    This construction is not, however, a technical parenthesis.
    B203 Κάμπτω τὰ γόνατά is a paraphrase for προσεύχομαι. The conjunction ἵνα is
    used in v. 16 to denote the content of the prayer ("I pray . . . that").

15 M94 Does πᾶς with an anarthrous noun invariably mean "every," or can it mean
    "the whole, the entire?" It was formerly claimed that it meant "every" and
    not "the whole." Πᾶσα πατριά is not to be translated "the whole family" (A.V.)
    but "every family" (R.V.) raising interesting speculations as to angelic or
    demonic families or tribes in heaven (cf. 2:21).

16 R593 Εἰς is used in a pregnant sense for ἐν, "in" (cf. T256).
    M175 The adjectival genitive may have a semitic sense. Does τὸ πλοῦτος τῆς

δόξης αὐτοῦ mean "his wealth of glory" (so Goodspeeds's translation) or "glorious wealth." [Ed. The principle to keep in mind is that it is incorrect to claim a semitic genitive where a good Greek genitive makes better sense. In view of this and the similar construction in 1:7, the best translation seems to be, "the wealth of his glory."]

17 R1090 The infinitives κραταιωθῆναι and κατοικῆσαι are used with the notion of result (hypothetical here), "that he may."
TGr166 The participles are used as imperatives, meaning "(be ye) rooted and grounded in love."

18 T55 Καταλαμβάνω appears in the middle voice where one expects the active, since it has a transitive sense, "apprehend" (mentally).
H310 Ἐξισχύω with the infinitive is a striking perfective, "be strong enough" to apprehend, a strength exerted till its object is attained.

19 R519 The comparative idea is predominant in γνώσεως, "which surpasses knowledge."

20 M26 The meaning of the voice used in κατα την δύναμιν την ἐνεργουμένην ἐν ἡμῖν is, in itself, ambiguous. [Ed. Paul uses ἐνεργουμένην with a middle sense, meaning "operative" or "effective"; cf. Gal. 5:6.]
M42 Ὑπερεκπερισσοῦ ὧν means "exceedingly much more than" and is an adverb of comparison (although here the preceding ὑπερ πάντα ποιῆσαι confuses the construction: is πάντα a direct object of ποιῆσαι and ὑπέρ an adverb, reiterated by ὑπερεκπερισσοῦ? Or is ὑπέρ a preposition governing πάντα, and ὧν a grammatical laxity for ἅ, perhaps partly suggested by the idea of comparison with its genitive association? [Ed. In the N.T., ὑπέρ is seldom used as an adverb. Also, since ὑπέρ is so closely connected to the accusative πάντα, it would be unusual to translate ὑπέρ as an adverb. In addition to these factors, attraction of the relative pronoun occurs frequently in the N.T. Consequently, the latter suggestion seems more probable.]

EPHESIANS 4

1 TGr121 St. Paul describes himself in Eph. 4:1 as "the prisoner in the Lord" (A.V.). He lived in Christ, in hope, in consecration, in peace. They are spheres or atmospheres, air, which the Christian breathes. St. Paul is precise in his use of prepositions where the finer points of theology are at stake (ἐν κυρίῳ is attributive to ὁ δέσμιος; cf. R783).
BD337(1) The exhortation in the aorist tense is used to express the coming about of conduct which contrasts with prior conduct (ingressive, "I exhort . . . to walk").

2 R807 In ἀνεχόμενοι ἀλλήλων the direct middle voice is used, "holding yourselves back from one another."
R946 The participle ἀνεχόμενοι is used as an imperative. ("be ye forgiving towards one another"--TGr166; the participle is used as an imperative [although the participle may depend on the verb immediately before it]--T343; this participle and σπουδάζοντες in v. 3 are used as imperatives--BD468[2]; cf. MT181). [Ed. The participles seem to gain their imperatival sense from the preceding

verb of exhortation (in v. 1).]

4   T263 'Εν is used with a sense similar to εἰς, meaning "into."

6   R567 The variation of the preposition is a skillful way of condensing thought,
    each preposition adding a new idea. Paul is especially fond of this idiom,
    "over all and through all and in all."

9   TGr171 The obscure cosmogony in Eph. 4:9 has the comparative adjective κατώ-
    τερα followed by γῆς, which should be interpreted as "the lower parts than the
    earth" (like the margin of N.E.B.) rather than the "the lowest level of the
    earth" (τῆς γῆς may be partitive, or appositive, "the lower regions, that is,
    the earth:--T215; τῆς γῆς is a genitve of content, with the meaning "the re-
    gions under the earth"--BD167). [Ed. It seems preferable to take τῆς γῆς as
    a comparative genitive, because it follows a comparative adjective.]
    T182 Τό introduces a proverbial phrase (used as a relative pronoun--R735),
    "what."

10 R647 'Υπέρ -- ἄνω is a simple compound that in the late Greek gradually
    displaced ὑπέρ. Here it occurs literally of place, "above."
    T25 םִיַמָשׁ is behind οὐρανοῦ: but here again, following a Jewish idea, the plu-
    ral of seven heavens may be intended, especially in 2 Cor. 12:2 and Eph. 4:10.
    In the material sense of the sky the singular predominates.
    T55 Some verbs appear in the middle where one expects the active, since they
    have a transitive sense. Πληρόω is controversial: it appears in the active in
    Eph 4:10, "fill," but is this the same as the middle in 1:23? The A.V. and
    R.V. translations take it so, but some take it as passive, of Christ being
    filled. [Ed. If an active verb can be translated with good sense as such,
    it is unnecessary to translate it as if it were a middle verb.]

14 M53 When πρός is used in transferred senses, it means "tending towards, leading
    to, concerning, against, in view of." 'Εν . . . πλάνης apparently is to be
    translated "by craftiness in accordance with the wiles of error."
    H339 In the papyri μεθοδεία reverted in meaning to "method" (cf. J.A. Robinson
    in location).

16 R589 In the phrase ἐν μέτρῳ the preposition means "in the sphere of."
    M94 Πᾶν το σῶμα should be translated "the whole body" (cf. T200, and also
    2:21, 3:15).

17 R407 When adjectives and participles are not in concord with their antecedent
    noun in number or gender, it is due to the sense, instead of mere grammar (so
    ἐσκοτωμένοι changes from the neuter [ἔθνη] to the masculine, because reference
    is made to people).
    R700 Μηκέτι περιπατεῖν is in apposition to τοῦτο, with the idea of command.

18 BD352 Periphrasis may be used for the participle itself (ἐσκοτωμένοι . . .
    ὄντες; cf. Col. 1:21); it is used to express still more forcibly the persis-
    tence of the new state of things (the durative aspect of the perfect is accen-
    ted--R910).

19 M89 Many prepositions compounded with verbs have a sense which defies exact
    explanation. 'Απαλγέω means "to cease to feel."

21 M112 Does καθώς ἐστιν ἀλήθεια ἐν τῷ 'Ιησοῦ mean "just as Truth is (to be
     found) in Jesus: (as though it had been ἡ ἀλήθεια)?   [Ed. The clause καθώς
     ἐστιν ἀλήθεια seems to describe the nature or manner of the instruction ("in
     accordance with the truth"), while the following clause, i.e., vv. 22ff., ex-
     presses its substance.]

22 R283 Προτέραν is used as an adjective, meaning "the former."
     R1038 The use of an accusative with an infinitive where a nominative (and
     finite verb) could have occurred is rare in classical Greek, but common in
     the N.T. Consequently, ἀπόθεσθαι ὑμᾶς occurs here (the infinitive may repre-
     sent merely the content and not clearly either result or purpose--R10890,
     "that you put off."
     H485 Τὰς ἐπιθυμίας τῆς ἀπάτης means "deceitful lusts" (an adjectival genitive).

24 M59 There is an unique usage of κατά in the clause τὸν . . . κτισθέντα which
     means "the new man who has been created in accordance with God" (i.e., in God's
     image, cf. Col. 3:10).

26 R1173 Generally οὐ follows καί rather than μή. [Ed. But μή occurs here be-
     cause it is the negative generally used to negate imperatives.]
     BD387(1) The imperative is by no means confined to commands, but also expresses
     a request or a concession (in the N.T. or classical Greek). 'Οργίζεσθε καὶ
     μὴ ἁμαρτάνετε most probably means "you may be angry as far as I am concerned
     (if you can't help it), but do not sin thereby" (sometimes as in this verse
     two imperatives are connected by καί when the first suggests concession--
     R949).

28 BD339(3) The present participle is occasionally used (as in classical Greek)
     for something which happened previously (representing the imperfect) thus ὁ
     κλέπτων "who stole up to now" (cf. T81; the present participle has an itera-
     tive sense, "the rogue"--R892; ὁ κλέπτων is not "he who stole" or "he who
     steals," but simply "the stealer" differing from ὁ κλεπτής "the thief" only
     in being more closely associated with the verb κλεπτέτω--MT127; cf. a generic
     articular participle--T151).

29 R753 In πᾶς-μή the denial is universal, "let no corrupt word."
     R994 'Ινα with the subjunctive is used for the imperative here. [Ed. The
     imperatival idea is carried on from the preceding verb ἐκπορευέσθω, with the
     resultant meaning "let not . . ., that it may."]
     T25 Τοῦ στόματος ὑμῶν is the distributive singular. Something belonging to
     each person in a group is placed in the singular.
     T274 Πρός with the accusative has the sense of purpose--result, "for building
     up."

32 R594 Εἰς is used in this verse where disposition or attitude of mind is set
     forth, "to one another."

                              EPHESIANS 5

2   T75 The present imperative περιπατεῖτε has the meaning "go on walking."

2 R753 Πᾶς μή expresses a universal denial (cf. 4:29), "let not any."
R1173 Μηδέ means "not even."
R714 The singular relative pronoun ὅ could have occurred because of the preceding connective ἥ (cf. v. 5), with the meaning "which is."

4 BD358(2) The imperfect is used in expressions of necessity or obligation. "Α οὐκ ἀνῆκεν (D and E have τὰ οὐκ ἀνήκοντα) may mean "what is (really) not proper (but yet happens)."

5 R406 With ἥ connecting subjects the verb is usually in the singular in the New Testament (thus ἐστιν occurs with more than one subject).
R753 In πᾶς . . . οὐ the denial about πᾶς is complete (cf. T196; as a rule the negative precedes that which is negated, but not here--T287).
R786 In τοῦ Χριστοῦ καὶ θεοῦ one person may be described because the article is not repeated (but θεοῦ often occurs without the article; we must seriously consider the possibility of departing from all our English versions by translating the final part of vs. 5 as, "in the kingdom of Christ who is God"--TGr16).
M130 Sometimes a neuter relative pronoun (ὅ) is used where strictly a masculine or feminine might have been expected, presumably with reference to the whole idea of the preceding clause rather than to the single word which is the immediate antecedent of the relative (the pronoun has the general notion of thing, "which thing is being an idolater"--R713; ὅ ἐστιν means "that is to say"--BD132[2]).

7 M61n.3 Συμμέτοχος scarcely seems to mean more than "participant" (cf. Eph. 3:6).

8 T75 The present imperative περιπατεῖτε means "go on walking."
M174 The adjectival genitive seems to be a Semitic idiom. "Sons of light" means simply "people worthy of" or "associated with light."

12 R530 In κρυφῇ the dative of manner is used, "which things are done in secret."

13 T55 Some verbs appear in the middle voice where one expects the active. Thus φανεροῦται appears to mean "that which illuminates," or is it passive? [Ed. It is best to translate a passive verb as such, if good sense can be maintained; such is the case here, "becomes visible."]

14 M25 Does πᾶν γὰρ τὸ φανερούμενον φῶς ἐστιν mean "whatever illuminates is light" (not a very illuminating remark), or "whatever is illuminated becomes light" (which would embody the hopeful doctrine that the darkness of sin, once illuminated by the Gospel, may be converted into light). [Ed. The latter is more probable; cf. the note on vs. 13.]
T180 A generic article may accompany plurals like νεκρῶν, "the dead."

16 H309 Ἐξαγοράζομαι means "ransom (from bondage)."

18 R533 The dative οἴνῳ is used as a dative of means, "do not get drunk with wine."
R854 The present prohibition μὴ μεθύσκεσθε may imply that some of them were getting drunk (cf. even at the Lord's Table, 1 Cor. 11:21; in the prohibition μὴ μεθύσκεσθε the apostle was uttering urgent warnings against sins which were sure to reappear in the Christian community or were as yet only imperfectly expelled--MT126).

19 R690 The reflexive pronoun ἑαυτοῖς is used in a reciprocal sense in which it
        does not really differ in idea from ἀλλήλων, "speaking to one another."

21 R500 Χριστοῦ is used as an objective genitive, "reverence for Christ."
        BD468(2) Ὑποτασσόμενοι is greatly detached from the finite verb and approaches
        the imperatival usage, "be subject."

23 R399 Αὐτός is used in emphatic apposition here, "he himself is."
        R782 In κεφαλὴ . . ., κεφαλὴ . . ., σωτὴρ it is possible that the qualitative
        force of anarthrous nouns is prevalent, "is head . . . "

26 R521 Τῷ λουτρῷ is an instance of the pure locative dative without the preposi-
        tion ἐν. Blass does not think that the pure locative occurs in the N.T. [Ed.
        The noun λουτρῷ may have the meaning of "washing," consequently the whole
        phrase may be taken as instrumental, with the resultant meaning "by the washing
        of water."]
        M78 Ἐν is occasionally used in the sense of accompaniment. Thus ἐν ῥήματι
        perhaps means "accompanied by the formula" (or is it instrumental?). [Ed. A
        prepositional phrase generally modifies a verb or verbal idea rather than a
        noun (cf. R784). Thus it should be taken as adverbial unless there is speci-
        fic indication that it modifies a noun. In this verse, the prepositional phrase
        modifies the participle καθαρίσας and seems to have an instrumental sense, "by
        the word."]

27 H361 Σπίλος originally meaning "rock," came to signify successively "porous
        rock, rotten stone, clay, and clay stain," until Paul could employ it metaphor-
        ically as in Eph. 5:27, with the meaning "spot."

29 R1147 Ποτέ here does not have the notion of "once upon a time" but that of
        "ever."
        H311 Ἐκτρέφω means "rear up." In our idiom it is decidely perfective; in Eph.
        5:29, "nourisheth" is too weak.

31 R574 Ἀντὶ τούτου is used in the sense of "because (therefore)."
        H463 Εἰς with an accusative is used in place of a predicate nominative, "the
        two shall become one flesh."

32 BD277(1) The nominative pronoun ἐγώ is employed according to the standards of
        good style as in classical Greek for contrast or other emphasis. Here there is
        contrast between speaker and subject.

33 R933 There are examples in the N.T. where ἵνα seems to be merely an introduc-
        tory expletive with the volitive subjunctive. Ἵνα φοβῆται is parallel with
        the imperative ἀγαπάτω (cf. R994, Eph. 4:29; cf. BD389, T95, MT179; "and let
        the wife revere"--M144).
        R1187 Paul uses πλήν at the end of an argument to single out the main point
        (vs. 33 presents the culmination of the discussion in vv. 22-32).
        M60 Οἱ καθ' ἕνα means "individually" ("as individuals"--T15).

                                    EPHESIANS 6

2   M113 Does ἥτις ἐστὶν ἐντολὴ πρώτη ἐν ἐπαγγελίᾳ mean "which is the first com-

                                    356

mandment with a promise" (attached to it, which is not literally true, and in which the omission of the article would be curious); or does it mean "which is a foremost commandment, and has a promise attached to it" (which is an unlikely sense for πρώτη in such a context)? The case for the former alternative certainly strengthened by the ommission of the article in Mark 12:28, since the article is usually absent in temporal expressions (the ordinal [πρώτη] was felt to be definite enough even though anarthrous--R793). [Ed. Consequently, the former suggestion seems most probable.]

3 R875 The deliberative question is used with ἵνα (O.T. quotation). Deliberative questions ask not for the facts, but about the possibility, desirability or necessity of a proposed course of action (cf. T100; it shows purpose--BD369 [3]). [Ed. Since ἵνα is more readily used in the N.T. to indicate purpose than to introduce a deliberative question, this particle apparently portrays the notion of purpose in both the clause in which it actually occurs and in the clause in which it is implied.]

4 H311 Ἐκτρέφω means "nurture" (cf. 5:29).

9 R502 Both genitives αὐτῶν and ὑμῶν precede the noun κυριός (the usual order of a genitive is after the substantive). [Ed. Thus, the position in this verse denotes some degree of emphasis.]

10 R550 Τοῦ λοιποῦ is not technically an adverb though adverbial in force ("hence forth, finally, for the rest"--M39; cf. T235).
   R816 It is difficult to tell whether the verb ἐνδυναμοῦσθε is middle or passive. [Ed. The verb appears to have a passive sense, "be strengthened," cf. Acts 9:22; Rom. 4:20; 2 Tim. 2:1 and Heb. 11:34.]

11 R991 Πρὸς τὸ δύνασθαι is a pure purpose clause (cf. R1003, T144, and B414).
   T28 Plurals with the abstract nouns may imply "cases of." Thus μεθοδεῖαι means "astuteness."

13 R563 In this verse στῆναι ("stand") is stronger in force than the compound ἀντιστῆναι, "withstand."
   R777 With the repeated article in ἐν τῇ ἡμέρᾳ τῇ πονηρᾷ both substantive and adjective receive emphasis and the adjective is added as a sort of climax in apposition with a separate article, "in the day that is the evil one."

16 M77 Ἐν ᾧ means "with which."
   M78 Ἐν πᾶσιν perhaps means "in the midst," or "in spite of all these things" (cf. Neh. 10:1 [LXX 20:1], etc.)

17 B295 The second half of this verse should be translated "the sword of the Spirit which is the Word of God" (ὅ ἐστιν is explanatory without regard to the gender of the antecedent--R411).

18 R618 The two prepositions περί and ὑπέρ differ very little in meaning in vv. 18ff., "for" (cf. M63 and T270).
   M57 Διά is used with the genitive to express environment and attendant circumstance. Διὰ πάσης προσευχῆς καὶ δεήσεως means "with all (possible) prayer and petition" (cf. T267; "every"--M94).
   M76 The preposition in ἐν παντὶ καιρῷ is used with a temporal sense, meaning

"again, constantly" ("in every time"?--M78).

19 R1090 Γνωρίσαι is a consecutive (result) infinitive although it is hypothetical and not actual, "that I may make known."
H485 A secondary Hebraism may lurk behind the phrase ἐν ἀνοίξει, "when I open."

21 R608 Κατά is more than a lengthy way of expressing the genitive. [Ed. The
phrase τὰ κατ᾽ ἐμέ appears to have the sense of "my circumstances"; cf. Ph.
1:12; Col. 4:7.]
T344 Normally the dependent clause follows the main clause. But the purpose
clause with ἵνα precedes the main clause here, "Tychicus will make known . . .
for the purpose that you also may know my circumstances."

22 R846 Ἔπεμψα is an epistolary aorist ("whom I send to you for this very purpose"
--B21; cf. M12).

24 M197 Ἐν ἀφθαρσίᾳ may be intended to mean both "sincerely" (in the incorrup-
tion) and "eternally" (in incorruptibility).

Philippians

2   R795 Κύριος in the Gospels usually means "God," similar to the O.T. "Lord," but in Paul's writings it almost always means "Lord Jesus."

3   R604 The meaning of ἐπί in this verse wavers between occasion and time, "at."
R772 Πάσῃ τῇ means "all."
T207 The genitive ὑμῶν is quite ambiguous; it may be (a) subjective, "whenever you remember me," or (b) objective, "whenever I think of you" (perhaps ὑμῶν includes the idea of both subjective and objective genitive. Paul gives thanks to God both when he remembers them and they him--TGr91).

5   TGr91 The preposition εἰς involves movement toward a goal. The R.V. translation, "your fellowship in furtherance of the Gospel," is better although it still does not quite show the implication of εἰς.

6   T246 Αὐτὸ τοῦτο means "in just this confidence," equivalent to "I am sure."
BD290(4) The perfect participle πεποιθώς seems to refer to the constancy emphasized in vs. 5 (or to the following ὅτι?).   [Ed. The perfect participle with αὐτὸ τοῦτο seems to refer to confidence in what God will do with the Philippian Christians, rather than the past fellowship of the Philippian believers with Paul. There is much more of a point in having confidence in a future event than in something past. In addition, ὅτι appears to be used to denote the content of αὐτὸ τοῦτο.]

7   M65 Τοῦτο φρονεῖν ὑπὲρ πάντων ὑμῶν seems to mean "to entertain these thoughts about all of you" (cf. R632).
T143 Διά τό with an infinitive is almost equal to ὅτι or διότι denoting cause. This is the only instance of such a construction in Paul's writings (the preceding καθώς is parallel to the infinitive clause--R966).

9   T29 μᾶλλον means "still more greatly."

10 R594 The preposition εἰς marks either the limit or accents the duration expressed by the accusative, "until the day of Christ."
T143 Εἰς τό with the infinitive equals ἵνα or ὥστε as indicating purpose or result. Usually it denotes purpose in Pauline literature (cf. R991 and 1071), "so that you may approve."
T151 The meaning of τὰ διαφέροντα is ambiguous. It may refer to "different values" (moral distinctions--N.E.B.) or "superior things" (R.V. and R.S.V. translations). [Ed. "Discriminating between different values" does not appear to do justice to the context. Paul's deep concern for the Philippian believers is that they continue to grow toward maturity (cf. vv. 5 - 7 and 3:12 - 16).]

11   T247 Πληρόω takes the accusative rather than the genitive in the passive,
       "filled with fruit."
     R595 Εἰς indicates aim or purpose.

12   T15 Τὰ κατ' ἐμέ means "what concerns me" (cf. Eph. 6:21).

13   R463 'Εν has a causal sense (under Septuagintal influence), "because of Christ."
     R540 "Ωστε with the infinitive expresses actual result here, "so that it has
       become known."

14   M45 A causal use of the dative may be seen in πεποιθότας τοῖς δεσμοῖς μου if
       this really means "having grown confident as a result of," "encouraged by the
       witness of my imprisonment" (cf. T242; "confident because of my imprisonment").
     M108 Τῶν ἀδελφῶν ἐν κυρίῳ clearly means "the brothers who are in the Lord" (un-
       less the ἐν κυρίῳ goes with the πεποιθότας which follows, although this is ex-
       tremely unlikely).

18   R487 Παντὶ τρόπῳ is used as an instrumental dative, "by every way."
     R1180 'Αλλά is not contradictory but climatic (cf. T330; "yes, indeed," intro-
       ducing a strong addition; emphatic--BD448[6]).
     B60 Χαρήσομαι is used as a progressive future, "and therein I rejoice, yea, and
       will continue to rejoice" (cf. M10).
     BD449(2) Πλήν means "only in any case" and is used to conclude a discussion and
       emphasize what is essential.

19   R787 Since the article τῆς is not repeated the two categories of aid are treat-
       ed together.
     M70 The preposition εἰς in this verse may mean either "with a view to," or "re-
       sulting in." [Ed. In this context, the preposition is used to describe what
       the result will be, not what the purpose is.]
     M89 'Αποβήσεται carries the meaning of "eventuate."

21   R1059 Both infinitives in this verse are used as subjects of the implied verb,
       "to live is Christ, and to die is gain."

22   R810 The middle verb αἱρήσομαι means "I take for myself."
     T264 Τὸ ζῆν ἐν σαρκί means "to live in the sphere of the flesh."
     H422 Καί has a consecutive meaning, "but if . . . then what shall I choose?"

23   R628 The preposition σύν has the notion of fellowship (the preposition denotes
       spiritual contact with Christ, cf. 1 Thess. 4:17 and 5:10--M81).
     T29 The phrase πολλῷ μᾶλλον κρεῖσσον means "much more better" (all this empha-
       sis is due to Paul's struggling emotion--R664).
     T143 Εἰς τό with an infinitive in Paul expresses purpose almost always, but
       here it limits a noun, "the desire to depart."

24   R1059 The articular infinitive τὸ ἐπιμένειν is used as a subject of the implied
       verb, "to remain in the flesh is more necessary."

25   R613 The preposition in the compound verb παραμενῶ simply means "beside."

26   R588 The prepositional phrase ἐν ἐμοί is used as a simple dative, "for me."
     M53 Πρός denotes position, "with" (cf. H467).

28 R729 The antecedent of ἥτις is the general idea of the preceding clause.
    BD468(2) The participle πτυρόμενοι is similar to an imperative in actual
    meaning. [Ed. Actually, the participle gains this sense from the previous im-
    perative, "only let your manner of life be worthy of the gospel of Christ . .
    without being frightened."]

29 R632 Ὑπέρ means "for the sake of."
    R777 The two articular infinitives are used to explain the initial article τό,
    "that is for the sake of Christ, not only to believe . . ., but also to suffer."

PHILIPPIANS 2

1   R410 There is a difficulty with the indefinite pronoun varying in gender from
    its noun (τι should be written throughout--BD137[2]). [Ed. In view of the
    nouns used, we would expect τις . . . τι . . . τις . . τι. A few later manu-
    scripts correct the last pronoun.]

2   B217 Ἵνα is used to denote content, "fulfill ye my joy, that ye be of the same
    mind" (the ἵνα- clause is descriptive of what the writer means by completing
    his joy, "complete my joy by having the same outlook"--M145).

4   BD306(2) Τὰ ἑτερῶν is correctly used in contrast to τα ἑαυτῶν (cf. T197), "his
    own . . . of others."

6   R407 The plural adjective ἵσα differs little from ἵσον in the adverbial sense,
    "to be on equality with."
    R1059 The articular infinitive το εἶναι is used as the direct object of the
    verb ἡγήσατο (cf. B394 and 2:24).

7   T220 The dative of respect ὁμοιώματι becomes almost an adverb.
    B145 Γενόμενος is related to λαβών as a participle of identical action; the
    relation of λαβών to ἐκένωσεν is less certain. It may denote the same action
    as ἐκένωσεν viewed from the opposite point of view (identical), or may be
    thought of as an additional fact (subsequent) to ἐκένωσεν (the aorist partici-
    ple λαβών does not indicate subsequent action--R1114). [Ed. When an aorist
    participle occurs with an aorist verb, the participle may refer to action that
    is simultaneous with that of the main verb, especially if the participle fol-
    lows the verb (cf. Matt. 2:8; Acts 15:8 and Rom. 4:20), "but emptied himself,
    while taking."]

8   BD447(8) Δέ is used to denote an explanation or an intensification, "even death
    on a cross."

9   R629 Ὑπέρ in the compound verb carries the notion of excess, "more than."

10 M78 The preposition ἐν portrays the idea of accompaniment or attendant circum-
    stance, with the meaning "when the name of Jesus is spoken" or "at the name."

11 T302 P.F. Regard thinks that the omission of the stative verb in ὅτι κύριος
    Ἰησοῦς Χριστός emphasizes κύριος, since this type of phrase has the copula
    elsewhere (eg. 1 John 4:15).

12   R564 Κατεργάζομαι accents the carrying of the work through, "outworking" or
     "development," whereas ἐνεργῶν has the idea of in-working.
     M144 Ὥστε is used as an inferential particle meaning "and so, accordingly."
     MT174 The present imperative has a conative idea, "set to working out."

13   R1059 The two infinitives in this verse give the object of ἐνεργῶν, "for God
     is in-working both to will and to do."
     M65 It is uncertain whether θεὸς . . . εὐδοκίας means "with a view to (perform-
     ing) his good pleasure," or whether we are to connect ὑπὲρ τῆς εὐδοκίας with
     the following πάντα ποιεῖτε and translate "for the sake of pleasing him" (ὑπέρ
     suggests the object at which one is aiming, "for"--R632). [Ed. It seems
     best to take the prepositional phrase with the preceding θεὸς γάρ ἐστιν ὁ
     ἐνεργῶν, since the punctuation with a full stop after εὐδοκίας is virtually
     undisputed in the manuscripts. In addition, the more common use of the prepo-
     sition favors Moule's former suggestion (cf. 2 Cor. 1:6).]

15   BD296 There is a change in gender from the feminine noun γενεᾶς to the mascu-
     line pronoun οἷς. This occurs because of the actual reference to people (cf.
     R713).

17   R787 Since the article τῇ is not repeated, both θυσίᾳ and λειτουργίᾳ are taken
     together, "the sacrifice and service."
     B284 Εἰ is used in a concessive clause here, corresponding to the first class
     conditional clause (denoting a statement of fact), "although I am being poured."

18   M34 Τὸ αὐτὸ is used as an adverbial accusative meaning "in the same way" (cf.
     Matt. 27:44; T246 and BD154).

20   T270 Τὰ περὶ ὑμῶν means "your affairs" (cf. M63).
     BD379 Ὅστις is used to introduce a qualitative consecutive clause (denoting
     the result of the previous statement; cf. R961).

22   R441 Note the lack of parallelism in πατρὶ τέκνον σὺν ἐμοί. Paul purposely
     adds the preposition σύν to avoid carrying out the figure of speech too liter-
     ally.

23   T15 In τὰ περὶ ἐμὲ the preposition has a meaning similar to κατά. Consequent-
     ly the phrase refers to "my circumstances" and not "my surroundings" (cf. M62
     and M63).
     MT167 Ὡς ἂν means "whenever" (similar to ὅταν--BD455[2]).

24   R895 The perfect verb πέποιθα is almost purely durative, "I trust."

25   R418 Sharp contrast may be expressed by close proximity of two genitives as
     with μου and ὑμῶν ("my fellow worker . . . but your messenger").

26   R964 Διότι has a causal meaning, "because," whereas ὅτι has a declarative
     sense, "that."
     H452 The imperfect periphrastic construction (ἐπιποθῶν ἦν . . , καὶ ἀδημονῶν)
     occurs twice in this verse (cf. R888; the participles are actually adjectival
     rather than periphrastic--MT227). [Ed. On occasion it is difficult to deter-
     mine whether a participle with a stative verb is adjectival or periphrastic.
     But because of the close proximity of the participle and verb, the periphras-
     tic rendering seems preferable here, "he was longing . . , and in distress."]

27 BD235(3) The preposition ἐπί means "in addition to" (this is similar to the
multipliative use of   --H173).

28 T30 The comparative adverb σπουδαιοτέρως is used as an elative superlative,
"very zealous."
T73 Ἔπεμψα is used as an epistolary aorist: the action will have been completed when the letter reaches them (cf. B44 and M12).

29 R481 The double accusative occurs in καὶ τοὺς τοιούτους ἐντίμους ἔχετε ("regard someone as honored"--BD168[1]). [Ed. Τοὺς τοιούτους is the direct object of the verb, while ἐντίμους is in apposition to (predicates) the direct
object.]

30 T218 The joining together of several genitives is characteristic of Paul's
style of writing, although it is quite rare to have two genitives depend on
the same noun, which then usually stands between them, as in τὸ ὑμῶν ὑστέρημα
τῆς πρός με λειτουργίας (cf. BD168[1]), "your lack of service toward me."

PHILIPPIANS 3

1 R420 Ὑμῶν ἐμοί is an instance of unusual word order. [Ed. The two pronouns
are brought together in order to indicate sharp contrast (cf. 2:25).]
R487 Τὸ λοιπόν is used as an adverbial accusative with the meaning "finally."
B96 The present infinitive portrays the linear sense, "to be writing the same
things to you, to me indeed is not irksome" (the infinitive is used in this
sentence construction as the subject of the implied verb--R1058).

2 BD488(1b) In the repetition of περιτομή after κατατομήν (Jewish circumcision),
Paul seizes upon the word in which his opponents take pride and in a rhetorical manner uses it to their discredit.

3 M46 Οἱ πνεύματι θεοῦ λατρεύοντες may refer to those whose divine service is of
a spiritual (and not material) sort, with an adverbial sense of the dative.
This meaning becomes more plausible if, with p[46], we omit θεοῦ. The reading
with θεῷ appears to be a correction (cf. T239; the dative has an instrumental
sense--R540). [Ed. The former suggestion seems preferable since the contrast
that Paul presents is between true spiritual worship and mere external ordinances.]

4 R1129 Καίπερ is used to make the concessive idea evident, "although."
M179 The participle occurs in καίπερ ἐγὼ ἔχων where the finite verb ἔχω (with
a corresponding alternative to καίπερ) would have been strictly correct. [Ed.
The participle is used with a concessive sense and the particle καίπερ is employed to give added force to the concession. Actually, there is nothing
grammatically wrong with this construction (cf. Heb. 5:8 and 7:5).]

5 T220 Περιτομῇ is used as a dative of respect, "with respect to circumcision"
(cf. "with regard to circumcision"--M46 and "with respect to circumcision an
eight day one"--BD197).

7 R480 In the double accusative ταῦτα . . . ζημίαν, the latter is used as the

predicate of the former (in essence it has the sense of apposition), "I considered these things as loss."

8   R1036 Εἶναι is used as an infinitive of indirect discourse following ἡγοῦμαι
    (the infinitive is used as a direct object of ἡγοῦμαι--T137). [Ed. Both of
    these descriptions have a similar meaning. The infinitive is complementing
    the verb, "I consider . . . to be."]
    R1148 The particles μεν, οὖν and γε have a climatic force (cf. T138 "much more,
    in fact").

9   T191 The possessive adjective usually occurs in post-position, consequently
    when it occurs in the pre-position (i.e., before the noun it modifies) it gen-
    erally indicates emphasis. Here it is used predicatively (anarthrous), "right-
    eousness which is my own" (cf. BD285[2], "a righteousness of my own").

10 M128f. Τοῦ with the infinitive γνῶναι may denote a final sense (i.e., purpose),
    parallel to the preceding ἵνα clause; or it may be consecutive, expressing the
    result of the previous conditions (equivalent to ὥστε with an infinitive); or
    it may even be epexegetic, further explaining the previous statement (it is ep-
    exegetic--R1002 and BD400[8]). [Ed. Paul generally employs some construction
    other than τοῦ with an infinitive to express a purpose clause (cf. R1088 and
    MT217). The usual meaning of this construction is epexegetic (cf. Phil. 3:21).
    Consequently, it is preferable to consider it is epexegetic in this passage.]

11 B253 Εἴ πως with the subjunctive here has the subjective sense, "but I press
    on, if so be that I may apprehend."
    M109 There are many instances in the N.T. that strike the English reader as an
    almost pedantic repetition of the article. [Ed. The article τήν is repeated
    here to show that the prepositional phrase ἐκ νεκρῶν is attributive to the pre-
    ceding noun, "the resurrection that is the resurrection from the dead."]

12 R901 The aorist verb ἔλαβον denies the sufficiency of Paul's achievement, where-
    as the perfect verb τετελείωμαι denies it as a present reality.
    M132 It may be that καταλάβω is used absolutely (cf. 1 Cor. 9:24), in which
    case ἐφ' ᾧ means "inasmuch as" or possibly the phrase implies an object for
    καταλάβω, "that I may grasp that (achievement) with a view to which I have
    been grasped" (the phrase seems to indicate aim or purpose--R605). [Ed. The
    translation which includes the rendering "with a view to which" is in essence
    indicating the aim, which seems preferable here.]
    BD368 Εἰ is used to introduce a deliberative question meaning "whether" (cf. BD
    375, an expression of expectation).

13 R807 The middle voice in ἐπεκτεινόμενος has the resultant meaning "stretching
    myself forward."
    T137 The infinitive κατειληφέναι is used as the direct object of the verb λογ-
    ίζομαι (in essence the infinitive is supplementing or complementing the verb,
    "I do not consider that I have made it my own").

16 R1187 Paul uses πλήν at the end of an argument to single out the main point.
    T75 The present infinitive στοιχεῖν is used as an imperative ("go on walking"),
    parallel to the hortatory subjunctive φρονῶμεν (cf. R944; B364; M126; MT179).

18 BD151(1) The simple construction of λέγω with an accusative has the meaning "to
    mention in speaking."

20 T190 The position of the personal pronoun ἡμῶν indicates that it carries strong
emphasis (cf. BD284[2]), "our citizenship."

21 M129 The articular infinitive τοῦ δύνασθαι has an epexegetical sense (explanatory or extensive of a preceding idea), with the meaning "by virtue of the power by which he can," or "the power, namely his ability to" (cf. R996, T141 and
MT217; there is a very loose relationship between the noun ἐνέργειαν and the
infinitive, with a slight tendency toward a consecutive sense--BD400[2]).
T214 The addition of the personal pronoun to the genitive when properly it belongs to the first noun (τὸ σῶμα τῆς ταπεινώσεως ἡμῶν) is the result of semitic influence. Consequently the meaning is "our body of humiliation" (equivalent to "our humble body").

PHILIPPIANS 4

1 M144 Ὥστε is used simply as an inferential particle meaning "and so," "accordingly."

3 BD442(13) Μετὰ καί is actually pleonastic with the meaning "together with."

6 M45 Τῇ προσευχῇ and τῇ δεήσει should be understood as datives of accompaniment rather than instrumental datives, "with prayer and supplication."

7 R499 Τοῦ θεοῦ is used as a subjective genitive, "the peace that God has and
gives."
R1183 After the initial καί in this verse, we may supply "so"; this is equivalent to a consecutive use of καί, "and so."

8 M161 Τὸ λοιπόν means "finally" (or "and so"; the adverb is similar to an emphatic particle--R1146).

10 R1147 Ἤδε ποτέ denotes more the notion of culmination ("now at last") than
that of time.
T270 Φρονέω with the preposition ὑπέρ means "think upon."
M132 Does the phrase ἐφ' ᾧ mean "inasmuch as" or, more probably, "with regard
to which" (i.e., τὸ ὑπὲρ ἐμοῦ φρονεῖν)? (The prepositional phrase has a causal sense in this verse--R963.) [Ed. Moule's second suggestion seems the most
favorable, since Paul uses this prepositional phrase to introduce a clause
which alleviates the harshness of the previous statement.]

11 R835 Ἔμαθον is used as a culminative aorist with emphasis laid on the end of
the action as opposed to the beginning ("I have learned").
R1041 Ἔμαθον with the infinitive has the meaning "learn how" not "learn that"
(cf. T146 and MT229).
R965 In this verse, οὐχ ὅτι may be either objective or causal, "I do not mean
to say that," or "I say this not because" (something like ἔστιν should be supplied before οὐχ ὅτι--T303; this introductory phrase is obscure, unless it is
to be understood to mean "so I say"--BD480[5]). [Ed. Paul generally uses
this construction to introduce an objective clause (cf. 2 Cor. 1:24, 3:5; Phil.
3:12 and 4:17), which appears to be its usage here. The suggestion that ἔστιν
should be supplied is equivalent with this rendering.]

T37 Ἐγω occurs without much emphasis here.

12 R1181 In οἶδα καὶ . . . οἶδα καὶ, the καὶ occurs with both parts of the comparison, a studied balancing of the two members of the sentence is apparent
(the first καὶ may also have the meaning "even"--BD444[3]).
M75 The phrase ἐν παντι καὶ ἐν πᾶσιν is used to indicate emphasis, "in any and
all things."

13 M77 The preposition ἐν in ἐν τῷ ἐνδυναμοῦντι apparently should be considered
as similar to the preposition in the ἐν Χριστῷ formula (which occurs frequently in Paul's writings; the repeated ἐν in the compound verb may portray the
idea of intensity--M88).

14 R1187 Paul uses πλήν at the end of an argument to single out the main point.
T189 The personal pronoun μου carries a degree of emphasis because of its unusual position (before the noun rather than following it), "my trouble."

15 M167 Ὑμεῖς does not seem to be emphatic here.

16 R1183 Καὶ . . . καὶ . . . καὶ has the meaning "even . . . both . . . and."

17 R594 Εἰς is used with a sense similar to the dative, with an attitude of mind
set forth (similar to the ethical dative, "to" or "for your credit").
R965 Οὐχ ὅτι may be objective or causal (ἔστιν should be supplied before οὐχ
ὅτι--T303). [Ed. The objective rendering, which is also compatible with
Turner's suggestion, appears to be preferable (cf. 4:11).]

18 M52 Τὰ παρ' ὑμῶν literally means "the things from beside her," with a possible
suggestion of emphasis on the movement of the Philippians away from their possessions.

22 BD437 The preposition ἐκ in this verse denotes membership.

Colossians

2   T181 The article may be carried over (in sense) from the first noun to the second, thus meaning "the saints and the faithful brethren" (the same group).
T263 Πιστος ἐν means either "the belief of those who are in Christ," or
"Christ's own personal faith." [Ed. The former suggestion is more probable
in this context, since Paul uses the adjective to further describe his recipients. Thus, it is equivalent to τοῖς ἐν Χριστῷ (cf. M108).]

3   T28 The letter writer's plural is frequent in Paul's writings, especially where
he seems to be writing on behalf of a group (as it seems here).
T228 An adverb usually follows the adjective or verb which it determines in the
N.T. Greek. Therefore, it will be more natural to take παντότε with the former
verb εὐχαριστοῦμεν than with the subsequent participle προσευχόμενοι with the
resultant meaning "we always give thanks to God."

4   R783 The need for another article with the attributive prepositional phrase was
not felt. Consequently, ἐν Χριστῷ is to be taken with the noun πίστιν, "your
faith in Christ."
R1128 The participle ἀκούσαντες is used in a causal sense (stating the ground
for the action of the main verb).

5   T213 'Αληθείας may be a genitive of quality, thus the phrase means "of the
true Gospel" (or is εὐαγγελίου a genitive of apposition meaning "of the Truth
which is the Gospel?" cf. R498). [Ed. The difficulty seems to arise over
the problem whether ἀληθείας modifies εὐαγγελίου or vice versa. Considering
the word order here, it seems more probable that εὐαγγελίου is modifying (i.e.,
in apposition to) ἀληθείας, "the Truth, that is, the Gospel"; cf. Eph. 1:13.]
T252 The preposition ἐν with τῷ λόγῳ may mean "by means of" (or perhaps it has
a temporal sense, "when"). [Ed. It appears to have a temporal sense here, especially since the previous verb has a temporal designation.]

6   R978 'Αφ' ἧς ἡμέρας literally means "from which day," thus the meaning "since"
is arrived at (the phrase is virtually a conjunction--T17).
T55 In the use of καρποφορούμενον, can there be significance in the contrast
between the active in v. 10 and the middle in v. 6? The middle is rare but
there seems to be no difference; "bearing fruit."

7   R172 'Επαφρᾶ is an abbreviation of Ἐπαφρόδιτας (Ph. 2:25; 4:18), but it does
not necessarily follow that, if true, the same man is indicated in Philippians
and Colossians.
R781 In διάκονος τοῦ Χριστοῦ, the idea is "a minister of the Christ," not "the
minister of Christ."
T259 'Από stands for παρά with the genitive after μανθάνω, "to learn from."

9 R485 The true passive of many verbs retains the accusative of the thing. This
   is true of verbs that have two accusatives in the active ("filled with knowledge"--T247).
   R600 The preposition ἐπί compounded with the noun has the perfective idea,
   "true knowledge."
   R784 The prepositional phrase (ἐν . . .) is predicate rather than attributive
   (i.e., it is used with the verb rather than the noun, with the resultant meaning "that you may be filled . . . in all spiritual wisdom").
   R993 Ἵνα is used after αἰτούμενοι to show the contents of the asking (the requests of the prayers), "asking that."

10 BD337(1) Where the new life of the Christian is meant, corresponding to the divine call which creates a new beginning, the aorist imperative is used. [Ed.
   Actually, an imperative is not used here, but an infinitive denoting the content
   of the entreaty.]

13 M175 Τοῦ υἱοῦ τῆς ἀγάπης αὐτοῦ probably is equivalent to τοῦ ἀγαπητοῦ υἱοῦ
   αὐτοῦ, meaning "his beloved son."

15 TGr122ff. Πάσης κτίσεως is a partitive genitive, "among" (rather than comparative or objective), identifying Christ as our Archetype, "among all creation"
   (cf. Rev. 3:14).
   H279 Πρωτότοκος means "bearing a firstborn."

16 R896 In v. 16, the aorist verb ἐκτίσθη is merely punctiliar, while in the same
   verse the perfect verb ἔκτισται adds the durative idea, whereas in v. 17, again,
   συνέστηκεν has lost the puntiliar and is only durative, "were created . . .
   have been created" (the perfect is used to denote a continuing effect on the
   subject, although the effect need not always be expressed even though it is
   present--BD341[1]).
   TGr125 This verse should be translated as follows: "in (ἐν, with an instrumental sense--T253 and BD219[1]) him were once created all things that are in
   heaven and upon earth, the visible and the invisible, thrones, lordships, powers, authorities; all these have been created (and now exist) by his continual
   support (διά) and he is their goal (εἰς)."

17 R534 The usual way of expressing the agent in the N.T. is ὑπό for the direct
   agent and διά for the intermediate agent. But ἐν is used here, "by him."
   R774 Πάντα is used to describe the sum total of things.
   M74 Πρό is perhaps used in a metaphorical sense meaning "above all" (or temporal, "before"; probably temporal--R622). [Ed. Paul uses the preposition
   πρό twelve times in the N.T., and in each instance, time is designated. When
   he desires to show the superiority of rank, he generally employs the prepositions ἐπί or ὑπέρ.]

18 T41 In vv. 17 and 18, αὐτός refers to "he himself" (alone; the pronoun indicates emphasis--R679).

20 M119 In δι' αὐτοῦ ἀποκαταλλάξαι τὰ πάντα εἰς αὐτόν, it is surprising that there
   appears to be no variant ἑαυτον and that editors do not print αὐτόν, which
   seems in order to distinguish Christ, referred to in δι' αὐτοῦ, from God, to
   whom (probably) the reconciliation is made.

T212 Σταυροῦ seems to be a genitive of place (blood shed on the cross; cf.
2 Cor. 11:26).

21 R777 With the repetition of the article and the order of τοῖς ἐργοῖς τοῖς
πονηροῖς, both the substantive and adjective receive emphasis and the adjective
is added as a sort of climax in apposition with a separate article ("the works,
that is the evil ones").
B155 The effect of the periphrastic construction is that of a perfect participle clearly marked as one of existing state (cf. R375; used to express still
more forcibly the persistence of the new state of things--BD352).
B420 The participle in this verse is used as an adjective. This is clear especially since it is joined by καί to the adjective ἐχθρούς. [Ed. Actually,
it seems that the participle ἀπηλλοτριωμένους is used with a periphrastic sense.
But regardless of its usage, ὄντας emphasizes this state as continuous.]

22 M56 The preposition διά is used in the sense of "by means of."

23 T200 Πᾶς with the anarthrous noun here has the meaning of "all" or "the whole
of."

24 R574 In the verb ἀνταναπληρόω, Paul uses ἀντί in the sense of "in his turn"
(answering over to Christ). As Christ, so Paul fills up the measure of suffering.
M71 Notice the compound verb, where the ἀντί may merely imply that fulness replaces lack, or may anticipate the force of the ὑπέρ which follows. [Ed. The
latter suggestion seems more probable, since ὑπέρ both precedes and follows
this verb (cf. R574).]

29 R714 The neuter relative pronoun ὅ is used to refer to a verbal idea or to the
whole sentence. [Ed. The antecedent appears to be the whole preceding verse,
with the meaning "for this I toil."]

COLOSSIANS 2

1 R886 Notice the force of the present tense in θέλω (a continual desire).
R908 The infinitive εἰδέναι is used in indirect discourse, "for I want you to
know."

2 R1382 The ἵνα clause should be rendered as a wish.
TGr166 The participle is used as an imperative; "They (supply "must be") knit
together in love" (as an optative--MT182). [Ed. The participle has an imperatival sense, whether it is to be taken as an imperative or volitive optative.]

T206 Χριστοῦ is in apposition to θεοῦ (despite the fact that it presents an
exception to the use of the article with the noun in apposition), "of God, that
is Christ."

4 M145 In many cases ἵνα is virtually imperatival: v. 4 seems to be an example,
for τοῦτο λέγω ἵνα μηδεὶς παραλογίζηται makes better sense as "what I mean is
this: nobody is to talk you round," than as "this I say in order to prevent
anybody . . ." (ἵνα may be final, but equally possible is an imperatival sense

--T102). [Ed. It is difficult to determine the sense of ἵνα here, although ἵνα may be used to denote the content of τοῦτο λέγω similar to ὅτι in 1 Cor. 1:12, thus giving it an imperatival sense; cf. Col. 4:16.]

5   B284 Concessive clauses of the class corresponding to the first class of conditional sentences are most frequent in the N.T. The event referred to in the concessive clause (εἰ καί . . .) is in general not contingent, but conceived of as actual (εἰ καί means "if also" and introduces a conditional clause--R1026). [Ed. In essence there is very little difference in meaning between "although" corresponding to a first class condition, and "since."]
M46 Clearly in v. 5, τῇ σαρκί means "physically" as contrasted with τῷ πνεύματι meaning "spiritually."
BD448(5) When ἀλλά is used in a clause after εἰ, it means "yet, certainly, at least."
BD471(5) The awkward co-ordination of participles is seen in v. 5; χαίρων καὶ βλέπων   means "viewing with joy" or "rejoicing to see."

6   T75 The present imperative περιπατεῖτε should be translated "go on walking."

8   R1116 The present tense of συλαγωγῶν is used with an iterative sense, "that no one makes a prey of you repeatedly."
R1159 The negative μή is used because the clause is final (purpose; an object clause is introduced--B206; μή is used in a cautious assertion and the whole clause should be translated "take heed! perhaps there will be someone who . ." --MT192). [Ed. When Paul uses βλέπετε μή, the negative introduces an object clause (cf. 1 Cor. 8:9 and Gal. 5:15); although here it may denote some subjective or cautious notion as well.]
M106 The first part of this verse should be translated "Beware that there is nobody to despoil you" (or "to make spoil of you").
MT228 The use of the articular participle instead of a relative clause gives directness and individuality to the reference, "someone who will."

11 H310 The noun ἀπέκδυσις connotes complete stripping, of oneself or another in one's own interest.

12 T218 In the accumulation of several genitives the governing genitive will generally precede the dependent one, "through faith in the working of God."

13 R1205 The pronoun ὑμᾶς is repeated in this verse for the sake of clarity.

14 R648 Ἐκ τοῦ μέσου means "out of the way," "aside."
M45 Τὸ . . . χειρόγραφον τοῖς δόγμασιν means "the document with its decrees" (apparently a document "containing" or "consisting of" decrees; cf. Eph. 2:15).
T219 Verse 14 may have an example of a noun with a dative attribute, "a subscription to the ordinances."
T242 The dative of cause occurs here (transposing τοῖς δόγμασιν after ὃ ἦν), thus the phrase should be translated "which was against us because of the decrees" (but Eph. 2:15 adds ἐν, suggesting that this is a dative of attendant circumstance, even instrumental; i.e., take the phrase closely with the verb implied in χειρόγραφον--"written in . . ."). [Ed. This last suggestion seems to be the most probable, in view of the Ephesians reference (cf. M45).]

15 R805 Ἀπεκδυσάμενος does not mean "to undress," but "to throw off from one's

self" (the middle voice is used with an active sense--BD316[1]; cf. T55).
[Ed. An active sense meaning "to disarm" seems to fit the context more readily, especially since the accusatives ἀρχάς and ἐξουσίας immediately follow.
Also, θεός appears to be the continuing subject from v. 13.]
T40 The form αὐτούς is used after ἀρχάς, in accord with the sense rather than
grammatical concord (i.e., masculine referring to people).
T265 A variety of interpretations is possible for ἐν αὐτῷ; local "in him" or
"on it" (the cross), instrumental "by means of him" or "by means of it" (the
cross; cf. Eph. 2:16). [Ed. The nearest antecedent of αὐτῷ is σταυρῷ in v. 14.
In addition to this, v. 15 seems to present the procedure of victory rather
than the outcome of victory. Consequently, this phrase means "on the cross."]
BD148(1) θριαμβεύω is only transitive in meaning, "to lead in triumphal proces-
sion; to mock; deride" (cf. H400).

18 R65 Ramsay finds ἐμβατεύω used in the technical sense of "entering in" on the
part of initiates in the sanctuary of Apollos at Claros in an inscription there.
R500 In v. 18, θρησκεία τῶν ἀγγέλων, refers to "worship paid to angels" (an objective genitive).
M183 θέλων ἐν ταπεινοφροσύνη looks as though it were better taken as a semitism
("delighting in humility") than as though θέλων were used absolutely, separate
from the prepositional phrase; cf. Ps. 112:1 (the participle means "intentionally"--BD148[2]). [Ed. Both of these suggestions give θέλων an adverbial
force, which is probably correct (cf. R551). But Moule's suggestion is more
accurate since θέλω does not have the meaning of "intentionally" elsewhere in
the N.T.]
T246 ᾍ may be taken to show content or internal object. Thus the relative
clause would mean "upon what he vainly imagined in the vision of his initiation"
(making the conjectural emendations unnecessary; the relative clause should
be translated "vainly conceited over what he beheld at his initiation"--BD154).
[Ed. In essence there is very little difference in meaning between these suggestions.]

19 R478 Τὴν αὔξησιν is an accusative of inner content, "grow with the growth."
R1138 In general it may be said of the koine that the presence of οὐ with the
participle means that the negative is clear-cut and decisive. [Ed. The negative οὐ is employed here because the author stresses the fact that the false
teachers were not only losing their grasp of Christ, but completely rejecting
Him.]

20 R807 The use of the voice in δογματίζεσθε is probably direct middle meaning
"subject yourselves to ordinances" (passive, "let yourselves be regulated"--
BD314; the verb is intransitive active in idea, "submit to rules"--T57). [Ed.
According to form this verb may be either middle or passive, and either translation may fit the context. In essence, Turner actually arrives at a passive
sense.]
M210 J.B. Lightfoot (in reference to ἀποθνήσκειν and θνήσκειν) stated that when
the aorist is desired the compound verb is used; when the perfect is desired
the simple verb is used. This rule holds universally in the Greek New Testament.
T251 The prepositional phrase ἀπό . . . is used for the dative (the phrase denotes alienation--BD211). [Ed. This use of ἀπό following ἀπεθάνετε expresses
the idea of severance more than the dative would.]

21 R853 In v. 21, μὴ ἅψῃ (aorist prohibition) is a warning to the Colossian Chris-
    tians not to be led astray by the gnostic asceticism.

22 R714 The neuter plural relative pronoun ἅ is used to cover a vague general idea,
    "referring to things which all perish."
    BD145(1) Εἶναι εἰς means "to serve for."

23 R626 Πρός does not of itself mean "against," although that may be the resultant
    idea (as here).
    R1152 In this verse the antithesis is really stated in οὐκ . . . without an
    adversative particle (such as ἀλλά).

                          COLOSSIANS 3

1   R881 The relative pronoun οὗ introduces an explanatory clause, "where Christ is."

3   R587 Ἐν τῷ θεῷ may be compared with Paul's frequent mystical use of
    (cf. John 15:4).
    R628 As applied to Christ σύν, like ἐν may express the intimate mystical union.

4   TGr119 According to this verse, Christ is life (the appositional noun ζωή).

5   R727 The pronoun ἥτις is merely explanatory (causal--R960). [Ed. It is forcing
    this pronoun to make it have a causal sense, especially since it is more usually
    used in the N.T. to express mere explanation; cf. Eph. 5:5.]
    TGr105 The adjective μέλη should be taken as a vocative noun. Thus, an adjec-
    tival phrase ("which are upon the earth") is changed into a noun phrase ("the
    things which . . .") and becomes the object of the imperative verb, "mortify."
    The phrase reads "members of my body, mortify the things that are on earth;
    fornication, uncleanness, inordinate affection . . ." It may be perhaps more
    significant, in this context, to understand "members" as members of the Body of
    Christ. St. Paul may refer to Christians in general and to his readers in par-
    ticular.
    BD258 The article is often absent from abstracts, but it occurs with the last
    noun here, meaning "and that chief vice, covetousness" (the addition of the re-
    lative clause occasions the use of the article by making the preceding noun de-
    finite; cf. Acts 19:13, 26:27; 2 Cor. 8:18).

6   T208 The translation of the genitive, "of disobedience" is equivalent to "dis-
    obedient" (i.e., similar to an adjective).

7   R971 The temporal conjunction ὅτε occurs with the imperfect ἐζῆτε to show the
    custom of the people.
    M79 Both instances of ἐν with the dative are used of accompaniment here, "with."

9   MT126 The apostle uses the present imperative to utter an urgent warning against
    a sin which was sure to reappear in the Christian community, or was as yet only
    imperfectly expelled, "do not lie."

10 M59 The prepositional phrase with κατά has the sense of "in God's image."
    M70 Εἰς is used in the sense of "with a view to," or "resulting in."

11 R1188 Dissimilar things may be united by καί as here, but we do not have to
    take καί as equivalent to ή.
    M75 Is ἐν with the dative here to be classed as a local usage (as though the
    meaning were "in all persons" or "permeating the whole of things," cf. 1 Cor.
    15:28)? Or is πάντα ἐν πᾶσιν a mere phrase of emphasis (such as the A. V.
    translation has -- "all in all")?
    M160 Here at least πάντα and ἐν πᾶσιν seem necessarily to stand for two distin-
    guishable ideas; and 1 Cor. 9:22 shows how close these phrases lie to quite or-
    dinary terms of human conduct, "Christ is all and is in all."

13 R690 The reflexive pronoun ἑαυτός occurs side by side with ἀλλήλων as if by
    way of variety (the reflexive pronoun means "one another").
    R742 As a substantive τις may be equal to "anyone."
    R1418 The present participles are used as present imperatives. [Ed. Actually
    the participles here are dependent upon the imperative verb in v. 12, "put on
    therefore . . ., forbearing . . ., forgiving."

14 R605 The notion of addition is seen in ἐπί with the dative ("in addition to"--
    BD235[3]).
    R713 The neuter relative pronoun ὅ comes in between a feminine antecedent and
    a masculine predicate substantive (it gathers the general notion of "thing").
    T212 The objective genitive is used here meaning "the bond producing perfection"
    (cf. BD163).

15 R499 In this verse τοῦ Χριστοῦ is probably subjective and means "the peace that
    Christ has and gives," but the meaning is richer than any phrase.
    M70 The preposition εἰς is used in the sense of "with a view to," or "resulting"
    (i.e., final or consecutive). [Ed. The context seems to support the final ren-
    dering, indicating the goal.]

16 R690 The reflexive pronoun ἑαυτούς is used in a reciprocal sense (i.e., for
    ἀλλήλων; cf. T43 and 3:13).
    M45 The datives ψαλμοῖς, ὕμνοις, and ᾠδαῖς seem more like datives of accompani-
    ment than instrumentality, "with . . ."
    M75 It is difficult to describe whether ἐν means "within" (an individual) or
    "among" (a number of persons), in the phrase ἐν ὑμῖν. [Ed. The exhortation
    seems to be given to a corporate group of believers, especially in view of the
    following clauses in the plural and the sense of ἑαυτούς. Thus, ἐν ὑμῖν more
    probably means "among you."]
    M78 The phrase ἐν πάσῃ σοφίᾳ is adverbial if joined with the words which follow
    it: otherwise it has a different shade of meaning -- of accompaniment. Whereas
    the phrase ἐν τῇ χάριτι perhaps means "gratefully" (an adverbial usage). [Ed.
    The prepositional phrase ἐν πάσῃ σοφίᾳ appears to go more readily with the fol-
    lowing clause rather than with the previous one; because the adverb πλουσίως
    sufficiently qualifies the previous imperative, and the noun σοφίᾳ makes much
    better sense if it modifies διδάσκοντες rather than ἐνοικείτω]
    TGr166 The participles are used as imperatives and should be translated, "in
    all wisdom (supply "be ye") teachers and exhorters of yourselves; in psalms,
    hymns, and songs (supply "be ye") joyful choristers" (cf. R946; BD468[2] and
    MT181).

17 M79 The preposition ἐν is used with a descriptive sense. Thus the first part
    of the verse should be translated "whatever you do, whether it is a matter of
    words or actions . . ."

18   R807   Ὑποτάσσεσθε may be a direct middle, "subject yourselves . . ." (cf. MT 163).

        R887   The imperfect tense of ἀνῆκεν may be used to show an obligation which is not lived up to, or has not been met (it is used simply to express a present obligation—B32; cf. T90; "as is fitting"—BD358[2]). [Ed. The final suggestion is most probable since the imperfect may be used to refer to a present obligation in the N.T.; cf. Acts 22:22 and Eph. 5:4.]

19   H402   Πικραίνομαι means "to show bitterness."

20   T263   It is misleading to render the last part of v. 20 by "pleasing <u>to</u> the Lord"; Paul means that obedience to parents is fit and proper in that state of grace in which the Christian now lives. In the Pauline Corpus "to" after εὐάρεστος is expressed by the simple dative, not ἐν, and we would expect only the dative here if "to" is meant; moreover, the parallel with ἐν κυρίῳ, in the command to women just above, would be lost; for in v. 18 it can only mean "in the Lord."

COLOSSIANS 4

2   T265   The first occurrence of ἐν in this verse has the meaning "occupied in" (cf. 1 Tim. 4:15).

3   R407   Ἡμῖν appears to be a literary plural (referring to Paul himself; cf. the singular verb δέδεμαι).

        R1090   The infinitive λαλῆσαι is used to express the notion of result (hypothetically), "that I may speak" (cf. Eph. 6:19).

        R1140   Ἅμα with the participle suggests simultaneous or immediate sequence in relation to the main verb ("at the same time also for us"—BD425[2]).

        T212   Does ἡ θύρα τοῦ λόγου mean "the door leading to the word" (objective) or "the door where the word enters" (subjective: "where the word enters"—BD166). [Ed. Apparently Paul uses the noun θύρα with ἀνοίγω in a metaphorical sense, referring to an opportunity to preach the Gospel, cf. Acts 14:27; 1 Cor. 16:9 and 2 Cor. 2:12.]

5   R625   The preposition πρός with the accusative case seems to be employed for a living relationship or intimate converse.

        R810   The indirect middle is used here; τὸν καιρὸν ἐξαγοραζόμενοι means "buying the opportunity for yourselves out of the open market" (this verb means "redeeming what has fallen into bad hands"—H309).

        T75   The present imperative means "go on walking."

6   R1045   In v. 6, πῶς after εἰδέναι ("know how to do") is to be distinguished from the use of the infinitive after οἶδα (cf. Luke 11:13).

        R1090   The infinitive εἰδέναι is used to express the notion of result (hypothetically; "that you may know").

7   T15   Τὰ κατ' ἐμέ means "what concerns me."

8   R846   Ἔπεμψα is an epistolary aorist (the event will be perceived of as past by the recipients, cf. B44 and M12).

12 R172 'Επαφρᾶς is an abbreviation of 'Επαφρόδιτας, but it does not follow that
     the same man is indicated in Philippians and Colossians (cf. 1:7).
     R772 The anarthrous πᾶς here means "every," with the resultant meaning "what-
     ever be the will of God for you."
     R994 "Ινα is used to introduce an object.
     H275 Πληροφορέω means "to bring in full."

15 R608 The phrase κατ' οἶκον has the notion of rest, "in" or "at her house."

16 R600 In τὴν ἐκ Λαοδικίας the ἐκ assumes, of course, that an epistle had been
     sent to Laodicea, and suggests that the Colossians get it from (ἐκ) them (ἐκ
     is used for ἐν[τὴν ἐκ -- "the one that is at"]--BD437). [Ed. The preposition
     ἐκ should be considered as signifying origin or source, i.e., "from," rather
     than indicating a local sense (i.e., "at"), because ἐκ is more commonly used
     as such. Before a preposition is to be taken as having an unusual meaning
     (i.e., used instead of another preposition), the more general idea of the pre-
     position has to have very little meaning in the context. The letter had al-
     ready been written to Laodicea, now it would come from Laodicea.]
     T95 "Ινα . . . ἀναγνωσθῇ is used in an imperatival sense meaning "see that it
     is read" (in vv. 16 and 17, ἵνα is used in an object clause [cf. v. 12]--B205).
     [Ed. In both verse 16 and 17, the ἵνα clause follows an imperative. In each
     instance the clause is used to denote the content of the command, giving it an
     imperatival force. But actually the ἵνα clause is used as an object clause.]

I Thessalonians

3 T211 The genitives πίστεως, ἀγάπης, and ἐλπίδος are subjective and mean, "work
    done from faith and love" and "the sustaining patience which hope brings" (cf.
    BD163).

5 R1045 Οἷοι is used in an indirect question here, "you know what kind of men."
    M78 In ἐν λόγῳ μόνον, the preposition is used in the sense of accompaniment,
    "merely as so much talking."

7 T25 Τύπον is used as a distributive singular with the plural pronoun ὑμᾶς, "you
    became an example."
    T182 In ἐν τῇ Μακεδονίᾳ καὶ ἐν τῇ Ἀχαΐᾳ, the two provinces are viewed sepa-
    rately (repeated article), then in the following verse they are grouped to-
    gether (ἐν τῇ Μακεδονίᾳ καὶ Ἀχαΐᾳ) and contrasted with ἀλλ' ἐν παντὶ τόπῳ.

8 B369 Ὥστε with the infinitive expresses the result of the principal verb, "in
    every place your faith to God-ward is gone forth, so that we do not need to
    say anything."
    T187 The article ἡ is used with the prepositional phrase here to avoid ambi-
    guity (the article ἡ indicates that πρὸς τὸν θεόν modifies the noun πίστις).

9 R732 Ὁποίαν is used in an indirect question, "they report . . . what kind of
    welcome."
    R1032 Πῶς is used for ὅτι (in a declarative sense, although it is best tran-
    slated "how") after the verb ἀπαγγέλουσιν.

10 R475 ἀναμένω has the sense of "wait for" when it is used with an accusative.
    R426 In this verse, ῥυόμενον is explanatory, and ἐρχομένης is restrictive, with
    the resultant meaning "who delivers us from the wrath to come."

I THESSALONIANS 2

4 M32 Note the retained accusative with the passive infinitive, "we have been
    approved to be entrusted with the Gospel" (cf. 1 Cor. 9:17). [Ed. Οὐ is used
    with the participle here because of the οὐ . . . ἀλλά contrast.]

5 M78 Ἐν is used in the sense of accompaniment, "we neither . . . used words of
    flattery."

6 T259 There isn't much significance in the change of prepositions from ἐκ to
    ἀπό here (both prepositions mean "from" in this context).

7 M78 Ἐν βάρει εἶναι means "to be burdensome" (ἐν with the dative has an adverbial sense).

9 R1075 Πρὸς τό with the infinitive expresses subjective purpose, "that we might not burden."
M69 Εἰς ὑμας is used as a simple dative (S* has ὑμῖν, "to you").

10 R1032 Ὡς is used in a declarative sense (similar to ὅτι), although it really means "how." When used with a declarative meaning, ὅτι expresses the thing itself and ὡς the manner or quality of the thing.
T239 The dative pronoun ὑμῖν is used with ἐγενήθημεν in the sense of credit, "for you believers."

12 R787 Although βασιλείαν and δόξαν may be distinct, they are considered as one here, because the article τήν is not repeated.
R1072 Εἰς τό with the infinitive περιπατεῖν is used as the object of the participle of command or entreaty giving the content of those participles (it is equivalent to ἵνα with a subjunctive verb after verbs of exhorting; cf. (B412 and T143), "encouraging . . . you to live lives worthy of."

13 M167 Characteristic, it would seem, of Paul is the displacement of καί which ought logically to cohere closely with the verb, as in καὶ διὰ τοῦτο καὶ ἡμεῖς εὐχαριστοῦμεν. Here the context points to εὐχαριστοῦμεν rather than ἡμεῖς as the proper focus, with the resultant meaning "that is in fact (καί)why we give thanks" (διὰ τοῦτο καί is a phrase so fixed that καί can even be separated from the verb which it emphasizes--BD442[12]).

14 T212 As a genitive of relationship, θεοῦ is used to express an ill-defined relationship which may be called "mystical" and seems to be interchangeable with the ἐν Χριστῷ formula, "the churches of God which are in Judea in Christ Jesus." BD111(2) Συμφυλέτης means "tribesman."

15 R1205 Note Paul's use of hyperbole in "oppose all men."

16 M70 Εἰς τέλος means "completely" (a phrase probably influenced by Hebrew: "in full"--BD207[3]).
T143 Εἰς τὸ ἀνακληρῶσαι refers to the purpose of God (cf. MT219; the result is conceived or actual--B411). [Ed. Possibly both elements of purpose and result are involved, cf. Rom. 1:11.]
T189 The possessive pronoun αὐτῶν occurs in an unusual position here (occurring before the noun rather than after it, consequently indicating emphasis).

17 M156 In ἀπορφανισθέντες . . . προσώπῳ οὐ καρδίᾳ, the negative οὐ is, strictly, construed with the participle, though remote in position. [Ed. Actually, οὐ negates the noun καρδίᾳ not the participle, with the resultant meaning "when we were torn away from you, in person, not in heart."]

18 M119 Does ἠθελήσαμεν . . . ἐγὼ μὲν Παῦλος mean "we (all) wanted . . . (at least I did)," or does it mean simply "I wanted (though others did not)"? (Paul uses the plural verb to refer to himself--R407). [Ed. Moule's latter suggestion seems to be preferable since Paul frequently uses the literary plural.]

19 T190 The possessive pronoun ἡμῶν occurs before the nouns that it is used with

to avoid repetition (rather than the usual position of following the noun).

I THESSALONIANS 3

1 M119 The plural in this verse must certainly be epistolary (by the very meaning of μόνος), referring to Paul himself.

2 M65 Ὑπέρ with the genitive has the meaning "concerning, about," thus the last part of this verse should be translated "to encourage you about your faith" (cf. T270).
M119 Ἐπέμψαμεν appears to be identical in meaning with ἔπεμψα in v. 5 (thus the plural refers to Paul himself, cf. v. 1).
MT68 Ἐν τῷ εὐαγγελίῳ means "in the sphere of the Gospel."

3 R686 In this verse, αὐτοῦ means "you for yourselves."
BD399(3) Τὸ μηδένα with the infinitive expresses the notion of purpose here (cf. M140).

4 H467 Πρός has the meaning "with" (due to semitic influences).

5 R458 Εἰς with the accusative κενόν seems to denote the idea of purpose.
R988 Paul's use of μή πως ἐπείρασεν . . . γένηται is in accord with the Attic idiom where in pure final sentences a past tense of the indicative was used if it was distinctly implied that the purpose was not attained (that in fact is the case here, because the tempter did not succeed with the Thessalonians).
R1071 Εἰς τό with the infinitive has the idea of purpose, "in order to know" (cf. M140 and T143).
M167 Κἀγώ appears to be displaced, thus the verse does not begin with "therefore I also sent," but with "therefore I actually sent," or "that is in fact why I sent."

6 R579 One should not read too much into the preposition ἀπό. It does not mean "authority from," although Timothy undoubtedly claimed it.

7 R605 Ἐφ' ὑμῖν seems to be a simple use of the dative case with ἐπί supplementing it, meaning "in you" (cf. 2 Cor. 9:14).
T190 The attributive pronoun ὑμῶν in this context is emphatic (it precedes the noun πίστεως), "your faith."

8 BD372(1a) Ἐάν appears for εἰ (equivalent to ἐπεί) with the present indicative στήκετε in a causal sense, "since you stand."

10 R1072 Εἰς τὸ ἰδεῖν is used as the object of δεόμενοι (cf. 2:12), "praying . . . that we may see you."

11 B176 Notice the three optatives of wishing in vv. 11f. (indicating prayerful expectation).
T41 The pronoun αὐτός probably has some emphasis here ("God, himself").

I THESSALONIANS 4

1 R766 The article τό introduces an indirect question (thus there is no special
   meaning linked with the article, i.e., it is not to be translated).
   M161 Λοιπὸν οὖν means "finally, then" (or "and so").

2 M57f. Τίνας . . . ᾿Ιησοῦ means "what injunctions we (or perhaps I) gave you in
   the name of the Lord Jesus" (parallel to ἐν κυρίῳ ᾿Ιησοῦ in v. 1), or do both
   phrases mean "as those who are [or one who is] in contact with the Lord Jesus"?
   (cf. Acts 3:6 and 4:30; although Paul is the speaker he conceives of Jesus as
   also making the commands--R583). [Ed. It appears that Paul is concerned about
   presenting the authority of the commands which he had given, rather than the
   validity of his own position. Thus Moule's former suggestion is more favorable.]

3 R698, 1059 Both the noun ἁγιασμός and the infinitive ἀπέχεσθαι are in apposition to τοῦτο meaning, "this is the will of God, that is your sanctification,
   that you . . ." (cf. B386).

4 M78 ᾿Εν with the dative nouns ἁγιασμῷ and τιμῇ appears to have an adverbial
   sense, "holily (devoutly) and honorably."

6 R1059 Both the articular and anarthrous infinitives here are in apposition to
   τοῦτο in v. 3, "that no man transgress and wrong."

7 R605 ᾿Επί with the dative ἀκαθαρσίᾳ is used to express aim or purpose, "for
   uncleanness."
   M78 Is there a real distinction or mere overlapping of prepositions here (i.e.,
   ἐπί and ἐν)?
   TGr121 No one, having examined v. 7, would charge Paul with anything short of
   precision in his use of prepositions where the finer points of theology are at
   stake. In the same sentence, he distinguishes ἐπί from ἐν, but bluntly insen-
   sitive, as often, King James's bishops failed to make the same sort of distinctions in English. It is easy to make it: "God has not called us to uncleanness, but His call is addressed to us in our state of sanctification." The
   call to believe comes to us in the sphere of Christian sanctification and redemption.

9 R997 Εἰς τό with the infinitive is always final in the other N.T. writers. But
   Paul has non-final uses (εἰς τό with the infinitive is epexegetic with the verbal adjective θεοδίδακτοι--R1072), "taught by God to love."

12 T75 The present verb περιπατῆτε means "to continue on walking."

14 R817 The passive participle κοιμηθέντας means "those who were put to sleep"
    (this gives a strikingly beautiful sense--MT162).
    M57 Διά is used in the sense of accompaniment, with the resulting meaning "those
    who have died as Christians" (perhaps "in contact with Jesus," parallel with
    οἱ νεκροὶ ἐν Χριστῷ).

15 R618 The notion of "beyond" is in the compound participle περιλειπόμενοι.

M79 The prepositional phrase ἐν λόγῳ κυρίου means "as a message from the Lord."
BD101 Φθάνω is used with the meaning "to precede" only in this verse (for this
sense Matthew uses προφθάνω in 17:25).

16 R783 The prepositional phrase ἐν Χριστῷ is attributive to the preceding noun
(the repeated article was not necessary), "the dead in Christ."
M78 The preposition in ἐν κελεύσματι has the sense of attendant circumstance,
"at the word of command."
T41 Αὐτός is emphatic here, "the Lord Himself."

17 M82 In this verse and in 5:10, ἅμα σύν with the dative looks almost like a kind
of compound preposition (cf. R638); but there is nothing to prove that ἅμα is
there doing any of the duty of a preposition, any more than "simultaneously"
in the phrase "simultaneously with" (cf. "together with").

18 M144 Ὥστε is used simply as an inferential particle (as if it was ὥς τε),
meaning "and so, accordingly" (it introduces an independent sentence--B237).

I THESSALONIANS 5

1 T27 The plural noun καιρῶν refers to a period of time (the Messianic period).

4 R998 Ἵνα has a consecutive force in this verse (cf. Gal. 5:17), "but you are
not in darkness, brethren, that (with the result that) that day should overtake you like a thief" (cf. MT210; conceived result--B218).

5 T208 Figuratively υἱός is used with a noun in the genitive in order to express
a certain quality (this adjectival genitive simply means "people worthy of" or
"associated with light"--M175).

7 H383 Μεθύσκω in the middle voice means "to get drunk."

8 M103 The participle ὄντες has a causal sense, "but we" or "since we belong to
the day."

9 T55 Some verbs appear in the middle where one expects an active, since they
have a transitive sense (here the middle of τίθημι has an active sense), "God
has not appointed us."

10 B253 A preference for the more common εἴτε (over the somewhat unusual ἐάντε)
may have led to its use in spite of the fact that the meaning required a subjunctive verb ("whether . . . or").
BD369(2) The aorist verb ζήσωμεν means "live again" (i.e., at the parousia).

11 M120 Εἷς τὸν ἕνα is used as the reciprocal pronoun ἀλλήλους (cf. 1 Cor. 4:6),
"one another."

13 BD287 Ἐν ἑαυτοῖς appears to be used for ἐν ἀλλήλοις, "among one another" (cf.
Mark 9:50; it may also be translated as "among yourselves").

14 R625 Disposition towards one is often expressed by πρός, whether it be friendly
as in this verse or hostile as in Luke 23:12.

15 B206 The object clause may be introduced by the simple negative μή (as here)
     rather than ὅπως μή, because it follows a verb meaning "to take heed."

23 M136 The optative verbs in this verse express a wish, or prayerful expectation
     (i.e., volitive optatives, "may the God . . . sanctify you wholly, and may . .
     be kept").
     T41 Αὐτός is emphatic here.

25 M63 Περὶ ἡμῶν has the resultant meaning "for us."

27 R484 The causative verb ἐνορκίζω has two accusatives here. Actually the idea
     is "cause to swear by."

II Thessalonians

4   R287 Αὐτοὺς ἡμᾶς is intensive, not reflexive (emphasizing ἡμᾶς), "we ourselves."

5   BD480(6) Ὅ ἐστιν should be understood as preceding ἔνδειγμα, with the resultant meaning "which is evidence."

8   R787 Those that do not know God and those that disobey the Gospel of our Lord are referred to as two distinct groups, because the article τοῖς is repeated.
BD165 Φλογός is used as a genitive of quality, "flaming fire."

10 T57 Notice that the accusative is retained with the passive verb ἐπιστεύθη, "our testimony to you was believed."

11 R714 The relative pronoun ὅ refers either to a verbal idea or to the whole preceding sentence. [Ed. In this context εἰς ὅ refers to the following ἵνα clause.]

12 R786 Both nouns τοῦ θεοῦ and κυρίου may refer to the same person because the article is not repeated, but the fact that κυρίος is often anarthrous like a proper noun slightly weakens this argument ("our Lord and God Jesus Christ" would be the correct rendering for the latter part of this verse--T16).
R987 Ὅπως is used for the sake of variety (ἵνα is used just previously).

1   R632 Ὑπέρ is used with the sense of "concerning" or "in connection with" (for περί; cf. M65).

2   R964 Ὡς has a causal force here with ὅτι (cf. 2 Cor. 5:19).
R1072 Εἰς τό with the infinitive is used as the object of the verb ἐρωτῶμεν, "we ask you . . . not to be quickly shaken."
BD211 Ἀπό is used to designate separation or alienation, "shaken from."

3   R1202 Notice that there is no apodosis expressed here (supply "it cannot happen").
B166 In the New Testament, the prohibitory subjunctive occurs rarely in the third person (but it occurs here), "let no one deceive you."

4   B371 Ὥστε with the infinitive indicates a tendency, although by implication realized in actual result, "so that he sits."
M154 Ἀποδεικνύντα ἑαυτὸν ὅτι ἔστιν θεός means "declaring that he is a god" (ὅτι is declarative--R1034).

382

6 BD442(15) Καὶ νῦν with the assertions means "now then."

10 R499 Τῆς ἀληθείας is used as an objective genitive, "love the truth."
   M71 'Ανθ' ὧν means "since" or "because" (possibly from semitic influence).

13 R501 The genitive πίστει ἀληθείας is used in an objective sense, meaning
   "faith in the truth" (cf. v. 10).

14 R714 The pronoun ὅ refers to the whole preceding clause (cf. 1:11).

15 T77 The imperative κρατεῖτε means "go on preserving."

16 T41 The pronoun αὐτός is emphatic in this verse, "our Lord Jesus Christ himself."

17 B176 Note the two optatives of wishing in this verse and the one in 3:5 (denoting a prayerful expectation).
   T189 Note the unusual position of ὑμῶν (possible emphasis).

II THESSALONIANS 3

1 M161 Τὸ λοιπόν means "finally" or "and so" (the neuter accusative adjective
   is adverbial).

2 R1205 Note Paul's use of hyperbole by understatement in the latter part of the
   verse.

3 R961 The relative clause with ὅς expresses a result of the preceding characteristic of the Lord.

5 TGr122 Τοῦ Χριστοῦ is used as a mystical genitive, meaning "steadfast loyalty
   in the body of Christ" (similar to ἐν Χριστῷ) rather than "the patience of
   Christ."
   T211 Τοῦ θεοῦ is an objective genitive, "that your hearts may love God" (the
   pronoun ὑμῶν also occurs in an unusual position, indicating emphasis--T189).

6 R1047 The infinitive στέλλεσθαι is used to express the content of an indirect
   command (cf. the use of ἵνα in v. 12), "we command you . . ., that you keep
   away."

8 R1075 Πρὸς τό with an infinitive is used to express a subjective purpose,
   "that we might not."

9 R965 Οὐχ ὅτι may be used in an objective ("not that") or causal sense ("not
   because"). [Ed. In the New Testament, οὐχ ὅτι generally has the meaning "not
   that" or "not as if" (cf. 2 Cor. 1:24 and 3:5). But even with that rendering
   here the notion of reason or cause is retained.]

10 R1046 The recitative ὅτι with the imperative here is not an instance of indirect command, but simply the direct command preserved.

11 R564 The whole contrast in the participles is expressed by the use of περί,

where a free rendering may be "doing nothing but doing about."
B16 The present tense in ἀκούομεν is used as the perfect tense meaning "we are informed."

14 R944 The infinitive συναναμίγνυσθαι may be explained as expressing purpose or taken as equivalent to an imperative. [Ed. The infinitive denotes the purpose of the command (σημειοῦσθε) rather than the command itself.]

15 T161 The participle is omitted after ὡς, where the phrase means "as if he were an enemy" (cf. BD416[1]).

16 M136 The optative δῴη is used to express a prayerful expectation (or wish), "may the Lord of peace Himself give."
T41 Αὐτός has some degree of emphasis here ("the Lord of peace Himself").

I Timothy

1   T206 Σωτῆρος is in apposition to θεοῦ, with the resultant meaning "of God our Savior."

3   BD115(1) 'Ετεροδιδασκαλεῖν means "to teach a different doctrine."
    BD387(3) Perhaps ἵνα παραγγείλῃς is used as an imperative (or it may depend on παρεκάλεσα--T95). [Ed. Even though the idea of exhortation is predominant throughout this context, the ἵνα clause denotes the purpose for which Timothy was to remain in Ephesus.]
    BD467 In more complicated sentences, an interrupting clause or sentence sometimes causes the author to forget the original construction and substitute another for it in resuming the discussion. The construction in 1 Tim. 1:3ff. is reduced to utter chaos by interminable insertions and appended clauses (cf. T 343).

4   BD185(2) The genitive (of comparison) would not be appropriate in this verse especially since μᾶλλον ἤ is here the equivalent of a negative in meaning (a comparative adjective expressing exclusion, "rather than"; cf. T216).
    T221 It is very rare in the New Testament to have the article with the attributive prepositional phrase and not with the noun (as in οἰκονομίαν θεοῦ τὴν ἐν πίστει), "the training of God that is in faith."

6   M41 ῟Ων τινες ἀστοχήσαντες means "which things some having missed" (i.e., failed to hit; but 1 Tim. 6:2 has περί with an accusative--T235).

9   R699 Τοῦτο is expanded or explained in the ὅτι clause, "that the law . . ."
    R427 Sometimes the connective (καί) is used with part of the list (pairs) and not with the rest for the sake of variety (as in 1 Tim. 1:9ff.).

10 T197 ῎Αλλος and ἕτερος are found together for variety, showing there is little difference between them.

11 R485 The nominative with the passive here becomes the predicate accusative, "with which I have been entrusted." [Ed. Actually, this is a retained accusative with a passive verb, but it provides the same translation (cf. 1 Thess. 2:4 and Gal. 2:7).]

12 R1035 ῞Οτι has a declarative sense. [Ed. In this context ὅτι does not express the content of the previous verb, but rather the reason for the action in that verb. Thus it has a causal use here.]
    T80 θέμενος is more suitably interpreted as referring to an action which is coincident with the main verb, "he considered me faithful by appointing."

13 R1127 'Αγνοῶν is used as a participle of manner, "I did it ignorantly."

385

15 M198 In the Pastoral Epistles, does πιστὸς ὁ λόγος refer to what precedes or
    to what follows? [Ed. This construction occurs five times in these letters
    (1 Tim. 1:15; 3:1; 4:9; 2 Tim. 2:11; and Tit. 3:8). Generally it is used to
    introduce a significant point that Paul is about to make, as it appears to be
    used here.]

16 R771 ῾Απᾶς occurs only once in the New Testament in the attributive position
    and with the meaning "the total sum of his longsuffering" ("his entire patiencᵉ'
    --M94; "the almost [perfect] patience of which he is capable"--BD275[7]).
    M77 ῞Ινα ἐν ἐμοῖ πρώτῳ perhaps means "that in my case, as the foremost example."
    An extension of the instrumental use might be called exemplary (cf. R657).

18 BD308 ῾Ο προάγων means "the earlier, preceding."

19 R620 Only with the Philippian Epistle did Paul begin the use of περί with the
    accusative (cf. the genitive) in the sense of "concerning" (cf. T270; περί
    with the accusative is used in a metaphorical sense, "in respect of their (or
    the) faith"--M62).

20 M43 ῟Ων ἐστιν means "among whom is" (a partitive genitive; the partitive geni-
    tive may be used predicatively as well as attributively--T210).

I TIMOTHY 2

2   R581 Διά in the compound verb here has a perfective idea, "clear through their
    life."

3   R642 ᾿Ενώπιον has the notion of judgment here, "acceptable before."

6   R490 Τὸ μαρτύριον is in the accusative without any immediate connection unless
    it is in apposition with the preceding clause or is loosely united with δούς.
    [Ed. This noun is in apposition to the accusative in the previous clause,
    "the ransom . . ., that is the testimony" (or witness).]
    R573 Both ἀντί and ὑπέρ combine with λύτρον in expressing the idea of "instead
    of" (the substitutionary conception of Christ's death).

9   M57 Διά with the genitive is used to express environment, attendant circum-
    stance. Κοσμεῖν . . . ἀγαθῶν means "to adorn themselves . . . with good deeds"

12 BD257(3) A noun may be anarthrous in formula, thus γυναικί . . . ἀνδρός occurs
    with the meaning "over a man" (instead of: "over her husband").
    H278 Αὐθεντέω means "be master of, govern." The verb is branded as vulgar by
    Atticists, and is accordingly good vernacular, in the same sense as in this
    context.

15 M56 Διά may possibly mean "by means of" in this verse (see commentaries for
    the interpretation "saved by means of her (or the) childbearing"; but why not
    "brought safely through childbirth"? (Cf. 1 Pet. 3:20; it may be either--T267).
    [Ed. The latter rendering portrays the local sense of the preposition. Also
    the following clause with ἐάν is more easily understood with this rendering.]

I TIMOTHY 3

3   R1172 The negative μή is used with the two nouns, because they are dependent
      upon the construction δεῖ εἶναι (μή is the usual negative with the infinitive),
      "it is necessary to be . . . no drunkard, not violent."

6   R664 The bishop is not to be a neophyte (i.e., a new convert). The point, of
      course, lies more in length of experience than of age.

13   M81 In πίστις ἐν it is not certain that ἐν indicates the object so much as the
      sphere of faith (even with the repeated article; it means "the belief of those
      who are in Christ," or "Christ's own personal faith"--T263). [Ed. The con-
      text here supports the former suggestion.]

14   T30 Τάχιον means "quickly" (a comparative used for a positive).

15   R729 Ἥτις is not in concord with its antecedent οἴκῳ, but with its predicate
      nominative ἐκκλησία.

16   R534 Ἀγγέλοις may possibly be an instrumental dative, but is most probably a
      true dative (i.e., a simple dative), "appeared to angels."
      R713 The true text with ὅς is changed in the Western class of documents to ὅ
      to agree with the noun μυστήριον.
      M199 The hymn in this verse consists of six brief sentences, with the verbs
      all in the third singular aorist passive and therefore rhyming, and with a
      noun in the dative at the end of each (strongly stylized--BD488; balanced in
      Hebrew parallelism--R422).
      BD312(1) Ἐπιστεύθη means "be believed in." When a verb which takes a dative
      in the active is in the passive, the dative becomes the subject.

I TIMOTHY 4

1   R499 The noun δαιμονίων is used as a subjective genitive, "from demons."
      BD62 Ὕστερος occurs as a superlative only here, "in future times."

3   R785 The article τοῖς is not repeated because the epithets refer to the same
      people.

4   B436 The adverbial participle with a conditional sense occurs in this verse,
      "for **every creature of God is good, and nothing is to be rejected, if** it be
      received with thanksgiving."

5   M57 Διά is used in the sense of "by means of" (it has the meaning "in the
      presence of," cf. 1 Tim. 2:10--T267). [Ed. The former suggestion seems to be
      preferable since it is the more usual meaning of this preposition and it has
      a valid sense within the context.]

8   R1128 Ἔχουσα is used as a causal participle, "because it has promise" (cf.
      B439).

T274 Πρός with the accusative has the meaning of purpose or result (the idea
of purpose is retained here).

13 R976 Έως with the present indicative ἔρχομαι has the notion of "while" not
"until" and is a lively proleptic future in reference to the present (it probably means "while I am coming," the coming being conceived of as in progress
from the time of speaking—B328; since ἔως clauses are invariably post-positive, we must alter our punctuation here and take the clause with what precedes, "make yourself an example, until I come"—T344). [Ed. It is not
totally correct to say that ἔως is invariably post-positive (cf. Matt. 5:18
and 2 Cor. 3:15, as well as this exception). But the present verb ἔρχομαι
seems to be used as a futuristic present (cf. John 21:22ff.), with the resultant
meaning "until I come, apply yourself to . . ."]

14 R611 Μετά approaches the instrumental idea (it has the meaning "association
with"—M61).
M57 Διά has the sense of accompaniment, ". . . was given to you with accompanying prophecy," unless it means "through the medium of prophecy," i.e.,
an instrumental sense (the preposition means "in the presence of"—T267).
[Ed. It is difficult to determine how the preposition is used here, but the
most probable sense is that of Moule's first suggestion.]
T76 We might expect the aorist prohibition rather than the present μὴ ἀμέλει,
"don't start" (Paul makes frequent use of μή with the present imperative in an
inchoative sense, prohibiting a course of conduct—R890).

15 MT184 Ἐν τούτοις ἴσθι means "let us be wrapped up in these things" ("in the
sphere of"—R589; "occupied in"—T265).
T189 It is not very common to have the possessive pronoun preceding the substantive (consequently, σοῦ is being emphasized here).

I TIMOTHY 5

1 MT125 The aorist prohibition μὴ ἐπιπλήξῃς would be answered with "I will
avoid doing so."

5 R302 The adverb ὄντως is used as an adjective, "the real widow."

11 BD101 The active verb γαμεῖν is used with reference to a woman here and in a
few other instances in the New Testament. Otherwise, the passive is used with
a woman.

13 R617 The noun περίεργος for "busybody" has the sense "busy about trifles and
not about important matters" (περί has the notion of "beyond"—R618).
T160 Is the participle used with the verb or is εἶναι to be supplied? More
often the infinitive is used with μανθάνω (this is not an example of a participle with μανθάνω, for this could only mean "learn that they are going about"
—M229). [Ed. Εἶναι is to be supplied with ἀργαί.]

19 R603 Ἐπί with the genitive yields the resultant meaning of "before" or "in
the presence of."
M83 There is obviously a redundancy here, but it may be presumed that, without

the εἰ μή, ἐκτός would have been virtually a preposition; cf. the illiterate "without he interpret" (together it means "except if"--T321).

21 B447 The participle (ποιῶν) expressing manner or means denotes the same action as that of the principal verb (φυλάξης), describing it from a different point of view.

22 BD337(2) The present imperative in the construction σεαυτὸν ἁγνὸν τήρει has the sense of "(henceforth in all things) keep yourself pure."
MT125 In μηδὲ κοινώνει, was Timothy warned to stop what he was hitherto guilty of? (The present tense is used with an inchoative or conative sense [prohibiting a course of conduct], cf. 4:14--R890.)

24 R620 Πρόδηλος means "openly manifest," "before all."

I TIMOTHY 6

2 BD170(3) Ἀντιλαμβάνεσθαι means "to care for."

3 R609 Κατ᾽ εὐσέβειαν carries the notion of tendency or aim (promoting godliness).
BD115 Ἑτεροδιδασκαλεῖ means "to teach a different doctrine."

4 T270 Περί with the accusative, meaning "about, concerning," is used for περί with the genitive.

5 M41 Ἀποστερεῖν means "to deprive of," followed by the genitive of separation.
BD116(4) Διαπαρατριβαί has the sense of "constant disputations," from παρατριβή which means "dispute" (παρατριβή literally has the meaning "collision"--H303; the combined διά and παρά has the perfective idea of "clear through" or "thoroughly"--R582).

8 R871 The future verb ἀρκεσθησόμεθα is durative, "we shall be content continually" (the resolution is volitive, similar to an imperative--R889).
BD101 In Hellenistic Greek the passive deponent of ἀρκεῖν means "be satisfied with."

10 BD202 Περιπείρω . . . literally means "to pierce oneself with many pangs."

12 T77 The aorist imperative (ἐπιλαβοῦ) is used for a precept that is valid until the coming of Christ.

13 R603 Ἐπί and the genitive has the resultant meaning of "before" or "in the presence of."

15 R495 The accusative when used of time expresses duration over a period, the locative (dative) regards the period as a point even if it is of some length (as with καιροῖς ἰδίοις), while the genitive implies nothing as to duration.
R660 Κύριος τῶν κυριευόντων is a superlative, "the Lord of lords."

17 R783 In ἐν τῷ νῦν αἰῶνι another article was not necessary with the attributive prepositional phrase (i.e., τοῖς ἐν), "the rich in this world (age)."

B102 The perfect tense has intensive force, "charge them that are rich in this present world, that they be not high minded, nor have their hope set on the uncertainty of riches" (cf. R908).

18 H378 Κοινωνικός originally meant "social," but later acquired the meaning "ready to go shares," as here.

20 R810 Ἐκτρέπομαι is used as an indirect middle, "avoiding for yourselves." R856 The aorist imperative φύλαξον is used to show that the action, durative in itself, is treated as punctiliar, "guard what has been entrusted to you." BD146(1b) Ὦ is usually employed to express emotion. Here it introduces a strict command.

21 T270 Περί with the accusative is used for περί with the genitive (cf. v. 4), "concerning."

II Timothy

3   R963 'Ὡς may have almost the force of a causal participle ("when" or "since").

6   R722 The prepositional phrase δι' ἥν αἰτίαν acts as a causal conjunction, "wherefore, hence."

8   B426 The explanatory attributive participle occurs here, "according to the power of God; who saved us, and called us with a holy calling."
     MT125 The aorist prohibition (μὴ ἐπαισχυνθῇς) would be answered with "I will avoid doing so."

9   T27 Χρόνων does not quite mean "years," as in much later Greek, but advancing that way, it certainly has the meaning "period."

12   R594 Εἰς is used with expressions of time, where the preposition marks either the limit or accents the duration expressed by the accusative. Thus we find εἰς ἐκείνην τὴν ἡμέραν where "until" suits as a translation (cf. "against").
     MT204 Δυνατὸς φυλάξαι means "competent for guarding."

14   T77 The aorist imperative may be used for precepts which are valid until the coming of Christ (a durative action is expressed by a simple aorist, cf. 2:2 --R856).

18   TGr90f. The latter part of this verse should be translated "you are very well aware of all that Onesiphorus did for me at Ephesus." Hellenistic writers tended to depart from classical standards by using the comparative degree of the adjective in place of the superlative (cf. MT236 and H164; βέλτιον means "better than I"--R665; this adjective does not mean "better than I"--BD244[2]). [Ed. The comparative adjective βέλτιον is actually used as an adverb (cf. R277) with the meaning "very well."]

2   R856 In the verb παράθου the action, durative in itself, is treated as punctiliar (the aorist imperative here and in v. 3 is used for precepts, cf. 1:14-- T77).
     B376 The infinitive may be used to limit adjectives and adverbs. Thus we have "who shall be able to teach others also."
     M57 Διὰ πολλῶν μαρτύρων means "in the presence of (or perhaps "supported by") many witnesses" (i.e., διά of attendant circumstance; cf. T267).

5   B260 An example of the present general conditional clause occurs here. Thus

it means "and if also a man contends in the games, he is not crowned, unless
he contends lawfully."

6   M95 Τὸν κοπιῶντα γεωργόν perhaps means little more than "the industrious farmer"; but τὸν γεωργον κοπιῶντα would have meant "the farmer as he worked" (or
"works") a sense which a mere adjective could not have conveyed (cf. "working
men" and "men at work").

8   R1041 Ἐγηγερμένον is an adverbial participle used in indirect discourse with
the verb μνημόνευε ("remember that Jesus Christ has risen from the dead").

11 BD372(2a) Εἰ is used with the indicative of reality to produce the sense of
a disjunctive deduction, "if . . . then."

12 M149 Εἰ with the present and future indicative carries the meaning of a recur-
rent or future condition, whether real or hypothetical (although the form implies that the condition is considered as fulfilled; "if we shall deny him he
also will deny us"; cf. B254).

13 R1119 Πιστός is supplementary to the main verb μένει, "he remains faithful."
B287 The examples in the New Testament of concessive clauses corresponding to
conditional clauses (of a present general supposition) are few, and the concessive force is not strongly marked, "although we are faithless, he remains
faithful" (cf. 2:5).

14 R605 The idea of aim or purpose seems to be present in the preposition ἐπί
here (denoting purpose-result--BD235[4]; result--T272). [Ed. In this context
the preposition seems to denote the result rather than the purpose of disputing over words.]
B479 The negative of the imperative is μή. Some exceptions may be explained
as parenthetic non-imperatival phrases in the midst of imperatival sentences.
Thus we have "that they strive not about words, (a thing which is) profitable
for nothing" (ἐπ' οὐδὲν χρήσιμον; cf. R947).
T78 Μὴ λογομαχεῖν may depend on the participle διαμαρτυρόμενος, "charging them
before God to avoid disputing about words." [Ed. Since the imperative has a
direct object, the infinitive λογομαχεῖν is dependent upon the participle διαμαρτυρόμενος expressing the content of that which is to be charged.]

15 R856 In the aorist imperative σπούδασον, the action, durative in itself, is
treated as punctiliar, "do your best," or "make every effort" (cf. v. 2; used
for a precept--T77).
H274 Ὀρθοτομέω occurs in Prov. 3:6 and 11:5, of leveling or straightening a
road; "cutting straight the path of Truth," for the pilgrims' progress thereon,
would be an attractive meaning. But it is simpler to compare (with Grimm)
καινοτομεῖν, meaning "to innovate," where the second element has faded: ὀρθοτομέω will then be "to direct, apply faithfully," as men speak of "a straight
talk" (so practically the R.V. translation in this verse).

18 M62 Περί with the accusative is used with a metaphorical sense, meaning "in
respect of" ("concerning"--R626).

21 R597 In the compound verb, ἐκ has the perfective idea ("thoroughly cleanse").

22 BD227(3) Μετά means "in company with," not simply "with" (cf. T269).

24 H379 Διδακτικός means "apt at teaching" (cf. 1 Tim. 3:2).

25 R565 In a double compound verb each preposition as a rule adds something to the
    picture, hence "to place oneself in opposition" here.
    R988f. The reading in the Westcott and Hort text is μή ποτε δώῃ(optative) in
    2 Tim. 2:25. But even so, if true, it is not a pure final clause but a kind
    of indirect question as in Luke 3:15, only in this instance the optative occurs
    after a primary tense. It is hardly just to say with Moulton that here Paul
    misused an obsolete idiom, since the optative after primary tenses occurs oc-
    casionally with ἵνα in the papyri. But it is more likely, as Moulton argues,
    that we should read δώῃ (subjunctive) since ἀνανήψωσιν undoubtedly is subjunc-
    tive.
    B225 For the gentleness and meekness in dealing with those that oppose them,
    which he has enjoined, the apostle adds the argument, (fearing) "lest God may
    perchance grant them repentance," i.e., "lest on the assumption that they are
    past repentance, you be found dealing in harshness with those to whom God will
    yet grant repentance" (the subjunctive δώῃ is the correct text).
    T178 The anarthrous noun ἀληθεία does not refer specifically to Christ.

26 R707 Notice the distinction between ἐκείνου and αὐτοῦ (αὐτοῦ and ἐκείνου ap-
    pear to be synonymous--T194). [Ed. Ἐκείνου appears to be used for stylistic
    variation.]
    T266 The preposition εἰς portrays the idea of purpose, "to do the will of that
    one."

II TIMOTHY 3

1 R699 The pronoun τοῦτο is explained in the following ὅτι clause, "know this,
   that."

2 BD460(2) Asyndeton (the omission of the article) appears naturally in lengthy
   enumerations, and specifically here because the same men are referred to.

6 BD101 Ἐνδύνοντες means "creeping in."

7 R1173 Μηδέποτε is an intensifying negative compound, "never at all."

8 M62 Περί with the accusative is used in a metaphorical sense, "in respect of"
   (instead of with the genitive).
   BD475(3) Ὃν τρόπον is felt to be one word, which is equivalent to ὡς ("in the
   manner in which" is similar in meaning to "[just] as").

15 R879 In ἀπό βρέφους οἶδας, the past action is in progress at the present time,
    "you have known" (cf. M8).
    T263 Πίστις ἐν means either "the belief of those who are in Christ" or "Christ's
    own personal faith." [Ed. In view of the context here the former suggestion
    seems preferable, cf. 1 Tim. 3:13.]

16 M95 It is most unlikely that πᾶσα γραφή means "every inspired Scripture," and
    much more probably means "the whole of Scripture is inspired" ("every Scrip-

ture," if separate portions are referred to--R772; "whatever is Scripture"--
T199). [Ed. In this context, the primary issue is whether θεόπνευστος and
ώφέλιμος are attributive or predicative adjectives. The second adjective appears to be used with a predicative sense, and καί seems to present the two
adjectives as parallel. Consequently, the preferable rendering is "all Scripture is inspired."]

II TIMOTHY 4

1   BD442(16) Καί is used for the co-ordination of two ideas, one of which is de-
    pendent on the other (hendiadys). This serves in the New Testament to avoid
    a series of dependent genitives, "of (or "at") His appearing and His kingdom."

5   T37 Σύ is used for some sort of emphasis or antithesis in v. 5; the same is
    true of ἐγώ in v. 6 ("but you . . . for I").

7   BD342(1) The perfect tense here is used to denote a continuing effect on the
    subject, that is, up to now, from which the lasting result mentioned in v. 8
    is derived (durative punctiliar with a backward look--R895; "I have fought the
    good fight, I have finished the course, I have kept the faith"--B74).

8   M161 Λοιπὸν ἀπόκειταί μοι . . . means "it remains that there is reserved for
    me . . ." ("therefore" is possible--M207).

9   R1205 In σπούδασον ταχέως the redundancy may be due to the custom of the lan-
    guage with no thought of the repetition. Here it seems to be more for the
    sake of clarification, "Do your best to come to me quickly."

10 R858 'Αγαπήσας is an example of the ingressive aorist, "Demas deserted me hav-
    ing fallen in love with this present age" (only the inception of the action
    in the aorist participle ἀγαπήσας precedes that of the principal verb--B137).

13 R614 In the phrase παρὰ Κάρπῳ the noun has a locative sense, with the resultant
    meaning "with Carpus" (i.e., at his house).

15 T127 The adverb λίαν occurs in an unusual position, since an adverb usually
    follows the adjective or verb with which it goes. [Ed. This unusual position
    of λίαν apparently denotes emphasis.]
    BD458 The relative pronoun is used as a connective; it seems to be something
    intermediate between a relative clause and a demonstrative clause with the re-
    sultant meaning "and this," "but this," or "this very thing."

16 R854 The aorist optative λογισθείη is used to denote a wish, "may it not be
    counted against them."

17 BD217(3) The phrase ἐκ στόματος is "out of the jaws."

Titus

1 M112 It is difficult to determine the meaning of the anarthrous ἀληθείας (cf. Heb. 10:26; ἀληθείας without the article refers to truth in a general sense [not to Christ]--T176).

2 T27 The plural noun χρόνων here carries the meaning of a period of time (cf. 2 Tim. 1:9).

5 T37 Ὡς ἐγώ σοι διεταξάμην is a regular phrase in letters. Thus, ἐγώ does not show emphasis.

7 R1172 The occurrences of μή here are to be explained because the infinitival construction is carried on to the latter part of the verse.

10 BD119(2) Φρεναπάτης means "one who deceives his own mind" (i.e., "conceited").

11 R774 The plural ὅλους has the sense of "whole."
BD428(4) Relative clauses with the indicative have οὐ except in two instances (here and in 1 John 4:3, and there ὃ μὴ ὁμολογεῖ is a spurious reading for ὃ λύει). Ἃ μή is neither conditional nor generalizing-iterative, therefore it is unclassical; ἃ μὴ δεῖ is probably merely a mixture of τὰ μὴ δέοντα (1 Tim. 5:13) and ἃ οὐ δεῖ (ἃ μή . . . is an exception to the general rule for relative clauses, unless indeed the relative clause is to be taken as conditional--B474; the relative clause has the negative μή because the clause is indefinite--R962).

12 T191 Ἴδιος αὐτῶν . . . means "their own poet" (i.e., not of another nationality).

15 T190 The genitive pronoun αὐτῶν occurs before the noun to avoid repetition.

16 R1036 The declarative infinitive follows ὁμολογέω here (they confess to know God).
T146 The subject of the infinitive is not expressed because it is the same as that of the main verb.

2 M179 The imperatival infinitive is highly probable in vv. 2 - 10 (cf. R944).

3 H278 Καλοδιδάσκαλος may be taken as "noble teacher."

4 R943 Ἵνα with the subjunctive is used with an imperatival sense (purpose--T101). [Ed. The imperatival sense is prevalent in the initial part of v. 3,

but the notion of purpose (or result) is denoted here.]

5   H274 Οἰκουργός is a compound with locative dependence, meaning "home worker" (or "house guardian"--H273).

7   M62 Περί is used in a metaphorical sense, with the resultant meaning "in all respects."

8   R1087 Λέγειν is an epexegetical infinitive (i.e., it further explains μηδὲν ἔχων), "having nothing to say."

9   T192 Ἰδίοις is used as a mere possessive, differing little if at all from αὐτῶν, "their masters."

10 H408 Νοσφιζομένους has a special middle force, "to purloin" (νόσφι means "apart, aside").

11 M114 Ἐπεφάνη . . . σωτήριος means "God's favour has appeared with saving power," whereas the reading ἡ σωτήριος would, of course, make the adjective into a merely qualifying adjective, i.e., "God's saving favour . . ." (the adjective σωτήριος never developed a feminine ending, which would be expected in this context--R272; it is used as a predicate adjective here--R656).

13 M109 Does τῆς . . . Ἰησοῦ mean "the glory of our great God-and-Savior Jesus Christ" or " . . . of the great God, and of our Savior Jesus Christ" (a sense which would be guaranteed if the article were repeated with σωτῆρος, but which is possible in Koine Greek even without the repetition of the article)? In this particular instance, there is the ingenious but highly improbable alternative (see the discussion in W. Lock, I.C.C. and Hort on Jas. 2:1) of taking σωτῆρος as in apposition with τῆς δόξης, and καί as meaning "namely." The latter part of this verse would then mean "the glory of our great God, namely our Savior Jesus Christ," (cf. 2 Pet. 1:1; the repetition of the article was not strictly necessary to ensure that the items be considered separately. The relevant consideration on the other side is that the phrase "God and Savior" in contemporary language referred to only one person (in approximately A.D. 100). Moreover, the article could have been repeated to avoid the misunderstanding if separate individuals had been intended [the N.E.B. text is probably correct] --T181; cf. MT84; the same person is referred to--R786 and BD276[3]).

14 R618 In the compound adjective, περί has the notion of "beyond."
    R632 Ὑπέρ is used in place of ἀντί with the resultant idea of "instead."

TITUS 3

1   BD460(1) If the text is correct that omits καί between ἀρχαῖς and ἐξουσίαις, then it is to be understood in view of the following asyndeton, "rulers and authorities."

5   R681 Αὐτοῦ is in the attributive position (emphatic, "his"--BD284[3]).

9   T28 The plural of abstract nouns may imply cases of (e.g., μάχας νομικάς means "strife about the law").

14   R1041   With the infinitive, μανθάνω means "to learn how," not "to learn that."
     T266   Εἰς is used in a causal sense, with the resultant meaning "to maintain
     good works, because of the compelling need of them."

Philemon

5   R624 Lightfoot (in location) sees a propriety in the faith which is toward
     (πρός) Christ and the love excited upon (εἰς) men.
     T189 Note the position of σοῦ here (possibly indicating emphasis).

6   M41 Τῆς πίστεως appears to be used as an objective genitive, "sharing of your
     faith."

7   T267 Διά with the genitive is used to show agency, "by you."

8   M102 Ἔχων is used as a concessive participle, "although having."

9   R201 In πρεσβύτης the sense seems to demand πρεσβευτής, "ambassador" (it is
     debatable--H86). [Ed. Actually if Paul would have desired to portray him-
     self as an ambassador, he could have done so, as he did in 2 Cor. 5:20 and
     Eph. 6:20. Elsewhere in the New Testament, πρεσβύτης refers to an aged person.
     At this stage in life, Paul undoubtedly considered himself as such.]
     M102 Ὤν presents an ambiguity: is it concessive or causal? Does the clause
     mean "though I am none other . . ." or "because I am . . ."? In other words, is
     the second παρακαλῶ still equivalent to "I only entreat" (though I might com-
     mand, as in v. 8), or is it "I entreat (with all the more force because I am)
     none other than . . ."? [Ed. In view of the context, a concessive idea ap-
     pears to be preferred; although Paul had the authority to command, he only en-
     treats, cf. v. 8 and v. 14.]
     M113 In this verse an exegetical problem occurs as to the article. Does Παῦλος
     . . . mean "Paul the aged, and now also a prisoner . . ." (A.V. translation)?
     If so, the Greek might with less ambiguity have been Παῦλος ὁ πρεσβύτης, ὁ
     νυνὶ καὶ δέσμιος, the articles serving to place two qualifying concepts, "aged"
     and "prisoner," side by side. Middleton seems to miss the point when he claims
     that the translation "the aged" would imply a distinction from other people
     called "Paul," and is not possible without the article. Still more, if (with
     the R.V. margin) we take πρεσβύτης as meaning "ambassador" (for which the
     strict orthography seems to be πρεσβευτής), the two concepts "ambassador" and
     "prisoner" are in (paradoxical) parallelism. Or does it, alternatively, mean
     simply "the aged Paul -- who is now also a prisoner"? [Ed. The final sugges-
     tion seems to be the most probable, especially since νυνὶ δὲ καί is used as
     the connective.]

10   R713 The relative pronoun agrees with the real gender rather than the grammati-
     cal gender (the masculine gender is used referring to a person).

12   R846 Ἀνέπεμψα is used as an epistolary aorist (cf. B44, M12 and T73), in which
     the author views the letter from the perspective of the recipients.
     H435 This verse does not contain a semitism (ὅν . . . αὐτόν), since αὐτόν is
     emphatic, with the following clause in apposition to it, "him, that is . . ."

13   R886 Ἐβουλόμην (a past preference) is contrasted with οὐδεν ἠθέλησα (a past
     decision).

B33 An imperfect with verbs of wishing, without ἄν, is best explained as a
true progressive imperfect, describing a desire which the speaker for a time
felt, without affirming that he actually cherishes it at the time of his **present utterance.**   Thus, we have, "I was wishing . . ." or "I have sometimes
wished . . ." ("I should have liked, but I do not, or did not, do it"--BD359
[2]; the verb is not to be taken as Blass takes it because it maintains its
usual past sense--R919; Burton's translation is certainly complicated by the
epistolary aorist in v. 12--M9).   [Ed.   Even though Paul had not yet sent
Onesimus to Philemon, the desire to keep him was probably in the past but still
tentative.]
BD458 Ὅν means "and this," "but this," "this very thing" (cf. 2 Tim. 4:15).

14 BD263(1) The neuter singular adjective ἀγαθόν is used in an individual sense
of a particular definite thing or act, "your good deed."

16 R632 Ὑπέρ with the accusative has the metaphorical sense of "above" or "over"
(ὑπερ δοῦλον means "as one who is more than a slave"--BD230).
R663 In this verse we have a distinction drawn between μάλιστα and μᾶλλον,
"especially to me, but how much more to you."

19 R623 In the compound verb, πρός has the notion of "besides."
R845 Ἔγραψα usually refers to an epistle just finished, but even so the stand-
point veers naturally to that of the reader (cf. an epistolary aorist).
R1199 Paul's innate delicacy of feeling makes him take the reproach on himself
(thus ἵνα . . . occurs, cf. 2 Cor. 9:4).
M145 Ἵνα can be explained as more or less consciously final (it is imperatival
--T95).   [Ed.   This ἵνα μη λέγω construction appears to have a remote impera-
tival sense, "not to say," cf. 2 Cor. 9:4.]

20 R784 The prepositional phrases are predicative rather than attributive (thus
they are to be taken with the verbs).
M23 The only example of the first person optative in the New Testament to express a wish is here, "let me benefit."   All the others are in the third person
singular (it is imperatival in sense, "yes brother, let me have this benefit
from you in the Lord" [followed by an imperative]--M136).

22 M135 The present imperative here is apparently inappropriate (the sense seems
to prefer the aorist, "prepare a guest room").

Hebrews

2 R408 The plural αἰῶνες is used in the sense of "world," or "eternity."
   M114 The A.V. and the R.V. translations have "by his Son" for ἐν υἱῷ. Westcott's
   paraphrase is more correct, "One who is Son." Westcott remarks further that
   we should lose as much by omitting the article before προφήταις (in v. 1) as by
   inserting it here.
   MT107 Ἐπ᾽ ἐσχάτου is equivalent to the simple dative, "in these last days."

3 T214 In the phrase "His word of power" (equivalent to "his powerful word") the
   genitive personal pronoun αὐτοῦ occurs at the end of the phrase because of semitic influence.
   H298 The Biblical use of ἀπαύγασμα seems to mean "effulgence." The noun ἀπαύγασμα comes from ἀπαυγάζω, where we have to choose between ἀπό meaning "from,
   away" and ἀπό meaning "back," and between "radiance" and "reflexion," sunlight
   and moonlight. Philo's usage is divided. The Greek Fathers are unanimous for
   "radiance."
   H368 Originally χαρακτήρ referred to a tool for engraving, then of the die or
   mould, then of the stamp or impress, as on a coin or seal (as it does here).

4 BD473(2) Ἀγγελῶν and ὄνομα are in an emphatic position (emphasizing the contrast); ὄνομα also forms a link with the following clause.

5 H463 Εἰς with the accusative is used in place of a predicate nominative, "I
   will be a father to him . . . "

7 R626 Πρός with the accusative simply means "with reference to."

8 R465 In this verse it is not certain whether ὁ θεός is vocative or nominative
   (it may conceivably be a true nominative, construed so as to mean "Thy throne
   is God," but it is more probably a vocative, "Thy throne, O God"--M32; ὁ θεός
   is used as a vocative, consequently Jesus is understood to be God--TGr15).

9 M33 The construction here with the double accusative has the sense of "thy God
   hath anointed thee with oil."

2 M57 Διά with the genitive here has the sense "by means of."

3 R1023 The adverbial participle ἀμελήσαντες is used in a conditional sense, "if
   we neglect" (cf. B436).

6   R742 Although the author uses this ποῦ τις construction, the τις is really
    quite definite in his mind, "But one . . ."
    R1001 Both occurrences of ὅτι here have a consecutive sense, "so that" (this
    conjunction corresponds to the use of the Hebrew conjunction which is consecu-
    tive in the quotation, but ὅτι seems more likely to have the meaning "for what
    reason why"--BD456[2]). [Ed. There is no apparent reason to force this un-
    usual sense upon ὅτι, especially since the original Hebrew prefers a consecu-
    tive rendering.]

8   T145 Ἐν τῷ with the aorist infinitive may mean "putting everything in subjec-
    tion" (R.S.V.), not "having put" (N.E.B. has "in subjecting all things").
    BD447(1) The use of δέ here carries the sense of "but, however" (with an adver-
    sitive sense).

9   R632 Ὑπέρ has the meaning "instead of" (equivalent to ἀντί).

10 R583 The idea of cause ("for whom") and agency ("through whom") are distin-
    guished entirely by means of the cases here.
    B149 The aorist participle ἀγαγόντα expresses an action which is neither ante-
    cedent nor subsequent to τελειῶσαι (an infinitive complementary to the verb
    ἔπρεπεν), nor is it strictly identical with it (but simultaneous action is pos-
    sible at the same time), "when he brought" (the aorist participle should be
    translated "by bringing in"--T80).
    MT106 Διά with the genitive is used to refer to God, who is the final cause and
    the efficient cause of all things (denoting the originator rather than the agent
    --BD223[2]).

14 R687 Τῶν αὐτῶν means "the same."

15 R582 Διά is used in an expression of time here (seldom in the New Testament),
    "through the whole of life" (cf. M56).

16 BD491 Since ἐπιλαμβάνεται is repeated, it is more emphatic than if it had been
    omitted in the second occurrence.

17 R920 The imperfect verb ὤφειλεν is used to describe a past obligation, "it was
    necessary for him to be made."
    B409 Εἰς τό with the infinitive ἱλάσκεσθαι is used to express purpose (cf. T143).
    M33 Τά is used as an accusative of respect, "a faithful high priest in respect
    of things pertaining to God" (or perhaps "on the Godward side").

18 R721 Ἐν ᾧ has a causal force (equivalent to ἐν τούτῳ ἐν ᾧ; cf. 6:17 and T253;
    "wherefore"--BD219[2]).
    B443 Πειρασθείς is used as an adverbial participle of means (the instrumental
    and causal ideas are similar; cf. R1128), "He Himself has suffered by being
    tempted."

                                    HEBREWS 3

5   BD351(2) Λαληθησομένων is the only example of a future passive participle in
    the New Testament, "of those things which were to be spoken."

8   B162 The aorist subjunctive σκληρύντε is used in the second person with μή to
    express a prohibition, "harden not your hearts."

9   R717 Οὗ can be regarded as an adverb ("where") or as a relative pronoun ("where-
    with"). [Ed. The former suggestion seems preferable in view of the original
    rendering of this quotation in Psa. 95.]

11 R968 Ὡς is used in a consecutive sense, "so" (cf. 4:3).
    B272 Εἰ with the future indicative is used (by semitic influence) without an
    apodosis, with the force of an emphatic negative assertion or oath, "they cer-
    tainly shall not enter" (cf. M179).

12 M114 The phrase ἀπό θεοῦ ζῶντος is much more common in the anarthrous form than
    in the articular form and the anarthrous construction always fixes attention
    upon the character as distinguished from the person of God.
    T146 Ἐν τῷ with the infinitive is epexegetical, with the resultant meaning
    "the wicked faithless heart of a deserter" (cf. "in the form of an [accom-
    plished] apostasy"--BD404 [3]).

13 R975 Ἄχρις occurs with a present indicative verb, and has the meaning "so long"
    (linear) or "while" (cf. Gal. 3:19).
    BD200(1) Καθ' ἑκάστην ἡμέραν means "every day."

16 R583 Διά is used here with the sense of an intermediate agent, "under Moses'
    leadership" (cf. M57).

19 BD442(2) Καί is used in a consecutive sense, "and so we see" (cf. R1183).

                                   HEBREWS 4

1   B224 Μή (μήποτε) is used to introduce an object clause after the verb φοβηθῶμεν
    (this occurs in Luke's writings, Paul's writings, and Hebrews as a semi-liter-
    ary feature, rather than as popular style), "therefore, let us fear lest."
    BD337(1) The aorist subjunctive here means "let us begin to fear" (ingressive).

2   B84 The periphrastic perfect denotes a completed action here ("the good news
    was preached to us").
    M175 Τῆς ἀκοῆς is used as a descriptive genitive, meaning "the word which they
    heard."

3   R132 The perfect tense of εἴρηκεν is used to emphasize the permanence of the
    Scriptural record (it is similar to the aorist here), "as he said."
    R968 Ὡς may have a consecutive sense, "so" (cf. 3:11).
    R1129 The particle καίτοι is used to make the concessive idea in the participle
    more plain, "although his works were finished."
    B272 Εἰ with the future indicative in vv. 3 and 5 has the force of an emphatic
    negative assertion (cf. 3:11).
    M73 The preposition ἀπό is used in a temporal sense, "since the creation."

4   T52 Κατέπαυσεν means "took rest."
    BD102 Ποῦ means "approximately."

6   BD62 Πρότερον is used of the first of two acts, "the first time" with reference
    to the giving of the Law; contrast πάλιν in v. 7.

7   B475 The aorist subjunctive σκληρύνητε is used with μή in a prohibition meaning
    "harden not your hearts" (cf. 3:8).
    T261 The preposition ἐν has a local sense, "in David."

9   R541 Τῷ λαῷ is perhaps a dative of advantage, "for the people."

11 T257 Ἐν after πίπτω does not mean "into," but has the resultant meaning "lest
    any one fall after," or "by."

12 R633 Ὑπέρ is used here with a comparative sense, "than."

13 R625 Πρός is employed to denote a living relationship and intimate converse,
    "with whom we have to reckon."
    T331 After the foregoing negative here, δέ has the strong adversative force of
    ἀλλά.

14 T232 The verb κρατέω means "hold sway over."

15 R530 The dative ταῖς ἀσθενείαις is used with an associative idea, "with our
    weaknesses."

HEBREWS 5

1   B124 Λαμβανόμενος does not mean "one that is accustomed to being taken," but
    "that is taken." "Being once taken" is the mark of the class of people here
    referred to.

3   BD229(1) Περί is used here in the sense of ὑπέρ meaning "on account of, because
    of, for" (cf. M63).

5   M127 The infinitive γενηθῆναι is used in an epexegetical sense (i.e., it defines
    more closely the content of the action denoted by the previous verb), "Christ
    did not take for himself the honor of becoming high priest" (cf. B375; this
    infinitive expresses the idea of result--R1089). [Ed. The immediate context
    of this verse introduces the idea that one does not acquire the honorable posi-
    tion of high priest by human means, but it is only given to him by God. Conse-
    quently, Christ was given this position in his glorification (cf. Moule's trans-
    lation). In addition, the parallelism of the initial segments of vv. 4 and 5
    is more evident with this rendering.]

7   R580 The preposition ἀπό has the idea of cause here, "heard because of his piety"
    (cf. H461).
    R598 The use of ἐκ here may accentuate the power of God (δυνάμενον), although
    Christ had not yet entered into death.
    T18 Ἰκετηρίας means "earnest supplication."

8   R1129 Καίπερ is used to make the concessive idea of the participle more plain
    (the emphasis in the use of πέρ portrays the notion of in spite of opposition),
    "although he was a Son."

10 H399 Προσαγορεύω means "to address, hail."

11 R523 Ταῖς ἀκοαῖς is used as a locative (the dative of respect is more probable
      --T220). [Ed. In essence the translation "in the sphere of hearing" is simi-
      lar to "in reference to hearing."]
      R1076 The infinitive λέγειν is complementary to the adjective δυσερμήνευτος
      (the tense of this infinitive should not be stressed--R1081), "and hard of in-
      terpretation to state," i.e., "hard to state intelligibly" (cf. B377).

12 T141 Τοῦ and the infinitive διδάσκειν is epexegetical to the noun χρείαν, "you
      have need again that someone teach you."
      BD452(3) Καὶ γάρ simply means "for," καί having lost its force.

13 T213 Δικαιοσύνης is used as a genitive of quality, "incapable of understanding
      correct speech" (or "normal speech").

14 M204 The accusative case is used with διά, where the genitive seems at least
      as appropriate, if not more so, "by exercise."

                                    HEBREWS 6

1   R498 Μετανοίας is used as a genitive of apposition or definition, "consisting
      of repentance."

2   T218 Βαπτισμῶν διδαχῆς (the manuscripts p[46] and B with διδαχήν are probably
      correct) means "teaching concerning baptisms" (cf. BD474[4]).
      BD444[4] The author changes the conjunction from τε to καί in order to link
      ἀναστάσεως and κρίματος more closely together than the other aspects of this
      verse.

6   R539 Ἑαυτοῖς is used as a dative of disadvantage, "against themselves," or
      "to their loss."
      R613 The verb παραπίπτω was used as a commercial word, meaning "to fall below
      par."
      M70 The preposition εἰς is used in a final or consecutive sense, "with a view
      to" or "resulting in."
      MT230 The participle ἀνασταυροῦντας has a causal sense, "since they crucify."

10 R998 The infinitive ἐπιλαθέσθαι is used in a consecutive sense, "to the extent
      of forgetting."

12 T331 After the negative here, δέ has the strong adversative force of ἀλλά (cf.
      4:13).

13 M60 Κατά is used with the verb of swearing, to give the resultant meaning, "he
      swore by himself."
      T80 The aorist participle ἐπαγγειλάμενος is best interpreted as expressing co-
      incident action in reference to the main verb (i.e., the same action is ex-
      pressed), "when God made a promise."

14 B448 In quotations from the Old Testament a participle is sometimes placed be-
      fore a personal form of the same verb. The force of the participle is inten-

sive (i.e., intensifying the verbal idea), "certainly I will bless you . . ."
T336 Eἶ (K and L* correct to ἦ) μήν means "yes" (cf. BD441[1]).

17 M132 It is not certain whether ἐν ᾧ means "in which," or "and so" (the phrase
is causal, cf. 2:18--T253; it should be translated "wherefore"--BD219[2]).
[Ed. Moule's second suggestion is similar in meaning to the proposals of
the other two grammarians, and is the preferred rendering.]

18 R827 In οἱ καταφυγόντες, the perfective sense of κατά coincides with the
effective aorist, "we who have fled for refuge."
T72 Κρατῆσαι is used as an ingressive aorist, "begin to grasp" (cf. "to hold
fast to"--T232).

HEBREWS 7

3 M164 Εἰς τὸ διηνεκές in the New Testament occurs only in Hebrews (7:3, 10:1,
12 and 14) and means "uninterruptedly, continuously."
H276 Ἀπάτωρ means "father unknown," (so in the papyri for illegitimate
children), "with no recorded father."

4 H24 Notice the sudden touch of conversational audacity which introduces such
a word as πηλίκος into the majestic description of Melchizedek (this term
of exclamation occurs only twice in the New Testament, here and in Gal. 6:11
--R741).

6 R896 In vv. 6, 9, 11, 13, 16, 20 and 23, the perfect tense is used to explain
the permanence of the Jewish institutions (the perfect of allegory occurs in
the New Testament when the Old Testament is being expounded--M14), "blessed."

8 M104f. The anarthrous construction ἀποθνῄσκοντες ἄνθρωποι could mean "dying
men," but in the context here, it is virtually adjectival and means "mortal
men, men who are to die." In the same verse, μαρτυρούμενος ὅτι ζῇ is a bold
and rather unusual way of saying "one of whom witness is borne that he is alive."
MT114 The present tense of ἀποθνῄσκω has a frequentative notion (i.e., action
which recurs from time to time with different individuals; cf. 10:28).

9 B383 The infinitive used absolutely in a parenthetic clause (ὡς ἔπος εἰπεῖν)
occurs only once in the New Testament, meaning "so to speak" (this type of
construction occurs in literary language; cf. BD391).

11 M163 With μέν here οὖν is equivalent to an inferential particle; the resultant
meaning of both particles together is "therefore."
BD234(8) Ἐπ' αὐτῆς is not temporal, but means "on the basis of it."

12 R1129 The participle μετατιθεμένης is used with a conditional meaning, "for
it the priesthood changes."

13 M15 The perfect tense of the verbs in vv. 13f. initially appears to be used with
an allegorical sense (cf. v. 6); but since the verbs refer to the living Christ
it may be that they fall rather into the normal category of a past event which
is still operative--not merely still relevant as standing recorded in the
abiding Christian tradition.

15 T29 The two comparatives here are used to heighten the comparison meaning
     "still more manifest."
     T115 Εἰ is used with the present indicative to refer to a present reality, "as
     said before" (cf. v. 11).

16 M59 Κατά with the accusative here has the meaning "by virtue of a law . . .,
     by virtue of a power" (cf. T268).

18 T190 The pronoun αὐτῆς is not emphatic here regardless of the special position
     it has, "its weakness."
     BD308 Προαγούσης as an attributive participle means "the earlier, preceding."

20 R963 Καθ' ὅσον has a causal idea, "because."

24 R789 When the article occurs with the substantive, but not with the adjective,
     the result is the equivalent of a relative clause.
     M109 A delicate subtlety occurs in this verse in reference to the use of the ar-
     ticle. Ἀπαράβατον ἔχει τὴν ἱερωσύνην probably does not mean "is possessed of
     an inalienable priesthood" (as if the article was not used), but "has a priest-
     hood which is inalienable," the article suggesting that we know that he has a
     priesthood: it is "his (known, assumed) priesthood"; but we now add that he
     has it "as an inalienable one" (cf. 186).

25 M165 Εἰς τὸ παντελές seems best to be translated as "absolutely," with the re-
     sultant meaning "Christ is able to save absolutely."

26 R1181 The first Καί in this verse almost means "precisely" (it means "also"--
     BD442[12]). [Ed. Καί is used to portray a further description. Either of the
     proposed translations may be used to express this concept.]

27 R691 Ἰδίων has the sense of "private" here (an individual's sins as opposed to
     the peoples').

28 R418 Notice the emphatic climax in τετελειωμένον placed at the end of the sen-
     tence, "who has been made perfect forever."

                                  HEBREWS 8

1   R605 Ἐπί with the dative in this verse has the notion of "addition to" (cf.
     BD235[3]).

2   T27 The plural of ἅγιος means "temple" in this context.

3   R989 The relative clause ὅ προσενέγκῃ is used as a purpose clause, "something
     to offer" (cf. M139; the relative clause here is a complementary relative clause
     expressing that for which a person or thing is fitted--B318; cf. BD379 and T109).
     [Ed. In view of the fact that the subjunctive verb is used in this relative
     clause, the former rendering seems preferable (cf. Luke 11:6 and Acts 21:16).]
     T143 Εἰς τό with the infinitive here is used with the notion of purpose.

5   M14 The perfect verb Κεχρημάτισται is used in explaining the Old Testament (a

perfect of allegory, cf. 7:6), "he was admonished."

6   R728 The pronoun ἥτις has a causal sense.
     BD235(2) Ἐπί with the dative here has the meaning "on the basis of" (equiva-
     lent to "by virtue of," "in accordance with").

8   BD442(4) The first καί in this verse expresses a temporal designation, and
     means "when."

9   BD423(5) Ἐν ἡμέρᾳ ἐπιλαβομένου μου is a peculiar use of the genitive abso-
     lute construction. It is dependent on ἐν ἡμέρᾳ, meaning "on the day when I
     took." The participle is treated almost like an infinitive (i.e., as a sub-
     stantive in the genitive limiting another noun; the μοῦ should be taken with
     ἡμέρᾳ and the participle is used as a temporal adverb--R1123).

10   MT107 Καρδίας is best considered as accusative, but only because of εἰς τὴν
     διάνοιαν which precedes (cf. 10:16).
     MT224 The participle διδούς is parallel to the verb ἐπιγράψω (making the
     participle equivalent to an indicative verb; cf. 10:16 and R1135), "I will put."

11   T30 The simple adjective μικρός is used as a superlative, "the least."

12   T96 Οὐ μή is used with the aorist subjunctive for an emphatic denial here
     (cf. Rom. 4:8), "no more."

13   R895 The perfect tense of πεπαλαίωκεν denotes a completed state (i.e., an
     extensive perfect), "he has made the first old."
     R1073 Ἐν τῷ λέγειν has a causal notion, "because he says" (cf. T146).

                                 HEBREWS 9

1   R777 There is an apparent difficulty in translating τό τε ἅγιον κοσμικόν,
     which may be compared with ὁ ὄχλος πολύς (Jn. 12:9).   Perhaps both ἅγιον and
     κοσμικόν were felt to be adjectives (although the adjective κοσμικόν is in the
     predicate position here, it is used in an attributive sense), "earthly something."
     M163 Μὲν οὖν may be purely resumptive or transitional, "so then," or it may be
     adversative, "however, nay rather." [Ed. Μὲν οὖν appears to be transitional
     simply denoting continuation, cf. 7:11 and 8:4.]

3   M60 This is the only occurrence of μετά with a spatial sense in the New Testa-
     ment, "after (or "beyond") the second veil" (cf. R612; possibly a temporal
     notion is also included, "after the second curtain one comes to . ."--BD226).
     T31 Τὰ ἅγια ἁγίων means "the holiest place."

5   R154 In this verse ἱλαστήριον has the meaning of "place of propitiation" or
     "mercy seat."
     M60 Κατὰ μέρος means "in detail."

8   R700 The perfect infinitive πεφανερῶσθαι in indirect discourse is in apposi-
     tion to τοῦτο, "that the way . . . was not yet revealed."
     BD163 Τὴν τῶν ἁγίων ὁδόν means "the way into the sanctuary."

9   M59 Καθ' ἥν means "in accordance with."

10 BD235(2) The preposition ἐπί with the dative in this verse has the meaning
    "on the basis of" (cf. 8:6).

12 R809 In αἰωνίαν λύτρωσιν εὑράμενος, Jesus is represented as having found eternal
    redemption by himself (indirect middle voice).
    B145 It is best to take the aorist participle εὑράμενος as referring to an action
    subsequent to that of the verb εἰσῆλθεν. But it is possible that εἰσῆλθεν is
    used to describe the whole highpriestly act, including both the entrance into the
    holy place and the subsequent offering of the blood, and that εὑράμενος is thus
    a participle of identical action. In either case it should be translated not
    "having obtained" as in the R.V. translation, but "obtaining" or "and obtained."
    M57 Διά with the genitive αἵματος perhaps means "with blood" (parallel with ἐν
    αἵματι in v. 25; cf. T267).

15 BD235(2) In vv. 15 and 17, ἐπί with the dative has the meaning "on the basis of"
    (cf. 9:10).

17 BD428(5) Ἐπεί μήποτε is clearly interrogative (i.e., asking a question).

19 M95 Πάσης ἐντολῆς probably means "the whole commandment."

25 R589 Ἐν is used to refer to an accompanying circumstance, with the resultant
    meaning "with blood" (cf. BD198[2]).

26 R604 Ἐπί is used with the locative in an expression of time, "at the close of
    the ages" (cf. M50). This is not a common usage of this preposition.
    R920 In ἐπεί . . . παθεῖν there is an implied condition ("it would then have
    been necessary"--T90).

27 R963 The phrase καθ' ὅσον has a causal sense (cf. 7:20).

                                HEBREWS 10

1   M164 The phrase εἰς τὸ διηνεκές in vv. 1, 12 and 14 means "continuously" (cf.
    7:3).
    MT58 The plural verbs προσφέρουσιν and δύνανται (if correct) have an idiomatic
    usage, where there is such a suppression of the subject in bringing emphasis on
    the action, that we get the effect of a passive verb. The priests are certain-
    ly not prominent in the writer's thought, and a passive construction would have
    given the meaning exactly.

2   B230 The causal clause here (independent) has the meaning "since (if what was
    said previously was not true) they would have ceased to be offered."
    M151 In this verse there is an implied protasis, "would not (the offerings)
    have ceased to be offered (if the law could have perfected its adherents)?"

6   M63 The phrase περί ἁμαρτίας is used as the technical Septuagint term equiva-
    lent to "sin-offering" (cf. v. 26; the preposition περί is equivalent to ὑπέρ--
    BD229[1]; cf. v. 12).

7   T141 Τοῦ with the infinitive has a final sense (purpose), "I have come to do
     thy will."

8   M101 The present participle λέγων is used to denote an action which takes
     place previous to the action of the main verb εἴρηκεν ("after he said . . .
     then he said").

9   R895 The perfect tense is used in εἴρηκεν to denote the idea "it was spoken
     (punctiliar) and still is on record" (durative; the perfect verb probably con-
     veys the thought of existing result, though the use of an adverb of past time
     serves to give more prominence to the past action than is usually given by a
     perfect tense--B88).

10   H463 The preposition ἐν with the dative has a causal sense (semitic), "by that
     will," or "because of that will."

11   R617 The preposition in the compound verb περιελεῖν (περιαιρέω) has the per-
     fective force, "to take away altogether."

13   M34 Τὸ λοιπόν means "finally" or "henceforward" (adverbial, "thenceforth a-
     waiting . . ."; cf. BD451[6]).

14   R895 The perfect tense of the verb τετελείωκεν portrays a completed state (i.e.,
     an extensive perfect; cf. 8:13), "he has perfected for all time."
     MT127 Is τοὺς ἁγιαζομένους timeless, "the objects of sanctification," or itera-
     tive, "those who from time to time receive sanctification," or purely durative,
     "those who are in process of sanctification"? The latter, with the perfect verb
     τετελείωκεν, which tells (like the unique ἐστε σεσῳσμένοι of Eph. 2:5 and 8)
     of a work which is finished on its author's side, but progressively realized by
     its objects (thus the expression is similar to the recurrent οἱ σῳζόμενοι and
     οἱ ἀπολλύμενοι, in which durative action is obvious), involves a suggestive
     contrast.

16   MT224 The participle διδούς is parallel with the verb ἐπιγράφω (cf. 8:10), "I
     will put."

18   BD229(1) The preposition περί is actually used for ὑπέρ in this verse, "for."

19   BD163 The phrase εἰς τὴν εἴσοδον τῶν ἁγίων means "for entering the holy place"
     (instead of εἰς τὰ ἅγια; cf. T212).

25   T190 The reflexive pronoun ἑαυτῶν is used for ὑμῶν αὐτῶν (very emphatic), "of
     yourselves" (this pronoun is used for ἡμῶν αὐτῶν--BD284[2]). [Ed. The latter
     suggestion is preferable since this participial clause is dependent upon the
     verb κατανοῶμεν (first person plural), "not neglecting the assembling of our-
     selves."]

26   M63 The preposition περί is used instead of ὑπέρ in this verse (cf. vv. 6 and
     12), "for sins."
     T178 A peculiarity of Biblical Greek is that when ἀλήθεια is articular it re-
     fers to Christ as the real truth. But in this verse the reference is not to
     Christ, because the article is used by attraction.

27   R743 Τις actually intensifies φοβερά, "a certain fearful expectation" (cf.
     BD301[1]).

28   BD235(2) The prepositional phrase with ἐπί means "on the basis of the testi-
     mony."
     MT114 The present tense of ἀποθνῄσκει has a frequentative idea (i.e., it refers
     to action which recurs from time to time with different individuals; cf. 7:8).

29   M44 Πόσῳ . . . χείρονος means "by how much . . . worse" (cf. T220).

31   R1059 The articular infinitive is used as the subject of the verbal adjective,
     "it is a fearful thing to fall into the hands."

33   T215 The substantival adjective κοινωνός with a genitive of person means "an
     associate of."

35   R728 The pronoun ἥτις has a causal meaning.

36   B217 Although the purpose of ὑπομονή is contained in the ἵνα clause, yet the
     function is not telic (indicating purpose). Its office is not to express the
     purpose of the principal clause, but to set forth a result (conceived, not ac-
     tual) of which the possession of ὑπομονή is the necessary condition, "for you
     have need of patience, that having done the will of God, you may receive the
     promise."

37   T50 Ὅσον ὅσον is equivalent to "very little" or "how little."
     BD304 Ἔτι μικρον ὅσον ὅσον means "only for a very little while."

38   T43 Ἡ ψυχή μου is equivalent to ἐγω αὐτός, "I, myself."

                              HEBREWS 11

1   T307 The occurrence of ἔστιν seems to be exceptional in this verse, probably
     with the meaning "represents."
     BD426 It is unusual to have the negative οὐ with a participle in New Testament
     Greek. Οὐ occurs with the participle βλεπομένων in this verse because the nega-
     tive is equivalent to an a-privative. [Ed. The verb βλέπω generally denotes
     sense perception (i.e., it is the opposite of blindness, cf. Matt. 12:22 and
     Luke 7:21). The negative οὐ is used with a participial form of this verb to
     stress the fact that these things cannot be perceived through objective sense
     perception. But they are not incomprehensible.]

3   R423 In this verse the negative μή negates the prepositional phrase ἐκ . . .
     Generally the negative occurs before the word or words that are negated (cf.
     T287 and BD433[2]).
     B411 Εἰς το with the infinitive γεγονέναι expresses the idea of result, "so
     that what is seen hath not been made out of things which do appear" (cf. R1003;
     this verse indicates that one of the results or symptoms of faith is that we
     grasp (νοοῦμεν) that the worlds (αἰῶνες) were made by the word of God -- i.e.,
     the reference seems to be to the creation ex nihilo, the visible having come
     into being out of the invisible; but, if so, ἐκ μη φαινομένων is a much more

natural phrase--M168).
T25   The temporal noun αἰῶνες in this context means "world."

4   T146   A nominative noun occurs with the infinitive in ἐμαρτυρήθη εἶναι δίκαιος,
with the resultant meaning "certified to be righteous" (the nominative is used
here because it is the predicate of the subject of the verb--BD405[1 & 2]).

5   B390   The infinitive is used in indirect discourse here, "he had witness borne
to him that he had been well-pleasing unto God."

10   H278   The noun δημιουργός seems to originate from the meaning of "public worker"
which developed into "craftsman." From this the idea of "skill" grew stronger
and it becomes in philosophy a name for the Creator.

11   R616   The preposition παρά has the notion of "beyond" ("past the age").
R686   The pronoun αὐτή has an intensive sense, "Sarah herself."

12   T45   The conjunction and pronoun (καὶ ταῦτα) are used with an adverbial sense,
"and indeed" (this adverbial construction occurs with a concessive participle
--R705; the phrase means "and that even"--BD425[1]).

13   R833   Ἀπέθανον is used as a constative aorist (occurring in a summary statement),
"these all died."

15   R1015   The conditional clause of this verse refers to past time, "if they had
kept on remembering, they would have kept on having" (cf. B248).
T259   The preposition ἀπό in this verse has a meaning which is similar to ἐκ,
"out of."
MT204   The infinitive ἀνακάμψαι is used to complement (or further define) the
noun καιρόν, with the resultant meaning "opportunity for returning."

17   R885   Προσέφερεν has the sense of an interrupted imperfect ("he tried to offer"
--T65).
BD342(5)   The perfect verb προσενήνοχεν occurs with reference to an Old Testament event and implies that this event still retains its (exemplary) meaning
(an abiding example).

18   H463   The preposition ἐν has a causal sense in this verse (from Septuagint
influence).

19   M78   The prepositional phrase ἐν παραβολῇ is virtually an adverb, meaning "para-
bolically."

20   R788   The repeated article τόν emphasizes the distinction between the subject
and object.

21   R827   The compound participle ἀποθνήσκων has the simple notion of "dying" (the
present tense denotes the whole process leading up to an attained goal; cf.
MT114).

23   R833   The verb ἐκρύβη is used as a constative aorist, summing up a period of
time ("was hid for three months"). The verb ἐκαρτέρησεν also has the sense of
a constative aorist, summarizing an action.

28 BD342(4) The perfect verb πεποίηκεν is used to denote a continuing effect on
    the object (referring to a permanent institution, cf. v. 3), "he kept the pass-
    over."

32 R1126 The adverbial participle is used in ἐπιλείψει με γὰρ διηγούμενον ὁ χρόνος,
    where in a poetic way time is described as going off and leaving the writer
    discoursing about Gideon and the rest (the participle has a conditional sense,
    "if I tell"--T157).

33 MT116 The verb εἰργάσαντο is used as a constative aorist (summarizing a way of
    life).

34 R748 The pronoun ἀλλοτρίων has the notion of "aliens."
    T259 The preposition in ἀπὸ ἀσθενείας has a temporal sense, "after weakness"
    (cf. BD209[4]).
    MT116 Ἔφυγον is used as an ingressive aorist (i.e., denoting the beginning of
    an action) referring not to the goal of safety attained, but to the first and
    decisive step away from danger.

35 BD430(3) It is unusual to have the negative οὐ with a participle in New Testa-
    ment Greek. The negative οὐ occurs with the participle προσδεξάμενοι because
    of classical influence. [Ed. Οὐ is used with this participle in order to
    emphatically portray that these believers did not embrace the opportunity to
    gain freedom so as to avoid torture (cf. v. 1). Consequently, these people
    were victorious in another sense. They endured even until death.]

37 R590 The prepositional phrase ἐν φόνῳ μαχαίρης has an instrumental sense, "with
    murder by the sword."

39 R833 Ἐκομίσαντο is used as a constative aorist, summarizing the action of many
    people, "they did not receive."

                                    HEBREWS 12

1   R432 Chapter 11 has a splendid conclusion in 12:1f., which should belong to
    chapter 11 as the closing period in the discussion about the promises (this
    portrays a fluid oratorical style; τοσοῦτον and ὄγκον are emphatic--BD473[2]).
    R810 Ἀποθέμενοι is used as an indirect middle, "laying aside from yourselves
    every weight."
    B160 The verb τρέχωμεν is used as a hortatory subjunctive, with the resultant
    meaning "let us run with patience the race that is set before us."
    BD117(1) The double compounded verbal adjective εὐπερίστατον probably means
    "easily surrounding, ensnaring" (cf. H282; the p[46] manuscript has the variant
    εὐπερίσπαστον, which means "easily distracted, liable to distract").

2   M204 It is difficult to determine the meaning of the preposition ἀντί in this
    verse. Does this verse mean that Jesus chose a cross instead of the joy he
    might have had (cf. Ph. 2:6), or that he chose a cross for the sake of winning
    the joy which lay beyond and through it (cf. 11:25f. and 12:16)? (The rendering
    "Christ endured the cross instead of the joy that was set before him," seems
    more probable--TGr172; in this verse the cross and the joy face each other in

                                       412

the mind of Jesus and he takes both, the cross in order to get the joy--R574).
[Ed. The rendering of this verse depends not only on the sense of the preposition ἀντί, but also on the meaning of the participle προκειμένης. This participle seems to refer to "something that is set before" (cf. the similar usage
in Heb. 6:18). The joy that was set before him appears to be the glory that he
would experience after suffering on the cross (cf. Luke 24:26 and I Pet. 1:11).
The preposition ἀντί apparently has the same meaning here as it does in v. 16
of this chapter (i.e., "for the sake of").]

3   BD342(5) The perfect participle ὑπομεμενηκότα is used to refer to an abiding
    example from the life of Jesus.

4   R645 The adverbial preposition μέχρις in this context has the notion of "mea-
    sure" or "degree."

6   R1184 The conjunction δέ in this verse is not adversative, but continuative,
    "and punishes."

7   T174 Notice the anarthrous construction with υἱός, . . . πατήρ (and it is not
    ὁ πατήρ, "his father), "a father" (cf. BD257[3]); "what son is there whom his
    father, as a father, does not chasten?"-- MT82).
    T267 The preposition εἰς with the accusative has a causal sense here, "you are
    enduring because of discipline."

9   T334 Καί occurs with the imperfect verb ἐνετρεπόμεθα to express a further re-
    sult.

10 R625 In vv. 10f. the preposition πρός is used in a temporal expressions, in-
    dicating the extension of time.

13 R1413 Since the ἵνα μή construction is continued with δέ, the ἵνα μή is not re-
    peated, but the sense is retained, "so that . . . not . . ., but rather."

15 MT178 In this verse a clause of warning is introduced by μή, following the par-
    ticiple ἐπισκοποῦντες, "See to it that . . ."

16 M71 The preposition ἀντί has the meaning of "in exchange for" in this context,
    with the resultant rendering "he sold his birthright for one meal."

17 MT245 According to the form, ἴστε may be indicative or imperative. It seems
    preferable to take this verb as an imperative here (if it is indicative, it is
    a purely literary word).
    H310 The compound verb ἐκζητέω always seems to denote that the seeker finds, or
    at least exhausts his powers of seeking (as in this verse).

18 R1118 The present participle ψηλαφωμένῳ has the meaning of "touchable."

23 M170 Commentators are divided as to how to translate κριτῇ θεῷ πάντων, whether
    it should be "a God who is judge of all," or "a judge who is God of all."
    If the former is right, the order can only be explained as a trick of style.
    It comes in a highly rhetorical passage (cf. T350). [Ed. Moule's latter sug-
    gestion seems preferable in view of the word order and in view of the fact that
    usually a genitive immediately follows the noun that it modifies.]

24 R615 In the comparison here, the preposition παρά has the notion of "beyond"
    ("than that of Abel").

25 R810 Παραιτήσησθε is used as an indirect middle verb, meaning "beg off from
    yourselves" (i.e., "reject").
    B209 Μή with the subjunctive verb παραιτήσησθε may be co-ordinate with βλέπετε
    and consequently would be regarded as a prohibitory subjunctive (cf. R996).
    [Ed. The negative μή with a subjunctive verb generally occurs with an impera-
    tive form of βλέπω to denote the content of that imperative (cf. Luke 21:8;
    Acts 13:40; 1 Cor. 8:9; 10:12 and Gal. 5:15). Thus, in essence, it has a pro-
    hibitory sense, "See that you do not refuse."]

27 T182 The article τό is used to introduce the quotation in the initial part of
    this verse.

28 R955 In δι' ἧς λατρεύωμεν, the subjunctive verb appears to be volitive (i.e.,
    hortatory subjunctive; cf. BD377[3], "through which let us worship").

29 BD452(3) Καὶ γάρ in this verse simply means "for" (cf. 5:12).

                              HEBREWS 13

2   T226 The verb ἔλαθον expresses an adverbial idea, transferring the verbal idea
    to the participle, "they entertained angels unconsciously" (cf. R550).

4   M180 Simple adjectives may be used as imperatives in the New Testament, as is
    the case with the three adjectives and a participle in vv. 4f. (cf. R396),
    "let marriage be held in honor . . ."

5   B172 The use of οὐ μή with the aorist subjunctive here has the sense of an em-
    phatic negation with a future indicative, with the resultant translation "I
    will in no wise fail thee, neither will I in any wise forsake thee" (cf. R930;
    when a negative is followed by the double negative, the effect is a strengthen-
    ed negation--B489; cf. R1175).

6   MT150 The future passive verb φοβηθήσομαι has a durative sense. It seems to
    mean "be afraid" (durative), rather than "become afraid" (cf. M10).

9   R1166 Only the negative οὐ occurs in οὐ βρώμασιν to indicate the contrast in
    thought, "by grace, not by foods."
    MT125 The prohibition with the present tense μὴ παραφέρεσθε has an iterative
    sense, "do not be led away whenever different teachings arise."

11 M204 The preposition διά used in connection with a person has the sense of
    agency (cf. T267), "by the high priest."
    BD229(1) The preposition περί occurs with the sense of ὑπέρ, "for sin."

16 R532 The dative case in τοιαύταις θυσίαις has a causal idea ("because of such
    sacrifices"; cf. T242).

17 The particle ὡς with the participle ἀποδώσοντες expresses subjective motive,
    meaning "with the thought that they must."

18   T75 The present imperative προσεύχεσθε should be translated "keep praying" (cf.
     BD336[3]).
     BD322 Πειθόμεθα seems to be a perfective present verb, "we are convinced" (some
     manuscripts have included the perfect tense here).

19   BD244(1) The comparative adverb τάχιον appears to have a true comparative
     sense in this verse, "more quickly" or "sooner" (cf. v. 23).

20   M78 The preposition in ἐν αἵματι seems to have the notion of accompaniment,
     "with the blood."

21   B176 The aorist optative καταρτίσαι expresses the notion of wishing, "may God
     . . . make you complete."

22   R845 Ἐπέστειλα is used as an epistolary aorist, referring to the letter that
     is drawing to a close.
     M57 The prepositional phrase διὰ βραχέων denotes attendant circumstance, with
     the meaning "briefly."

23   T30 The comparative adverb τάχιον is used for the positive, with the meaning
     "soon" ("if he comes very soon"--BD244[1]).

24   T15 The articular prepositional phrase οἱ ἀπὸ τῆς Ἰταλίας simply means "the
     Italians" (from this phrase it is difficult to determine whether the persons
     are still in Italy or outside of Italy--R578).

James

1   B388 The infinitive χαίρειν in salutations is to be regarded as the object of
    an unexpressed verb of bidding, "James . . . to the twelve tribes which are of
    the Dispersion, greeting."

2   BD275(3) Πᾶσαν χαράν has the sense "all that joy means" (pure joy).

3   M96 Τὸ δοκιμεῖον (δοκίμιον) means "test" or "tested (genuine) part" (cf.
    TGr168f.).

4   B219 The idea of result is expressed by the ἵνα clause, "and let patience have
    its perfect work, that ye may be perfect and entire."

5   R1023 The imperative verb αἰτείτω is used as the apodosis of an expressed con-
    dition and the implied protasis of another conclusion, "let him ask God."
    M41 Λείπεται means "to fall short of."

7   T76 The present prohibition here means "he must stop thinking."

11 M12 The aorist verbs in this verse represent the Hebrew Perfect, which is used
    not gnomically, as is sometimes claimed, but to emphasize the suddenness and
    completeness of the withering: the grass has withered and the flower has faded
    before you can look around, as it were (thè aorist verbs are gnomic--R837; cf.
    B43, MT135 and H27; they may be gnomic aorists but they seem to render the
    Hebrew perfect too literally, unless we see in the aorist punctiliar a graphic
    picture of the fading of the grass and flower--T73). [Ed. Since the Septuagint
    has the aorist rendering of the Hebrew perfect for Isa. 40:7, that is what we
    expect to have in this reference (cf. 1 Pet. 1:24). Although what Moule sug-
    gests may very well have been the intent of the translator.]
    BD221 The prepositional phrase σὺν τῷ καύσωνι means "together with its scorch-
    ing heat."

12 T213 Στέφανον τῆς ζωῆς is a genitive of quality or an appositive genitive,
    "that crown which is life."

13 R579 In the clause ἀπὸ θεοῦ πειράζομαι, "tempted of God," temptation is pre-
    sented as coming from God (the preposition ἀπό is used for ὑπό, denoting the
    agent after the passive verb--T258). [Ed. Generally in the New Testament
    when ἀπό occurs with a passive verb, it has a sense similar to ὑπό (cf. Matt.
    16:21; Acts 2:22 and 4:36; especially note the use of ὑπό in the following
    verse).]
    M41 Ἀπείραστός may mean "untempted by."
    M8 There are several examples of Gnomic aorists in Jas. 1:13-15 (i.e., refer-
    ring to some thing well known).

BD182(3) Κακῶν appears to be used as a genitive of separation, meaning "not subject to temptation, unexperienced in evil, alien to evil."

14 BD493(3) A climax is evident in the taking up of the key word πειράζω from the previous sentence.

17 R501 Τροπῆς ἀποσκίασμα means "a shadow cast by turning."
M17 Ἄνωθεν ἐστιν καταβαῖνον may be translated "is from above, descending" (i.e., it need not be periphrastic at all).

18 BD301(1) Τις is used to soften the metaphorical expression, "so to say, a kind of."

19 B413 Εἰς τό with an infinitive is used like the simple infinitive to limit the adjectives ταχύς and βραδύς (cf. T143), "quick to hear, slow to speak."
H222 Ἴστε should be taken as an imperative, "know this" (rather than an indicative) **wherever** it occurs, except perhaps in Heb. 12:17 (cf. R329 and BD99[2]).

22 R947 The negative is used with μόνον because of the understood imperative γίνεσθε.

23 M105 Οὐ ποιητής is sort of a title, "the no doer."

24 M12 The aorist verbs κατενόησεν and ἐπελάθετο should be explained in a perfect sense (interrupted by a perfect), "no sooner has he looked . . . than he has gone away and . . . forgotten" (cf. T73).

25 R780 The article τόν is used with a sense similar to a demonstrative pronoun, "that is" (the article occurs after the anarthrous noun νόμον as a type of afterthought--T218).
M175 Notice the descriptive genitives, "forgetful hearer" and "active doer."

27 B386 The infinitive ἐπισκέπτεσθαι is in apposition to αὕτη, "pure religion and undefiled . . . is this to visit orphans and widows in their affliction."

                                    JAMES 2

1 R503 In this verse Ἰησοῦ Χριστοῦ is in apposition with κυρίου, the pronoun ἡμῶν also modifies κυρίου, which itself is an objective genitive with πίστιν, while τῆς δόξης is probably in apposition with Ἰησοῦ Χριστοῦ. The resultant rendering would be "the faith in our Lord Jesus Christ, the Lord of glory."

2 R124 Συναγωγή refers to a Christian assembly.

3 T37 The pronoun σύ has some degree of emphasis here.

4 M175 The construction κριταὶ διαλογισμῶν πονηρῶν has the meaning "judges with wicked ideas" ("who make evil decisions"--BD165).

5 M46 The dative τῷ κοσμῷ is best translated into English by an adverb, "the literally (i.e., materially) poor."

6   B139   The articular noun τὸν πτῶχον refers to the example in v. 2, "that beggar."

8   B67   Ἀγαπήσεις is used as a volitive future, "thou shalt love thy neighbor as
          thyself."
     M108   Βασιλικόν, by its very meaning ("royal" or "supreme"), practically implies
     definition, and one would accordingly expect τὸν νόμον τὸν βασιλικόν or τὸν
     βασιλικὸν νόμον. But Mayor is prepared to translate simply "you fulfill the
     royal law" (as though the article had been used). The strictly correct alter-
     native, "you fulfill the law as supreme," is rendered less likely by the con-
     text. Also "you fulfill a royal law" seems ruled out by the context. [Ed.
     Apparently the noun νόμον does not have to be articular to have a definite
     sense (cf. Jas. 4:11). In addition to this, an adjective may be attributive
     to a noun if both are anarthrous (cf. στρατιᾶς οὐρανίου in Luke 2:13). Conse-
     quently, the most probable rendering seems to be "fulfill the royal law" (es-
     pecially in view of Christ's reference to this law in Matt. 7:12 and 22:40).]
     BD450(1)   Μέντοι is weakened to "but" in this verse.

14 M111   Occasionally, the article is practically equivalent to a demonstrative
     pronoun. Μὴ δύναται ἡ πίστις σῶσαι αὐτόν is sometimes claimed to mean "can
     such faith save him?" But if αὐτόν is the emphatic word, then ἡ may (by a
     familiar idiom) mean "his"; "can his faith save him?" (the article is anaphoric,
     referring to the previous reference of πίστις--T173). [Ed. In this paragraph
     James is particularly concerned about the relationship of faith and works.
     Consequently, the emphasis doesn't appear to be upon the pronoun αὐτόν but upon
     the noun πίστις. The articular noun should then be translated as "such faith"
     or "that faith."]

15 R1121   The participle ὑπάρχωσιν carries the idea of "existing."

19 R404   Usually a neuter noun plural subject in the New Testament that has a per-
     sonal or collective meaning has a plural verb (this explains the occurrence
     of the neuter plural subject τὰ δαιμονία with the plural verb).

20 R878   θέλεις γνῶναι is a substitute for the future tense; this formula with the
     infinitive is polite, "Do you want to know?"
     BD146(16)   The vocative expression ὦ ἄνθρωπε indicates some degree of emotion.

25 R966   The participles ὑποδεξαμένη and ἐκβαλοῦσα are used to give the real reason;
     causal in meaning (cf. MT230).

                                    JAMES 3

1   R1172   The position of the negative μή may give the imperative γίνεσθε emphasis
     (generally the negative occurs directly before the word negated; cf. T287).

2   R1076   The infinitive here is complementary to the adjective δυνατός, "able to
     bridle."

3   R418   There is sharp emphasis expressed by τῶν ἵππων, because of the unusual
     position of the genitive (generally the genitive follows the noun it modifies).

4   T31 Τηλικαῦτα is used as an elative superlative, "very small."
     MT23 The participle ὄντα has a concessive sense, "big though they are" (cf.
     R1129).

5   R733 The examples of ἡλίκος in James may be regarded as exclamatory, "How
     great . . . !"

7   R533 Τῇ φύσει is used as a dative of means (cf. T240 and BD191[5]), "by human-
     kind."
     R902 The distinction between present and perfect is sharply drawn in the occur-
     rence of δαμάζεται and δεδάμασται, "are being tamed and have been tamed."

9   R590 The preposition ἐν has an instrumental sense here, "with it" or "by it."

12   R417 Emphasis is indicated from the position of the words in ἁλυκὸν γλυκὺ
     ποιῆσαι ὕδωρ (contrasting salt water with fresh water).

13   T49 Τίς is probably an interrogative pronoun in this verse, "who . . .?" (cf.
     BD298[4] and MT93).

14   R1173 The negative μή seems to negate both verbs connected by καί, rather than
     to employ μηδέ for the second verb.
     M152 There are two instances in the New Testament of conditional clauses which
     are perfectly correct in grammatical form, but which are logically inconsequent,
     as it would seem. Logically, the imperative clauses should be future indica-
     tive, "if you go on like this you will . . ."
     The sense of the sentence is scarcely mended by putting a question mark
     at the end, since μή would then make it a question expecting the answer "no."
     If only it could be a question expecting the answer "yes," it would make
     good sense, "If you have bitter rivalry . . . are you not exulting and lying
     against the truth?"

15   M17 The present periphrastic means "this wisdom is not one that descends from
     above."

18   T215 Καρπὸς δὲ δικαιοσύνης includes a genitive of apposition, "the harvest of
     a life devoted to the will of God."
     T238 Τοῖς ποιοῦσιν is used as a dative of advantage, "for those that make peace"
     (it is an instrumental dative, "by those who make peace"--BD191[4]). [Ed. The
     major point that James sets forth in this paragraph is that one's manner of life
     portrays whether or not he possesses Godly wisdom. In view of this, only those
     who make peace are sowing the fruit of righteousness. Consequently, Blass's
     rendering seems preferable.]

                                    JAMES 4

3   T55 The distinction between the active αἰτέω -- a simple requesting, and the
     middle αἰτέομαι -- an asking for what is done by contract, is not present in
     this verse (cf. MT160; the middle is used with the resultant meaning "you ask
     for yourselves amiss"--R805).

5 R626 Πρὸς φθόνον has an adverbial force, meaning "jealously."

9 T76 The aorist imperatives in vv. 9f. should be translated "start to be wretch-ed and mourn and weep, . . . start to humble yourselves" (cf. BD337[1]).

13 B294 The relative clause in vv. 13f. means "go to now, ye that say, 'Today or tomorrow we will go into this city, and spend a year there and trade and get gain,' whereas (i.e., although) ye know not of what sort your life will be on the morrow" (ἄγε is used as an interjection--R1193).
BD289 Εἰς τήνδε τὴν πόλιν means "into such and such a town."
H400 Ἐμπορεύομαι means "to travel as a merchant."

14 M124 Οἵτινες seems to be used adversatively, meaning "whereas actually."
BD266(3) The article τό (or τά) with τῆς αὔριον means "the things of the mor-row," "what happens tomorrow" (the manuscript B omits the article, in which case τῆς αὔριον is to be taken with ἡ ζωή). [Ed. Actually, τῆς doesn't have to be taken with ἡ ζωή, but may refer to an understood noun such as ἡμέρας. The resultant rendering would be "you know not on the day after tomorrow (or "on the morrow") of what nature **your life shall be." The text is uncertain** here, but the shorter text seems preferable.]
BD298(2) Ποία has a qualitative sense, "how miserable is your life."

15 R574 In this verse ἀντί has the idea of substitution, with the points of view contrasted ("instead of"--T144).
BD442(7) The use of καί to introduce an apodosis is due primarily to Hebrew influence, although it appears as early as Homer. Here, the second clause can be considered to begin with καὶ ζήσομεν, "both . . . and."

17 BD264(2) The anarthrous substantive adjective καλόν has the meaning "something good."

JAMES 5

1 R428 Winer finds asyndeton (i.e., the omission of connectives) frequent in cases of a climax in impassioned discourse (as with ἄγε . . ., κλαύσατε here; cf. R 949; ἄγε is exclamatory), "Come now, . . . weep."
R1116 The present participle ἐπερχομέναις has a futuristic sense, "that are coming."

3 M70 Εἰς has either the sense of "with a view to," or "resulting in" (i.e., final or consecutive). [Ed. The consecutive rendering seems preferable since this is a result of the rust rather than the purpose for it.]
TGr164f. The prepositional phrase ἐν ἐσχάταις ἡμέραις means "in the last days." The phrase is not used for a simple dative.

6 BD139 The articular expression τὸν δίκαιον denotes an individual example, "the righteous man."

8 R856 The action in the aorist imperative μακροθυμήσατε is durative in itself, but it is treated as punctiliar, "be patient" (considered as a precept--T77).

9 R621 Πρὸ denotes place, "before."

10   M35   The accusative τοὺς προφήτας is used predicatively, "take the prophets
     as an example."
     BD442(16)   The co-ordination of two ideas, one of which is dependent on the
     other, serves in the New Testament to avoid a series of dependent genitives,
     "of perserverance in suffering."

12   R622   Πρό occurs in the sense of superiority, "before" (preference).
     TGr31   James puts this prohibition in the present tense (μη ὀμνύετε), bidding
     his readers to refrain at once from the practice.

13   BD494   The resolution of a sentence into unconnected component parts produces
     a more powerful effect than would the periodic form proper.   The point of the
     sentence, moreover, is heightened by the brevity of the components in this
     verse.

16   M26   Πολὺ . . . ἐνεργουμένη perhaps means "the prayer of an upright man is
     very powerful in its effect," in which a transitive sense of the verb seems
     best.

17   M27n.1   Οὐκ ἔβρεξεν means "it did not rain."

I Peter

1   T170 The beginnings of letters are formula-like; consequently the article is missing from all the nouns and substantives in this salutation (although they are definite).
T235 The genitive διασπορᾶς has both a temporal and local meaning, "the sojourners in the diaspora."

2   B175 Πληθυνθείη is used as an optative of wishing, "grace to you and peace be multiplied."

4   R535 Εἰς ὑμᾶς has the sense of a simple dative, "for you" (cf. T236).

6   R978 'Εν ᾧ has its antecedent expressed in the preceding sentence and means "wherein" (there is ambiguity as to whether ἐν ᾧ is a genuine relative pronoun, meaning "in which circumstances you exult," or simply meaning "and so you exult"; cf. Heb. 6:17--M131f.). [Ed. Moule's former suggestion is preferable since that is the more usual meaning of ἐν ᾧ.]

7   M96 Τὸ δοκίμιον means "the tested (genuine) part" (cf. T14).

8   R1096 'Ανεκλάλητος is active in sense, "inexpressible."
R1138 Οὐ harmonizes with the sense of the participle ἰδόντες as an actual experience, while μή with ὁρῶντες is in accord with the concessive idea in contrast with πιστεύοντες (in the first instance, the inactuality is emphasized more--BD430[3]; the first is a direct statement of historical fact; the second is introduced as it were hypothetically, merely to bring out the full force of πιστεύοντες--MT232). [Ed. Why does Peter use οὐ with the first participle? Εἶδον is a verb of perception with two levels of meaning. It may have reference either to physical seeing (cf. Matt. 2:2 and 11), or to a deeper relationship such as actually experiencing (cf. Lk. 2:26, Acts 2:27 and 1 Pet. 3:10). Apparently the author wanted to be certain that the readers understood this verse to refer to the fact that they had not seen Christ in person and not to any lack in their spiritual relationship with Him. The use of μή with the second participle does not need to be explained. This negative is expected. Once the point was made that the seeing was objective, the author may have changed from οὐκ to μή for the sake of variety. This is plausible since μή is used with the participle to negate both objective and subjective aspects.]

10   R563 The preposition may be used with a verb but omitted with the second occurrence of that verb, but with the same sense (so ἐξηραύνησαν and ἐραυνῶντες here, cf. MT115).

11   R594 Here εἰς marks either the limit or accents the duration of the time expressed by the accusative.

T48 Τίνα . . . ποῖον is used as a tautology (i.e., a repetition) for emphasis
(cf. BD298[2]; there seems to be a distinction between the two pronouns--R735).
[Ed. There appears to be a distinction between the interrogative pronouns,
especially in view of the rarity that they occur together in the New Testament
(this is the only such example with a temporal reference). Ποῖον tends to have
more of a qualitative sense. Thus the searching in two areas; when and in what
circumstances salvation should come.]

16 T86 The volitive future ἔσεσθε expresses a command, "you shall be holy."

17 T247 Πατέρα is used as a predicate of τὸν . . . κρίνοντα, with the resultant
meaning "if you invoke as father the one who judges."
M79 Ἐν denotes the idea of accompaniment, "with fear."

18 R777 The adjective πατροπαραδότου is used in the predicate position but with
an attributive sense ("the futile ways inherited from your fathers"). This
may be explained because of the occurrence of an additional attributive.

19 R533 Τιμίῳ αἵματι is used as a dative of means, "by precious blood" (cf. M77).

21 M143 There is ambiguity as to whether ὥστε with the infinitive has a final or
consecutive (result) idea here. [Ed. Since the more usual rendering of ὥστε
with an infinitive is actual result, that appears to be the meaning in this
verse (cf. Acts 1:19; 2 Cor. 7:7 and Phil. 1:13). However, intended or contemplated result is possible.]

22 BD337(2) The aorist imperative ἀγαπήσατε has the meaning "direct your love."

24 M12 The aorist verbs in this verse (cf. Jas. 1:11) represent the Hebrew perfect
which is used <u>not</u> gnomically, as is sometimes claimed, but to emphasize the
suddenness and completeness of the withering: the grass has withered and the
flower has faded before you can look around, as it were (the aorist is used
with a gnomic sense, referring to a customary truth--R837, B43, T73 and MT135).
[Ed. Since the Septuagint has the aorist rendering of the Hebrew perfect for
Isa. 40:7, that is what we expect to have in this reference (cf. Jas. 1:11).
However, what Moule suggests may very well have been the intent of the translator.]

25 M69 The prepositional phrase εἰς ὑμᾶς is used as equivalent to a simple dative,
"to you."

I PETER 2

2 BD269(5) Τὸ λογικὸν ἄδολον γάλα occurs because ἄδολον γάλα was probably an
everyday expression, "pure spiritual milk."

6 R392 The subject of περιέχει is the following quotation (cf. M28; the verb
means "it is written"--BD308).
T237 Ἐπί following πιστεύω may mean either "to believe in" or "to believe on
the basis of" ("to believe in" is preferable here--BD187[6]).

BD258(2) Ἐν γραφῇ means "in a scriptural passage" (γραφῇ is definite even without the article--R772). [Ed. The article is not necessary to make the noun
definite in a prepositional phrase.]

7   R418 Sometimes the words in contrast are brought sharply together, as πιστεύου-
    σιν and ἀπιστοῦσιν are here.

8   R714 Ὅ is used to refer to the preceding clause.

9   Rxii Ἀρετή has the meaning "Thy Excellency."

11 H378 The termination ικος with σάρξ presents the idea of "made of," denoting
    an ethical relationship.

12 R789 When the article occurs with the substantive, but not with the adjective
    (τὴν ἀναστροφὴν . . . καλήν), the result is the equivalent of a relative clause.
    T260 Ἐκ has a causal sense, "because of good deeds."
    MT181 The participle ἔχοντες appears to have an imperatival sense (cf. R946;
    "maintain good conduct").

13 R772 Πᾶσα κτίσις means "every created thing" (the whole creation"--T200). [Ed.
    the usual meaning of πᾶς followed by an anarthrous noun is "every" which seems
    to be the case in this verse.]

17 T77 The aorist imperative is used for a precept until the coming of Christ
    (the reason for the use of the tense is difficult to determine. Πάντας τιμήσατε
    should be emended into πάντα ποιήσατε and taken with what precedes [. . .
    ὡς θεοῦ δοῦλοι], then it has the impressiveness of a climax, the aorist impera-
    tive sharpening the edge of the exhortation in accordance with the tone of ur-
    gency which the writer constantly expresses in this way. By the succeeding
    present imperatives he is indicating states of mind in a calmer tone--M21; the
    aorist imperative means "give to each his honor," completed in the present--
    BD237[2]). [Ed. Since the text has τιμήσατε it is incorrect to alter it to
    include ποιήσατε. The aorist imperative seems to express a simple all-inclu-
    sive statement, "give to each the honor due him." The present imperatives fol-
    low, specifying the action in a more detailed manner.]
    BD110(1) Ἀδελφότητα is used as a concrete collective noun meaning "brotherhood."

18 R946 The participle ὑποτασσόμενοι is used as an imperative, "be subject" (cf.
    Eph. 5:22 and MT181).

19 R500 Συνείδησιν θεοῦ denotes that it is a good conscience toward God (an ob-
    jective genitive).
    R704 The neuter pronoun τοῦτο occurs in place of the feminine αὕτη (agreeing
    with χάρις) to present a more separate and abstract notion than αὕτη would
    have done.
    BD372 Εἰ has the meaning of "that."

20 T115 Εἰ with the future ὑπομενεῖτε portrays a feeling of definiteness (almost
    causal in sense).

21 R633 In the compound noun ὑπογραμμός, ὑπό introduces the idea of "under."

24 T22 The idiomatic singular τῷ μώλωπι has a plural meaning, "wounds" or "bruis-
     es."
     MT237 Since the Greek of 1 Peter is remarkably good, it does not seem likely
     that οὗ τῷ μώλωπι αὐτοῦ is due to Peter's style. In the Septuagint, αὐτοῦ may
     well have been added by a scribe who did not notice that the οὗ made it unneces-
     sary (the whole clause should be rendered "by whose bruises you have been
     healed."--M44).
     M46 The datives here should be translated in the following way, "in order that,
     dead with regard to sins, we might live with regard to righteousness."

                                 I PETER 3

1   R946 The participle ὑποτασσόμεναι is used with an imperatival sense, "be sub-
     missive" (cf. v. 7 and M181).
     R1026 Καὶ εἴ is used in a supposition which is considered improbable. Since
     καὶ εἰ is employed the truth of the succeeding clause is stoutly affirmed in
     the face of this one objection.
     T192 The adjective τοῖς ἰδίοις is used as a simple pronoun (cf. v. 5).

3   B479 The use of οὐχ rather than μή in 1 Pet. 3:3 seems to indicate that the
     following words, ὁ . . . κόσμος , are excluded in a prohibition (i.e., they
     are parenthetic).
     BD168(2) When a genitive is dependent upon another genitive, the governing
     genitive always precedes the dependent one (the occurrence of a series of ad-
     juncts between the article and noun is rare in the New Testament, but it is
     common in classical Greek. The simplicity of New Testament style naturally
     causes less involved forms to be generally preferred--MT236).

4   M79 Ὁ κρυπτὸς τῆς καρδίας ἄνθρωπος with the following dative has the meaning
     "the secret nature of the heart, consisting of . . ."

7   R1071 Εἰς τό with the infinitive here denotes purpose (cf. B409).

8   R945 The imperative should be supplied with the adjectives here by implication,
     "have unity of spirit . . ."
     M34 Ὁ τέλος means "finally" (or perhaps "in short").

9   R573 In this context the preposition ἀντί means "for."

10 H450 Τοῦ with the infinitive denotes purpose. This is due to developing ten-
     dencies in Koine Greek, rather than to Hebrew influence.

12 M49 The first occurrence of ἐπί in this verse has the meaning of "towards"
     (favorably), whereas the second occurrence means "against" (unfavorably).

14 B286 The use of καί before πάσχοιτε suggests that the writer has in mind that
     suffering is apparently opposed to blessedness. Yet it is probable that he in-
     tends to affirm that blessedness comes, not in spite of, but through suffering
     for righteousness's sake. Thus, the protasis suggests, even intentionally, a
     concession, but it is a true causal conditional clause.

                                    425

M40 Grammatically, φόβον αὐτῶν could mean "do not be afraid as they are afraid" (subjective genitive) but the context makes it mean "do not be afraid with fear of them" (objective genitive; cf. T212 and BD153[1]).

17 B259 This verse should be translated "for it is better, if the will of God should so will, that ye suffer for well doing than for evil doing" ("if perchance"--BD385[2]).

18 B145 Ζφοποιηθείς is clearly subsequent (occurring later) to ἀπέθανεν (or ἔπαθεν), but is probably to be taken together with θανατωθείς as defining the whole of the preceding clause Χριστὸς . . . θεῷ (cf. R1114).
BD229 Περί is actually used for ὑπέρ, "for."

19 R778 The anarthrous participle ἀπειθήσασιν is used with a predicative sense (i.e., adverbial; this participle has an unclassical usage with the ellipsis of the article with an attributive participle, "the spirits who disobeyed"--T153). [Ed. The former suggestion seems to be supported grammatically. The occurrence of an adjectival or attributive anarthrous participle with an articular noun is very irregular, and Turner supplies no additional examples to support his claim.]
M131 Ἐν ᾧ may refer strictly to the grammatical antecedent πνεύματι; thus Christ went in spirit (as opposed to in the flesh) to the spirits in prison; or is it a vague resumptive phrase, "and so" (Selwyn takes a middle course -- "in which process" or "in the course of which").

20 M56 The preposition διά does not mean "by means of" but "through" (the preposition denotes attendant circumstances, "through"--T267).
BD205 Εἰς is used instead of ἐν with a local sense, "within which a few were saved" (cf. M68).

21 R714 The pronoun ὅ is used to refer to the previous clause.

I PETER 4

1 M44 The dative σαρκί has a metaphorically local sense "anyone who has suffered, physically" (as contrasted to τῷ πνεύματι, spiritually).

2 R1070 It is not necessary for the article to come next to the infinitive. Several words may intervene and the clause may be one of considerable extent. But the New Testament does not have the numerous extended clauses of this nature as the ancient Greek literature did, and the adverbs usually follow (εἰς τό goes with βιῶσαι).

3 BD405(2) The nominative adjective ἀρκετός does not influence the infinitive κατειργάσθαι, which has its own subject ("you").
BD460(2) If a series is not strictly a summary but merely an enumeration, asyndeton may be necessary, as in πεπορευμένος . . . εἰδωλολατρίαις (καί is necessary because of the adjective with the last noun); the insertion of καί each time would make the separate items too important.

4 M132 Does the relative clause ἐν ᾧ . . . mean "and so they are surprised when

you do not . . ." or "at which they are surprised, namely when you do not . . ?"
It is perhaps relevant that in Acts 24:16 ἐν τούτῳ . . . seems to represent a
similarly vague reference, but in its direct, not relative form (cf. 1:6).
BD126(2) The verb ζενίζω means "to surprise."

5   M161 The New Testament Greek uses ἔχω (the English language employs the verb
    "to be") with the adverb ἑτοίμως.

6   M56 Ἵνα . . . πνεύματι is difficult; perhaps it should be rendered "that they
    might be judged in the eyes of men (as men reckon judgment) physically, but
    might live as God lives spiritually" (it would be possible to assume that ἵνα
    is causal and that a second ἵνα [of purpose] has fallen out before ζῶσιν, or
    that we are to take ἵνα first as causal and then as telic--T102; cf. BD369).

8   R622 Πρὸ πάντων is used to indicate superiority (preference).
    R789 When the article occurs with the substantive but not with the adjective,
    the result is the equivalent of a relative clause, "the love which is out-
    stretched."
    R946 The participles in vv. 8ff. have an imperatival sense (ἔχοντες and
    διακονοῦντες), "have (or practice) . . ., serve."

10 M204(n.p. 69) The preposition εἰς may have a local sense, similar to ἐν with
    the dative. [Ed. This suggestion seems improbable, since the more usual
    meaning of εἰς makes good sense, "for (unto) one another."]

11 B425 Ὡς occurs in elliptical constructions from which the participle is
    dropped (the participle would have an imperatival sense here, "let him speak
    as one who utters oracles of God").

12 R532 The dative τῇ πυρώσει is used with a causal sense (cf. T242 and BD196).
    B440 Ὡς prefixed to a participle of cause implies that the action denoted by
    the participle is supposed (asserted, or professed by some one, usually the
    subject of the principal verb) to be the cause of the action of the principal
    verb. The speaker does not say whether the supposed or alleged cause actually
    exists, "as though (or because) something strange were happening."
    MT126 The present prohibition here has the meaning "stop being surprised."

14 R785 The second occurrence of the article τό is probably due to the second
    genitive (putting equal emphasis upon both genitives; the second part should
    be translated, "and therefore the Spirit of God"--T187).

15 T76 The present prohibition μὴ . . . πασχέτω means "let none of you ever
    suffer" (the manner or character of the action may be specifically denoted
    --BD336[2]).

16 M78 The preposition ἐν is possibly instrumental, but it more probably denotes
    the sphere in which, "by virtue of bearing the name."

17 B400 The articular infinitive τοῦ ἄρξασθαι modifies the noun καιρός, "the time
    is come."

18 R871 The future verb φανεῖται has a durative sense, "where will the ungodly
    and sinner appear?"
    M144 The particle ὥστε has a simple inferential sense in this context, meaning
    "and so."

427

I PETER 5

2   T77 The aorist imperative ποιμάνατε refers to a precept which is valid until
     the coming of Christ (cf. BD337[2]), "shepherd."
     BD101 'Επισκοπέω has the meaning "look out for."

4   R498 Τῆς δόξης is used as a genitive of definition, "the unfading crown of
     glory" (denoting quality--T213).

5   R808 'Εγκομβώσασθε is used as a direct middle verb, "gird yourselves with
     humility."

6   M65 The preposition ὑπό possibly indicates motion to beneath. If so, then the
     whole clause would be interpreted "humble yourselves therefore (to a position)
     beneath the strong hand of God" (otherwise it would mean "humble yourselves,
     being, as you are, beneath the strong hand of God"). [Ed. In view of the
     passive voice of the verb ταπεινώθητε, it seems preferable to render the clause
     "therefore allow yourselves to be humbled beneath the strong hand of God."]

7   R946 The participle ἐπιρίψαντες is not imperatival, but is dependent upon the
     imperative verb ταπεινώθητε (cf. M181n.2) "casting all your anxieties."
     M28 The impersonal verb with περί means "it matters to someone concerning"
     (i.e., "he cares about you").

8   R1085 There is no instance in the New Testament of the infinitive occurring
     in a subordinate clause, unless we consider the infinitive as the accurate
     reading here (ex., οἱ βλέπουσι [not βλέπειν] τὸν ἄνθρωπον). [Ed. This
     comment is difficult to understand, because in the next verse an infinitive
     is dependent upon a participle which introduces a subordinate clause.]
     T206 Is ὁ ἀντίδικος ὑμῶν διάβολος an example of apposition, or is ὁ ἀντίδικος
     adjectival? [Ed. Διάβολος is apparently in apposition to the previous sub-
     stantive, since διάβολος was commonly considered as a proper name (even a
     title) and an article was not necessary to show apposition, "your opponent
     the devil."]

9   R505 The pronoun with the genitive here refers to the same kinds of suffering
     rather than to the same suffering (cf. R687).
     M168 The latter part of this verse should mean "the brotherhood (brothers) in
     your world" (because of the position of the pronoun ὑμῶν), instead of "your
     brothers in the world."
     T55 'Επιτελεῖσθαι occurs in the middle voice with the meaning "to pay in full."

10   R606 In the compound verb here κατά has a perfective force (emphasizing the
     complete nature of the restoration).

12   R846 "Εγραψα seems to refer to the epistle just finished (an epistolary aorist).
     R1036 Εἶναι is used as an infinitive of indirect discourse following ἐπιμαρ-
     τυρῶν, "bearing witness that this is the true grace."
     T256 Εἰς has a metaphorical sense here, "in the sphere of" (similar to ἐν).

II Peter

1 M109f. In τοῦ θεοῦ ἡμῶν καὶ σωτῆρος Ἰησοῦ Χριστοῦ, the article has probably
been correctly omitted, and τοῦ (μεγαλοῦ) θεοῦ is intended to apply to Jesus,
meaning "our God even Jesus." B. S. Easton (in location) makes the point that
"God and Saviour" was a commonplace phrase in the religion of the day (i.e.,
according to him approximately A.D. 95-105) and meant without exception one
deity and not two (cf. 1:11 and Tit. 2:13). The implications for the date
and authorship are, of course, important (cf. R127 and TGr16).

3 R533 The datives ἰδίᾳ, δόξῃ and ἀρετῇ have an instrumental sense, "by . . ."

5 R1200 In this list of virtues (vv. 5ff) the repeated words give a cumulative
force.
BD290(4) The construction καὶ αὐτὸ δὲ τοῦτο has an adverbial sense "for this
very reason" (it may be corrupted from κατ' αὐτὸ δὲ τοῦτο).

9 R542 The relative pronoun ᾧ may be used as a possessive dative with πάρεστιν,
"to whom these are not."
R962 Occasionally when a relative clause is indefinite the subjective negative
μή occurs with the indicative (as here).
T190 The pronoun αὐτοῦ is not emphatic here regardless of its position.
H290 Μυωπάζω is formed from μύωψ meaning "short-sighted" (i.e., one who "screws
up [μύει] his eyes to see").

10 MT191 This verse provides the only example of οὐ μή with the subjunctive verb
in Peter's writings (an emphatic negation).

12 MT230 Καίπερ is used to make the concessive idea of the participle more distinct. Without this particle present, there may have been ambiguity, "although
you know."

16 BD442(16) Καί is used here to co-ordinate two ideas one of which is dependent
on the other. Thus the conjunction serves to avoid a series of dependent genitives, "the power of our Lord's appearing."
MT231 The negative οὐ occurs with the participle here because of the formal
contrast (οὐ . . . ἀλλά).

17 B55 The aorist verb εὐδόκησα may be explained in a variety of ways: 1) as an
historical aorist having reference to a specific event as its basis, "I was
well pleased with thee" (e.g., for receiving baptism); 2) as a comprehensive
historical aorist covering the period of Christ's preincarnate existence; 3)
as a comprehensive historical aorist having the force of an English perfect,
and referring to the period of Christ's earthly existence up to the time of
speaking; and 4) as an inceptive aorist referring to some indefinite, imagined

point of past time at which God is represented as becoming well pleased with
Jesus -- most probable (it is a timeless aorist and may also be gnomic [some-
thing well known]--R842).
M69 Εἰς with an accusative here is used with a sense equivalent to a pure dative, "with whom."

19 MT228 Προσέχοντες seems to be used as a complementary participle with the verb
ποιεῖτε, "you do well to pay attention to."

20 R772 The singular γραφή occurs twice in the New Testament as anarthrous but
with a definite sense (here and in 1 Pet. 2:6).

21 M73 Does ἐλάλησαν ἀπὸ θεοῦ mean "they spoke what was derived from God" (practically equivalent to τὰ ἀπὸ θεοῦ), or does ἀπὸ θεοῦ simply reinforce ὑπὸ πνεύματος ἁγίου and mean "controlled by God"? (The preposition ἀπὸ takes the place
of ὑπὸ in a causal sense [or perhaps it is used for τὰ ἀπὸ θεοῦ?]--T258). [Ed.
Generally when the preposition ἀπὸ is used in place of ὑπὸ with an instrumental
or causal sense, the passive voice of the verb is employed (cf. Acts 2:22; 20:19
Heb. 5:7 and Jas. 1:13). Consequently, Moule's first suggestion seems preferable.]

II PETER 2

3 BD148(1) Ἐμπορεύομαι occurs with a transitive sense, meaning "to defraud," "to
buy," "to import," "to make gain or business of."

6 M38 The genitives Σοδόμων and Γομόρρας represent nothing less than a second
noun in apposition to the first, "the city Sodom . . ."
T240 The dative καταστροφῇ has an instrumental sense "to extinction" (the classical would have expected a genitive construction, cf. BD195[2]).

10 BD415 The participle βλασφημοῦντες is supplementary to the verb, "they are not
afraid to blaspheme."

11 R665 Although the comparative adjective occurs without an object of comparison,
it still has a comparative sense, "greater."
BD456(3) Ὅπου seems to mean "in so far as."

12 M36 Φθαρήσονται, ἀδικούμενοι μισθὸν ἀδικίας might be equivalent to an accusative in apposition to a sentence, "they shall perish -- which is the proper recompense for their wickedness, wicked that they are," if only the middle, ἀδικούμενοι could be taken as transitive: but it is not so attested (the variant
reading with κομιούμενοι of course smooths out the construction, but robs the
sentence of some of its point).
BD152(1) Ἐν οἷς ἀγνοοῦσιν following βλασφημέω means "in matters of which they
are ignorant" (cf. the more intelligible expression in Jude 10).

14 M41 The adjective ἀκατάπαυστος, meaning "that has never had enough of" (i.e.,
"that never ceases from"), owes its construction with the genitive to the idea
of separation. In this context it refers to "eyes unceasingly looking for sin."
M41n.2 The phrase καρδίαν γεγυμνασμένην πλεονεξίας apparently means "a heart

trained in exhortation" (the genitive is difficult to define; it may be taken as Moule suggests or it may be a genitive of quality, giving further definition, meaning "a heart trained and greedy"--T233). [Ed. Moule's suggestion seems preferable in this context, especially in view of the textual emendation in a few manuscripts (changing πλεονεξίας to the dative).]

16 T192 Ἰδίας is equivalent to a mere possessive pronoun, "his transgression."

18 BD102(6) Ὀλίγως means "hardly" here.

19 T240 The dative pronoun ᾧ is used with an instrumental sense, meaning "by which" (cf. R533).

22 BD111(2) Κύνες refers to stray dogs.
BD266(3) The neuter article τό has a substantival sense, "that which is found in the true proverb."
MT155f. The middle participle λουσαμένη has a passive sense. Certainly, if the pig's ablutions are really reflexive rather than passive, sundry current notions need revising. To Peter at any rate λουσαμένη did not suggest willing coopera- tion.

II PETER 3

1 R714 The relative pronoun αἷς probably refers to both of Peter's epistles (cf. BD296).
M168 The pronoun ὑμῶν is displaced from εἰλικρινῆ διάνοιαν (indicating proba- ble emphasis).
T192 Ταύτην . . . δευτέραν . . . ἐπιστολήν means "this is the second letter."

2 R1086 The infinitive here is epexegetical (appositional) to the previous verse, "that you should remember."
M166 Τῆς τῶν ἀποστόλων ὑμῶν ἐντολῆς τοῦ κυρίου καὶ σωτῆρος sounds a little stilted (perhaps it means "of the commandment of the Lord and Saviour trans- mitted by the apostles to you"--T218; cf. BD168[1]).

3 R1039 The participle γινώσκοντες occurs instead of a finite verb because of anacoluthon (i.e., the failure to complete a sentence as originally conceived), "know this."
M166 Ἐπ' ἐσχάτων τῶν ἡμερῶν looks like a displacement for ἐπὶ τῶν ἐσχάτων ἡμερῶν; but Blass (BD264[5]) takes it as an instance of the neuter plural ἔσχα- τα as a noun (substantive). In that case Jude 18, ἐπ' ἐσχάτου τοῦ χρόνου, is either a deliberate displacement or a scribal slip. [Ed. Apparently ἔσχατος with the article was considered as definite enough without the use of the ar- ticle (cf. 1 Pet. 1:5 and 20), "in the last days."]

4 R880 The present verb διαμένει has a progressive sense in which the past and present time are gathered into one phrase, "all things have continued as they are."
R978 Ἀφ' ἧς means "since."

5 M55 In the expression γῆ ἐξ ὕδατος καὶ δι' ὕδατός συνεστῶσα, the preposition

διά with the genitive probably has a spatial sense, meaning "continuous land, rising out of and extending through water"; but δι' ὕδατος may mean "between water," and refer to the idea that there are waters above and below the earth. [Ed. The more regular use of διά seems to support Moule's former suggestion.]

9   R1128 The participle βουλόμενος has a causal sense.
BD180(5) The genitive ἐπαγγελίας is used here because the verb βραδύνω has an idea of separation, "the Lord is not holding back, delaying the fulfillment of his promise."

14   R542 Αὐτῷ is used as a dative of agency, "by him."

17   R993 ῞Ινα is used to express the content of φυλάσσεσθε (similar to ὅτι), "beware lest you."

I John

1 M34 The phrase ἀπ' ἀρχῆς means "from the beginning" (cf. John 8:25).
BD342(2) The perfect tense is used in vv. 1 and 3 to denote a continuing effect
on the subject, ἀκηκόαμεν and ἑωράκαμεν are **coordinated**, where hearing is e-
qually essential with seeing (cf. John 3:32).

3 M165 When the copula is sufficiently represented by δέ, a καί may be rendered
by some such phrase as "yes, and" or "moreover." Thus, in this verse we have
"yes, and our fellowship is."

4 R406 The literary plural occurs in this verse (an impersonal way to conceal
one's identity), where γράφομεν does not differ in reality from γράφω in 2:1
(cf. T28 and BD280).

5 R1033 Note that a declarative ὅτι occurs after the noun ἀγγελία, "this is the
message . . . that God is light."

9 B218 Ἵνα is used here to introduce a clause which expresses the notion of conceived result (cf. Heb. 6:10; ἵνα introduces a clause with the sense of actual
result--BD391[5]; cf. R998). [Ed. The actuality of the result clause is dependent upon the conditional clause at the beginning of v. 9.]
B263 The conditional clause here actually has a futuristic sense, "if we shall
confess our sins, (he will forgive us, for) he is faithful and righteous to forgive us our sins."

10 B88 The verb ἡμαρτήκαμεν is used as a true perfect of completed action, being
explained in v. 8.

1 TGr150f. The aorist tense of the verb ἁμάρτῃ describes a state, and has the
meaning "begins to be a sinner" (i.e., "committed an act of sin"); it is only
an initial step along a certain road (cf. 3:9).

2 R618 Περί has a sense similar to ὑπέρ in this verse, "for" (this is the usual
idea when the preposition is used with ἁμαρτία).

3 M77 Ἐν has an instrumental sense here, "by this."
TGr153 When the epexegesis (apposition) is fact, John preferred a subordinate
clause introduced by ὅτι (rather than ἵνα). Thus for this verse the translation should be, "knowledge consists of this: that we have gained our knowledge
of him if we keep his commandments" (cf. 5:2; ἐάν is in apposition with ἐν

τούτῳ--R700; ἐάν and ὅταν may be used in apposition if the fact is only assumed, cf. 5:2--BD394). [Ed. The ὅτι clause denotes the content of the verb
γινώσκομεν, whereas the ἐάν clause is in apposition to ἐν τούτῳ. Ἐάν is apparently used to avoid the repetition of ὅτι (cf. 4:13).]

5   B79 The perfect tense of τετελείωται apparently has a gnomic sense, referring
    to a state that commonly existed (gnomic, expressing a customary truth--R897;
    it refers to a general assertion with a futuristic sense--BD344).

6   R708 A definite contrast is denoted in this verse by the pronouns ἐκεῖνος and
    αὐτός.

7   B28 The imperfect verb εἴχετε refers to an action not separated from the time
    of speaking by a recognized interval, "which you have had from the beginning."

8   M130f Possibly the use of ὅ in this verse is parallel to that in Eph. 5:5. R.
    Law, in The Tests of Life (p. 376), prefers to construe it as a parenthetic
    clause in apposition, rather than taking ὅ ἐστιν ἀληθές as the direct object
    after γράφω, with ἐντολὴν καινήν as an accusative of nearer definition: "I
    write to you, as a new commandment, what is true in Him." On p. 235, he offers
    the paraphrase: "This commandment . . . is, nevertheless, a new, fresh, living
    commandment -- a fact that is realized first in Christ and then in you" (the
    relative pronoun ὅ in this verse agrees neither with the antecedent nor with a
    predicate substantive, but gathers the general notion of thing, "which thing
    is true"--R713). [Ed. Actually, Robertson's comment is similar to Moule's
    suggestion.]

9   R879 The present verb ἐστίν refers to a past action still in progress (it dif-
    fers from the perfect in that the action is still in progress--T62).
    R1182 Καί conveys the notion of "and yet."

12 M12 A thrice-repeated γράφω is followed by a thrice-repeated ἔγραψα in vv.
    12ff. Is this an instance of such absolute identity of meaning between the
    present and the epistolary aorist as to make the writer indifferent as to which
    he uses? Or are we to assume an interruption after the thrice-repeated γράφω,
    followed by a threefold retrospective aorist; or take the aorists as referring
    back to the Gospel; or assume displacement?
    T73 In vv. 12ff, γράφω occurs three times, then ἔγραψα three times (perhaps for
    the sake of novelty; the author of this epistle is fond of varying his tenses)
    which may refer back to some earlier writing. [Ed. Ἔγραψα appears to be used
    as an epistolary aorist referring to this epistle (cf. vv. 21, 26 and 5:13).
    The change of the tenses appears to denote a shift in the perspective from the
    writer's point of view to the readers' point of view (note the slight varia-
    tions). John's tendency was to be repetitive.]

16 T213 In ἡ ἐπιθυμία τῆς σαρκός the genitive is a genitive of quality (adjecti-
    val) describing the noun ἐπιθυμία, or is it subjective? (The genitive is sub-
    jective, "the lust proceeding from the flesh," parallel to the sentence ἡ σαρξ
    ἐπιθυμεῖ--M40.)

19 M145 The ἵνα clause should be taken as imperatival, "they had to be shown up"
    (cf. T95; elliptically, ἀλλ' ἵνα, meaning "on the contrary [but] this happened
    [or a similar verb], in order that" is equivalent to "rather they were to be
    --BD448[7]).

H433   It seems questionable whether the use of οὐ -- πάντες is a Hebraism, as
is usually believed.   The explanation of the idiom probably is, not that πᾶς
was used in a distributive sense, but that, in vernacular Greek, the negative
was attached in sense to the verb, where we attach it to the nominative ("all
are not" equals "none are").   The attachment of οὐ to what seems to us the
wrong word is not unusual in Greek (cf. R753).

21   R753   In πᾶν -- οὐ, the denial about πᾶν is complete (instead of οὐδείς--M182;
the πᾶν is positive, and the οὐ negates the verb--H434).
R845   Ἔγραψα may be used as an epistolary aorist (cf. v. 12).

24   BD466(1)   The pronoun ὑμεῖς is used in contrast to the previous ἀρνούμενος.

26   R845   With the aorist verb ἔγραψα, the reference may not be to the whole epistle
but to the portion in hand, although the standpoint is that of the reader (an
epistolary aorist; cf. v. 12).

27   B216   Ἵνα introduces a clause which is a complementary limitation to the noun
χρείαν (it expresses a conceived result--B218).   [Ed.   Since John frequently
uses ἵνα in apposition to a noun or demonstrative pronoun (cf. 3:11, 23; 4:21
and John 2:25, and the discussion on John 17:3), that is the preferred rendering here.]
BD466(1)   The word order of καὶ ὑμεῖς in this context emphasizes the exceptional position of the reader (cf. v. 20).

28   R1147   Notice καὶ νῦν τεκνία, where John's emotional appeal is sharpened by the
use of νῦν.
H460   Ἀπό with the genitive is used instead of an accusative after αἰσχυνθῶμεν
(possibly influenced by the Hebrew), "to be ashamed before."

29   BD372(1a)   Ἐὰν εἰδῆτε . . . γινώσκετε ὅτι καὶ . . . .   means "just as," or
"as soon as you know . . ., you also know that . . ."

I JOHN 3

1   R741   Ποταπός occurs in an indirect question here, with the meaning "of what
sort" (equivalent to ποῖος).
R999   Καὶ ἐσμέν accents the consecutive force of ἵνα (ἵνα has an epexegetical
usage--BD394).   [Ed.   Ἵνα is used to further explain ποταπὴν ἀγάπην (an especially common usage of ἵνα in John's first epistle), but the result of God's
love is also indicated.]

6   R880   In vv. 6 and 8, the present tense of ἁμαρτάνει has an iterative sense
(repeatedly).

8   T62   The present verb ἁμαρτάνει refers to past action still in progress, "the
devil has sinned from the beginning" (cf. 2:9).
T260   In vv. 8, 10, 12, and 19, ἐκ is used with the sense of "belonging to" (of
a sect or school).

9   T150f.   The present infinitive ἁμαρτάνειν expresses a state rather than an action.   The apostle affirms that a Christian can never be a sinner.   He will

start to be one, will take the first step by committing this or that sin (cf. 2:1), but he stops short of the condition of being a sinner. To be "in Christ" is not to be at once perfect, but whenever such a one disgraces himself, his actions never permanently remove him from that mystical union which is unbreakable (cf. T72).

11   R1079   Ἴνα introduces an appositional clause following αὕτη, "that we love."

13   R965   Εἰ is used after the verb of emotion θαυμάζετε to express a causal sense, because the issue is conceived of as an hypothesis rather than a direct reason (in which case ὅτι would have been used).

15   R753   In πᾶς -- οὐ, the denial in reference to πᾶς is complete (cf. 2:21).

16   T139   Ὅτι introduces an appositional clause in apposition to ἐν τούτῳ, "by this we know . . ., that" (cf. 2:3).

18   TGr10   John exhorts the Christians to love one another sincerely (i.e., "in truth," cf. III John 1).

19   R871   The future verb πεύσομεν has a durative sense, "we will be persuading."

20   R512   The genitive ἡμῶν appears to be used with the verb, although it may go with καρδία (cf. v. 21). [Ed. The pronoun ἡμῶν appears to be used with the verb, since this compound verb takes a genitive object and because ἡμῶν occurs in an unusual position to be taken with the articular noun, "if our heart condemns us."]

22   B299   The supposition here refers to any instance of asking in general, "whatsoever we ask, we receive."
      BD214(6)   "Pleasing in the eyes of someone" is equivalent to "pleasing to someone."

23   R850   The aorist subjunctive πιστεύσωμεν has an ingressive sense, "we should come to believe."

24   R679   The pronoun αὐτός is emphatic here.

I JOHN 4

1   MT125   The present imperative πιστεύετε has an iterative force, "do not believe every spirit that you happen to come in contact with."

2   R1123   The perfect tense here expresses the notion of perfected state.
      B460   The substantival participle forms a part of the object of the verb, equivalent to a clause of indirect discourse, with the resultant meaning "every spirit which confesses that Jesus Christ has come in the flesh is of God" (cf. III John 4).

3   R962   Occasionally when the relative pronoun is indefinite, μή occurs with the indicative verb, as here (cf. Tit. 1:11).

R964 Ὅτι is used as a co-ordinate relative pronoun, "that."

R1149 The use of ἤδη in καὶ νῦν . . . ἤδη is climactic and indicates that the point is now at last clear and may be assumed as true.

M182 The denial in reference to πᾶν is complete in πᾶν . . . οὐκ (occurring instead of οὐδείς; cf. 2:21).

6   M73 The prepositional phrase in ἐκ τούτου γινώσκομεν has a causal or instrumental sense, "by this we know" (cf. T260).

8   TGr5 John inserts the definite article in just the right position to give the sense, "God is love." Otherwise we are presented with an antitheistic idea that God is no more than the relationships which we experience in life (i.e., "love is God," cf. v. 16).

9   R777 The article is repeated with the adjective μονογενῆ, thus giving the adjective additional emphasis (cf. John 10:11).

M202 Lightfoot distinguishes between the tense of ἀπέσταλκεν and ἀπέστειλεν in vv. 9f. (the two verbs are evidently synonymous--M14). [Ed. There appears to be a distinction between the aorist and perfect tense in this context. The aorist tense indicates a simple fact dependent upon the stative verb ἐστιν, whereas the perfect tense refers to the permanence of Christ's mission. In both verses where the perfect tense occurs (vv. 9 and 14), verbs of observing are used.]

BD220(1) Ἐν ὑμῖν, with the meaning "in our case," occurs where a simple dative or accusative may have been used.

13 M72 Ἐκ with the genitive here has a partitive sense (cf. R599 and John 1:16), "of his Spirit."

14 R894 A real distinction exists between the perfect and present tense of τεθεά-μεθα and μαρτυροῦμεν, "we have seen and are witnessing."

16 R768 God and love are not convertible terms, thus θεός has the article (cf. v. 8 and John 1:1).

17 M61 The prepositional phrase μεθ' ἡμῶν is probably plain Greek, rather than semitic, with the resultant meaning "love is perfected among us" (i.e., "in our community"; cf. R610f.).

19 R549 Πρῶτος is used as a true adjective (rather than an adverb), thus "God is the first one who loves" (cf. John 20:4).

21 R699 Ἵνα is used in apposition to ταύτην τὴν ἐντολήν (cf. John 4:34), "this commandment . . . that."

I JOHN 5

3   R993 The appositional use of ἵνα is parallel to ὅτι here (cf. vv. 9, 11 and John 4:34), "that."

4   R698 Ἡ πίστις is in apposition to ἡ νίκη, "this is the victory . . ., that is our faith."

T21 The neuter gender may refer to a person, provided that the emphasis is
less on the individual than on some outstanding general quality; πᾶν is often
added to make this clear (as here).

6   M57 In δι' ὕδατος καὶ αἵματος the prepositional phrase has the notion of
attendant circumstance, parallel with ἐν τῷ ὕδατι . . . (it has the notion
of manner, "with"--T267; the phrase portrays the idea of means--R583).
[Ed. Both the idea of accompaniment and instrumentality appear to be present
in the prepositional phrases here.]

8   BD205 Εἰς with the accusative in this verse is used for the predicate nominative (cf. H462; A.E. Brooke, in location, takes this construction as meaning
"are for the one thing," "tend in the same direction" or "exist for the same
object"; the preposition εἰς is used in place of ἐν with the meaning "in" or
"at"--R593). [Ed. In essence Robertson's comment is in agreement with the
preceding rendering.]

13   R418 The verb ἔχετε comes between the adjective and substantive to give unity
to the clause (cf. Acts 1:5).
R845 Ἔγραψα is used as an epistolary aorist, referring to the epistle just
completed (cf. 2:26).

14   T55 The change in voice in αἰτώμεθα . . . αἰτώμεθα . . . ἠτήκαμεν may have
some significance, but what? (Αἰτέω is used for ordinary requests and
αἰτέομαι refers to business transactions--R805).

15   T116 Ἐάν with the indicative seems to have a causal sense (cf. BD372[1a]).

16   R477 The cognate accusative denotes the objective result, "sinning a sin."

18   M119 Ἑαυτόν (or αὐτόν) seems to be required by the sense here, instead of
αὐτόν (cf. Col. 1:20; the manuscript support for ἑαυτόν is very strong).

20   R707 The pronoun οὗτος refers to the preceding αὐτοῦ.
R776 The adjective ἀληθινός receives greater emphasis than the substantive,
because the article occurs only with the adjective, "the true God."
B198 In the construction ἵνα γινώσκομεν the indicative verb is probably pregnant in force, with the meaning "that we may know, and whereby we do know."

21   T77 The aorist imperative φυλάξατε is used for a precept which is valid until
the coming of Christ.
H460 Ἀπό with the genitive is used instead of an accusative after φυλάξατε
(cf. 2:28), "keep from."

II John

1   R713   The relative pronoun οὕς is masculine because of the sense (referring to
    people, rather than maintaining the neuter gender of τέκνοις).
    R1116   The perfect tense of ἐγνωκότες has lost the notion of completion but main-
    tains the linear idea alone in the present sense (cf. John 18:22), "all those
    who know."
    T178   The latter segment of this verse may be translated "whom I sincerely love,
    and . . . all who have sincere standards" (anaphoric use of τὴν ἀλήθειαν, re-
    ferring to previous reference).

3   T178   Ἐν ἀληθείᾳ means "with sincerity" (cf. v. 1).

4   TGr10   John rejoiced when he found Christians who behaved sincerely (i.e., "in
    truth"; "behaving with sincerity"--T178).
    T209   The prepositional phrase with ἐκ is used as a partitive genitive, "some
    of your children."

5   R1140   The concessive notion is dominant in οὐχ ὡς, which means "not as if" (cf.
    BD425[3]).

6   R699   The first ἵνα clause here is in apposition with the previous pronoun, αὕτη
    (cf. 1 John 3:11).

7   M101   K. and S. Lake construe ἐρχόμενον in a future sense; but it appears from
    the context that it is past, "as having come," equivalent clearly to the ἐλη-
    λυθότα of 1 John 4:2 (similar to an imperfect--T81; cf. John 9:25).

8   R1413   When a ἵνα clause is continued with ἀλλά, ἵνα is not repeated, but the
    sense is retained (cf. John 3:16).
    B209   The ἵνα clause following βλέπετε is probably objective, but may be pure
    final (purpose).   [Ed.   When βλέπετε is used in warnings it is generally fol-
    lowed by an object clause, which apparently is the case in this verse.   Conse-
    quently, the ἵνα clause indicates the content of the warning, "watch . . .,
    that."]
    MT116   The aorist verb εἰργάσασθαι has a constative sense, with stress on the
    activity rather than on its product.

9   T51   Προάγω means "to go forward."

10 R1093   The infinitive χαίρειν is the object of λέγετε, "do say a greeting."
    MT125   The present imperatives in this verse have an iterative force (cf. 1 John
    4:1), "whenever the occasion arises."

12 R625   Στόμα πρὸς στόμα contains the concept of face to face converse (cf. 3
    John 14).
    R919   The past tense of ἐβουλήθην is used to express courtesy, thus it does not
    mean "would have liked" (but "I do not want to"; cf. Phil. 3 and Gal. 4:20).

M56 Διά with the genitive has an instrumental sense, "with paper and ink" (cf.
T267   and 1 John 5:6).

III John

1   T178   The prepositional phrase with ἐν has an adverbial sense, "whom I sincerely love" (cf. 2 John 3).

2   M63   Περὶ πάντων is taken by many to mean simply "in all respects." The A.V. translation, "above all things" might conceivably be justified by the περισσός associations, but this seems improbable unless clear parallels can be found (cf. BD229[2]; the subject matter of the prayer is implied--R619).

3   R968   Καθώς has an epexegetical usage here (to introduce indirect discourse-- BD453[2]).
     TGr8   In this verse, ἀλήθεια occurs both as articular and anarthrous. The distinction has never been observed, since it is generally understood that the first occurrence (in spite of being articular) refers to an abstract characteristic of Gaius, his "sincerity" or "truthfulness," and it has escaped notice that this more intelligibly refers to Christ as the Truth. The difficulty in taking the first truth as a reference to Christ the Truth arises because it is not appreciated that σου need not be a personal possessive pronoun; it does not mean "your truth." The verb μαρτυρέω often has an indirect object in the genitive case. Consequently, the second section of this verse means "the brethren came and testified about you to (Christ) the Truth" (cf. John 14:6; it is difficult to build much on the presence of the article in vv. 3, 4, and 12--M112). [Ed. The article τῇ is possibly anaphoric, referring to the ἀλήθεια in v. 1, with the resultant meaning "the brethren testified to (concerning) your sincerity" (with the inherent idea of "a way of life"). This rendering is supported by the following explanatory clause introduced by καθώς and the similar construction in v. 6.]

4   R704   The plural τούτων refers to a single object, "than this."
     B460   The substantival participle forms a part of the object of the verb, equivalent to a clause of indirect discourse, "to hear that . . ." (cf. 1 John 4:2).
     TGr10   The article occurs with ἀλήθεια, referring back to a previous mention of the word (anaphoric, cf. v. 3), and it has the meaning "with that same sincerity" ("in the Truth [Christ]"--T178; cf. the discussion on v. 3).
     H166   The double comparative μειζότερος is best explained as the result of an effort to add fresh strength to a form, the comparative force of which was somewhat blunted since it did not have the normal termination.

5   MT116   The aorist verb ἐργάσῃ has a constative sense, surveying in perspective the continuous labor which is generally expressed by the present tense.

6   R861   The aorist participle προπέμψας refers to action which is simultaneous to that of the principal verb, "you will do well when you send them" (cf. Luke 9:25).

8   R633   The idea of hospitality (under one's roof) is natural with the compound verb ὑπολαμβάνω.
     T178   The articular ἀλήθεια refers to Christ (cf. the discussion on v. 3).

9   R846 The aorist verb ἔγραψα refers to a previous letter.

12   T178 Αὐτῆς τῆς ἀληθείας means "Christ himself" (cf. v. 3). [Ed. This may not
     be a mere personification of ἀληθεία, but it may refer to the Christian genuine-
     ness of Demetrius. The truth he professed was evident throughout his life.]

13   M56   Διά with the genitive has an instrumental sense, "with pen and ink" (cf.
     2 John 12).

14   R625 Στόμα πρὸς στόμα present the concept of face to face converse (cf. 2 John
     12).

Jude

1   T240 'Ιησοῦ Χριστῷ is used as an instrumental dative, "kept by Jesus Christ."
T264 The use of ἐν is difficult to determine: the preposition may be displaced, but "beloved in God" in the Christian mystical sense is reasonable (possibly ἐν θεῷ has a personal sense here, "in God's judgment"--MT103).

2   R940 The optative of wishing occurs here, "may mercy, peace and love be multiplied."

5   R1129 The participle εἰδότας has a concessive notion (not causal as Winer thinks), "although you were once for all fully informed" (cf. MT230).

7   R748 In this verse ἕτερος has the idea of difference of kind.
BD194(1) The dative τούτοις with the adjective of identity portrays the owner of the same thing.

8   BD450(1) The conjunction μέντοι merely means "but" in this verse.

9   R529 The dative τῷ διαβόλῳ has the associative idea, "with the devil."
M175 Κρίσιν . . . βλασφημίας means "an abusive verdict."

11   M39 Possibly μισθοῦ is used as a genitive of price, "they went headlong for a reward."
M47 This verse furnishes a curious study in the meanings of the Dative τῇ ὁδῷ (perhaps local), τῇ πλάνῃ (possibly "according to the wandering of"; "abandon themselves to"--T238) and τῇ αντιλογίᾳ (perhaps instrumental, "because of a contradicting [like that of] Korah"; cf. T242).

12   R704 Οὗτοι has the masculine gender because it refers to people.

13   BD253(2) θαλάσσης is anarthrous because it is part of the predicate; also the thing being emphasized is this particular characteristic ("wild waves") of the sea.

14   R589 The sense of ἐν here is similar to that of μετά and σύν (associative dative), "with."
M47 The difficulty in understanding τούτοις vanishes if the sense is "he prophesied _for_ these"; but the context seems to require "with reference to these," for which a plain dative is very odd and perhaps unparalleled (περί with the genitive would be more natural).

15   M35 'Ασεβεῖς is used as a predicate of the previous nominative (i.e., in apposition), "godless as they are."

17   B422 The articular participle is equivalent to a restrictive relative clause, "remember the words which have been spoken before."

Revelation

3   R764   The article οἱ is repeated with the participle here because different persons are referred to.

4   R414   In ἀπὸ ὁ ὢν καὶ ὁ ἦν καὶ ὁ ἐρχόμενος,. the nominative is evidently intentional to accent the unchangeableness of God (it is not that John did not know how to use the ablative after ἀπό).
R734   In ὁ ἦν the article is used as a relative pronoun, "who was" (cf. v. 8).
R764   The article ὁ is repeated with the participles here because different aspects of the same person are presented (cf. v. 3).
M103   The present participle ὁ ἐρχόμενος may be futuristic, meaning "the one who is to come" (indicating certainty).

5   R458   The nominative case is retained with μάρτυς instead of it being put in the case of the word with which it is in apposition (John appears to be unconcerned with agreement in concord in the Apocalypse).
M77   The preposition ἐν has an instrumental sense, "by his blood."

8   R785   Since the second article τό occurs, it accents sharply a different aspect of the person.

13   M54   Πρός with the dative here implies position, "by" or "at."

16   R414   The wrong case appears with ἔχων (almost a separate sentence) if it refers to αὐτοῦ; if it refers to φωνή it is the gender that presents problems. [Ed. The participle ἔχων refers to υἱόν in v. 13. The case changes from accusative to nominative because John begins to think of Christ as the subject of this extended sentence.]

18   B429   The participle ζῶν is used as the predicate of the verb εἰμί, "I am alive" (a periphrastic construction--B431).

20   MT9   In any other writer we might be tempted to spend time over τὰς λυχνίας, where τῶν λυχνιῶν is clearly necessary, although for John (at least in the Apocalypse) it is enough to say that the neighboring οὕς may have produced the aberration (he is perpetually indifferent to concord).

5   R1025   Εἰ δὲ μή has the sense of "but if not, otherwise."
M46   Σοί is used as a dative of disadvantage in vv. 5 and 16, "I am coming, to your cost" (cf. T238 and MT75).

8 M10 The aorist verbs in the last clause of this verse have an ingressive notion, "Christ died and sprang to life" (cf. TGr151).

10 T213 The genitive in στέφανον τῆς ζωῆς may be a genitive of quality (similar to an adjective) or an appositional genitive, "that crown which is life" (the appositional usage is preferable--R498).

11 R599 'Εκ following ἀδικηθῇ has a causal sense.

13 R614 In this verse παρά has the idea of "among" (cf. Matt. 28:15).

14 R1106 The anarthrous participle κρατοῦντας has an indefinite notion, "some who hold."

16 R534 The locative ἐν τῇ ρομφαίᾳ is equivalent to the instrumental in meaning, "with the sword."
    M61 The preposition μετά has the idea of "conflict with," "I will do battle against them" (cf. 1 Cor. 6:6).

17 R519 Τοῦ μάννα has the meaning "some of the manna."

19 T190 The possessive pronoun occurs before the first of a group of nouns to eliminate repetition (generally the possessive pronoun occurs after the noun it modifies).

24 R406 The verb λέγουσιν is used as a general indefinite plural (the present tense has an aoristic sense--R866), "as some say."

25 T77 The aorist imperative κρατήσατε is misused; the present tense would be preferred (the aorist imperative here is not ingressive, but perhaps complexive -- terminative--BD337[1]), "hold fast."

28 T70 Εἴληθα is used as a narrative perfect (aoristic--MT145). [Ed. These explanations have a similar meaning; cf. the discussion on 3:3.]

REVELATION 3

2 B28 The imperfect verb ἔμελλον refers to an action which is not separated from the time of speaking by a recognized interval of time (cf. 1 John 2:7; it is a progressive imperfect, looking forward--R884), "that were about to die."

3 R740 In its occurrence here ποῖος merely has the force of τίς (i.e., it does not indicate quality).
    R901 The perfect and aorist occur in close proximity here. If the aorist ἄκουσας had been ἀκήκοας no difficulty would exist. The perfect would emphasize the permanence of the obligation, although the reception may seem more a matter to be emphasized as durative, than the hearing (punctiliar; the perfect tense is similar to the aorist--T69; cf. MT145). [Ed. The perfect tense seems to have an aoristic sense, especially in view of the relatively few occurrences of the aorist indicative of λαμβάνω in Revelation.]

5   R589 Ἐν has the notion of accompanying circumstance, meaning "with."

8   R420 Μικράν occurs in the position that it does here because of the tendency
    in the New Testament to place pronouns (and on occasion nouns) forward in the
    sentence (because of the flexibility of the Greek language, vivid, impassioned
    speech easily gives rise to these dislocations—BD473[2]).

9   B205 Ἵνα is used with both a future indicative and aorist subjunctive in ob-
    ject clauses here, "behold, I will make them to come and worship before thy
    feet, and to know that I have loved thee" (both clauses portray the idea of
    purpose—BD369[2]).
    BD476(1) Αὐτούς is actually the subject of the ἵνα clause, but brought forward
    (cf. v. 8).

14 R759 The masculine gender is used with ἀμήν because Jesus is referred to (cf.
    1 Cor. 14:16).
    T210 It is debatable whether the genitive in ἡ ἀρχὴ τῆς κτίσεως is used as a
    partitive genitive, meaning "among," or whether the rule is not rather that
    of supremacy, "over" (cf. Col. 1:15). [Ed. In this context, the noun ἀρχή
    appears to have the notion of pre-eminence, cf. Col. 1:14-20, a passage which
    would have been familiar to the Laodicean Church.]

16 B232 Since the causal clause with ὅτι is subordinate, the intent of the sen-
    tence is to state why he will resort to such action (cf. John 16:3).

17 R785 When several epithets are applied to the same person, usually only one
    article is used with many adjectives (as here).
    T183 Usually a predicate adjective is anarthrous, but note ὁ ταλαίπωρος (this
    articular phrase means "that wretched man"—T173).

18 R1413 When the construction with ἵνα is continued in a further clause by μή,
    the negative alone is repeated (but with the sense retained).

20 R895 Ἕστηκα is almost a purely durative perfect, "I stand."

                            REVELATION 4

3   R644 Κυκλόθεν is used as a preposition in vv. 3f., "all around."

7   R201 The masculine participle ἔχων occurs in vv. 7f., although the substantive
    is neuter (ζῷον ; the masculine is used to indicate a personal sense.)

8   M66 Ἀνὰ has a distributive sense, "six wings apiece" ("each"—T266).
    BD493(1) Note the repetition of the word ἅγιος for emphasis.

9   T86 The future verbs in vv. 9f. seem to be entirely due to semitic influence
    when they "gave glory . . . they fell . . . worshipped . . . threw" (this is
    a possible literal rendering of the Hebrew imperfect, which can be future un-
    der some circumstances).

11 R758 It is interesting to observe that in the list of attributes of God in the
    songs in Rev. 4:11; 5:13; 7:12, the article is expressed with each quality,

while in 5:12 one article (τήν) is used with the whole list.
B376 The infinitive λαβεῖν is used to limit the adjective ἄξιος, "worthy to
receive."

REVELATION 5

5   R835 Ἐνίκησεν is used as an effective aorist (i.e., emphasis is laid on the
    end of the action as opposed to the beginning), "has conquered."
    R1001 The infinitive ἀνοῖξαι has a consecutive sense here (actual result--
    R1089; tendency, by implication realized in actual result--B371), "so that he
    can open."

6   M202 Perhaps the perfect tense in ἐσφαγμένος has a unique sense here, because
    there is a distinction between the death of Christ as a past event and as an
    abiding force.

7   BD343(1) The perfect verb εἴληθεν is used as an aorist (cf. MT145; a dramatic
    historical [aoristic] perfect, where John sees Jesus with the book in his
    hand--R897; cf. 3:3).

9   R589 The notion of price is indicated by the preposition ἐν here (an extension
    of the instrumental usage--M77), "by your blood."

10 BD177 The prepositional phrase ἐπὶ τῆς γῆς means "on the earth."

12 R427 In enumerations the repetition of καί gives a kind of solemn dignity (as
    here, cf. 4:11; rhetorical--BD460[3]).

REVELATION 6

1   BD247(1) The numeral μίαν means "the first."

6   R501 Notice the genitive of price, "for a denarius."

8   M66 In v. 8, the instruments "sword," "famine" and "death" are perhaps distin-
    guished deliberately from the "beasts" which are more like agents: ἐν ῥομθαίᾳ
    . . . , but ὑπὸ τῶν θηρίων. In this verse, the variety may be due merely to
    the fact that the ἐν is from Ezekiel, while the ὑπό seems to fall outside the
    quotation. And note that here ὑπὸ τῶν θηρίων actually follows an active verb,
    ἀποκτεῖναι, so that in a sense the beasts are only the instruments wielded by
    the subject of that verb. Normally ὑπό is used of the agent after a passive
    verb or its equivalent.

REVELATION 7

1   R752 Μὴ πᾶς has the sense of "not any."
    R1413 When the construction with ἵνα is continued in a further clause by μή,

the negative alone is repeated (but the sense is retained; cf. 3:18).
BD233(1) The prepositional phrase ἐπὶ τῆς γῆς (and θαλάσσης) means "on the
face of the earth (and sea)," whereas ἐπὶ πᾶν δένδρον means "upon every tree."

3   R609 The compound noun μέτ-ωπον has the sense of "the space between the eyes."
B164 The aorist tense of ἀδικήσητε is used in the prohibition to forbid an action which has not begun (cf. MT125).

12   R427 The repetition of καί represents a solemn dignity in the enumeration here
(cf. 5:12).

14   B80 The perfect indicative εἴρηκα ("I said") refers to a simple past fact, where
it is scarcely possible to suppose that the thought of existing result was in
the writer's mind (an aoristic perfect; cf. BD343[1]).
M75 Does the prepositional phrase ἐν τῷ αἵματι have a local or instrumental
sense? [Ed. This phrase is figurative since one does not generally make something white with blood. Ἐν τῷ αἵματι occurs frequently in the New Testament
with an instrumental sense, "through the blood of Christ," as it appears to be
used in this verse; cf. 1:5; Rom. 3:25 and 1 Pet. 1:19.]

16   R752 Οὐ πᾶς has the idea of "not any."
B487 Note the negatives here, "they shall hunger no more, neither thirst any
more, neither shall the sun strike upon them at all" (a double negative).

17   T218 Occasionally two genitives may depend on the same noun, which then usually stands between them (ἐπὶ ζωῆς πηγὰς ὑδάτων), "to fountains of living water."

REVELATION 8

1   R958 Ὅταν is used in a definite sense here (as in Homer; cf. B316 and BD382
[4]; it is unusual to have the adverb ὅταν used for a single definite past action, cf. Mark 11:19—R973; this adverb suggests that the Lamb's breaking of
the seals was a repetitive performance, in spite of the aorist—T93). [Ed.
The occurrence of ὅταν with the aorist here appears to refer to a definite action in the past. When the Lamb opened this particular seal there was silence
for about an half an hour.]

4   R529 The dative ταῖς προσευχαῖς is used as an associative-instrumental with
ἀνέβη (cf. MT75; a dative of advantage, "in favor of their prayers," although
it may be temporal—T238; of advantage—BD188[1]; in vv. 3f., ταῖς προσευχαῖς
may be considered as temporal, "simultaneously with prayers"—M43). [Ed. The
temporal and associative rendering have a similar sense, such as "together with
prayers," which appears to be the meaning in this verse; cf. Acts 10:4 where
prayers are offered with the giving of alms.]

5   R899 Εἴληθεν is used as a dramatic historical perfect (cf. 5:7; "the angel
took").

11   R598 The prepositional phrase ἐκ τῶν ὑδάτων portrays the notion of cause, "because of the water."
H462 Εἰς with the accusative is used for the predicate nominative after ἐγένετο,
"a third of the waters became wormwood."

12 R1413 When the construction with ἵνα is continued in a further clause by μή, the negative alone is repeated (but with the sense retained; cf. 3:18 and 9:15).

13 R1193 Οὐαί is used with the accusative, as the object of thought, "woe to those" (cf. 12:12; possibly an adverbial accusative--R487).
    M73 Ἐκ has a causal sense here, "for" (cf. v. 11).
    BD247(2) The numeral ἑνός is equivalent to the indefinite pronoun here, "an eagle."
    H278 Μεσουράνημα, meaning "mid-heaven," is derived from the verb μεσουρανέω, "to culminate," of heavenly bodies crossing the meridian.

REVELATION 9

1   R1123 The notion of perfected state is predominate in the perfect participle πεπτωκότα (John observed the star in its fallen state).

4   R752 Οὐ πᾶς has the resultant meaning "not any" (cf. 7:16).
    R992 Ἵνα with the future indicative is used as the subject of the verb ἐρρέθη (cf. B212; and v. 5), "it was told to them that".

6   R709 The independent use of the singular pronoun ἐκεῖνος is almost confined to the Gospel of John (and the First Epistle). On the other hand, the pronoun ἐκεῖνος occurs only twice in the Apocalypse (9:6 and 11:13) and in both instances it is dependent upon a substantive (i.e., it is used as an adjective), "those days."
    R870 The futuristic present φεύγει portrays a sense of certainty.
    B60 The future verbs have a progressive sense, "will be seeking . . ." (cf. ζητήσουσιν, εὑρήσουσιν and ἐπιθυμήσουσιν).

14 R412 Note the construction according to sense in φωνὴν . . . λέγοντα (the masculine participle personifies the voice).
    R604 Ἐπί is used with the locative dative here, "at the great river."

20 B218 Ἵνα introduces a clause that expresses the idea of conceived result (cf. MT210), "that."

REVELATION 10

4   R853 The aorist prohibition μὴ αὐτὰ γράψῃς means "do not begin to write."

6   M60 Ἐν is used with the dative here to designate the guarantee of an oath (not common in Koine Greek--M183), "swore by him."

7   T53 Occasionally a causative sense is given to intransitive verbs, so that they may have an object (so with εὐηγγέλισεν in this verse; the active verb here does not mean "cause the good news to be preached," but as elsewhere in Hellenistic Greek it's equivalent to εὐαγγελίζομαι--BD309[1]). [Ed. The unusual usage of the active verb εὐηγγέλισεν in this verse appears to support Turner's suggestion.]

7   H422 Καί has a consecutive sense here, "as a result," or "then."

10 MT115 In New Testament Greek, the preposition in a compound verb may be omit-
    ted, without weakening the sense, when the verb is repeated. Consequently,
    ἔφαγον seems to be the continuation of κατέφαγον in this verse (cf. John 1:12).

                              REVELATION 11

1   TGr188n. The participle λέγων is used in an unusual sense-construction, "a
    reed was given to me, saying" (λέγων appears to be indeclinable here--T315;
    cf. H454). [Ed. Actually, these explanations are only attempts to explain
    the lack of concord, which is prevalent in the Apocalypse.]

5   R1026 Καὶ εἰ in this verse means "and if," not "even if."

6   R973 Ὁσάκις occurs four times in the New Testament (1 Cor. 11:25f.; Rev. 11:6),
    each time with ἐάν and the subjunctive, and having the notion of indefinite
    repetition, "as often as."
    T101 Ἵνα μή with the subjunctive introduces a purpose clause here (as opposed
    to the usual rendering of "lest").

9   R599 Ἐκ is used with the partitive genitive here, "men from" (cf. T209).

10 R565 Note the two uses of ἐπί, with the genitive and dative, "upon the earth
    . . . over them."

17 R834 Ἐβασίλευσας is used as an ingressive aorist, "assumed rule" ("you have
    become king"--B54).

18 R414 The accusative τοὺς μικρούς is in apposition with the dative τοῖς δούλοις
    (cf. 1:5), "servants . . , the small . . ."
    R757 The article is repeated to specify different classes of people in τοῖς
    προφήταις καὶ τοῖς ἁγίοις καὶ τοῖς φοβουμένοις.
    T313 The neuter plural subject has a plural verb (the subject τὰ ἔθνη has a
    personal sense).
    MT118 Ὠργίσθησαν may mean "were angry," but the ingressive sense, "waxed an-
    gry," (at the accession of the King), suits the context better.

                              REVELATION 12

6   R579 Ἀπό has the notion of agency here, similar to ὑπό (ἀπό may be purely in-
    strumental, or does it carry the connotation "derived from God?"--M74). [Ed.
    The construction here appears to mean "prepared by God's command" not by him-
    self, with ἀπό denoting that God was the source of the command.]

7   R1066 Τοῦ with the infinitive is in explanatory apposition with πόλεμος,
    "there was war . . . Michael . . . fighting" (it is doubtful if any less bar-
    barous Greek than that of Revelation would have tolerated the subjects of the
    infinitive to be in the nominative case--M129).

11 M55 Διά with the accusative here seems to be used in the sense of "through"
    (cf. 13:14; it has the usual causal sense—R584; "by force of"—BD222). [Ed.
    The preposition διά is used with the accusative to denote the efficient cause,
    meaning "by" or "through," cf. 13:14.]

12 R1193 Οὐαί is used with the accusative, as the object of thought (cf. 8:13),
    "woe to the earth and sea."

REVELATION 13

3   R818 'Εθαυμάσθη has an active sense here, "wondered," or "was astonished."
    T214 "His plague of death" (equivalent to "his mortal wound") becomes "the
    plague of death" (because of semitic influence).

8   M73 The preposition ἀπό has a temporal sense here, "since the foundation of the
    world."

10 R590 'Εν has an instrumental sense, "with the sword."
    H450 The second occurrence of the simple infinitive ἀποκτανθῆναι occurs with
    a jussive sense, denoting an imperatival notion, "he must be killed with the
    sword."

12 B205 "Ινα is used with a future indicative in an object clause, "he makes the
    earth and its inhabitants worship" (the clause portrays an idea of purpose—
    T100).

13 B222 This verse is the most probable instance of ἵνα denoting actual result;
    ἵνα . . . ποιῇ is probably equivalent to ὥστε ποιεῖν, and is explanatory of
    μεγάλα (epexegetical). It would be best translated "so as even to make" (cf.
    R998 and BD391[5]).

14 M55 Διά with the accusative in this verse seems to be used with the sense of
    "through" (cf. 12:11).
    T71 "Εζησεν is used as an ingressive aorist, "he sprang to life."

REVELATION 14

4   BD339(3) The present participle is used here to refer to something which hap-
    pened previously (representing the imperfect), thus οἱ ἀκολουθοῦντες means
    "who (always) followed."

6   T53 Εὐαγγελίσαι with an object has a causative sense, cf. 10:7. [Ed. Actually
    the accusative εὐαγγέλιον αἰώνιον is used as the direct object of the partici-
    ple ἔχοντα, not the object of the infinitive εὐαγγελίσαι. Thus, εὐαγγελίζω
    has its usual intransitive sense.]

8   T218 In a construction with several genitives (τοῦ οἴνου τοῦ θυμοῦ τῆς πορνείας
    αὐτῆς), usually the governing genitive will precede the dependent one (cf. BD
    168[2]), "the vengeful wine of her fornication."

BD493(1) The repetition here and in 18:2 emphasizes the verb ἔπεσεν (the aorist tense is used here to refer to what has just happened--MT135).

10 R680 If there is any emphasis in the use of the pronoun αὐτός, it is very slight.
H422 The initial καί in this verse has a consecutive sense, "then" (cf. 10:7).

13 B124 The present participle οἱ ἀποθνήσκοντες refers to an act, the single doing of which is the mark of the class of people, "blessed are the dead which die in the Lord."
TGr48 Ἵνα ἀναπαήσονται may have a causal sense here (p[47] has ὅτι), although an imperatival sense is more suitable (ἵνα may be imperatival here, "they shall rest"--M207; cf. MT248; this clause may express the idea of conceived result--B218). [Ed. Ἵνα ἀναπαήσονται apparently has an imperatival meaning, since occasionally ἵνα introduces such a rendering in the New Testament and the future tense adds a volitive notion.]
BD12(3) In this verse ἀπ' ἄρτι means "exactly, certainly."

15 T334 The καί preceding θέρισον here has a final sense, denoting purpose (cf. BD442[2]).

18 T215 Τῆς γῆς is used as an appositional genitive, "the grapes which are the earth." [Ed. Turner actually gives an incorrect rendering of his grammatical observation. Τῆς γῆς is not in apposition with τοὺς βότρυας, but with τῆς ἀμπέλου, because of the word order and the concord in number and case. The resultant rendering should then be "the vine which is the earth."]

20 R575 The preposition ἀπό has the idea of "off" or "away from" (cf. John 11:18), "for a distance of."

REVELATION 15

2 R475 Νικάω is generally transitive with an accusative, but here it uses ἐκ with the ablative (τοὺς νικῶντας ἐκ τοῦ θηρίου is probably a compressed phrase; supply "by separating themselves from" or "and delivered themselves from"--T260; cf. BD212).
R881 The present participle νικῶντας has the sense of completion (similar to a perfect).
R529 Πυρί is used as an associative dative (it is an instrumental dative, "to mix with fire"--T240). [Ed. In essence, the dative of association is similar to the associative-instrumental. But in this context (with μεμιγμένην) the concept of association is more predominant than that of instrumentality.]

REVELATION 16

9 R1001 The infinitive δοῦναι has a consecutive sense here, "to give him glory" (cf. T136 and BD391[4]; tendency or conceived result--B371).
H445 The intensive cognate accusative occurs here, "burnt with the fierce heat."

10   R598   The preposition ἐκ conveys a causal notion here, "they gnawed their tongues
for (because of) their pain" (cf. M73 and T260).

11   R598   In ἐκ τῶν ἔργων the preposition has the sense of separation, "from their
deeds."

15   R1413 Neither ἵνα nor μή is repeated, although the concept of ἵνα μή is carried
on by the second subjunctive verb, "that he may not."

18   R978   'Αφ' οὗ is the simple equivalent of ἀπὸ τούτου ὅτε, with the resultant
meaning "since."

19   T218   In the construction with several genitives, τοῦ οἴνου τοῦ θυμοῦ τῆς ὀργῆς
αὐτοῦ, the governing genitive precedes the dependent ones, "the cup of the wine
of the wrath of his anger" (cf. 14:8).
H462   Εἰς τρία μέρη is used as a predicate nominative after ἐγένετο (cf. 8:11;
"the great city became three parts").

21   R599   The second occurrence of ἐκ here has a causal sense, "because of the
plague" (cf. v. 10).

REVELATION 17

3   R414   The masculine participle ἔχων is not in agreement with the gender of its
antecedent θηρίον (a frequent incident in the Apocalypse; the masculine gender
indicates a personification of the beast).
T213   Βλασφημίας is used as a genitive of quality, "blasphemous names" (similar
to an adjective).

8   M73   'Από has a temporal meaning here, "since."

10   R764   With the numerals here (ἑπτά -- οἱ πέντε -- ὁ εἷς -- ὁ ἄλλος) the article
points out a certain number, placing the number in the foreground.

16   R590   'Εν has an instrumental sense here, "by," or "with."

17   R975   "Αρχι is used with the future to refer to an indefinite future time, "until
the words of God shall be fulfilled."

18   R604   The preposition ἐπί has the idea of "over."

REVELATION 18

2   BD493(1) The repetition of the verb ἔπεσεν emphasizes the defeat of Babylon
(cf. 14:8).

3   R599   The preposition in ἐκ τῆς δυνάμεως has a causal sense, "because of the
wealth of" (the causal idea may be expressed by the rendering "grew rich on her
enormous luxury"--M73).

12   T31   Τιμιώτατος is used as an elative superlative, "most rare" or "very rare"

(cf. R670).

14   R873 Εὑρήσουσιν is used as a predictive future, "they shall find these things
no more" (the negative οὐ μή with the future is very emphatic--MT192).

17   R474 Τὴν θάλασσαν ἐργάζονται is somewhat unusual; since this verb is usually
intransitive, the resultant meaning is "those that work on the sea for their
livelihood."

21   H432 Εἷς is used for τις with an indefinite sense, "a certain mighty angel."

REVELATION 19

3   B80 Εἴρηκαν is used as an aoristic perfect, denoting a simple past fact (cf.
7:14), "they said."

9   R1396 The use of the demonstrative οὗτοι in this verse means "these are," but
in 21:5 and 22:6 it means "these words are."

10   MT178 In 19:10 and 22:9, μή stands alone after ὅρα (cf. our colloquial expression "don't!").

11   BD219(4) The prepositional phrase with ἐν has the sense of manner (i.e., ἐν
δικαιοσύνῃ is equivalent to δικαίως; "righteously").

13   R533 Αἵματι is used as an instrumental dative, "by blood."
B75 The perfect tense is used in περιβεβλημένος to denote the whole attention
to the present resulting state, "he is clothed."

14   R407 The participle ἐνδεδυμένοι is in the masculine gender because of the
sense (referring to people).

15   R680 If there is any emphasis in the occurrence of the pronoun αὐτός, it is
very slight (cf. 14:10).
R960 Ἵνα occurs where a relative pronoun may have been used, "with which to
smite" (cf. H436).

16   H443 Βασιλεὺς βασιλέων means "ruler over kings" (a sort of superlative in sense).

21   R599 With the verb ἐχορτάσθησαν the preposition ἐκ has the notion of cause or
occasion, "were gorged (fed) because of their flesh."

REVELATION 20

2   R414 The nominative noun ὁ ὄφις is in apposition with the accusative noun τον
δράκοντα, "the dragon, that ancient snake" (cf. 1:5).

4   R833 In this verse ἔζησαν is probably ingressive, but ἐβασίλευσαν is clearly
constative, "reigned" (the former means "sprang to life"--TGr151).

5   BD62 Πρῶτος is used for πρότερος, referring to the first of two (cf. 21:1 and
      the discussion on Acts 1:1).

10   M206 The present participle πλανῶν refers to action which precedes that of the
      principal verb, thus representing a frequentative or durative sense ("who de-
      ceived them"--T81).

REVELATION 21

1   BD62 Πρῶτος is used for the comparative, referring to the first of two (cf. 20:
      5).

2   R539 Τῷ ἀνδρί is used as a dative of advantage, "for her husband."

3   R611 In this verse, μετά has the notion of "fellowship with."

11   T31 Τιμιώτατος is used as an elative superlative, "most rare" or "very rare"
      (cf. 18:12).
      BD108(3) Κρυσταλλίζω means "to look like crystal, to glisten."

13   MT73 The ablative occurs with the idea of place expressed in the prepositional
      phrases of this verse with ἀπό, "on."

16   T240 Τῷ καλάμῳ is used as an instrumental dative, "to measure with the measuring
      rod."

17   BD165 Ἑκατὸν τεσσαράκοντα τεσσάρων πηχῶν means "as amounting to one hundred
      and forty-four cubits."

18   H307 Ἐνδώμησις means "building in."

19   H376 Χαλκηδών is the name given to a copper silicate found in the mines near
      Chalcedon. The place name itself is a derivative of χαλκός, "copper."

23   B216 Ἵνα with the subjunctive is a complementary limitation to the preceding
      nouns (the clause further explains the nouns, "to shine").

24   T313 The neuter plural subject τὰ ἔθνη has the plural verb περιπατήσουσιν,
      which is contrary to the classical rule (this occurs occasionally in the New
      Testament, especially with nouns that have a personal sense).

25   M39 The genitive ἡμέρας means "by day."

27   R1187 In this verse εἰ μή means "but only" (εἰ μή occurs for ἀλλά--H468).
      T196 Οὐ μή . . . πᾶν means "not one thing."

REVELATION 22

2   T198 Ἕκαστος rarely occurs in an attributive position in the New Testament,

455

but it does in this verse (with emphasis), "each specific month."

4   R871 The future verb ὄφονται has a durative sense, "they will continue to see
    his face."

9   MT178 Ὅρα μή occurs here with the simple meaning "don't!" (cf. 19:10).

14 B218 Ἵνα with the future indicative introduces a clause of conceived result
    "that they may" (the clause seems to have an imperatival sense, "may they have
    right to the tree of life"--TGr48). [Ed. In the two subordinate clauses of
    this verse, the future verb ἔσται is parallel to the aorist subjunctive εἰσέλ-
    θωσιν. Within this context, the future verb is used to point to the certainty
    of the result rather than to portray an imperatival sense.]

18 BD488(1c) A word in the preceding conversation may be taken up and its meaning
    turned to a metaphorical sense, as with ἐπιθῇ . . . ἐπιθήσει here, with the
    meaning "add to . . . add to."